Jaime Balmes Pbro.

European Civilization.

Protestantism and Catholicity

COMPARED IN THEIR EFFECTS ON THE CIVILIZATION OF EUROPE.

BY REV. J. BALMES.

SIXTEENTH EDITION.

BALTIMORE:
PUBLISHED BY JOHN MURPHY & CO.
182 BALTIMORE STREET.

AUTHOR'S PREFACE.

AMONG the many and important evils which have been the necessary result of the profound revolutions of modern times, there appears a good extremely valuable to science, and which will probably have a beneficial influence on the human race,—I mean the love of studies having for their object man and society. The shocks have been so rude, that the earth has, as it were, opened under our feet; and the human mind, which, full of pride and haughtiness, but lately advanced on a triumphal car amid acclamations and cries of victory, has been alarmed and stopped in its career. Absorbed by an important thought, overcome by a profound reflection, it has asked itself, "What am I? whence do I come? what is my destination?" Religious questions have regained their high importance; and when they might have been supposed to have been scattered by the breath of indifference, or almost annihilated by the astonishing development of material interests, by the progress of the natural and exact sciences, by the continually increasing ardour of political debates,—we have seen that, so far from having been stifled by the immense weight which seemed to have overwhelmed them, they have reappeared on a sudden in all their magnitude, in their gigantic form, predominant over society, and reaching from the heavens to the abyss.

This disposition of men's minds naturally drew their attention to the religious revolution of the sixteenth century; it was natural that they should ask what this revolution had done to promote the interests of humanity. Unhappily, great mistakes have been made in this inquiry. Either because they have looked at the facts through the distorted medium of sectarian prejudice, or because they have only considered them superficially, men have arrived at the conclusion, that the reformers of the sixteenth century conferred a signal benefit on the nations of Europe, by contributing to the development of science, of the arts, of human liberty, and of every thing which is comprised in the word *civilization.*

What do history and philosophy say on this subject? How has man, either individually or collectively, considered in a religious, social, political, or literary point of view, been benefited by the reform of the sixteenth century? Did Europe, under the exclusive influence of Catholicity, pursue a prosperous career? Did Catholicity impose a single fetter on the movements of civilization? This is the examination which I propose to make in this work. Every age has its peculiar wants; and it is much to be wished that all Catholic writers were convinced, that the complete examination of these questions is one of the most urgent necessities of the times in which we live. Bellarmine and Bossuet have done what was required for their times; we ought to do the same for ours I am fully aware of the immense extent of the questions I have adverted to, and I do not flatter myself that I shall be able to elucidate them as they deserve; but, however this may be, I promise to enter on my task with the courage which is inspired by a love of truth; and when my strength shall be exhausted, I shall sit down with tranquillity of mind, in expectation that another, more vigorous than myself, will carry into effect so important an enterprise.

PREFACE TO THE AMERICAN EDITION.

The work of Balmes on the comparative influence of Protestantism and Catholicity on European civilization, which is now presented to the American public, was written in Spanish, and won for the author among his own countrymen a very high reputation. A French edition was published simultaneously with the Spanish, and the work has since been translated into the Italian and English languages, and been widely circulated as one of the most learned productions of the age, and most admirably suited to the exigencies of our times. When Protestantism could no longer maintain its position in the field of theology, compelling its votaries by its endless variations to espouse open infidelity, or to fall back upon the ancient church, it adopted a new mode of defence, in pointing to its pretended achievements as the liberator of the human mind, the friend of civil and religious freedom, the patron of science and the arts; in a word, the active element in all social ameliorations. This is the cherished idea and boasted argument of those who attempt to uphold Protestantism as a system. They claim for it the merit of having freed the intellect of man from a degrading bondage, given a nobler impulse to enterprise and industry, and sown in every direction the seed of national and individual prosperity. Looking at facts superficially, or through the distorted medium of prejudice, they tell us that the reformers of the 16th century contributed much to the development of science and the arts, of human liberty, and of every thing which is comprised in the word *civilization.* To combat this delusion, so well calculated to ensnare the minds of men in this materialistic and utilitarian age, the author undertook the work, a translation of which is here presented to the public. "What do history and philosophy say on this subject? How has man, either individually or collectively, considered in a religious, social, political, or literary point of view, been benefited by the reform of the 16th century? Did Europe, under the exclusive influence of Catholicity, pursue a prosperous career? Did Catholicity impose a single fetter on the movements of civilization?" Such is the important investigation which the author proposed to himself, and it must be admitted that he has accomplished his task with the most brilliant success? Possessed of a penetrating mind, cultivated by profound study and adorned with the most varied erudition, and guided by a fearless love of truth, he traverses the whole Christian era, comparing the gigantic achievements of Catholicity, in curing the evils of mankind, elevating human nature, and diffusing light and happiness, with the results of which Protestantism may boast; and he proves, with the torch of history and philosophy in his hand, that the latter, far from having exerted any beneficial influence upon society, has retarded the great work of civilization which Catholicity commenced, and which was advancing so prosperously under her auspicious guidance. He does not say that nothing has been done for civilization by *Protestants;* but he asserts and proves that *Protestantism* has been greatly unfavorable, and even injurious to it.

By thus exposing the short-comings, or rather evils of Protestantism, in a social and political point of view, as Bossuet and others had exhibited them under the theological aspect, Balmes has rendered a most important service to Catholic literature. He has supplied the age with a work, which is peculiarly adapted to its wants, and which must command a general attention in the United States. The Catholic, in perusing its pages, will learn to admire still more the glorious character of the faith which he professes: the Protestant, if sincere, will open his eyes to the incompatibility of his principles with the happiness of mankind: while the scholar in general will find in it a vast amount of information, on the most vital and interesting topics, and presented in a style of eloquence seldom equalled.

"The reader is requested to bear in mind that the author was a native of Spain, and therefore he must not be surprised to find much that relates more particularly to that country. In fact, the fear that Protestant ism might be introduced there seems to have been the motive which induced him to undertake the work. He was evidently a man of strong national as well as religious feeling, and he dreaded its introduction both politically and religiously, as he considered that it would be injurious to his country in both points of view. He thought that it would destroy the national unity, as it certainly did in other countries.

"A very interesting part of the work is that where he states the relations of religion and political freedom; shows that Catholicity is by no means adverse to the latter, but, on the contrary, highly favorable to it; and proves by extracts from St. Thomas Aquinas and other great Catholic divines, that they entertained the most enlightened political views On the other hand, he shows that Protestantism was unfavorable to civil liberty, as is evidenced by the fact, that arbitrary power made great progress in various countries of Europe soon after its appearance. The reason of this was, that the moral control of religion being taken away, physical restraint became the more necessary." The author, on this subject, naturally expresses a preference for monarchy, it being a cherished inheritance from his forefathers; but, it will be noticed that the principles which he lays down as essential to a right administration of civil affairs, regard the substance and not the form of government; are as necessary under a republican as under the monarchical system; and, if duly observed, they cannot fail to ensure the happiness of the people. This portion of the volume will be read with peculiar interest in this country, and ought to command an attentive consideration.

In preparing this edition of the work from the English translation by Messrs. Hanford and Kershaw, care has been taken to revise the whole of it, to compare it with the original French, and to correct the various errors, particularly the mistakes in translation. A biographical notice of the illustrious writer has also been prefixed to the volume, to give the reader an insight into his eminent character, and the valuable services he has rendered to his country and to society at large.

BALTIMORE, November 1, 1850.

NOTICE OF THE AUTHOR

James Balmes was born at Vich, a small city in Catalonia, in Spain, on the 28th of August, 1810. His parents were poor, but noted for their industry and religion, and they took care to train him from his childhood to habits of rigid piety. Every morning, after the holy sacrifice of mass, his mother prostrate before an altar dedicated to St. Thomas of Aquin, implored this illustrious doctor to obtain for her son the gifts of sanctity and knowledge. Her prayers were not disappointed.

From seven to ten years of age, Balmes applied himself with great ardor to the study of Latin. The two following years were devoted to a course of rhetoric, and three years more were allotted to philosophy; a ninth year was occupied with the prolegomena of theology. Such was the order of studies in the seminary of Vich. While thus laboring to store his mind with knowledge, Balmes preserved an irreproachable line of conduct. Called to the ecclesiastical state, he submitted readily to the strict discipline which this vocation required, and he was seen nowhere but under the parental roof, at the church, in some religious community, or in the episcopal library. At the age of fourteen he was admitted to a benefice, the revenue of which, though small, enabled him to complete his education. In 1826, he went to the University of Cervera, which at that time was the centre of public instruction in that part of Spain. It numbered four colleges, in all of which an enlightened piety prevailed, affording the young Balmes a most favorable opportunity of developing his rare qualities. Here, the frame and habit of his mind were observable to all, in his deep and animated look, in his grave and modest demeanor, and in his method of study. He would read a few pages over a table, his head resting upon his hands; then, wrapt in his mantle, he would spend a long time in reflection. "The true method of study," he used to say, "is to read little, to select good authors, and to think much. If we confined ourselves to a knowledge of what is contained in books, the sciences would never advance a step. We must learn what others have not known. During my meditations in the dark, my thoughts ferment, and my brain burns like a boiling cauldron."

Devoted to the acquisition of knowledge, he cultivated retirement as a means of facilitating the attainment of his object. His thirst for learning was so intense, that it held him under absolute sway, and he found it necessary at a later period to offer a systematic resistance to its exclusive demands. Pursuing his favorite method of study, Balmes remained four years at the University of Cervera, reading no other works than the Sum of St. Thomas, and the commentaries upon it by Bellarmine, Suarez and Cajetan. If he made any exception from this rule, it was in favor of Chateaubriand's *Gènie du Christanisme.* "Every thing," said he, "is to be found in St. Thomas; philosophy, religion, politics: his writings are an inexhaustible mine." Having thus strengthened his mind by a due application to philosophical and theological studies, he proceeded to enlarge his sphere of knowledge by reading a greater variety of authors. In taking up a work, he first looked at the table of contents, and when it suggested an idea or fact which seemed to open before him a new path, he read that part of the volume which developed this idea or fact; the rest was overlooked. In this way, he accumulated a rich store of varied erudition. At the age of twenty-two he knew by memory the tabular contents of an extraordinary number of volumes; he had learned the French language; he spoke and wrote Latin better than his native tongue, and had been admitted successively to the degrees of bachelor and licentiate in theology. The virtues of his youth, far from having been weakened by these studies, had acquired greater strength and maturity. As he approached the solemn period of his ordination, he became still more remarkable for the gravity and modesty of his deportment. He prepared himself for his elevation to the priesthood by a retreat of one hundred days. After his promotion to the sacerdotal dignity, which took place in his native city, he returned to the University of Cervera, where he continued his studies, and performed the duties of assistant professor. Here also he began to manifest his political views; but, always with that discretion and moderation for which the Spanish clergy have been with few exceptions distinguished during the last twenty years. At that period Spain was agitated by two conflicting parties, that of Maria Christina and the other of Don Carlos. Balmes avoided all questions which were rather calculated to encourage the spirit of faction than promote the general interest of the country. In 1835 he evinced this circumspection in a remarkable degree, when the doctorate which had been conferred upon him, required him to deliver an address in honor of the reigning monarch. Maria Christina was then the queen regent, and civil war was about to commence in the mountains of Catalonia; but Balmes performed his task without allusion to politics, and without offending the adherents of either party.

After two years of study at Cervera, where he applied himself to theology and law, our author returned to Vich, where he determined to spend four years more in retirement, for the purpose of maturing his character and knowledge. In this solitude, he devoted himself to his tory, poetry and politics, but principally to mathematics, of which he obtained a professorship in 1837. During all these literary labors, Balmes was actuated by a lively faith, and a sincere, unassuming piety. Religious meditation, intermingled with scientific reflections, was the constant occupation of his mind; he did not neglect, however, the exterior practices of devotion. Besides the celebration of the holy sacrifice, he frequently visited the blessed sacrament, and paid his homage to the B. Virgin in some solitary chapel. The *Following of Christ*, the *Sum* of the angelic doctor, and the Holy Scriptures, were always in his hands, and he took pleasure in reading the ascetic writers of his own country. In this way did he prepare himself, until the age of thirty, to become one of the most solid and gifted minds of our time, and to act the important part to which he was called by Divine Providence.

The first literary effort of Balmes before the public, was a prize essay which he wrote on clerical celibacy. This was soon followed by another production of his pen, entitled "Observations on the Property of the Clergy, in a social, political, and commercial point of view," which was elicited by the clamoring of the revolutionary army under Espartero for the spoliation of the clergy. The learning, philosophy and eloquence of the writer in this work, excited the wonder and admiration of the most distinguished statesmen in the country. Some months after, he published his "Political Considerations on the Condition of Spain," in which he had the courage to defend the rights of both parties in the country, and to suggest means of a conciliatory nature for restoring public order and tranquillity.

Amidst these political efforts, Balmes did not lay aside his peculiar functions as a minister of God. The edification of the faithful, the religious instruction of youth, and the defence of the faith against the assaults of heresy and rationalism, were constant objects of his attention. During the same year, 1840, he translated and published the "Maxims of St. Francis of Sales for every day in the year;" he also composed a species of catechism for the instruction of young persons, which was very extensively circulated. At the same time he undertook the preparation of the present work, in order to counteract the pernicious influence exerted among his countrymen by Guizot's lectures on European civilization, and to neutralize the facilities offered under the regime of Espartero for the success of a Protestant Propagandism in Spain. The occasion and object of this work rendered it expedient that it should be published simultaneously in Spanish and in French, and with this view our author visited France, and afterwards, to extend his observations, passed into England.

On his return to Barcelona, towards the close of 1842, Balmes became a collaborator in the editing of the *Civilizacion*, a monthly periodical of great merit, devoted to literary reviews, and to solid instruction on the current topics of the day. His connection with this work lasted only eighteen months. He then commenced a review of his own, entitled the *Sociedad*, a philosophical, political, and religious journal, which acquired a great reputation during the one year of its existence. Driven soon after into retirement by the disturbances of the times, Balmes composed another philosophical work, *El Criterio*, which is a course of logic adapted to every capacity.

From the national uprising that overthrew the government of Espartero, there arose a general feeling of patriotic independence, which called for the cessation of civil strife, and the harmonizing of the two parties that divided the nation. Many of the adherents of Maria Christina, who were the nobility and the bourgeoisie, recognized the excesses of the revolutionary faction which they had called to their aid, while the Carlists were not all in favor of absolute monarchy, and numbered an imposing majority among the lower classes. All these men of wise and moderate views longed to see a remedy applied to the wounds of their afflicted country; and with one accord they turned their eyes upon Balmes, as the only individual capable of conducting this important affair. He had already, in his *Political Considerations*, indicated the principal idea of his policy for putting an end to the national evils; it was a matrimonial alliance between the Queen and the son of Don Carlos. Under these circumstances he commenced in February, 1844, a new journal, entitled *Pensamiento de la Nacion*, the object of which was to denounce the revolutionary spirit as the enemy of all just and peaceful government, and to inspire the Spanish people with a proper reverence for the religious, social and political inheritance received from their ancestors, and with a due respect for the reasonable ameliorations of the age. In this spirit the different questions of the day were discussed with energy and calmness, and especially the project of an alliance between the Queen and the son of Don Carlos, which Balmes considered of the utmost importance. This measure, such as he proposed it, was, to use the language of his biographer, "the reconciliation of the past and the future, of authority and liberty, of monarchy and representative government." Such was the patriotism, dignity and force, with which our author conducted his hebdomadal, that it won the esteem of a large portion of the most distinguished men among the Carlists, while it also acquired favor among an immense number in the opposite party. To support its views a daily journal, the *Conciliador*, was started by a body of young but fervid and brilliant writers, and nothing it would seem was wanting to insure a triumph for the friends of Spain. Prudence, energy, moderation, reason and eloquence, with a majority of the people on their side, deserved and should have commanded success; but they could not prevail against diplomatic influence and court intrigue. Balmes learned with equal surprise and affliction, in the retirement of his native mountains, that the government had resolved to offer the Queen in marriage to the infant Don Francisco, and the infanta to the Duke of Montpensier This was a severe stroke to the sincere and ardent patriotism of Balmes. He might have resisted this policy with the power and eloquence of his pen, but he preferred a silent resignation to the heat of political strife, and the *Pensamiento de la Nacion*, although a lucrative publication, was discontinued on the 31st of December, 1846.

During that same year, our author collected into one volume his various essays on politics, as well for his own vindication as for the diffusion of sound instruction on the condition of Spain. The following year he completed his "Elementary course of Philosophy." But his physical strength was not equal to these arduous labors. To re-establish in some degree his declining health, he travelled in Spain and France, and remained several weeks in Paris. The intellectual and moral corruption which was gnawing at the very vitals of the French nation, and threatened all Europe with its infection, filled him with increased anxiety. He predicted the dissolution of society, and a return to barbarism, unless things would take some unexpected turn through the special interposition of Providence. This last hope was the only resource left, in his opinion, for the salvation of society and civilization, and he exulted when he beheld Pius IX opening a new career for Italy, and consecrating the aspirations and movements of all who advocated legitimate reform and rational liberty. The political ameliorations, however, of the sovereign Pontiff appeared to the opponents of liberalism in Spain, at variance with the great opposition which Balmes had always exhibited to the revolutionary spirit. Hence, it became necessary for him to pay the just tribute of his admiration to the illustrious individual who sat in the chair of Peter, and to proclaim the eminent virtues of the prince and the pontiff. This he did with surpassing eloquence, in a brochure entitled *Pius IX*, the brilliant style of which is only equalled by its wisdom of thought. In this work, he sketches with graphic pen, the acts of the papal policy, showing that the holy see is the best guide of men in the path of liberty and progress, that Pius IX shows a profound knowledge of the evils that afflict society, and possesses all the energy and firmness necessary to apply their proper remedy. Balmes was full of hope for the future, in contemplating the course of the great head of the church, and he cherished this hope to the last moment of his life. His essay on the policy of Pius IX was the last production of his pen. His career in literature was brief, but brilliant and effective. Eight years only had elapsed since his appearance as a writer, and he had labored with eminent success in every department of knowledge. The learned divine, the profound philosopher, the enlightened publicist, he has stamped upon his age the impress of his genius, and bequeathed to posterity a rich legacy in his immortal works. In the moral as well as in the intellectual point of view, his merit may be summed up in those words of *Wisdom*: "Being made perfect in a short space, he fulfilled a long time." chap. iv.

This distinguished ecclesiastic, the boast of the Spanish clergy and the Catalan people, died at Vich, his native city, on the 9th of July, 1848, in the same spirit of lively faith and fervent piety which had always marked his life. His funeral took place on the 11th, with all the pomp that could be furnished by the civil and ecclesiastical authorities The municipality decreed that one of the public places should be named after him.

Balmes was little below the middle height, and of weak and slender frame. But the appearance of feeble health which he exhibited, was combatted by the animation of his looks. His forehead and lips bore the impress of energy, which was to be seen also in his eyes, black, deep-set, and of unusual brightness. The expression of his countenance was a mixture of vivacity, openness, melancholy and strength of mind. A careful observer of all his sacerdotal duties, he found in the practices of piety, the vigor which he displayed in his intellectual labors. The distribution of his time was extremely methodical, and his pleasures consisted only in the society of his friends. To the prospect of temporal honors and the favor of the great, he was insensible; neither did he seek after ecclesiastical dignities or literary distinctions. His aim was the diffusion of truth, not the acquisition of a great reputation. These qualities, however, with his eminent talents, varied erudition, and invaluable writings, have won for him a universal fame.

TABLE OF CONTENTS.

CHAPTER LIII.

OF THE FACULTIES OF THE CIVIL POWER.

CHAPTER LIV.

ON RESISTANCE TO THE CIVIL POWER.

CHAPTER LV.

ON RESISTANCE TO DE FACTO GOVERNMENTS.

CHAPTER LVI.

HOW IT IS ALLOWED TO RESIST THE CIVIL POWER.

CHAPTER LVII.

ON POLITICAL SOCIETY IN THE SIXTEENTH CENTURY.

CHAPTER LVIII.

ON MONARCHY IN THE SIXTEENTH CENTURY.

CHAPTER LIX.

ON ARISTOCRACY IN THE SIXTEENTH CENTURY.

CHAPTER LX.

ON DEMOCRACY IN THE SIXTEENTH CENTURY.

CHAPTER LXI.

VALUE OF DIFFERENT POLITICAL FORMS—CHARACTER OF MONARCHY IN EUROPE.

CHAPTER LXII.

HOW MONARCHY WAS STRENGTHENED IN EUROPE.

CHAPTER LXIII.

TWO SORTS OF DEMOCRACY.

CHAPTER LXIV.

CONTEST BETWEEN THE THREE SOCIAL ELEMENTS.

CHAPTER LXV.

POLITICAL DOCTRINES BEFORE THE APPEARANCE OF PROTESTANTISM.

CHAPTER LXVI.

OF POLITICAL DOCTRINES IN SPAIN.

CHAPTER LXVII.

POLITICAL LIBERTY AND RELIGIOUS INTOLERANCE.

CHAPTER LXVIII.

UNITY IN FAITH RECONCILED WITH POLITICAL LIBERTY.

CHAPTER LXIX.

INTELLECTUAL DEVELOPMENT UNDER THE INFLUENCE OF CATHOLICITY.

CHAPTER LXX.

HISTORICAL ANALYSIS OF INTELLECTUAL DEVELOPMENT.

CHAPTER LXXI.

RELIGION AND THE HUMAN INTELLECT IN EUROPE.

CHAPTER LXXII.

PROGRESS OF THE HUMAN MIND FROM THE ELEVENTH CENTURY TO THE PRESENT TIME.

CHAPTER LXXIII.

SUMMARY OF THE WORK—DECLARATION OF THE AUTHOR.

TABLE OF NOTES.

PROTESTANTISM

COMPARED WITH

CATHOLICITY.

CHAPTER I.

NAME AND NATURE OF PROTESTANTISM.

THERE is a fact in existence among civilized nations, very important on account of the nature of the things which it affects—a fact of transcendent importance, on account of the number, variety, and consequence of its influences—a fact extremely interesting, because it is connected with the principal events of modern history. This fact is Protestantism.

Like a clap of thunder, it attracted at once the attention of all Europe; on one side it spread alarm, and on the other excited the most lively sympathy: it grew so rapidly, that its adversaries had not time to strangle it in its cradle. Scarcely had it begun to exist, and already all hope of stopping, or even restraining it, was gone; when, emboldened by being treated with respect and consideration, it became every day more daring; if exasperated by rigour, it openly resisted measures of coercion, or redoubled and concentrated its forces, to make more vigorous attacks. Discussions, the profound investigations and scientific methods which were used in combating it, contributed to develope the spirit of inquiry, and served as vehicles to propagate its ideas.

By creating new and prevailing interests, it made itself powerful protectors; by throwing all the passions into a state of fury, it aroused them in its favor It availed itself, by turns, of stratagem, force, seduction, or violence, according to the exigencies of times and circumstances. It attempted to make its way in all directions; either destroying impediments, or taking advantage of them, if they were capable of being turned to account.

When introduced into a country, it never rested until it had obtained guarantees for its continued existence; and it succeeded in doing so everywhere. After having obtained vast establishments in Europe—which it still retains—it was transported into other parts of the world, and infused into the veins of simple and unsuspecting nations.

In order to appreciate a fact at its just value, to embrace it in all its relations, and to distinguish properly between them, it is necessary to examine whether the constituting principle of the fact can be ascertained, or at least whether we can observe in its appearance any characteristic trait capable of revealing its inward nature. This examination is very difficult when we have to do with a fact of the kind and importance of that which now occupies our attention. In matters of this sort, numbers of opinions accumulate in the course of time, in favor of all which arguments have been sought. The inquirer, in the midst of so many and such various objects, is perplexed, disconcerted, and confounded; and if he wish to place himself in a more advantageous point of view, he finds the ground so covered with fragments, that he cannot make his way without risk of losing himself at every step.

The first glance which we give to Protestantism, whether we consider its actual condition, or whether we regard the various phases of its history, shows us that it is very difficult to find any thing constant in it, any thing which can be assigned as its constituent character. Uncertain in its opinions, it modifies them continually, and changes them in a thousand ways. Vague in its tendencies, and fluctuating in its desires, it attempts every form, and essays every road. It can never attain to a well-defined existence; and we see it every moment enter new paths, to lose itself in new labyrinths.

Catholic controversialists have pursued and assailed it in every way; ask them what has been the result? They will tell you that they had to contend with a new Proteus, which always escaped the fatal blow by changing its form. If you wish to assail the doctrines of Protestantism, you do not know where to direct your attacks, for they are unknown to you, and even to itself. On this side it is invulnerable, because it has no tangible body. Thus, no more powerful argument has ever been urged, than that of the immortal Bishop of Meaux —viz. "You change; and that which changes is not the truth." An argument much feared by Protestantism, and with justice; because all the various forms which are assumed to evade its force, only serve to strengthen it. How just is the expression of that great man! At the very title of his book, Protestantism must tremble: The History of the Variations! A history of variations must be a history of error. (See note at the end of the vol.)

These unceasing changes, which we ought not to be surprised at finding in Protestantism, because they essentially belong to it, show us that it is not in possession of the truth; they show us also, that its moving principle is not a principle of life, but an element of dissolution. It has been called upon, and up to this time in vain, to fix itself, and to present a compact and uniform body. How can that be fixed, which is, by its nature, kept floating about in the air? How can a solid body be formed of an element, the essential tendency of which is towards an incessant division of particles, by diminishing their reciprocal affinity, and increasing their repellent force?

It will easily be seen that I speak of the right of private judgment in matters of faith, whether it be looked upon as a matter of human reason alone, or as an individual inspiration from heaven.

If there be any thing constant in Protestantism, it is undoubtedly the substitution of private judgment for public and lawful authority. This is always found in union with it, and is, properly speaking, its fundamental principle: it is the only point of contact among the various Protestant sects,—the basis of their mutual resemblance. It is very remarkable that this exists, for the most part, unintentionally, and sometimes against their express wishes.

However lamentable and disastrous this principle may be, if the coryphæi of Protestantism had made it their rallying point, and had constantly acted up to it in theory and practice, they would have been consistent in error. When men saw them cast into one abyss after another, they would have recognised a system,—false undoubtedly; but, at any rate, a system. As it is, it has not been even that: if you examine the words and the acts of the first Reformers, you will find that they made use of this principle as a means of resisting the authority which controlled them, but that they never dreamed of establishing it permanently; that if they labored to upset lawful authority, it was for the purpose of usurping the command themselves; that is to say, that they followed, in this respect, the example of revolutionists of all kinds, of all ages, and of all countries. Everybody knows how far Luther carried his fanatical intolerance; he who could not bear the slightest contradiction, either from his own disciples or anybody else, without giving way to the most senseless fits of passion, and the most unworthy outrages. Henry VIII. of England, who founded there what is called the liberty of thinking, sent to the scaffold those who did not think as he did; and it was at the instigation of Calvin that Servetus was burnt alive at Geneva.

I insist upon this point, because it seems to me to be of great importance. Men are but too much inclined to pride; and if they heard it constantly repeated, without contradiction, that the innovators of the sixteenth century proclaimed the freedom of thought, a secret interest might be excited in their favor; their violent declamations might be regarded as the expressions of a generous movement, and their efforts as a noble attempt to assert the rights of intellectual freedom. Let it be known, never to be forgotten, that if these men proclaimed the principle of free examination, it was for the purpose of making use of it against legitimate authority; but that they attempted, as soon as they could, to impose upon others the yoke of their own opinions. Their constant endeavour was, to destroy the authority which came from God, in order to estalish their own upon its ruins. It is a painful necessity to be obliged to give proofs of this assertion; not because they are difficult to find, but because one cannot adduce the most incontestable of them without calling to mind words and deeds which not only cover with disgrace the founders of Protestantism, but are of such a nature, that they cannot be mentioned without a blush on the cheek, or written without a stain upon the paper. (2)

Protestantism, when viewed in a mass, appears only a shapeless collection of innumerable sects, all opposed to each other, and agreeing only in one point, viz. in protesting against the authority of the Church. We only find among them particular and exclusive names, commonly taken from the names of their founders; in vain have they made a thousand efforts to give themselves a general name expressive of a positive idea; they are still called after the manner of philosophical sects. Lutherans, Calvinists, Zuinglians, Anglicans, Socinians, Arminians, Anabaptists, all these names, of which I could furnish an endless host, only serve to exhibit the narrowness of the circle in which these sects are enclosed; and it is only necessary to pronounce them, to show that they contain nothing universal, nothing great.

Everybody who knows any thing of the Christian religion must be convinced by this fact alone, that these sects are not truly Christian. But what occurred when Protestantism attempted to take a general name, is singularly remarkable. If you examine its history, you will see that all the names which it attempted to give itself failed, if they contained any positive idea, or any mark of Christianity; but that it adopted a name taken by chance at the Diet of Spires; a name which carries with it its own condemnation, because it is repugnant to the origin, to the spirit, to the maxims, to the entire history of the Christian religion; a name which does not express that unity—that union which is inseparably connected with the Christian name; a name which is peculiarly becoming to it, which all the world gives to it by acclamation, which is truly its own—viz. *Protestantism.* (3)

Within the vast limits marked out by this name, there is room for every error and for every sect. You may deny with the Lutherans the liberty of man, or renew with the Arminians the errors of Pelagius. You may admit with some that real presence, which you are free to reject with the Calvinists and Zuinglians; you may join with the Socinians in denying the divinity of Jesus Christ; you may attach yourself to Episcopalians, to Puritans, or, if you please, to the extravagances of the Quakers; it is of no consequence, for you always remain a Protestant, for you protest against the authority of the Church; your field is so extensive, that you can hardly escape from it, however great may be your wanderings; it contains all the vast extent that we behold on coming forth from the gates of the Holy City. (4)

CHAPTER II.

CAUSES OF PROTESTANTISM.

WHAT, then, were the causes of the appearance of Protestantism in Europe, of its development, and of its success? This is a question well worthy of being examined to the bottom, because it will lead us to inquire into the origin of this great evil, and will put us in a condition to form the best idea of this phenomenon, so often but so imperfectly described.

It would be unreasonable to look for the causes of an event of this nature and importance, in circumstances either trivial in themselves, or circumscribed by places and events of a limited kind. It is a mistake to suppose that vast results can be produced by trifling causes; and if it be true that great events sometimes have their commencement in little ones, it is no less certain that the commencing point is not the cause; and that to be the commencement of a thing, and to be its real cause, are expressions of a widely different meaning. A spark produces a dreadful conflagration, but it is because it falls upon a heap of inflammable materials. That which is general must have general causes; and that which is lasting and deeply rooted must have lasting and profound causes.

This law is true alike in the moral as in the physical order; but its applications cannot be perceived without great difficulty, especially in the moral order, where things of great importance are sometimes clothed in a mean exterior; where each effect is found allied with so many causes at once, connected with them by ties so delicate, that, possibly, the most attentive and piercing eye may miss altogether, or regard as a trifle, that which perhaps has produced very great results: trifling things, on the other hand, are frequently so covered with glitter, tinsel, and parade, that it is very easy to be deceived by them. We are always too much inclined to judge by appearances.

It will appear from these principles, that I am not disposed to give great importance to the rivalry excited by the preaching of indulgences, or to the excesses which may have been committed by some inferiors in this matter; these things may have been an occasion, a pretext, a signal to commence the contest, but they were of too little importance in themselves to put the world in flames. There would be, perhaps, more apparent plausibility in seeking for the causes of Protestantism in the characters and positions of the first reformers; but this also would be unsatisfactory.

People lay great stress on the violence and fury of the writings and speeches of Luther, and show how apt this savage eloquence was to inflame men's minds, and drag them into the new errors by the deadly hatred against Rome with which it inspired them. Too much stress also is laid on the sophistical art, the order and elegance of the style of Calvin; qualities which served to give an appearance of regularity to the shapeless mass of new errors, and make them more acceptable to men of good taste. The talents and other qualities of the various innovators are described in the same way with more or less truth.

I will not deny to Luther, Calvin, and the other founders of Protestantism, the titles on which their sad celebrity is founded; but I venture to assert that we cannot attribute to their personal qualities the principal influence upon the development of this evil, without palpably mistaking and underrating the importance of the evil itself, and forgetting the instructions of universal history.

If we examine these men with impartiality, we shall find that their qualities were not greater than those of other sectarian leaders, if so great. Their talents, their learning, and their knowledge, have passed through the crucible of criticism, and there is, even among Protestants, no well-instructed and impartial person who does not now consider the extravagant eulogiums which have been lavished upon them, as the exaggerations of party. They are classed among the number of those turbulent men who are well fitted to excite revolutions; but the history of all times and countries, and the experience of every day, teach that men of this kind are not uncommon, and that they arise everywhere when a sad combination of events affords them a fit opportunity.

When causes more in proportion to Protestantism, by their extent and importance, are sought for, two are commonly pointed out: the necessity of reform, and the spirit of liberty. "There were numerous abuses," says one party, "legitimate reform was neglected: this negligence produced revolution." "The human intellect was in fetters," says another; "the mind longed to break its chains; Protestantism was only a grand effort for the freedom of human thought, a great movement towards liberating the human mind." It is true, that these two opinions point out causes of great importance and of wide extent: both are well adapted to make partisans. The one, by establishing the necessity of reform, opens a wide field for the censure of neglected laws and relaxed morals; this theme always finds sympathy in the heart of man,—indulgent towards its own defects, but stern and inexorable towards the faults of others. With respect to the other opinion, which raises the cry of the movement of religious liberty and the freedom of the human mind, it is sure to be widely adopted: there are always a thousand echoes to a cry which flatters our pride.

I do not deny that a reform was necessary; to be convinced of this, I need only glance at history, and listen to the complaints of several great men, justly regarded by the Church as among the most cherished of her sons. I read in the first decree of the Council of Trent, that one of the objects of the Council was the reform of the Christian clergy and people; I learn from the mouth of Pius IV., when confirming the said Council, that one of the objects for which it was assembled, was the correction of morals, and the re-establishment of discipline. Notwithstanding all this, I am not inclined to give to abuses so much influence as has been attributed to them. I must also say, that it appears to me that we give a very bad solution of the question, when, to show the real cause of the evil, we insist on the fatal results produced by these abuses. These words also, "a new movement of liberty," appear to me altogether insufficient. I shall say, then, with freedom, in spite of my respect for those who entertain the first opinion, and my esteem for the talents of those who refer all to the spirit of liberty, that I cannot find in either that analysis, at once philosophical and historical, which, without wandering from the ground of history, examines facts, clears them up, shows their inward nature, their relations and connections.

If men have wandered so much in the definition and explanation of Protestantism, it is because they have not sufficiently observed that it is not only a fact common to all ages of the history of the Church, but that its importance and its particular characteristics are owing to the epoch when it arose. This simple consideration, founded on the constant testimony of history, clears up every thing; we have no longer to seek in the doctrines of Protestantism for any thing singular or extraordinary; all its characteristics prove that it was born in Europe, and in the sixteenth century. I shall develope these ideas, not by fanciful reasonings or gratuitous suppositions, but by adducing facts which nobody can deny.

It is indisputable that the principle of submission to authority in matters of faith has always encountered a vigorous resistance in the human mind. I shall not point out here the causes of this resistance; I propose to do so in the course of this work; I shall content myself at present with stating this fact, and reminding those who may be inclined to call it in question, that the history of the Church has always been accompanied by the history of heresies. This fact has presented different phases according to the changes of time and place. Sometimes making a rude mixture of Judaism and Christianity, sometimes combining the doctrines of Jesus Christ with the dreams of the East, or corrupting the purity of faith by the subtilties and chicaneries of Grecian sophistry; this fact presents us with as many different aspects as there are conditions of the mind of man. But we always find in it two general characteristics, which clearly show that it has always had the same origin, notwithstanding the variation in its object and in the nature of its results: these two characteristics are, hatred of the authority of the Church, and the spirit of sect.

In all ages sects have arisen, opposing the authority of the Church, and establishing as dogmas the errors of their founders: it was natural for the same thing to happen in the sixteenth century. Now, if that age had been an exception to the general rule, it seems to me, looking at the nature of the human mind, that we should have had to answer this very difficult question, How is it possible that no sect appeared in that age? I say, then, error having once arisen in the sixteenth century, no matter what may have been its origin, occasion, and pretext—a certain number of followers having assembled around its banner—Protestantism forthwith presents itself before me in all its extent, with its transcendent importance, its divisions, and subdivisions; I see it, with boldness and energy, making a general attack on all the doctrines and discipline taught and observed by the Church. In place of Luther, Zuinglius, and Calvin, let us suppose Arius, Nestorius, and Pelagius; in place of the errors of the former, let them teach the errors of the latter; it will all lead to the same result. The errors will excite sympathy; they will find defenders; they will animate enthusiasts; they will spread, they will be propagated with the rapidity of fire, they will be diffused, they will throw sparks in all directions; they will all be defended with a show of knowledge and erudition; creeds will change unceasingly; a thousand professions of faith will be drawn up; the liturgy will be altered,—will be destroyed; the bonds of discipline will be broken; we shall have to sum up all in one word, Protestantism.

How did it happen that the evil in the sixteenth century was necessarily so extensive, so great, and so important? It was because the society of that time was different from any other that had preceded it; that which at other times would only have produced a partial fire, necessarily caused in the sixteenth century a frightful conflagration. Europe was then composed of a number of immense states, cast, so to speak, in the same mould, resembling each other in ideas, manners, laws and institutions, drawn together incessantly by an active communication which was kept up alternately by rival and common interests; knowledge found in the Latin language an easy means of diffusion; in fine, most important of all, there had become general over all Europe a rapid means of disseminating ideas and feelings, a creation which had flashed from the human mind like a miraculous illumination, a presage of colossal destinies, viz. the press.

Such is the activity of the mind of man, and the ardour with which it embraces all sorts of innovation, that when once the standard of error was planted, a multitude of partisans were sure to rally round it. The yoke of authority once thrown off, in countries where investigation was so active, where so many discussions were carried on, where ideas were in such a state of effervescence, and where all the sciences began to germinate, it was impossible for the restless mind of man to remain fixed on any point, and a swarm of sects was necessarily produced. There is no middle path; either civilized nations must remain Catholic, or run through all the forms of error. If they do not attach themselves firmly to the anchor of truth, we shall see them make a general attack upon it, we shall see them assail it in itself, in all that it teaches, in all that it prescribes. A man of free and active mind will remain tranquil in the peaceful regions of truth, or he will seek for it with restlessness and disquietude. If he find only false principles to rest on,—if he feel the ground move under his feet, he will change his position every moment, he will leap from error to error, and precipitate himself from one abyss to another. To live amid errors, and be contented with them, to transmit error from generation to generation, without modification or change, is peculiar to those who vegetate in debasement and ignorance; there the mind of man is not active, because it is asleep.

From the point of view where we have now placed ourselves, we can see Protestantism such as it is. From this commanding position we see every thing in its place, and it is possible for us to appreciate its dimensions, to perceive its relations, calculate its influence, and explain its anomalies. Men there assume their true position; as they are seen in close proximity with the great mass of events, they appear in the picture as very small figures, for which others may be substituted without inconvenience; which may be placed nearer or farther off, and the features and complexion of which are not of any consequence. Of what importance, then, are the energy of character, the passion, and boldness of Luther, the literary polish of Melancthon, and the sophistical talents of Calvin? We are convinced, that to lay stress upon all this, is to lose our time, and explain nothing.

What were these men, and the other coryphæi of Protestantism? Was there any thing really extraordinary about them? We shall find men like them everywhere. There are some among them who did not surpass mediocrity; and it may be said of almost all, that if they had not obtained an unhappy celebrity, they would hardly have been celebrated at all. Why, then, did they effect such great things? They found a mass of combustibles, and they set them on fire. Certainly this was not difficult, and yet it was all they did. When I see Luther, mad with pride, commit those extravagances which were the subject of so many lamentations on the part of his friends—when I see him grossly insult all who oppose him, put himself in a passion, and vomit forth a torrent of impure words against all those who do not humble themselves in his presence, I am scarcely moved by any other feeling than pity. This man, who had the extraordinary mania of calling himself the *Notharius Dei*, became delirious; but he breathed, and his breath was followed by a terrible conflagration: it was because a powder-magazine was at hand on which he threw a spark. Nevertheless, like a man blinded by insanity, he cried out, "Behold my power! I breathe, and my breath puts the world in flames!"

But, you will ask me, what was the real influence of abuses? If we take care not to leave the point of view where we now are, we shall see that they were an occasion, and that they sometimes afforded food, but that they did not exercise all the influence which has been attributed to them. Do I wish, then, to deny, or to excuse them? Not at all. I can appreciate the complaints of some men, who are worthy of the most profound respect; but while lamenting the evil, these men never pretended to detail the consequences. The just man when he raises his voice against vice, the minister of the sanctuary when he is burning with zeal for the house of the Lord, express themselves in accents so loud and vehement, that they must not always be taken literally. Their whole hearts are opened, and, inflamed as they are with a zealous love of justice, they make use of burning words. Men without faith interpret their expressions maliciously, exaggerating and misrepresenting them.

It appears to me to be clear, from what I have just shown, that the principal cause of Protestantism is not to be found in the abuses of the middle ages. All that can be said is, that they afforded opportunities and pretexts for it. To assert the contrary would be to maintain that there were always numerous abuses in the Church from the beginning, even in the time of her primitive fervor, and of that proverbial purity of which our opponents have said so much; for even then there were swarms of sects who protested against her doctrines, denied her divine authority, and called themselves the true Church. The case is the same, and the inference cannot be denied. If you allege the extent and rapid propagation of Protestantism, I will remind you that such was also the case with other sects; I will repeat to you the words of St. Jerome, with regard to the ravages of Arianism: "All the world groans, and is full of astonishment at finding itself Arian." I will repeat, again, that if you observe any thing remarkable and peculiar belonging to Protestantism, it ought not to be attributed to abuses, but to the epoch when it appeared.

I believe I have said enough to give an idea of the influence which abuses could exert; yet, as it is a subject which has occupied much attention, and on which many mistakes have been made, it will be well to revert to it once more, to make our ideas on the subject still clearer. That lamentable abuses had crept in during the course of the middle ages, that the corruption of manners had been great, and that, consequently, reform was required, is a fact which cannot be denied. This fact is proved to us, with respect to the eleventh and twelfth centuries, by irreproachable witnesses, such as St. Peter Damien, St. Gregory VII., and St. Bernard. Some centuries later, even after many abuses had been corrected, they were still but too considerable, as is witnessed by the complaints of men who were inflamed with a desire of reform. We cannot forget the alarming words addressed by Cardinal Julian to Pope Eugenius IV., on the subject of the disorders of the clergy, especially those of Germany.

Having fully avowed the truth on this point, and my opinion that the cause of Catholicity does not require dissimulation or falsehood to defend it, I shall devote a few words to examining some important questions. Are we to blame the court of Rome or the bishops for these great abuses? I venture to think that they were to be attributed to the evils of the time alone. Let us call to mind the events which had taken place in the midst of Europe; the dissolution of the decrepit and corrupt empire of Rome; the irruption and inundation of northern barbarians; their fluctuations, their wars, sometimes with each other, and sometimes with the conquered nations, and that for so many ages; the establishment and absolute reign of feudalism, with all its inconveniences, its evils, its troubles, and disasters; the invasion of the Saracens, and their dominion over a large portion of Europe; now, let any reflecting man ask himself whether such revolutions must not of necessity produce ignorance, corruption of morals, and the relaxation of all discipline. How could the ecclesiastical society escape being deeply affected by this dissolution, this destruction of the civil society? Could she help participating in the evils of the horrible state of chaos into which Europe was then plunged?

But were the spirit and ardent desire of reforming abuses ever wanting in the Church? It can be shown that they were not. I will not mention the saints whom she did not cease to produce during these unhappy periods; history proves their number and their virtues, which, so vividly contrasting with the corruption of the age, show that the divine flames which descended on the Apostles had not been extinguished in the bosom of the Catholic Church. This fact proves much; but there is another still more remarkable, a fact less subject to dispute, and which we cannot be accused of exaggerating; a fact which is not limited to individuals, but which is, on the contrary, the most complete expression of the spirit by which the whole body of the Church was animated; I mean, the constant meeting of councils, in which abuses were reproved and condemned, and in which sanctity of morals and the observance of discipline were continually inculcated. Happily this consoling fact is indisputable; it is open to every eye; and to be aware of it, one only needs to consult a volume of ecclesiastical history, or the proceedings of councils. There is no fact more worth our attention; and I will add, that perhaps all its importance has not been observed.

Let us remark what passes in other societies: we see that in proportion to the change of ideas and manners, laws everywhere undergo a rapid modification;

and if manners and ideas come to be directly opposed to laws, the latter, reduced to silence, are soon either abolished or trodden under foot. Nothing of this sort has happened in the Church. Corruption has extended itself everywhere to a lamentable degree; the ministers of religion have allowed themselves to be carried away by the stream, and have forgotten the sanctity of their vocation; but the sacred fire did not cease to burn in the sanctuary; the law was there constantly proclaimed and inculcated; and, wonderful spectacle! the men who themselves violated it frequently assembled to condemn themselves, to censure their own conduct, and thus to render more public and more palpable the contrast which existed between their instructions and their actions. Simony and incontinence were the prevailing vices; if you open the canons of councils, you will find them everywhere anathematized Nowhere do you find a struggle so prolonged, so constant, so persevering, of right against wrong; you always see, throughout so many ages, the law, opposed face to face to the irregular passions, maintain itself firm and immovable, without yielding a single step, without allowing them a moment of repose or peace until they were subjugated. And this constancy and tenacity of the Church were not useless. At the commencement of the sixteenth century, at the time when Protestantism appeared, we find abuses comparatively less numerous, morals perceptibly improved, discipline become more strict, and observed with sufficient regularity. The time when Luther declaimed was not like that when St. Peter Damien and St. Bernard deplored the evils of the Church. The chaos was reduced to form; order, light, and regularity had made rapid progress; and an incontestable proof that the Church was not then plunged in such ignorance and corruption as is alleged, is, that she produced the great assemblage of saints who shed so much lustre on the age, and the men who displayed their eminent wisdom at the Council of Trent. Let us remember that great reforms require much time, that they met with much resistance both from the clergy and laity; that for having undertaken them with firmness, and urged them with vigour, Gregory VII. has been charged with rashness. Let us not judge of men without regard to times and places; and let us not pretend to measure every thing according to our own limited ideas; ages move in an immense orbit, and the variety of circumstances produces situations so strange and complicated that we can hardly form an idea of them.

Bossuet, in his History of the Variations, after having differently classed the spirit which guided certain men, before the thirteenth century, in their attempts at reform, and having cited the threatening words of Cardinal Julian on the subject of abuses, adds: "It is thus that, in the fifteenth century, this cardinal, the greatest man of his times, deplored these evils, and foresaw their fatal effects; by which he seems to have predicted those that Luther was about to bring on all Christianity, and in the first place on Germany; and he was not deceived when he thought that the neglect of reformation, and the increased hatred against the clergy, was about to produce a sect more dangerous to the Church than the Bohemians." (*Hist. des Variat.* liv. i.) It is inferred from these words that the illustrious Bishop of Meaux found one of the principal causes of Protestantism in the omission of a legitimate reform made in time. Nevertheless, we must not suppose from this that Bossuet meant, in any degree, to excuse the promoters of it, or that he had any idea of sanctioning their intentions; on the contrary, he ranked them as turbulent innovators, who, far from promoting the real reform which was desired by wise and prudent men, only served to render it more difficult, by introducing, by the means of their erroneous doctrines, the spirit of disobedience, schism, and heresy.

In spite of the authority of Bossuet, I cannot persuade myself to look upon abuses as one of the principal causes of Protestantism; but it is not necessary to repeat what I have said in support of this opinion. It may not, however, be useless to repeat, that the authority of Bossuet is misapplied when used to justify the intentions of the reformers, since the illustrious prelate is the first to declare them highly culpable, and to observe, that if abuses were in existence, their intention was not to correct them, but rather to make them a pretext for abandoning the faith of the Church, throwing off the yoke of lawful authority, breaking the bands of discipline, and introducing thereby disorder and licentiousness.

How, indeed, can we attribute to the reformers the real spirit of reform, when almost all of them proved the contrary by the ignominy of their own conduct? If they had condemned, by the austerity of their morals, or by devoting themselves to a severe asceticism, the relaxations of which they complained, there might be a question whether their extravagances were not the effects of exaggerated zeal, and if some excess in the love of virtue had not drawn them into error. But they did nothing of the kind. Let us hear on this point an eye-witness, a man who certainly cannot be accused of fanaticism, since the connection which he had with the leaders of Protestantism has rendered him culpable in the eyes of many. Behold what Erasmus said, with his usual wit and bitterness: "The reform, as far as it has gone, has been limited to the secularization of a few nuns and the marriage of a few priests; and this great tragedy finishes with an event altogether comic, since every thing is wound up, as in comedies, by a marriage."

This shows to conviction the true spirit of the innovators of the sixteenth century. It is clear that, far from wishing the reformation of abuses, they wished rather to increase them. This bare consideration of facts has led M. Guizot, on this point, into the path of truth, when he rejects the opinion of those who pretend, that the Reformation was "an attempt conceived and executed simply with the intention of reconstructing a pure and primitive Church. The Reformation," he said, "was not a mere attempt at religious amelioration, or the fruit of a Utopian humanity and virtue." (*Histoire Générale de la Civilisation en Europe*, douzième leçon.)

We shall have now no difficulty in appreciating at its just value the explanation which the same writer gives of this phenomenon. "The Reformation," says M. Guizot, "was a great attempt at the liberation of human thought—an uprising of the mind of man." This attempt, according to M. Guizot, arose out of the energetic movement given to the human mind, and the state of inaction into which the Roman Church had fallen; it arose from this, that the human mind advanced rapidly and impetuously, while the Church remained stationary. Explanations of this kind, and this one in particular, are very apt to draw admirers and proselytes; these ideas are high, and placed on a level so lofty and extended, that they cannot be looked at closely by the generality of readers; and, moreover, they appear in brilliant imagery, which blinds the sight and prejudices the judgment.

That which restrains freedom of thought, as understood by M. Guizot and other Protestants is, authority in matters of faith: it was, then, against this authority that the uprising of the mind declared itself; or, in other words, the mind rebelled, because it advanced, while the Church, immovable in her doctrines, was, according to the expression of M. Guizot, "in a stationary state."

Whatever may be the disposition of mind of M. Guizot towards the dogmas of the Catholic Church, he ought, as a philosopher, to have seen that it was a great mistake to point out as the distinctive characteristic of one period, that which had been at every time a glorious title for the Church. For more than eighteen hundred years the Church has been stationary in her dogmas, and it is no equivocal proof that she possesses the truth: the truth is unchangeable, because it is one.

What the Church was in the sixteenth century, she had been before, and she has been since. She had nothing particular, she adopted no new characteristic. The reason, then, by which it is attempted to explain this phenoménon, viz. the uprising of the mind, cannot advance the explanation a single step; and if this be the reason why M. Guizot compares the Church to governments grown old, we will tell him that she has had this old age from her cradle. M. Guizot, as if he had himself felt the weakness of his reasoning, presents his thoughts in groups, and as it were *pêle-mêle;* he parades before his readers ideas of different kinds, without taking pains to classify or distinguish them; one would be inclined to think that he meant to distract them by variety, and confound them by mixture. Judging, indeed, from the context of his discourse, the epithets *inert and stationary*, which he applies to the Church, do not appear, according to his intention, to relate to matters of faith; and he gives us to understand that he speaks rather of the pretensions of the Church with regard to politics and state economy. He has taken pains, elsewhere, to repel as calumnies, the charges of tyranny and intolerance which have been so often made against the court of Rome.

We find here an incoherence of ideas which was not to be expected in so clear a mind; and as many persons may scarcely be inclined to believe how far this incoherence extends, it is necessary to give his words literally: they will show us into what inconsistencies great minds can fall when they are placed in a false position.

"The government of the human mind, the spiritual power," says M. Guizot, "had fallen into an inert and stationary condition. The political influence of the Church, of the court of Rome, was much diminished; European society no longer was ruled by it; it had passed under the control of lay governments. Nevertheless, the spiritual power preserved all its pretensions, all its *éclat*, all its external importance. There happened in this respect, what has more than once happened to old governments. The greater part of the complaints made against it were hardly better founded."

It is evident that M. Guizot, in this passage, does not point out any thing which is at all connected with liberty, any thing which is not quite of another kind: why does he not do so? The court of Rome, he tells us, had seen its political influence diminished, and yet it preserved its pretensions; the direction of European society no longer belonged to it, but Rome kept its pomp and its external importance. Is any thing here meant besides the rivalries of which political affairs had been the subject? Did M. Guizot forget what he himself said some pages before, viz. that it did not appear to him to be reasonable to assign the rivalry of kings with the ecclesiastical power as the cause of Protestantism, and that such a cause was not adequate to the extent and importance of the event?

Although all this has no direct connection with freedom of thought, still, if any one be inclined to attribute the uprising of the mind to the intolerance of the court of Rome, let him listen to M. Guizot: "It is not true," says he, "that in the sixteenth century the court of Rome was very tyrannical; that abuses, properly so called, were then more numerous, more crying, than they had been at other times; never, perhaps, on the contrary, had the ecclesiastical power been more easy, more tolerant, more disposed to let things go their own way. Provided that it was not itself called in question, provided that the rights which it had formerly enjoyed were allowed in theory, that the same existence was secured, and the same tributes were paid to it, it would willingly have allowed the human mind to remain at peace, if the human mind had done the same in respect to it."

Thus M. Guizot seems to have forgotten what he had urged with the view of showing that the Protestant Reformation was a great attempt at the liberation of human thought—a rebellion of the mind of man. He does not allege any thing which was an obstacle to the freedom of man's thoughts; and he himself acknowledges that there was nothing to provoke this rebellion, as, for example, intolerance or cruelty; he has himself just told us that the ecclesiastical government of the sixteenth century, far from being tyrannical, was easy and tolerant, and that, if left to itself, it would willingly have allowed the human mind to remain tranquil.

It is, then, evident, that the great attempt at the liberation of the human mind is, in M. Guizot's mouth, only a vague, undefined expression,—a brilliant veil with which he seems to have wished to cover the cradle of Protestantism, even at the risk of being inconsistent with his own opinions. He reverts to the political rivalries which he before rejected. Abuses have no importance in his eyes; he cannot find in them the real cause; and he forgets what he had just asserted in the preceding lecture, viz. that if necessary reform had been made in time, the religious revolution might have been avoided.

He tries to give a picture of the obstacles to the liberty of thought, and endeavours to rise to the general considerations which embrace all the importance and influences of the human mind; but he stops at *éclat*, at *external importance*, and *political rivalries;* he lowers his flight to the level of tributes and services.

This incoherence of ideas, this weakness of reasoning, and forgetfulness of assertions previously made, will appear strange only to those who are accustomed rather to admire the high flights of talented men than to study their aberrations. It is true that M. Guizot was in a position in which it was very difficult to avoid being dazzled and deceived. If it be true that we cannot observe attentively what passes on the ground around us without narrowing our view of the horizon,—if this method leads the observer to form a collection of isolated facts rather than compare general maxims, it is not less certain that, by extending our observations over a larger space, we run the risk of many illusions. Too great generalization borders on hypothesis and fancy. The mind, when taking an immoderate flight in order to get a general view of things, no longer sees them as they really are; perhaps sometimes even loses sight of them altogether. Therefore it is that the loftiest minds should frequently remember the words of Bacon: "We do not want wings, but lead." Too impartial not to confess that abuses had been exaggerated,—too good a philosopher not to see that they could not have had so great an effect,—M. Guizot, who was prevented by his sense of dignity and decency from joining the crowd who incessantly raise the cry of cruelty and intolerance, has made an effort to do justice to the Church of Rome; but, unfortunately, his prejudices against the Church would not allow him to see things in their true light. He was aware that the origin of Protestantism must be sought in the human mind itself; but, knowing the age and epoch when he was speaking, he thought it was necessary to propitiate his audience by frequent appeals to liberty, in order that his discourse might be well received. This is the reason why, after having tempered the bitterness of his reproaches against the Church by a few soft words, he reserves all that is noble, grand, and generous for the ideas which produced the Reformation, and throws on the Church all the shadows of the picture.

While acknowledging that the principal cause of Protestantism is to be found in the human mind, it is easy to abstain from these unjust comparisons; and M. Guizot might have avoided the inconsistency to which we have alluded. He might have discovered the origin of the fact in the character of the human mind; he might, at the same time, have shown the greatness and importance of it, while simply explaining the nature and position of the societies in which it appeared. In fine, he might have observed that it was no *extraordinary effort,* but a mere repetition of what has happened in every age; and a phenomenon, the character of which depended on the particular state of the atmosphere in which it was produced.

This way of considering Protestantism as an ordinary event, increased and developed by the circumstances in which it arose, appears to me to be as philosophical as it is little attended to. I shall support it by another observation, which will supply us with reasons and examples at the same time.

The state of modern society for three hundred years has been such, that all the events that have occurred have acquired a character of generalization, and consequently an importance, which distinguishes them from all the events of a similar kind which occurred at other times and in a different social state. If we examine the history of antiquity, we shall see that all the events therein occurring were isolated in some sort from each other; this was what rendered them less beneficial when they were good, and less injurious when they were bad. Carthage, Rome, Sparta, Athens, all these nations more or less advanced in the career of civilization, each followed its own path, and progressed in a different way. Ideas, manners, political constitutions, succeeded each other, without our being able to perceive any influence of the ideas of one nation on those of another, or of the manners of one nation on those of another; we do not find any evidence of a tendency to bring nations to one common centre.

We also remark that, except when forced to intermix, ancient nations could be a long time in close proximity without losing their peculiarities, or suffering any important change by the contact.

Observe how different is the state of things in Europe in modern times. A revolution in one country affects all others; an idea sent forth from the schools agitates nations and alarms governments. Nothing is isolated, every thing is general, and acquires by expansion a terrible force. It is impossible to study the history of one nation without seeing all the others make their appearance on the stage; and we cannot study the history of a science or an art without discovering a thousand connections with objects which do not belong to science or to art.

All nations are connected, objects are assimilated, relations increase. The affairs of one nation are interesting to all the others, and they wish to take part in them. This is the reason why the idea of *non-intervention* in politics is, and always will be, impracticable; it is, indeed, natural for us to interfere in that in which we are interested.

These examples, although taken from things of a different kind, appear to me very well calculated to illustrate my idea of the religious events of that period. Protestantism, it is true, is thereby stripped of the philosophic mantle by which it has been covered from its infancy; it loses all right to be considered as full of foresight, magnificent projects, and high destinies, from its cradle; but I do not see that its importance and extent are thereby diminished; the fact itself, in a word, is unimpaired, but the real cause of the imposing aspect in which it has presented itself to the world is explained.

Every thing, in this point of view, is seen in its just dimensions; individuals are scarcely perceived, and abuses appear only what they really are—opportunities and pretexts; vast plans, lofty and generous ideas, and efforts at independence of mind, are only gratuitous suppositions. Thence ambition, war, the rivalry of kings, take their position as causes more or less influential, but always in the second rank. All the causes are estimated at their real value; in fine, the principal causes being once pointed out, it is acknowledged that the fact was sure to be accompanied in its development by a multitude of subordinate agents. There remains still an important question in this matter, viz. what was the cause of the hatred, or rather the feeling of exasperation, on the part of sectarians against Rome? Was it owing to some great abuse, some great wrong on the part of Rome? There is but one answer to make, viz. that in a storm, the waves always dash with fury against the immovable rock which resists them.

So far from attributing to abuses all the influence which has been assigned to them on the birth and development of Protestantism, I am convinced, on the contrary, that all imaginable legitimate reforms, and the greatest degree of willingness on the part of the Church authorities to comply with every exigence, would not have been able to prevent that unhappy event.

He has paid little attention to the extreme inconstancy and fickleness of the human mind, and studied its history to little purpose, who does not recognise in the event of the sixteenth century one of those great calamities which God alone can avert by a special intervention of his providence. (5)

CHAPTER III.

EXTRAORDINARY PHENOMENON IN THE CATHOLIC CHURCH.

THE proposition contained in the concluding lines of the last chapter suggests a corollary, which, if I am not mistaken, offers a new demonstration of the divine origin of the Catholic Church. Her existence for eighteen centuries, in spite of so many powerful adversaries, has always been regarded as a most extraordinary thing. Another prodigy, too little attended to, and of not less importance when the nature of the human mind is taken into account, is, *the unity of the Church's doctrines, pervading, as it does, all her various instructions, and the number of great minds which this unity has always enclosed within her bosom.*

I particularly call the attention of all thinking men to this point; and although I cannot hope to develope this idea in a suitable manner, I am sure they will find in it matter for very serious reflection. This method of considering the Church may perhaps recommend itself to the taste of some readers on another account, viz. because I shall lay aside Revelation, in order to consider Catholicity, not as a Divine religion, but as a school of philosophy.

No one who has studied the history of letters can deny that the Church has, in all ages, possessed men illustrious for science. The history of the Fathers of the first ages of the Church is nothing but the history of the most learned men in Europe, in Africa, and in Asia; the list of learned men who preserved, after the irruption of the Barbarians, some remains of ancient knowledge, is composed of churchmen. In modern times you cannot point out a branch of human knowledge, in which a considerable number of Catholics have not figured in the first rank. Thus there has been, for eighteen hundred years, an uninterrupted chain of learned men, who were Catholics, that is, men united in the profession of the doctrines taught by the Catholic Church. Let us lay aside for a moment the divine characteristics of Catholicity, to consider it only as a school or sect; I say, that in the fact which I have pointed out, we find a phenomenon so extraordinary, that its equal cannot be found elsewhere, and that no effort of reason can explain it, according to the natural order of human things.

It is certainly not new in the history of the human mind for a doctrine, more or less reasonable, to be professed for a time by a certain number of learned and enlightened men; this has been shown in schools of philosophy both ancient and modern. But for a creed to maintain itself for many ages, by preserving the adhesion of men of learning of all times and of all countries—of minds differing among themselves on other points—of men opposed in interests and divided by rivalries, is a phenomenon new, unique, and not to be found anywhere but in the Catholic Church. It always has been, and still is, the practice of the Church, while one in faith and doctrine, to teach unceasingly—to excite discussion on all subjects—to promote the study and examination of the foundations on which faith itself reposes—to scrutinize for this purpose the ancient languages, the monuments of the remotest times, the documents of history, the discoveries of scientific observation, the lessons of the highest and most analytic sciences, and to present herself with a generous confidence in the great lyceums, where men replete with talents and knowledge concentrate, as in a focus, all that they have learned from their predecessors, and all that they themselves have collected: and nevertheless we see her always persevere with firmness in her faith and in the unity of her doctrines; we see her always surrounded by illustrious men, who, with their brows crowned with the laurels of a hundred literary contests, humble themselves, tranquil and serene, before her, without fear of dimming the brightness of the glory which surrounds their heads.

We ask those who see in Catholicity only one of the innumerable sects by which the earth has been covered, to point out elsewhere a similar fact; to explain to us how the Church has been able to show us a phenomenon, constantly existing, so opposed to the ever-varying spirit of the human mind; let them tell us by what secret talisman the Sovereign Pontiffs have been able to do what other men have found impossible. Those men, who bowed their heads at the command of the Vatican, who have laid aside their own opinions to adopt those of a man called the Pope, were not simple and ignorant men. Look at them attentively; you will see in the boldness of their mien their knowledge of their own intellectual power; you will read in their bright and penetrating eyes the flame of genius which burns in their breasts. They are the same men who have filled the highest places in the academies of Europe; who have spread their fame over the world, and whose names have been handed down to future generations. Examine the history of all ages, search all the countries of the world, and if you find anywhere such an extraordinary combination of knowledge in union with faith, of genius in submission to authority, and of discussion without breach of unity, you will have made an important discovery, and science will have to explain a new phenomenon. But you know well that you cannot do so. This is the reason why you have recourse to new stratagems in order to cast a shade on the brightness of this fact; for you feel that impartial reason and common sense must draw from it the conclusion that there is in the Catholic Church something which is not to be found elsewhere.

These facts, say our adversaries, are certain; the reflections which they suggest are dazzling at first sight; but if we examine the subject thoroughly, we shall see the difficulties they raise disappear. This phenomenon, which we have seen realized in the Catholic Church, and which is not found elsewhere, only proves that there has always been in the Church a fixed system, which has been developed with uniform regularity. The Church knew that union is the source of strength; that union cannot exist without unity of doctrine; and that unity cannot be preserved without submission to authority. This simple observation established, and constantly maintained, the principle of submission. Such is the explanation of the phenomenon. The idea, we grant, is profoundly wise, the scheme is grand, the system is extraordinary; but they do not prove any thing in favor of the Divine origin of Catholicism.

This is the best reply which they can make; it is easy to show that the difficulty remains entire. Indeed, if it be true that there has existed a society on earth which has been for eighteen centuries guided by one fixed and constant principle—a society which has known how to bind to this principle eminent men of all ages and countries, the following questions must be asked of our adversaries:—Why has the Church alone possessed this principle, and monopolized this idea? If other sects have been in possession of it, why have they not acted on it? All the philosophic sects have disappeared, one after another;

the Church alone remains. Other religions, in order to preserve some sort of unity, have been compelled to shun the light, to avoid discussion, to hide themselves in the thickest shades. Why has the Church preserved her unity while seeking the light, while publishing her books in open day, while lavishing all sorts of instruction, and founding everywhere colleges, universities, and establishments of every description, where all the splendor of knowledge and erudition has been concentrated?

It is not enough to say that there was a plan—a system; the difficulty lies in the existence of this plan and this system; it consists in explaining how they were conceived and executed. If we had to do with a small number of men, in limited circumstances, times, and countries, for the execution of a limited project, there would be nothing extraordinary; but we have to do with a period of eighteen hundred years, with all the countries of the world, with circumstances the most varied, the most different, and the most opposed to each other; we have to do with a multitude of men who did not meet together, or act in concert. How is all this to be explained? If it were a plan and a system devised by man, we should ask, What was the mysterious power of Rome which enabled her to unite around her so many illustrious men of all times and of all countries? How did the Roman Pontiff, if he be only the chief of a sect, manage to fascinate the world to this extent? What magician ever did such wonders? Men have long declaimed against his religious despotism; why has no one been found to wrest the sceptre from his grasp? why has not a pontifical throne been raised capable of disputing the pre-eminence with his, and of maintaining itself with equal splendor and power? Shall we attribute it to his temporal power? This power is very limited. Rome was not able to contend in arms with any of the other European powers. Shall we attribute it to the peculiar character, to the knowledge or the virtues of the men who have occupied the Papal throne? There has been, during these eighteen hundred years, an infinite variety in the characters and in the talents and virtues of the Popes. For those who are not Catholics, who do not see in the Roman Pontiff the vicar of Jesus Christ,—the rock on which He has built His Church,—the duration of this authority must be the most extraordinary phenomenon; and it is certainly one of the questions most worthy of being examined by the science which devotes itself to the history of the human mind; how there existed for many centuries an uninterrupted series of learned men, always faithful to the doctrines of the Roman See?

M. Guizot himself, in comparing Protestantism with the Roman Church, seems to have felt the force of this truth; and its light appears to have made him confused in his remarks. Let us listen again to this writer, whose talents and renown have dazzled, on this point, so many readers, who do not examine the solidity of proofs when they are clothed in brilliant images, and who applaud all kinds of ideas when they are conveyed to them in a torrent of enchanting eloquence; men who, pretending to intellectual independence, subscribe, without inquiry, to the decisions of the leaders of their school; who receive their doctrines with submission, and dare not even raise their heads to ask for the titles of their authority. M. Guizot, like all the great men among Protestants, was aware of the immense void which exists amid its various sects, and of the force and vigour which is contained in Catholicity; he has not been able to free himself from the rule of great minds,—a rule which is explicitly confirmed by the writings of the greatest men of the Reformation. After pointing out the inconstant progress of Protestantism, and the error which it has introduced into the organization of intellectual society, M. Guizot proceeds thus: "People have not known how to reconcile the rights and necessities of tradition with those of liberty; and the cause of it undoubtedly has been, that the Reformation did not fully understand and accept either its principles or its effects." What sort of a religion must that be which does not fully understand and accept its principles or its effects?

Did a more formal condemnation of the Reformation ever issue out of the mouth of man? could any thing of the kind ever be said of the sects of philosophers, ancient or modern? Can the Reformation, then, after this, pretend to direct men or society? "Thence arises," continues M. Guizot, "a certain air of inconsistency and narrowness of spirit, which has often given advantages over it to its opponents. The latter knew very well what they did and what they wished; they ascended to the principles of their conduct, and avowed all their consequences. There never was a government more consistent, more systematic than that of the Church of Rome." But whence was the origin of a system so consistent? When we consider the fickleness and inconstancy of the human mind, do not this system, this consistency, and these fixed principles, speak volumes to the philosopher and man of good sense?

We have observed those terrible elements of dissolution which have their source in the mind of man, and which have acquired so much force in modern society; we have seen with what fatal power they destroy and annihilate all institutions, social, political, and religious, without ever succeeding in making a breach in the doctrines of Catholicity,—without altering that system, so fixed and so consistent. Is there no conclusion to be drawn from all this in favour of Catholicity? To say that the Church has done that which no schools, or governments, or societies, or religions could do, is it not to confess that she is wiser than every thing human? And does it not clearly prove that she does not owe her origin to human thought, and that she is derived from the bosom of the Creator? This society—formed, you say, by men—this government, directed by men, has endured for eighteen hundred years; it extends to all countries, it addresses the savage in the forest, the barbarian in his tent, the civilized man in the most populous cities; it reckons among its children the shepherd clothed in skins, the laborer, the powerful nobleman; it makes its laws heard alike by the simple mechanic at his work, and the man of learning in his closet absorbed in the profoundest speculations. This government has always had, according to M. Guizot, a full knowledge of its actions and its wishes; it has always been consistent in its conduct. Is not this avowal its most convincing apology, its most eloquent panegyric; and shall it not be considered a proof that it contains within itself something more than human?

A thousand times have I beheld this prodigy with astonishment; a thousand times have my eyes been fixed upon that immense tree which extends its branches from east to west, from north to south; I see beneath its shade a multitude of different nations, and the restless genius of man reposing in tranquillity at its feet.

In the East, at the period when this divine religion first appeared, I see, amidst the dissolutions of all sects, the most illustrious philosophers crowd to hear her words. In Greece, in Asia, on the banks of the Nile, in all the countries where, a short time before, swarmed innumerable sects, I see appear on a sudden a generation of great men, abounding in learning, in knowledge, in eloquence, and all agreeing in the unity of Catholic doctrine.

In the West, a multitude of barbarians throw themselves on an empire falling to decay; a dark cloud descends upon an horizon charged with calamities and disasters; there, in the midst of a people submerged in the corruption of morals, and having lost even the remembrance of their ancient grandeur, I see the only men who can be called worthy heirs of the Roman name, seek, in the retirement of their temples, an asylum for the austerity of their morals; it is there that they preserve, increase, and enrich the treasure of ancient knowledge. But my admiration reaches its height, when I observe that sublime intellect, worthy heir of the genius of Plato, which, after having sought the truth in all the schools, in all the sects, and with indomitable boldness run through all human errors, feels itself subjugated by the authority of the Church, and transforms the freethinker into the great Bishop of Hippo. In modern times the series of great men who shone in the times of Leo X. and Louis XIV. passes before my eyes. I see the illustrious race still continue throughout the calamities of the eighteenth century; and in the nineteenth I see fresh heroes, who, after having followed error in all directions, come to hang their trophies at the gates of the Catholic Church. What, then, is this prodigy? Has a sect or religion like it ever before been seen? These men study every thing, dispute on every thing, reply to every thing, know every thing; but always agreeing in unity of doctrine, they bend their noble and intellectual brows in respectful obedience to faith. Do we not seem to behold another planetary system, where globes of fire revolve in their vast orbits in the midst of immensity, always drawn to their centre by a mysterious attraction? That central force, which allows no aberration, takes from them nothing of their extent, or of the grandeur of their movement; but it inundates them with light, while giving to their motion a more majestic regularity. (6)

CHAPTER IV.

PROTESTANTISM AND THE MIND.

THIS fixedness of idea, this unanimity of will, this wisdom and constancy of plan, this progress with a firm step towards a definite object and end; and, in fine, this admirable unity, acknowledged in favor of Catholicism by M. Guizot himself, have not been imitated by Protestantism, either in good or evil. Protestantism, indeed, has not a single idea, of which it can say: "This is my own." It has attempted to appropriate to itself the principle of private judgment in matters of faith; and if several of its opponents have been too willing to accord it, it was because they were unable to find therein any other constitutive element; it was also because they felt that Protestantism, in boasting of having given birth to such a principle, labored to throw disgrace on itself, like a father who boasts of having unworthy and depraved sons. It is false, however, that Protestantism produced this principle of private judgment, since it was itself the offspring of that principle. That principle, before the Reformation, was formed in the bosom of all sects; it is the real germ of all errors; in proclaiming it, Protestants only yielded to a necessity which is common to all the sects separated from the Church.

There was therein no plan, no foresight, no system. The mere resistance to the authority of the Church included the necessity of unlimited private judgment, and the establishment of the understanding as supreme judge; even had the coryphæi of Protestantism wished from the first to oppose the consequences and applications of this right, the barrier was broken, and the torrent could not have been confined.

"The right of examining what we ought to believe," says a celebrated Protestant, (*Germany*, by Mad. de Staël, part iv. chap. 2), "is the foundation of Protestantism. The first Reformers did not think thus; they thought themselves able to place the pillars of Hercules of the mind according to their own lights; but they were mistaken in hoping to make those who had rejected all authority of this kind in the Catholic religion submit to their decisions as infallible." This resistance on their part proves, that they were not led by any of those ideas, which, although erroneous, show, in some measure, nobleness and generosity of heart; and that it is not of them that the human mind can say: "They have erred, but it was in order to give me more liberty of action."

"The religious revolution of the sixteenth century," says M. Guizot, "did not understand the true principles of intellectual liberty; it liberated the human mind, and yet pretended to govern it by law."

But it is in vain for man to struggle against the nature of things: Protestantism endeavored, without success, to limit the right of private judgment. It raised its voice against it, and sometimes appeared to attempt its total destruction; but the right of private judgment, which was in its own bosom, remained there, developed itself, and acted there in spite of it. There was no middle course for Protestantism to adopt: it was compelled either to throw itself into the arms of authority, and thus acknowledge itself in the wrong, or else allow the dissolving principle to exert so much influence on its various sects, as to destroy even the shadow of the religion of Jesus Christ, and debase Christianity to the rank of a school of philosophy.

The cry of resistance to the authority of the Church once raised, the fatal results might be easily imagined; it was thus easy to foresee that that poisoned germ, in its development, must cause the ruin of all the Christian truths; and what could prevent its rapid development in a soil where fermentation was so active? Catholics were not wanting to proclaim loudly the greatness and imminence of the danger; and it must be allowed that many Protestants foresaw it clearly. No one is ignorant that the most distinguished men of the sect gave their opinions on this point, even from the beginning. Men of the greatest talent never found themselves at ease in Protestantism. They always felt that there was an immense void in it; this is the reason why they have constantly inclined either towards irreligion or towards Catholic unity.

Time, the best judge of opinions, has confirmed these melancholy prognostics. Things have now reached such a pass, that those only who are very ill instructed, or who have a very limited grasp of mind, can fail to see that the Christian religion, as explained by Protestants, is nothing more than an opinion—a system made up of a thousand incoherent parts, and which is degraded to the level of the schools of philosophy. If Christianity still seems to surpass these schools in some respects, and preserves some features which cannot be found in what is the pure invention of the mind of man, it ought not to be a matter of astonishment. It is owing to that sublimity of doctrine and that sanctity of morality which, more or less disfigured, always shines while a trace is preserved of the words of Jesus Christ. But the feeble light which struggles with darkness after the sun has sunk below the horizon, cannot be compared to that of day: darkness advances and spreads; it extinguishes the expiring reflection, and night comes on. Such is the doctrine of Christianity among Protestants. A glance at these sects shows us that they are not purely philosophical, but it shows us at the same time that they have not the characters of true religion. Christianity has no authority therein; and is there like a being out of its proper element,—a tree deprived of its roots: its face is pale and disfigured like that of a corpse. Protestantism talks of faith, and its fundamental principle destroys it; it endeavors to exalt the gospel, and its own principle, by subjecting that gospel to private judgment, weakens its authority. If it speak of the sanctity and purity of Christian morality, it is reminded that some of its dissenting sects deny the divinity of Jesus Christ; and that they all may do so according to the principle on which it rests. The Divinity of Jesus Christ once doubted, the God-made man is reduced to the rank of a great philosopher and legislator; He has no longer the authority necessary to give to His laws the august sanction which renders them so holy in the eyes of men; He can no longer imprint upon them the seal which raises them above all human thoughts, and His sublime instructions cease to be lessons flowing from the lips of uncreated Wisdom.

If you deprive the human mind of the support of authority of some kind or other, on what can it depend? Abandoned to its own delirious dreams, it is forced again into the gloomy paths which led the philosophers of the ancient schools to chaos. Reason and experience are here agreed. If you substitute the private judgment of Protestants for the authority of the Church, all the great questions respecting God and man remain without solution. All the difficulties are left; the mind is in darkness, and seeks in vain for a light to guide it in safety: stunned by the voices of a hundred schools, who dispute without being able to throw any light on the subject, it relapses into that state of discouragement and prostration in which Christianity found it, and from which, with so much exertion, she had withdrawn it. Doubt, pyrrhonism, and indifference become the lot of the greatest minds; vain theories, hypothetical systems, and dreams take possession of men of more moderate abilities; the ignorant are reduced to superstitions and absurdities.

Of what use, then, would Christianity have been on the earth, and what would have been the progress of humanity? Happily for the human race, the Christian religion was not abandoned to the whirlwind of Protestant sects. In Catholic authority she has found ample means of resisting the attacks of sophistry and error. What would have become of her without it? Would the sublimity of her doctrines, the wisdom of her precepts, the unction of her counsels, have been now any thing more than a beautiful dream, related in enchanting language by a great philosopher? Yes, I must repeat, without the authority of the Church there is no security for faith; the divinity of Jesus Christ becomes a matter of doubt; His mission is disputed; in fact, the Christian religion disappears. If she cannot show us her heavenly titles, give us full certainty that she has come from the bosom of the Eternal, that her words are those of God Himself, and that He has condescended to appear on earth for the salvation of men, she has then lost her right to demand our veneration. Reduced to the level of human ideas, she must, then, submit to our judgment like other mere opinions; at the tribunal of philosophy she may endeavor to maintain her doctrines as more or less reasonable; but she will always be liable to the reproach of having wished to deceive us, by passing herself off as divine when she was only human; and in all discussions on the truth of her doctrines, she will have this fatal presumption against her, viz. that the account of her origin was an imposture.

Protestants boast of their independence of mind, and reproach the Catholic religion with violating the most sacred rights, by demanding a submission which outrages the dignity of man. Here extravagant declamation about the strength of our understanding is introduced with good effect; and a few seductive images and expressions, such as "*bold flights*" and "*glittering wings,*" &c., are enough to delude many readers.

Let the human mind enjoy all its rights; let it boast of possessing that spark of divinity called the intellect; let it pass over all nature in triumph, observing all the beings by which it is surrounded, and congratulate itself on its own immense superiority, in the midst of the wonders with which it has known how to embellish its abode; let it point out, as proofs of its strength and grandeur, the changes which are everywhere worked by its presence; by its intellectual force and boldness it has acquired the complete mastery over nature. Let us acknowledge the dignity and elevation of our minds to show our gratitude to our Creator, but let us not forget our weakness and defects. Why should we deceive ourselves by fancying that we know what we are really ignorant of? Why forget the inconstancy and variableness of our minds, and conceal the fact, that with respect to many things, even of those with which we are supposed to be acquainted, we have but confused ideas? How delusive is our knowledge, and what exaggerated notions we have of our progress in information? Does not one day contradict what another had affirmed? Time runs its course, laughs at our predictions, destroys our plans, and clearly shows how vain are our projects.

What have those geniuses who have descended to the foundations of science, and risen by the boldest flights to the loftiest speculations, told us? After having reached the utmost limits of the space which it is permitted to the human mind to range over,—after having trodden the most secret paths of science, and sailed on the vast ocean of moral and physical nature, the greatest minds of all ages have returned dissatisfied with the results. They have seen a beautiful illusion appear before their eyes,—the brilliant image which enchanted them has vanished; when they thought they were about to enter a region of light, they have found themselves surrounded with darkness, and they have viewed with affright the extent of their ignorance. It is for this reason that the greatest minds have so little confidence in the strength of the human intellect, although they cannot but be fully aware that they are superior to other men. The sciences, in the profound observation of Pascal, have two extrêmes which meet each other: the first is, the pure natural state of ignorance in which men are at their birth; the other extreme is, that at which great minds arrive when, having reached the utmost extent of human knowledge, they find that they know nothing, and that they are still in the same state of ignorance as at first. (*Pensées*, 1 partie, art. 6.)

Catholicism says to man, "Thy intellect is weak, thou hast need of a guide in many things." Protestantism says to him, "Thou art surrounded by light, walk as thou wilt; thou canst not have a better guide than thyself." Which of the two religions is most in accordance with the lessons of the highest philosophy?

It is not, therefore, surprising that the greatest minds among Protestants have all felt a certain tendency towards Catholicism, and have seen the wisdom of subjecting the human mind, in some things, to the decision of an infallible authority. Indeed, if an authority can be found uniting in its origin, its duration, its doctrines, and its conduct, all the characteristics of divinity, why should the mind refuse to submit to her; and what has it to gain by wandering, at the mercy of its illusions, on the most serious subjects, in paths where it only meets with recollections of errors, with warnings and delusions?

If the human mind has conceived too great an esteem for itself, let it study its own history, in order to see and understand how little security is to be found in its own strength. Abounding in systems, inexhaustible in subtilties; as ready in conceiving a project as incapable of maintaining it; full of ideas which arise, agitate, and destroy each other, like the insects which abound in lakes; now raising itself on the wings of sublime inspiration, and now creeping like a reptile on the face of the earth; as able and willing to destroy the works of others, as it is impotent to construct any durable ones of its own; urged on by the violence of passion, swollen with pride, confounded by the infinite variety of objects which present themselves to it; confused by so many false lights and so many deceptive appearances, the human mind, when left entirely to itself, resembles those brilliant meteors which dart at random through the immensity of the heavens, assume a thousand eccentric forms, send forth a thousand sparks, dazzle for a moment by their fantastic splendour, and disappear without leaving even a reflected light to illuminate the darkness.

Behold the history of man's knowledge! In that immense and confused heap of truth, error, sublimity, absurdity, wisdom, and folly, are collected the proofs of my assertions, and to that do I refer any one who may be inclined to accuse me of having overcharged the picture. (7)

CHAPTER V.

INSTINCT OF FAITH IN THE SCIENCES.

THE truth of what I have just advanced with respect to the weakness of our intellect, is proved by the fact that the hand of God has placed at the bottom of our souls a preservative against the excessive changeability of our minds, even in things which do not regard religion. Without this preservative all social institutions would be destroyed, or rather never would have had existence; without it the sciences would not have advanced a step, and when it had disappeared from the human heart, individuals and society would have been swallowed up by chaos.' I allude to a certain tendency to defer to authority—to the *instinct of faith*, if I may so call it—an instinct which we ought to examine with great attention, if we wish to know any thing of the human mind, and the history of its development.

It has often been observed that it is impossible to comply with the most urgent necessities, or perform the most ordinary acts of life, without respecting the authority of the statement of others; it is easy to understand that, without this faith, all the treasures of history and experience would soon be dissipated, and that even the foundation of all knowledge would disappear.

These important observations are calculated to show how vain is the charge against the Catholic religion, of requiring nothing but faith; but this is not my only object here; I wish to present the matter under another aspect, and place the question in such a position as to make this truth gain in extent and interest, without losing any thing of its immovable firmness. In looking over the history of human knowledge, and glancing at the opinions of our contemporaries, we constantly observe that the men who boast the most of their spirit of inquiry and freedom of thought, only echo the opinions of others. If we examine with attention that great study which, under the name of science, has made so much noise in the world, we shall observe that it contains at bottom a large portion of authority; and that if a perfectly free spirit of inquiry were to be introduced into it, even with respect to points of pure reason, the greatest part of the edifice of science would be destroyed, and very few men would remain in possession of its secrets.

No branch of knowledge, whatever may be the clearness and exactitude of which it boasts, is an exception to this rule. Do not the natural and exact sciences, rich as they are in evident principles, rigorous in their deductions, abounding in observation and experience, depend, nevertheless, for a great many of their truths, upon other truths of a higher nature; the knowledge of which necessarily requires a delicacy of observation, a power of calculation, a clear and penetrating *coup d'œil*, which belongs to few?

When Newton proclaimed to the scientific world the fruit of his profound calculations, how many of his disciples could flatter themselves that they were able to confirm them by their own convictions? I do not except from this question many of those who, by laborious efforts, had been able to comprehend something of this great man; they had followed the mathematician in his calculations, they had a full knowledge of the mass of facts and experience which the naturalist exposed to their view; they had listened to the reasons on which the philosopher rested his conjectures; in this way they thought that they were *fully convinced*, and that they did not owe their assent to any thing but the force of reason and evidence. Well, take away the name of Newton, efface from the mind the profound impression made by the authority of the man who made so extraordinary a discovery, and has employed so much genius in supporting it,—take away, I repeat it, the shade of Newton, and you will directly see, in the minds of his disciples, their principles vacillate, their reasonings become less convincing and exact, and their observations appear less in accordance with the facts. Then, he who thought himself a perfectly impartial observer, a perfectly independent thinker, will see and understand to how great an extent he was enthralled by the force of authority, by the ascendency of genius; he will find that, on a variety of points, he *assented* without being *convinced;* and that, instead of being a perfectly independent philosopher, he was only an obedient and accomplished pupil.

I appeal with confidence to the testimony, not of the ignorant, not of those who have only a smattering of scientific knowledge, but of real men of learning, of those who have devoted much time to the various branches of study. Let them look into their own minds, let them examine anew what they call their scientific convictions, let them ask themselves, with perfect calmness and impartiality, whether, even on those subjects in which they consider themselves the most advanced, their minds are not frequently controlled by the ascendency of some author of the first rank. I believe they will be compelled to acknowledge that, if they strictly applied the method of Descartes even to some of the questions which they have studied the most, they would find that they believe rather than are convinced. Such always has been, and such always will be, the case. It is a thing deeply rooted in the nature of our minds, and it cannot be prevented. Perhaps the regulation is a matter of absolute necessity; perhaps it contains much of that instinct of preservation which God, with so much wisdom, has diffused throughout society; perhaps it is intended to counteract the many elements of dissolution which society contains within its bosom. Undoubtedly, it is often very much to be regretted that men servilely follow in the footsteps of others, and injurious consequences not unfrequently are the result. But it would be still worse, if men constantly held themselves in an attitude of resistance to all others, for fear of deception. Woe to man and to society, if the philosophic mania of wishing to submit all matters to a rigorous examination were to become general in the world; and woe to science, if this rigorous, scrupulous, and independent scrutiny were extended to every thing.

I admire the genius of Descartes, and acknowledge the signal services which he has rendered to science; but I have more than once thought that, if his method of doubting became general for any time, society would be destroyed. And it seems to me that, among learned men themselves, among impartial philosophers, this method would do great harm; at least, it may be supposed that the number of men devoid of sense in the scientific world would be considerably increased.

Happily there is no danger of this being the case. If it be true that there is always in man a certain tendency towards folly, there is also always to be found there a fund of good sense which cannot be destroyed. When certain individuals of heated imaginations attempt to involve society in their delirium, society answers with a smile of derision; or if it allows itself to be seduced for a moment, it soon returns to its senses, and repels with indignation those who have endeavored to lead it astray. Passionate declamation against vulgar prejudice, against docility in following others and willingness to believe all without examination, is only considered as worthy of contempt by those who are intimately acquainted with human nature Are not these feelings participated in by many who belong not to the vulgar? Are not the sciences full of gratuitous suppositions, and have they not their weak points, with which, however, we are satisfied, as if they afforded a firm basis to rest upon?

The right of possession and prescription is also one of the peculiarities which the sciences present to us; and it is well worthy of remark that, without ever having borne the name, this right has been acknowledged by a tacit but unanimous consent. How can this be? Study the history of the sciences, and you will find at every step this right acknowledged and established. How is it, amid the continual disputes which have divided philosophers, that we see an old opinion make a long resistance to a new one, and sometimes succeed in preventing its establishment? It is because the old opinion was in possession, and was strengthened by the right of prescription. It is of no importance that the words were not used, the result was the same; this is the reason why discoverers have so often been despised, opposed, and even persecuted.

It is necessary to make this avowal, although it may be repugnant to our pride, and may scandalize some sincere admirers of the progress of knowledge These advances have been numerous; the field over which the human mind has exercised itself, and its sphere of action, are immense; the works by which it has proved its power are admirable; but there is always in all this a large portion of exaggeration, and it is necessary to make a considerable allowance, especially in the moral sciences. It cannot justly be inferred, from these exaggerated statements, that our intellect is capable of advancing in every path with perfect ease and activity; no deduction can be drawn from it to contradict the fact which we have just established, viz. the mind of man is almost always in subjection, even imperceptibly, to the authority of other men.

In every age there appear a small number of privileged spirits, who, by nature superior to all the rest, serve as guides in the various careers; a numerous crowd, who think themselves learned, follow them with precipitation, and, fixing their eyes on the standard which has been raised, rush breathlessly after it; and yet, strange as it is, they all boast of their independence, and flatter themselves that they are distinguishing themselves by pursuing the new path; one would imagine that they had discovered it, and that they were walking in it guided by their own light and inspirations. Necessity, taste, or a thousand other circumstances, lead us to cultivate this or that branch of knowledge; our own weakness constantly tells us that we have no creative power; that we cannot produce any thing of our own, and that we are incapable of striking out a new path; but we flatter ourselves that we share some part of the glory belonging to the illustrious chief whose banner we follow; we sometimes will succeed in persuading ourselves, in the midst of these reveries, that we do not fight under anybody's standard, and that we are only rendering homage to our own convictions, when, in reality, we are the proselytes of others.

Herein common sense shows itself to be wiser than our weak reason; and thus language, which gives such deep expression to things, where we find, without knowing whence they come, so much truth and exactitude, gives us a severe admonition on the subject of these vain pretensions. In spite of us, language calls things by their right names, and knows how to class us and our opinions according to the leader that we follow. What is the history of science but the history of the contests of a small number of illustrious men? If we glance over ancient and modern times, and bring into view the various branches of knowledge, we shall see a number of schools founded by a philosopher of the first rank, and then falling under the direction of another whose talents have made him worthy to succeed the founder. Thus the thing goes on, until circumstances having changed, or the spirit of vitality being gone, the school dies a natural death, unless a man of bold and independent mind appears, who takes the old school and destroys it, in order to establish his own doctrines on the ruins.

When Descartes dethroned Aristotle, did he not immediately take his place? Then philosophers pretended to independence—an independence which was contradicted by the very name they bore, that of Cartesians. Like nations who, in times of rebellion, cry out for liberty, dethrone their old king, and afterwards submit to the first man who has the boldness to seize the vacant throne.

It is thought in our age, as it has been in times gone by, that the human mind acts with perfect independence, owing to declamation against authority in scientific matters, and the exaltation of the freedom of thought. The opinion has become general that, in these times, the authority of any one man is worth nothing; it has been thought that every man of learning acts according to his own convictions alone. Moreover, systems and hypotheses have lost all credit, and a great desire for examination and analysis has become prevalent. This has made people believe not only that authority in scientific matters is completely gone, but that it is henceforth impossible.

At first sight there appears to be some truth in this; but if we look attentively around us, we shall observe that the number of leaders is only somewhat increased, and the time of their command somewhat shortened. Our age is truly one of commotions, literary and scientific revolutions, like those in politics, where nations imagine that they possess more liberty because the government is placed in the hands of a greater number of persons, and because they find more facility in getting rid of their rulers. They destroy those men to whom but a short time before they have given the names of fathers and liberators; then, the first transport being passed, they allow other men to impose upon them a yoke in reality not less heavy. Besides the examples afforded us by the history of the past century, at the present day we see only great names succeed each other, and the leaders of the human mind take each other's places.

In the field of politics, where one would imagine the spirit of freedom ought to have full scope, do we not see men who take the lead; and are they not looked upon as the generals of an army during a campaign? In the parliamentary arena, do we see any thing but two or three bodies of combatants, performing their evolutions under their respective chiefs with perfect regularity and discipline? These truths are well understood by those who occupy these high positions! They are acquainted with our weakness, and they know that men are commonly deceived by mere words. A thousand times must they have been tempted to smile, when, contemplating the field of their triumphs, and seeing themselves surrounded by followers who, proud of their own intelligence, admire and applaud them, they have heard one of the most ardent of their disciples boast of his unlimited freedom of thought, and of the complete independence of his opinions and his votes.

Such is man, as shown to us by history and the experience of every day. The inspiration of genius, that sublime force which raises the minds of some privileged men, will always exercise, not only over the ignorant, but even over the generality of men who devote themselves to science, a real fascination. Where, then, is the insult which the Catholic religion offers to reason when, presenting titles which prove her divinity, she asks for that faith which men grant so easily to other men in matters of various kinds, and even in things with which they consider themselves to be the best acquainted? Is it an insult to human reason to point out to him a fixed and certain rule with respect to matters of the greatest importance, while, on the other hand, she leaves him perfectly free to think as he pleases on all the various questions which God has left to his discretion? In this the Church only shows herself to be in accordance with the lessons of the highest philosophy. She shows a profound knowledge of the human mind, and she delivers it from all the evils which are inflicted by its fickleness, its inconstancy, and its ambition, combined as these qualities are with an extraordinary tendency to defer to the opinions of individuals. Who does not see that the Catholic Church puts thereby a check on the spirit of proselytism, of which society has had so much reason to complain? Since there is in man this irresistible tendency to follow the footsteps of another, does she not confer an eminent service on humanity, by showing it a sure way of following the example of a God incarnate? Does she not thus take human liberty under her protection, and at the same time save from shipwreck those branches of knowledge which are the most necessary to individuals and to society? (8)

CHAPTER VI.

DIFFERENCES IN THE RELIGIOUS WANTS OF NATIONS—MATHEMATICS—MORAL SCIENCES.

THE progress of society, and the high degree of civilization and refinement to which modern nations have attained, will no doubt be urged against the authority which seeks to exercise jurisdiction over the mind. In this way men will attempt to justify what they call the emancipation of the human mind. For my own part, this objection seems to have so little solidity, and to be so little supported by facts, that, from the progress of society, I should, on the contrary, conclude that there is the more need of that living rule which is deemed indispensable by Catholics.

To say that society in its infancy and youth may have required this authority as a check, but that this check has become useless and degrading since the human mind has reached a higher degree of development, is completely to mistake the connection which exists between the various conditions of our mind and the objects over which this authority extends. The true idea of God, the origin, the end, and the rule of human conduct, together with all the means with which God has furnished us to attain to our high destiny, such are the subjects with which faith deals, and with respect to which Catholics contend that it is necessary to have an infallible rule. They maintain that without this it would be impossible to avoid the most lamentable errors, and to protect truth from the effects of human passions.

This consideration will suffice to show, that private judgment would be much less dangerous among nations still less advanced in the career of civilization. There is, indeed, in a young nation, a great fund of natural candor and simplicity, which admirably disposes it to receive with docility the instructions contained in the sacred volume. Such a people will relish those things which are easily to be understood, and will bow with humility before the sublime obscurity of those pages which it has pleased God to cover with a veil of mystery. Moreover, the condition of this people, as yet exempt from the pride of knowledge, would create a sort of authority, since there would be found within its bosom only a small number of men able to examine divine revelation; and thus a centre for the distribution of instruction would be naturally formed.

But it is far otherwise with a nation far advanced in the career of knowledge. With the latter, the extension of knowledge to a greater number of individuals, by augmenting pride and fickleness, multiplies sects, and ends by revolutionizing ideas and corrupting the purest traditions. A young nation is devoted to simple occupations; it remains attached to its ancient customs; it listens with respect and docility to the aged, who, surrounded by their children and grandchildren, relate with emotion the histories and the maxims which they have received from their ancestors. But when society has reached a great degree of development, when respect for the fathers of families and veneration for gray hairs have become weakened; when pompous titles, scientific display, and grand libraries make men conceive a high idea of their intellectual powers; when the multitude and activity of communications widely diffuse those ideas, which, when put in motion, have an almost magical power of affecting men's minds, then it is necessary,—it is indispensable to have an authority, always living, always ready to act whenever it is wanted,—to cover with a protecting ægis the sacred deposit of truths which are the same in all times and places; truths without the knowledge of which man would be left to the mercy of his own errors and caprices from the cradle to the grave; truths on which society rests as its surest foundation; truths which cannot be destroyed without shaking to pieces the whole social edifice. The literary and political history of Europe for the last three hundred years affords but too many proofs of this. Religious revolution broke out at the moment when it was capable of doing the most harm: it found society agitated by all the activity of the human mind, and it destroyed the control when it was most necessary.

Undoubtedly, it is necessary to guard against depreciating the mind of man by charging it with faults which it has not, or by exaggerating those which it has; but it is no less improper to puff it up by exalting its strength too much. The latter would be injurious to it in several ways, and would be little likely to advance its progress; it would also, if properly understood, be little conformable to that gravity and discretion which ought to distinguish true science. Indeed, to merit the name, science ought to show the folly of being vain of what does not rightly belong to it; it ought to know its limits, and have sufficient candor and generosity to acknowledge its weakness.

There is a fact in the history of science, which, by revealing the intrinsic weakness of the mind, palpably shows the flattery of those unmeasured eulogies which are sometimes lavished on it, and also demonstrates to us how dangerous it would be to abandon it to itself without any guide. This fact is, the obscurity which increases in proportion as we approach the first principles of science; so that even in those sciences the truth, evidence, and exactness of which are considered the best established, it seems that no firm ground is to be obtained when we attempt to go to the bottom of them; and the mind, not finding any security, recoils in the fear of meeting with something to throw doubt and uncertainty on the truths of which it was convinced.

I do not participate in the ill-humor of Hobbes against the mathematics. Devoted to their progress, and deeply convinced as I am of the advantages which their study confers on the other sciences and on society, I shall not attempt to underrate their merit, or deny any of their great claims; but who can say that they are an exception to the general rule? Have they not their weak points and their darksome paths?

It is true that, when we confine ourselves to the explanation of the first principles of these sciences, and the deduction from them of the most elementary propositions, the mind is on firm ground, where no fear of making a false step occurs to it. I put aside at present the obscurity which would be found in idealogy and metaphysics, if they were to discuss certain points according to the writings of the most distinguished philosophers. Let us confine ourselves to the circle to which the mathematics are naturally confined. Who that has studied them is ignorant that you may reach a point in their theories, where the mind finds nothing but obscurity? The demonstration is before our eyes; it has been developed in all its parts; and yet the mind wavers, feeling within itself a kind of uncertainty which it cannot well describe. It sometimes happens that, after reasoning a long time, the truth rushes upon us like the light of day; but it is not until we have walked in darkness for a long period. When we fix our attention upon those thoughts which wander in our minds like moving lights, on those almost imperceptible emotions which, on these occasions, arise, and then die away in the soul, we observe that the mind, in the midst of its fluctuations, seeks instinctively for the anchor which is to be found in the authority of another. To reassure ourselves completely, we then invoke the authority of some great mathematicians, and we rejoice that the fact is placed beyond a doubt by the series of great men who have always viewed it in the same light. But perhaps our ignorance and pride will not admit the truth of these reflections. Let us, then, study these sciences, or at least read their history, and we shall be convinced that they afford numerous proofs of the weakness of the intellect.

Did not the extraordinary invention of Newton and Leibnitz find many opponents in Europe? Were there not required to establish it, both the sanction of time and the touchstone of experience, which made manifest the truth of their principles and the exactness of their reasonings? Do you believe that, if this invention were again, for the first time, to make its appearance in the field of science, even fortified with all the proofs which have been brought forward to strengthen it, and surrounded with all the light which so many explanations have shed upon it,—do you believe, I say, that it would not need a second time the right of prescription, to regain its tranquil and undisturbed empire?

It is easy to suppose that the other sciences have no little share in this uncertainty arising from the weakness of the human mind; as I do not imagine that this assertion will be called in question, I pass on to a few remarks on the peculiar character of the moral sciences.

The fact has not been sufficiently attended to, that there is no study more deceptive than that of the moral sciences; I say deceptive, because this study, seducing the mind by an appearance of facility, draws it into difficulties which it is no easy matter to overcome. It may be compared to those tranquil waters which, although apparently but shallow, are in reality unfathomably deep. Familiarized from our infancy with the language of this science, surrounded by its continual applications, and having before our eyes its truths under a palpable form, we possess a certain facility of speaking readily on many parts of the subject; and we have the rashness to suppose that it would not be difficult to master its highest principles and its most delicate relations. But wonderful as it is, scarcely have we quitted the path of common sense, and attempted to go beyond those simple impressions which we have received from our mothers, when we find ourselves in a labyrinth of confusion. If the mind gives itself up to subtilties, it ceases to listen to the voice of the heart, which speaks to it with equal simplicity and eloquence; if it does not repress its pride, and attend to the wise counsels of good sense, it will be guilty of despising those salutary and necessary truths, which have been preserved by society to be transmitted from generation to generation: it is then, while groping its way in the dark, that it falls into the wildest extravagances, the lamentable effects of which are so often exemplified in the history of the sciences.

If we observe attentively, we shall find something of the same kind in all the sciences. The Creator has taken care to supply us with knowledge necessary for the purposes of life, and for the attainment of our destiny; but it has not pleased Him to gratify our curiosity by discovering to us what was not necessary. Nevertheless, in some things he has communicated to the mind a power which renders it capable of constantly adding to its knowledge; but, with respect to moral truths, it has been left sterile. What man is required to know, has been deeply engraven on his heart, in characters simple and intelligible; or is contained in the sacred volume; and moreover, he has had pointed out to him, in the authority of the Church, a fixed rule, to which he can apply to have his doubts explained. With respect to the rest, man has been placed in such a position, that if he attempt to enter into matters which are too subtle, he only wanders backwards and forwards in the same road, at the extremities of which he finds on the one side skepticism, on the other pure truth.

Perhaps some modern idealogists will urge, in opposition to this, the result of their own analytical labours. "Before men began to analyze facts," they will say, "and while they indulged in fanciful systems, and satisfied themselves with verbal disputes without critical examination, all this might be true; but now that we have explained all the ideas of moral good and evil, in so perfect a way, and have separated the prejudice in them from the true philosophy; now that the whole system of morality is based upon the simple principles of pleasure and pain, and we have given the clearest ideas of these things, such, for example, as the sensations produced in us by an orange; to maintain your assertion, is to be ungrateful towards science, and to underrate the fruit of our labours."

I am aware of the labours of some moral idealogists, and I know with what deceptive simplicity they develope their theories, by giving to the most difficult things an easy turn, which affects to make them intelligible to the most limited minds. This is not the place to examine these analytical investigations, and their results. I shall, however, remark that, in spite of their promised simplicity, it does not appear that either society or science makes much progress through their means, and that these opinions, although but a short time broached, are already superannuated. This is not a matter of astonishment to us; for it was easy to perceive that, in spite of their positiveness, if I may be allowed to use the expression, these idealogists are as hypothetical as many of their predecessors, who are loaded by them with sarcasms and contempt. They are a poor, narrow-minded school, devoid of the truth, and not even adorned by the brilliant dreams of great men; a proud and deluded school, who fancy they explain a fact, when they only obscure it; and prove a thing, when they only assert it; and imagine that they analyze the human heart, when they take it to pieces.

If such is the human mind; if such is its inability in matters of science, whether physical or moral, that it has not advanced a single step beyond the limit prescribed by a beneficent Providence; what service has Protestantism rendered to modern society, by impairing the force of authority, that power which could alone present an effectual barrier to man's unhappy wanderings? (9)

CHAPTER VII.

INDIFFERENCE AND FANATICISM.

In rejecting the authority of the Church, and in adopting this resistance as its only principle, Protestantism was compelled to seek its whole support in man; thus to mistake the true character of the human mind, and its relations with religious and moral truth, was to throw itself, according to circumstances, into the opposite extremes of fanaticism and indifference.

It may seem strange that these opposite errors should emanate from the same source; and yet nothing is more certain. Protestantism, by appealing to man alone in religious matters, had only two courses to adopt; either to suppose men to be inspired by Heaven for the discovery of truth, or to subject all religious truths to the examination of reason. To submit religious truths to the judgment of reason was sooner or later to produce indifference; on the other hand, private inspiration must engender fanaticism.

There is a universal and constant fact in the history of the human mind—viz. its decided inclination to invent systems in which the reality of things is completely laid aside, and where we only see the workings of a spirit which has chosen to quit the ordinary path in order to give itself up to its own inspirations. The history of philosophy is little else than a perpetual repetition of this phenomenon, which the human mind shows, in some shape or other, in all things which admit of it. When the mind has conceived a peculiar idea, it regards it with that blind and exclusive predilection which is found in the love of the father for his children. Under the influence of this prejudice, the mind developes its ideas and accommodates facts to suit it; that which at first was only an ingenious and extravagant idea, becomes the germ of important doctrines; and if it arise in a person of an ardent disposition, fanaticism, the cause of so much madness, is the consequence.

The danger is very much increased when the new system applies to religious matters, or is immediately connected with them. The extravagances of a diseased mind are then looked upon as inspirations from Heaven; the fever of delirium as a divine flame; and a mania of being singular as an extraordinary vocation. Pride, unable to brook opposition, rises against all that it finds established; it insults all authority; it attacks all institutions; it despises everybody; it conceals the grossest violence under the mantle of zeal, and ambition under the name of apostleship. The dupe of himself rather than an impostor, the wretched maniac sometimes becomes deeply persuaded that his doctrines are true, and that he has received the commands of Heaven. As there is something extraordinary and striking in the fiery language of the madman, he communicates to those who listen to him a portion of his insanity, and makes, in a short time, a considerable number of proselytes. The men capable of playing the first part in this scene of madness are not numerous, it is true; but unhappily the majority of men are foolish enough to be easily led away. History and experience sufficiently prove that the crowd are easily attracted, and that to form a party, however criminal, extravagant, or ridiculous, it is only necessary to raise a standard.

I wish to take this opportunity of making an observation which I have never seen pointed out—viz. that the Church, in her contest with heresy, has rendered an important service to the science which devotes itself to the examination of the true character, tendency, and power of the human mind. The zealous guardian of all great truths, she has always known how to preserve them unimpaired; she was fully acquainted with the weakness of the mind of man, and its extreme proneness to folly and extravagance; she has followed it closely in all its steps, has watched it in all its movements, and has constantly resisted it with energy, when it attempted to pollute the pure fountain of which she is the guardian. During the long and violent contests which she has had with it, the Church has made manifest its incurable folly; she has exhibited it on every side, and has shown it in all its forms. Thus it is that, in the history of heresies, she has made an abundant collection of facts, and has painted an extremely interesting picture of the human mind, where its characteristic physiognomy is faithfully represented; a picture which will doubtless be of great service in the composition of the important work which is yet unwritten—viz. the true history of the human mind. (10)

Certain it is that the ravings and extravagances of fanaticism have not been wanting in the history of Europe for the last three hundred years. Their monuments still remain; in whatever direction we turn our steps, we find bloody traces of the fanatical sects produced by Protestantism, and engendered by its fundamental principle. Nothing could confine this devastating torrent, neither the violent character of Luther, nor the furious efforts which he made to oppose every one who taught doctrines different from his own. Impiety succeeded impiety, extravagance extravagance, fanaticism fanaticism. The pretended Reformation was soon divided into as many sects as there were found men with the ingenuity to invent and the boldness to maintain a system of their own. This was necessarily the case; for besides the danger of leaving the human mind without a guide on all questions of religion, there was another cause fruitful in fatal results, I mean the private interpretation of the sacred books.

It was then found that the best things may be abused, and that these divine volumes, which contain so much instruction for the mind, and so much consolation for the heart, are full of danger to the proud. How great will this be, if you add to the obstinate resolution of resisting all authority in matters of faith, the false persuasion that the meaning of the Scriptures is everywhere clear, and that, in all cases, the inspirations of Heaven may be expected to solve every doubt? What will happen to those who turn over their pages with a longing desire to find some text which, more or less tortured, may seem to authorize their sophisms, subtilties, and absurdities?

There never was a greater mistake than that which was committed by the

Protestant leaders, when they placed the Bible in the hands of all for self-interpretation; never was the nature of that sacred volume more completely lost sight of. It is true that Protestantism had no other method to pursue, and that every objection which it could make to the private interpretation of the sacred text would be a striking inconsistency, an apostasy from its own principles, and a denial of its own origin; but at the same time, this is its most decided condemnation. What claim, indeed, can that religion have to truth and sanctity whose fundamental principle contains the germ of sects the most fanatical—the most injurious to society?

It would be difficult to collect into so narrow a space, in opposition to this essential error of Protestantism, so many facts and convincing proofs of this, as are contained in the following lines, written by a Protestant, O'Callaghan, which, I have no doubt, my readers will thank me for quoting here. "Led away," says O'Callaghan, "by their spirit of opposition to the Church of Rome, the first Reformers loudly proclaimed the right of interpreting the Scriptures according to each one's private judgment; but in their eagerness to emancipate the people from the authority of the Pope, they proclaimed this right without explanation or restriction: and the consequences were fearful. Impatient to undermine the papal jurisdiction, they maintained without exception, that each individual has an incontestable right to interpret the Scriptures for himself; and as this principle, carried to the fullest extent, was not sustainable, they were obliged to rely for support upon another, viz. that the Bible is an easy book, within the comprehension of all minds, and that the divine revelations contained in it are always clear to all; two propositions which, whether we consider them together or apart, cannot withstand a serious attack.

"The private judgment of Muncer found in the Scriptures that titles of nobility and great estates are impious usurpations, contrary to the natural equality of the faithful, and he invited his followers to examine if this were not the case. They examined into the matter, praised God, and then proceeded by fire and sword to extirpate the impious and possess themselves of their properties. Private judgment made the discovery in the Bible that established laws were a permanent restriction on Christian liberty; and, behold, John of Leyden, throwing away his tools, put himself at the head of a mob of fanatics, surprised the town of Munster, proclaimed himself king of Sion, and took fourteen wives at a time, asserting that polygamy is Christian liberty, and the privilege of the saints. But if the criminal madness of these men in another country is afflicting to the friends of humanity and of real piety, certainly the history of England, during a great part of the seventeenth century, is not calculated to console them. During that period an immense number of fanatics appeared, sometimes together and sometimes in succession, intoxicated with extravagant doctrines and mischievous passions, from the fierce ravings of Fox to the more methodical madness of Barclay; from the formidable fanaticism of Cromwell to the silly profanity of 'Praise God Barebones.' Piety, reason, and good sense seemed to be extinct on earth, and to be succeeded by an extravagant jargon, a religious frenzy, and a zeal without discretion. All quoted the Scriptures, all pretended to have had inspirations, visions, and spiritual ecstasies, and all, indeed, had equal claims to them. It was strongly maintained that it was proper to abolish the priesthood and the royal dignity, because priests were the ministers of Satan, and kings the delegates of the whore of Babylon, and that the existence of both were inconsistent with the reign of the Redeemer. The fanatics condemned science as a Pagan invention, and universities as seminaries of antichristian impiety. Bishops were not protected by the sanctity of their functions, or kings by the majesty of the throne; both, as objects of contempt and hatred, were mercilessly put to death by these fanatics, whose only book was the Bible, without note or comment. During this time, the enthusiasm for prayer, preaching, and the reading of the sacred books was at the highest point; everybody prayed, preached, and read, but nobody listened. The greatest atrocities were justified by the Scriptures; in the most ordinary transactions of life, scriptural language was made use of; national affairs, foreign and domestic, were discussed in the phraseology of Holy Writ. There were scriptural plots, conspiracies, and proscriptions; and all this was not only justified but even sanctified by quotations from the word of God. These facts, attested by history, have often astonished and alarmed men of virtue and piety, *but the reader, too much imbued with his own ideas, forgets the lesson to be learnt by this fatal experience; namely, that the Bible without note or comment was not intended to be read by rude and ignorant men.*

"The majority of mankind must be content to receive the instructions of others, and are not enabled to trust themselves. The most important truths in medicine, in jurisprudence, in physics, in mathematics, must be received from those who drink at the fountain head. The same plan has in general been pursued with respect to Christianity; and whenever the departure from it has been wide enough, '*society has been shaken to its foundation.*'"

These words of O'Callaghan do not require any comment. It cannot be said that they are hyperbolical or declamatory, as they are only a simple and faithful narration of acknowledged facts. The recollection of these events should suffice to prove the danger of placing the sacred Scriptures, without note or comment, into the hands of all, as Protestantism does, under the pretence, that the authority of the Church is useless for understanding the holy books; and that every Christian has only to listen to the dictates which generally emanate from his passions and heated imagination. By this error alone, if it had committed no other, Protestantism is self-reproved and condemned; for it is a religion which has established a principle destructive to itself. In order to appreciate the madness of Protestantism on this point, and to see how false and dangerous is the position which it has assumed with regard to the human mind, it is not necessary to be a theologian, or a Catholic; it is enough to have read the Scriptures with the eyes of a philosopher or a man of literature. Here is a book which comprises, within a limited compass, the period of four thousand years, and advances further towards the most distant future, by embracing the origin and destiny of man and the universe—a book which, with the continued history of a chosen people, intermingles, in its narrations and prophecies, the revolutions of mighty empires—a book which, side by side with the magnificent pictures of the power and splendor of Eastern monarchs, describes, in simple colors, the plain domestic manners, the candor, and innocence of a young nation—a book in which historians relate, sages proclaim their maxims of wisdom, apostles preach, and doctors instruct—a book in which prophets, under the influence of the divine Spirit, thunder against the errors and corruptions of the people, and announce the vengeance of the God of Sinai, or pour forth inconsolable lamentations on the captivity of their brethren, and the desolation and solitude of their country; where they relate, in wonderful and sublime language, the magnificent spectacles which are presented to their eyes; where, in moments of ecstasy, they see pass before them the events of society and the catastrophes of nature, although veiled in mysterious figures and visions of obscurity—a book, or rather a collection of books, where are to be found all sorts of styles and all varieties of narrative, epic majesty, pastoral simplicity, lyric fire, serious instruction, grave historical narrative, and lively and rapid dramatic action; a collection of books, in fine, written at various times and in various languages, in various countries, and under the most peculiar and extraordinary circumstances. Must not all this confuse the heads of men who, puffed up with their own conceit, grope through these pages in the dark, ignorant of climates, times, laws, customs, and manners? They will be puzzled by allusions, sur prised by images, deceived by expressions; they will hear the Greek and Hebrew, which was written in those remote ages, now spoken in a modern idiom. What effects must all these circumstances produce on the minds of readers who believe that the Bible is an easy book, to be understood without difficulty by all? Persuaded that they do not require the instructions of others, they must either resolve all these difficulties by their own reflections, or trust to that individual inspiration which they believe will not be wanting to explain to them the loftiest mysteries. Who, after this, can be astonished that Protestantism has produced so many absurd visionaries and furious fanatics? (11)

CHAPTER VIII.

FANATICISM—ITS DEFINITION.—FANATICISM IN THE CATHOLIC CHURCH.

It would be unjust to charge a religion with falsehood, merely because fanatics are to be found within its bosom. This would be to reject all, because none are to be found exempt from them. A religion, then, is not to be condemned because it has them, but because it produces them, urges them on, and opens a field for them. If we observe closely, we shall find at the bottom of the human heart an abundant source of fanaticism; the history of man affords us many proofs of this incontestable truth. Imagine whatever delusion you please, relate the most extravagant visions, invent the most absurd system, if you only take care to give to all a religious coloring, you may be sure that you will have enthusiastic followers, who will heartily devote themselves to the propagation of your doctrines, and will espouse your cause blindly and ardently; in other words, you will have under your standard a troop of fanatics.

Philosophers have devoted many pages to declamation against fanaticism; they have, as it were, assumed the mission of banishing it from the earth. They have tired mankind with philosophical lectures, and have thundered against the monster with all the vigor of their eloquence. They used the word, however, in so wide a sense as to include all kind of religion. But, if they had confined themselves to attacking real fanaticism, I believe they would have done much better if they had devoted some time to the examination of this matter in an analytic spirit, and had treated it, after so doing, maturely, calmly, and without prejudice.

Inasmuch as these philosophers were aware that fanaticism is a natural infirmity of the human mind, they could, if they were men of sense and wisdom, have had little hope of banishing the accursed monster from the world by reasoning and eloquence; for I am not aware that, up to the present time, philosophy has remedied any of the important evils that afflict humanity. Among the numerous errors of the philosophy of the eighteenth century, one of the principal was the mania for types; there was formed in the mind a type of the nature of man, of society, in a word, of every thing; and every thing that could not be adjusted to this type, every thing that could not be moulded into the required form, was so subjected to the fury of philosophers, as to make it certain, at least, that the want of pliability did not go unpunished.

But do I mean to deny the existence of fanaticism in the world? There is much of it. Do I deny that it is an evil? It is a very great one. Can it be extirpated? It cannot. How can its extent be diminished, its force weakened, and its violence checked? By directing man wisely. Can this be done by philosophy? We shall presently see. What is the origin of fanaticism? We must begin by defining the real meaning of the word. By fanaticism is meant, taking the word in its widest signification, the strong excitement of a mind powerfully acted on by a false or exaggerated opinion. If the opinion be true, if it be confined within just limits, there is no fanaticism; or, if there *be* any, it is only with respect to the means employed in defending the opinion. But in that case there is an erroneous judgment, since it is believed that the truth of the opinion authorizes the means; that is to say, there is already error or exaggeration. If a true opinion be sustained by legitimate means, if the occasion be opportune, whatever may be the excitement or effervescence of mind, whatever may be the energy of the efforts and the sacrifices made, then there is enthusiasm of mind and heroism of action, but no fanaticism. Were it otherwise, the heroes of all times and countries might be stigmatized as fanatics.

Fanaticism, in this general sense, extends to all the subjects which occupy the human mind; thus there are fanatics in religion, in politics, even in science and literature. Nevertheless, according to etymology and custom, the word is properly applied to religious matters only; therefore the word, when used alone, means fanaticism in religion, whilst, when applied to other things, it is always accompanied by a qualifying epithet; thus we say political fanatics, literary fanatics, &c.

There is no doubt that in religious matters men have a strong tendency to give themselves to a dominant idea, which they desire to communicate to all around them, and propagate everywhere. They sometimes go so far as to attempt this by the most violent means. The same fact appears, to a certain extent, in other matters; but it acquires in religious things a character different from what it assumes elsewhere. It is there that the human mind acquires increased force, frightful energy, and unbounded expansion; there are no more difficulties, obstacles, or fetters; material interests entirely disappear; the greatest sufferings acquire a charm; torments are nothing; death itself is a seductive illusion.

This phenomenon varies with individuals, with ideas, with the manners of the nation in whose bosom it is produced; but at bottom it is always the same. If we examine the matter thoroughly, we shall find that the violences of the followers of Mahomet, and the extravagant disciples of Fox, have a common origin.

It is with this passion as with all others; when they produce great evils, it is because they deviate from their legitimate objects, or because they strive at those objects by means which are not conformable to the dictates of reason and prudence. Fanaticism, then, rightly understood, is nothing but misguided religious feeling; a feeling which man has within him from the cradle to the tomb, and which is found to be diffused throughout society in all periods of its existence. Vain have been the efforts made up to this time to render men irreligious; a few individuals may give themselves up to the folly of complete irreligion; but the human race always protests against those who endeavor to stifle the sentiment of religion. Now this feeling is so strong and active, it exercises so unbounded an influence on man, that no sooner has it been diverted from its legitimate object, and quitted the right path, than it is seen to produce lamentable results; then it is that two causes, fertile in great disasters, are found in combination, complete blindness of the understanding and irresistible energy of the will.

In declaiming against fanaticism, many Protestants and philosophers have thought proper to throw a large share of blame on the Catholic Church; certainly they ought to have been more moderate in this respect if their philosophy had been good. It is true the Church cannot boast of having cured all the follies of man; she cannot pretend to have banished fanaticism so completely as not to have some fanatics among her children; but she may justly boast that no religion has taken more effectual means of curing the evil. It may, moreover, be affirmed, that she has taken her measures so well, that when it does make its appearance, she confines it within such limits that it may exist for a time, but cannot produce very dangerous results.

Its mental errors and delirious dreams, which, if encouraged, lead men to the commission of the greatest extravagances and the most horrible crimes, are kept under control when the mind possesses a salutary conviction of its own weakness and a respect for infallible authority. If they be not extinguished at their birth, at least they remain in a state of isolation, they do not injure the deposit of true doctrine, and the ties which unite all the faithful as members of the same body are not broken. With respect to revelations, visions, prophecies, and ecstasies, as long as they preserve a private character and do not affect the truths of faith, the Church, generally speaking, tolerates them and abstains from interference, leaving the discussion of the facts to criticism, and allowing the faithful an entire liberty of thinking as they please; but if the affair assumes a more important aspect, if the visionary calls in question points of doctrine, she immediately shows her vigilance. Attentive to every voice raised against the instructions of her Divine Master, she fixes an observant eye on the innovator. She examines whether he be a man deceived in matters of doctrine or a wolf in sheep's clothing; she raises her warning voice, she points out to all the faithful the error or the danger, and the voice of the Shepherd recalls the wandering sheep; but if he refuse to listen to her, and prefer to follow his own caprices, she separates him from the flock, and declares him to resemble the wolf. From that moment all those who are sincerely desirous of continuing in the bosom of the Church, can no more be infected with the error.

Undoubtedly, Protestants will reproach Catholics with the number of visionaries who have existed in the Church; they will recall the revelations and visions of a great number of saints who are venerated on our altars; they will accuse us of fanaticism,—a fanaticism, they will say, which, far from being limited in its effects to a narrow circle, has been able to produce the most important results. "Do not the founders of religious orders alone," they will say, "afford us a spectacle of a long succession of fanatics, who, self-deluded, exercised upon others, by their words and example, the greatest fascination that was ever seen?"

As this is not the place to enlarge upon the subject of religious communities, which I propose to do in another part of this work, I shall content myself with the observation, that even supposing that all the visions and revelations of our saints and the heavenly inspirations with which the founders of religious orders believed themselves to have been favored were delusions, our opponents would not be in any way justified in throwing on the Church the reproach of fanaticism. And, first, it is easy to see that, as far as individual visions are concerned, as long as they are thus limited, there may be delusion, or, if you will, fanaticism; but this fanaticism will not be injurious to any one, or create confusion in society. If a poor woman believe herself to be peculiarly favoured by Heaven, if she fancy that she hears the words of the Blessed Virgin, that she converses with angels who bring her messages from God, all this may excite the credulity of some and the raillery of others, but certainly it will not cost society a drop of blood or a tear. As to the founders of religious orders, in what way are they subject to the charge of fanaticism? Let us pass in silence the profound respect which their virtues deserve, and the gratitude which humanity owes them for the inestimable benefits conferred; let us suppose that they were deceived in all their inspirations; we may certainly call this delusion, but not fanaticism. We do not find in them either frenzy or violence; they are men diffident in themselves, who, when they believe that they are called by Heaven to a great design, never commence the work without having prostrated themselves at the feet of the Sovereign Pontiff; they submit to his judgment the rules for the establishment of their orders, they ask his instruction, listen to his decision with docility, and do nothing without having obtained his permission. How, then, do these founders of orders resemble the fanatics, who putting themselves at the head of a furious multitude, kill, destroy, and leave everywhere behind them traces of blood and ruin? We see in the founders of religious orders men who, deeply impressed with an idea, devote themselves to realize it, however great may be the sacrifice. Their conduct constantly shows a fixed idea, which is developed according to a preconcerted plan, and is always highly social and religious in its object: above all, this is submitted to authority, maturely examined and corrected by the counsels of prudence. An impartial philosopher, whatever may be his religious opinions, may find in all this more or less illusion and prejudice, or prudence and address; but he cannot find fanaticism, for there is nothing there which resembles it. (12)

CHAPTER IX.

INFIDELITY AND INDIFFERENCE IN EUROPE, THE FRUITS OF PROTESTANTISM.

THE fanaticism of sects, which is excited, kept alive, and nourished in Europe, by the private judgment of Protestantism, is certainly an evil of the greatest magnitude; yet it is not so mischievous or alarming as the infidelity and religious indifference for which modern society is indebted to the pretended Reformation. Brought on by the scandalous extravagances of so many sects of *soidisant* Christians, infidelity and religious indifference, which have their root even in the very principle of Protestantism, began to show themselves with alarming symptoms in the sixteenth century; they have acquired with time great diffusion, they have penetrated all the branches of science and literature, have produced an effect on languages, and have endangered all the conquests which civilization had gained during so many ages.

Even during the sixteenth century, and amid the hot disputes and religious wars which Protestantism had enkindled, infidelity spread in an alarming manner; and it is probable that it was even more common than it appeared to be, as it was not easy to throw off the mask at a period so near to the time when religious convictions had been so deeply rooted. It is very likely that infidelity was propagated disguised under the mantle of the Reformation, and that sometimes enlisting under the banner of one sect and sometimes of another, it labored to weaken them all, in order to set up its own throne on the general ruin of faith.

It does not require a great effort of logic to pass from Protestantism to Deism; from Deism to Atheism, there is but a step; and there must have been, at the time when these errors were broached, a large number of persons with reasoning powers enough to carry them out to the fullest extent. The Christian religion, as explained by Protestants, is only a kind of philosophic system more or less reasonable; as, when fully examined, it has no divine character. How, then, can it govern a reflecting and independent mind? Yes, one glance at the first exhibitions of Protestantism must have been enough to incline all those to religious indifference who, naturally disinclined to fanaticism, had lost the anchor of the Church's authority. When we consider the language and conduct of the sectarian leaders of that time, we are strongly inclined to suspect that they laughed at all Christian faith; that they concealed their indifference or their Atheism under strange doctrines which served as a standard, and that they propagated their writings with very bad faith, while they disguised their perfidious intention of preserving in the minds of their partisans sectarian fanaticism.

Thus, listening to the dictates of good sense, the father of the famous Montaigne, although he had seen as yet only the preludes of the Reformation, said, "that this beginning of evil would easily degenerate into execrable Atheism." A very remarkable testimony, which has been preserved to us by his son himself, who was certainly neither weak nor hypocritical. (*Essais de Montaigne*, liv. ii. chap. 12.) When this man pronounced so wise a judgment on the real tendency of Protestantism, did he imagine that his own son would confirm the justness of his prediction? Everybody knows that Montaigne was one of the first skeptics that became famous in Europe. It was requisite, at that time, for men to be cautious in declaring themselves Atheists or indifferentists, among Protestants themselves; and it may readily be imagined that all unbelievers had not the boldness of Gruet; yet we may believe the celebrated theologian of Toledo, Chacon, who said at the beginning of the last third of the sixteenth century, "that the heresy of the Atheists, of those who believed nothing, had great strength in France and in other countries."

Religious controversy continued to occupy the attention of all the savans of Europe, and during this time the gangrene of infidelity made great progress. This evil, from the middle of the seventeenth century, assumed a most alarming aspect. Who is not dismayed at reading the profound thoughts of Pascal on religious indifference? and who has not felt, in reading them, the emotion which is caused in the soul by the presence of a dreadful evil?

Things were now much advanced, and unbelievers were not far from being in a position, to take their rank among the schools who disputed for the upper hand in Europe. With more or less of disguise, they had already for a long time shown themselves under the form of Socinianism; but that did not suffice, for Socinianism bore at least the name of a religious sect, and irreligion began to feel itself strong enough to appear under its own name. The last part of the seventeenth century presents a crisis which is very remarkable with respect to religion;—a crisis which perhaps has not been well examined, although it exhibits some very remarkable facts; I allude to a lassitude of religious disputes, marked by two tendencies diametrically opposed to each other, and yet very natural: one towards Catholicity and the other towards Atheism.

Every one knows how much disputing there had been up to this time on religion; religious controversies were the prevailing taste, and it may be said that they formed the principal occupation not only of ecclesiastics, both Catholic and Protestant, but even of the well-educated laity. This taste penetrated the palaces of kings and princes. The natural result of so many controversies was to disclose the radical error of Protestantism: then the mind, which could not remain firm on such slippery ground, was obliged, either to adopt authority, or abandon itself to Atheism or complete indifference. These tendencies made themselves very perceptibly felt; thus it was that at the very time when Bayle thought Europe sufficiently prepared for his infidelity and skepticism, there was going on an animated and serious correspondence for the reunion of the German Protestants with the Catholic Church. Men of education are acquainted with the discussions which took place between the Lutheran Molanus, abbot of Lockum, and Christopher, at first Bishop of Tyna, and afterwards of Newstad. The correspondence between the two most remarkable men at that time in Europe of both communions, Bossuet and Leibnitz, is another monument of the importance of these negotiations. The happy moment was not yet come; political considerations, which ought to have vanished in the presence of such lofty interests, exercised a mischievous influence on the great soul of Leibnitz, and he did not preserve, throughout the progress of the discussions and negotiations, the sincerity, good faith, and elevation of view, which he had evinced at the commencement. The negotiation did not succeed, but the mere fact of its existence shows clearly enough the void which was felt in Protestantism; for we cannot believe that the two most celebrated men of that communion,

Molanus and Leibnitz, would have advanced so far in so important a negotiation, unless they had observed among themselves many indications of a disposition to return to the bosom of the Church. Add to this, the declaration of the Lutheran university of Helmstad in favor of the Catholic religion, and the fresh attempts at a reunion made by a Protestant prince, who addressed himself to Pope Clement XI., and you have strong reasons for believing that the Reformation felt itself mortally wounded. If God had been willing to permit that so great a result should appear to have been effected in any way by human means, the deep convictions prevalent among the most distinguished Protestants might perhaps have greatly contributed to heal the wounds which had been inflicted upon religious unity by the revolutionists of the sixteenth century.

But the profound wisdom of God had decided otherwise. In allowing men to pursue their own opposite and perverse inclinations, He was pleased to chastise them by means of their own pride. The tendency towards unity was no longer dominant in the next century, but gave place to a philosophic skepticism, indifferent towards all other religions, but the deadly enemy of the Catholic. It may be said that at that time there was a combination of the most fatal influences to hinder the tendency towards unity from attaining its object. Already were the Protestant sects divided and subdivided into numberless parties, and although Protestantism was thereby weakened, yet, nevertheless, it was diffused over the greater part of Europe; the germ of doubt in religious matters had inoculated the whole of European society. There was no truth which had escaped attack; no error or extravagance which had not had apostles and proselytes; and it was much to be feared that men would fall into that state of fatigue and discouragement which is the result of great efforts made without success, and into that disgust which is always produced by endless disputes and great scandals.

To complete the misfortune, and to bring to a climax the state of lassitude and disgust, there was another evil, which produced the most fatal results. The champions of Catholicity contended, with boldness and success, against the religious innovations of Protestants. Languages, history, criticism, philosophy, all that is most precious, rich, and brilliant in human knowledge, had been employed in the noblest way in this important struggle; and the great men who were most prominent among the defenders of the Church seemed to console her for the sad losses which she had sustained by the troubles of another age. But while she embraced in her arms these zealous sons, those who boasted the most of being called her children, she observed in some of them, with surprise and dread, an attitude of disguised hostility; and in their thinly veiled language and conduct she could easily perceive that they meditated giving her a fatal blow. Always asserting their submission and their obedience, but never submitting or obeying; continually extolling the authority and divine origin of the Church, and carefully concealing their hatred of her existing laws and institutions under cover of professed zeal for the re-establishment of ancient discipline; they sapped the foundations of morality, while they claimed to be its earnest advocates; they disguised their hypocrisy and pride under false humility and affected modesty; they called obstinacy firmness, and wilful blindness strength of mind. This rebellion presented an aspect more dangerous than any heresy; their honeyed words, studied candor, respect for antiquity, and the show of learning and knowledge, would have contributed to blind the best informed, if the innovators had not been distinguished by the constant and unfailing characteristic of all erroneous sects, viz, hatred of authority.

They were seen from time to time struggling against the declared enemies of the Church, defending, with great display of learning, the truth of her sacred dogmas, citing, with respect and deference, the writings of the holy fathers, and declaring that they adhered to tradition, and had a profound veneration for the decisions of councils and Popes. They particularly prided themselves on being called Catholics, however much their language and conduct were inconsistent with the name. Never did they get rid of the marvellous infatuation with which they denied their existence as a sect; and thus did they throw in the way of ill-informed persons the unhappy scandal of a dogmatical dispute, going on apparently within the bosom of the Church herself. The Pope declared them heretics; all true Catholics bowed to the decision of the Vicar of Jesus Christ; from all parts of the world a voice was unanimously raised to pronounce anathema against all who did not listen to the successor of St. Peter; but they themselves, denying and eluding all, persisted in considering themselves as a body of Catholics oppressed by the spirit of relaxation, abuse, and intrigue.

This scandal gave the finishing stroke to the leading of men astray, and the fatal gangrene which was infecting European society soon developed itself with frightful rapidity. The religious disputes, the multitude and variety of sects, the animosity which they showed against each other, all contributed to disgust with religion itself whoever were not held fast by the anchor of authority. To establish indifference as a system, atheism as a creed, and impiety as a fashion, there was only wanting a man laborious enough to collect, unite, and present in a body all the numerous materials which were scattered in a multitude of works; a man who knew how to give to all this a philosophical complexion suitable to the prevailing taste, and who could give to sophistry and declamation that seductive appearance, that deceptive form and dazzling show, by which the productions of genius are always marked, in the midst even of their wildest vagaries. Such a man appeared in the person of Bayle. The noise which his famous dictionary made in the world, and the favor which it enjoyed from the beginning, show how well the author had taken advantage of his opportunity. The dictionary of Bayle is one of those books which, considered apart from their scientific and literary merit, always serve to denote a remarkable epoch, because they present, together with the fruits of the past, the clear perception of a long future. The author of such a work is not distinguished so much on account of his own merit, as because he has known how to become the representative of ideas previously diffused in society, but floating about in a state of uncertainty; and yet his name recalls a vast history, of which he is the personification. The publication of Bayle's work may be regarded as the solemn inauguration of the chair of infidelity in Europe. The sophists of the eighteenth century found at hand an abundant repository of facts and arguments; but to render the thing complete, there was wanting a hand capable of retouching the old paintings, of restoring their faded colors, and of shedding over all the charms of imagination and the refinement of wit; there was wanting a guide to lead mankind by a flowery path to the borders of the abyss. Scarcely had Bayle descended into the tomb, when there appeared above the literary horizon a young man, whose great talents were equalled by his malice and audacity; Voltaire.

It was necessary to draw the reader's attention to the period which I have just described, to show him how great was the influence exercised by Protestantism in producing and establishing in Europe the irreligion, atheism, and fatal indifference which have caused so many evils in modern society. I do not mean to charge all Protestants with impiety; and I willingly acknowledge the sincerity and firmness of many of their most illustrious men, in struggling against the progress of irreligion. I am not ignorant that men sometimes adopt a principle and repudiate its consequences, and that it would, therefore, be very unjust to class them with those who openly accept those consequences; but on the other hand, however painful it may be to Protestants to avow that their system leads to atheism, it is nevertheless a fact which cannot be denied. All that they can claim of me on this point is, not to criminate their intentions;

after that, they cannot complain if, guided by the instructions of history and philosophy, I develope their fundamental principle to the fullest extent.

It would be useless to sketch, even in the most rapid manner, what has passed in Europe since the appearance of Voltaire: the events are so recent, and have been so often discussed, that all that I could say would be only a useless repetition. I shall better attain my object by offering some remarks on the actual state of religion in Protestant countries. Amid so many revolutions, and when so many heads were turned; when all the foundations of society were shaken, and the strongest institutions were torn out of the soil in which they had been so deeply rooted; when even Catholic truth itself could not have been sustained without the manifest aid of the arm of the Most High, we may imagine the fate of the fragile edifice of Protestantism, exposed, like all the rest, to so many and such violent attacks. No one is ignorant of the numberless sects which abound in Great Britain, of the deplorable condition of faith among the Swiss Protestants, even on the most important points. That there might be no doubt as to the real state of the Protestant religion in Germany, that is, in its native country, where it was first established as in its dearest patrimony, the Protestant minister, Baron Starck, has taken care to tell us, that "*in Germany there is not one single point of Christian faith which has not been openly attacked by the Protestant ministers themselves.*" The real state of Protestantism appears to me to be truly and forcibly depicted by a curious idea of J. Heyer, a Protestant minister. Heyer published, in 1818, a work entitled *Coup d'œil sur les Confessions de Foi;* not knowing how to get out of the difficulty in which all Protestants found themselves placed when they had to choose a symbol, he proposed the simple expedient of *getting rid of all symbols.*

The only way that Protestantism has of preserving itself, is to violate as much as possible its own fundamental principle, by withdrawing the right of private judgment, inducing the people to remain faithful to the opinions in which they have been educated, and carefully concealing from them the inconsistency into which they fall, when they submit to the authority of a private individual, after having rejected the authority of the Catholic church. But things are not taking this course; and in spite of the efforts of some Protestants to follow it, Bible Societies, working with a zeal worthy of a better cause, in promoting among all classes the private interpretation of the Bible, would suffice to keep alive always the spirit of inquiry. This diffusion of the Bible operates as a constant appeal to private judgment, which, after perhaps causing many days of sorrow and mourning to society, will eventually destroy the remains of Protestantism. All this has not escaped the notice of its disciples; and some of the most remarkable among them have raised their voices to point out the danger. (13)

CHAPTER X.

CAUSES OF THE CONTINUANCE OF PROTESTANTISM.

After having clearly shown the intrinsic weakness of Protestantism, it is natural to ask this question: If it be so feeble, owing to the radical defects of its constitution, why has it not by this time completely disappeared? If it bear in its own breast the seeds of death, how has it been able so long to withstand such powerful adversaries, as Catholicity, on the one hand, and irreligion or Atheism, on the other? In order to resolve this question satisfactorily, it is necessary to consider Protestantism in two points of view; as embodying a fixed creed, and as expressing a number of sects, who, in spite of their numerous mutual differences, agree in calling themselves Christians, and preserve a shadow of Christianity, although they reject the authority of the Church. It, is necessary to consider Protestantism in this double point of view, since its founders, while endeavoring to destroy the authority and dogmas of the Roman Church, were compelled to form a system of doctrines to serve as a symbol for their followers. Considered in the first aspect, it has almost entirely disappeared; we should rather say it scarcely ever had existence. This truth is sufficiently evident from what I have said of the variations and actual condition of Protestantism in the various countries of Europe; time has shown how much the pretended Reformers were deceived, when they fancied that they could fix the columns of Hercules of the human mind, to repeat the expression of Madame de Staël.

Who now defends the doctrines of Luther and Calvin? Who respects the limits which they prescribed? What Protestant Church distinguishes itself by the ardor of its zeal in preserving any particular dogmas? What Protestant now holds the divine mission of Luther, or believes the Pope to be Antichrist? Who watches over the purity of doctrine, and points out errors? Who opposes the torrent of sectarianism?

Do we find, in their writings, or in their discourses, the energetic tones of conviction, or the zeal of truth? In fine, what a wide difference do we find when we compare the Protestant Church with the Catholic! Inquire into the faith of the latter, and you will hear from the mouth of Gregory XVI., the successor of St. Peter, the same that Luther heard from Leo X. Compare the doctrine of Leo X. with that of his predecessors, you will always find it the same up to the Apostles, and to Jesus Christ himself. If you attempt to assail a dogma, if you try to attack the purity of morals, the voice of the ancient Fathers will denounce your errors, and in the middle of the nineteenth century you will imagine that the old Leos and Gregories are risen from the tomb. If your intentions are good, you will find indulgence; if your merits are great, you will be treated with respect; if you occupy an elevated position in the world, you will have attention paid to you. But if you attempt to abuse your talents by introducing novelty in doctrine; if, by your power, you aspire to demand a modification of faith; and if, to avoid troubles or prevent schism, or conciliate any one, you ask for a compromise or even an ambiguous explanation; the answer of the successor of St. Peter will be, "Never! faith is a sacred deposit which we cannot alter; truth is immutable; it is one:" and to this reply of the Vicar of Jesus Christ, which with a word will banish all your hopes, will be added those of the modern Athanasiuses, Gregories of Nazianzen, Ambroses, Jeromes, and Augustins. Always the same firmness in the same faith, the same unchangeableness, the same energy in preserving the sacred deposit intact, in defending it against the attacks of error, in teaching it to the faithful in all its purity, and in transmitting it unaltered to future generations. Will it be said that this is obstinacy, blindness, and fanaticism? But, eighteen centuries gone by, the revolutions of empires, the most fearful catastrophes, an infinite variety of ideas and manners, the most severe persecutions, the darkness of ignorance, the conflicts of passion, the lights of knowledge,—none of these have been able to enlighten this blindness, to bend this obstinacy, or extinguish this fanaticism. Certainly a reflecting Protestant, one of those who know how to rise above the prejudices of education, when fixing his eyes on this picture, the truth of which he cannot but acknowledge, if he is well informed on the question, will feel strong doubts arise within him as to the truth of the instruction he has received; he will at least feel a desire of examining more closely this great prodigy which the Catholic Church presents to us. But to return.

We see the Protestant sects melting away daily, and this dissolution must constantly increase; nevertheless, we have no reason to be astonished that Protestantism, inasmuch as it consists of a number of sects who preserve the name and some remains of Christianity, does not wholly disappear; for how could it disappear? Either Protestant nations must be completely swallowed up by irreligion or atheism, or they must give up Christianity and adopt one of the religions which are established in other parts of the world. Now both these suppositions are impossible; therefore this false form of Christianity has been and will be preserved, in some shape or other, until Protestants return to the bosom of the Church.

Let us develope these ideas. Why cannot Protestant nations be completely swallowed up by irreligion and atheism, or indifference? Because such a misfortune may happen to an individual, but not to a nation. By means of false books, erroneous reasonings, and continual efforts, some individuals may extinguish the lively sentiments of their hearts, stifle the voice of conscience, and trample under foot the dictates of common sense; but a nation cannot do so. A people always preserves a large fund of candor and docility, which, amid the most fatal errors and even the most atrocious crimes, compels it to lend an attentive ear to the inspirations of nature. Whatever may be the corruption of morals, whatever may be the errors of opinion, there will never be more than a small number of men found capable of struggling for a long time against themselves, in the attempt to eradicate from their hearts that fruitful germ of good feelings, that precious seed of virtuous thoughts, with which the beneficent hand of the Creator has enriched our souls. The conflagration of the passions, it is true, produces lamentable prostration, and sometimes terrible explosions; but when the fire is extinguished, man returns to himself, and his mind becomes again accessible to the voice of reason and virtue. An attentive study of society proves that the number of men is happily very small who are, as it were, steeled against truth and virtue; who reply with frivolous sophistry to the admonitions of good sense; who oppose with cold stoicism the sweetest and most generous inspirations of nature, and venture to display, as an illustration of philosophy, firmness, and elevation of mind, the ignorance, obstinacy, and barrenness of an icy heart. The generality of mankind, more simple, more candid, more natural, are consequently ill-suited to a system of atheism, or indifference. Such a system may take possession of the proud mind of a learned visionary; it may be adopted, as a convenient opinion, by dissipated youth; and in times of agitation, it may influence a few fiery spirits; but it will never be able to establish itself in society as a normal condition.

No, by no means. An individual may be irreligious, but families and society never will. Without a basis on which the social edifice must rest; without a great creative idea, whence will flow the ideas of reason, virtue, justice, obligation, and right, which are as necessary to the existence and preservation of society as blood and nourishment are to the life of the individual, society would be destroyed; without the sweet ties by which religious ideas unite together the members of a family, without the heavenly harmony which they infuse into all its connections, the family would cease to exist, or at least would be only a rude and transient union, resembling the intercourse of animals. God has happily gifted all his creatures with a marvellous instinct of self-preservation. Guided by that instinct, families and society repudiate with indignation those degrading ideas which, blasting by their fatal breath all the germs of life, breaking all ties, upsetting all laws, make both of them retrograde towards the most abject barbarism, and finish by scattering their members like dust before the wind.

The repeated lessons of experience ought to have convinced certain philosophers that these ideas and feelings, engraven on the heart of man by the finger of the Author of nature, cannot be eradicated by declamation or sophistry. If a few ephemeral triumphs have occasionally flattered their pride, and made them conceive false hopes of the result of their efforts, the course of events has soon shown them. that to pride themselves on these triumphs was to act like a man who, on account of having succeeded in infusing unnatural sentiments into the hearts of a few mothers, would flatter himself that he has banished maternal love from the world. Society (I do not mean the populace or the commonalty)—society will be religious, even at the risk of being superstitious; if it does not believe in reasonable things, it will in extravagant ones; and if it have not a divine religion, it will have a human one: to suppose the contrary, is to dream; to struggle against this tendency, is to struggle against an eternal law; to attempt to restrain it, is to attempt to restrain with a weak arm a body launched with an immense force—the arm will be destroyed, but the body will continue its course. Men may call this superstition, fanaticism, the result of error; but to talk thus can only serve to console them for their failure.

Since, then, religion is a real necessity, we have therein an explanation of the phenomenon which history and experience present to us, namely, that religion never wholly disappears, and that when changes take place, the two rival religions, during their struggles, more or less protracted, occupy successively the same ground. The consequence is, that Protestantism cannot entirely disappear unless another religion takes its place. Now, as in the actual state of civilization, no religion can replace it but the Catholic, it is evident that Protestant sects will continue to occupy, with more or less variation, the countries which they have gained.

Indeed, how is it possible, in the present state of civilization among Protestant nations, that the follies of the Koran, or the absurdities of idolatry, should have any chance of success among them? The spirit of Christianity circulates in the veins of modern society; its seal is set upon all legislation; its light is shed upon all branches of knowledge; its phraseology is found in all languages; its precepts regulate morals; habits and manners have assumed its form; the fine arts breathe its perfume, and all the monuments of genius are full of its inspirations. Christianity, in a word, pervades all parts of that great, varied, and fertile civilization, which is the glory of modern society. How then, is it possible for a religion entirely to disappear which possesses, with the most venerable antiquity, so many claims to gratitude, so many endearing ties, and so many glorious recollections? How could it give place, among Christian nations, to one of those religions which, at the first glance, show the finger of man, and indicate, as their distinctive mark, degradation and debasement? Although the essential principle of Protestantism saps the foundations of the Christian religion, although it disfigures its beauty, and lowers its sublimity, yet the remains which it preserves of Christianity, its idea of God, and its maxims of morality, raise it far above all the systems of philosophy, and all the other religions of the world.

If, then, Protestantism has preserved some shadow of the Christian religion, it was because, looking at the condition of the nations who took part in the schism, it was impossible for the Christian name wholly to disappear; and not on account of any principle of life contained in the bosom of the pretended Reformation. On the other hand, consider the efforts of politicians, the natural attachment of ministers to their own interests, the illusions of pride which flatter men with the freedom they will enjoy in the absence of all authority, the remains of old prejudices, the power of education, and such like causes, and you will find a complete solution of the question. Then you will no longer be surprised that Protestantism continues to retain possession of many of those countries where it unfortunately became deeply rooted.

CHAPTER XI.

THE POSITIVE DOCTRINES OF PROTESTANTISM REPUGNANT TO THE INSTINCT OF CIVILIZATION.

THE best proof of the extreme weakness of Protestantism, considered as a body of doctrine, is the little influence which its positive doctrines have exercised in European civilization. I call its positive doctrines those which it attempts to establish as its own; and I distinguish them thus from its other doctrines, which I call negative, because they are nothing but the negation of authority. The latter found favor on account of their conformity with the inconstancy and changeableness of the human mind; but the others, which have not the same means of success, have all disappeared with their authors, and are now plunged in oblivion. The only part of Christianity which has been preserved among Protestants, is that which was necessary to prevent European civilization from losing among them its nature and character; and this is the reason why the doctrines which had too direct a tendency to alter the nature of this civilization have been repudiated, we should rather say, despised by it.

There is a circumstance here well worthy of attention, and which has not perhaps been noticed, viz. the fate of the doctrine held by the first reformers with respect to free-will. It is well known that one of the first and most important errors of Luther and Calvin consisted in denying free-will. We find this fatal doctrine professed in the works which they have left us. Does it not seem that this doctrine ought to have preserved its credit among the Protestants, and that they ought to have fiercely maintained it, since such is commonly the case with errors which serve as a nucleus in the formation of a sect? It seems, also, that Protestantism being widely spread, and deeply rooted in several countries of Europe, this fatalist doctrine ought to have exercised a strong influence on the legislation of Protestant nations. Wonderful as it is, such has not been the case; European moralists have despised it; legislation has not adopted it as a basis; civilization has not allowed itself to be directed by a principle which sapped all the foundations of morality, and which, if once applied to morals and laws, would have substituted for European civilization and dignity the barbarism and debasement of Mahometanism.

There is no doubt that this fatal doctrine has perverted some individuals; it has been adopted by sects more or less numerous; and it cannot be denied that it has affected the morality of some nations. But it is also certain, that, in the generality of the great human family, governments, tribunals, administration, legislation, science, and morals, have not listened to this horrible doctrine of Luther,—a doctrine which strips man of his free will, which makes God the author of sin, which charges the Creator with the responsibility of all the crimes of His creatures, and represents Him as a tyrant, by affirming that His precepts are impossible; a doctrine which monstrously confounds the ideas of good and evil, and removes all stimulus to good deeds, by teaching that faith is sufficient for salvation, and that all the good works of the just are only sins.

Public opinion, good sense, and morality here side with Catholicity. Those even who in theory embrace these fatal religious doctrines, usually reject them in practice; this is because Catholic instruction on these important points has made so deep an impression on them; because so strong an instinct of civilization has been communicated to European society by the Catholic religion. Thus the Church, by repudiating the destructive errors taught by Protestantism, preserved society from being debased by these fatalist doctrines. The Church formed a barrier against the despotism which is enthroned wherever the sense of dignity is lost; she was a fence against the demoralization which always spreads whenever men think themselves bound by blind necessity, as by iron chain; she also freed the human mind from the state of abjection into which it falls whenever it thinks itself deprived of the government of its own conduct, and of the power of influencing the course of events. In condemning those errors of Luther, which were the bond of Protestantism at its birth, the Pope raised the alarm against an irruption of barbarism into the order of ideas; he saved morality, laws, public order, and society; the Vatican, by securing the noble sentiment of liberty in the sanctuary of conscience, preserved the dignity of man; by struggling against Protestant ideas, by defending the sacred deposit confided to it by its Divine Master, the Roman See became the tutelary divinity of future civilization.

Reflect on these great truths, understand them thoroughly, you who speak of religious disputes with cold indifference, with apparent mockery and pity, as if they were only scholastic puerilities. Nations *do not live on bread alone;* they live also on ideas, on maxims, which, converted into spiritual aliment, give them greatness, strength, and energy, or, on the contrary, weaken them, reduce them, and condemn them to stupidity. Look over the face of the globe, examine the periods of human history, compare times with times, and nations with nations, and you will see that the Church, by giving so much importance to the preservation of these transcendent truths, by accepting no compromise on this point, has understood and realized better than any other teacher, the elevated and salutary maxim, that truth ought to reign in the world; that on the order of ideas depends the order of events, and that when these great problems are called in question, the destinies of humanity are involved.

Let us recapitulate what we have said; the essential principle of Protestantism is one of destruction; this is the cause of its incessant variations, of its dissolution and annihilation. As a particular religion it no longer exists, for it has no peculiar faith, no positive character, no government, nothing that is essential to form an existence; Protestantism is only a negative. If there is any thing to be found in it of a positive nature, it is nothing more than vestiges and ruins; all is without force, without action, without the spirit of life. It cannot show an edifice raised by its own hands; it cannot, like Catholicity, stand in the midst of its vast works and say, "These are mine." Protestantism can only sit down on a heap of ruins, and say with truth, "I have made this pile."

As long as sectarian fanaticism lasted, as long as this flame, enkindled by furious declamation, was kept alive by unhappy circumstances, Protestantism showed a certain degree of force, which, although it was not the sign of vigorous life, at least indicated the convulsive energy of delirium. But that period has passed, the action of time has dispersed the elements that fed the flame, and none of the attempts which have been made to give to the Reformation the character of a work of God, have been able to conceal the fact that it was the work of human passions. Let us not be deceived by the efforts which are now being made; what is acting under our eyes is not living Protestantism, it is the operation of false philosophy, perhaps of policy, sometimes of sordid interest disguised under the name of policy. Every one knows how powerful Protestantism was in exciting disturbances and causing disunion. It is on this account that evil-minded men search in the bed of this exhausted torrent for some remains of its impure waters, and knowing them to contain a deadly poison, present them to the unsuspecting in a golden cup.

But it is in vain for weak man to struggle against the arm of the Almighty, God will not abandon His work. Notwithstanding all his attempts to deface the work of God, man cannot blot out the eternal characters which distinguish truth from error. Truth in itself is strong and robust: as it is the ensemble of the relations which unite things together, it is strongly connected with them, and cannot be separated either by the efforts of man or by the revolution of time. Error, on the contrary, the lying image of the great ties which bind together the compact mass of the universe, stretches over its usurped domain like those dead branches of the forest which, devoid of sap, afford neither freshness nor verdure, and only serve to impede the advance of the traveller.

Confiding men, do not allow yourselves to be seduced by brilliant appearances, pompous discourse, or false activity. Truth is open, modest, without suspicion, because it is pure and strong; error is hypocritical and ostentatious, because it is false and weak. Truth resembles a woman of real beauty, who, conscious of her charms, despises the affectation of ornament; error, on the contrary, paints and ornaments herself, because she is ugly, without expression, without grace, without dignity. Perhaps you may be pleased with its laborious activity. Know, then, that it has no strength but when it is the rallying cry of a faction; then, indeed, it is rapid in action and fertile in violent measures. It is like the meteor which explodes and vanishes, leaving behind it nothing but darkness, death, and destruction; truth, on the contrary, like the sun, sends forth its bright and steady beams, fertilizes with its genial warmth, and sheds on every side life, joy, and beauty.

CHAPTER XII.

THE EFFECTS WHICH THE INTRODUCTION OF PROTESTANTISM INTO SPAIN WOULD HAVE PRODUCED.

In order to judge of the real effect which the introduction of Protestant doctrines would have had in Spain, we shall do well, in the first place, to take a survey of the present state of religion in Europe. In spite of the confusion of ideas which is one of the prevailing characteristics of the age, it is undeniable that the spirit of infidelity and irreligion has lost much of its strength, and that where it still exists it has merged into indifference, instead of preserving its systematic form of the last century. With the lapse of time declamation ceases; men grow tired of continually repeating the same insulting language; their minds resist the intolerance and bad faith of sects; systems betray their emptiness, opinions their erroneousness, judgments their precipitation, and reasonings their want of exactitude. Time shows their counterfeit intentions, their deceptive statements, the littleness of their ideas, and the mischievousness of their projects; truth begins to recover its empire, things regain their real names, and, thanks to the new direction of the public mind, that which before was considered innocent and generous is now looked upon as criminal and vile. The deceitful masks are taken off, and falsehood is discovered surrounded by the discredit which ought always to have accompanied it.

Irreligious ideas, like all those which are prevalent in an advanced state of society, would not, and could not be confined to mere speculation; they invaded the domain of practice, and labored to gain the upper hand in all branches of administration and politics. But the revolution which they produced in society became fatal to themselves; for there is nothing which better exposes the faults and errors of a system, and undeceives men on the subject, than the touchstone of experience. There is in our minds a certain power of viewing an object under a variety of aspects, and an unfortunate aptitude for supporting the most extravagant proposition by a multitude of sophisms. In mere disputation, it is difficult for the most reasoning minds to keep clear of the snares of sophistry. But when we come to experience, it is otherwise; the mind is silent, and facts speak; and if the experience has been on a large scale, and applied to objects of great interest and importance, it is difficult for the most specious arguments to counteract the convincing eloquence of the result. Hence it is that a man of much experience obtains an instinct so sure and delicate, that when a system is but explained he can point out all its inconveniences. Inexperience, presumptuous and prejudiced, appeals to argument in support of its doctrines; but good sense, that precious and inestimable quality, shakes its head, shrugs its shoulders, and with a tranquil smile leaves its prediction to be tested by time.

It is not necessary now to insist on the practical results of those doctrines of which infidelity was the motto; we have said enough on that subject. Suffice it to say, that those same men who seem to belong to the last century by their principles, interests, recollections, or for other reasons, have been obliged to modify their doctrines, to limit their principles, to palliate their propositions, to cool the warmth and passion of their invectives; and when they wish to give a mark of their esteem and veneration for those writers who were the delight of their youth, they are compelled to declare "that those men were great philosophers, but philosophers of the cabinet;" as if in reality what they call the knowledge of the cabinet was not the most dangerous ignorance.

It is certain that these attempts have had the effect of throwing discredit on irreligion as a system. If people do not regard it with horror, at least they look upon it with mistrust. Irreligion has labored in all the branches of science, in the vain hope that the heavens would cease to relate the glories of God, that the earth would disown Him who laid its foundations, and that all nature would give testimony against the Lord who gave it existence and life. These same labors have banished the scandalous division which had begun between religion and science; so that the ancient accents of the man of Hus have again resounded, without dishonor to science, in the mouths of men in the nineteenth century, and what shall we say of the triumphs of religion in all that is noble, tender, and sublime on earth? How grand are the operations of Providence displayed therein! Admirable dispensation! The mysterious hand which governs the universe seems to hold in reserve for every great crisis of society an extraordinary man. At the proper moment this man presents himself; he advances, himself ignorant whither he is going, but he advances with a firm step towards the accomplishment of the high mission for which Providence has destined him.

Atheism was bathing France in a sea of tears and blood; an unknown man silently traverses the ocean. While the violence of the tempest rends the sails of his vessel, he listens attentively to the hurricane—he is lost in the contemplation of the majesty of the heavens. Wandering in the solitudes of America, he asks of the wonders of creation the name of their Author; the thunder on the confines of the desert, the low murmuring of the forests, and the beauties of nature answer him with canticles of love and harmony. The view of a solitary cross reveals to him mysterious secrets; the traces of an unknown missionary awaken important recollections which connect the new world with the old; a monument in ruins, the hut of a savage, excite in his mind thoughts which penetrate to the foundations of society and to the heart of man. Intoxicated with these spectacles, his mind full of sublime conceptions, and his heart inundated with the charms of so much beauty, this man returns to his native soil. What does he find there? The bloody traces of Atheism; the ruins and ashes of ancient temples devoured by the flames or destroyed by violence; the remains of a multitude of innocent victims, buried in the graves which formerly afforded an asylum to persecuted Christians. He observes, however, that something is in agitation; he sees that religion is about to redescend upon France, like consolation upon the unfortunate, or the breath of life upon a corpse. From that moment he hears on all sides a concert of celestial harmony; the inspirations of meditation and solitude revive and ferment in his great soul; transported out of himself, and ravished into ecstasy, he sings with a tongue of fire the glories of religion, he reveals the delicacy and beauty of the relations between religion and nature, and in surpassing language he points out to astonished men the mysterious golden chain which connects the heavens and the earth. That man was Chateaubriand.

It must, however, be confessed, that the confusion which has been introduced into ideas cannot be corrected in a short time, and that it is not easy to eradicate the deep traces of the ravages of irreligion. Men's minds, it is true, are tired of the irreligious system; society, which had lost its balance, is generally ill at ease; the family feels its ties relaxed, and individuals sigh after a ray of light, a drop of hope and consolation. But where shall the world find the remedy which is wanting? Will it follow the best road—the only road? Will it re-enter the fold of the Catholic Church? Alas! God alone knows the secrets of the future; He alone has clearly unfolded before His eyes the great events which are no doubt awaiting humanity. He alone knows what will be the result of that activity, of that energy, which again urges men to the examination of great political and religious questions; and He alone knows what, to future generations, will be the result of the triumphs obtained by religion, in the fine arts, in literature, in science, in politics, in all the operations carried on by the human mind.

As to us, carried away as we are by the rapid and precipitate course of revolution, hardly have we time to cast a fleeting glance upon the chaos in which our country is involved. What can we confidently predict? All that we can be sure of is, that we are in an age of disquietude, of agitation, of transition; that the multiplied examples and warnings of so many disappointed expectations, the fruits of fearful revolutions and unheard-of catastrophes, have everywhere thrown discredit upon irreligious and disorganizing doctrines, without having established the legitimate empire of true religion. Hearts sick of so many misfortunes are willingly open to hope; but minds are in a state of great uncertainty as to the future: perhaps they even anticipate a new series of calamities. Owing to revolutions, to the efforts of industry, to the activity and extension of commerce, to the progress and prodigious diffusion of printing, to scientific discoveries, to the ease, rapidity, and universality of communication, to the taste for travelling, to the dissolving action of Protestantism, of incredulity, and skepticism, the human mind certainly now presents one of the most singular phases of its history. Reason, imagination, and the heart are in a state of agitation, of movement, and of extraordinary development, and show us at the same time the most singular contrasts, the most ridiculous extravagances, and the most absurd contradictions. Observe the sciences, and you will no longer find those lengthened labors, that indefatigable patience, that calm and tranquil progress, which characterized these studies at other epochs; but you will find there a spirit of observation, and a tendency to place questions in that transcendental point of view where may be discovered the relations subsisting between them, the ties by which they are connected, and the way in which they throw light upon each other. Questions of religion, of politics, of legislation, of morals, of government, are all mingled, stand prominently forward, and give to the horizon of science a grandeur and immensity which it did not previously possess. This progress, this confusion, this chaos, if you like to call it so, is a fact which must be taken into account in studying the spirit of the age, in examining the religious condition of the time; for it is not the work of a single man, or the effect of accident; it is the result of a multitude of causes, the fruit of a great number of facts; it is an expression of the present state of intelligence; a symptom of strength and disease, an announcement of change and of transition, perhaps a sign of consolation, perhaps a presage of misfortune. And who has not observed the fertility of imagination and unbounded reach of thought in that literature, so various, so irregular, and so vague, but at the same time so rich in fine images, in delicate feeling, and in bold and generous thought? You may talk as much as you please of the debasement of science, of the falling off in study. You may speak in a tone of derision of the *lights of the age*, and turn with regret to ages more studious and more learned; there will be some exaggeration, truth and error, in all this, as there always is in declamation of this kind; but whatever may be the degree of utility belonging to the present labors of the human mind, never, perhaps, was there a time when it displayed more activity and energy, never was it agitated by a movement so general, so lively, so various, and never, perhaps, did it desire, with a more excusable curiosity and impatience, to raise a part of the veil which covers the boundless future. What will be able to govern elements so powerful and so opposite? What can calm this tempestuous sea? What will give the union, the connection, the consistency necessary to form, out of these repulsive and discordant elements, a whole compact and capable of resisting the action of time? Will this be done by Protestantism, with its fundamental principle which establishes and diffuses and sanctions the dissolving principle of private interpretation in matters of religion, and realizes this unhappy notion by circulating among all classes of society copies of the Bible?

Nations numerous, proud of their power, vain of their knowledge, rendered dissipated by pleasure, refined by luxury, continually exposed to the powerful influence of the press, and possessing means of communication which would have appeared fabulous to their ancestors; nations in whom all the violent passions have an object, all intrigues an existence, all corruptions a veil, all crimes a title, all errors an advocate, all interests a support; nations which, warned and deceived, still vacillate in a state of dreadful uncertainty between truth and falsehood; sometimes looking at the torch of truth as if they meant to be guided by its light, and then again seduced by an *ignis fatuus;* sometimes making an effort to rule the storm, and then abandoning themselves to its violence; modern nations show us a picture as extraordinary as it is interesting, where hopes, fears, prognostics, and conjectures have free scope, and nobody can pretend to predict with accuracy, and the wise man must await in silence the *dénouement* marked out in the secret decrees of God, where alone are clearly written the events of all time, and the future destinies of men.

But it may be easily understood that Protestantism, on account of its essentially dissolving nature, is incapable of producing any thing in morals or religion to increase the happiness of nations, for it is impossible for this happiness to exist as long as men's minds are at war on the most important questions which can occupy them.

When the observer, amid this chaos and obscurity, seeks for a ray of light to illuminate the world—for a powerful principle capable of putting an end to so much confusion and anarchy, and of bringing back men's minds to the path of truth, Catholicity immediately presents herself to him, as the only source of all these benefits. When we consider with what *écla* and with what power Catholicity maintains herself against all the unprecedented attempts which are made to destroy her, our hearts are filled with hope and consolation; and we feel inclined to hail this divine religion, and to congratulate her on the new triumph which she is about to achieve on earth.

There was a time when Europe, inundated by a torrent of barbarians, saw at once overwhelmed all the monuments of ancient civilization and refinement. Legislators and their laws, the empire and its power and splendor, philosophers and the sciences, the arts and their *chef-d'œuvres*, all disappeared; and those immense regions, where had flourished all the civilization and refinement that had been gained during so many ages, were suddenly plunged into ignorance and barbarism. Nevertheless, the spark of light which had appeared to the world in Palestine, continued to shine amid the chaos: in vain did whirlwinds threaten to extinguish it; kept alive by the breath of the Eternal, it continued to shine. Ages rolled away, and it appeared with greater brilliancy; and when, perchance, the nations only expected a beam of light to guide them in the darkness, they found a resplendent sun, everywhere diffusing life and light: and who shall say that there is not reserved for her in the secrets of the Eternal, another triumph more difficult, but not less useful, not less brilliant? If in other times that religion instructed ignorance, civilized barbarism, polished rudeness, softened ferocity, and preserved society from being always the prey of the fiercest brutality and the most degrading stupidity, will it be less glorious for her to correct ideas, to harmonize and refine feelings, to establish the eternal principles of society, to curb the passions, to remove animosities, to remove excesses, to govern all minds and hearts? How honorable will it be to her, if, while regulating all things, and unceasingly stimulating all kinds of knowledge and improvement, she can inspire with a proper spirit of moderation that society which so many elements, devoid of central attraction, threaten every moment with dissolution and death!

It is not given to man to penetrate the future; but in the same way as the physical world would be broken up by a terrible catastrophe, if it were deprived for a moment of the fundamental principle which gives unity, order, and concert to the various movements of the system; in the same way, if society, full as it is of motion, of communication, and life, were not placed under the direction of a constant and universal regulating principle, we could not fix our eyes on the lot of future generations without the greatest alarm.

There is, however, a fact which is consoling in the highest degree, viz. the wonderful progress which Catholicity has made in different countries. It is gaining strength in France and Belgium: the obstinacy with which it is combated in the north of Europe shows how much it is feared. In England its progress has been recently so great that it would not be credited without the most irresistible evidence; and in the foreign missions it has shown an extent of enterprise and fruitfulness, worthy of the time of its greatest ascendency and power.

When other nations tend towards unity, shall we commit the gross mistake of adopting schism? at a time when other nations would be happy to find within their bosoms a vital principle capable of restoring the power which incredulity has destroyed, shall Spain, which preserves Catholicity, and alone possesses it full and complete, allow the germ of death to be introduced into her bosom thereby rendering impossible the cure of her evils, or rather entailing on herself complete and certain ruin? Amid the moral regeneration towards which nations are advancing, seeking to quit the painful position in which they have been placed by irreligious doctrines, is it possible to overlook the immense advantage which Spain still preserves over most of them? Spain is one of those least affected by the gangrene of irreligion; she still preserves religious unity, that inestimable inheritance of a long line of ages. Is it possible to overlook the advantage of that unity if properly made use of, that unity which is mixed up with all our glories, which awakens such noble recollections, and which may be made so wonderful an instrument in the regeneration of social order?

If I am asked my opinion of the nearness of the danger, and if I think the present attempts of Protestants have any probability of success, I must draw a distinction in my reply. Protestantism is extremely weak, both on account of its own nature, and of its age and decaying condition. In endeavoring to introduce itself into Spain, it will have to contend with an adversary full of life and strength, and deeply rooted in the soil. This is the reason why I think that its direct action is not to be feared; and yet, if it should succeed in establishing itself in any part of our country, however limited may be its domain, it is sure to produce fearful results. It is evident that we shall then have in the midst of us a new apple of discord, and it is not difficult to foresee that collisions will frequently arise. Protestantism in Spain, besides its intrinsic weakness, will labor under the disadvantage of not finding its natural aliment. Hence it will be obliged to take advantage of any support that is offered; it will immediately become the point of reunion for the discontented; and although failing in its intended object, it will succeed in becoming the nucleus of new parties and the banner of factions. Scandal, strife, demoralization, troubles, and perhaps catastrophes,—such will be the immediate and infallible results of the introduction of Protestantism among us. On this point I appeal to the candid opinion of every man who is well acquainted with Spain. But this is not all: the question is enlarged, and acquires an incalculable importance, if we consider it with reference to foreign politics. What a lever will be afforded to foreigners for all kinds of attempts in our unhappy country! How gladly will those, who are perhaps on the look-out for such an aid, avail themselves of it!

There is in Europe a nation remarkable for her immense power, and worthy of respect on account of the great progress which she has made in the arts and sciences; a nation that holds in her hands powerful means of action in all parts of the world, and knows how to use them with wonderful discretion and sagacity. As that nation has taken the lead in modern times in passing through all the phases of political and religious revolution, and has seen, during fearful convulsions, the passions in all their nakedness, and crime in all its forms, she is better acquainted than all others with their causes.

Not misled by the vain names under which, at such periods, the lowest passions and the most sordid interests disguise themselves, she is too much on her guard to allow the troubles which have inundated other countries with tears and blood, to be easily excited within herself. Her internal peace is not disturbed by the agitation and heat of disputes; although she may expect to have to encounter, sooner or later, difficulties and embarrassments, she enjoys, in the mean time, the tranquillity which is secured to her by her constitution, her manners, her riches,—and, above all, by the ocean which surrounds her. Placed in so advantageous a position, that nation watches the progress of others, for the purpose of attaching them to her car by golden chains, if they are simple enough to listen to her flattery; at least she attempts to hinder their advance, when a noble independence is about to free them from her influence. Always attentive to her own aggrandizement, by means of commerce and the arts, and by a policy eminently mercantile, she hides her self-interest under all sorts of disguises; and although religion and politics, where she has to do with another people, are quite indifferent to her, she knows how to make an adroit use of these powerful arms, to make friends, to defeat her enemies, and to enclose all within the net of commerce, which she is always extending in all quarters of the world. Her sagacity must necessarily have perceived how much progress she will have made in adding Spain to the number of her colonies, when she has persuaded the Spanish people to fraternize with her in religion; not so much on account of the sympathy which such a fraternization would establish between them, as because she would find therein a sure method of stripping the Spanish people of that peculiar character and grave appearance which distinguishes them from all others, by depriving them of the only national and regenerative idea which remains to them after so many convulsions; from that moment, in truth, Spain, that proud nation, would be rendered accessible to all kinds of foreign impressions, docile and pliable in bending to all opinions, and subject to the interests of her astute protectors. Let it not be forgotten that there is no other nation that conceives her plans with so much foresight, prepares them with so much prudence, executes them with so much ability and perseverance. As she has remained since her great revolutions, that is, since the end of the seventeenth century, in a settled condition, and entirely free from the convulsions undergone since that time by other European nations, she has been able to follow a regular political system, both internal and external; and her politicians have been formed to the perfect science of government, by constantly inheriting the experience and views of their predecessors. Her statesmen well know how important it is to be prepared beforehand for every event. They deeply study what may aid or impede them in other nations. They go out of the sphere of politics: they penetrate to the heart of every nation over which they propose to extend their influence: they examine what are the conditions of its existence; what is its vital principle; what are the causes of the strength and energy of every people.

During the autumn of 1805, Pitt gave a dinner in the country to some of his friends. While thus engaged, a despatch was brought to him announcing the surrender of Mack at Ulm, with 40,000 men, and the march of Napoleon on Vienna. Pitt communicated the fatal news to his friends, who cried out, "All is lost; there is no longer any resource against him." "There is one still left," replied the minister, "if I can excite a national war in Europe; and that war must begin in Spain." "Yes, gentlemen," he added, "Spain will be the first country to commence the patriotic war which shall give liberty to Europe." Such was the importance attributed by this profound statesman to a national idea; he expected from it what the strength of all the governments could not effect, the downfall of Napoleon, and the liberation of Europe. But it not uncommonly happens that the march of events is such, that these same national ideas, which one time were the powerful auxiliaries of ambitious cabinets, become, at another, the greatest obstacles; and then, instead of encouraging, it becomes their interest to extinguish them. As the nature of this work will not allow me to enter into the details of politics, I must content myself with appealing to the judgment of those who have observed the line of conduct pursued by England during our war and revolution, since the death of Ferdinand VII. If we consider what the interests of that powerful nation require for the future, we may conjecture the part which she will take.

The means of saving a nation, by delivering it from interested protectors, and of securing her real independence, are to be found in great and generous ideas, deeply rooted in the people; in feelings engraved on their hearts by the action of time, by the influence of powerful institutions, by ancient manners and customs; in fine, in that unity of religious thought, which makes a whole people as one man. Then the past is united with the present, the present is connected with the future; then arises in the mind that enthusiasm which is the source of great deeds; then are found disinterestedness, energy, and constancy; because ideas are fixed and elevated, because hearts are great and generous.

It is not impossible that during one of the convulsions which disturb our unhappy country, men may arise amongst us blind enough to attempt to introduce the Protestant religion into Spain. We have had warnings enough to alarm us; we have not forgotten events which showed plainly enough how far some would sometimes have gone, if the great majority of the nation had not restrained them by their disapprobation. We do not dread the outrages of the reign of Henry VIII.; but what we do fear is, that advantage may be taken of a violent rupture with the Holy See, of the obstinacy and ambition of some ecclesiastics, of the pretext of establishing toleration in our country, or some other pretext, to attempt to introduce amongst us, in some shape or other, the doctrines of Protestantism. We certainly have no need of importing toleration from abroad; it already exists amongst us so fully, that no one is afraid of being disturbed on account of his religious opinions. What would be thus introduced and established in Spain, would be a new system of religion, provided with every thing necessary for gaining the upper hand; and for weakening, and, if possible, destroying Catholicity. Then would resound in our ears, with a force constantly increasing, the fierce declamation which we have heard for several years; the vain threatenings of a party who are delirious, because they are on the point of expiring. The aversion with which the nation regards the pretended Reformation, we have no doubt, would be looked upon as rebellion; the pastorals of bishops would be treated as insidious persuasions, and the fervent zeal of our priests as sedition; the unanimity of Catholics to preserve themselves from contagion would be denounced as a diabolical conspiracy, devised by intolerance and party spirit, and executed by ignorance and fanaticism. Amid the efforts of the one party, and the resistance of the other, we should see enacted, in a greater or less degree, the scenes of times gone by; and although the spirit of moderation, which is one of the characteristics of this age, would not allow the perpetration of excesses which have stained the annals of other nations, they would not be without imitators. We must not forge that, with respect to religion in Spain, we cannot calculate on the coldness and indifference which other nations would now display on a similar occasion. With the latter, religious feelings have lost much of their force, but in Spain they are still deep, lively, and energetic; and if they were to come into open and avowed opposition to each other, the shock would be violent and general. Although we have witnessed lamentable scandals, and even fearful catastrophes in religious matters, yet, up to this time, perverse intentions have been always concealed by a mask, more or less transparent. Sometimes the attack was made against a person charged with political machinations; sometimes against certain classes of citizens, who were accused of imaginary crimes. If, at times, the revolution exceeded its bounds, it was said that it was impossible to restrain it, and thus the vexations, the insults, the outrages heaped upon all that was most sacred upon earth, were only the inevitable results, and the work of a mob that nothing could restrain. There has always been more or less of disguise; but if the dogmas of Catholicity were attacked deliberately, and with *sang froid;* if the most important points of discipline were trodden under foot; if the most august mysteries were turned into ridicule, and the most holy ceremonies treated with public contempt; if church were raised against church, and pulpit against pulpit, what would be the result? It is certain that minds would be very much exasperated; and if, as might be feared, alarming explosions did not ensue, at least religious controversy would assume a character so violent that we should believe ourselves transferred to the sixteenth century.

It is a common thing among us for the principles which prevail in politics to be entirely opposed to those which rule in society; it may then easily happen that a religious principle, rejected by society, may find support among influential statesmen. We should then see reproduced, under more important circumstances, a phenomenon which we have witnessed for so many years, viz. governments attempting to alter the course of society by force. This is one of the principal differences between our revolution and those of other countries; it is, at the same time, a key which explains the greatest anomalies. Everywhere else revolutionary ideas took possession of society, and afterwards extended themselves to the sphere of politics; with us they first ruled in the political sphere, and afterwards strove to descend into the social sphere; society was far from being prepared for such innovations; this was the cause of shocks so violent and so frequent. It is on account of this want of harmony that the government of Spain exercises so little influence over the people; I mean by influence, that moral ascendency which does not require to be accompanied by the idea of force. There is no doubt that this is an evil, since it tends to weaken that authority which is indispensably necessary for all societies. But on more than one occasion it has been a great benefit. It is no slight advantage that in presence of a senseless and inconstant government there is found a society full of calmness and wisdom, and that that society pursues its quiet and majestic march, while the government is carried away by rashness. We may expect much from the right instinct of the Spanish nation, from her proverbial gravity, which so many misfortunes have only augmented, and from that fact, which teaches her so well how to discern the true path to happiness, by rendering her deaf to the insidious suggestions of those who seek to lead her astray. Although for so many years, owing to a fatal combination of circumstances, and a want of harmony between the social and political order, Spain has not been able to obtain a government which understands her feelings and instincts, follows her inclinations, and promotes her prosperity, we still cherish the hope that the day will come when from her own bosom, so fertile in future life, will come forth the harmony which she seeks, and the equilibrium which she has lost. In the mean time, it is of the highest importance that all men who have a Spanish heart in their breasts, and who do not wish to see the vitals of their country torn to pieces, should unite and act in concert to preserve her from the genius of evil. Their unanimity will prevent the seeds of perpetual discord from being scattered upon our soil, will ward off this additional calamity, and will preserve from destruction those precious germs, whence may arise, with renovated vigor, our civilization, which has been so much injured by disastrous events.

The soul is overwhelmed with painful apprehensions at the thought that a day may come when religious unity will be banished from among us; that unity which is identified with our habits, our customs, our manners, our laws; which guarded the cradle of our monarchy in the cavern of Covadonga, and which was the emblem on our standard during a struggle of eight centuries against the formidable crescent; that unity which developed and illustrated our civilization in times of the greatest difficulty; that unity which followed our terrible *tercios*, when they imposed silence upon Europe; which led our sailors when they discovered the new world, and guided them when they for the first time made the circuit of the globe; that unity which sustains our soldiers in their most heroic exploits, and which, at a recent period, gave the climax to their many glorious deeds in the downfall of Napoleon. You who condemn so rashly the work of ages; you who offer so many insults to the Spanish nation, and who treat as barbarism and ignorance the regulating principle of our civilization, do you know what it is you insult? Do you know what inspired the genius of Gonzalva, of Ferdinando Cortez, of the conqueror of Lepanto? Do not the shades of Garcilazo, of Herrara, of Ercilla, of Fray Luis de Leon, of Cervantes, of Lope de Vega, inspire you with any respect? Can you venture to break the tie which connects us with them, to make us the unworthy posterity of these great men? Do you wish to place an impassable barrier between their faith and ours, between their manners and ours, to make us destroy all our traditions, and to forget our most inspiring recollections? Do you wish to preserve the great and august monuments of our ancestors' piety among us only as a severe and eloquent reproach? Will you consent to see dried up the most abundant fountains to which we can have recourse to revive literature, to strengthen science, to reorganize legislation, to re-establish the spirit of nationality, to restore our glory, and replace this nation in the high position which her virtues merit, by restoring to her the peace and happiness which she seeks with so much anxiety, and which her heart requires?

CHAPTER XIII.

CATHOLICITY AND PROTESTANTISM IN RELATION TO SOCIAL PROGRESS. PRELIMINARY COUP D'ŒIL.

After having placed Catholicity and Protestantism in contrast, in a religious point of view, in the picture which I have just drawn; after having shown the superiority of the one over the other, not only in certainty, but also in all that regards the instincts, the feelings, the ideas, the characteristics of the human mind, it seems to me proper to approach another question, certainly not less important, but much less understood, and in the examination of which we shall have to contend against strong antipathies, and to dissipate many prejudices and errors. Amid the difficulties by which the question that I am about to undertake is surrounded, I am supported by a strong hope that the interest of the subject, and its analogy with the scientific taste of the age, will invite a perusal; and that I shall thereby avoid the danger which commonly threatens those who write in favor of the Catholic religion, that of being judged without being heard. The question may be stated thus: "When we compare Catholicity and Protestantism, which do we find the most favorable to real liberty, to the real progress of nations, to the cause of civilization?" Liberty! This is one of those words which are as generally employed as they are little understood; words which, because they contain a certain vague idea, easily perceived, present the deceptive appearance of perfect clearness, while, on account of the multitude and variety of objects to which they apply, they are susceptible of a variety of meanings, and, consequently, are extremely difficult to comprehend. Who can reckon the number of applications made of the word liberty? There is always found in this word a certain radical idea, but the modifications and graduations to which the idea is subject are infinite. The air circulates with liberty; we move the soil around the plant, to enable it to grow and increase with liberty; we clean out the bed of a stream to allow it to flow with liberty; when we set free a fish in a net, or a bird in a cage, we give them their liberty; we treat a friend with freedom; we have free methods, free thoughts, free expressions, free successions, free will, free actions; a prisoner has no liberty; nor have boys, girls, or married people; a man behaves with greater freedom in a foreign country; soldiers are not free; there are men free from conscription, from contributions; we have free votes, free acknowledgments, free interpretation, free evidence; freedom of commerce, of instruction, of the press, of conscience; civil freedom, and political freedom; we have freedom just, unjust, rational, irrational, moderate, excessive, limited, licentious, seasonable, unseasonable. But I need not pursue the endless enumeration. It seemed to me necessary to dwell upon it for a moment, even at the risk of fatiguing the reader; perhaps the remembrance of all this may serve to engrave deeply on our minds the truth, that when, in conversation, in writing, in public discussions, in laws, this word is so frequently employed as applied to objects of the highest importance, it is necessary to consider maturely the number and nature of the ideas which it embraces in the particular case, the meaning that the subject needs, the modifications which the circumstances require, and the precaution demanded in the case.

Whatever may be the acceptation in which the word liberty is taken, it is apparent that it always implies the absence of a cause restraining the exercise of a power. Hence it follows that, in order to fix in each case the real meaning of the word, it is indispensable to pay attention to the circumstances as well as to the nature of the power, the exercise of which is to be prevented or limited, without losing sight of the various objects to which it applies, the conditions of its exercise, as also the character, power, and extent of the means which are employed to restrain it. To explain this matter, let it be proposed to form a judgment on the proposition, "Man ought to enjoy liberty of thought."

It is here affirmed that freedom of thought in man ought not to be restrained; but do you speak of physical force exercised directly on thought itself? In that case the proposition is entirely vain; for as such an application of force is impossible, it is useless to say that it ought not to be employed. Do you mean to say that it is not allowable to restrain the expression of thought; that is to say, that the liberty of manifesting thought ought not to be hindered or restrained? You have, then, made a great step, you have placed the question on a different footing. Or if you do not mean to say that every man, at all times, in all places, and on all subjects, has a right to give utterance to all that comes into his head, and that in any way he may think proper, you must then specify the things, the persons, the places, the times, the subjects, the conditions; in short, you must note a variety of circumstances, you must prohibit altogether in some cases, limit in others, bind in some, loosen in others; in fine, make so many restrictions, that you will make little progress in establishing your general principle of freedom of thought, which at first appeared so simple and so clear. Even in the sanctuary of thought, where human sight does not extend, and which is open to the eye of God alone, what means the liberty of thought? Is it owing to chance that laws are imposed on thought to which it is obliged to submit under pain of losing itself in chaos? Can it despise the rules of sound reason? Can it refuse to listen to the counsels of good sense? Can it forget that its object is truth? Can it disregard the eternal principles of morality? Thus we find, in examining the meaning of the word liberty, even as applied to what is certainly freer than any thing else in man, viz. thought—we find such a number and variety of meanings that we are forced to make many distinctions, and necessity compels us to limit the general proposition, if we wish to avoid saying any thing in opposition to the dictates of reason and good sense, the eternal laws of morality, the interests of individuals, and the peace and preservation of society. And what may not be said of so many claims of liberty which are constantly propounded in language intentionally vague and equivocal?

I avail myself of these examples to prevent a confusion of ideas; for in defending the cause of Catholicity, I have no need of pleading for oppression, or of applauding tyranny, or of approving the conduct of those who have trodden under foot men's most sacred rights. Yes, I say, sacred; for after the august religion of Jesus Christ has been preached, man is sacred in the eyes of other men on account of his origin and divine destiny, on account of the image of God which is reflected in him, and because he has been redeemed with ineffable goodness and love by the Son of the Eternal. This divine religion declares the rights of man to be sacred; for its august Founder threatens with eternal punishment not only those who kill a man, those who mutilate or rob him, but even those who offend him in words: "He who shall say to his brother, Thou fool, shall be in danger of hell-fire." (Matt. v. 22.) Thus speaks our divine Lord.

Our hearts swell with generous indignation, when we hear the religion of Jesus Christ reproached with a tendency towards oppression. It is true that, if you confound the spirit of real liberty with that of demagogues, you will not find it in Catholicity; but, if you avoid a monstrous misnomer, if you give to the word liberty its reasonable, just, useful, and beneficial signification, then the Catholic religion may fearlessly claim the gratitude of the human race, *for she has civilized the nations who embraced her, and civilization is true liberty.*

It is a fact now generally acknowledged, and openly confessed, that Christianity has exercised a very important and salutary influence on the development of European civilization; if this fact has not yet had given to it the importance which it deserves, it is because it has not been sufficiently appreciated. With respect to civilization, a distinction is sometimes made between the influence of Christianity and that of Catholicity; its merits are lavished on the former, and stinted to the latter, by those who forget that, with respect to European civilization, Catholicity can always claim the principal share; and, for many centuries, an exclusive one; since, during a very long period, she worked alone at the great work. People have not been willing to see that, when Protestantism appeared in Europe, the work was bordering on completion; with an injustice and ingratitude which I cannot describe, they have reproached Catholicity with the spirit of barbarism, ignorance, and oppression, while they were making an ostentatious display of the rich civilization, knowledge, and liberty, for which they were principally indebted to her.

If they did not wish to fathom the intimate connection between Catholicity and European civilization, if they had not the patience necessary for the long investigations into which this examination would lead them, at least it would have been proper to take a glance at the condition of countries where the Catholic religion has not exerted all her influence during centuries of trouble, and compare them with those in which she has been predominant. The East and the West, both subject to great revolutions, both professing Christianity, but in such a way that the Catholic principle was weak and vacillating in the East, while it was energetic and deeply rooted in the West; these, we say, would have afforded two very good points of comparison to estimate the value of Christianity without Catholicity, when the civilization and the existence of nations were at stake. In the West, the revolutions were multiplied and fearful; the chaos was at its height; and, nevertheless, out of chaos came light and life. Neither the barbarism of the nations who inundated those countries, and established themselves there, nor the furious assaults of Islamism, even in the days of its greatest power and enthusiasm, could succeed in destroying the germs of a rich and fertile civilization. In the East, on the contrary, all tended to old age and decay; nothing revived; and, under the blows of the power which was ineffectual against us, all was shaken to pieces. The spiritual power of Rome, and its influence on temporal affairs, have certainly borne fruits very different from those produced, under the same circumstances, by its violent opponents.

If Europe were destined one day again to undergo a general and fearful revolution, either by a universal spread of revolutionary ideas or by a violent invasion of social and proprietary rights by pauperism; if the colossus of the North, seated on its throne amid eternal snows, with knowledge in its head, and blind force in its hands, possessing at once the means of civilization, and unceasingly turning towards the East, the South, and the West that covetous and crafty look which in history is the characteristic march of all invading empires; if, availing itself of a favorable moment, it were to make an attempt on the independence of Europe, then we should perhaps have a proof of the value of the Catholic principle in a great extremity; then we should feel the power of the unity which is proclaimed and supported by Catholicity, and while calling to mind the middle ages, we should come to acknowledge one of the causes of the weakness of the East and the strength of the West. Then would be remembered a fact, which, though but of yesterday, is falling into oblivion, viz. that the nation whose heroic courage broke the power of Napoleon was proverbially Catholic; and who knows whether, in the attempts made in Russia against Catholicity, attempts which the Vicar of Jesus Christ has deplored in such touching language—who knows whether there be not the secret influence of a presentiment, perhaps even a foresight of the necessity of weakening that sublime power, which has been in all ages, when the cause of humanity was in question, the centre of great attempts? But let us return.

It cannot be denied that, since the sixteenth century, European civilization has shown life and brilliancy; but it is a mistake to attribute this phenomenon to Protestantism. In order to examine the extent and influence of a fact, we ought not to be content with the events which have followed it; it is also necessary to consider whether these events were already prepared; whether they are any thing more than the necessary result of anterior facts; and we must take care not to reason in a way which is justly declared to be sophistical by logicians, *post hoc, ergo propter hoc:* after that, therefore on account of it. Without Protestantism, and before it, European civilization was already very much advanced, thanks to the labors and influence of the Catholic religion; the greatness and splendor which it subsequently displayed were not owing to it, but arose in spite of it.

Erroneous ideas on this matter have arisen from the fact, that Christianity has not been deeply studied; and that, without entering into a serious examination of Church history, men have too often contented themselves with taking a superficial view of the principles of brotherhood which she has so much recommended. In order fully to understand an institution, it is not enough to remain satisfied with its leading ideas; it is necessary to follow all its steps, see how it realizes its ideas, and how it triumphs over the obstacles that oppose it. We shall never form a complete idea of an historical fact, unless we carefully study its history. Now the study of Church history in its relations with civilization, is still incomplete. It is not that ecclesiastical history has not been profoundly studied; but it may be said that since the spirit of social analysis has been developed, that history has not yet been made the subject of those admirable labors which have thrown so much light upon it in a critical and dogmatical point of view.

Another impediment to the complete comprehension of this matter is, that an exaggerated importance is given to the intentions of men, and the great march of events is too much neglected. The greatness of events is measured, and their nature judged of, by the immediate means which produces them, and the objects of the men whose actions are treated of; this is a very important error. The eye ought to range over a wider field; we ought to observe the successive development of ideas, the influence which they have exercised on events, the institutions which have sprung from them; but it is necessary to see all these things as they are in themselves, that is, on a large scale, without stopping to consider particular and isolated facts. It is an important truth, which ought to be deeply engraven on the mind, that when one of those great facts which change the lot of a considerable portion of the human race is developed, it is rarely understood by those who take part in it, and figure as the principal actors. The march of humanity is a grand drama; the parts are played by persons who pass by and disappear: man is very little; God alone is great. Neither the actors who figured on the scene in the ancient empires of the East, nor Alexander invading Asia and reducing numberless nations into servitude, nor the Romans subjugating the world, nor the barbarians overturning the empire and breaking it in pieces, nor the Mussulmen ruling Asia and Africa and menacing the independence of Europe, knew, or could know, that they were the instruments in the great designs whereof we admire the execution.

I mean to show from this, that when we have to do with Christian civilization, when we collect and analyze the facts which distinguish its march, it is not necessary, or even often proper, to suppose that the men who have contributed to it in the most remarkable manner understood, to the full extent, the results of their own efforts. It is glory enough for a man to be pointed out as the chosen instrument of Providence, without the necessity of attributing to him great ability or lofty ambition. It is enough to observe that a ray of light has descended from heaven and illumined his brow; it is of little importance whether he foresaw that this ray, by reflection, was destined to shed a brilliant light on future generations. Little men are commonly smaller than they think themselves, but great men are often greater than they imagine; if they do not know all their grandeur, it is because they are ignorant that they are the instruments of the high designs of Providence. Another observation which we ought always to have present in the study of these great events is, that we should not expect to find there a system, the connection and harmony of which are apparent at the first *coup d'œil.* We must expect to see some irregularities and objects of an unpleasant aspect; it is necessary to guard against the childish impatience of anticipating the time; it is indispensable to abandon that desire which we always have, in a greater or less degree, and which always urges us to seek every thing in conformity with our own ideas, and to see every thing advance in the way most pleasing to us.

Do you not see nature herself so varied, so rich, so grand, lavish her treasures in disorder, hide her inestimable precious stones and her most valuable veins of metal in masses of earth? See how she presents huge chains of mountains, inaccessible rocks, and fearful precipices, in contrast with her wide and smiling plains. Do you not observe this apparent disorder, this prodigality, in the midst of which numberless agents work, in secret concert, to produce the admirable whole which enchants our eyes and ravishes the lover of nature? So with society; the facts are dispersed, scattered here and there, frequently offering no appearance of order or concert; events succeed each other, act on each other, without the design being discovered; men unite, separate, co-operate, and contend, and nevertheless time, that indispensable agent in the production of great works, goes on, and all is accomplished according to the destinies marked out in the secrets of the Eternal.

This is the march of humanity; this is the rule for the philosophic study of history; this is the way to comprehend the influence of those productive ideas, of those powerful institutions, which from time to time appear among men to change the face of the earth. When in a study of this kind we discover acting at the bottom of things a productive idea, a powerful institution, the mind, far from being frightened at meeting with some irregularities, is inspired, on the contrary, with fresh courage; for it is a sure sign that the idea is full of truth, that the institution is fraught with life, when we see them pass through the chaos of ages, and come safe out of the frightful ordeals. Of what importance is it that certain men were not influenced by the idea, that they did not answer the object of the institution, if the latter has survived its revolutions, and the former has not been swallowed up in the stormy sea of the passions? To mention the weaknesses, the miseries, the faults, the crimes of men, is to make the most eloquent apology for the idea and the institution.

In viewing men in this way, we do not take them out of their proper places, and we do not require from them more than is reasonable. We see them enclosed in the deep bed of the great torrent of events, and we do not attribute to their intellects, or to their will, any thing that exceeds the sphere appointed for them; we do not, however, fail to appreciate in a proper manner the nature and the greatness of the works in which they take part, but we avoid giving to them an exaggerated importance, by honoring them with eulogiums which they do not deserve, or reproaching them unjustly. Times and circumstances are not monstrously confounded; the observer sees with calmness and *sang froid* the events which pass before his eyes; he speaks not of the empire of Charlemagne as he would of that of Napoleon, and is not hurried into bitter invectives against Gregory VII. because he did not adopt the same line of political conduct as Gregory XVI.

Observe that I do not ask from the philosophical historian an impassive indifference to good and evil, to justice and injustice; I do not claim indulgence for vice, nor would I refuse to virtue its eulogy. I have no sympathy with that school of historic fatalism, which would bring back to the world the destiny of the ancients; a school which, if it acquired influence, would corrupt the best part of history, and stifle the most generous emotions. I see in the march of society a plan, a harmony, but not a blind necessity; I do not believe that events are mingled up together indiscriminately in the dark urn of destiny, nor that fatalism holds the world enclosed in an iron circle. But I see a wonderful chain stretching over the course of centuries, a chain which does not fetter the movements of individuals or of nations, and which accommodates itself to the ebb and flow which are required by the nature of things; at its touch great thoughts arise in the minds of men: this golden chain is suspended by the hand of the Eternal, it is the work of infinite intelligence and ineffable love.

CHAPTER XIV.

DID THERE EXIST AT THE EPOCH WHEN CHRISTIANITY APPEARED ANY OTHER PRINCIPLE OF REGENERATION?

In what condition did Christianity find the world? This is a question which ought to fix all our attention, if we wish to appreciate correctly the blessings conferred by that divine religion on individuals and on society, if we are desirous of knowing the real character of Christian civilization. Certainly at the time when Christianity appeared, society presented a dark picture. Covered with fine appearances, but infected to the heart with a mortal malady, it presented an image of the most repugnant corruption, veiled by a brilliant garb of ostentation and opulence. Morality was without reality, manners without modesty, the passions without restraint, laws without authority, and religion without God. Ideas were at the mercy of prejudices, of religious fanaticism, and philosophical subtilties. Man was a profound mystery to himself; he did not know how to estimate his own dignity, for he reduced it to the level of brutes; and when he attempted to exaggerate its importance, he did not know how to confine it within the limits marked out by reason and nature: and it is well worthy of observation, that while a great part of the human race groaned in the most abject servitude, heroes, and even the most abominable monsters, were elevated to the rank of gods.

Such elements must, sooner or later, have produced social dissolution. Even if the violent irruption of the barbarians had not taken place, society must have been overturned sooner or later, for it did not possess a fertile idea, a consoling thought, or a beam of hope, to preserve it from ruin.

Idolatry had lost its strength; it was an expedient exhausted by time and by the gross abuse which the passions had made of it. Its fragile tissue once exposed to the dissolving influence of philosophical observation, idolatry was entirely disgraced; and if the rooted force of habit still exercised a mechanical influence on the minds of men, that influence was neither capable of re-establishing harmony in society, nor of producing that fiery enthusiasm which inspires great actions—enthusiasm which in virgin hearts may be excited by superstition the most irrational and absurd. To judge of them by the relaxation of morals, by the enervated weakness of character, by the effeminate luxury, by the complete abandonment to the most repulsive amusements and the most shameful pleasures, it is clear that religious ideas no longer possessed the majesty of the heroic age; no longer efficacious, they only exerted on men's minds a feeble influence, while they served in a lamentable manner as instruments of dissolution. Now it was impossible for it to be otherwise: nations who had obtained the high degree of cultivation of the Greeks and Romans;

nations who had heard their great sages dispute on the grand questions of divinity and man, could not continue in the state of simplicity which was necessary to believe with good faith the intolerable absurdities of which Paganism is full; and whatever may have been the disposition of mind among the ignorant portion of the people, assuredly those who were raised above the common standard did not believe them—those who listened to philosophers as enlightened as Cicero, and who daily enjoyed the malicious railleries of their satirical poets.

If religion was impotent, was there not another means, viz. knowledge? Before we examine what was to be hoped from this, it is necessary to observe, that knowledge never founded a society, nor was it ever able to restore one that had lost its balance. In looking over the history of ancient times, we find at the head of some nations eminent men who, thanks to the magic influence which they exercised over others, dictated laws, corrected abuses, rectified ideas, reformed morals, and established a government on wise principles; thus securing, in a more or less satisfactory manner, the happiness and prosperity of those who were confided to their care. But we should be much mistaken if we imagined that these men proceeded according to what we call scientific combinations. Generally simple and rude, they acted according to the impulses of their generous hearts, only guided by the wisdom and good sense of the father of a family in the management of his domestic affairs: never did these men adopt for their rule the wretched subtilties which we call theories, the crude mass of ideas which we disguise under the pompous name of science. Were the most distinguished days of Greece those of Plato and Aristotle? The proud Romans, who conquered the world, certainly had not the extent and variety of knowledge of the Augustan age; and yet who would exchange the times or the men?

Modern times also can show important evidences of the sterility of science in creating social institutions; which is the more evident as the practical effects of the natural sciences are the more visible. It seems that in the latter sciences man has a power which he has not in the former; although, when the matter is fully examined, the difference does not appear so great as at the first view.

Let us briefly compare their respective results.

When man seeks to apply the knowledge which he has acquired of the great laws of nature, he finds himself compelled to pay respect to her; as, whatever might be his wishes, his weak arm could not cause any great *bouleversement*, he is obliged to make his attempts limited in extent, and the desire of success induces him to act in conformity with the laws which govern the bodies he has to do with. It is quite otherwise with the application made of the social sciences. There man is able to act directly and immediately on society itself, on its eternal foundations; he does not consider himself necessarily bound to make his attempts on a small scale, or to respect the eternal laws of society; he is able, on the contrary, to imagine those laws as he pleases, indulge in as many subtilties as he thinks proper, and bring about disasters which humanity laments. Let us remember the extravagances which have found favor, with respect to nature, in the schools of philosophy, ancient and modern, and we shall see what would have become of the admirable machine of the universe, if philosophers had had full power over it. Descartes said, "Give me matter and motion, and I will form a world!" He could not derange an atom in the system of the universe. Rousseau, in his turn, dreamed of placing society on a new basis, and he upset the social state. It must not be forgotten that science, properly so called, has little power in the organization of society: this ought to be remembered in modern times, when it boasts so much of its pretended fertility. It attributes to its own labors what is the fruit of the lapse of ages, of the instinctive law of nations, and sometimes of the inspirations of genius; now neither this instinct of nations nor genius at all resembles science.

But without pushing any further these general considerations, which are, nevertheless, very useful in leading us to a knowledge of man, what could be hoped from the false light of science which was preserved in the ruins of the ancient schools at the time we are speaking of? However limited the knowledge of the ancient philosophers, even the most distinguished, may have been on these subjects, we must allow that the names of Socrates, Plato, and Aristotle command some degree of respect, and that amid their errors and mistakes they give us thoughts which are really worthy of their lofty genius. But when Christianity appeared, the germs of knowledge planted by them had been destroyed; dreams had taken the place of high and fruitful thoughts, the love of disputation had replaced that of wisdom, sophistry and subtilties had been substituted for mature judgment and severe reasoning. The ancient schools had been upset, others as sterile as they were strange had been formed out of their ruins; on all sides there appeared a swarm of sophists like the impure insects which announce the corruption of a dead body. The Church has preserved for us a very valuable means of judging of the science of that time, in the history of the early heresies. Without speaking of what therein deserves all our indignation, as, for example, their profound immorality, can we find any thing more empty, absurd, or pitiable? (14)

The Roman legislation, so praiseworthy for its justice and equity, its wisdom and prudence, and much as it deserves to be regarded as one of the most precious ornaments of ancient civilization, was yet incapable of preventing the dissolution with which society was threatened. Never did it owe its safety to jurisconsults; so great a work is beyond the sphere of action of jurisprudence. Let us suppose the laws as perfect as possible, jurisprudence carried to the highest point, jurisconsults animated by the purest feelings and guided by the most honest intentions, what would all this avail if the heart of society is corrupt, if moral principles have lost their force, if manners are in continual opposition with laws? Let us consider the picture of Roman manners such as their own historians have painted them; we shall not find even a reflection of the equity, justice, and good sense which made the Roman laws deserve the glorious name of written reason.

To give a proof of impartiality, I purposely omit the blemishes from which the Roman law was certainly not exempt, for I do not desire to be accused of wishing to lower every thing which is not the work of Christianity. Yet I must not pass over in silence the important fact, that it is by no means true that Christianity had no share in perfecting the jurisprudence of Rome; I do not mean merely during the period of the Christian emperors, which does not admit of a doubt, but even at a prior period. It is certain that some time before the coming of Jesus Christ the number of the Roman laws was very considerable, and that their study and arrangement already occupied the attention of many of the most illustrious men. We know from Suetonius (*In Cæsar.* c. 44) that Julius Cæsar had undertaken the extremely useful task of condensing into a small number of books those which were the most select and necessary among the immense collection of laws; a similar idea occurred to Cicero, who wrote a book on the methodical digest of the civil law (*de jure civili in arte redigendo*), as Aulus Gellius attests. (*Noct. Att.* lib. i. c. 22.) According to Tacitus, this work also occupied the attention of the Emperor Augustus. Certainly these projects show that legislation was not in its infancy; but it is not the less true that the Roman law, as we possess it, is in great part the product of later ages. Many of the most famous jurists, whose opinions form a considerable part of the law, lived long after the coming of Jesus Christ. As to the constitutions of the emperors, their very names remind us of the time when they were digested.

These facts being established, I shall observe that it does not follow that because the emperors and jurists were pagans, the Christian ideas had no influence on their works. The number of Christians was immense in all places; the cruelty alone with which they had been persecuted, the heroic courage which they had displayed in the face of torments and death, must have drawn upon them the attention of the whole world; and it is impossible that this should not have excited, among men of reflection, curiosity enough to examine what this new religion taught its proselytes. The reading of the apologies for Christianity already written in the first ages with so much force of reasoning and eloquence, the works of various kinds published by the early Fathers, the homilies of Bishops to their people, contain so much wisdom, breathe such a love for truth and justice, and proclaim so loudly the eternal principles of morality, that it was impossible for their influence not to be felt even by those who condemned the religion of Christ. When doctrines having for their object the greatest questions which affect man are spread everywhere, propagated with fervent zeal, received with love by a considerable number of disciples, and maintained by the talent and knowledge of illustrious men, these doctrines make a profound impression in all directions, and affect even those who warmly combat them. Their influence in this case is imperceptible, but it is not the less true and real. They act like the exhalations which impregnate the atmosphere; with the air we inhale sometimes death, and sometimes a salutary odor which purifies and strengthens us.

Such must necessarily have been the case with a doctrine which was preached in so extraordinary a manner, propagated with so much rapidity, and the truth of which, sealed by torrents of blood, was defended by writers such as Justin, Clement of Alexandria, Irenæus, and Tertullian. The profound wisdom, the ravishing beauty of these doctrines, explained by the Christian doctors, must have called attention to the sources whence they flowed; it was natural that curiosity thus excited should put the holy Scriptures into the hands of many philosophers and jurists. Would it be strange if Epictetus had imbibed some of the doctrines of the Sermon on the Mount, and if the oracles of jurisprudence had imperceptibly received the inspiration of a religion whose power, spreading in a wonderful manner, took possession of all ranks of society? Burning zeal for truth and justice, the spirit of brotherhood, grand ideas of the dignity of man, the continued themes of Christian instruction, could not remain confined among the children of the Church. More or less rapidly they penetrated all classes; and when, by the conversion of Constantine, they acquired political influence and imperial authority, it was only the repetition of an ordinary phenomenon; when a system has become very powerful in the social order, it ends by exerting an empire, or at least an influence, in the political.

I leave these observations to the judgment of thinking men with perfect confidence; I am sure that if they do not adopt them, at least they will not consider them unworthy of reflection. We live at a time fruitful in great events, and when important revolutions have taken place; therefore we are better able to understand the immense effects of indirect and slow influences, the powerful ascendency of ideas, and the irresistible force with which doctrines work their way.

To this want of vital principles capable of regenerating society, to all those elements of dissolution which society contained within itself, was joined another evil of no slight importance,—the vice of its political organization. The world being under the yoke of Rome, hundreds of nations differing in manners and customs were heaped together in confusion, like spoils on the field of battle, and constrained to form a factitious body, like trophies placed upon a spear. The unity of the government being violent, could not be advantageous; and moreover, as it was despotic, from the emperor down to the lowest pro-consul, it will be seen that it could not produce any other result than the debasement and degradation of nations, and that it was impossible for them to display that elevation and energy of character which are the precious fruit of a feeling of self-dignity and love for national independence. If Rome had preserved her ancient manners, if she had retained in her bosom warriors as celebrated for the simplicity and austerity of their lives as for the renown of their victories, some of the qualities of the conquerors might have been communicated to the conquered, as a young and robust heart reanimates with its vigor a body attenuated by disease. Unfortunately such was not the case. The Fabiuses, the Camilluses, the Scipios, would not have acknowledged their unworthy posterity; Rome, the mistress of the world, like a slave, was trodden under the feet of monsters who mounted to the throne by perjury and violence, stained their sceptres with corruption and cruelty, and fell by the hands of assassins. The authority of the Senate and people had disappeared; only vain imitations of them were left, *vestigia morientis libertatis*, as Tacitus calls them, vestiges of expiring liberty; and this royal people, who formerly disposed of kingdoms, consulships, legions, and all, then thought only of two things, food and games,

> "Qui dabat olim
> Imperium, fasces, legiones, omnia, nunc se
> Continet, atque duas tantum res anxius optat,
> Panem et Circenses."—JUVENAL, *Satire* x.

At length, in the plenitude of time Christianity appeared; and without announcing any change in political forms, without intermeddling in the temporal and earthly, it brought to mankind a twofold salvation, by calling them to the path of eternal felicity, but at the same time bountifully supplying them with the only means of preservation from social dissolution, the germ of a regeneration slow and pacific, but grand, immense, and lasting, and secure from the revolutions of ages; and this preservative against social dissolution, this germ of invaluable improvements, was a pure and lofty doctrine, diffused among all mankind, without exception of age, sex, and condition, as the rain which falls like a mild dew on an arid and thirsty soil. No religion has ever equalled Christianity in knowledge of the hidden means of influencing man; none has ever, when doing so, paid so high a compliment to his dignity; and Christianity has always adopted the principle, that the first step in gaining possession of the whole man is that of gaining his mind; and that it is necessary, in order either to destroy evil or to effect good, to adopt intellectual means: thereby it has given a mortal blow to the systems of violence which prevailed before its existence; it has proclaimed the wholesome truth, that in influencing men, the weakest and most unworthy method is force; a fruitful and beneficial truth, which opened to humanity a new and happy future. Only since the Christian era do we find the lessons of the sublimest philosophy taught to all classes of the people, at all times and in all places. The loftiest truths relating to God and man, the rules of the purest morality, are not communicated to a chosen number of disciples in hidden and mysterious instructions; the philosophy of Christianity has been bolder; it has ventured to reveal to man the whole naked truth, and that in public, with a loud voice, and that generous boldness which is the inseparable companion of the truth. "That which I tell you in the dark, speak ye in the light; and that which you hear in the ear, preach ye upon the housetop." (Matt. x. 27.)

As soon as Christianity and Paganism met face to face, the superiority of the former was rendered palpable, not only by its doctrines themselves, but by the manner in which it propagated them. It might easily be imagined that a religion so wise and pure in its teachings, and which, in propagating them, addressed itself directly to the mind and heart, must quickly drive from its usurped dominion the religion of imposture and falsehood. And, indeed, what did Paganism do for the good of man? What moral truths did it teach? How did it check the corruption of manners? "As to morals," says St. Augustine, "why have not the gods chosen to take care of those of their adorers, and prevent their irregularities? As to the true God, it is with justice that He has neglected those who did not serve Him. But whence comes it that those gods, the prohibition of whose worship is complained of by ungrateful men, have not established laws to lead their adorers to virtue? Was it not reasonable that, as men undertook their mysteries and sacrifices, the gods, on their side, should undertake to regulate the manners and actions of men? It is replied, that no one is wicked but because he wishes to be so. Who doubts this? but the gods ought not on that account to conceal from their worshippers precepts that might serve to make them practise virtue. They were, on the contrary, under the obligation of publishing those precepts aloud, of admonishing and rebuking sinners by their prophets; of publicly threatening punishment to those who did evil, and promising rewards to those who did well. Was there ever heard, in the temples of the gods, a loud and generous voice teaching any thing of the kind?" (*De Civit.* lib. ii. c. 4.) The holy doctor afterwards paints a dark picture of the infamies and abominations which were committed in the spectacles and sacred games celebrated in honor of the gods—games and shows at which he had himself assisted in his youth; he continues thus: "Thence it comes that these divinities have taken no care to regulate the morals of the cities and nations who adore them, or to avert by their threats those dreadful evils which injure not only fields and vineyards, houses and properties, or the body which is subject to the mind, but the mind itself, the directress of the body, which was drenched with their iniquities. Or if it be pretended that they did make such menaces, let them be shown and proved to us. But let there not be alleged a few secret words whispered in the ears of a small number of persons, and which, with a great deal of mystery, were to teach virtue. It is necessary to point out, to name the places consecrated to the assemblies—not those in which were celebrated games with lascivious words and gestures; not those feasts called *fuites*, and which were solemnized with the most unbridled license; but the assemblies where the people were instructed in the precepts of the gods for the repression of avarice, moderating ambition, restraining immodesty; those where these unfortunate beings learn what Perseus desires them to know, when he says, in severe language, 'Learn, O unhappy mortals, the reason of things, what we are, why we come into the world, what we ought to do, how miserable is the term of our career, what bounds we ought to prescribe to ourselves in the pursuit of riches, what use we ought to make of them, what we owe to our neighbor, in fine, the obligations we owe to the rank we occupy among men.' Let them tell us in what places they have been accustomed to instruct the people in these things by order of the gods; let them show us these places, as we show them churches built for this purpose wherever the Christian religion has been established." (*De Civit.* lib. ii. c. 6.) This divine religion was too deeply acquainted with the heart of man ever to forget the weakness and inconstancy which characterize it; and hence it has ever been her invariable rule of conduct unceasingly to inculcate to him, with untiring patience, the salutary truths on which his temporal well-being and eternal happiness depend. Man easily forgets moral truths when he is not constantly reminded of them; or if they remain in his mind, they are there like sterile seeds, and do not fertilize his heart. It is good and highly salutary for parents constantly to communicate this instruction to their children, and that it should be made the principal object of private education; but it is necessary, moreover, that there should be a public ministry, never losing sight of it, diffusing it among all classes and ages, repairing the negligences of families, and reviving recollections and impressions which the passions and time constantly efface.

This system of constant preaching and instruction, practised at all times and in all places by the Catholic Church, is so important for the enlightenment and morality of nations, that it must be looked upon as a great good, that the first Protestants, in spite of their desire to destroy all the practices of the Church, have nevertheless preserved that of preaching. We need not be insensible on this account to the evils produced at certain times by the declamation of some factious or fanatical ministers; but as unity had been broken, as the people had been precipitated into the perilous paths of schism, we say that it must have been extremely useful for the preservation of the most important notions with respect to God and man and the fundamental maxims of morality, that such truths should be frequently explained to the people by men who had long studied them in the sacred Scriptures. No doubt the mortal blow given to the hierarchy by the Protestant system, and the degradation of the priesthood which was the consequence, have deprived its preachers of the sacred characteristics of the Holy Spirit; no doubt it is a great obstacle to the efficacy of their preachers, that they cannot present themselves as the anointed of the Lord, and that they are only, as an able writer has said, *men clothed in black, who mount the pulpit every Sunday to speak reasonable things;* but at least the people continue to hear some fragments of the excellent moral discourses contained in the sacred Scriptures, they have often before their eyes the edifying examples spread over the Old and New Testament, and, what is still more precious, they are reminded frequently of the events in the life of Jesus Christ,—of that admirable life, the model of all perfection, which, even when considered in a human point of view, is acknowledged by all to be the purest sanctity *par excellence,* the noblest code of morality that was ever seen, the realization of the finest *beau ideal* that philosophy in its loftiest thoughts has ever conceived under human form, and which poetry has ever imagined in its most brilliant dreams. This we say is useful and highly salutary; for it will always be salutary for nations to be nourished with the wholesome food of moral truths, and to be excited to virtue by such sublime examples.

CHAPTER XV.

DIFFICULTIES WHICH CHRISTIANITY HAD TO OVERCOME IN THE WORK OF SOCIAL REGENERATION.—OF SLAVERY.—COULD IT BE DESTROYED WITH MORE PROMPTNESS THAN IT WAS BY CHRISTIANITY?

ALTHOUGH the Church attached the greatest importance to the propagation of truth, although she was convinced that to destroy the shapeless mass of immorality and degradation that met her sight, her first care should be to expose error to the dissolving fire of true doctrines, she did not confine herself to this; but, descending to real life, and following a system full of wisdom and prudence, she acted in such a manner as to enable humanity to taste the precious fruit which the doctrines of Jesus Christ produce even in temporal things. The Church was not only a *great and fruitful school; she was also a regenerative association;* she did not diffuse her general doctrines by throwing them abroad at hazard, merely hoping that they would fructify with time; she developed them in all their relations, applied them to all subjects, inoculated laws and manners with them, and realized them in institutions which afforded silent but eloquent instructions to future generations. Nowhere was the dignity of man acknowledged, slavery reigned everywhere; degraded woman was dishonored by the corruption of manners, and debased by the tyranny of man. The feelings of humanity were trodden under foot, infants were abandoned, the sick and aged were neglected, barbarity and cruelty were carried to the highest pitch of atrocity in the prevailing laws of war; in fine, on the summit of the social edifice was seen an odious tyranny, sustained by military force, and looking down with an eye of contempt on the unfortunate nations that lay in fetters at its feet.

In such a state of things it certainly was no slight task to remove error, to reform and improve manners, abolish slavery, correct the vices of legislation, impose a check on power, and make it harmonize with the public interest, give new life to individuals, and reorganize family and society; and yet nothing less than this was done by the Church. Let us begin with slavery. This is a matter which is the more to be fathomed, as it is a question eminently calculated to excite our curiosity and affect our hearts. What abolished slavery among Christian nations? Was it Christianity? Was it Christianity alone, by its lofty ideas on human dignity, by its maxims and its spirit of fraternity and charity, and also by its prudent, gentle, and beneficent conduct? I trust I shall prove that it was. No one now ventures to doubt that the Church exercised a powerful influence on the abolition of slavery; this is a truth too clear and evident to be questioned. M. Guizot acknowledges the successful efforts with which the Church labored to improve the social condition. He says: "No one doubts that she struggled obstinately against the great vices of the social state; for example, against slavery." But, in the next line, and as if he were reluctant to establish without any restriction a fact which must necessarily excite in favor of the Catholic Church the sympathies of all humanity, he adds: "It has been often repeated that the abolition of slavery in the modern world was entirely due to Christianity. I believe that this is saying too much; slavery existed for a long time in the bosom of Christian society without exciting astonishment or much opposition." M. Guizot is much mistaken if he expects to prove that the abolition of slavery was not due exclusively to Christianity, by the mere representation that slavery existed for a long time amid Christian society. To proceed logically, he must first see whether the sudden abolition of it was possible, if the spirit of peace and order which animates the Church could allow her rashly to enter on an enterprise which, without gaining the desired object, might have convulsed the world. The number of slaves was immense; slavery was deeply rooted in laws, manners, ideas, and interests, individual and social; a fatal system, no doubt, but the eradication of which all at once it would have been rash to attempt, as its roots had penetrated deeply and spread widely in the bowels of the land.

In a census of Athens there were reckoned 20,000 citizens and 40,000 slaves; in the Peloponnesian war no less than 20,000 passed over to the enemy. This we learn from Thucydides. The same author tells us, that at Chio the number of slaves was very considerable, and that their defection, when they passed over to the Athenians, reduced their masters to great extremities. In general, the number of slaves was so very great everywhere that the public safety was often compromised thereby. Therefore it was necessary to take precautions to prevent their acting in concert. "It is necessary," says Plato (*Dial.* 6, *de Leg.*), "that slaves should not be of the same country, and that they should differ as much as possible in manners and desires; for experience has many times shown, in the frequent defections which have been witnessed, among the Messenians, and in other cities that had a great number of slaves of the same language, that great evils commonly result from it." Aristotle in his Government (b. i. c. 5) gives various rules as to the manner in which slaves ought to be treated; it is remarkable that he is of the same opinion as Plato, for he says: "That there should not be many slaves of the same country." He tells us in his Politics (b. ii. c. 7), "That the Thessalians were reduced to great embarrassments on account of the number of their Penestes, a sort of slaves; the same thing happened to the Spartans on account of the Helotes. The Penestes have often rebelled in Thessaly; and the Spartans, during their reverses, have been menaced by the plots of the Helotes." This was a difficulty which required the serious attention of politicians. They did not know how to prevent the inconveniences induced by this immense multitude of slaves. Aristotle laments the difficulty there was in finding the best way of treating them; and we see that it was the subject of grave cares; I will transcribe his own words: "In truth," he says, "the manner in which this class of men ought to be treated is a thing difficult and full of embarrassment; for if they are treated mildly, they become insolent, and wish to become equal to their masters; if they are treated harshly, they conceive hatred, and conspire."

At Rome, the multitude of slaves was such that when, at a certain period, it was proposed to give them a distinctive dress, the Senate opposed the measure, fearing that if they knew their own numbers the public safety would be endangered; and certainly this precaution was not vain, for already, a long time before, the slaves had caused great commotions in Italy. Plato, in support of the advice which I have just quoted, states, "That the slaves had frequently devastated Italy with piracy and robbery." In more recent times Spartacus, at the head of an army of slaves, was the terror of that country for some time, and engaged the best generals of Rome. The number of slaves had reached such an excess, that many masters reckoned them by hundreds. When the Prefect of Rome, Pedanius Secundus, was assassinated, four hundred slaves who belonged to him were put to death. (*Tac. Ann.* b. xiv.) Pudentila, the wife of Apuleius, had so many that she gave four hundred to her son. They became a matter of pomp, and the Romans vied with each other in their number. When asked this question, *quod pascit servos*, how many slaves does he keep, according to the expression of Juvenal (*Sat.* 3, v. 140), they wished to be able to show a great number. The thing had reached such a pass that, according to Pliny, the cortege of a family resembled an army.

It was not only in Greece and Italy that this abundance of slaves was found; at Tyre they arose against their masters, and, by their immense numbers, they were able to massacre them all. If we turn our eyes towards barbarous nations, without speaking of some the best known, we learn from Herodotus that the Scythians, on their return from Media, found their slaves in rebellion, and were compelled to abandon their country to them. Cæsar in his Commentaries (*de Bello Gall.* lib. vi.) bears witness to the multitude of slaves in Gaul. As their number was everywhere so considerable, it is clear that it was quite impossible to preach freedom to them without setting the world on fire. Unhappily we have, in modern times, the means of forming a comparison which, although on an infinitely smaller scale, will answer our purpose. In a colony where black slaves abound, who would venture to set them at liberty all at once? Now how much are the difficulties increased, what colossal dimensions does not the danger assume, when you have to do, not with a colony, but with the world? Their intellectual and moral condition rendered them incapable of turning such an advantage to their own benefit and that of society; in their debasement, urged on by the hatred and the desire of vengeance which ill-treatment had excited in their minds, they would have repeated, on a large scale, the bloody scenes with which they had already, in former times, stained the pages of history; and what would then have happened? Society, thus endangered, would have been put on its guard against principles favoring liberty; henceforth it would have regarded them with prejudice and suspicion, and the chains of servitude, instead of being loosened, would have been the more firmly riveted. Out of this immense mass of rude, savage men, set at liberty without preparation, it was impossible for social organization to arise; for social organization is not the creation of a moment, especially with such elements as these; and in this case, since it would have been necessary to choose between slavery and the annihilation of social order, the instinct of preservation, which animates society as well as all beings, would undoubtedly have brought about the continuation of slavery where it still existed, and its re-establishment where it had been destroyed. Those who complain that Christianity did not accomplish the work of abolishing slavery with sufficient promptitude, should remember that, even supposing a sudden or very rapid emancipation possible, and to say nothing of the bloody revolutions which would necessarily have been the result, the mere force of circumstances, by the insurmountable difficulties which it would have raised, would have rendered such a measure absolutely useless. Let us lay aside all social and political considerations, and apply ourselves to the economical question. First, it was necessary to change all the relations of property. The slaves played a principal part therein; they cultivated the land, and worked as mechanics; in a word, among them was distributed all that is called labor; and this distribution being made on the supposition of slavery, to take away this would have made a disruption, the ultimate consequences of which could not be estimated. I will suppose that violent spoliations had taken place, that a repartition or equalization of property had been attempted, that lands had been distributed to the emancipated, and that the richest proprietors had been compelled to hold the pickaxe and the plough; I will suppose all these absurdities and mad dreams to be realized, and I say that this would have been no remedy; for we must not forget that the production of the means of subsistence must be in proportion to the wants of those they are intended to support, and that this proportion would have been destroyed by the abolition of slavery. The production was regulated, not exactly according to the number of the individuals who then existed, but on the supposition that the majority were slaves; now we know that the wants of a freeman are greater than those of a slave.

If at the present time, after eighteen centuries, when ideas have been corrected, manners softened, laws ameliorated; when nations and governments have been taught by experience; when so many public establishments for the relief of indigence have been founded; when so many systems have been tried for the division of labor; when riches are distributed in a more equitable manner; if it is still so difficult to prevent a great number of men from becoming the victims of dreadful misery, if that is the terrible evil, which, like a fatal nightmare, torments society, and threatens its future, what would have been the effect of a universal emancipation, at the beginning of Christianity, at a time when slaves were not considered by the law as *persons*, but as *things;* when their conjugal union was not looked upon as a marriage; when their children were property, and subject to the same rules as the progeny of animals; when, in fine, the unhappy slave was ill-treated, tormented, sold, or put to death, according to the caprices of his master? Is it not evident that the cure of such evils was the work of ages? Do not humanity and political and social economy unanimously tell us this? If mad attempts had been made, the slaves themselves would have been the first to protest against them; they would have adhered to a servitude which at least secured to them food and shelter; they would have rejected a liberty which was inconsistent even with their existence. Such is the order of nature: man, above all, requires wherewith to live; and the means of subsistence being wanting, liberty itself would cease to please him. It is not necessary to allude to the individual examples of this, which we have in abundance; entire nations have given signal proofs of this truth. When misery is excessive, it is difficult for it not to bring with it degradation, stifle the most generous sentiments, and take away the magic of the words independence and liberty. "The common people," says Cæsar, speaking of the Gauls (lib. vi. *de Bello Gall.*), "are almost on a level with slaves; of themselves they venture nothing; their voice is of no avail. There are many of that class, who, loaded with debts and tributes, or oppressed by the powerful, give themselves up into servitude to the nobles, who exercise over those who have thus delivered themselves up the same rights as over slaves." Examples of the same kind are not wanting in modern times; we know that in China there is a great number of slaves whose servitude is owing entirely to the incapacity of themselves or their fathers to provide for their own subsistence.

These observations, which are supported by facts that no one can deny, evidently show that Christianity has displayed profound wisdom in proceeding with so much caution in the abolition of slavery.

It did all that was possible in favor of human liberty; if it did not advance more rapidly in the work, it was because it could not do so without compromitting the undertaking—without creating serious obstacles to the desired emancipation. Such is the result at which we arrive when we have thoroughly examined the charges made against some proceedings of the Church. We look into them by the light of reason, we compare them with the facts, and in the end we are convinced that the conduct blamed is perfectly in accordance with the dictates of the highest wisdom and the counsels of the soundest prudence. What, then, does M. Guizot mean, when, after having allowed that Christianity labored with earnestness for the abolition of slavery, he accuses it of having consented for a long time to its continuance? Is it logical thence to infer that it is not true that this immense benefit is due exclusively to Christianity? That slavery endured for a long time in presence of the Church is true; but it was always declining, and it only lasted as long as was necessary to realize the benefit without violence—without a shock—without compromitting its universality and its continuation. Moreover, we ought to subtract from the time of its continuance many ages, during which the Church was often proscribed, always regarded with aversion, and totally unable to exert a direct influence on the social organization. We ought also, to a great extent, to make exception of later times, as the Church had only begun to exert a direct and public influence, when the irruption of the northern barbarians took place, which, together with the corruption which infected the empire and spread in a frightful manner, produced such a perturbation, such a confused mass of languages, customs, manners, and laws, that it was almost impossible to make the regulating power produce salutary fruits. If, in later times, it has been difficult to destroy feudality; if there remain to this day, after ages of struggles, the remnants of that constitution; if the slave-trade, although limited to certain countries and circumstances, still merits the universal reprobation which is raised throughout the world against its infamy; how can we venture to express our astonishment—how can we venture to make it a reproach against the Church, that slavery continued some ages after she had proclaimed men's fraternity with each other, and their equality before God?

CHAPTER XVI.

IDEAS AND MANNERS OF ANTIQUITY WITH RESPECT TO SLAVERY.—THE CHURCH BEGINS BY IMPROVING THE CONDITION OF SLAVES.

HAPPILY the Catholic Church was wiser than philosophers; she knew how to confer on humanity the benefit of emancipation, without injustice or revolution. She knew how to regenerate society, but not in rivers of blood. Let us see what was her conduct with respect to the abolition of slavery. Much has been already said of the spirit of love and fraternity which animates Christianity, and that is sufficient to show that its influence in this work must have been great. But perhaps sufficient care has not been taken in seeking the positive and practical means which the Church employed for this end. In the darkness of ages, in circumstances so complicated or various, will it be possible to discover any traces of the path pursued by the Catholic Church in accomplishing the destruction of that slavery under which a large portion of the human race groaned? Will it be possible to do any thing more than praise her Christian charity? Will it be possible to point out a plan, a system, and to prove the existence and development of it, not by referring to a few expressions, to elevated thoughts, generous sentiments, and the isolated actions of a few illustrious men, but by exhibiting positive facts, and historical documents, which show what were the *esprit de corps* and tendency of the Church? I believe that this may be done, and I have no doubt that I shall be able to do it, by availing myself of what is most convincing and decisive in the matter, viz. the monuments of ecclesiastical legislation.

In the first place, it will not be amiss to remember what I have already pointed out, viz. that when we have to do with the conduct, designs, and tendencies of the Church, it is by no means necessary to suppose that these designs were conceived in their fullest extent by the mind of any individual in particular, nor that the merit and all the prudence of that conduct was understood by those who took part in it. It is not even necessary to suppose that the first Christians understood all the force of the tendencies of Christianity with respect to the abolition of slavery. What requires to be shown is, that the result has been obtained by the doctrines and conduct of the Church, as with Catholics, (although they know how to esteem at their just value the merit and greatness of each man,) individuals, when the Church is concerned, disappear. Their thoughts and will are nothing; the spirit which animates, vivifies, and directs the Church, is not the spirit of man, but that of God himself. Those who belong not to our faith will employ other names; but at least we shall agree in this, that facts, considered in this way, above the mind and the will of individuals, preserve much better their real dimensions; and thus the great chain of events in the study of history remains unbroken. Let it be said that the conduct of the Church was inspired and directed by God; or that it was the result of instinct; that it was the development of a tendency contained in her doctrines; we will not now stay to consider the expressions which may be used by Catholics, or by philosophers; what we have to show is, that this instinct was noble and well-directed; that this tendency had a great object in view, and knew how to attain it.

The first thing that Christianity did for slaves, was to destroy the errors which opposed, not only their universal emancipation, but even the improvement of their condition; that is, the first force which she employed in the attack was, according to her custom, the *force of ideas*. This first step was the more necessary, as the same thing applies to all other evils, as well as to slavery; every social evil is always accompanied by some error which produces or foments it. There existed not only the oppression and degradation of a large portion of the human race, but, moreover, an accredited error, which tended more and more to lower that portion of humanity. According to this opinion, slaves were a mean race, far below the dignity of freemen: they were a race degraded by Jupiter himself, marked by a stamp of humiliation, and predestined to their state of abjection and debasement. A detestable doctrine, no doubt, and contradicted by the nature of man, by history and experience; but which, nevertheless, reckoned distinguished men among its defenders, and which we see proclaimed for ages, to the shame of humanity and the scandal of reason, until Christianity came to destroy it, by undertaking to vindicate the rights of man. Homer tells us (*Odys.* 17) that "Jupiter has deprived slaves of half the mind." We find in Plato a trace of the same doctrine, although he expresses himself, as he is accustomed to do, by the mouth of another; he ventures to advance the following: "It is said that, in the mind of slaves, there is nothing sound or complete; and that a prudent man ought not to trust that class of persons; which is equally attested by the wisest of our poets." Here Plato cites the above-quoted passage of Homer (*Dial.* 8, *de Legibus*). But it is in the Politics of Aristotle that we find this degrading doctrine in all its deformity and nakedness. Some have wished to excuse this philosopher, but in vain; his own words condemn him without appeal. In the first chapter of his work, he explains the constitution of the family, and attempts to state the relations of husband and wife, of master and slave; he states that, as the wife is by nature different from the husband, so is the slave from the master. These are his words: "Thus the woman and the slave are distinguished by nature itself." Let it not be said that this is an expression that escaped from the pen of the writer; it was stated with a full knowledge, and is a *résumé* of his theory. In the third chapter, where he continues to analyze the elements which compose the family, after having stated "that a complete family is formed of free persons and slaves," he alludes particularly to the latter, and begins by combating an opinion which he thinks too favorable to them: "There are some," he says, "who think that slavery is a thing out of the order of nature, since it is the law itself which makes some free and others slaves, while nature makes no distinction." Before combating this opinion, he explains the relations between master and slave, by using the comparison of artist and instrument, and that of the soul and body; he continues thus: "If we compare man to woman, we find that the first is superior, therefore he commands; the woman is inferior, therefore she obeys. The same thing ought to take place among all men. *Thus it is that those among them who are as inferior with respect to others, as the body is with respect to the soul, and the animal to man; those whose powers principally consist in the use of the body, the only service that can be obtained from them, they are naturally slaves.*" We should imagine, at first sight, that the philosopher spoke only of idiots; his words would seem to indicate this; but we shall see, by the context, that such is not his intention. It is evident that if he spoke only of idiots, he would prove nothing against the opinion which he desires to combat; for the number of them is nothing with respect to the generality of men. If he spoke only of idiots, of what use would be a theory founded on so rare and monstrous an exception?

But we have no need of conjectures as to the real intention of the philosopher, he himself takes care to explain it to us, and tells us at the same time for what reason he ventures to make use of expressions which seem, at first, to place the matter on another level. His intention is nothing less than to attribute to nature the express design of producing men of two kinds; one born for slavery, the other for liberty. The passage is too important and too curious to be omitted. It is this: "Nature has taken care to create the bodies of free men different from those of slaves; the bodies of the latter are strong, and proper for the most necessary labors: those of freemen, on the contrary, well formed, although ill adapted for servile works, are proper for civil life, which consists in the management of things in war and peace. Nevertheless, the contrary often happens. To a free man is given the body of a slave; and to a slave the soul of a free man. There is no doubt that, if the bodies of some men were as much more perfect than others, as we see is the case in the image of the Gods, all the world would be of opinion that these men should be obeyed by those who had not the same beauty. If this is true in speaking of the body, it is still more so in speaking of the soul; although it is not so easy to see the beauty of the soul as that of the body. Thus it cannot be doubted that there are some men born for liberty, as others are for slavery; a slavery which is not only useful to the slaves themselves, but, moreover, just." A miserable philosophy, which, in order to support that degraded state, was obliged to have recourse to such subtilties, and ventured to impute to nature the intention of creating different castes, some born to command and others to obey; a cruel philosophy, which thus labored to break the bonds of fraternity with which the

Author of nature has desired to knit together the human race, pretending to raise a barrier between man and man, and inventing theories to support inequality; not that inequality which is the necessary result of all social organization, but an inequality so terrible and degrading as that of slavery.

Christianity raises its voice, and by the first words which it pronounces on slaves, declares them equal to all men in the dignity of nature, and in the participation of the graces which the Divine Spirit diffuses upon earth. We must remark the care with which St. Paul insists on this point; it seems as if he had in view those degrading distinctions which have arisen from a fatal forgetfulness of the dignity of man. The Apostle never forgets to inculcate to the faithful that there is no difference between the slave and the freeman. "For in one Spirit were we all baptized into one body, whether Jews or Gentiles, whether bond or free." (1 Cor. xii. 13.) "For you are all children of God, by faith in Jesus Christ. For as many of you as have been baptized in Christ have put on Christ. There is neither Jew nor Greek; *there is neither bond or free;* there is neither male or female. For you are all one in Christ Jesus." (Gal. iii. 26–28.) "Where there is neither Gentile nor Jew, circumcision nor uncircumcision, barbarian or Scythian, bond or free; but Christ is all and in all." (Colos. iii. 11.) The heart dilates at the sound of the voice thus loudly proclaiming the great principles of holy fraternity and equality. After having heard the oracles of Paganism inventing doctrines to degrade still more the unhappy slaves, we seem to awake from a painful dream, and to find ourselves in the light of day in the midst of the delightful reality. The imagination delights to contemplate the millions of men who, bent under degradation and ignominy, at this voice raised their eyes towards Heaven, and were animated with hope.

It was with this teaching of Christianity as with all generous and fruitful doctrines; they penetrate the heart of society, remain there as a precious germ, and, developed by time, produce an immense tree which overshadows families and nations. When these doctrines were diffused among men, they could not fail to be misunderstood and exaggerated. Thus there were found some who pretended that Christian freedom was the proclamation of universal freedom. The pleasing words of Christ easily resounded in the ears of slaves: they heard themselves declared children of God, and brethren of Jesus Christ; they saw that there was no distinction made between them and their masters, between them and the most powerful lords of the earth; is it, then, strange that men only accustomed to chains, to labor, to every kind of trouble and degradation, exaggerated the principles of Christian liberty, and made applications of them which were neither just in themselves, nor capable of being reduced to practice? We know, from St. Jerome, that many, hearing themselves called to Christian liberty, believed that they were thereby freed. Perhaps the Apostle alluded to this error when, in his first epistle to Timothy, he said, "Whosoever are servants under the yoke, let them count their masters worthy of all honor; lest the name of the Lord and His doctrines be blasphemed." (1 Timothy vi. 1.) This error had been so general, that after three centuries it was still much credited; and the Council of Gangres, held about 324, was obliged to excommunicate those who, under pretence of piety, taught that slaves ought to quit their masters, and withdraw from their service. This was not the teaching of Christianity; besides, we have clearly shown that it would not have been the right way to achieve universal emancipation. Therefore this same Apostle, from whose mouth we have heard such generous language in favor of slaves, frequently inculcates to them obedience to their masters; but let us observe, that while fulfilling this duty imposed by the spirit of peace and justice which animates Christianity, he so explains the motives on which the obedience of slaves ought to be based, he calls to mind the obligations of masters in such affecting and energetic words, and establishes so expressly and conclusively the equality of all men before God, that we cannot help seeing how great was his compassion for that unhappy portion of humanity, and how much his ideas on this point differed from those of a blind and hardened world. There is in the heart of man a feeling of noble independence, which does not permit him to subject himself to the will of another, except when he sees that the claims to his obedience are founded on legitimate titles. If they are in accordance with reason and justice, and, above all, if they have their roots in the great objects of human love and veneration, his understanding is convinced, his heart is gained, and he yields. But if the reason for the command is only the will of another, if it is only man against man, these thoughts of equality ferment in his mind, then the feeling of independence burns in his heart, he puts on a bold front, and his passions are excited. Therefore, when a willing and lasting obedience is to be obtained, it is necessary that the man should be lost sight of in the ruler, and that he should only appear as the representative of a superior power, or the personification of the motives which convince the subject of the justice and utility of his submission; thus he does not obey the will of another because it is that will, but because it is the representative of a superior power, or the interpreter of truth and justice; then man no longer considers his dignity outraged, and obedience becomes tolerable and pleasing.

It is unnecessary to say that such were not the titles on which was founded the obedience of slaves before Christianity: custom placed them in the rank of brutes; and the laws, outdoing it if possible, were expressed in language which cannot be read without indignation. Masters commanded because such was their pleasure, and slaves were compelled to obey, not on account of superior motives or moral obligations, but because they were the property of their masters, horses governed by the bridle, and mere mechanical machines. Was it, then, strange that these unhappy beings, drenched with misfortune and ignominy, conceived and cherished in their hearts that deep rancor, that violent hatred, and that terrible thirst for vengeance, which at the first opportunity exploded so fearfully? The horrible massacre of Tyre, the example and terror of the universe, according to the expression of Justin; the repeated revolts of the Penestes in Thessaly, of the Helotes in Sparta; the defections of the slaves of Chio and Athens; the insurrection under the command of Herdonius, and the terror which it spread in all the families of Rome; the scenes of blood, the obstinate and desperate resistance of the bands of Spartacus; was all this any thing but the natural result of the system of violence, outrage, and contempt with which slaves were treated? Is it not what we have seen repeated in modern times, in the catastrophes of the negro colonies? Such is the nature of man, whoever sows contempt and outrage will reap fury and vengeance. Christianity was well aware of these truths; and this is the reason why, while preaching obedience, it took care to found it on Divine authority. If it confirmed to masters their rights, it also taught them an exalted sense of their obligation. Wherever Christian doctrines prevailed, slaves might say: "It is true that we are unfortunate; birth, poverty, or the reverses of war have condemned us to misfortune; but at least we are acknowledged as men and brethren; between us and our masters there is a reciprocity of rights and obligations." Let us hear the Apostle: "You, slaves, obey those who are your masters according to the flesh, with fear and trembling, in the simplicity of your hearts, as to Jesus Christ himself. *Not serving to the eye, as it were pleasing men*, but, as the servants of Christ, doing the will of God from the heart. With a good will serving, as to the Lord, and not to men. Knowing that whatsoever good things any man shall do, the same shall he receive from the Lord, *whether he be bond or free*. And you, masters, do the same thing to them, forbearing threatenings, knowing that the Lord both of them and you is in heaven, and *there is no respect of persons with Him*." (Eph. vi. 5–9.) In the Epistle to the Colossians he inculcates the same doctrine of obedience anew, basing it on the same motives; for, to console the unfortunate slaves, he tells them: "You shall receive of the Lord the reward of inheritance: serve ye the Lord Christ. For he that doth wrong shall receive for that which he hath done wrongfully, and there is no respect of persons with God" (Colos. iii. 24, 25); and lower down, addressing himself to masters: "Masters, do to your servants that which is just and equal, knowing that you also have a Master in heaven." (iv. 1.)

The diffusion of such beneficent doctrines necessarily tended to improve greatly the condition of slaves; their immediate effect was to soften that excessive rigor, that cruelty which would be incredible if it were not incontrovertibly proved. We know that the master had the right of life and death, and that he abused that power even to putting a slave to death from caprice, as Quintus Flaminius did in the midst of a festival. Another caused one of these unfortunate beings to be thrown to the fishes, because he broke a glass of crystal This is related of Vedius Pollio; and this horrible cruelty was not confined to the circle of a few families subject to a master devoid of compassion; no, cruelty was formed into a system, the fatal but necessary result of erroneous notions on this point, and of the forgetfulness of the sentiments of humanity. This violent system could only be supported by constantly trampling upon the slave; and there was no cessation of tyranny until the day when he, with superior power, attacked his master and destroyed him. An ancient proverb said, "So many slaves, so many enemies." We have already seen the ravages committed by men thus rendered savage by revenge, whenever they were able to break their chains; but certainly, when it was desired to terrify them, their masters did not yield to them in ferocity. At Sparta, on one occasion when they feared the ill-will of the Helotes, they assembled them all at the temple of Jupiter, and put them to death. (*Thucyd.* b. iv.) At Rome, whenever a master was assassinated, all his slaves were condemned to death. We cannot read in Tacitus without a shudder (*Ann.* l. xiv. 43) the horrible scene which was witnessed when the prefect of the town, Pedanius Secundus, was assassinated by one of his slaves. Not less than four hundred were to die; all, according to the ancient custom, were to be led to punishment. This cruel and pitiable spectacle, in which so many of the innocent were to suffer death, excited the compassion of the people, who raised a tumult to prevent this horrid butchery. The Senate, in doubt, deliberated on the affair, when an orator named Cassius maintained with energy that it was necessary to complete the bloody execution, not only in obedience to the ancient custom, but also because without it it would be impossible to preserve themselves from the ill-will of the slaves. His words are all dictated by injustice and tyranny; he sees on all sides dangers and conspiracies; he can imagine no other safeguards than force and terror. The following passage is above all remarkable in his speech, as showing in a few words the ideas and manners of the ancients in this matter: "Our ancestors," says the senator, "always mistrusted the character of slaves, even of those who, born on their possessions and in their houses, might be supposed to have conceived from their cradle an affection for their masters; but as we have slaves of foreign nations, differing in customs and religion, this rabble can only be restrained by terror." Cruelty prevailed, the boldness of the people was repressed, the way was filled with soldiers, and the four hundred unfortunate beings were led to punishment.

To soften this cruel treatment, to banish these frightful atrocities, ought to have been the first effect of the Christian doctrines; and we may rest assured that the Church never lost sight of so important an object. She devoted all her efforts to improve as much as possible the condition of slaves; in punishments she caused mildness to be substituted for cruelty; and what was more important than all, she labored to put reason in the place of caprice, and to make the impetuosity of masters yield to the calmness of judges; that is to say, she every day assimilated the condition of slaves more and more to that of freemen, by making right and not might reign over them. The Church never forgot the noble lesson which the Apostle gave when writing to Philemon, and interceding in favor of a fugitive slave named Onesimus; he spoke in his favor with a tenderness which this unhappy class had never before inspired: "I beseech thee," he says to him, "for my son Onesimus. Receive him as my own bowels; no more as a slave, but as a most dear brother. If he hath wronged thee in any thing, or is in thy debt, put that to my account." (Epis. to Phil.) The Council of Elvira, held in the beginning of the fourth century, subjects the woman who shall have beaten her slave so as to cause her death in three days to many years of penance; the Council of Orleans, held in 549, orders that if a slave guilty of a fault take refuge in a church, he is to be restored to his master, but not without having exacted from the latter a promise, confirmed by oath, that he will not do him any harm; that if the master, in violation of his oath, maltreat the slave, he shall be separated from the communion of the faithful and the sacraments. This canon shows us two things: the habitual cruelty of masters, and the zeal of the Church to soften the treatment of slaves. To restrain this cruelty, nothing less than an oath was required; and the Church, always so careful in these things, yet considered the matter important enough to justify and require the invocation of the sacred name of God.

The favor and protection which the Church granted to slaves rapidly extended. It seems that in some places the custom was introduced of requiring a promise on oath, not only that the slave who had taken refuge in the church should not be ill-treated in his person, but even that no extraordinary work should be imposed on him, and that he should wear no distinctive mark. This custom, produced no doubt by zeal for humanity, but which may have occasioned some inconveniences by relaxing too much the ties of obedience, and allowing excesses on the part of slaves, appears to be alluded to in a regulation of the Council of Epaone (now Abbon, according to some), held about 517. This Council labors to stop the evil by prescribing a prudent moderation; but without withdrawing the protection already granted. It ordains, in the 39th canon, "That if a slave, guilty of any atrocious offence, takes refuge in a church, he shall be saved from corporal punishment; but the master shall not be compelled to swear that he will not impose on him additional labor, or that he will not cut off his hair, in order to make known his fault." Observe that this restriction is introduced only in the case when the slave shall have committed a heinous offence, and even in this case all the power allowed to the master consists in imposing on the slave extraordinary labor, or distinguishing him by cutting his hair.

Perhaps such indulgence may be considered excessive; but we must observe that when abuses are deeply rooted, they cannot be eradicated without a vigorous effort. At first sight it often appears as if the limits of prudence were passed; but this apparent excess is only the inevitable oscillation which is observed before things regain their right position. The Church had therein no wish to protect crime, or give unmerited indulgence; her object was to check the violence and caprice of masters; she did not wish to allow a man to suffer torture or death because such was the will of another. The establishment of just laws and legitimate tribunals, the Church has never opposed; but she has never given her consent to acts of private violence. The spirit of opposition to the exercise of private force, which includes social organization, is clearly shown to us in the 15th canon of the Council of Merida, held in 666. I have already shown that slaves formed a large portion of property. As the division of labor was made in conformity with this principle, slaves were absolutely necessary to those who possessed property, especially when it was considerable. Now the Church found this to be the case; and as she could not change the organization of society on a sudden, she was obliged to yield to necessity, and admit slavery. But if she wished to introduce improvements in the lot of slaves in general, it was good for her to set the example herself: this example is found in the canon I have just quoted. There, after having forbidden the bishops and priests to maltreat the servants of the Church by mutilating their limbs, the Council ordains that if a slave commit an offence, he shall be delivered to the secular judges, but so that the bishops shall moderate the punishment inflicted on him. We see by this canon that the right of mutilation exercised by private masters was still in use; and perhaps it was still more strongly established, since we see that the Council limits itself to interdicting that kind of punishment to ecclesiastics, without saying any thing as to laymen. No doubt, one of the motives for this prohibition made to ecclesiastics, was to prevent their shedding human blood, and thus rendering themselves incapable of exercising their lofty ministry, the principal act of which is the august sacrifice in which they offer a victim of peace and love; but this does not in any way detract from the merit of the regulation, or at all diminish its influence on the improvement of the condition of slaves. It was the substitution of public vengeance for private; it was again to proclaim the equality of slaves and freemen with respect to the effusion of their blood; it was to declare that the hands which had shed the blood of a slave, had contracted the same stain as if they had shed that of a freeman. Now, it was necessary to inculcate these salutary truths on men's minds in every way, for they ran in direct contradiction to the ideas and manners of antiquity; it was necessary to labor assiduously to destroy the shameful and cruel exceptions which continued to deprive the majority of mankind of a participation in the rights of humanity. There is, in the canon which I have just quoted, a remarkable circumstance, which shows the solicitude of the Church to restore to slaves the dignity and respect of which they had been deprived. To shave the hair of the head was among the Goths a very ignominious punishment; which, according to Lucas de Tuy, was to them more cruel than death itself. It will be understood, that whatever was the force of prejudice on this point, the Church might have allowed the shaving of the hair without incurring the stain which was attached to the shedding of blood. Yet she was not willing to allow it, which shows us how attentive she was to destroy the marks of humiliation impressed on slaves. After having enjoined priests and bishops to deliver criminal slaves to the judges, she commands them "not to allow them to be shaved ignominiously." No care was too great in this matter; to destroy one after another the odious exceptions which affected slaves, it was necessary to seize upon all favorable opportunities. This necessity is clearly shown by the manner in which the eleventh Council of Toledo, held in 675, expresses itself. This Council, in its 6th canon, forbids bishops themselves to judge crimes of a capital nature, as it also forbids them to order the mutilation of members. Behold in what terms it was considered necessary to state that this rule admitted of no exception; "not even," says the Council, "with respect to the slaves of the Church." The evil was great, it could not be cured without assiduous care. Even the right of life and death, the most cruel of all, could not be extirpated without much trouble; and cruel applications of it were made in the beginning of the sixth century, since the Council of Epaone, in its 34th canon, ordains that "the master who, *of his own authority*, shall take away the life of his slave, shall be cut off for two years from the communion of the Church." After the middle of the ninth century, similar attempts were still made, and the Council of Worms, held in 868, labored to repress them, by subjecting to two years of penance the master who, of his own authority, shall have put his slave to death.

CHAPTER XVII.

MEANS EMPLOYED BY THE CHURCH TO ENFRANCHISE SLAVES.

WHILE improving the condition of slaves and assimilating it as much as possible to that of freemen, it was necessary not to forget the universal emancipation; for it was not enough to ameliorate slavery, it was necessary to abolish it. The mere force of Christian notions, and the spirit of charity which was spread at the same time with them over the world, made so violent an attack on the state of slavery, that they were sure sooner or later to bring about its complete abolition. It is impossible for society to remain for a long time under an order of things which is formally opposed to the ideas with which it is imbued. According to Christian maxims, all men have a common origin and the same destiny; all are brethren in Jesus Christ; all are obliged to love each other with all their hearts, to assist each other in their necessities, to avoid offending each other even in words; all are equal before God, for they will all be judged without exception of persons. Christianity extended and took root everywhere —took possession of all classes, of all branches of society; how, then, could the state of slavery last—a state of degradation which makes man the property of another, allows him to be sold like an animal, and deprives him of the sweetest ties of family and of all participation in the advantages of society? Two things so opposite could not exist together; the laws were in favor of slavery, it is true; it may even be said that Christianity did not make a direct attack on those laws. But, on the other hand, what did it do? It strove to make itself master of ideas and manners, communicated to them a new impulse, and gave them a different direction. In such a case, what did laws avail? Their rigor was relaxed, their observance was neglected, their equity began to be doubted, their utility was disputed, their fatal effects were remarked, and they gradually fell into desuetude, so that sometimes it was not necessary to strike a blow to destroy them. They were thrown aside as things of no use; or, if they deserved the trouble of an express abolition, it was only for the sake of ceremony; it was a body interred with honor.

But let it not be supposed, after what I have just said, that in attributing so much importance to Christian ideas and manners, I mean that the triumph of these ideas and manners was abandoned to that force alone, without that co-operation on the part of the Church which the time and circumstances required. Quite the contrary: the Church, as I have already pointed out, called to her aid all the means the most conducive to the desired result. In the first place, it was requisite, to secure the work of emancipation, to protect from all assault the liberty of the freed—liberty which unhappily was often attacked and put in great danger. The causes of this melancholy fact may be easily found in the remains of ancient ideas and manners, in the cupidity of powerful men, the system of violence made general by the irruptions of the barbarians, in the poverty, neglect, and total want of education and morality in which slaves must have been when they quitted servitude. It must be supposed that a great number of them did not know all the value of liberty, that they did not always conduct themselves, in their new state, according to the dictates of reason and the exigences of justice; and that, newly entered on the possession of the rights of freemen, they did not know how to fulfil all their new obligations. But these different inconveniences, inseparable from the nature of things, were not to hinder the consummation of an enterprise called for both by religion and humanity, and it was proper to be resigned to them from the consideration of the numerous motives for excusing the conduct of the enfranchised; the state which these men had just quitted had checked the development of their moral and intellectual faculties.

The liberty of newly-emancipated slaves was protected against the attacks of injustice, and clothed with an inviolable sanctity, from the time that their enfranchisement was connected with things which then exercised the most powerful ascendency. Now the Church, and all that belonged to her, was in this influential position; therefore the custom, which was then introduced, of performing the *manumission in the churches*, was undoubtedly very favorable to the progress of liberty. This custom, by taking the place of ancient usages, caused them to be forgotten; it was, at the same time, a tacit declaration of the value of human liberty in the sight of God, and a proclamation, with additional authority, of the equality of men before Him; for the manumission was made in the same place where it was so often read, that before Him there was no exception of persons; where all earthly distinctions disappeared, and all men were commingled and united by the sweet ties of fraternity and love. This method of manumission more clearly invested the Church with the right of defending the liberty of the enfranchised. As she had been witness to the act, she could testify to the spontaneity and the other circumstances which assured its validity; she could even insist on its observance, by representing that the promised liberty could not be violated without profaning the sacred place, without breaking a pledge which had been given in the presence of God himself. The Church did not forget to turn these circumstances to the advantage of the freed. Thus we see that the first Council of Orange, held in 441, ordains, in its 7th canon, that it was necessary to check, by ecclesiastical censures, whoever desired to reduce to any kind of servitude slaves who had been emancipated within the enclosure of the church. A century later we find the same prohibition repeated in the 7th canon of the fifth Council of Orleans, held in 549.

The protection given by the Church to freed slaves was so manifest and known to all, that the custom was introduced of especially recommending them to her. This recommendation was sometimes made by will, as the Council of Orange, which I have just quoted, gives us to understand; for it orders that the emancipated who had been recommended to the Church by will, shall be protected from all kinds of servitude, by ecclesiastical censures.

But this recommendation was not always made in a testamentary form. We read in the sixth canon of the sixth Council of Toledo, held in 589, that when any enfranchised persons had been recommended to the Church, neither they nor their children could be deprived of the protection of the Church: here they speak in general, without limitation to cases in which there had been a will. The same regulation may be seen in another Council of Toledo, held in 633, which simply says, that the Church will receive under her protection only the enfranchised of individuals who shall have taken care to recommend them to her.

In the absence of all particular recommendation, and even when the manumission had not been made in the Church, she did not cease to interest herself in defending the freed, when their liberty was endangered. He who has any regard for the dignity of man, and any feeling of humanity in his heart, will certainly not find it amiss that the Church interfered in affairs of this kind; indeed, she acted as every generous man should do, in the exercise of the right of protecting the weak. We shall not be displeased, therefore, to find in the twenty-ninth canon of the Council of Agde in Languedoc, held in 506, a regulation commanding the Church, in case of necessity, to undertake the defence of those to whom their masters had given liberty in a lawful way.

The zeal of the Church in all times and places for the redemption of captives has no less contributed to the great work of the abolition of slavery. We know that a considerable portion of slaves owed their servitude to the reverses of war. The mild character which we see in modern wars would have appeared fabulous to the ancients. Woe to the vanquished! might then be said with perfect truth; there was nothing but slavery or death. The evil was rendered still greater by a fatal prejudice, which was felt with respect to the redemption of captives—a prejudice which was, nevertheless, founded on a trait of remarkable heroism. No doubt the heroic firmness of Regulus is worthy of all admiration. The hair stands upon our head when we read the powerful description of Horace; the book falls from our hands at this terrible passage:

> "Fertur pudicæ conjugis osculum
> Parvosque natos, ut capitis minor,
> Ab se removisse, et virilem
> Torvus humi posuisse vultum."—Lib. iii. od. 5.

Nevertheless, if we lay aside the deep impression which such heroism produces on us, and the enthusiasm at all that shows a great soul, we must confess that this virtue bordered on ferocity; and that, in the terrible discourse of Regulus, that is a cruel policy, against which the sentiments of humanity would strongly recoil, if the mind were not, as it were, prostrated at the sight of the sublime disinterestedness of the speaker. Christianity could not consent to such doctrines; it could not allow the maxim to be maintained that, in order to render men brave in battle, it was necessary to deprive them of hope. The wonderful traits of valor, the magnificent scenes of force and constancy, which shine in every page of the history of modern nations, eloquently show that the Christian religion was not deceived; gentleness of manners may be united with heroism. The ancients were always in excess, either in cowardice or ferocity; between these two extremes there is a middle way, and that has been taught to mankind by the Christian religion. Christianity, in accordance with its principles of fraternity and love, regarded the redemption of captives as one of the worthiest objects of its charitable zeal. Whether we consider the noble traits of particular actions, which have been preserved to us by history, or observe the spirit which guided the conduct of the Church, we shall find therein one of the most distinguished claims of the Christian religion to the gratitude of mankind.

A celebrated writer of our times, M. de Chateaubriand, has described to us a Christian priest who, in the forests of France, voluntarily made himself a slave, who devoted himself to slavery for the ransom of a Christian soldier, and thus restored a husband to his desolate wife, and a father to three unfortunate orphan children. The sublime spectacle which Zachary offers us, when enduring slavery with calm serenity for the love of Jesus Christ, and for the unhappy being for whom he has sacrificed his liberty, is not a mere fiction of the poet. More than once, in the first ages of the Church, such examples were seen; and he who has wept over the sublime disinterestedness and unspeakable charity of Zachary, may be sure that his tears are only a tribute to the truth. "We have known," says St. Clement the Pope, "many of ours who have devoted themselves to captivity, in order to ransom their brethren." (*First Letter to the Corinth.* c. 55.) The redemption of captives was so carefully provided for by the Church that it was regulated by the ancient canons, and to fulfil it, she sold, if necessary, her ornaments, and even the sacred vessels. When unhappy captives were in question, her charity and zeal knew no bounds, and she went so far as to ordain that, however bad might be the state of her affairs, their ransom should be provided for in the first instance. (*Caus.* 12, 5, 2.) In the midst of revolutions produced by the irruption of barbarians, we see that the Church, always constant in her designs, forgot not the noble enterprise in which she was engaged. The beneficent regulations of the ancient canons fell not into forgetfulness or desuetude, and the generous words of the holy Bishop of Milan, in favor of slaves, found an echo which ceased not to be heard amid the chaos of those unhappy times. We see by the fifth canon of the Council of Mâcon, held in 585, that priests undertook the ransom of captives by devoting to it the Church property. The Council of Rheims, held in 625, inflicts the punishment of suspension from his functions on the bishop who shall have destroyed the sacred vessels; but with generous foresight, it adds, "for any other motive than the redemption of captives;" and long afterwards, in the twelfth canon of the Council of Verneuil, held in 844, we find that the property of the Church was used for that merciful purpose. When the captive was restored to liberty, the Church did not deprive him of her protection; she was careful to continue it, by giving him letters of recommendation, for the double purpose of protecting him from new trouble during his journey, and of furnishing him with the means of repairing his losses during his captivity. We find a proof of this new kind of protection in the second canon of the Council of Lyons, held in 583, which ordains that bishops shall state in the letters of recommendation which they give to captives, the date and price of their ransom. The zeal for this work was displayed in the Church with so much ardor, that it went so far as to commit acts of imprudence which the ecclesiastical authority was compelled to check. These excesses, and this mistaken zeal, prove how great was the spirit of charity. We know by a Council, called that of St. Patrick, held in Ireland in the year 451 or 456, that some of the clergy ventured to procure the freedom of captives by inducing them to run away. The Council, by its thirty-second canon, very prudently checks this excess, by ordaining that the ecclesiastic who desires to ransom captives must do so with his own money; for to steal them, by inducing them to run away, was to expose the clergy to be considered as robbers, which was a dishonor to the Church. A remarkable document, which, while showing us the spirit of order and equity which guides the Church, at the same time enables us to judge how deeply was engraved on men's minds the maxim, that *it is holy, meritorious, and generous to give liberty to captives;* for we see that some persons had persuaded themselves that the excellence of the work justified seizing them forcibly. The disinterestedness of the Church on this point is not less laudable. When she had employed her funds in the ransom of a captive, she did not desire from him any recompense, even when he had it in his power to discharge the debt. We have a certain proof of this in the letters of St. Gregory, where we see that that Pope reassures some persons who had been freed with the money of the Church, and who feared that after a time they would be called upon to pay the sum expended for their advantage. The Pope orders that no one, at any time, shall venture to disturb either them or their heirs, seeing that the sacred canons allow the employment of the goods of the Church for the ransom of captives. (L. 7, ep. 14.)

The zeal of the Church for so holy a work must have contributed in an extraordinary way to diminish the number of slaves; the influence of it was so much the more salutary, as it was developed precisely at the time when it was most needed, that is, in those ages when the dissolution of the Roman empire, the irruption of the barbarians, the fluctuations of so many peoples, and the ferocity of the invading nations, rendered wars so frequent, revolutions so constant, and the empire of force so habitual and prevailing. Without the beneficent and liberating intervention of Christianity, the immense number of slaves bequeathed by the old society to the new, far from diminishing, would have been augmented more and more; for wherever the law of brute force prevails, if it be not checked and softened by a powerful element, the human race becomes rapidly debased, the necessary result of which is the increase of slavery. This lamentable state of agitation and violence was in itself very likely to render the efforts which the Church made to abolish slavery useless; and it was not without infinite trouble that she prevented what she succeeded in preserving on one side, from being destroyed on the other. The absence of a central power, the complication of social relations, almost always badly determined, often affected by violence, and always deprived of the guarantee of stability and consistency, was the reason why there was no security either for things or persons, and that while properties were unceasingly invaded, persons were deprived of their liberty. So that it was at that time necessary to fight against the violence of individuals, as had been formerly done against manners and legislation. We see that the third canon of the Council of Lyons, held about 566, excommunicates those who unjustly retain free persons in slavery; in the seventeenth canon of the Council of Rheims, held in 625, it is forbidden, under the same penalty, to pursue free persons in order to reduce them to slavery: in the twenty-seventh canon of the Council of London, held in 1102, the barbarous custom of dealing in men, like animals, is proscribed: and in the seventh canon of the Council of Coblentz, held in 922, he who takes away a Christian to sell him is declared guilty of homicide; a remarkable declaration, when we see liberty valued at as high a price as life itself. Another means of which the Church availed herself to abolish slavery was, to preserve for the unfortunate who had been reduced to that state by misery, a sure means of quitting it.

We have already remarked above that indigence was one of the causes of slavery, and we have seen that this was frequently the cause among the Gauls, as is evidenced by a passage of Cæsar. We also know that by virtue of an ancient law, he who had fallen into slavery could not recover his liberty without the consent of his master; as the slave was really property, no one could dispose of him without the consent of his master, and least of all himself. This law was in accordance with Pagan doctrines, but Christianity regarded the thing differently; and if the slave was still in her eyes a property, he did not cease to be a man. Thus on this point the Church refused to follow the strict rules of other properties; and when there was the least doubt, at the first favorable opportunity she took the side of the slave. These observations make us understand all the value of the new law introduced by the Church, which ordained that persons who had been sold by necessity should be able to return to their former condition by restoring the price which they had received. This law, which is expressly laid down in a French Council, held about 616 at Boneuil, according to the common opinion, opened a wide field for the conquests of liberty; it supported in the heart of the slave a hope which urged him to seek and put into operation the means of obtaining his ransom, and it placed his liberty within the power of any one who, touched with his unhappy lot, was willing to pay or lend the necessary sum. Let us remember what we have said of the ardent zeal which was awakened in so many hearts for works of this kind; let us call to mind that the property of the Church was always considered as well employed when it was used for the succor of the unfortunate, and we shall understand the incalculable influence of the regulation which we have just mentioned. We shall see that it was to close one of the most abundant sources of slavery, and prepare a wide path to universal emancipation.

CHAPTER XVIII.

CONTINUATION OF THE SAME SUBJECT.

THE conduct of the Church with respect to the Jews also contributed to the abolition of slavery. This singular people, who bear on their forehead the mark of proscription, and are found dispersed among all nations, like fragments of insoluble matter floating in a liquid, seek to console themselves in their misfortune by accumulating treasures, and appear to wish to avenge themselves for the contemptuous neglect in which they are left by other nations, by gaining possession of their wealth by means of insatiable usury. In times when revolutions and so many calamities must necessarily have produced distress, the odious vice of unfeeling avarice must have had a fatal influence. The harshness and cruelty of ancient laws and manners concerning debtors were not effaced, liberty was far from being estimated at its just value, and examples of persons who sold it to relieve their necessities were not wanting; it was therefore important to prevent the power of the wealthy Jews from reaching an exorbitant extent, to the detriment of the liberty of Christians. The unhappy notoriety which, after so many centuries, attaches to the Jews in this matter, proves that this danger was not imaginary; and facts of which we are now witnesses are a confirmation of what we advance. The celebrated Herder, in his *Adrastus*, ventures to prognosticate that the children of Israel, from their systematic and calculating conduct, will in time make slaves of all Christians. If this extraordinary and extravagant apprehension could enter the head of a distinguished man, in circumstances which are certainly infinitely less favorable to the Jews, what was to be feared from this people in the unhappy times of which we speak? From these considerations, every impartial observer, every man who is not under the influence of the wretched desire of taking the part of every kind of sect, in order to have the pleasure of accusing the Catholic Church, even at the risk of speaking against the interests of humanity; every observer who is not one of those who are less alarmed by an irruption of Caffres than by any regulation by which the ecclesiastical power appears in the smallest degree to extend the circle of its prerogative; every man, I say, who is neither thus bitter, little, nor pitiful, will see, not only without being scandalized, but even with pleasure, that the Church, with prudent vigilance, watched the progress of the Jews, and lost no opportunity of favoring their Christian slaves, until they were no longer allowed to have any.

The third Council of Orleans, held in 538, by its 13th canon, forbids Jews to compel Christian slaves to do things contrary to the religion of Jesus Christ. This regulation, which guarantied the liberty of the slave in the sanctuary of conscience, rendered him respectable even in the eyes of his master: it was besides a solemn proclamation of the dignity of man, it was a declaration that slavery could not extend its dominion over the sacred region of the mind. Yet this was not enough; it was proper also that the recovery of their liberty should be facilitated to the slaves of Jews. Three years only pass away; a fourth Council is held at Orleans; let us observe the progress which the question had made in so short a time. This Council, by its 30th canon, allows the Christian slaves who shall take refuge in the church to be ransomed, on paying to their Jewish master the proper price. If we pay attention, we shall see that such a regulation must have produced abundant results in favor of liberty, as it gave Christian slaves the opportunity of flying to the churches, and there imploring, with more effect, the charity of their brethren, to gain the price of their ransom. The same Council, in its 31st canon, ordains that the Jew who shall pervert a Christian slave shall be condemned to lose all his slaves; a new sanction given to the security of the slave's conscience—a new way opened to liberty. The Church constantly advanced with that unity of plan—that admirable consistency—which even her enemies have acknowledged in her. In the short interval between the period alluded to and the latter part of the same century, her progress was more perceptible. We observe, in the canonical regulations of the latter period, a wider scope, and, if we may so speak, greater boldness. In the Council of Mâcon, held in 581 or 582, canon 16, Jews are expressly forbidden to have Christian slaves; and it is allowed to ransom those who are in their possession for twelve sous. We find the same prohibition in the 14th canon of the Council of Toledo, held in 589; so that at this time the Church shows what her desire is; she is unwilling that a Christian should be in any way the slave of a Jew. Constant in her design, she checked the evil by all the means in her power; if it was necessary, limiting the right of selling slaves, when there was danger of their falling into the hands of Jews.

Thus we see that, by the 9th canon of the Council of Châlons, held in 650, it is forbidden to sell slaves out of the kingdom of Clovis, lest they should fall into the power of Jews. Yet the intention of the Church on this point was not understood by all, and her views were not seconded as they ought to have been; but she did not cease to repeat and inculcate them. In the middle of the seventh century there were found clergy and laity who sold their Christian slaves to Jews. The Church labored to check this abuse. The tenth Council of Toledo, held in 657, by its 7th canon, forbids Christians, and especially clerics, to sell their slaves to Jews; the Council adds these noble words: "They cannot be ignorant that these slaves have been redeemed by the blood of Jesus Christ; wherefore they ought rather to buy than sell them."

This ineffable goodness of a God made man, who had shed His blood for the redemption of all men, was the powerful motive which urged the Church to interest herself with so much zeal in the enfranchisement of slaves; and, indeed, was it not enough to inspire horror for so degrading an inequality, to think that these same men, reduced to the level of brutes, had been, as well as their masters, as well as the most powerful monarchs upon earth, the objects of the merciful intentions of the Most High? "Since our Redeemer, the Creator of all things," said Pope S. Gregory, "has deigned, in His goodness, to assume the flesh of man, in order to restore to us our pristine liberty, by breaking, through the means of His Divine grace, the bonds of servitude, which held us captives, it is a salutary deed to restore to men, by enfranchisement, their native liberty; for, in the beginning, nature made them all free, and they have only been subjected to the yoke of servitude by the law of nations." (L. 5, lett. 72.)

During all times the Church has considered it very necessary to limit, as much as possible, the alienation of her property; and it may be said that the general rule of her conduct in this point was to trust very little to the discretion of any one of her ministers individually; she thus endeavored to prevent dilapidations, which otherwise would have been frequent. As her possessions were dispersed on all sides, and intrusted to ministers chosen from all classes of the people, and exposed to the various influences which the relations of blood, friendship, and a thousand other circumstances, the effects of difference of character, knowledge, prudence, and even of times and places, always exercise, the Church showed herself very watchful in giving her sanction to the power of alienation; and, when requisite, she knew how to act with salutary rigor against those ministers who, neglecting their duty, wasted the funds confided to them. We have seen that, in spite of all this, she was not stopped by any consideration when the ransom of captives was in question; it may be also shown that, with respect to property in slaves, she saw things in a different light, and changed her rigor into indulgence. When slaves had faithfully served the Church, the Bishops could grant them their liberty, and add a gift to assist them in maintaining themselves. This judgment as to the merit of slaves appears to have been confided to the discretion of the Bishops; and it is evident that such a regulation opened a wide door to their charity; at the same time, it stimulated the slaves to behave themselves, so as to deserve so precious a recompense. As it might happen that the succeeding Bishop might raise doubts as to the sufficiency of the motives which induced his predecessor to give liberty to a slave, and attempt afterwards to call it in question, it was ordained that they should respect the appointments of their predecessors on this point, and leave to the enfranchised not only their liberty, but also the gratuity which had been given to them in lands, vineyards, or houses: this is prescribed in the 7th canon of the Council of Agde in Languedoc, held in the year 506. Let it not be objected that manumission is forbidden by the canons of this Council in other places; they speak only in general terms, and allude not to cases where slaves had merited well. Alienations or mortgages made by a Bishop who left no property were to be revoked. This regulation itself shows that it alludes to cases in which the Bishops had acted against the canons. Yet if he had given liberty to any slaves, the rigor of the law was mitigated in their favor, and it was ordained that the enfranchised should continue to enjoy their liberty. This is ordained by the 9th canon of the Council of Orleans, held in 541. This canon only imposes on the enfranchised the obligation of lending their services to the Church; services which were evidently only those of the enfranchised. On the other hand, she recompensed them with the protection which she always granted to men in this condition.

As another proof of the indulgence of the Church with respect to slaves, may be cited the 10th canon of the Council of Celchite, in England, held in 816, the result of which must have been to enfranchise, in a few years, all the English slaves of the Churches existing in the countries where the Council was observed. Indeed, this canon ordained that, at the death of a Bishop, all his English slaves should be set at liberty; it added, that each of the other Bishops and Abbots might enfranchise three slaves on the occasion, by giving each of them three sous. Such regulations smoothed the way more and more, and prepared circumstances and men's minds, so that, some time later, was witnessed that noble scene, where, at the Council of Armagh, in 1172, liberty was given to all the English who were slaves in Ireland.

The advantageous conditions enjoyed by the slaves of the Church were so much the more valuable, because a regulation newly introduced prevented their losing them. If they could have passed into the hands of other masters, in this case they would have lost the benefits which they derived from living under the rule of so kind a mistress. But happily, it was forbidden to exchange them for others; and if they left the power of the Church, it was for freedom. We have a positive proof of this regulation in the decretals of Gregory IX. (l. 3, t. 19, chaps. 3 and 4). It should be observed that in this document the slaves of the Church are regarded as consecrated to God; thereon is founded the regulation which prevents their passing into other hands and leaving the Church, except as freemen. We also see there that the faithful, for the good of their souls, had the custom of offering their slaves to God and the Saints. By placing them thus in the power of the Church, they put them out of common dealing and prevented their again falling into profane servitude. It is useless to enlarge on the salutary effect which must have been produced by these ideas and manners, in which we see religion so intimately allied with the cause of humanity; it is enough to observe, that the spirit of that age was highly religious, and that which was attached to the cause of religion was sure to ride in safety.

Religious ideas, by constantly developing their strength and directing their action to all branches, were intended in a special manner to relieve men by all possible means from the yoke of slavery. On this subject we may be allowed to remark a canonical regulation of the time of Gregory the Great. In a Council at Rome, held in 595, and presided over by that Pope, a new means of escaping from their degraded state was offered to slaves, by deciding that liberty should be given to all those who desired to embrace the monastic life. The words of the holy Pope are worthy of attention; they show the ascendency of religious motives, and how much these motives preponderated over considerations and interests of a worldly nature. This important document is found in the letters of St. Gregory; it may be read in the notes at the end of the volume.

To imagine that such regulations would remain barren, is to mistake the spirit of those times: on the contrary, they produced the most important effects. We may form an idea of them by reading in the decree of Gratian (*Distin.* 54, c. 12), that they led to scandal; slaves fled from the houses of their masters and took

K

refuge in monasteries, under pretext of religion. It was necessary to check this abuse, against which complaints arose on all sides. Without waiting to consider what these abuses themselves indicate, is it difficult to imagine that these regulations of the Church must have had valuable results? They not only gained liberty for a great many slaves, but also raised them very much in the eyes of the world, for they placed them in a state which every day gained importance and acquired an immense prestige and a powerful influence. We may form an idea of the profound change which took place every day in the organization of society, thanks to these various means, by fixing our attention for a moment on what resulted with respect to the ordination of slaves. The discipline of the Church on this point was in accordance with her doctrines. The slave was a man like other men, and he could be ordained as well as the greatest noble. Yet while he was subject to the power of his master, he was devoid of the independence necessary for the dignity of the sacred ministry; therefore it was required that he should not be ordained until he had been previously set at liberty. Nothing could be more just, reasonable, and prudent, than the limit thus placed on a discipline otherwise so noble and generous—a discipline which was in itself an eloquent protest in favor of the dignity of man. The Church solemnly declared that the misfortune of being a slave did not reduce him below the level of other men, for she did not think it unworthy of her to choose her ministers from among those who had been in servitude. By placing in so honorable a sphere those who had been slaves, she labored with lofty generosity to disperse the prejudices which existed against those who were placed in that unhappy condition, and created strong and effective ties between them and the most venerated class of freemen. The abuse which then crept in of conferring orders on slaves, without the consent of their masters, is above all worthy of our attention; an abuse, it is true, altogether contrary to the sacred canons, and which was checked by the Church with praiseworthy zeal, but which is not the less useful in enabling the observer duly to appreciate the profound effect of religious ideas and institutions. Without attempting in any way to excuse what was blamable therein, we may very well make use of the abuse itself, by considering that it frequently happens that abuses are only exaggerations of a good principle. Religious ideas accord but ill with slavery, although supported by laws; thence the incessant struggle, repeated under different aspects, but always directed towards the same end, viz. universal emancipation. It appears to us that we may now the more confidently avail ourselves of this kind of argument, as we have seen the most dreadful attempts at revolution treated with indulgence, on account of the principles with which the revolutionists were imbued and the objects which they had in view; objects which, as every one knows, were nothing less than an entire change in the organization of society. The abuse to which we have alluded, is attested by the curious documents which are found collected in the decree of Gratian (*Dist.* 54, c. 9, 10, 11, 12). When we examine these documents with attention, we find, 1st, that the number of slaves thus freed was very considerable, since the complaints on this subject were almost universal: 2d, that the Bishops were generally in favor of the slaves; that they carried their protection very far; that they labored in all ways to realize these doctrines of equality; indeed, it is affirmed in these documents that there was hardly a Bishop who could not be charged with this reprehensible compliance: 3d, that slaves were aware of this spirit of protection, and were eager to throw off their chains and cast themselves into the arms of the Church: 4th, that this combination of circumstances must have produced in men's minds a movement very favorable to liberty; and that this affectionate communication established between slaves and the Church, then so powerful and influential, must soon have weakened slavery, and rapidly have promoted the advance of nations towards that liberty which completely triumphed a few centuries later.

The Church of Spain, whose civilizing influence has received so many eulogiums from men certainly but little attached to Catholicity, equally displays her lofty views and consummate prudence on this point. Charitable zeal in favor of slaves was so ardent, the tendency to raise them to the sacred ministry so decided, that it was necessary to allow free scope to this generous impulse, while reconciling it as much as possible with the sacredness of the ministry. Such was the two-fold object of the discipline introduced into Spain, by virtue of which it was allowed to confer sacred orders on the slaves of the Church, on their being previously enfranchised. This is ordered by the 74th canon of the fourth Council of Toledo, held in 633; it is also inferred from the 11th canon of the ninth Council of Toledo, which ordains that Bishops shall not introduce the slaves of the Church among the clergy without having previously given them their liberty.

It is remarkable that this regulation was extended by the 18th canon of the Council of Merida, in 666, which gives to parish-priests the right of selecting clerks among the slaves of their own church, with the obligation of maintaining them according to their means. This wise discipline prevented, without any injustice, all the difficulties that might have ensued from the ordination of slaves; while it was a very mild way of effecting the most beneficent results, since in conferring orders on the slaves of the Church, it was easy to choose from among them such as were most deserving by their intellectual and moral qualifications. At the same time, it was affording the Church a most favorable and honorable mode of liberating her slaves, by enrolling them among her ministers. Finally, the Church by her generous conduct towards slaves, gave a salutary example to the laity. We have seen that she allowed the parochial clergy, as well as the bishops, the privilege of setting them free; and this must have rendered it less painful for laymen to emancipate their slaves, when circumstances seemed to call the latter to the sacred ministry.

CHAPTER XIX.

DOCTRINES OF S. AUGUSTINE AND S. THOMAS AQUINAS ON THE SUBJECT OF SLAVERY.—RÉSUMÉ OF THE SUBJECT.

Thus did the Church, by a variety of means, break the chains of slavery, without ever exceeding the limits marked out by justice and prudence: thus did she banish from among Christians that degrading condition, so contrary to their exalted ideas on the dignity of man, and their generous feelings of fraternity and love. Wherever Christianity shall be introduced, chains of iron shall be turned into gentle ties, and humiliated men shall raise their ennobled heads. With what pleasure do we read the remarks of one of the greatest men of Christianity, S. Augustine, on this point (*De Civit. Dei*, l. xix. c. 14, 15, 16). He establishes in a few words the obligation incumbent upon all who rule—fathers, husbands, and masters—to watch over the good of those who are under them: he lays down the advantage of those who obey, as one of the foundations for obedience; he says that the just do not rule from ambition or pride, but from duty and the desire of doing good to their subjects: "Neque enim dominandi cupiditate imperant, sed officio consulendi, nec principandi superbia, sed providendi misericordia;" and by these noble maxims he proscribes all opinions which tend to tyranny, or found obedience on any degrading notions; but on a sudden, as if this great mind apprehended some reply in violation of human dignity, he grows warm, he boldly faces the question; he rises to his full height, and, giving free scope to the noble thoughts that ferment in his mind, he invokes the idea of nature and the will of God in favor of the dignity of man thus menaced. He says: "Thus wills the order of nature; thus has man been created by God. He has given him to rule over the fishes of the sea, the birds of the air, and the reptiles that crawl on the face of the earth. *He has ordained that reasoning creatures, made according to His own image, shall rule only over creatures devoid of reason. He has not established the dominion of man over man, but that of man over the brute.*" This passage of S. Augustine is one of those bold features which shine forth in writers of genius, when grieved by the sight of a painful object, they allow their generous ideas and feelings to have free scope, and cease to restrain their daring energies. Struck by the force of the expression, the reader, in suspense and breathless, hastens to read the succeeding lines; he fears that the author may be mistaken, seduced by the nobleness of his heart, and carried away by the force of his genius. But, with inexpressible pleasure, he finds that the writer has in no degree departed from the path of true doctrine, when, like a brave champion, he has descended into the arena to defend the cause of justice and humanity. Thus does S. Augustine now appear to us: the sight of so many unfortunate beings groaning in slavery, victims of the violence and caprice of their masters, afflicted his generous mind. By the light of reason and the doctrines of Christianity, he saw no reason why so considerable a portion of the human race should be condemned to live in such debasement; wherefore, when proclaiming the doctrines of submission and obedience, he labors to discover the cause of such ignominy; and not being able to find it in the nature of man, he seeks for it in sin, in malediction. "The primitive just men," says he, "were rather established as pastors over their flocks, than as kings over other men; whereby God gives us to understand what was called for by the order of creation, and what was required by the punishment of sin; for the condition of slavery has, with reason, been imposed on the sinner. Thus we do not find the word slave in the Scriptures before the day when the just man, Noah, gave it as a punishment to his guilty son; whence it follows that this word came from sin, and not from nature." This manner of considering slavery as the offspring of sin, as the fruit of the Divine malediction, was of the highest importance. By protecting the dignity of human nature, that doctrine completely destroyed all the prejudices of natural superiority which the pride of free men could entertain. Thereby also, slavery was deprived of all its supposed value as a political principle or means of government: it could only be regarded as one of the numberless scourges inflicted on the human race by the anger of the Most High. Henceforth slaves had a motive for resignation, while the absolute power of masters was checked, and the compassion of all free men was powerfully excited. All were born in sin, all might have been in a state of slavery. To make a boast of liberty would have been like the conduct of a man who, during an epidemic, should boast of having preserved his health, and imagine that on that account he had a right to insult the unhappy sick. In a word, the state of slavery was a scourge, nothing more; like pestilence, war, famine, or any thing else of the kind. The duty of all men was to labor to remedy and abolish it. Such doctrines did not remain sterile. Proclaimed in the face of day, they were heard in all parts of the Catholic world; and not only were they put in practice, as we have seen by numberless examples, but they were carefully preserved as a precious theory, throughout the confusion of the times. After the lapse of eight centuries, we see them repeated by one of the brightest lights of the Catholic Church, S. Thomas Aquinas (I. p. q. xcvi. art. 4). That great man does not see in slavery either difference of race or imaginary inferiority or means of government; he only considers it as a scourge inflicted on humanity by the sins of the first man.

Such is the repugnance with which Christians have looked upon slavery: we see from this, how false is the assertion of M. Guizot: "It does not seem that Christian society was surprised or much offended by it." It is true there was not that blind disturbance and irritation which, despising all barriers and paying no attention to the rules of justice or the counsels of prudence, ran with foolish haste to efface the mark of degradation and ignominy. But if that disturbance and irritation are meant which are caused by the sight of oppression and outrages committed against man, sentiments which can well accord with longanimity and holy resignation, and which, without checking for a moment the action of charitable zeal, nevertheless avoid precipitating events, preferring mature arrangement in order to secure a complete result; how can this perturbation of mind and holy indignation be better proved to have existed in the bosom of the Church than by the facts and doctrines which we have just quoted? What more eloquent protest against the continuance of slavery can you have than the doctrine of these two illustrious doctors? They declare it, as we have just seen, to be the fruit of malediction, the chastisement of the prevarication the human race; and they only acknowledge its existence by considering it as one of the great scourges that afflict humanity.

of I have explained, with sufficient evidence, the profound reasons which induced the Church to recommend obedience to slaves, and she cannot be reproached on that account with forgetting the rights of humanity. We must not suppose on that account that Christian society was wanting in the boldness necessary for telling the whole truth; but it told only the pure and wholesome truth. What took place with respect to the marriages of slaves is a proof of what I advance. We know that their union was not regarded as a real marriage, and that even that union, such as it was, could not be contracted without the consent of their masters, under pain of being considered as void. Here was a flagrant violation of reason and justice. What did the Church do? She directly reprobated so gross a violation of the rights of nature. Let us hear what Pope Adrian I. said on this subject: "According to the words of the Apostles, as in Jesus Christ we ought not to deprive either slaves or freemen of the sacraments of the Church, so it is not allowed in any way to prevent the marriage of slaves; and if their marriages have been contracted in spite of the opposition and repugnance of their masters, nevertheless they ought not to be dissolved in any way." (*De Conju. Serv.*, lib. iv. tom. 9, c. 1.) And let it not be supposed that this regulation, which secured the liberty of slaves on one of the most important points, was restricted to particular circumstances; no, it was something more; it was a proclamation of their freedom in this matter. The Church was unwilling to allow that man, reduced to the level of the brute, should be forced to obey the caprice or the interest of another, without regard to the feelings of his heart. St. Thomas was of the same opinion, for he openly maintains that, with respect to the contracting of marriage, slaves are not obliged to obey their masters (2ª. 2, q. 104, art. 5).

In the hasty sketch which I have given, I believe that I have kept the promise which I made at the beginning, not to advance any proposition without supporting it by undeniable documents, and not to allow myself to be misled by enthusiasm in favor of Catholicity, so as to concede to it that to which it is not entitled. By passing, rapidly it is true, the course of ages, we have shown, by convincing proofs, which have been furnished by times and places the most various, that it was Catholicity that abolished slavery, in spite of ideas, manners, interests, and laws, which opposed obstacles apparently invincible; and that it has done so without injustice, without violence, without revolutions,—with the most exquisite prudence and the most admirable moderation. We have seen the Catholic Church make so extensive, so varied, and so efficacious an attack on slavery, that that odious chain was broken without a single violent stroke.

Exposed to the action of the most powerful agents, it gradually relaxed and fell to pieces. Her proceedings may be thus recapitulated :—

First, she loudly teaches the truth concerning the dignity of man; she defines the obligations of masters and slaves; she declares them equal before God, and thus completely destroys the degrading theories which stain the writings even of the greatest philosophers of antiquity. She then comes to the application of her doctrines: she labors to improve the treatment of slaves; she struggles against the atrocious right of life and death; she opens her temples to them as asylums, and when they depart thence, prevents their being ill-treated; she labors to substitute public tribunals for private vengeance. At the same time that the Church guarantees the liberty of the enfranchised, by connecting it with religious motives, she defends that of those born free; she labors to close the sources of slavery, by displaying the most active zeal for the redemption of captives, by opposing the avarice of the Jews, by procuring for men who were sold, easy means of recovering their liberty. The Church gives an example of mildness and disinterestedness; she facilitates emancipation, by admitting slaves into monasteries and the ecclesiastical state; she facilitates it by all the other means that charity suggests; and thus it is that, in spite of the deep roots of slavery in ancient society—in spite of the perturbation caused by the irruptions of the barbarians—in spite of so many wars and calamities of every kind, which in great measure paralyzed the effect of all regulating and beneficent action—yet we see slavery, that dishonor and leprosy of ancient civilization, rapidly diminish among Christians, until it finally disappears. Surely in all this we do not discover a plan conceived and concerted by men. But we do observe therein, in the absence of that plan, such unity of tendencies, such a perfect identity of views, and such similarity in the means, that we have the clearest demonstration of the civilizing and liberating spirit contained in Catholicity. Accurate observers will no doubt be gratified in beholding, in the picture which I have just exhibited, the admirable concord with which the period of the empire, that of the irruption of the barbarians, and that of feudality, all tended towards the same end. They will not regret the poor regularity which distinguishes the exclusive work of man; they will love, I repeat it, to collect all the facts scattered in the seeming disorder, from the forests of Germany to the fields of Bœotia—from the banks of the Thames to those of the Tiber. I have not invented these facts; I have pointed out the periods, and cited the Councils. The reader will find, at the end of the volume, in the original and in full, the texts of which I have just given an abstract—a *résumé:* thus he may fully convince himself that I have not deceived him. If such had been my intention, surely I should have avoided descending to the level ground of facts; I should have preferred the vague regions of theory; I should have called to my aid high sounding and seductive language, and all the means the most likely to enchant the imagination and excite the feelings; in fine, I should have placed myself in one of those positions where a writer can suppose at his pleasure things which have never existed, and made the best use of the resources of imagination and invention. The task which I have undertaken is rather more difficult, perhaps less brilliant, but certainly more useful.

We may now inquire of M. Guizot what were the *other causes*, the *other ideas*, the *other principles of civilization,* the great development of which, to avail myself of his words, was necessary "to abolish this evil of evils, this iniquity of iniquities." Ought he not to explain, or at least point out, these causes, ideas, and principles of civilization, which, according to him, assisted the Church in the abolition of slavery, in order to save the reader the trouble of seeking or divining them? If they did not arise in the bosom of the Church, *where* did they arise? Were they found in the ruins of ancient civilization? But could these remains of a scattered and almost annihilated civilization effect what that same civilization, in all its vigor, power, and splendor, never did or thought of doing?—Were they in the *individual independence of the barbarians?* But that individuality, the inseparable companion of violence, must consequently have been the source of oppression and slavery. Were they found in the *military patronage* introduced, according to M. Guizot, by the barbarians themselves; patronage which laid the foundation of that aristocratical organization which was converted at a later period into feudality? But what could this patronage —an institution likely, on the contrary, to perpetuate slavery among the indigent in conquered countries, and to extend it to a considerable portion of the conquerors themselves—what could this patronage do for the abolition of slavery? Where, then, is the idea, the custom, the institution, which, born out of Christianity, contributed to the abolition of slavery? Let any one point out to us the epoch of its formation, the time of its development; let him show us that it had not its origin in Christianity, and we will then confess that the latter cannot exclusively lay claim to the glorious title of having abolished that degraded condition; and he may be sure that this shall not prevent our exalting that idea, custom, or institution which took part in the great and noble enterprise of liberating the human race.

We may be allowed, in conclusion, to inquire of the Protestant churches, of those ungrateful daughters who, after having quitted the bosom of their mother, attempt to calumniate and dishonor her, where were you when the Catholic Church accomplished in Europe the immense work of the abolition of slavery? and how can you venture to reproach her with sympathizing with servitude, degrading man, and usurping his rights? Can you, then, present any such claim entitling you to the gratitude of the human race? What part can you claim in that great work which prepared the way for the development and grandeur of European civilization? Catholicity alone, without your concurrence, completed the work; and she alone would have conducted Europe to its lofty destinies, if you had not come to interrupt the majestic march of its mighty nations, by urging them into a path bordered by precipices,—a path the end of which is concealed by darkness which the eye of God alone can pierce. (15)

CHAPTER XX.

CONTRAST BETWEEN TWO ORDERS OF CIVILIZATION.

We have seen that European civilization owes to the Catholic Church its finest ornament, its most valuable victory in the cause of humanity, the abolition of slavery. It was the Church that, by her doctrines, as beneficent as elevated, by a system as efficacious as prudent, by her unbounded generosity, her indefatigable zeal, her invincible firmness, abolished slavery in Europe; that is to say, she took the first step towards the regeneration of humanity, and laid the first stone for the wide and deep foundation of European civilization; we mean the emancipation of slaves, the abolition for ever of so degrading a state, —universal liberty. It was impossible to create and organize a civilization full of grandeur and dignity, without raising man from his state of abjection, and placing him above the level of animals. Whenever we see him crouching at another's feet, awaiting with anxiety the orders of his master or trembling at the lash; whenever he is sold like a beast, or a price is set upon his powers and his life, civilization will never have its proper development, it will always be weak, sickly, and broken; for thus humanity bears a mark of ignominy on its forehead.

After having shown that it was Catholicity that removed that obstacle to all social progress, by, as it were, cleansing Europe of the disgusting leprosy with which it was infected from head to foot, let us examine what it has done towards creating and erecting the magnificent edifice of European civilization. If we seriously reflect on the vitality and fruitfulness of this civilization, we shall find therein new and powerful claims on the part of the Catholic Church to the gratitude of nations. In the first place, it is proper to glance at the vast and interesting picture which European civilization presents to us, and to sum up in a few words its principal perfections; thereby we shall be enabled the more easily to account to ourselves for the admiration and enthusiasm with which it inspires us.

The individual animated by a lively sense of his own dignity, abounding in activity, perseverance, energy, and the simultaneous development of all his faculties; woman elevated to the rank of the consort of man, and, as it were, recompensed for the duty of obedience by the respectful regards lavished upon her; the gentleness and constancy of family ties, protected by the powerful guarantees of good order and justice; an admirable public conscience, rich in maxims of sublime morality, in laws of justice and equity, in sentiments of honor and dignity; a conscience which survives the shipwreck of private morality, and does not allow unblushing corruption to reach the height which it did in antiquity; a general mildness of manners, which in war prevents great excesses, and in peace renders life more tranquil and pleasing; a profound respect for man, and all that belongs to him, which makes private acts of violence very uncommon, and in all political constitutions serves as a salutary check on governments; an ardent desire of perfection in all departments; an irresistible tendency, sometimes ill-directed, but always active, to improve the condition of the many; a secret impulse to protect the weak, to succour the unfortunate—an impulse which sometimes pursues its course with generous ardor, and which, whenever it is unable to develop itself, remains in the heart of society, and produces there the uneasiness and disquietude of remorse; a cosmopolitan spirit of universality, of propagandism, an inexhaustible fund of resources to grow young again without danger of perishing, and for self-preservation in the most important junctures; a generous impatience, which longs to anticipate the future, and produces an incessant movement and agitation, sometimes dangerous, but which are generally the germs of great benefits, and the symptoms of a strong principle of life; such are the great characteristics which distinguish European civilization; such are the features which place it in a rank immensely superior to that of all other civilizations, ancient and modern.

Read the history of antiquity; extend your view over the whole world; wherever Christianity does not reign, and where the barbarous or savage life no longer prevails, you will find a civilization which in nothing resembles our own, and which cannot be compared with it for a moment. In some of these states of civilization, you will perhaps find a certain degree of regularity and some marks of power, for they have endured for centuries; but how have they endured? Without movement, without progress; they are devoid of life; their regularity and duration are those of a marble statue, which, motionless itself, sees the waves of generations pass by. There have also been nations whose civilization displayed motion and activity; but what motion and what activity? Some, ruled by the mercantile spirit, never succeeded in establishing their internal happiness on a firm basis; their only object was to invade new countries which tempted their cupidity, to pour into their colonies their superabundant population, and establish numerous factories in new lands: others, continually contending and fighting for a few measures of political freedom, forgot their social organization, took no care of their civil liberty, and acted in the narrowest circle of time and space; they would not be even worthy of having their names preserved for posterity, if the genius of the beautiful had not shone there with indescribable charm, and if the monuments of their knowledge, like a mirror, had not preserved the bright rays of Eastern learning: others, great and terrible, it is true, but troubled by intestine dissensions, bear inscribed upon their front the formidable destiny of conquest; this destiny they fulfilled by subjugating the world, and immediately their rapid and inevitable ruin approached: others, in fine, excited by violent fanaticism, raged like the waves of ocean in a storm; they threw themselves upon other nations like a devastating torrent, and threatened to involve Christian civilization itself in their deafening uproar; but their efforts were vain; their waves broke against insurmountable barriers; they repeated their attempts, but, always compelled to retire, they fell back again, and spread themselves on the beach with a sullen roar: and now look at the Eastern nations; behold them like an impure pool, which the heat of the sun is about to dry up; see the sons and successors of Mahomet and Omar on their knees at the feet of the European powers, begging a protection, which policy sometimes affords them, but only with disdain. Such is the picture presented to us by every civilization, ancient and modern, except that of Europe, that is, the Christian. It alone at once embraces every thing great and noble in the others; it alone survives the most thorough revolutions; it alone extends itself to all races and climates, and accommodates itself to forms of government the most various; it alone, in fine, unites itself with all kinds of institutions, whenever, by circulating in them its fertile sap, it can produce its sweet and salutary fruits for the good of humanity. And whence comes the immense superiority of European civilization over all others? How has it become so noble, so rich, so varied, so fruitful; with the stamp of dignity, of nobility, and of loftiness; without castes, without slaves, without eunuchs, without any of those miseries which prey upon other ancient and modern nations? It often happens that we Europeans complain and lament more than the most unfortunate portion of the human race ever did; and we forget that we are the privileged children of Providence, and that our evils, our share of the unavoidable patrimony of humanity, are very slight, are nothing in comparison with those which have been, and still are, suffered by other nations. Even the extent of our good fortune itself renders us difficult to please, and exceedingly fastidious. We are like a man of high rank, accustomed to live respected and esteemed in the midst of ease and pleasure, who is indignant at a slighting word, is filled with disquietude and affliction at the most trifling contradiction, and forgets the multitude of men who are plunged in misery, whose nakedness is covered with a few rags, and who meet with a thousand insults and refusals before they can obtain a morsel of bread to satisfy the cravings of hunger.

The mind, when contemplating European civilization, experiences so many different impressions, is attracted by so many objects that at the same time claim its attention and preference, that, charmed by the magnificent spectacle, it is dazzled, and knows not where to commence the examination. The best way in such a case is to simplify, to decompose the complex object, and reduce it to its simplest elements. *The individual, the family, and society;* these we have thoroughly to examine, and these ought to be the subjects of our inquiries. If we succeed in fully understanding these three elements, as they really are in themselves, and apart from the slight variations which do not affect their essence, European civilization, with all its riches and all its secrets, will be presented to our view, like a fertile and beautiful landscape lit up by the morning sun.

European civilization is in possession of the principal truths with respect to the individual, to the family, and to society; it is to this that it owes all that it is and all that it has. Nowhere have the true nature, the true relations and object of these three things been better understood than in Europe; with respect to them we have ideas. sentiments, and views which have been wanting in other civilizations. Now, these ideas and feelings, strongly marked on the face of

European nations, have inoculated their laws, manners, institutions, customs, and language; they are inhaled with the air, for they have impregnated the whole atmosphere with their vivifying aroma. To what is this owing? To the fact, that Europe, for many centuries, has had within its bosom a powerful principle which preserves, propagates, and fructifies the truth; and it was especially in those times of difficulty, when the disorganized society had to assume a new form, that this regenerating principle had the greatest influence and ascendency. Time has passed away, great changes have taken place, Catholicity has undergone vast vicissitudes in its power and influence on society; but civilization, its work, was too strong to be easily destroyed; the impulse which had been given to Europe was too powerful and well secured to be easily diverted from its course. Europe was like a young man gifted with a strong constitution, and full of health and vigor; the excesses of labor or of dissipation reduce him and make him grow pale; but soon the hue of health returns to his countenance, and his limbs recover their suppleness and vigor.

CHAPTER XXI.

OF THE INDIVIDUAL—OF THE FEELING OF INDIVIDUAL INDEPENDENCE ACCORDING TO M. GUIZOT.

The individual is the first and simplest element of society. If the individual is not well constituted, if he is ill understood and ill appreciated, there will always be an obstacle to the progress of real civilization. First of all, we must observe, that we speak here only of the individual, of man as he is in himself, apart from the numerous relations which surround him when we come to consider him as a member of society. But let it not be imagined from this, that I wish to consider him in a state of absolute isolation, to carry him to the desert, to reduce him to the savage state, and analyze the individuality as it appears to us in a few wandering hordes, a monstrous exception, which is only the result of the degradation of our nature. Equally useless would it be to revive the theory of Rousseau, that pure Utopianism which can only lead to error and extravagance. We may separately examine the pieces of a machine, for the better understanding of its particular construction; but we must take care not to forget the purpose for which they are intended, and not lose sight of the whole, of which they form a part. Without that, the judgment we should form of them would certainly be erroneous. The most wonderful and sublime picture would be only a ridiculous monstrosity, if its groups and figures were considered in a state of isolation from its other parts; in this way, the prodigies of Michael Angelo and Raffael might be taken for the dreams of a madman. Man is not alone in the world, nor is he born to live alone. Besides what is he in himself, he is a part of the great scheme of the Universe. Besides the destiny which belongs to him in the vast plan of creation, he is raised, by the bounty of his Maker, to another sphere, above all earthly thoughts. Good philosophy requires that we should forget nothing of all this. It now remains for us to consider the individual and individuality.

In considering man, we may abstract from his quality of citizen,—an abstraction which, far from leading to any extravagant paradoxes, is likely to make us thoroughly understand a remarkable peculiarity of European civilization, one of the distinctive characteristics, which will be alone sufficient to enable us to avoid confounding it with others. All will readily understand that there is a distinction to be made between the man and the citizen, and that these two aspects lead to very different considerations; but it is more difficult to say how far the limits of this distinction should extend; to what extent the feeling of independence should be admitted; what is the sphere which ought to be assigned to purely individual development; in fine, whatever is peculiar to our civilization on this point. We must justly estimate the difference which we find herein between our state of society and that of others; we must point out its source, and its result; we must carefully weigh its real influence on the advance of civilization. This task is difficult; I repeat it,—for we have here various questions, great and important, it is true, but delicate and profound, and very easily mistaken,—it is not without much trouble that we can fix our eyes with certainty on these vague, indeterminate, and floating objects, which are connected together by no perceptible ties.

We here meet with the famous *personal independence*, which, according to M. Guizot, was brought by the barbarians from the North, and played so important a part, that we ought to look upon it as one of the chief and most productive principles of European civilization. This celebrated publicist, analyzing the elements of this civilization, and pointing out the share which the Roman empire and the Church had therein, in his opinion, finds a remarkable principle of productiveness in the feeling of individuality, which the Germans brought with them, and inoculated into the manners of Europe. It will not be useless to discuss the opinion of M. Guizot on this important and delicate matter. By thus explaining the state of the question, we shall remove the important errors of some persons, errors produced by the authority of this writer, whose talent and eloquence have unfortunately given plausibility and semblance of truth to what is in reality only a paradox. The first care we ought to take, in combating the opinions of this writer, is not to attribute to him what he has not really said; besides, as the matter we are treating of is liable to many mistakes, we shall do well to transcribe the words of M. Guizot at length. "What we require to know," he says, "is the general condition of society among the barbarians. Now it is very difficult, now-a-days, to give an account of it. We can understand, without too much trouble, the municipal system of Rome, and the Christian Church; their influence has continued down to our times; we find traces of them in many institutions and existing facts. We have a thousand means of recognising and explaining them. The manners, the social condition of the barbarians, have entirely perished; we are compelled to divine them, by the most ancient historical documents, or by an effort of imagination."

What has been preserved to us of the manners of the barbarians is, indeed, little; this is an assertion which I will not deny. I will not dispute with M. Guizot about the authority which ought to belong to facts which require to be filled up by an effort of the imagination, and which compel us to have recourse to the dangerous expedient of divining. As for the rest, I am aware of the nature of these questions; and the reflections which I have just made, as well as the terms which I have used, prove that I do not think it possible to proceed with rule and compass in such an examination. Nevertheless, I have thought it proper to warn the reader on this point, and combat the delusion into which he might be led by a doctrine which, when fully examined, is, I repeat it, only a brilliant paradox. "There is a feeling, a fact," continues M. Guizot, "which it is above all necessary to understand well, in order to represent to ourselves with truth what a barbarian was: this is, the pleasure of individual independence—the pleasure of playing amid the chances of the world and of life, with power and liberty; the joys of activity without labor; the taste for an adventurous destiny, full of surprises, vicissitudes, and perils. Such was the ruling feeling of the barbarian state, the moral necessity which put these masses of men in motion. To-day, in the regular society in which we live, it is difficult to represent to one's self this feeling, with all the influence which it exercised over the barbarians of the fourth and fifth centuries. There is only one work, in my opinion, in which this character of barbarism is described with all its force, viz. *The History of the Conquest of England by the Normans,* of M Thierry—the only book where the motives, the inclinations, the impulses which actuate man in a social state bordering on barbarism, are felt and described with a truth really Homeric. Nowhere do we see so clearly what a barbarian was, and what was his life. We also find something of this, although in a very inferior degree, in my opinion, in a manner much less simple, much less true, in the romances of Mr Cooper on the American savages. There is in the life of the savages of America, in the relations and feelings which exist in those forests, something which reminds one, to a certain extent, of the manners of the ancient Germans. No doubt these pictures are a little ideal, a little poetical; the unfavorable side of barbarian life and manners is not displayed in all its crudity. I do not speak merely of the evils which these manners produce in the individual social condition of the barbarian himself. In this passionate love of personal independence, there was something more rude and coarse than one would imagine from the work of M. Thierry; there was a degree of brutality, of indolence, of apathy, which is not always faithfully described in his pictures Nevertheless, when one examines the thing to the bottom, in spite of brutality, coarseness, and this stupid *egotism,* the taste for individual independence is a noble moral feeling, which draws its power from the moral nature of man: it is the pleasure of feeling himself a man—the sentiment of personality, of spontaneous action in his free development. Gentlemen, it was by the German barbarians that this feeling was introduced into the civilization of Europe; it was unknown to the Roman world, unknown to the Christian Church, unknown to almost all the ancient civilizations:—when you find liberty in the ancient civilizations, it is political liberty, the liberty of the citizen. It is not with his personal liberty that the man is prepossessed, but with his liberty as a citizen. He belongs to an association—he is devoted to an association—he is ready to sacrifice himself for an association. It was the same with the Christian Church: there prevailed a feeling of great attachment to the Christian corporation—of devotion to its laws—a strong desire of extending its empire; the religious feeling produced a reaction on the man himself—on his soul—an internal struggle to subdue his own will, and make it submit to the demands of his faith. But the feeling of personal independence, the taste for liberty showing itself at any hazard, with hardly any other object than its own satisfaction—this feeling, I repeat, was unknown to the Roman and Christian society. It was brought in by the barbarians, and placed in the cradle of modern civilization. It has played so great a part, it has produced such noble results, that it is impossible not to bring it to light as one of the fundamental elements thereof." (*Histoire Générale de la Civilisation en Europe,* leçon 2.) This feeling of personal independence, exclusively attributed to a nation—this vague, undefinable feeling—a singular mixture of nobleness and brutality, of barbarism and civilization—is in some degree poetical, and is very likely to seduce the fancy; but, unfortunately, there is in the contrast, intended to increase the effect of the picture, something extraordinary, I will even say contradictory, which excites the suspicion of cool reason that there is some hidden error which compels it to be on its guard. If it be true that this phenomenon ever existed, what was its origin? Will it be said that it was the result of climate? But how can it be imagined that the snows of the north protected what was not found in the ardent south? How comes it that the feeling of personal independence was wanting precisely in those southern countries of Europe, where the feeling of political independence was developed with so much force? and would it not be a strange thing, not to say an absurdity, if these different climates had divided these two kinds of liberty between them, like an inheritance? It will be said, perhaps, that this feeling arose from the social state. But in that case, it cannot be made the characteristic mark of one nation: it must be said, in general terms, that the feeling belonged to all the nations who were in the same social condition as the Germans. Besides, even according to this hypothesis, how could that which was peculiar to barbarism have been a germ, a fruitful principle of civilization? This feeling, which must have been effaced by civilization, could not even preserve itself in the midst thereof, much less contribute to its development. If its perpetuation in some form was absolutely necessary, why did not the same thing take place in the bosom of other civilizations? Surely the Germans were not the only people who passed from barbarism to civilization. But I do not pretend to say that the barbarians of the north did not present some remarkable peculiarity in this point of view; and I do not deny that we find in European civilization a feeling of personality, if I may so speak, unknown to other civilizations. But what I venture to affirm is, that it is little philosophical to have recourse to mysteries and enigmas to explain the *individuality* of the Germans, and that it is useless to seek in their barbarism the cause of the superiority which European civilization possesses in this respect. To form a clear idea of this question, which is as complicated as it is important, it is first of all necessary to specify, in the best way we can, the real nature of the barbarian *individuality.* In a pamphlet which I published some time ago, called *Observations Sociales, Politiques, et Economiques, sur les Biens du Clergé,* I have incidentally touched upon this individuality, and attempted to give clear ideas on this point. As I have not changed my opinion since that time, but, on the contrary, as it has been confirmed, I will transcribe what I then said, as follows: "What was this feeling? Was it peculiar to those nations? Was it the result of the influence of climate, of a social position? Was it perchance a feeling formed in all places and at all times, but which is here modified by particular circumstances? What was its force, its tendency? How far was it just or unjust, noble or degrading, profitable or injurious? What benefits did it confer on society; what evils? How were these evils combated, by whom, by what means, and with what result? These questions are numerous, but they are not so complicated as they appear at first sight; when once the fundamental idea shall be cleared up, the others will be understood without difficulty, and the theory, when simplified, will immediately be confirmed and supported by history. There is a strong, active, an indestructible feeling in the human heart which urges men to self-preservation, to avoid evils, and to attain to their well-being and happiness. Whether you call it self-love, instinct of preservation, desire of happiness or of perfection, egotism, *individuality,* or whatever name you give to it, this feeling exists; we have it within us. We cannot doubt of its existence; it accompanies us at every step, in all our actions, from the time when we first see the light till we descend into the tomb. This feeling, if you will observe its origin, its nature, and its object, is nothing but a great law of all beings applied to man; a law which, being a guarantee for the preservation and perfecting of individuals, admirably contributes to the harmony of the universe. It is clear that such a feeling must naturally incline us to hate oppression, and to suffer with impatience what tends to limit and fetter the use of our faculties. The cause is easily found; all this gives us uneasiness, to which our nature is repugnant; even the tenderest infant bears with impatience the tie that fastens him in his cradle; he is uneasy, he is disturbed, he cries.

"On the other hand, the individual, when he is not totally devoid of knowledge of himself, when his intellectual faculties are at all developed, will feel another sentiment arise in his mind which has nothing in common with the instinct of self-preservation with which all beings are animated, a sentiment which belongs exclusively to intelligence; I mean, the feeling of dignity, of value of ourselves, of that fire which, enkindled in our hearts in our earliest years is nourished, extended, and supported by the aliment afforded to it by time, and acquires that immense power, that expansion which makes us so restless, active, and agitated during all periods of our life. The subjection of one man to another wounds this feeling of dignity; for even supposing it to be reconciled with all possible freedom and mildness, with the most perfect respect for the person subjected, this subjection reveals a weakness or a necessity which compels him in some degree to limit the free use of his faculties. Such is the second origin of the feeling of personal independence. It follows from what I have just said, that man always bears within himself a certain love of independence, that this feeling is necessarily common to all times and countries, for we have found its roots in the two most natural feelings of man—viz. *the desire of well-being and the consciousness of his own dignity.* It is evident that these feelings may be modified and varied indefinitely, on account of the infinity of situations in which the individual may be placed, morally and physically. Without leaving the sphere which is marked out for them by their very essence, these feelings may vary as to strength or weakness on the most extensive scale; they may be moral or immoral, just or unjust, noble or vile, advantageous or injurious. Consequently they may contribute to the individual the greatest variety of inclinations, of habits, of manners; and thereby give very different features to the physiognomy of nations, according to the particular and characteristic manner in which they affect the individual. These notions being once cleared up by a real knowledge of the constitution of the heart of man, we see how all questions which relate to the feeling of individuality must be resolved; we also see that it is useless to have recourse to mysterious language or poetical explanations, for in all this there is nothing that can be submitted to a rigorous analysis. The ideas which man forms of his own well-being and dignity, the means which he employs to promote the one and preserve the other, these are what will settle the degrees of energy, will determine the nature and signalize the tendency of all these feelings; that is to say, all will depend on the physical and moral state of society and the individual. Now, supposing all other circumstances to be equal, give a man true ideas of his own well-being and dignity, such as reason and above all the Christian religion teach, and you will form a good citizen; give false, exaggerated, absurd ideas, such as are entertained by perverted schools and promulgated by agitators at all times and in all countries, and you spread the fruitful seeds of disturbance and disorder.

"In order to complete the clearing up of the important point which we have undertaken to explain, we must apply this doctrine to the particular fact which now occupies us. If we fix our attention on the nations who invaded and overturned the Roman empire, confining ourselves to the facts which history has preserved of them, to the conjectures which are authorized by the circumstances in which they were placed, and to the general data which modern science has been able to collect from the immediate observation of the different tribes of America, we shall be able to form an idea of what was the state of society and of the individual among the invading barbarians. In their native countries, among their mountains, in their forests covered with frost and snow, they had their family ties, their relationships, their religion, traditions, customs, manners, attachment to their hereditary soil, their love of national independence, their enthusiasm for the great deeds of their ancestors, and for the glory acquired in battle; in fine, their desire of perpetuating in their children a race strong, valiant, and free; they had their distinctions of family, their division into tribes, their priests, chiefs, and government. Without discussing the character of their forms of government, and laying aside all that might be said of their monarchy, their public assemblies, and other similar points, questions which are foreign to our subject, and which besides are always in some degree hypothetical and imaginary, I shall content myself with making a remark which none of my readers will deny, viz. that among them the organization of society was such as might have been expected from rude and superstitious ideas, gross habits, and ferocious manners; that is to say, that their social condition did not rise above the level which had naturally been marked out for it by two imperious necessities: first, that complete anarchy should not prevail in their forests; and second, that in war they should have some one to lead their confused hordes. Born in rigorous climates, crowding on each other by their rapid increase, and on that account obtaining with difficulty even the means of subsistence, these nations saw before their eyes the abundance and the luxuries of ample and well-cultivated regions; they were at the same time urged on by extreme want, and strongly excited by the presence of plunder. There was nothing to oppose them but the feeble legions of an effeminate and decaying civilization; their own bodies were strong, their minds full of courage and audacity; their numbers augmented their boldness; they left their native soil without pain; a spirit of adventure and enterprise developed itself in their minds, and they threw themselves on the Empire like a torrent which falls from the mountains, and inundates the neighboring plains. However imperfect was their social condition, and however rude were its ties, it sufficed, nevertheless, in their native soil, and amid their ancient manners; if the barbarians had remained in their forests, it may be said that that form of government, which answered its purpose in its way, would have been perpetuated; for it was born of necessity, it was adapted to circumstances, it was rooted in their habits, sanctioned by time, and connected with traditions and recollections of every kind. But these ties were too weak to be transported without being broken. These forms of government were, as we have just seen, so suited to the state of barbarism, and consequently so circumscribed and limited, that they could not be applied without difficulty to the new situation in which these nations found themselves almost suddenly placed. Let us imagine these savage children of the forest precipitated on the south; their fierce chiefs precede them, and they are followed by crowds of women and children; they take with them their flocks and rude baggage; they cut to pieces numerous legions on their way; they form intrenchments, cross ditches, scale ramparts, ravage the country, destroy forests, burn populous cities, and take with them immense numbers of slaves captured on the way. They overturn every thing that opposes their fury, and drive before them multitudes who flee to avoid fire and sword. In a short time see these same men, elated with victory, enriched by immense booty, inured by so many battles, fires, sackings, and massacres, transported, as if by enchantment, into a new climate, under another sky, and swimming in abundance, in pleasure, in new enjoyments of every kind. A confused mixture of idolatry and Christianity, of truth and falsehood, is become their religion; their principal chiefs are dead in battle; families are confounded in disorder, races mixed, old manners and customs altered and lost. These nations, in fine, are spread over immense countries, in the midst of other nations, differing in language, ideas, manners, and usages; imagine, if you can, this disorder, this confusion, this chaos, and tell me whether the ties which formed the society of these nations are not destroyed and broken into a thousand pieces, and whether you do not see barbarian and civilized society disappear together, and all antiquity vanish without any thing new taking its place? And at this moment, fix your eyes upon the gloomy child of the North, when he feels all the ties that bound him to society suddenly loosened, when all the chains that restrained his ferocity break; when he finds himself alone, isolated, in a position so new, so singular, so extraordinary, with an obscure recollection of his late country and without affection for that which he has just occupied; without respect for law, fear of man, or attachment to custom. Do you not see him, in his impetuous ferocity, indulge without limit his habits of violence, wandering, plunder, and massacre? He confides in his strong arm and activity of foot, and led by a heart full of fire and courage, by an imagination excited by the view of so many different countries and by the hazards of so many travels and combats, he rashly undertakes all enterprises, rejects all subjection, throws off all restraint, and delights in the dangers of fresh struggles and adventures. Do you not find here the mysterious individuality, the feeling of personal independence, in all its philosophical reality and all the truth which is assigned to it by history? This brutal individuality, this fierce feeling of independence, which was not reconcileable with the well-being or with the true dignity of the individual, contained a principle of eternal war and a continually wandering mode of life, and must necessarily produce the degradation of man and the complete dissolution of society. Far from containing the germ of civilization, it was this that was best adapted to reduce Europe to the savage state; it stifled society in its cradle; it destroyed every attempt made to reorganize it, and completed the annihilation of all that remained of the ancient civilization."

The observations which have just been made may be more or less well founded, more or less happy, but at least they do not present the inexplicable inconsistency, not to say contradiction, of allying barbarism and brutality with civilization and refinement; they do not give the name of an eminent and fruitful principle of European civilization to that which a little further on is pointed out as one of the strongest obstacles to the progress of social organization. As M. Guizot, on this last point, agrees with the opinion which I have just stated, and shows the incoherence of his own doctrines, the reader will allow me to quote his own words. "It is clear," he says, "that if men have no ideas extending beyond their own existence, if their intellectual horizon is limited to themselves, if they give themselves up to the caprices of their own passions and wills, if they have not among them a certain number of common notions and feelings, around which they rally; it is clear, I say, that no society can be possible among them; that such individual, when he enters into any association, will be a principle of disturbance and dissolution. Whenever individuality almost absolutely prevails, or man only considers himself, or his ideas do not extend beyond himself, or he obeys only his own passions, society, I mean one with any thing of extent or permanency, becomes almost impossible. Now such was the moral condition of the conquerors of Europe at the period of which we speak. I have pointed out, in the last lecture, that we owe the energetic feeling of individual liberty and humanity to the Germans. Now, in a state of extreme rudeness and ignorance, this feeling is egotism in all its brutality, in all its unsociability. From the fifth to the eighth century, such was the case among the Germans. They consulted only their own interests, their own passions, their own wills; how could this accord with the social state? It was attempted to make them enter it; they attempted it themselves; they soon left it from some sudden act, some sally of passion or misunderstanding. Every moment we see society attempted to be formed; every moment we see it broken by the act of man, by the want of the moral conditions necessary for its subsistence. Such, gentlemen, were the two prevailing causes of the state of barbarism. As long as they lasted, barbarism continued." (*Histoire Générale de la Civilisation en Europe,* leçon 3.)

With respect to his theory of *individuality*, M. Guizot has met with the common fate of men of great talents. They are forcibly struck by a singular phenomenon, they conceive an ardent desire of finding its cause, and they fall into frequent errors, led away by a secret tendency always to point out a new, unexpected, astonishing origin. In his vast and penetrating view of European civilization, in his parallel between this and the most distinguished ones of antiquity, he discovered a very remarkable difference between the individuals of the former and of the latter. He saw in the man of modern Europe, something nobler, more independent than in the Greek or Roman; it was necessary to point out the origin of this difference. Now this was not an easy task, considering the peculiar situation in which the philosophical historian found himself. From the first glance which he took at the elements of European civilization, the Church presented herself to him as one of the most powerful and the most influential agents on the organization of society; and he saw issue from her the impulse which was most capable of leading the world to a great and happy future. He had already expressly acknowledged this, and had paid homage to the truth in magnificent language; in order to explain this phenomenon, should he again have recourse to Christianity, to the Church? This would have been conceding to her the whole of the great work of civilization; and M. Guizot was desirous, at all hazards, of giving her coadjutors. Therefore, fixing his eyes upon the barbarian hordes, he expects to discover in the swarthy brows, the savage countenances, and the menacing looks of these children of the forest, a type, somewhat rude but still very just, of the noble independence, the elevation, and dignity which the European bears in his features.

After having explained the mysterious personality of the Germans, and shown that, far from being an element of civilization, it was a source of disorder and barbarism; it is besides necessary to examine the difference which exists between the civilization of Europe and other civilizations, with respect to the feeling of dignity; it is necessary to determine with precision what modifications have been undergone by a feeling, which, considered by itself, is, as we have seen, common to all men. In the first place, there is no foundation for this assertion of M. Guizot, *that the feeling of personal independence, the taste for liberty, displaying itself at all hazards, with scarcely any other object than its own satisfaction, was unknown to Roman society.* It is clear that in such a comparison, it is not meant to allude to the feeling of independence in the savage state, in the state of barbarism; for as well might it be said that civilized nations could not have the distinctive character of barbarism. But laying aside that circumstance of ferocity, we will say that the feeling was very active, not only among the Romans, but also among the other most celebrated nations of antiquity. "When you find in ancient civilization," says M. Guizot, "liberty, it is political liberty, the liberty of the citizen. It is not with his personal liberty that the man is prepossessed, it is with his liberty as a citizen; he belongs to an association, he is devoted to an association, he is ready to sacrifice himself for an association." I will not deny that this spirit of sacrifice for the benefit of an association did exist among ancient nations; I acknowledge also that it was accompanied by remarkable peculiarities, which I intend to explain further on; yet it may be doubted whether *the taste for liberty, with scarcely any other object than its own satisfaction,* was not more active with ancient nations than with us. Indeed, what was the object of the Phœnicians, the Greeks of the Archipelago and of Asia Minor, the Carthaginians, when they undertook those voyages which, for such remote times, were as bold and perilous as those of our most intrepid sailors? Was it, indeed, to sacrifice themselves for an association that they sought new territories with so much ardour, in order to amass there money, gold, and all kinds of articles of value? Were they not led by the desire of acquiring *to gratify themselves?* Where, then, is the association? Where do you find it here? Do you see any thing but the individual, with his passions and tastes, and his ardour in satisfying them? And the Greeks—those Greeks so enervated, so voluptuous, so spoiled by pleasures, had they not the most lively feeling of personal independence, the most ardent desire of living with perfect freedom, with no other object but to gratify themselves? Their poets singing of nectar and of love; their free courtesans receiving the homage of the most illustrious citizens, and making sages forget their philosophical moderation and gravity; and the people celebrating their festivals amid the most fearful dissoluteness; did they also only sacrifice on the altars of association? Had they not the desire of gratifying themselves? With respect to the Romans, perhaps it would not be so easy to demonstrate this, if we had to speak of what are called the glorious times of the Republic; but we have to deal with the Romans of the empire, with those who lived at the time of the irruption of the barbarians; with those Romans, greedy of pleasures, and devoured by that thirst for excess of which history has preserved such shameful pictures. Their superb palaces, their magnificent villas, their delicious baths, their splendid festive halls, their tables loaded with riches, their effeminate dresses, their voluptuous dissipation; do they not show us individuals who, without thinking of the association to which they belonged, only thought of gratifying their own passions and caprices; lived in the greatest luxury, with every delicacy and all imaginable splendour; had no care but to enjoy society, to lull themselves asleep in pleasure, to gratify all their passions, and give way to a burning love of their own satisfactions and amusements?

It is not easy, then, to imagine why M. Guizot exclusively attributes to the barbarians *the pleasure of feeling themselves men, the feeling of personality, of human spontaneousness in its free development.* Can we believe that such sentiments were unknown to the victors of Marathon and Platæa, to those nations who have immortalized their names by so many monuments? When, in the fine arts, in the sciences, in eloquence, in poetry, the noblest traits of genius shone forth on all sides, had they not among them the pleasure of feeling themselves men, the feeling and the power of the free development of all their faculties? and in a society where glory was so passionately loved, as we see it was among the Romans, in a society which shows us men like Cicero and Virgil, and which produced a Tacitus, who still, after nineteen centuries, makes every generous heart thrill with emotion, *was there no pleasure in feeling themselves men, no pride in appreciating their own dignity? Was there no feeling of the spontaneousness of man in his own free development?* How can we imagine that the barbarians of the north surpassed the Greeks and Romans in this respect? Why, then, these paradoxes, this confusion of ideas? Of what avail are these brilliant expressions meaning nothing? Of what use are these observations, of a false delicacy, where the mind at first sight discovers vagueness and inexactitude; and where it finds, after a complete examination, nothing but incoherency and revery?

CHAPTER XXII.

HOW THE INDIVIDUAL WAS ABSORBED BY ANCIENT SOCIETY.

If we profoundly study this question, without suffering ourselves to be led into error and extravagance, by the desire of passing for deep observers; if we call to our aid a just and cool philosophy, supported by the facts of history, we shall see that the principal difference between the ancient civilizations and our own with respect to the individual is, that, in antiquity, *man, considered as man, was not properly esteemed.* Ancient nations did not want either *the feeling of personal independence, or the pleasure of feeling themselves men*; the fault was not in the heart, but in the head. What they wanted was the comprehension of the dignity of man; the high idea which Christianity has given us of ourselves, while, at the same time, with admirable wisdom, it has shown us our infirmities. What ancient societies wanted, what all those, where Christianity does not prevail, have wanted, and will continue to want, is the respect and the consideration which surround every individual, *every man, inasmuch as he is a man.* Among the Greeks the Greeks are every thing; strangers, barbarians, are nothing: in Rome, the title of Roman citizen makes the man; he who wants this is nothing. In Christian countries, the infant who is born deformed, or deprived of some member, excites compassion, and becomes an object of the tenderest solicitude; it is enough that he is man, and unfortunate. Among the ancients, this human being was regarded as useless and contemptible; in certain cities, as for example at Lacedæmon, it was forbidden to nourish him, and, by command of the magistrates charged with the regulation of births, horrible to relate! he was thrown into a ditch. He was a *human being;* but what matter? He was a human being who would be of no use; and society, without compassion, did not wish to undertake the charge of his support. If you read Plato and Aristotle, you will see the horrible doctrine which they professed on the subject of abortion and infanticide; you will see the means which these philosophers imagined, in order to prevent the excess of population; and you will be sensible of the immense progress which society has made, under the influence of Christianity, in all that relates to man. Are not the public games, those horrible scenes where hundreds of men were slaughtered to amuse an inhuman multitude, an eloquent testimony to the little value attached to man, when he was sacrificed with so much barbarism for reasons so frivolous?

The right of the strongest was exercised among the ancients in a horrible manner; and this is one of the causes to which must be attributed the state of annihilation, so to speak, in which we see the individual with respect to society. Society was strong, the individual was weak; society absorbed the individual, and arrogated to itself all imaginable rights over him; and if ever he made opposition to society, he was sure to be crushed by it with an iron hand. When we read the explanation which M. Guizot gives us of this peculiarity of ancient civilizations, we might suppose that there existed among them a patriotism unknown to us; a patriotism which, carried to exaggeration, and stripped of the feeling of personal independence, produced a kind of annihilation of the individual in presence of society. If he had reflected deeply on the matter, M. Guizot would have seen that the difference is not in the feelings of antiquity, but in the immense fundamental revolution which has taken place in ideas; hence he would easily have concluded, that the difference observed in their feelings must have been owing to the differences in the ideas themselves. Indeed, it is not strange that the individual, seeing the little esteem in which he was held, and the unlimited power which society arrogated to itself over his independence and his life, (for it went so far as to grind him to powder, when he opposed it,) on his side formed an exaggerated idea of society and the public authority, so as to annihilate himself in his own heart before this fearful colossus. Far from considering himself as a member of an association the object of which was the safety and happiness of every individual, the benefits of which required from him some sacrifices in return, he regarded himself as a thing devoted to this association, and compelled, without hesitation, to offer himself as a holocaust on its altars. Such is the condition of man; when a power acts upon him, for a long time, unlimitedly, his indignation is excited against it, and he rejects it with violence; or else he humbles, he debases, he annihilates himself before the strong influence which binds and prostrates him. Let us see if this be not the contrast which ancient societies constantly afford us; the blindest submission and annihilation on the one hand, and, on the other, the spirit of insubordination, of resistance, showing itself in terrible explosions. It is thus, and thus only, that it is possible to understand how societies, whose normal condition was confusion and agitation, present us with such astonishing examples as Leonidas with his three hundred Spartans perishing at Thermopylæ, Sævola thrusting his hand into the fire, Regulus returning to Carthage to suffer and die, and Marcus Curtius, all armed, leaping into the chasm which had opened in the midst of Rome. All these phenomena, which at first sight appear inexplicable, are explained when we compare them with what has taken place in the revolutions of modern times Terrible revolutions have thrown some nations into confusion; the struggle of ideas and interests, inflaming their passions, has made them forget their true social relations, during intervals of greater or less duration. What has happened? At the same time that unlimited freedom was proclaimed, and the rights of individuals were incessantly extolled, there arose in the midst of society a cruel power, which, concentrating in its own hands all public authority, inflicted on them the severest blows. At such periods, when the formidable maxim of the ancients, the *salus populi*, that pretext for so many frightful attempts was in full force, there arose, on the other hand, that mad and ferocious patriotism which superficial men admire in the citizens of ancient republics.

Some writers have lavished eulogiums on the ancients, and, above all, on the Romans. It seemed as if, to gratify their ardent wishes, modern civilization must be moulded according to the ancient. They made absurd attempts; they attacked the existing social system with unexampled violence; they labored to destroy, or at least to stifle, Christian ideas concerning the individual and society, and they sought their inspiration from the shades of the ancient Romans. It is remarkable that, during the short time that the attempt lasted, there were seen, as in ancient Rome, admirable traits of strength, of valor, of patriotism, in fearful contrast with cruelties and crimes without example. In the midst of a great and generous nation there appeared again, to affright the human race, the bloody spectres of Marius and Sylla; so true it is that man is everywhere the same, and that the same order of ideas in the end produces the same order of events. Let the Christian ideas disappear, let old ones regain their force, and you will see that the modern world will resemble the ancient one. Happily for humanity, this is impossible. All the attempts hitherto made to produce such a result have been necessarily of short continuance, and such will be the case in future. But the bloody page which these criminal attempts have left in history offers an abundant subject for reflection to the philosopher who desires to become thoroughly acquainted with the intimate and delicate relations between ideas and facts. There he will see fully exhibited the vast scheme of social organization, and he will be able to appreciate at its just value the beneficial or injurious influence of the various religious and the different philosophical systems.

The periods of revolutions, that is to say, those stormy times when governments are swallowed up one after another like edifices built upon a volcanic soil, have all this distinctive character, the *tyranny of the interests of public authority over private interests.* Never is this power feebler, or less lasting; but never is it more violent, more mad. Every thing is sacrificed to its safety or its vengeance; the shade of its enemies pursues it and makes it continually tremble; its own conscience torments it and leaves it no repose; the weakness of its organization, its instable position, warn it at every step of its approaching fall, and in its impotent despair it makes the convulsive efforts of one dying in agony. What, then, in its eyes are the lives of citizens, if they excite the slightest, the most remote suspicion? If the blood of thousands of victims could procure for it a moment of security, and add a few days to its existence, "Perish my enemies," it says; "this is required for the safety of the state, that is, for mine!" Why this frenzy, this cruelty? It is because the ancient government, having been overturned by force, and the new having been enthroned in the same way, the idea of right has disappeared from the sphere of power. Legitimacy does not protect it, even its novelty betrays its little value; every thing forebodes its short existence. Stripped of the reason and justice which it is obliged to invoke in its own support, it seeks for both in the *very necessity of power*, a social necessity, which is always visible, and it proclaims that the safety of the people is the supreme care. Then the property and lives of individuals are nothing; they are annihilated in the presence of the bloody spectre which arises in the midst of society; armed with force, and surrounded by guards and scaffolds, it says, "I am the public power; to me is confided the safety of the people; it is I who watch over the interests of society."

Now, do you know what is the result of this absolute want of respect for the individual, of this complete annihilation of man in presence of the alarming power which claims to represent society? It is that the feeling of association reappears in different directions; no longer a feeling directed by reason, foresight, and beneficence, but a blind, instinctive feeling, which urges man not to remain alone, without defence, in the midst of a society which is converted into a field of battle and a vast conspiracy; men then unite either to sustain power, when, influenced by the whirlwind of revolution, they are identified with it, and regard it as their only rampart, or to overturn it, if, some motive having urged them into the opposite ranks, they see their most terrible enemy in the existing power, and a sword continually suspended over their heads. These men belong to an association, are devoted to an association, are ready to sacrifice themselves for it, for they cannot live alone; they know, they comprehend, at least instinctively, that the individual is nothing; for as the restraints that maintain social order have been broken, the individual no longer has a tranquil sphere where he can live in peace and independence, confident that a power founded on legitimacy and guided by reason and justice watches over the preservation of public order and the respect due to individual rights. Then timid men are alarmed and humbled, and begin to represent that first scene of servitude where the oppressed is seen to kiss the hand of the oppressor, and the victim to reverence the executioner. Daring men resist and contend, or rather, conspiring in the dark, they prepare terrible explosions. No one then belongs to himself; the individual is absorbed on all sides, either by the force which oppresses or by that which conspires. The tutelary divinity of individuals is justice; when justice vanishes, they are no more than imperceptible grains of dust carried away by the wind, or drops of water in the stormy waves of ocean. Imagine to yourself societies where this passing frenzy does not prevail, it is true, but which are yet devoid of true ideas on the rights and duties of individuals, and of those of public authority; societies where there are some wandering, uncertain, obscure, imperfect notions thereon, stifled by a thousand prejudices and errors; societies under which, nevertheless, public authority is organized under one form or another, and has become consolidated, thanks to the force of habit, and the absence of all other government better calculated to satisfy urgent necessities; you will then have an idea of the ancient societies, we should rather say, societies without Christianity, and you will understand the annihilation of the individual before the force of public power, either under an Asiatic despotism or the turbulent democracy of the ancient republics. And what you will then see will be precisely what you have observed in modern societies at times of revolution, only with this difference, that in these the evil is transitory and noisy, like the ravages of the tempest, while among the ancients it was the normal state, like the vitiated atmosphere which injures and corrupts all that breathe it.

Let us examine the cause of these two opposite phenomena, the lofty patriotism of the Greeks and Romans, and the state of prostration and political degradation in which other nations lay, and in which those still lie who are not under the influence of Christianity; what is the cause of this individual abnegation which is found at the bottom of two feelings so contrary? and why do we not find among any of those nations that individual development which is observed in Europe, and which with us is connected with a reasonable patriotism, from which the feeling of a legitimate personal independence is not excluded? It is because in antiquity man did not know himself, or what he was; it is because his true relations with society were viewed through a thousand prejudices and errors, and consequently were very ill understood. This will show that admiration for the patriotism, disinterestedness, and heroic self-denial of the ancients has been sometimes carried too far, and that these qualities, far from revealing in the men of antiquity a greater perfection of the individual, a superior elevation of mind to that of the men of modern times, rather indicate ideas less elevated and feelings less independent than our own. Perhaps some blind admirers of the ancients will be astonished at these assertions. Let them consider the women of India throwing themselves on the funeral-pile after the death of their husbands, and slaves putting themselves to death because they could not survive their masters, and they will see that personal self-denial is not an infallible sign of elevation of mind. Sometimes man does not understand his own dignity; he considers himself devoted to another being, absorbed by him, and then he regards his own existence only as a secondary thing, which has no object but to minister to the existence of another. We do not wish to underrate the merit which rightly belongs to the ancients; we do not wish to lower their heroism, as far as it is just and laudable, any more than we wish to attribute to the moderns an egotistical individuality, which prevents their sacrificing themselves for their country: our only object is to assign to every thing its place, by dissipating prejudices which are excusable up to a certain point, but do lamentable mischief by falsifying the principal features of ancient and modern history.

This annihilation of the individual among the ancients arose also from the weakness and imperfection of his moral development, and from his want of a rule for his own guidance, which compelled society to interfere in all that concerned him, as if public reason was called upon to supply the defect of private reason. If we pay attention, we shall observe that in countries where political liberty was the most cherished, civil liberty was almost unknown. While the citizens flattered themselves that they were very free, because they took part in the public deliberations, they wanted that liberty which is most important to man, that which we now call civil liberty. We may form an idea of the thoughts and manners of the ancients on this point, by reading one of their most celebrated writers, Aristotle. In the eyes of this philosopher, the only title which renders a man worthy of the name of citizen, seems to be the participation in the government of the republic; and these ideas, apparently very democratic and calculated to extend the rights of the most numerous class, far from proceeding, as one would suppose, from an exaggeration of the dignity of man, was connected in his mind with a profound contempt for man himself. His system was to reserve all honor and consideration for a very limited number; the classes of citizens who were thus condemned to degradation and nullity were all laborers, artisans, and tradesmen. (*Pol.* l. vii. c. 9, 12; l. viii. c. 1, 2; l. iii. c. 1.) This theory supposed, as may be seen, very curious ideas on individuals and society, and is an additional confirmation of what I have said respecting the eccentricities, not to say monstrosities, which we see in the ancient republics. Let us never forget that one of the principal causes of the evil was the want of an intimate knowledge of man; it was the little value which was placed upon his dignity as man; the individual, deprived of guides to direct him, could not conciliate esteem; in a word, there was wanting the light of Christianity, which was alone capable of illuminating the chaos.

The feeling of the dignity of man is deeply engraven on the heart of modern society; we find everywhere, written in striking characters, this truth, that man, by virtue of his title of man, is respectable and worthy of high consideration; hence it is that all the schools of modern times that have foolishly undertaken to exalt the individual, at the imminent risk of producing fearful perturbations in society, have adopted as the constant theme of their instructions, this dignity and nobility of man. They thus distinguish themselves in the most decided manner from the democrats of antiquity; the latter acted in a narrow sphere, without departing from a certain order of things, without looking beyond the limits of their own country; in the spirit of modern democrats, on the contrary, we find a tendency to invade all branches, an ardent propagandism which embraces the whole world. They never invoke mean ideas; *man, his reason, his imprescriptible rights*, these are their perpetual theme. Ask them what is their design, and they will tell you that they desire to level all things, to avenge the sacred cause of humanity. This exaggeration of ideas, the pretext and motive for so many crimes, shows us a valuable fact, viz. the immense progress which Christianity has given to ideas with relation to the dignity of our nature. When they have to mislead societies which owe their civilization to Christianity, they find no better means than to invoke the dignity of human nature. The Christian religion, the enemy of all that is criminal, could not consent to see society overturned, under the pretence of defending and raising the dignity of man; this is the reason why a great number of the most ardent democrats have indulged in insults and sarcasms against religion. On the other hand, as history loudly proclaims that all our knowledge and feeling of what is true, just, and reasonable on this point, is due to the Christian religion, it has been recently attempted to make a monstrous alliance between Christian ideas and the most extravagant of democratic theories. A celebrated man has undertaken this enterprise; but true Christianity, that is, Catholicity, rejects these adulterous alliances; it ceases to acknowledge its most eminent apologists when they have quitted the path of eternal truth. De Lamennais now wanders in the darkness of error, embracing a deceitful shadow of Christianity; and the voice of the supreme Pastor of the Church has warned the faithful against being dazzled by the illusion of a name illustrious by so many titles. (16)

CHAPTER XXIII.

THE PROGRESS OF INDIVIDUALITY UNDER THE INFLUENCE OF CATHOLICITY

If we give a just and legitimate meaning to the word individuality, taking the feeling of personal independence in an acceptation which is not repugnant to the perfection of the individual, and does not oppose the constitutive principles of all society; moreover, if we seek the various causes which have influenced the development of this feeling, without speaking of that which we have already pointed out as one of the most important, viz. the true notion of man, and his connections with his fellows, we shall find many of them which are quite worthy of attention in Catholicity. M. Guizot was greatly deceived when, putting the faithful of the Church in the same rank with the ancient Romans, he asserted that both were equally wanting in the feeling of personal independence. He describes the faithful as absorbed by the association of the Church, entirely devoted to her, ready to sacrifice themselves for her; so that, according to him, it was the interests of the association which induced them to act. There is an error here; but as this error has originated in a truth, it is our duty to distinguish the ideas and the facts with much attention.

There is no doubt that from the cradle of Christianity the faithful have had an extreme attachment to the Church, and it was always well understood among them, that they could not leave the communion of the Church without ceasing to be numbered among the true disciples of Jesus Christ. It is equally undeniable that, in the words of M. Guizot, "There prevailed in the Christian Church a feeling of strong attachment to the Christian corporation, of devotion to its laws, and an ardent desire to extend its empire;" but it is not true that the origin and source of all these feelings was the spirit of association alone, to the exclusion of all development of real individuality. The Christian belonged to an association, but that association was regarded by him as a means of obtaining eternal happiness, as the ship in which he was embarked, amid the tempests of the world, to arrive safe in the port of eternity: and although he believed it impossible to be saved out of the Church, he did not understand from that that he was devoted to the Church, but to God. The Roman was ready to sacrifice himself for his country; the Christian, for his faith. When the Roman died, he died for his country; the faithful did not die for the Church, but for God. If we open the monuments of Church history, and read the acts of the martyrs, we shall then see what passed in that terrible moment, when the Christian, fully arousing himself, showed in the presence of the instruments of torture, burning piles, and the most horrible punishments, the true principle which acted on his mind. The judge asks his name; he declares it, and adds, "I am a Christian." He is asked to sacrifice to the gods. "We only sacrifice to one God, the Creator of heaven and earth." He is reproached with the disgrace of following a man who has been nailed to the cross; for him the ignominy of the cross is a glory, and he loudly proclaims that the Crucified is his Saviour and his God. He is threatened with tortures; he despises them, for they are passing, and rejoices in being able to suffer something for his Master. The cross of punishment is already prepared, the pile is lighted before his eyes, the executioner raises the fatal axe to strike off his head; what does it matter to him? all this is but for a moment, and after that moment comes a new life of ineffable and endless happiness. We thus see what influenced his heart; it was the love of his God and the interest of his eternal happiness. Consequently, it is utterly false that the Christian, like men of the ancient republics, destroyed his individuality in the association to which he belonged, allowing himself to be absorbed in that association like a drop of water in the immensity of ocean. The Christian belonged to an association which gave him the rule of his faith and conduct; he regarded that association as founded and directed by God himself; but his mind and his heart were raised to God, and when following the voice of the Church, he believed that he was engaged with his own individual affair, which was nothing less than his eternal happiness. This distinction is quite necessary in an affair which has relations so various and delicate that the slightest confusion may produce considerable errors. Here a hidden fact reveals itself to us, which is infinitely precious, and throws much light upon the development and perfecting of the individual in Christian civilization. It is absolutely necessary that there should be a social order to which the individual must submit; but it is also proper that he should not be absorbed by society to such an extent that he cannot be conceived but as forming part of it, and remains deprived of his own sphere of action. If this were the case, never would true civilization be completely developed; as it consists in the simultaneous perfecting of the individual and of society, it is necessary, for its existence, that both should have a well determined sphere, where their peculiar and respective movements may not check and embarrass each other.

After these reflections, to which I especially call the attention of all thinking men, I will point out a thing which has, perhaps, not yet been remarked; it is, that Christianity has eminently contributed to create that individual sphere in which man, without breaking the ties which connect him with society, is free to develop all his peculiar faculties. From the mouth of an Apostle went forth that generous expression which strictly limits political power: "We ought to obey God rather than man." (Acts v. 29.) "Obedire oportet Deo magis quam hominibus." The Apostle thereby proclaims that the individual should cease to acknowledge power, when power exacts from him what he believes to be contrary to his conscience. It was among Christians that this great example was witnessed for the first time; individuals of all countries, of all ages, of both sexes, of all conditions, braving the anger of authority, and all the fury of popular passions, rather than pronounce a single word contrary to the principles which they professed in the sanctuary of conscience; and this, not with arms in their hands, in the midst of popular commotions, where their impetuous passions are excited, which communicate to the mind temporary energy, but in the solitude and obscurity of dungeons, amid the fearful calmness of the tribunals, that is, in that situation where man, alone and isolated, cannot show force and dignity without revealing the elevation of his ideas, the nobleness of his feelings, the unalterable firmness of his conscience, and the greatness of his soul. Christianity engraved this truth deeply on the heart of man, that individuals have duties to perform, even when the whole world is aroused against them; that they have an immense destiny to fulfil, and that it is entirely their own affair, the responsibility of which rests upon their own free will. This important truth, unceasingly inculcated by Christianity at all times, to both sexes, to all conditions, must have powerfully contributed to excite in man an active and ardent feeling of personality. This feeling, with all its sublimity, combining with the other inspirations of Christianity, all full of dignity and grandeur, has raised the human mind from the dust, where ignorance and rude superstitions, and systems of violence, which oppressed it on all sides, had placed and retained it. How strange and surprising to the ears of Pagans must have been those energetic words of Justin, which nevertheless expressed the disposition of mind of the majority of the faithful, when, in his Apology, addressed to Antoninus Pius, he said, "As we have not placed our hopes on present things, we contemn those who kill us, death being, moreover, a thing which cannot be avoided."

This full and entire self-consciousness, this heroic contempt of death, this calm spirit of a man who, supported by the testimony of intimate feeling, sets at defiance all the powers of earth, must have tended the more to enlarge the mind, as they did not emanate from that cold stoical impassibility, the constant effort of which was to struggle against the nature of things without any solid motive. The Christian feeling had its origin in a sublime freedom from all that is earthly, in a profound conviction of the holiness of duty, and in that undeniable maxim, that man, in spite of all the obstacles which the world places in his way, should walk with a firm step towards the destiny which is marked out for him by his Creator. These ideas and feelings together communicated to the soul a strong and vigorous temper, which, without reaching in any thing the savage harshness of the ancients, raised man to all his dignity, nobleness, and grandeur. It must be observed that these precious effects were not confined to a small number of privileged individuals, but that, in conformity with the genius of the Christian religion, they extended to all classes; for one of the noblest characters of that divine religion is the unlimited expansion which it gives to all that is good; it knows no distinction of persons, and makes its voice penetrate the obscurest places of society. It was not only to the elevated classes and philosophers, but to the generality of the faithful, that St. Cyprian, the light of Africa, addressed himself, when, summing up in a few words all the grandeur of man, he marked with a bold hand the sublime position where our soul ought to maintain itself with constancy. "Never," he says, "never will he who feels himself to be the child of God admire the words of man. *He falls from his noblest state who can admire any thing but God.*" (*De Spectaculis.*) Sublime words, which make us boldly raise our heads, and fill our hearts with noble feelings; words which, diffusing themselves over all classes, like a fertilizing warmth, were capable of inspiring the humblest of men with what previously seemed exclusively reserved for the transports of the poet:

> Os homini sublime dedit, cœlumque tueri
> Jussit, et erectos ad sidera tollere cultus.

M

The development of the moral life, the interior life, that life in which man, reflecting on himself, is accustomed to render a circumstantial account of all his actions, of the motives which actuate him, of the goodness or the wickedness of those motives, and the object to which they tend, is principally due to Christianity, to its unceasing influence on man in all his conditions, in all situations, in all moments of his life. Such a progress of the individual life in all that it has most intimate, most active, and most interesting for the heart of man, was incompatible with that absorption of the individual by society, with that blind self-denial, in which man forgot himself, to think only of the association of which he formed a part. This moral and interior life was unknown to the ancients, because they wanted principles for supporting, rules for guiding, and inspirations for exciting and nourishing it. Thus at Rome, where the political element tries its ascendency over minds, when enthusiasm becomes extinguished by the effect of intestine dissensions, when every generous feeling becomes stifled by the insupportable despotism which succeeds to the last agitations of the republic, we see baseness and corruption develope themselves with fearful rapidity. The activity of mind which before occupied itself in debates of the Forum and the glorious exploits of war, no longer finding food, gave itself up to sensual pleasures with an abandonment which we can hardly imagine now-a-days, in spite of the looseness of morals which we so justly deplore. Thus we see among the ancients only these two extremes, either the most exalted patriotism, or the complete prostration of the faculties of the soul, which abandons itself without reserve to the dictates of its irregular passions; there man was the slave either of his own passions, of another man, or of society.

Since the moral tie which united men to Catholic society has been broken, since religious belief has been weakened, in consequence of the individual independence which Protestantism has proclaimed in religious matters, it has unhappily become possible for us to conceive, by means of examples found in European civilization, what man still deprived of real knowledge of himself, his origin and destiny, must have been. We will indicate in another place the points of resemblance which are found between ancient and modern society in the countries where the influence of religious ideas is enfeebled. It is enough now to remark, that if Europe had completely lost Christianity, according to the insane desires of some men, a generation would not have passed away without there being revived among us the individual and society such as they were among the ancients, except the modifications which the difference of the material state of the two civilizations would necessarily produce.

The doctrine of free will, so loudly proclaimed by Catholicity, and sustained by her with such vigour, not only against the old Pagan teaching, but particularly against sectarians at all times, and especially against the founders of the pretended Reformation, has also contributed more than is imagined to develope and perfect the individual, to raise his ideas of independence, nobleness, and dignity. When man comes to consider himself as constrained by the irresistible force of destiny, and attached to a chain of events over which he has no control—when he comes to suppose that the operations of his mind, those active proofs of his freedom, are but vain illusions—he soon annihilates himself; he feels himself assimilated to the brute; he ceases to be the prince of living beings, the ruler of the earth; he is nothing more than a machine fixed in its place, which is compelled to perform its part in the great system of the universe. The social order ceases to exist; merit and demerit, praise and blame, reward and punishment, are only unmeaning words. If man enjoys or suffers, it is only in the same way as a shrub, which is sometimes breathed upon softly by the zephyrs, and sometimes blasted by the north wind. How different it is when man is conscious of his liberty! Then he is master of his destiny; good and evil, life and death, are before his eyes; he can choose, and nothing can violate the sanctuary of his conscience. There the soul is enthroned, there she is seated, full of dignity, and the whole world raging against her, the universe falling upon her fragile body, cannot force her will. The moral order is displayed before us in all its grandeur; we see good in all its beauty, and evil in all its deformity; the desire of doing well stimulates, and the fear of doing ill restrains us; the sight of the recompense which can be obtained by an effort of free will, and which appears at the end of the path of virtue, renders that path more sweet and peaceful, and communicates activity and energy to the soul. If man is free, there remains something great and terrible, even in his crime, in his punishment, and even in the despair of hell. What is man deprived of liberty and yet punished? What is the meaning of this absurd proposition, a chief dogma of the founders of Protestantism? This man is a weak and miserable victim, in whose torture a cruel omnipotence delights; a God who has created him in order to see him suffer; a tyrant with infinite power, that is, the most dreadful of monsters. But if man is free, when he suffers, he suffers because he has deserved it; and if we contemplate him in the midst of despair, plunged into an ocean of horrors, his brow furrowed by the just lightnings of the Eternal, we seem to hear him still pronounce those terrible words with a haughty bearing and proud look, *non serviam, I will not obey.*

In man, as in the universe, all is wonderfully united; all the faculties of man have delicate and intimate relations with each other, and the movement of one chord in the soul makes all the others vibrate. It is necessary to call attention to this reciprocal dependence of all our faculties on each other, in order to anticipate an objection which may be made. We shall be told, all that has been said only proves that Catholicity has developed the individual in a mystical sense. No, the observations which I have made show something more than this; they prove that we owe to Catholicity the clear idea and lively feeling of moral order in all its greatness and beauty; they prove that we owe her the real strength of what we call conscience, and that if the individual believes himself to be called to a mighty destiny, confided to his own free will, and the care of which belongs entirely to him, it is to Catholicity he owes that belief; they prove that Catholicity has given man the true knowledge which he has of himself, the appreciation of his dignity, the respect which is paid to him as man; they prove that she has developed in our souls the germs of the noblest and most generous feelings; for she has raised our thoughts by the loftiest conceptions, dilated our hearts by the assurance of a liberty which nothing can take away, by the promise of an infinite reward, eternal happiness, while she leaves in our hands life and death, and makes us in a certain manner the arbiters of our own destiny. In all this there is more than mere mysticism; it is nothing less than the development of the entire man; nothing less than the true, the only noble, just, and reasonable individuality; nothing less than the collected powerful impulses which urge the individual towards perfection in every sense; it is nothing less than the first, the most indispensable, the most fruitful element of real civilization.

CHAPTER XXIV.

OF THE FAMILY.—MONOGAMY.—INDISSOLUBILITY OF THE CONJUGAL TIE.

We have seen what the individual owes to Catholicity; let us now see what the family owes her. It is clear that the individual, being the first element of the family, if it is Catholicity which has tended to perfect him, the improvement of the family will thus have been very much her work; but without insisting on this inference, I wish to consider the conjugal tie in itself, for which purpose it is necessary to call attention to woman. I will not repeat here what she was among the Romans, and what she is still among the nations who are not Christians; history, and still more the literature of Greece and Rome, afford us sad or rather shameful proofs on this subject; and all the nations of the earth offer us too many evidences of the truth and exactness of the observation of Buchanan, viz. that wherever Christianity does not prevail, there is a tendency to the degradation of woman. Perhaps on this point Protestantism will be unwilling to give way to Catholicity; it will assert that in all that affects woman the Reformation has in no degree prejudiced the civilization of Europe. We will not now inquire what evils Protestantism has occasioned in this respect; this question will be discussed in another part of the work; but it cannot be doubted, that when Protestantism appeared, the Catholic religion had already completed its task as far as woman is concerned. No one, indeed, is ignorant that the respect and consideration which are given to women, and the influence which they exercise on society, date further back than the first part of the 16th century. Hence it follows that Catholicity cannot have had Protestantism as a coadjutor; it acted entirely alone in this point, one of the most important of all true civilization; and if it is generally acknowledged that Christianity has placed woman in the rank which properly belongs to her, and which is most conducive to the good of the family and of society, this is a homage paid to Catholicity; for at the time when woman was raised from abjection, when it was attempted to restore her to the rank of companion of man, as worthy of him, those dissenting sects that also called themselves Christians did not exist, and there was no other Christianity than the Catholic Church.

It has been already remarked in the course of this work, that when I give titles and honours to Catholicity, I avoid having recourse to vague generalities, and endeavour to support my assertions by facts. The reader will naturally expect me to do the same here, and to point out to him what are the means which Catholicity has employed to give respect and dignity to woman; he shall not be deceived in his expectation. First, and before descending to details, we must observe that the grand ideas of Christianity with respect to humanity must have contributed, in an extraordinary manner, to the improvement of the lot of woman. These ideas, which applied without any difference to woman as well as to man, were an energetic protest against the state of degradation in which one-half of the human race was placed. The Christian doctrine made the existing prejudices against woman vanish for ever; it made her equal to man by unity of origin and destiny, and in the participation of the heavenly gifts; it enrolled her in the universal brotherhood of man, with his fellows and with Jesus Christ; it considered her as the child of God, the coheiress of Jesus Christ; as the companion of man, and no longer as a slave and the vile instrument of pleasure. Henceforth that philosophy which had attempted to degrade her, was silenced; that unblushing literature which treated women with so much insolence found a check in the Christian precepts, and a reprimand no less eloquent than severe in the dignified manner in which all the ecclesiastical writers, in imitation of the Scriptures, expressed themselves on woman. Yet, in spite of the beneficent influence which the Christian doctrines must have exercised by themselves, the desired end would not have been completely attained, had not the Church undertaken, with the warmest energy, to accomplish a work the most necessary, the most indispensable for the good organization of the family and society, I mean the reformation of marriage. The Christian doctrine on this point is very simple: *one with one exclusively, and for ever.* But the doctrine would have been powerless, if the Church had not undertaken to apply it, and if she had not carried on this task with invincible firmness; for the passions, above all those of man, rebel against such a doctrine; and they would undoubtedly have trodden it under foot, if they had not met with an insurmountable barrier, which did not leave them the most distant hope of triumph. Can Protestantism, which applauded with such senseless joy the scandal of Henry VIII., and accommodated itself so basely to the desires of the Landgrave of Hesse-Cassel, boast of having contributed to strengthen that barrier? What a surprising difference! During many centuries, amid circumstances the most various, and sometimes the most terrible, the Catholic Church struggles with intrepidity against the passions of potentates, to maintain unsullied the sanctity of marriage. Neither promises nor threats could move Rome; no means could obtain from her any thing contrary to the instructions of her Divine Master: Protestantism, at the first shock, or rather at the first shadow of the slightest embarrassment, at the mere fear of displeasing a prince who certainly was not very powerful, yields, humbles itself, consents to polygamy, betrays its own conscience, opens a wide door to the passions, and gives up to them the sanctity of marriage, the first pledge for the good of the family, the foundation-stone of true civilization.

Protestant society on this point, wiser than the miscalled reformers who attempted to guide it, with admirable good sense repudiated the consequences of the conduct of its chiefs; although it did not preserve the doctrines of Catholicity, it at least followed the salutary impulse which it had received from them, and polygamy was not established in Europe. But history records facts which show the weakness of the pretended reformation, and the vivifying power of Catholicity. It tells us to whom it is owing that the law of marriage, that palladium of society, was not falsified, perverted, destroyed, amid the barbarous ages, amid the most fearful corruption, violence, and ferocity, which prevailed everywhere, as well at the time when invading nations passed pell-mell over Europe, as in that of feudality, and when the power of kings had already been preponderant,—history will tell what tutelary force prevented the torrent of sensuality from overflowing with all its violence, with all its caprices, from bringing about the most profound disorganization, from corrupting the character of European civilization, and precipitating it into that fearful abyss in which the nations of Asia have been for so many centuries.

Prejudiced writers have carefully searched the annals of ecclesiastical history for the differences between popes and kings, and have taken occasion therein to reproach the Court of Rome with its intolerant obstinacy respecting the sanctity of marriage; if the spirit of party had not blinded them, they would have understood that, if this intolerant obstinacy had been relaxed for a moment, if the Roman Pontiff had given way one step before the impetuosity of the passions, this first step once made, the descent into the abyss would have been rapid; they would have admired the spirit of truth, the deep conviction, the lively faith with which that august see is animated; no consideration, no fear, has been able to silence her, when she had occasion to remind all, and especially kings and potentates, of this commandment: "They shall be two in one flesh; man shall not separate what God has joined." By showing themselves inflexible on this point, even at the risk of the anger of kings, not only have the popes performed the sacred duty which was imposed on them by their august character as chiefs of Christianity, but they have executed a political *chef d'œuvre*, and greatly contributed to the repose and well-being of nations. "For," says Voltaire, "the marriages of princes in Europe decide the destiny of nations; and never has there been a court entirely devoted to debauchery, without producing revolutions and rebellions." (*Essai sur l'Histoire générale*, t. iii. c. 101.)

This correct remark of Voltaire will suffice to vindicate the pope, together with Catholicity, from the calumnies of their wretched detractors: it becomes still more valuable, and acquires an immense importance, if it is extended beyond the limits of the political order to the social. The imagination is affrighted at the thought of what would have happened, if these barbarous kings, in whom the splendor of the purple ill disguised the sons of the forest, if those haughty seigneurs, fortified in their castles, clothed in mail, and surrounded by their timid vassals, had not found a check in the authority of the Church; if at the first glance at a new beauty, if at the first passion which, when enkindled in their hearts, would have inspired them with a disgust for their legitimate spouses, they had not had the always-present recollection of an inflexible authority. They could, it is true, load a bishop with vexations; they could silence him with threats or promises; they might control the votes of a particular Council by violence, by intrigue, by subornation; but, in the distance, the power of the Vatican, the shadow of the Sovereign Pontiff, appeared to them like an alarming vision; they then lost all hope; all struggles became useless; the most violent endeavors would never have given them the victory; the most astute intrigues, the most humble entreaties, would have obtained the same reply: "One with one only, and for ever."

If we read but the history of the middle ages, of that immense scene of violence, where the barbarian, striving to break the bonds which civilization attempted to impose on him, appears so vividly; if we recollect that the Church was obliged to keep guard incessantly and vigilantly, not only to prevent the ties of a marriage from being broken, but even to preserve virgins (and even those who were dedicated to God) from violence; we shall clearly see that, if she had not opposed herself, as a wall of brass, to the torrent of sensuality, the palaces of kings and the castles of seigneurs would have speedily become their seraglios and harems. What would have happened in the other classes? They would have followed the same course; and the women of Europe would have remained in the state of degradation in which the Mussulman women still are. As I have mentioned the followers of Mohammed, I will reply in passing to those who pretend to explain monogamy and polygamy by climate alone. Christians and Mohammedans have been for a long time under the same sky, and their religions have been established, by the vicissitudes of the two races, sometimes in cold and sometimes in mild and temperate climates; and yet we have not seen the religions accommodate themselves to the climates; but rather, the climates have been, as it were, forced to bend to the religions. European nations owe eternal gratitude to Catholicity, which has preserved monogamy for them, one of the causes which undoubtedly have contributed the most to the good organization of the family, and the exaltation of woman. What would now be the condition of Europe, what respect would woman now enjoy, if Luther, the founder of Protestantism, had succeeded in inspiring society with the indifference which he shows on this point in his commentary on Genesis? "As to whether we may have several wives," says Luther, "the authority of the patriarchs leaves us completely free." He afterwards adds that "*it is a thing neither permitted nor prohibited, and that he does not decide any thing thereupon.*" Unhappy Europe! if a man, who had whole nations as followers, had uttered such words some centuries earlier, at the time when civilization had not yet received an impulse strong enough to make it take a decided line on the most important points, in spite of false doctrines. Unhappy Europe! if at the time when Luther wrote, manners had not been already formed, if the good organization given to the family by Catholicity had not been too deeply rooted to be torn up by the hand of man Certainly the scandal of the Landgrave of Hesse-Cassel would not then have remained an isolated example, and the culpable compliance of the Lutheran doctors would have produced bitter fruits. What would that vacillating faith, that uncertainty, that cowardice with which the Protestant Church was seen to tremble at the mere demand of such a prince as the Landgrave, have availed, to control the fierce impetuosity of barbarous and corrupted nations? How would a struggle, lasting for ages, have been sustained by those who, at the first menace of battle, gave way, and were routed before the shock?

Besides monogamy, it may be said that there is nothing more important than the indissolubility of marriage. Those who, departing from the doctrine of the Church, think that it is useful in certain cases to allow divorce, so as to dissolve the conjugal tie, and permit each of the parties to marry again, still will not deny that they regard divorce as a dangerous remedy, which the legislator only avails himself of with regret, and only on account of crime or faithlessness; they will see, also, that a great number of divorces would produce very great evils, and that in order to prevent these in countries where the civil laws allow the abuse of divorce, it is necessary to surround this permission with all imaginable precaution; they will consequently grant that the most efficacious manner of preventing corruption of manners, of guarantying the tranquillity of families, and of opposing a firm barrier to the torrent of evils which is ready to inundate society, is to establish the indissolubility of marriage as a moral principle, to base it upon motives which exercise a powerful ascendency over the heart, and to keep a constant restraint on the passions, to prevent them from slipping down so dangerous a declivity. It is clear that there is no work more worthy of being the object of the care and zeal of the true religion. Now, what religion but the Catholic has fulfilled this duty? What other religion has more perfectly accomplished so salutary and difficult a task? Certainly not Protestantism, for it did not even know how to penetrate the depth of the reasons which guided the conduct of the Church on this point. I have taken care to do justice in another place to the wisdom which Protestant society has displayed in not giving itself up entirely to the impulse which its chiefs wished to communicate to it. But it must not be supposed from this that Protestant doctrines have not had lamentable consequences in countries calling themselves reformed. Let us hear what a Protestant lady, Madame de Staël, says in her book on Germany, speaking of a country which she loves and admires: "Love," she says, "is a religion in Germany, but a poetical religion which tolerates very freely all that sensibility can excuse. It cannot be denied that in the Protestant provinces the facility of divorce is injurious to the sanctity of marriage. *They change husbands as quietly as if they were arranging the incidents of a drama:* the good nature of the man and woman prevents the mixture of any bitterness with their easy ruptures; and as there is among the Germans more imagination than real passion, the most curious events take place with singular tranquillity. Yet it is thus that manners and characters lose all consistency; the paradoxical spirit destroys the most sacred institutions, and there are no well established rules on any subject." (*De l'Allemagne*, p. 1, c. 3.) Misled by their hatred against the Roman Church, and excited by their rage for innovation in all things, the Protestants thought they had made a great reform in secularizing marriage, if I may so speak, and in rejecting the Catholic doctrine, which declared it a real sacrament. This is not the place to enter upon a dogmatical discussion of this matter; I shall content myself with observing, that by depriving marriage of the august seal of a sacrament, Protestantism showed that it had little knowledge of the human heart. To consider marriage, not as a simple civil contract, but as a real sacrament, was to place it under the august shade of religion, and to raise it above the stormy atmosphere of the passions; and who can doubt that this was absolutely necessary to restrain the most active, capricious, and violent passion of the heart of man? The civil laws are insufficient to produce such an effect. Motives are required, which, being drawn from a higher source, exert a more efficacious influence. The Protestant doctrine overturned the power of the Church with respect to marriage, and gave up matters of this kind exclusively to the civil power. Some one will perhaps think that the increase of the secular power on this point could not but serve the cause of civilization, and that to drive the ecclesiastical authority from this ground was a magnificent triumph gained over exploded prejudices, a valuable victory over unjust usurpation. Deluded man! If your mind possessed any lofty thought, if your heart felt the vibration of those harmonious chords which display the passions of man with so much delicacy and exactness, and teach the best means of directing them, you would see, you would feel, that to place marriage under the mantle of religion, and to withdraw it as much as possible from profane interference, was to purify, to embellish, and to surround it with the most enchanting beauty; for thus is that precious treasure, which is blasted by a look, and tarnished by the slightest breath, inviolably preserved. Would you not wish to have the nuptial bed veiled and strictly guarded by religion?

CHAPTER XXV.

OF THE PASSION OF LOVE.

BUT it will be said to Catholics, "Do you not see that your doctrines are too hard and rigorous? They do not consider the weakness and inconstancy of the human heart, and require sacrifices above its strength. Is it not cruel to attempt to subject the most tender affections, the most delicate feelings, to the rigor of a principle? Cruel doctrine, which endeavors to hold together, bound to each other by a fatal tie, those who no longer love, who feel a mutual disgust, who perhaps hate each other with a profound hatred! When you answer these two beings who long to be separated, who would rather die than remain united, with an eternal Never, showing them the divine seal which was placed upon their union at the solemn moment, do you not forget all the rules of prudence? Is not this to provoke despair? Protestantism, accommodating itself to our infirmity, accedes more easily to the demands, sometimes of caprice, but often also of weakness; its indulgence is a thousand times preferable to your rigor." This requires an answer; it is necessary to remove the delusion which produces these arguments, too apt, unhappily, to mislead the judgment, because they begin by seducing the heart. In the first place, it is an exaggeration to say that the Catholic system reduces unhappy couples to the extremity of despair. There are cases in which prudence requires that they should separate, and then neither the doctrines nor the practice of the Catholic Church oppose the separation. It is true that this does not dissolve the conjugal tie, and that neither of the parties can marry again. But it cannot be said that one of them is subject to tyranny; they are not compelled to live together, consequently they do not suffer the intolerable torment of remaining united when they abhor each other. Very well, we shall be told, the separation being pronounced, the parties are freed from the punishment of living together; but they cannot contract new ties, consequently they are forbidden to gratify another passion which, perhaps, their heart conceals, and which may have been the cause of the disgust or the hatred whence arose the unhappiness or discord of their first union. Why not consider the marriage as altogether dissolved? Why should not the parties become entirely free? Permit them to obey the feelings of their hearts, which, newly fixed on another object, already foresee happier days. Here, no doubt, the answer seems difficult, and the force of the difficulty becomes urgent; but, nevertheless, it is here that Catholicity obtains the most signal triumph; it is here it clearly shows how profound is its knowledge of the heart of man, how prudent its doctrines, and how wise and provident its conduct. Its rigor, which seems excessive, is only necessary severity; this conduct, far from meriting the reproach of cruelty, is a guarantee for the repose and well-being of man. But it is a thing which it is difficult to understand at first sight; thus we are compelled to develope this matter by entering into a profound examination of the principles which justify by the light of reason the conduct pursued by the Catholic Church; let us examine this conduct, not only in respect to marriage, but in all that relates to the direction of the heart of man.

In the direction of the passions there are two systems, the one of compliance, the other of resistance. In the first of these they are yielded to as they advance; an invincible obstacle is never opposed to them; they are never left without hope. A line is traced around them which, it is true, prevents them from exceeding a certain boundary; but they are given to understand that if they come to place their foot upon this limit, it will retire a little further; so that the compliance is in proportion to the energy and obstinacy of their demands. In the second system, a line is equally marked out to the passions which they cannot pass; but it is a line fixed, immovable, and everywhere guarded by a wall of brass. In vain do they attempt to pass it; they have not even the shadow of hope; the principle which resists them will never change, will never consent to any kind of compromise. Therefore, no resource remains but to take that course which is always open to man, that of sin. The first system allows the fire to break out, to prevent an explosion; the second hinders the beginning of it, in the fear of being compelled to arrest its progress. In the first, the passions are feared and regulated at their birth, and hopes of restraining them when they have grown up are entertained; in the second, it is thought that, if it is difficult to restrain them when they are feeble, it will be still more so when they are strengthened. In the one, they act on the supposition that the passions are weakened by indulgence; in the other, it is believed that gratification, far from satiating, only renders them every day more devouring.

It may be said, generally speaking, that Catholicity follows the second of these systems; that is to say, with respect to the passions, her constant rule is to check them at the first step, to deprive them of all hope from the first, and to stifle them, if possible, in their cradle. It must be observed, that we speak here of the severity with respect to the passions themselves, not with respect to man, who is their prey; it is very consistent to give no truce to passion, and to be indulgent towards the person under its influence; to be inexorable towards the offence, and to treat the offender with extreme mildness. With respect to marriage, this system has been acted on by Catholicity with astonishing firmness; Protestantism has taken the opposite course. Both are agreed on this point, that divorce, followed by the dissolution of the conjugal tie, is a very great evil; but there is this difference between them, that the Catholic system does not leave even the hope of a conjuncture in which this dissolution will be permitted; it forbids it absolutely, without any restriction; it declares it impossible: the Protestant system, on the contrary, consents to it in certain cases. Protestantism does not possess the divine seal which guaranties the perpetuity of marriage, and renders it sacred and inviolable; Catholicity does possess this seal, impresses it on the mysterious tie, and from that moment marriage remains under the shadow of an august symbol. Which of the two religions is the most prudent in this point? Which acts with the most wisdom? To answer this question, let us lay aside the dogmatical reasons, and the intrinsical morality of the human actions which form the subject of the laws which we are now examining; and let us see which of the two systems is the most conducive to the difficult task of managing and directing the passions. After having considered the nature of the human heart, and consulted the experience of every day, it may be affirmed that the best way to repress a passion is to leave it without hope; to comply with it, to allow it continual indulgences, is to excite it more and more; it is to play with fire amid a heap of combustibles, by allowing the flame to be lit, from time to time, in the vain confidence of being always able to put out the conflagration. Let us take a rapid glance at the most violent passions of the heart of man, and observe what is their ordinary course, according to the system which is pursued in their regard. Look at the gambler, who is ruled by an indefinable restlessness, which is made up of an insatiable cupidity and an unbounded prodigality, at the same time. The most enormous fortune will not satisfy him; and yet he risks all, without hesitation, to the hazard of a moment. The man who still dreams of immense treasures amid the most fearful misery, restlessly pursues an object which resembles gold, but which is not it, for the possession thereof does not satisfy him. His heart can only exist amid uncertainty, chances, and perils. Suspended between hope and fear, he seems to be pleased with the rapid succession of lively emotions which unceasingly agitate and torment him. What remedy will cure this malady—this devouring fever? Will you recommend to him a system of compliance? will you tell him to gamble, but only to a certain amount, at certain times, and in certain places? What will you gain by this? Nothing at all. If these means were good for any thing, there would be no gambler in the world who would not be cured of his passion; for there is no one who has not often marked out for himself these limits, and often said to himself, "You shall only play till such an hour, in such a place, and to such an amount." What is the effect of these palliations—of these impotent precautions—on the unhappy gambler? That he miserably deceives himself. The passion consents, only in order to gain strength, and the better to secure the victory: thus it gains ground; it constantly enlarges its sphere; and leads its victim again into the same, or into greater excesses. Do you wish to make a radical cure? If there be a remedy, it must be to abstain completely; a remedy which may appear difficult at first, but will be found the easiest in practice. When the passion finds itself deprived of all hope, it will begin to diminish, and in the end will disappear. No man of experience will raise the least doubt as to the truth of what I have said; every one will agree with me, that the only way to destroy the formidable passion of gambling is to deprive it at once of all food, to leave it without hope.

Let us pass to another example, more analogous to the subject which I intend to explain. Let us suppose a man under the influence of love. Do you believe that the best way to cure his passion will be to give him opportunities, even though very rare, of seeing the object of his passion? Do you think that it will be salutary to authorize him to *continue*, while you forbid him to *multiply*, these dangerous interviews? Will such a precaution quench the flame which burns in his heart? You may be sure that it will not. The limits will even augment its force. If you allow it any food, even with the most parsimonious hand, if you permit it the least success, you see it constantly increase, until it upset every thing that opposes it. But take away all hope, send the lover on a long journey, or place before him an impediment which precludes the probability, or even the possibility, of success; then, except in very rare cases, you will obtain at first distraction, and then forgetfulness. Is not this the daily teaching of experience? Is it not the remedy which necessity every day suggests to the fathers of families? The passions resemble fire. They are extinguished by a large quantity of water; but a few drops only render them more ardent. Let us raise our thoughts still higher; let us observe the passions acting in a wider field, in more extended regions. Whence comes it that so many strong passions are awakened at times of public disturbance? It is, because then they all hope to be gratified; it is, because the highest ranks, the oldest and most powerful institutions, having been overturned, and replaced by others, which were hitherto imperceptible, all the passions see a road open before them, amid the tempest and confusion; the barriers apparently insurmountable, the sight of which prevented their existence, or strangled them in the cradle, do not exist; as all is then unprotected and defenceless, it is only required to have boldness and intrepidity enough to stand amid the ruins of all that was old.

Regarding things in the abstract, there is nothing more strikingly absurd than hereditary monarchy, the succession secured to a family which may at any time place on the throne a child, a fool, or a wretch: and yet in practice there is nothing more wise, prudent, and provident. This has been taught by the long experience of ages, it has been shown by reason, and proved by the sad warnings of those nations who have tried elective monarchy. Now, what is the cause of this? It is what we are endeavoring to explain. Hereditary monarchy precludes all the hopes of irregular ambition; without that, society always contains a germ of trouble, a principle of revolt, which is nourished by those who conceive a hope of one day obtaining the command. In quiet times, and under an hereditary monarchy, a subject, however rich, however distinguished he may be for his talent or his valour, cannot, without madness, hope to be king; and such a thought never enters his head. But change the circumstances, —admit, I will not say, the probability, but the possibility of such an event, and you will see that there will immediately be ardent candidates.

It would be easy to develope this doctrine more at length, and apply it to all the passions of man; but enough has been said to show that the first thing to be done when you have to subdue a passion, is to oppose to it an insurmountable barrier, which it can have no hope of passing. Then the passion rages for a little time, it rebels against the obstacle that resists it; but when it finds that to be immovable, it recedes, it is cast down, and, like the waves of the sea, it falls back murmuring to the level which has been marked out for it.

There is a passion in the heart of man, a passion which exerts a powerful influence on the destinies of his life, and too often, by its deceitful illusions, forms a long chain of sadness and misfortune. This passion, which has for its necessary object the preservation of the human race, is found, in some form, in all the beings of nature; but, inasmuch as it resides in the soul of an intelligent being, it assumes a peculiar character in man. In brutes, it is only an instinct, limited to the preservation of the species; in man, the instinct becomes a passion; and that passion, enlivened by the fire of imagination, rendered subtile by the powers of the mind, inconstant and capricious, because it is guided by a free will, which can indulge in as many whims as there are different impressions for the senses and the heart, is changed into a vague, fickle feeling, which is never contented, and which nothing can satisfy. Sometimes it is the restlessness of a man in a fever; sometimes the frenzy of a madman; sometimes a dream, which ravishes the soul into regions of bliss; sometimes the anguish and the convulsions of agony. Who can describe the variety of forms under which this deceitful passion presents itself? Who can tell the number of snares which it lays for the steps of unhappy mortals? Observe it at its birth, follow it in its career, up to the moment when it dies out like an expiring lamp. Hardly has the down appeared on the face of man, when there arises in his heart a mysterious feeling, which fills him with trouble and uneasiness, without his being aware of the cause. A pleasing melancholy glides into his heart, thoughts before unknown enter his mind, seductive images pervade his imagination, a secret attraction acts on his soul, unusual gravity appears in his features, all his inclinations take a new direction. The games of childhood no longer please him; every thing shows a new life, less innocent, less tranquil; the tempest does not yet rage, the sky is not darkened, but clouds, tinged with fire, are the sad presage of what is to come. When he becomes adolescent, that which was hitherto a feeling, vague, mysterious, incomprehensible, even to himself, becomes, from that time, more decided; objects are seen more clearly, they appear in their real nature; the passion sees, and seizes on them. But do not imagine that it becomes more constant on that account. It is as vain, as changeable, as capricious as the multitude of objects which by turns present themselves to it. It is constantly deluded, it pursues fleeting shadows, seeks a satisfaction which it never finds, and awaits a happiness which it never attains With an excited imagination, a burning heart, with his whole soul transported, and all his faculties subdued, the ardent young man is surrounded by a brilliant chain of illusions; he communicates these to all that environs him; he gives greater splendor to the light of heaven, he clothes the earth with richer verdure and more brilliant coloring, he sheds on all the reflection of his own enchantment.

In manhood, when the thoughts are more grave and fixed, when the heart is more constant, the will more firm, and resolutions more lasting; when the conduct which governs the destinies of life is subjected to rule, and, as it were, confirmed in its faith, this mysterious passion continues to agitate the heart of man, and it torments him with unceasing disquietude. We only observe that the passion is become stronger and more energetic, owing to the development of the physical organization; the pride which inspires man with independence of life, the feeling of greater strength, and the abundance of new powers, render him more decided, bold, and violent; while the warnings and lessons of experience have made him more provident and crafty. We no longer see the candor of his earlier years. He now knows how to calculate; he is able to approach his object by covert ways, and to choose the surest means. Woe to the man who does not provide in time against such an enemy! His existence will be consumed by a fever of agitation; amid disquietudes and torments, if he does not die in the flower of his age, he will grow old still ruled by this fatal passion; it will accompany him to the tomb, surrounding him, in his last days, with those repulsive and hideous forms which are exhibited in a countenance furrowed by years, and in eyes which are already veiled by the shades of death.

What plan should be adopted to restrain this passion, to confine it within just limits, and prevent its bringing misfortune to individuals, disorder to families, and confusion to society? The invariable rule of Catholicity, in the morality which she teaches, as well as in the institutions which she establishes, is *repression;* Catholicism does not allow a desire she declares to be culpable in the eyes of God; even a look, when accompanied by an impure thought. Why this severity? For two reasons; on account of the intrinsic morality which there is in this prohibition; and also, because there is profound wisdom in stifling the evil at its birth. It is certainly easier to prevent a man's consenting to evil desires, than it is to hinder his gratifying them when he has allowed them to enter his inflamed heart. There is profound reason in securing tranquillity to the soul, by not allowing it to remain, like Tantalus, with the water at his burning lips. "Quid vis videre, quod non licet habere?" Why do you wish to see that which you are forbidden to possess? is the wise observation of the author of the admirable Imitation of Christ; thus summing up, in a few words, all the prudence which is contained in the holy severity of the Christian doctrine.

The ties of marriage, by assigning a legitimate object to the passions, still do not dry up the source of agitation and the capricious restlessness which the heart conceals. Possession cloys and disgusts, beauty fades and decays, the illusions vanish, and the charms disappear; man, in the presence of a reality which is far from reaching the beauty of the dreams inspired by his ardent imagination, feels new desires arise in his heart; tired with what he possesses, he entertains new illusions; he seeks elsewhere the ideal happiness which he thought he had found, and quits the unpleasing reality which thus deceives his brightest hopes.

Give, then, the reins to the passions of man; allow him in any way to entertain the illusion that he can make himself any new ties; permit him to believe that he is not attached for ever, and without recall, to the companion of his life; and you will see that disgust will soon take possession of him, that discord will be more violent and striking, that the ties will begin to wear out before they are contracted, and will break at the first shock. Proclaim, on the contrary, a law which makes no exception of poor or rich, weak or powerful, vassals or kings, which makes no allowance for difference of situation, of character, health, or any of those numberless motives which, in the hands of passions, and especially those of powerful men, are easily changed into pretexts; proclaim that this law is from heaven, show a divine seal on the marriage tie, tell the murmuring passions that if they will gratify themselves they must do so by immorality; tell them that the power which is charged with the preservation of this divine law will never make criminal compliances, that it will never dispense with the infraction of the divine law, and that the crime will never be without remorse; you will then see the passions become calm and resigned; the law will be diffused and strengthened, will take root in customs; you will have secured the good order and tranquillity of families for ever, and society will be indebted to you for an immense benefit. Now this is exactly what Catholicity has done, by efforts which lasted for ages; it is what Protestantism would have destroyed, if Europe had generally followed its doctrine and example, if the people had not been wiser than their deceitful guides.

Protestants and false philosophers, examining the doctrines and institutions of the Catholic Church through their prejudices and animosity, have not understood the admirable power of the two characteristics impressed at all times and in all places on the ideas and works of Catholicity, viz. *unity and fixity; unity* in doctrines, and *fixity* in conduct. Catholicity points out an object, and wishes us to pursue it straight forward. It is a reproach to philosophers and Protestants, that after having declaimed against unity of doctrine, they also declaimed against fixity of conduct. If they had reflected on man, they would have understood that this fixity is the secret of guiding and ruling him, and, when desirable of restraining his passions, of exalting his mind when necessary, and of rendering him capable of great sacrifices and heroic actions. There is nothing worse for man than uncertainty and indecision; nothing that weakens and tends more to make him useless. Indecision is to the will what skepticism is to the mind. Give a man a definite object, and if he will devote himself to it, he will attain it. Let him hesitate between two different ways, without a fixed rule to guide his conduct; let him be ignorant of his intention; let him not know whither he is going, and you will see his energy relax, his strength diminish, and he will stop. Do you know by what secret great minds govern the world? Do you know what renders them capable of heroic actions? And how all those who surround them are rendered so? It is that they have a fixed object, both for themselves and for others; it is that they see that object clearly, desire it ardently, strive after it directly, with firm hope and lively faith, without allowing any hesitation in themselves or in others. Alexander, Cæsar, Napoleon, and the other heroes of ancient and modern times, no doubt exercised a fascinating influence by the ascendency of their genius; but the secret of this ascendency, the secret of their power, and of that force of impulse by which they surmounted all, was the unity of thought, the fixity of plan, which produced in them that invincible, irresistible character which gave them an immense superiority over other men. Thus Alexander passed the Granicus, undertook and completed his wonderful conquest of Asia; thus Cæsar passed the Rubicon, put Pompey to flight, triumphed at Pharsalia, and made himself master of the world; thus did Napoleon disperse those who parleyed about the fate of France, conquered his enemies at Marengo, obtained the crown of Charlemagne, alarmed and astonished the world by the victories of Austerlitz and Jena.

Without unity there is no order, without fixity there is no stability; and in the moral as in the physical world, without order and stability nothing prospers. Protestantism, which has pretended to advance the individual and society by destroying religious unity, has introduced into creeds and institutions the multiplicity and fickleness of private judgment; it has everywhere spread confusion and disorder, and has altered the nature of European civilization by inoculating it with a disastrous principle which has caused and will continue to cause lamentable evils. And let it not be supposed, that Catholicity, on account of the unity of her doctrines and the fixity of her conduct, is opposed to the progress of ages. There is nothing to prevent that which is *one* from advancing, and there may be movement in a system which has some fixed points. The universe whose grandeur astonishes us, whose prodigies fill us with admiration, whose beauty and variety enchant us, is united, is ruled by laws constant and fixed. Behold some of the reasons which justify the strictness of Catholicity, behold why she has not been able to comply with the demands of a passion which, once let loose, has no boundary or barrier, introduces trouble into hearts, disorder into families, takes away the dignity of manners, dishonors the modesty of women, and lowers them from the noble rank of the companions of men. I do not deny that Catholicity is strict on this point; but she could not give up this strictness without renouncing at the same time the sublime functions of the depository of sound morality, the vigilant sentinel which guards the destinies of humanity. (17)

CHAPTER XXVI.

VIRGINITY IN ITS SOCIAL ASPECT.

We have seen, in the fifteenth chapter, with what jealousy Catholicity endeavors to veil the secrets of modesty; with what perseverance she imposes the restraint of morality on the most impetuous passion of the human heart. She shows us all the importance which belongs to the contrary virtue, by crowning with peerless splendor the total abstinence from sensual pleasure, viz. virginity. Frivolous minds, and principally those who are inspired by a voluptuous heart, do not understand how much Catholicity has thus contributed to the elevation of woman; but such will not be the case with reflecting men who are capable of seeing that all that tends to raise to the highest degree of delicacy the feeling of modesty, all that fortifies morality, all that contributes to make a considerabl[illegible] of women models of the most heroic virtue, equally tends to place wo[illegible] the atmosphere of gross passion. Woman then ceases to be presented to the eyes of man as the mere instrument of pleasure; none of the attractions with which nature has endowed her are lost or diminished, and she has no longer to dread becoming an object of contempt and disgust, after having been the unhappy victim of profligacy.

The Catholic Church is profoundly acquainted with these truths; and while she watched over the sanctity of the conjugal tie, while she created in the bosom of the family this admirable dignity of the matron, she covered with a mysterious veil the countenance of the Christian virgin, and she carefully guarded the spouses of the Lord in the seclusion of the sanctuary. It was reserved for Luther, the gross profaner of Catharine de Boré, to act in defiance of the profound and delicate wisdom of the Church on this point. After the apostate monk had violated the sacred seal set by religion on the nuptial bed, his was the unchaste hand to tear away the sacred veil of virgins consecrated to God: it was worthy of his hard heart to excite the cupidity of princes, to induce them to seize upon the possessions of these defenceless virgins, and expel them from their abodes. See him everywhere excite the flame of sensuality, and break through all control. What will become of virgins devoted to the sanctuary? Like timid doves, will they not fall into the snares of the libertine? Is this the way to increase the respect paid to the female sex? Is this the way to increase the feeling of modesty and to advance humanity? Was this the way in which Luther gave a generous impulse to future generations, perfected the human mind, and gave vigor and splendor to refinement and civilization? What man with a tender and sensitive heart can endure the shameless declamation of Luther, especially if he has read the Cyprians, the Ambroses, the Jeromes, and the other shining lights of the Catholic Church, on the sublime honor of the Christian virgin? Who, then, will object to see, during ages when the most savage barbarism prevailed, those secluded dwellings where the spouses of the Lord secured themselves from the dangers of the world, incessantly employed in raising their hands to heaven, to draw down upon the earth the dews of divine mercy? In times and countries the most civilized, how sad is the contrast between the asylums of the purest and loftiest virtue, and the ocean of dissipation and profligacy! Were these abodes a remnant of ignorance, a monument of fanaticism, which the coryphæi of Protestantism did well to sweep from the earth? If this be so, let us protest against all that is noble and disinterested; let us stifle in our hearts all enthusiasm for virtue; let every thing be reduced to the grossest sensuality; let the painter throw away his pencil, the poet his lyre; let us forget our greatness and our dignity; let us degrade ourselves, saying, "Let us eat and drink, for to-morrow we die!"

No; true civilization can never forgive Protestantism for this immoral and impious work; true civilization can never forgive it for having violated the sanctuary of modesty and innocence, for having employed all its efforts to destroy respect for virginity; thus treading under foot a doctrine professed by all the human race. It did not respect what was venerated by the Greeks in the priestesses of Ceres, by the Romans in their vestals, by the Gauls in their druidesses, by the Germans in their prophetesses. It has carried the want of respect for modesty farther than was ever done by the dissolute nations of Asia, and the barbarians of the new world. It is certainly a disgrace for Europe to have attacked what was respected in all parts of the world, to have treated as a mistaken prejudice the universal belief of the human race, sanctioned, moreover, by Christianity. What invasion of barbarians was equal to this attack of Protestantism on all that ought to be most inviolable among men? It has set the fatal example in modern revolutions of the crimes which have been committed.

When we see, in warlike rage, the barbarity of the conquerors remove all restraint from a licentious soldiery, and let them loose against the abodes of virgins consecrated to God, there is nothing but what may be conceived. But when these holy institutions are persecuted by system, when the passions of the populace are excited against them, by grossly assailing their origin and object, this is more than brutal and inhuman. It is a thing which cannot be described, when those who act in this way boast of being Reformers, followers of the pure Gospel, and proclaim themselves the disciples of Him who, in His sublime councils, has pointed out virginity as one of the noblest virtues that can adorn the Christian's crown. Now, who is ignorant that this was one of the works to which Protestantism devoted itself with the greatest ardor?

Woman without modesty will be an incentive to sensuality, but will never attract the soul by the mysterious feeling which is called love. It is very remarkable, that although the most urgent desire of the heart of woman is to please, yet as soon as she forgets modesty she becomes displeasing and disgusting. Thus it is wisely ordained that what wounds her heart the most sharply, becomes the punishment of her fault. Hence, every thing that maintains in woman the delicate feeling of modesty, elevates her, adorns her, gives her greater ascendency over the heart of man, and creates for her a distinguished place in the domestic as well as in the social order. These truths were not understood by Protestantism when it condemned virginity. It is true this virtue is not a necessary condition of modesty, but it is its *beau ideal* and type of perfection; and certainly we cannot destroy this model, by denying its beauty, by condemning its imitation as injurious, without doing great injury to modesty itself, which, continually struggling against the most powerful passion of the heart of man, cannot be preserved in all its purity, unless it be accompanied by the greatest precautions. Like a flower of infinite delicacy, of ravishing colours, of the sweetest perfume, it can scarcely support the slightest breath of wind; its beauty is destroyed with extreme facility, and its perfume readily evaporates.

But you will perhaps urge against virginity the injury which it does to population; you will consider the offerings which are made on the altar by this virtue as so much taken from the multiplication of the human race. Fortunately the observations of the most distinguished political economists have destroyed this delusion, originated by Protestantism, and supported by the incredulous philosophy of the 18th century. Facts have shown, in a convincing manner, two truths of equal importance in vindicating Catholic doctrines and institutions; 1, that the happiness of nations is not necessarily in proportion to the increase of their population; 2, that the augmentation and diminution of the population depend on many concurrent causes; that religious celibacy, if it be among them, has an insignificant influence.

A false religion and an illegitimate and egotistical philosophy have attempted to assimilate the secrets of this increase of the human race to that of other living beings. All idea of religion has been taken away; they have seen in humanity only a vast field where nothing was to be left sterile. Thus they have prepared the way for the doctrine which considers individuals as machines from which all possible profit should be drawn. No more was thought of charity, or the sublime instructions of religion with respect to the dignity and destinies of man; thus industry has become cruel, and the organization of labor, established on a basis purely material, increases the present, but fearfully menaces the future well-being of the rich.

How profound are the designs of Providence! The nation which has carried these fatal principles to the fullest extent now finds itself overcharged with men and products. Frightful misery devours her most numerous classes, and all the ability of her rulers will not be able to avoid the rock she is running on, urged by the power of the elements to which she has abandoned herself. The eminent professors of Oxford who, it seems, begin to see the radical vices of Protestantism, would find here a rich subject for meditation, if they would examine how far the pretended reformers of the 16th century have contributed, in preparing the critical situation in which England finds herself, in spite of her immense progress.

In the physical world all is disposed by number, weight, and measure; the laws of the universe show infinite calculation—infinite geometry; but let us not imagine that we can express all by our imperfect signs, and include every thing in our limited combinations; let us, above all, avoid the foolish error of assimilating too much the moral and the physical world—of applying indiscriminately to the first what only belongs to the second, and of upsetting by our pride the mysterious harmony of the creation. Man is not born simply for multiplication of his species; this is not the only part which he is intended to perform in the great machine of the universe; he is a being according to the image and likeness of God—a being who has his proper destiny—a destiny superior to all that surrounds him on earth. Do not debase him, do not level him with the earth, by inspiring him with earthly thoughts alone; do not oppress his heart, by depriving him of noble and elevated sentiments—by leaving him no taste for any but material enjoyments. If religious thoughts lead him to an austere life—if the inclination to sacrifice the pleasures of this life on the altar of the

God whom he adores takes possession of his heart—why should you hinder him? What right have you to despise a feeling which certainly requires greater strength of mind than is necessary for abandoning one's self to pleasure?

These considerations, which affect both sexes, have still greater force when they are applied to the female. With her lively imagination, her feeling heart, and ardent mind, she has greater need than man of serious inspiration, of grave, solemn thoughts, to counterbalance the activity with which she flies from object to object, receiving with extreme facility impressions of every thing she touches, and, like a magnetic agent, communicating them in her turn to all that surrounds her. Allow, then, a portion of that sex to devote itself to a life of contemplation and austerity; allow young girls and matrons to have always before their eyes a model of all the virtues—a sublime type of their noblest ornament, which is modesty. This will certainly not be without utility. Be assured, these virgins are not taken away from their families, nor from society—both will recover with usury what you imagine they have lost.

In fact, who can measure the salutary influence which the sacred ceremonies with which the Catholic Church celebrates the consecration of a virgin to God, must have exercised on female morals! Who can calculate the holy thoughts, the chaste inspirations which have gone forth from those silent abodes of modesty, erected sometimes in solitary places, and sometimes in crowded cities! Do you not believe that the virgin whose heart begins to be agitated by an ardent passion, that the matron who has allowed dangerous feelings to enter her soul, have not often found their passions restrained by the remembrance of a sister, a relative, a friend, who, in one of these silent abodes, raises her pure heart to Heaven, offering as a holocaust to the Divine Son of the blessed Virgin all the enchantments of youth and beauty? All this cannot be calculated, it is true; but this, at least, is certain, that no thought of levity, no inclination to sensuality has arisen therefrom. All this cannot be estimated; but can we estimate the salutary influence exercised by the morning dew upon plants? can we estimate the vivifying effect of light upon nature? and can we understand how the water which filters through the bowels of the earth fertilizes it by producing fruits and flowers?

There is, then, an infinity of causes of which we cannot deny the existence and the power, but which it is nevertheless impossible to submit to rigorous examination. The cause of the impotence of every work exclusively emanating from the mind of man is, that his mind is incapable of embracing the *ensemble* of the relations which exist in facts of this kind; it is impossible for him to appreciate properly the indirect influences—sometimes hidden, sometimes imperceptible—which act there with an infinite delicacy. This is the reason why time dispels so many illusions, belies so many prognostics, proves the weakness of what was reckoned strong, and the strength of what was considered weak. Indeed, time brings to light a thousand relations, the existence of which was not suspected, and puts into action a thousand causes which were either unknown or despised: the results advance in their development, appearing every day in a more evident manner, until at length we find ourselves in such a situation that we can no longer shut our eyes to the evidence of facts, or any longer evade their force.

One of the greatest mistakes made by the opponents of Catholicity is this. They can only see things under one aspect; they do not understand how a force can act otherwise than in a straight line; they do not see that the moral world, as well as the physical, is composed of relations infinitely varied, and of indirect influences, sometimes acting with more force than if they were direct. All form a system correlative and harmonious, the parts of which it is necessary to avoid separating, more than is absolutely needful for becoming acquainted with the hidden and delicate ties which connect the whole. It is necessary, moreover, to allow for the action of time, that indispensable element in all complete development, in every lasting work.

I trust I shall be pardoned for this short digression, necessary for the inculcation of the great truths which have not been sufficiently attended to in examining the great institutions founded by Catholicity. Philosophy is now compelled to withdraw propositions advanced too boldly, and to modify principles applied too generally. It would have avoided this trouble and mortification by being cautious and circumspect in its investigations. In league with Protestantism, it declared deadly war against the great Catholic institutions; it loudly appealed against moral and religious centralization. And now a unanimous shout is raised from all quarters of the world in favour of the principle of unity The instinct of nations seeks for it; philosophers examine the secrets of science to discover it. Vain efforts! No other foundation can be established than that which is already laid; duration depends upon solidity.

CHAPTER XXVII.

OF CHIVALRY AND BARBARIAN MANNERS, IN THEIR INFLUENCE ON THE CONDITION OF WOMEN.

An indefatigable zeal for the sanctity of marriage, and an anxious solicitude to carry the principle of modesty to the highest degree of delicacy, are the two rules which have guided Catholicity in her efforts for the elevation of woman. These are the two great means she has employed in attaining her object, and hence comes the influence and importance of women in Europe. M. Guizot is, therefore, wrong in saying that "it is to the development, to the necessary preponderance of domestic manners in the feudal system, that this change, this improvement in their condition is chiefly owing." I will not discuss the greater or less influence of the feudal system on the development of European manners. Undoubtedly when the feudal lord "shall have his wife, his children, and scarcely any others in his house, they alone will form his permanent society; they alone will share his interests, his destiny. It is impossible for domestic influence not to acquire great power." (*Leçon* 4.) But if the lord, returning to his castle, found one wife there, and not many, to what was that owing? Who forbade him to abuse his power by turning his house into a harem? Who bridled his passions and prevented his making victims of his timid vassals? Surely these were the doctrines and morals introduced into Europe, and deeply rooted there by the Catholic Church; it was the strict laws which she imposed as a barrier to the invasions of the passions; therefore, even if we suppose that feudality did produce this good, it is still owing to the Catholic Church.

That which has no doubt tended to exaggerate the influence of feudality in all that raises and ennobles women, is a fact that appears very evidently at that period, and is dazzling at first sight. This is the brilliant spirit of chivalry, which, rising out of the bosom of the feudal system, and rapidly diffusing itself, produced the most heroic actions, gave birth to a literature rich in imagination and feeling, and contributed in great measure to soften and humanize the savage manners of the feudal lords. This period is particularly distinguished for the spirit of gallantry; not the gallantry which consists generally in the tender relations of the two sexes, but a greatly exaggerated gallantry on the part of man, combining, in a remarkable way, the most heroic courage with the most lively faith and the most ardent religion. God and his lady; such is the constant thought of the knight; this absorbs all his faculties, occupies all his time, and fills up all his existence. As long as he can obtain a victory over the infidels, and is supported by the hope of offering at the feet of his lady the trophies of his triumph, no sacrifice costs him any thing, no journey fatigues, no danger affrights, no enterprise discourages him. His excited imagination transports him into a world of fancy; his heart is on fire; he undertakes all, he finishes all; and the man who has just fought like a lion on the plains of Spain, or of Palestine, melts like wax at the name of the idol of his heart; then he turns his eyes amorously towards his country, and is intoxicated with the idea that one day, sighing under the castle of his beloved, he may obtain a pledge of her affection, or a promise of love. Woe to any one who is bold enough to dispute his treasure, or indiscreet enough to fix his eyes on those battlements. The lioness who has been robbed of her cubs is not more terrible, the forest torn to pieces by the hurricane is not more agitated than his heart; nothing can stop his vengeance, *he must destroy his rival or die.* In examining this mixture of mildness and ferocity, of religion and passion, which, no doubt, has been exaggerated by the fancies of chroniclers and troubadours, but which must have had a real type, we shall observe that it was very natural at that time, and that it is not so contradictory as it appears at first sight. Indeed, nothing was more natural than violent passions among men whose ancestors, not long before, had come from the forests of the north to pitch their bloody tents on the site of ruined cities; nothing was more natural than that there should be no other judge than strength of arm among men whose only profession was war, and who lived in an embryo society, where there was no public law strong enough to restrain private passions. Nothing, too, was more natural to those men than a lively sense of religion, for religion was the only power which they acknowledged; she had enchanted their imaginations by the splendour and magnificence of her temples, by the majesty and pomp of her worship. She had filled them with astonishment, by placing before their eyes the most sublime virtue, by addressing them in language as lofty as it was sweet and insinuating; language, no doubt, imperfectly understood by them, but which, nevertheless, convinced them of the holiness and divinity of the Christian mysteries and precepts, inspired them with respect and admiration, and also exercising a powerful influence on their minds, enkindled enthusiasm and produced heroism. Thus we see that all that was good in this exalted sentiment emanated from religion; if we take away faith, we shall find nothing but the barbarian, who knew no other law than his spear, and no other rule of conduct than the inspirations of his fiery soul.

The more we penetrate into the spirit of chivalry and examine in particular the feelings which it professed towards women, the more we shall see that, instead of raising them, it supposes them already raised and surrounded by respect. Chivalry does not give a new place to women; it finds them already honoured and respected; and indeed, if it were not so, how could it imagine a gallantry so exaggerated, so fantastical? But if we imagine to ourselves the beauty of a virgin covered by the veil of Christian modesty; if we imagine this charm increased by illusion, we shall then understand the madness of the knight. If we imagine, at the same time, the virtuous matron, the companion of man, the mother of a family, the only woman in whom were concentrated all the affections of husband and children, the Christian wife, we shall understand why the knight was intoxicated at the mere idea of obtaining so much happiness, why his love was more than a sensual feeling, it was a respect, a veneration, a worship.

It has been attempted to find the origin of this kind of worship in the manners of the Germans; on the strength of some expressions of Tacitus, the social amelioration of woman's lot has been attributed to the respect with which the barbarians surrounded her. M. Guizot rejects this assertion, and justly combats it by observing that what Tacitus tells us of the Germans was not exclusively applicable to them, since "phrases similar to those of Tacitus, and sentiments and customs analogous to those of the ancient Germans, are met with in the statements of many observers of savage or barbarous nations." Yet in spite of this wise remark, the same opinion has been maintained: it is necessary, then, to combat it again.

The passage of Tacitus is this: "Inesse quin etiam sanctum aliquid et providum putant, nec aut consilia eorum aspernantur, aut responsa negligunt. Vidimus sub Divo Vespasiano Velledam diu apud plerosque numinis loco habitare." (*De Mor. Germ.*) "They go so far as to think that there is in women something holy and prophetical; they do not despise their counsels, and they listen to their predictions. In the time of the divine Vespasian, we have seen the greater part of them for a long time regard Velleda as a goddess." It seems to me that it is mistaking the passage of Tacitus, to extend its meaning to domestic manners, and to see in it a trait of married life. If we attend to the historian's words, we shall see that such an explanation is far from his idea. His words only relate to the superstition which made the people attribute to some women the prophetic character. Even the example chosen by Tacitus serves to show the truth and justness of this observation. "Velleda," he says, "was regarded as a goddess." In another part of his works, Tacitus explains his idea by telling us, of this same Velleda, "that this girl of the nation of Bructeres enjoyed great power, owing to an ancient custom among the Germans, which made them look upon many women as prophetesses, and, in fine, with the progress of superstition, as real divinities." "Ea virgo nationis Bructeræ late imperitabat, vetere apud Germanos more quo plerasque fœminarum fatidicas et augescente superstitione arbitrantur deas." (*Hist.* 4.) The text which I have just quoted proves to demonstration that Tacitus speaks of superstition and not of family regulations, very different things; as it might easily happen that some women were regarded as divinities, while the rest of their sex only occupied a place in society inferior to that which belonged to them. At Athens, great importance was given to the priestesses of Ceres; at Rome to the Vestals, the Pythonesses; and the history of the Sibyls shows that it was not peculiar to the Germans to attribute the prophetical character to women. It is not for me now to explain the cause of these facts; it is enough for my purpose to state them; perhaps, on this point, physiology might throw light on the philosophy of history.

When Tacitus, in the same work, describes the severity of the manners of the Germans with respect to marriage, it is easy to observe that the order of superstition and the order of the family were among them very different. We have no longer here any thing of the *sanctum et providum;* we find only a jealous austerity in maintaining the line of duty; and we see woman, instead of being regarded as a goddess, given up to the vengeance of the husband, if she has been unfaithful. This curious passage proves that the power of man over woman was not much limited by the customs of the Germans. "Accisis crinibus," says Tacitus, "nudatam coram propinquis expellit domo maritus, ac per omnem vicum verbere agit." "After having cut off her hair, the husband drives her from his house in presence of her relations, and beats her with rods ignominiously through the village." Certainly this punishment gives us an idea of the infamy which was attached to adultery among the Germans; but it was little calculated to increase the respect entertained for them publicly; this would have been greater had they been stoned to death.

When we read in Tacitus the description of the social state of the Germans, we must not forget that some traits of their manners are purposely embellished by him, which is very natural for a writer of his sentiments. We must not forget that Tacitus was indignant and afflicted at the sight of the fearful corruption of manners at that time in Rome. He paints, it is true, in glowing colours, the sanctity of marriage among the Germans; but who does not see that, when doing so, he had before his eyes matrons who, according to Seneca, reckoned their years not by the succession of consuls, but by change of husbands, and women without a shadow of modesty, given up to the greatest profligacy? We can easily see to whom he alludes when he makes these severe remarks: "Nemo enim illic vitia ridet, nec corrumpere et corrumpi sæculum vocatur." "There vice is not laughed at, and corruption is not called the fashion." A strong expression, which describes the age, and explains to us the secret joy with which Tacitus cast in the face of Rome, so refined and so corrupted, the pure image of German manners. That which sharpened the raillery of Juvenal and evenomed his bitter satires, excited the indignation of Tacitus, and drew from his grave philosophy these severe reprimands. Other information which we possess shows us that the pictures of Tacitus are embellished, and that the manners of this people were far from being as pure as he wishes to persuade us. Perhaps they may have been strict with respect to marriage; but it is certain that polygamy was not unknown among them. Cæsar, an eye-witness, relates, that the German king Ariovistus had two wives (*de Bello Gallico*, l. i.); and this was not a solitary instance, for Tacitus himself tells us that a few of them had several wives at once, not on account of sensuality, but for distinction. "Exceptis admodum paucis, qui non libidine, sed ob nobilitatem, pluribus nuptiis ambiuntur." This distinction, *non libidine sed ob nobilitatem*, is amusing; but it is clear that the kings and nobles, under one pretence or another, allowed themselves greater liberty than the severe historian would have approved of.

Who can tell what was the state of morality among those forests? If we may be allowed to conjecture by analogy, from the resemblance which may naturally be supposed to exist among the different nations of the North, what an idea might we conceive of it from certain customs of the Britons, who, in bodies of ten or twelve, had their wives in common; chiefly brothers with brothers, and fathers with sons; so that they were compelled to distinguish the families conventionally, by giving the children to him who had first married the woman! It is from Cæsar, an eye-witness, that we also learn this: "Uxores habent (Britanni) deni duodenique inter se communes, et maxime fratres cum fratribus et parentes cum liberis; sed si qui sunt ex his nati, eorum habentur liberi a quibus primum virgines quæque ductæ sunt." (*De Bello Gallico*, l. v.)

However this may have been, it is at least certain that the principle of monogamy was not so much respected among the Germans as people have been willing to suppose; an exception was made in favour of the nobles, that is, of the powerful; and that was enough to deprive the principle of all its force, and to prepare its ruin. In such a matter, to establish an exception to the law in favour of the powerful, is almost to abrogate it. It may be said, I admit, that the powerful will never want means of violating it; but it is one thing for the powerful to violate the law, and another for the law itself to retire before them, leaving the way open: in the first case, the employment of force does not destroy the law—the very shock which breaks it, makes its existence felt, and visibly shows the wrong and injustice; in the second case, the law prostitutes itself, if I may so speak; the passions have no need of force to open for themselves a passage, the law itself opens the door for them. From that time it remains degraded and disgraced; its own baseness has undermined the moral principle on which it was founded; and, owing to its own fault, it becomes itself the subject of animadversion to those who are still compelled to observe it. Thus the right of polygamy, once recognised among the Germans in favour of the great, must, with time, have become general among the other classes of the people; and it is very probable that this was the case when the conquest of more productive countries, the enjoyment of more genial climates, and some improvement in their social condition furnished them more abundantly with the means of gratifying their inclinations. An evil so great could only be withstood by the inflexible severity of the Catholic Church. Nobles and kings still had a strong inclination towards the privileges which we have seen their predecessors enjoying before they embraced the Christian religion. Thence it came that, in the first centuries after the irruption of the barbarians, the Church had so much trouble in restraining their violent inclinations. Would not those who have endeavored to find among the Germans so large a portion of the constitutive elements of modern civilization have shown more wisdom, if they had recognised, in the manners which we have been examining, one of the causes which made the struggles between the secular princes and the Church so frequent?

I do not see why we should seek in the forests of the barbarians for the origin of one of the finest attributes of our civilization, or why we should give to those nations virtues of which they showed so little evidence when they invaded the countries of the south.

Without monuments, without history—almost without any index as to their social condition—it is difficult, not to say impossible, to know any thing certain with respect to their manners; but I ask, what must have been their morality, in the midst of such ignorance, such superstition, and such barbarism?

The little that we know about these nations has been necessarily taken from the Roman historians; and unfortunately this is not one of the purest sources. It almost always happens that observers, especially when they are conquerors, only give some slight notions with regard to the political state of a people, and are almost silent as to their social and domestic condition. In order to form an idea of this part of the condition of a nation, it is necessary to mingle with them, and be intimate with them; now this is generally prevented by their different states of civilization, especially when the observers and the observed are exasperated against each other by long years of war and slaughter. Add to this, that, in such cases, the attention is particularly attracted by what favors or opposes the designs of the conquerors, who for the most part attach no great importance to moral subjects; this will show us how it is that nations who are observed in this way are only superficially known, and why such statements with respect to religion and manners are unworthy of much confidence.

The reader will judge whether these reflections are out of place in estimating the value of what the Romans have told us about the state of the barbarians. It is enough to fix our eyes on the scenes of blood and horror prevailing for centuries, which show us, on the one hand, the ambition of Rome, which, not content with the empire of the then known world, wished to extend its power over the most distant forests of the North; and, on the other, the indomitable spirit of barbarian independence, breaking in pieces the chains which were attempted to be imposed upon them, and destroying, by their bold incursions, the ramparts which the skill of the Roman generals labored to raise against them. See, then, what we ought to think of barbarian society, as described by Roman historians. What shall we think, if we consult the few traits which the barbarians themselves have left us, of their manners and maxims with respect to their social condition? It is always risking much to seek in barbarism for the origin of one of the most beautiful results of civilization, and to attribute to vague and superstitious feelings what, during centuries, forms the normal state of the most advanced nations. If these noble sentiments, which are represented to us as emanating from the barbarians, really existed among them, how did they avoid perishing in the midst of their migrations and revolutions? How did they alone remain, when every thing relating to the social condition of the barbarians disappeared?

These sentiments would not have been preserved in a stationary state, but we should have seen them stripped of their superstition and grossness, purified, ennobled, and made reasonable, just, salutary, chivalrous, and worthy of civilized nations. Such assertions have, from the first sight, the character of bold paradoxes. Certainly, when we have to explain great phenomena in the social order, it is rather more philosophical to seek for their origin in ideas which for a long time have exercised a powerful influence on society, in manners and institutions emanating from them, in laws, in fine, which have been recognised and respected for many centuries as established by Divine power.

Why, then, attempt to explain the respect in which women are held in Europe, by the superstitious veneration which barbarous nations offered in their forests to Velleda, Aurinia, and Gauna? Reason and good sense tell us that the real origin of this wonderful phenomenon is not to be found there, and that we must seek elsewhere for the causes which have contributed to produce it. History reveals to us these causes, and renders them palpable to us, by showing us facts which leave no doubt as to the source whence this powerful and salutary influence emanated. Before Christianity, woman, oppressed by the tyranny of man, was scarcely raised above the rank of slavery; her weakness condemned her to be the victim of the strong. The Christian religion, by its doctrines of fraternity in Jesus Christ, and equality before God, destroys the evil in its root, by teaching man that woman ought not to be his slave, but his companion. From that moment the amelioration of woman's lot was felt wherever Christianity was spread; and woman, as far as the degradation of ancient manners allowed, began to gather the fruit of a doctrine which was to make a complete change in her condition, by giving her a new existence. This is one of the principal causes of the amelioration of woman's lot: a sensible, palpable cause, which is easily shown without making any gratuitous supposition, a cause which is not founded on conjecture, but which appears evident on the first glance at the most notorious facts of history.

Moreover, Catholicity, by the severity of its morality, by the lofty protection which it affords to the delicate feeling of modesty, corrected and purified manners; thus it very much elevated woman, whose dignity is incompatible with corruption and licentiousness. In fine, Catholicity itself, or the Catholic Church, (and observe, I do not say Christianity,) by its firmness in establishing and preserving monogamy and the indissolubility of the marriage tie, restrained the caprices of man, and made him concentrate his affections on one wife, who could not be divorced. Thus woman passed from a state of slavery to that of the companion of man. The instrument of pleasure was changed into the mother of a family, respected by her children and servants. Thus was created in the family identity of interests; thus was guarantied the education of children, which produced the close intimacy which among us unites husband and wife, parents and children. The atrocious right of life and death was destroyed; the father had not even the right to inflict punishments too severe; and all this admirable system was strengthened by ties strong but mild, was based on the principles of sound morality, sustained by prevailing manners, guarantied and protected by the laws, fortified by reciprocal interests, sanctioned by time, and endeared by love. This is the truly satisfactory explanation of the enigma; this is the origin of the honor and dignity of woman in Europe; thence we have derived the organization of the family,—an inestimable benefit which Europeans possess without appreciating it, without being sufficiently acquainted with it, and watching over its preservation as they ought.

In treating of this important matter, I have purposely distinguished between Christianity and Catholicity, in order to avoid a confusion in words, which would have entailed a confusion in things. In reality, the true, the only Christianity is Catholicity; but, unfortunately, we cannot now employ these words indiscriminately, not only on account of Protestantism, but also on account of the monstrous philosophico-Christian nomenclature which ranks Christianity among philosophical sects, as if it were nothing more than a system imagined by man. As the principle of charity plays a great part wherever the religion of Jesus Christ is found, and as this principle is evident even to the eyes of the incredulous, philosophers who have wished to persevere in their incredulity without incurring the scandalous epithet of disciples of Voltaire, have adopted the words fraternity and humanity, to make them the theme of their instructions; they have consented to give to Christianity the chief glory of originating its sublime ideas and generous sentiments: thus they appear not to contradict the history of the past as the philosophy of the age gone by in its madness did; but they pretend to accommodate all to the present time, and prepare the way for a greater and happier future. For these philosophers Christianity is not a divine religion; by no means. With them it is an idea, fortunate, magnificent, and fruitful in grand results, but purely human; it is the result of long and painful human labors. Polytheism, Judaism, the philosophy of the East, of Egypt, of Greece, were all preparatory to that great work. Jesus Christ, according to them, only moulded into form an idea which was in embryo in the bosom of humanity. He fixed and developed it, and, by reducing it to practice, made the human race to take a step of great importance in the path of progress into which it has entered. But, He is always, in the eyes of these philosophers, nothing more than a philosopher of Judea, as Socrates was of Greece, and Seneca of Rome. Still we should rejoice that they grant to Him this human existence, and do not transform Him into a mythological being, by considering the Gospel narrative as a mere allegory.

Thus, at the present time, it is of the first importance to distinguish between Christianity and Catholicity, whenever we have to bring to light and present to the gratitude of mankind the unspeakable benefits for which they are indebted to the Christian religion. It is necessary to show that what has regenerated the world was not an idea thrown at hazard among all those who have struggled for preference and pre-eminence; but that it was a collection of truths sent from Heaven, transmitted to the human race by a God made Man, by means of a society formed and authorized by Himself, in order to perpetuate to the end of time the work which His word had established, which His miracles had sanctioned, and which He had sealed with His blood. It is consequently necessary to exhibit this society, that is, the Catholic Church, realizing in her laws and institutions the inspirations and instructions of her Divine Master, and accomplishing the lofty mission of leading men towards eternal happiness, while ameliorating their condition here below, and consoling them in this land of misfortune. In this way we form a correct idea of Christianity, if we may so speak, or rather we show it as it really is, not as men vainly represent it. And observe, that we ought never to fear for the truth, when the facts of history are fully and searchingly examined. If in the vast field into which our investigations lead us, we sometimes find ourselves in obscurity, walking for a long time in dark vaults which the rays of the sun do not visit, and where the soil under our feet threatens to swallow us up, let us fear nothing, let us advance with courage and confidence; amid the darkest windings we shall discover at a distance the light that shines upon the end of our journey; we shall see truth seated on the threshold, placidly smiling at our terrors and anxieties.

To philosophers, as well as to Protestants, we would say, if Christianity were not realized in a visible society, always in contact with man, and provided with the authority necessary for teaching and guiding him, it would be only a theory, like all others that have been and still are seen on the earth; consequently it would be either altogether sterile, or at least unable to produce any of those great works which endure unimpaired for ages. Now one of these is undoubtedly Christian marriage, and the family organization which has been its immediate consequence. It would have been vain to advance notions favorable to the dignity of woman and tending to improve her lot, if the sanctity of marriage had not been guarantied by a power generally acknowledged and revered. That power is continually struggling against the passions which labor to overcome it; what would have happened if they had had to contend with no other obstacle than a philosophic theory, or a religious idea without reality in society, and without power to obtain submission and obedience?

We have, then, no need of recurring to that extravagant philosophy which seeks for light in the midst of darkness, and which, on seeing order arise out of chaos, has conceived the singular notion of affirming that it was produced by it. If we find in the doctrines, in the laws of the Catholic Church the origin of the sanctity of marriage and the dignity of woman, why should we seek for it in the manners of brutal barbarians, who had no veil for modesty and the privacy of the nuptial couch? Let us hear Cæsar speaking of the Germans: "Nulla est occultatio, quod et promiscui in fluminibus perluuntur, et pellibus aut rhenorum tegumentis utuntur, magna corporis parte nuda." (*De Bello Gall.* l. vi.)

I have been obliged to oppose authority to authority; I was under the necessity of destroying the fantastical systems into which men have been seduced by an over love of subtilty, by the mania of finding extraordinary causes for phenomena, the origin of which may easily be discovered when we have recourse, in good faith and sincerity, to the concurring instructions of philosophy and history. It was highly necessary, in order to clear up one of the most delicate questions in the history of the human race, and to find the source of one of the most fruitful elements of European civilization. My task was nothing less than to explain the organization of families, that is, to fix one of the poles on which the axis of society turns.

Let Protestantism boast of having introduced divorce, of having deprived marriage of the beautiful and sublime character of a sacrament, of having withdrawn from the care and protection of the Church the most important act of human life; let it rejoice in having destroyed the sacred asylums of virgins consecrated to God; let it declaim against the most angelic and heroic virtue; let us, after having defended the doctrine and conduct of the Catholic Church at the tribunal of philosophy and history, conclude by appealing to the judgment, not indeed of high philosophy, but of good sense and feeling. (18)

CHAPTER XXVIII.

OF THE PUBLIC CONSCIENCE IN GENERAL.

When enumerating, in the twentieth chapter, the characteristics which mark European civilization, I pointed out, as one of them, "an admirable public conscience, rich in sublime maxims of morality, in rules of justice and equity, in sentiments of honor and dignity, a conscience which survives the shipwreck of private morality, and does not allow the open corruption to go so far as it did in ancient times." We must now explain more at length in what this public conscience consists, what is its origin, what are its results, showing at the same time what share Catholicity and Protestantism have had in its formation. This delicate and important question is, I will venture to say, untouched; at least I do not know that it has yet been attempted. Men constantly speak of the excellence of Christian morality, and on this point all the sects, all the schools of Europe are agreed; but they do not pay sufficient attention to the way in which that morality has become predominant, by first destroying Pagan corruption, then by maintaining itself for centuries in spite of the ravages of infidelity, so as to form an admirable public conscience; a benefit which we now enjoy without appreciating it as we ought, and without even thinking of it.

In order fully to comprehend this matter, it is above all necessary to form a clear idea of what is meant by conscience. Conscience in the general, or rather idealogical sense of the word, means the knowledge which each man has of his own acts. Thus we say that the soul is conscious of its thoughts, of the acts of its will, and of its sensations; so that the word conscience, taken in this sense, expresses a perception of what we do and feel. Applied to the moral order, this word signifies the judgment which we ourselves form of our actions as good or evil. Thus, when we are about to perform an action, conscience points it out to us as good or bad, and consequently lawful or unlawful; and it thus directs our conduct. The action being performed, it tells us whether we have done well or ill, it excuses or condemns us, it rewards us with peace of mind, or punishes us with remorse.

This explanation being given, we shall easily understand what is meant by public conscience; it is nothing but the judgment formed of their actions by the generality of men. It results from this that, like private conscience, the public conscience may be right or wrong, strict or relaxed; and that there must be differences on this point among societies of men, the same as there are among individuals; that is to say, that, as in the same society we find men whose consciences are more or less right or wrong, more or less strict or relaxed, we must also find societies superior to others in the justice of the judgment which they form on actions, and in the delicacy of their moral appreciation.

If we observe closely, we shall see that individual conscience is the result of widely different causes. It is an error to suppose that conscience resides solely in the intelligence; it is also rooted in the heart. It is a judgment, it is true; but we judge of things in a very different way according to the manner in which we feel them. Add to this, that the feelings have an immense influence on moral ideas and actions; the result is, that conscience is formed under the influence of all the causes which forcibly act on our hearts. Communicate to two children the same moral principles, by teaching them from the same book and under the same master; but suppose that one in his own family sees what he is taught constantly practised, while the other sees there nothing but indifference to it; suppose, moreover, that these two children grow up with the same moral and religious conviction, so that as far as the intellect is concerned there is no difference between them; nevertheless, do you believe that their judgment of the morality of actions will be the same? By no means; and why? Because the one has only convictions, while the other has also feelings. In the one, the doctrine enlightens the mind; while, in the other, example engraves it constantly on the heart. Thus what one regards with indifference, the other looks upon with horror; what the one does with negligence, the other performs with the greatest care; and the same subject that to one is of slight interest, is to the other of the highest importance.

Public conscience, which, in fact, is the sum of private consciences, is subject to the same influences as they are; so that mere instruction is not enough for it, and it requires the concurrence of other causes to act on the heart, as well as the mind. When we compare Christian with pagan society, we instantly see that the former must be infinitely superior to the latter on this point; not only on account of the purity of its morality, and the strength of the principles and motives sanctioning it, but also because it follows the wise course of continually inculcating this morality, and impressing it strongly on the mind by constant repetition. By this constant repetition of the same truths, Christianity has done what other religions never could do; none of them, indeed, have ever succeeded in organizing and putting into practice so important a system. But I have said enough on this point in the fourteenth chapter; it is useless to repeat it here; I pass on to some observations on the public conscience in Europe.

It cannot be denied that, generally speaking, reason and justice prevail in that public conscience. If you examine laws and actions, you will not find those shocking acts of injustice or those revolting immoralities which are to be met with among other nations. There are certainly evils, and very grave ones, but they are at least acknowledged, and called by their right names. We do not hear good called evil, or evil good; that is to say, society, in certain things, is like those persons of good principles and bad morals who are the first to acknowledge that their conduct is blamable, and that their words and deeds contradict each other. We often lament the corruption of morals, the profligacy of our large towns; but what is all the corruption and profligacy of modern society compared with the debauchery of the ancients? It certainly cannot be denied that there is a fearful extent of dissoluteness in some of the capitals of Europe. The records of the police, as well as those of the benevolent establishments where the fruits of crime are received, show shocking demoralization. In the highest classes dreadful ravages are caused by conjugal infidelity, and all sorts of dissipation and disorder; yet these excesses are very far from reaching the extent which they did among the best-governed nations of antiquity, the Greeks and Romans. So that our society, which we so bitterly lament, would have appeared to them a model of modesty and decorum. Need we call to mind the infamous vices then so common and so public, and which have scarcely a name among us now, whether it be because they are so rarely committed, or because the fear of public conscience forces them to hide themselves in the dark places, and, so to speak, in the bowels of the earth? Need we recall to mind the infamies which stain the writings of the ancients as often as they describe the manners of their times? Names illustrious in science and in arms have passed down to posterity with stains so black that we cannot consent to describe them. Now, how corrupt must have been the state of the other classes, when such degradation was attributed to men who, by their elevated positions or other circumstances, were the lights of society!

You talk of the avarice which is so prevalent now-a-days; but look at the usurers of antiquity who sucked the blood of the people everywhere; read the satirical poets, and you will see what was the state of manners on this point; consult, in fine, the annals of the Church, and you will see what pains she took to diminish the effects of this vice; read the history of ancient Rome, and you will find the *cursed thirst for gold*, and lenders without mercy, who, after having impudently robbed, carried in triumph the fruits of their rapine to live with scandalous ostentation, and buy votes again to raise them to command. No, in European civilization, among nations taught and elevated by Christianity, such evils would not be long tolerated. If we suppose administrative disorder, tyranny, and corruption of morals carried as far as you please, still public opinion would raise its voice and frown on the oppressors. Partial injustice may be committed, but rapine will never be formed into a shameless system, or be regarded as the rule of government. Rely upon it, the words *justice, morality, humanity*, which constantly resound in our midst, are not vain words; this language produces great results; it destroys immense evils. These ideas impregnate the atmosphere we breathe; they frequently restrain the arm of criminals, and resist with incredible force materialistic and utilitarian doctrines; they continue to exert an incalculable influence on society. We have among us a feeling of morality which mollifies and governs all; which is so powerful that vice is compelled to assume the appearance of virtue, and cover itself with many veils, in order to escape becoming the subject of public execration.

Modern society, it would seem, ought to have inherited the corruption of the old, since it was formed out of its ruins, at a time when its morals were most dissolute. We must observe, that the irruption of the barbarians, far from improving society, contributed, on the contrary, to make it worse; and this, not only on account of the corruption belonging to their fierce and brutal manners, but also on account of the disorder introduced among the nations they invaded, by violating laws, throwing their manners and customs into confusion, and destroying all authority. Whence it follows, that the improvement of public opinion among modern nations is a very singular fact; and that this progress can only be attributed to the influence of the active and energetic principle which has existed in the bosom of Europe for so many centuries.

Let us observe the conduct of the Church on this point—it is perhaps one of the most important facts in the history of the middle ages. Imagine an age when corruption and injustice most unblushingly raised their heads, and you will see that, however impure and disgusting the fact may be, the law is always pure; that is to say, that reason and justice always found some one to proclaim them, even when they appeared to be listened to by nobody. The state of ignorance was the darkest, licentious passions were uncontrolled; but the instructions and admonitions of the Church were never wanting; it is thus that, amidst the darkest night, the lighthouse shines from afar, to guide the mariners in safety.

When in reading the history of the Church we see on all sides assembled councils proclaiming the principles of the gospel morality, while at every step we meet with the most scandalous proceedings; when we constantly hear inculcated the laws which are so often trodden under foot, it is natural to ask, of what use was all this, and of what benefit were instructions thus unheeded? Let us not believe that these proclamations were useless, nor lose courage if we have to wait long for their fruits.

A principle which is proclaimed for a long time in society will in the end acquire influence; if it is true, and consequently contains an element of life, it will prevail in the end over all that opposes it, and will rule over all around it. Allow, then, the truth to speak—allow it to protest continually; this will prevent the prescription of vice. Thus vice will preserve its proper name; and you will prevent misguided men from deifying their passions, and placing them on their altars after having adored them in their hearts. Be confident that this protest will not be useless. Truth in the end will be victorious and triumphant; for the protests of truth are the voice of God condemning the usurpations of His creatures. This is what really happened; Christian morality, first contending with the corrupt manners of the empire, and afterwards with the brutality of the barbarians, had for centuries rude shocks to sustain; but at last it triumphed over all, and succeeded in governing legislation and public morals. We do not mean to say that it succeeded in raising law and morals to the degree of perfection which the purity of the gospel morality required, but at least it did away the most shocking injustice; it banished the most savage customs; it restrained the license of the most shameless manners; it everywhere gave vice its proper name; it painted it in its real colors, and prevented its being deified as impudently as it was among the ancients. In modern times, it has had to contend against the school which proclaims that private interest is the only principle of morals; it has not been able, it is true, to prevent this fatal doctrine from causing great evils, but at least it has sensibly diminished them. Unhappy for the world will be the day when men shall say without disguise, "*My own advantage is my virtue; my honor is what is useful to myself; all is good or evil, according as it is pleasing or displeasing to me.*" Unhappy for the world will be the day when such language will no longer be repudiated by public conscience. The opportunity now presenting itself, and wishing to explain so important a matter as fully as possible, I will make some observations on an opinion of Montesquieu respecting the censors of Greece and Rome. This digression will not be foreign to the purpose.

CHAPTER XXIX.

OF THE PRINCIPLE OF PUBLIC CONSCIENCE ACCORDING TO MONTESQUIEU—HONOR—VIRTUE.

MONTESQUIEU has said that republics are preserved by virtue, and monarchies by honor. He observes, moreover, that honor renders the censors, who were required among the ancients, unnecessary among us. True it is, that in modern times there are no censors charged with watching over the public morals; but the cause of this is not as stated by this famous publicist. Among Christian nations, the ministers of religion are the natural censors of public morals. The plenitude of this office belongs to the Church, with this difference, that the censorial power of the ancients was purely civil, while that of the Church is a religious power, which has its origin and sanction in divine authority. The religion of Greece and Rome neither did, nor could, exercise this censorial power over morals. To be convinced of this, it is enough to read the passage from St. Augustine, quoted in the fourteenth chapter—a passage so interesting on this matter, that I will venture to ask the reader to peruse it again. This is the reason why we find among the Greeks and Romans censors who are not seen among Christian nations. These censors were an addition to the Pagan religion, the impotence of which they clearly showed—a religion which was mistress of society, and yet could not fulfil one of the first duties of all religions—that of watching over the public morals. What I assert is so perfectly true, that in proportion as the influence of religion and the ascendency of its ministers have been lowered among modern nations, the ancient censors have reappeared in some sort in the institution of police. When moral means are wanting, it is necessary to have recourse to physical ones; violence is substituted for persuasion, and instead of a zealous and charitable missionary, delinquents fall into the hands of the ministers of public justice.

Much has been already written of the system of Montesquieu, with respect to the principles on which the different forms of government are based; but perhaps sufficient attention has not been paid to the phenomenon which has served to mislead him. As this question is intimately connected with the point which I have just touched upon, in relation to the existence of the censorial authority, I shall explain myself at some length. In the time of Montesquieu, the Christian religion was not so fully understood as it now is with respect to its social importance; and although on this point the author of the *Esprit des Lois* has done homage to her, it is well to remember what were his antichristian prejudices during his youth, and also that this work is still far from rendering to the true religion what is due to her. The ideas of an irreligious philosophy which, some years later, misled so many fine intellects, had begun at that time to gain the ascendant, and Montesquieu had not sufficient strength of mind to make a decided opposition to the prejudices which threatened universal dominion. To this cause we must add another, which, although distinct from the last, yet had the same origin, viz. a prejudice in favor of all that was old, and a blind admiration for every thing Roman or Grecian. It seemed to the philosophers of that time, that social and political perfection had reached their greatest height among the ancients, that there was nothing to be added to or taken from it, and that even in religion the fables and festivals of antiquity were a thousand times preferable to the faith and worship of the Christian religion. In the eyes of the new philosophers, the heaven of the Apocalypse could not sustain a comparison with that of the Elysian fields; the majesty of Jehovah was inferior to that of Jupiter; all the loftiest Christian institutions were a legacy of ignorance and fanaticism; the most holy and beneficent institutions were the work of tortuous and interested views—the vehicle and expression of sordid interests; public authority was only an atrocious tyranny; and the only noble, just, and salutary institutions were those of Paganism. There every thing was wise, and evinced profound designs highly advantageous to society; the ancients alone had enjoyed social advantages, and had succeeded in organizing public authority, with guarantees for the liberty of citizens. Modern nations should bitterly lament not being able to mingle in the agitation of the forum, being deprived of such orators as Demosthenes and Cicero,—having no Olympic games, or contests of athletæ; in fine, they must always regret a religion which, although full of illusion and falsehood, gave to all nature a dramatic interest, gave life to fountains, rivers, cascades, and seas, peopled the fields, the meadows, and the woods with beautiful nymphs, gave to man gods as the companions of his hearth, and above all, knew how to render life pleasant and charming, by giving full scope to all the passions, and deifying them under the most enchanting forms.

How, in the midst of such prejudices, was it possible to discover the truth in modern institutions? Every thing was in the most deplorable state of confusion; all that was established was condemned without appeal, and every one who attempted to defend it was considered a fool or a knave. Religion and political constitutions, which seemed destined soon to disappear, could reckon on no other support than the prejudices or the interests of governments. Lamentable aberration of the human mind! What would these writers now say if they could arise from their tombs? And yet a century has not yet elapsed since the epoch when their school began to acquire its influence. They have, for a long time, ruled the world at their pleasure; and they have only shed torrents of blood, heaping lesson upon lesson, and deception upon deception, in the history of humanity.

But let us return to Montesquieu. This publicist, who was so much affected by the atmosphere in which he lived, and who had no small share in perverting the age, saw the facts which are here so apparent; he recognised the results of that public opinion which has been created among European nations by the influence of Christianity. But while observing the effects, he did not ascertain the real causes, and labored in every way to accommodate them to his own system. In comparing ancient with modern society, he discovered between them a remarkable difference in the conduct of men; he observed that we see accomplished among us the noblest and most heroic actions, while we avoid a great part of the vices which defile the ancients; but, on the other hand, Montesquieu, like others, could not help seeing that men among us have not always that high moral aim which ought to be the motive of their laudable conduct. Avarice, ambition, love of pleasure, and other passions, still reign in the world, and are easily discovered everywhere. Still these passions do not reach the excess they did among the ancients; there is a mysterious power which restrains them; before giving way to their impulses, they throw a cautious glance around them, and do not indulge in certain excesses unless they are sure of being able to do so in secret. They have great dread of being seen by man; they can only live in solitude and darkness. The author of the *Esprit des Lois* asked himself what is the cause of this phenomenon. Men, he said to himself, often act, not from moral virtue, but from respect for the judgment which other men will pass upon their actions; this is to act from honor. Now, this is the case in France and in the other monarchies of Europe; it must be, therefore, the distinctive characteristic of monarchical governments; it must be the base of that form of government, the distinction between a republic and despotism. Let us hear the author himself: "Dans quel governement," says he, "faut il des censeurs? Il en faut dans une république, où le principe du governement est la vertu. Ce ne sont pas seulement les crimes qui detruisent la vertu, mais encore les negligences, les fautes, une certaine tiédeur dans l'amour de la patrie, des exemples dangereux, des semences de corruption; ce qui ne choque point les lois, mais les élude; ce qui ne les détruit pas, mais les affaiblit. Tout cela doit être corrigé par les censeurs. * * * Dans les monarchies il ne faut point de censeurs, elles sont fondées sur l'honneur; et la nature de l'honneur est d'avoir pour censeur tout l'univers. Tout homme qui y manque est soumis aux reproches de ceux mêmes qui n'en ont point." (*De l'Esprit des Lois*, liv. v. chap. 19.) Such is the opinion of this publicist. But if we reflect on the matter, we shall see that he was wrong in transferring to politics, and explaining by simply political causes, a fact purely social. Montesquieu points out, as the distinguishing characteristic of monarchies, what is the general characteristic of all modern European society; he seems not to have understood why the institution of censors was not necessary in Europe, any more than he did the real reason why they were required among the ancients. Monarchical forms have not exclusively prevailed in Europe. Powerful republics have existed there; and there are still some not to be despised. Monarchy itself has undergone numerous modifications; it has been allied sometimes with democracy, sometimes with aristocracy; sometimes its power has been very limited, and sometimes it has been unbounded; and yet we always find this restraint which Montesquieu speaks of, and which he calls honor; that is, a powerful influence stimulating to good deeds and deterring from bad, and all this from respect for the judgments which other men will pass.

"Dans les monarchies," says Montesquieu, "il ne faut point de censeurs, elles sont fondées sur l'honneur; et la nature de l'honneur est d'avoir pour censeur tout l'univers;" remarkable words, which reveal to us the ideas of the writer, and at the same time show us the origin of his mistake. They will assist us in solving the enigma. In order to explain this point as fully as the importance of the subject requires, and with as much clearness as the multitude and intricacy of its relations demand, I shall endeavour to convey my ideas with as much precision as possible.

Respect for the judgment of others is a feeling innate in man; consequently it is in his nature to do or avoid many things on account of this judgment. All this is founded on the simple fact of self-love: this is nothing but love of our own good fame, the desire of appearing to advantage, and the fear of appearing to disadvantage, in the eyes of our fellows. These things are so simple and clear, that they do not require or even admit of proofs or comments. Honor is a stimulant more or less active, or a restraint more or less powerful, according to the degree of severity which we expect in the judgments of others. Thus it is that the miser, when among the generous, makes an effort to appear liberal; the prodigal restrains himself in the presence of the lovers of strict economy; in meetings where decorum generally reigns we see that even libertines control themselves, while men whose manners are usually correct allow themselves certain freedoms in licentious societies. Now the society in which we live is, as it were, one vast company. If we know that strict principles prevail there, if we hear everywhere proclaimed the rules of sound morality, if we think that the generality of the men with whom we live give the right name to every action, without allowing the irregularity of their conduct to falsify their judgment, we see ourselves surrounded on all sides by witnesses and judges who cannot be corrupted; and this checks us at every step when we wish to do evil, and urges us on when we wish to do good. It will be far otherwise if we have reason to expect indulgence from the society in which we move. In this case, and, supposing us all to entertain the same convictions, vice will not appear to us so horrible, crime so detestable, or corruption so disgusting; our ideas with regard to the morality of our conduct will be very different, and in the end our actions will show the fatal influence of the atmosphere in which we live. It follows from this, that, in order to infuse into our hearts a feeling of honor strong enough to produce good, it is necessary that principles of sound morality should regulate society and that they should be generally and fully believed. This being granted, social habits will be formed, which will regulate manners; and even if these habits do not succeed in hindering the corruption of a great number of individuals, they will, nevertheless, be sufficient to compel vice to adopt certain disguises, which, although hypocritical, will not fail to add to the decorum of manners. The salutary effects of these habits will still continue after the faith on which their moral principles are based has been considerably weakened, and society will still gather in abundance the beneficent fruits of the despised or forgotten tree. This is the history of the morality of modern nations: although lamentably corrupt, they are still not so bad as the ancients. They preserve in their legislation, and in their morals, a fund of morality and dignity which the ravages of irreligion have not been able to destroy. Public opinion never dies; every day it censures vice, and extols the beauty and advantages of virtue; it reigns over governments and nations, and exercises the powerful ascendency of an element which is found universally diffused.

"Outre l'Aréopage," says Montesquieu, "il y avait à Athènes des gardiens des mœurs et des gardiens des lois. A Lacédémone, tous les vieillards étaient censeurs. A Rome, deux magistrats particuliers avaient la censure. Comme le Senat veille sur le peuple, il faut que des censeurs aient les yeux sur le peuple et sur le Senat. Il faut qu'ils rétablissent dans la république tout ce qui a été corrumpu, qu'ils notent la tiédeur, jugent les négligences, et corrigent les fautes, comme les lois punissent les crimes." (*De l'Esprit des Lois*, liv. v. chap. 7.) In describing the duties of the censors of antiquity, the author seems to state the functions of religious authority. To penetrate where the civil laws do not extend; to correct, and in some measure to chastise, what they leave unpunished; to exercise over society an influence more delicate and minute than that which belongs to legislation,—such are the objects of the censorial power; and who does not see that that power has been replaced by religious authority? and that if the former has been unnecessary among modern nations, it is owing to the existence of the latter, or to the influence which it has exercised for many centuries?

It cannot be denied that religious authority has for a long time gained a decided ascendency over men's minds and hearts; this fact is written in every page of the history of Europe. As to the results of that influence, so calumniated and ill understood, we meet with them every day,—we who see the principles of justice and sound morality still reigning over public conscience, in spite of the ravages which irreligion and immorality have committed among individuals.

The powerful influence of public conscience will be best explained by some examples. Let us suppose that the richest of nobles, or the most powerful of monarchs, indulged in the abominable excesses of a Tiberius, a Nero, or the other monsters who disgraced the imperial throne, what would happen? We will not predict; but we are confident that the universal shout of indignation and horror would be so loud, and the monster would be so crushed under the load of public execration, that it appears to us impossible for him to exist. It seems to us an anachronism, an impossibility at this time. Even if we admit that there might be men immoral enough to commit such enormities, sufficiently perverted in mind and heart to exhibit such depravity, we see that it would be an outrage against universal morals, and that such a spectacle could not stand for a moment in presence of public opinion. I could draw numberless contrasts, but I shall content myself with one, which, while it reminds us of a fine trait in ancient history, exhibits, with the virtue of a hero, the manners of the time and the melancholy condition of the public conscience. Let us suppose that a general of modern Europe captures by assault a town in which a distinguished lady, the wife of one of the principal leaders of the enemy, falls into the hands of the soldiers. The beautiful prisoner is brought to the general; what should be his conduct? Every one will immediately say, that she ought to be treated with the most delicate attention, that she ought to be immediately set at liberty and allowed to rejoin her husband. Such conduct appears to us so strictly obligatory, so much according to the order of things, and so conformable to our ideas and sentiments, that there certainly does not appear to us to be any peculiar merit in adopting it. We should say that the general had performed a strict and sacred duty, which he could not evade without covering himself with shame and ignominy. We certainly should not immortalize such an action in history; we should allow it to pass unnoticed in the ordinary course of events. Now, this is what Scipio did with respect to the wife of Mardonius at the taking of Carthagena; and ancient history records this generosity as an eternal monument of his virtues. This parallel explains better than any commentary the immense progress of morality and public conscience under the influence of Christianity. Now, such conduct, which among us is considered as simple, natural, and strictly obligatory, does not flow from the honor belonging to monarchies, as Montesquieu asserts, but from more lofty notions of human dignity, from a clearer knowledge of the true state of society, from a morality the purer and more powerful because it is established on eternal foundations. This, indeed, is found and felt everywhere, it governs the good and is respected even by the bad; this is what would stop the licentious man, who, in a case of this sort, would be inclined to indulge his cruelty or his other passions. The author of the *Esprit des Lois* would doubtless have perceived these truths if he had not been prejudiced by the favorite distinction established at the beginning of his work, and which throughout bound him to an inflexible system. We know what a preconceived system is—one that serves as the mould for a work. Like the bed of Procrustus, ideas and facts, right or wrong, are accommodated to the system; what is too much is taken away, and what is wanting is added. Thus Montesquieu finds in political motives, founded on the republican form of government, the reason for the power exercised over Roman women by their husbands. The cruel rights given to fathers over their children, the unlimited paternal power established by the Roman laws, also appeared to him to flow from political causes, as if it were not evident that these two regulations of the ancient Roman law were owing to causes purely domestic and social, altogether independent of the form of government. (19)

CHAPTER XXX.

ON THE DIFFERENT INFLUENCE OF PROTESTANTISM AND CATHOLICITY ON THE PUBLIC CONSCIENCE.

We have defined the nature of public conscience; we have pointed out its origin and effects. It now remains to examine whether Protestantism has had any share in forming it, and whether it is fairly entitled to the glory of having been of any service to European civilization on this point. We have already shown that the origin of this public conscience is to be found in Christianity. Now Christianity may be considered under two aspects—as a doctrine, and as an institution intended to realize that doctrine; that is to say, Christian morality may be considered in itself, or as taught and inculcated by the Church. To form the public conscience, and make Christian morality regulate it, it was not enough to announce this doctrine; there was still required a society, not only to preserve it in all its purity, that it might be transmitted from generation to generation, but to preach it incessantly to man, and apply it continually to all the acts of life. We must observe that ideas, however powerful they may be, have only a precarious existence until they are realized, and become embodied, as it were, in an institution which, while it is animated, moved, and guided by them, serves them as a rampart against the attacks of other ideas and other interests. Man is formed of body and soul; the whole world is a collection of spiritual and corporeal beings—a system of moral and physical relations; thus it is that all ideas, even the greatest and the loftiest, begin to fall into oblivion when they have no outward expression—no organ by which they make themselves heard and respected. They are then confounded and overwhelmed amid the confusion of the world, and in the end disappear altogether. Therefore, all ideas that are to have a lasting influence on society, necessarily tend to create an institution to represent them, in which they may be personified; not satisfied with addressing themselves to the mind, and with descending to practice by indirect means, they seek to give form to matter, they present themselves to the eyes of humanity in a palpable manner. These observations, which I submit with confidence to the judgment of sensible men, contain a condemnation of the Protestant system. So far from the pretended Reformation being able to claim any part in the salutary events which we are explaining, we should rather say that, by its principles and conduct, it would have been an obstacle in their way, if, as was happily the case, Europe had not been of adult age in the sixteenth century, and consequently almost incapable of losing the doctrines, feelings, habits, and tendencies which the Catholic Church had communicated to it during an education of so many centuries. Indeed, the first thing that Protestantism did was to attack authority, not by a mere act of resistance, but by proclaiming resistance to be a real right, by establishing private judgment as a dogma. From that moment Christian morality remained without support, for there was no longer a society which could claim the right of explaining and teaching it; that is to say, it was reduced to the level of those ideas which, not being represented or supported by an institution, and not having any authorized organ to explain them, possessed no direct means of acting on society, and had no means of protection when attacked.

But I shall be told that Protestantism *has* preserved the institution which realizes this idea; for it has preserved its ministers, worship, and preaching—in a word, all that truth requires in dealing with man.

I will not deny that there is some truth in this, and I will repeat what I have not hesitated to affirm in the fourteenth chapter of this work, "That we ought to regard it as a great good, that the first Protestants, in spite of their desire to upset all the practices of the Church, have yet preserved that of preaching." I added in the same place: "It is not necessary to deny on this account the evils produced at certain times by the declamation of some ministers, either furious or fanatical; but as unity was broken, and as the people had been hurried into the perilous path of schism, we say that it must have been very conducive to the preservation of the most important ideas concerning God and man, and the fundamental maxims of morality, for such truths to be frequently explained to the people by men who had long studied them in the Holy Scriptures." I repeat here what I there said: preaching practised among Protestants must have had very good effects; but this only amounts to saying, that it did not do so much mischief as was to be feared from its own principles. On this point, they were like men of immoral opinions, who are not so bad as they would be, were their hearts in accordance with their minds: they had the good fortune to be inconsistent. Protestantism had proclaimed the abolition of authority, and the right of private judgment without limit; but in practice it did not quite act up to these doctrines. Thus, it devoted itself with ardor to what it called gospel preaching, and its ministers were called gospellers. So that, at the very time when they just established the principle that every individual had the free right of private judgment, and ought to be guided by reason or private inspiration alone, without listening to any external authority, Protestant ministers were seen spreading themselves everywhere, and claiming to be the legitimate organs of the divine word.

The better to understand the strange nature of such a doctrine, we must remember the maxims of Luther with respect to the priesthood. We know that this heresiarch, embarrassed by the hierarchy which constitutes the ministry of the Church, pretended to overturn it at one blow, by maintaining that all Christians are priests, and that, to exercise the sacred ministry, a simple appointment is necessary, which adds nothing essential or characteristic to the quality of priests, which is the universal patrimony of all Christians. It follows from this doctrine, that the Protestant preacher wanting a mission is not distinguished from other Christians by any characteristic; he cannot, consequently, speak to them with any authority; he is not allowed, like Jesus Christ, to speak *quasi potestatem habens* (as having authority); he is nothing more than an orator who addresses the people with no other right than what he derives from his education, knowledge, or eloquence.

This preaching without authority, which, in reality and according to the preacher's own principles, was only human, although it committed the glaring inconsistency of pretending to be divine, may, no doubt, have contributed something to the preservation of good moral principles when they were already everywhere established; but it would certainly have been unable to establish them in a society where they were unknown, especially if it had had to struggle with other principles directly opposed to it, and supported by ancient prejudices, by deeply rooted passions, and by strong interests.

Yes, we repeat it, this preaching would have been unable to introduce its principles into such a society; unable to preserve them in safety amid the most alarming revolutions and the most unexampled catastrophes; unable to impart them to barbarous nations, who, proud of their triumph, listened to no other voice than that of their ferocious instinct; unable to make the conquerors and the conquered bow before these principles, to mould the most different nations into one people, by stamping on their laws, institutions, and manners the same seal, in order to form from them that admirable society, that assemblage of nations, or rather that one great nation, which is called Europe. In a word, Protestantism, from its very constitution, would have been incapable of realizing what the Catholic Church has done.

Moreover, this attempted preaching preserved by Protestantism is, at bottom, an effort to imitate the Church, that it may not remain unarmed in the presence of so redoubtable an adversary. It required a means of influencing the people,—a channel open to communicate, at the will of each usurper of religious authority, different interpretations of the Bible; this is the reason why, in spite of violent declamation against all that emanated from the chair of St. Peter, it preserved the valuable practice of preaching.

But the best way to feel the inferiority of Protestantism in regard to the knowledge and comprehension of the means proper to extend and strengthen morality, and make it prevail in all the acts of life, is to observe, that it has interrupted all communication between the conscience of the faithful and the direction of the priest; it only leaves to the latter a general direction, which, owing to its being extended over all at the same time, is exerted with effect over none. If we confine ourselves to the consideration of the abolition of the sacrament of Penance among Protestants, we may rest assured that they have thereby given up one of the most legitimate, powerful, and gentle means of rendering human conduct conformable to the principles of sound morality. Its action is legitimate; for nothing can be more legitimate than direct and intimate communication between the conscience of man who is to be judged by God, and the conscience of the man who represents God on earth;—an action which is powerful, because this intimate communication, established between man and man, between soul and soul, identifies, as it were, the thoughts and affections; because, in the presence of God alone, to the exclusion of every other witness, admonitions have more force, precepts more authority, and advice more unction and sweetness to penetrate into the inmost soul;—an action full of gentleness, for it supposes the voluntary manifestation of the conscience which seeks guidance—a manifestation which is commanded, it is true, by authority, but which cannot be enforced by violence, as God alone is the judge of its sincerity; —an action, I repeat, which is gentle, for the minister is compelled to the strictest secrecy; all imaginable precautions have been taken by the Church to prevent a betrayal, and man may rest with tranquillity in the assurance that the secrets of his conscience will never be revealed.

But you will ask me, do you believe all this is necessary to establish and preserve a good state of morality? If morality is to be any thing more than a mere worldly probity, which is exposed to destruction at the first shock of interest, or easily seduced by the passions; if it is to be a morality delicate, strict, and profound, extending over all the acts of life, guiding and ruling the heart of man, and transforming it into that *beau idéal* which we admire in Catholics who are really devoted to the observances and practices of their religion; if this is the morality which you mean, it is necessary, undoubtedly, that, placed under the inspection of religious authority, it should be directed and guided by a minister of the sanctuary, by a faithful communication of the secrets of our hearts and the numberless temptations which continually assail our weak nature. This is the doctrine of the Catholic Church; and I will add, that it is pointed out by experience and taught by philosophy. I do not mean to say, that Catholics alone are capable of performing virtuous actions; this would be to contradict the experience of every day. I only wish to prove the efficacy of a Catholic institution which is despised by Protestants. I speak of the great influence which this institution has in infusing into our hearts, and preserving in them, a morality which is cordial, constant, and applicable to all the acts of our souls.

No doubt, there is in man a monstrous mixture of good and evil; I know that it is not given him to attain in this life to that ineffable degree of perfection which consists in a perfect conformity with Divine truth and holiness—a perfection which he will not be able even to conceive until the moment when, stripped of his mortal body, he will be plunged into the pure ocean of light and love. But we cannot be permitted to doubt that man, in this earthly abode, in the land of misery and darkness, can, nevertheless, attain to the universal, delicate, and profound state of morality which I have just described; and, however much the present corruption of the world may be a too legitimate subject of affliction, it must be allowed that we still find, in our own days, a considerable number of honorable exceptions in the multitude of persons who conform to the strict rule of gospel morality in their conduct, their wishes, and even in their thoughts and inmost affections. To attain to this degree of morality (and observe, I do not say of evangelical perfection, but of mere morality), it is necessary that the religious principle should be visibly present to the eyes of the soul, that it should act continually upon her, urging on or restraining her in an infinite variety of circumstances which, in the course of life, occur to mislead from the path of duty. The life of man is, as it were, a chain composed of an infinite variety of acts, which cannot be constantly in accordance with reason and the eternal law, unless it remains constantly in the hands of a fixed and universal regulator. And let it not be said that such a state of morality is a *beau idéal*, the existence of which would bring such confusion into the acts of the soul, and complication of the whole life, as in the end to make it insupportable. No, this is not a mere fancy; it is a reality which is frequently seen by our eyes, not only in the cloister and the sanctuary, but amid the confusion and distractions of the world. That which establishes a fixed rule cannot bring confusion into the acts of the soul, or complicate the affairs of life. Quite the contrary; instead of confusion, it serves to distinguish and illuminate; instead of complicating, it puts in order and simplifies. Establish this rule, and you will have unity; and with unity general order.

Catholicity is always distinguished by its extreme vigilance with respect to morality, by its care in regulating all the acts of life, and even the most secret movements of the heart. Superficial observers have declaimed against the prolixity of moralists—against the minute and detailed study which they make of human actions considered under a moral aspect; they should have observed, that if Catholicity is the religion in the bosom of which has appeared so great a number of moralists, by whom all human actions have been examined in the greatest detail, it is because this religion has for its object to moralize for the whole man, as it were, in all his relations with God, with his neighbor, and with himself. It is clear that such an enterprise requires a more profound and attentive examination than would be necessary, if it had only to give to man an imperfect morality, stopping at the surface of actions, and not penetrating to the bottom of the heart. With respect to Catholic moralists, and without attempting to excuse the excess into which some among them have fallen, either by too great subtility, or by a spirit of party and dispute (excesses which cannot be imputed to the Catholic Church, since she has testified her displeasure when she has not expressly condemned them), it must be observed, that this abundance, this superfluity, if you will, of moral studies, has contributed more than people think to direct minds to the intimate study of man, by furnishing a multitude of facts and observations to those who have subsequently wished to devote themselves to this important science. Now, can there be a more worthy or more useful object for our labors? In another part of this work, I propose to develope the relations of Catholicity with the progress of science and literature; I shall not, therefore, enter more fully on the matter now. Still I may be allowed briefly to observe, that the development and education of the human mind have been principally theological; and that on this point, as well as on many others, philosophers are more indebted to theologians than they seem to imagine.

Let us return to the comparison of the Protestant and Catholic influence on the formation and preservation of a sound public conscience. We have showed that Catholicity, having constantly maintained the principle of authority which Protestantism rejects, has given to moral ideas a force and influence which Protestantism could not. Protestantism, indeed, by its nature and fundamental principles, has never given to these ideas any other support than they might have derived from a school of philosophy. But you will perhaps ask me, do you not acknowledge the force of these ideas; a force peculiar to them, and inherent in their nature, and which frequently changes the face of the world, by deciding its doctrines? Do you not know that they always, in the end, force a passage, in spite of every obstacle, and of all resistance? Have you forgotten the teaching of all history; and do you pretend to deprive human thought of that vital, creative force, which renders man superior to all that surrounds him? Such is the common panegyric on the strength of ideas; thus we see them transformed every moment into all-powerful beings, whose magical wand is capable of changing every thing at their pleasure.

However this may be, I am full of respect for human thought, and allow that there is much truth in what is called the force of an idea; yet I must beg leave to offer a few observations to these enthusiasts, not directly to combat their opinion, but to make some necessary modifications. In the first place, ideas, in the point of view in which we are now considering them, must be divided into two orders; some flattering our passions, the others checking them. It cannot be denied that the former have an immense expansive force. They have a motion of their own; they act in all places; they exert a rapid, violent power; one would say that they overflow with life and activity. The latter have great difficulty in making their way; they advance slowly, they cannot pursue their career without an institution to secure their stability. And why? Because it is not the ideas themselves which act in the former case, but the passions which accompany them, and assume their names; thus masking what is repulsive in them at first sight. In the latter case, on the contrary, it is the truth that speaks. Now, in this land of misfortune, the truth is but little attended to; for it leads to good; and the heart of man, as the Scripture says, is inclined to evil from his youth. Those who vaunt so much the native force of ideas, should point out to us, in ancient or modern history, one idea which, without going out of its own circle, that of the purely philosophical order, is entitled to the glory of having materially contributed to the amelioration of individuals and society.

It is commonly said that the force of ideas is immense; that once shown among men, they will fructify sooner or later; that once deposited in the bosom of humanity, they will remain there as a precious legacy, and contribute wonderfully to the improvement of the world, to the perfection towards which the human race advances. No doubt these assertions contain some truth; as man is an intelligent being, all that immediately affects his mind must certainly influence his destiny. Thus no great change is worked in society without being first realized in the order of ideas; all that is established contrary to our ideas, or without them, must be weak and passing. But it is by no means to be supposed that every useful idea contains in itself a conservative force capable of dispensing with all institutions; that is to say, with support and defence, even during times of social disorder: between these two propositions there is a gulf which cannot be closed without contradicting all history. Now humanity, considered by itself, and given up to its own strength, as it appears to philosophers, is not so safe a depositary as people wish to suppose. Unhappily we have melancholy proofs of this truth: we see too clearly that the human race, far from being a faithful trustee, has but too much imitated the conduct of a foolish spendthrift. In the cradle of the human race, we find great ideas on the unity of God, on man, on relations of man with God and their fellow-men. These ideas were certainly true, salutary, and fruitful: and yet, what did man do with them? Did he not lose them by modifying, mutilating, and distorting them in the most deplorable way? Where were they when Jesus Christ came into the world? What had humanity done with them? One nation alone preserved them; but in what way? Fix your attention on the chosen people, the Jews, and you will see that there was a continual struggle between truth and error; you will see that, by an inconceivable blindness, they incessantly inclined to idolatry; they had a constant tendency to substitute the abominations of the Gentiles for the sublime law of Mount Sinai. And do you know how the truth was preserved among this people? Observe it well; it was supported by the strongest institutions that can be imagined; it was armed with all the means of defence with which an inspired legislator could surround it. It will be said that they were a hard-hearted nation, in the language of the Scriptures; unhappily, since the fall of our first parent, this hardness of heart is become the patrimony of humanity; *the heart of man is inclined to evil from his youth;* ages before the existence of the Jews, God had covered the earth with the waters of heaven, and had blotted out man from the face of the world; *for all flesh had corrupted its way.* We must conclude from this, that the preservation of great moral ideas requires powerful institutions; it is evident, therefore, that they cannot be abandoned to the fickleness of the human mind without being disfigured, or even lost. I will say, moreover, that institutions are not only necessary to teach, but also to apply them. Moral ideas, especially those which openly contradict the passions, are never reduced to practice without great efforts; now the ideas themselves do not suffice to make these great efforts, and means of action are required capable of connecting ideas with facts; this is one of the reasons of the impotence of philosophical schools when they attempt to construct any thing. They are often powerful in destroying; momentary action is enough for this, and this action may be easily acquired in a moment of enthusiasm. But when they wish to establish and reduce their conceptions to practice, they are impotent; their only resource is what is called the force of ideas. Now, as ideas constantly vary and change—an inconstancy of which these schools themselves afford the first example—it happens that what we hear them announce one moment as an infallible means of human progress, is the next reduced to a mere object of curiosity.

These last observations anticipate the objection that may be urged against us with respect to the immense force which printing has given to ideas. But this is so far from being a preserver, that it may be said to be the best destroyer of all opinions. If we measure the immense orbit which the human mind has passed through since that important discovery, we shall see that the *consummation* of opinions (if I may be allowed the expression) is increased in a prodigious degree. The history of the human race, especially since the press has become periodical, appears to be the representation of a rapid drama, where the decorations change every moment, where the scenes succeed each other, scarcely allowing the spectator to catch any of the author's words. Half of this century has not yet passed away, and already it seems as if many centuries had elapsed, so great has been the number of schools which have been born and are dead, of reputations which, after being raised to the highest pitch of renown, have been soon forgotten. This rapid succession of ideas, so far from contributing to increase their force, necessarily renders them weak and unproductive. The natural order in the progress of ideas is this: at first to make their appearance, then to be realized in an institution representing them, and in fine to exert their influence on facts by means of an institution in which they are personified. Now, it is necessary that during these transformations, which essentially require time, ideas should preserve their credit, if they are to produce any favorable result. But when they succeed each other too rapidly, time is wanting for their successive transformations; new ideas strive to discredit the old ones, and consequently to render them useless. This is the reason why the strength of ideas, that is, of philosophy, was never so little to be relied on as now, to produce any thing durable and consistent in the moral order: in this respect, the gain to modern society may well be questioned. More is conceived, but less matured; what the mind gains in extent, it loses in depth, and the pretension in theory makes a sad contrast with the impotence of practice. Of what importance is it that our predecessors were not so ready as we are in *improvising* a discussion on great social and political questions, if they nevertheless organized and founded such admirable institutions? The architects who raised the astonishing monuments of ages which we call barbarous, were certainly not so learned or so cultivated as those of our time; and yet who has the boldness even to commence what they have finished? Thus it is in the social and political order. Let us remember that great thoughts are produced rather by intuition than by reasoning; in practice, success depends more upon the invaluable quality called tact, than upon enlightened reflection; and experience often teaches that he who knows much, sees little. The genius of Plato would not have been the best guide for Solon or Lycurgus; and all the knowledge of Cicero would not have succeeded in doing what was done by the tact and good sense of two unlettered men like Romulus and Numa. (20)

CHAPTER XXXI.

ON GENTLENESS OF MANNERS IN GENERAL.

A CERTAIN general gentleness of manners, which in war prevents great atrocities, and in peace renders life more quiet and agreeable:—such is one of the valuable qualities which I have pointed out as forming the distinguishing characteristics of European civilization. This is a fact which does not require proof; we see and feel it everywhere when we look around; it is evident to all who open the pages of history, and compare our times with any others. Wherein does this gentleness of manners in modern times consist? what is the cause of it? what has favoured it? what has opposed it? These interesting questions directly apply to our present subject; for they lead straight to the examination of other questions, such as the following: has Catholicity contributed in any way to this gentleness of manners; or, on the other hand, has it opposed or retarded it? in fine, what part has Protestantism played in the work, for good or evil? First of all, we must determine wherein gentleness of manners consists. Although we have here to deal with an idea which every one sees, or rather feels, we must still endeavor to explain and analyze it by a definition as complete and exact as possible. Gentleness of manners consists *in the absence of force;* so that manners will be more or less gentle according as force is less or more employed. Thus, we must not confound gentle with charitable manners; the latter work good, the former only exclude the idea of force. We must also distinguish gentle manners from those that are pure, and conformable to reason and justice. Immorality is often gentle, when, instead of resorting to force, it makes use of seduction and stratagem. This gentleness of manners consists in directing the human mind, not by violence which constrains the body, but by reasons which address themselves to the intellect, or by appeals to the passions. Thus it is that gentle manners are not always under the influence of reason; but their rule is always intellectual, although they are often made the slaves of the passions by golden chains of their own formation.

If gentleness of manners consists in not making use, in human transactions, of other means than those of conviction, persuasion, or seduction, it is clear that the most advanced society—that is, that in which intelligence has been most developed—should always participate more or less in this social advantage. There the mind rules, because it is strong; while material force disappears, because the body has less strength. Moreover, in societies very much advanced, where relations and interests are necessarily much multiplied, there is an indispensable want of means capable of acting in a universal and lasting manner, and applicable to all the details of life. These means are, unquestionably, moral and intellectual: the mind operates without destruction, while force dashes violently against obstacles, and breaks itself to pieces, if it cannot overturn them. Thus it is the cause of continual commotions, which cannot subsist in a society which has numerous and complicated relations, without throwing into confusion and destroying society itself.

We always observe in young nations a lamentable abuse of force. Nothing is more natural: the passions ally themselves with force, because they resemble it; they are energetical as violence, and rude as its shocks. When society has reached a great degree of development, the passions are divorced from force, and become allied with the intelligence; they cease to be violent, in order to become artful. In the first case, if it is the people who struggle, they make war on, they contend with, and destroy each other; in the second case, they contend with the arms of industry, commerce, and contraband. Governments attack, in the first case, by arms and invasions; and in the second by diplomacy. In the first epoch, warriors are every thing; in the second, they are nothing; they have not a very important part to play when negotiation, and not fighting, is required. When we look at ancient civilization, we observe a remarkable difference between the character of its manners and the gentleness of ours. Neither the Greeks nor Romans ever regarded this precious quality in the light in which we regard it, for the honor of European civilization. Those nations became enervated, but they did not become gentle; we may say that their manners were made effeminate, but they were not softened; for we see them make use of force on all occasions, when neither vigor of body nor energy of mind was required. There is nothing more worthy of observation than this peculiarity of ancient civilization, especially of that of Rome. Now this phenomenon, which at first sight appears to us to be very strange, has very deep causes. Besides the principal of these causes, which is, the want of an element of civilization such as that which modern nations have had in Christian charity, we shall find among the ancients, if we descend to the details of their social organization, certain causes which necessarily hindered this gentleness of manners being established among them.

In the first case, slavery, one of the constituent elements of their social and domestic organization, was an eternal obstacle to the introduction of this precious quality. The man who has the power of throwing another to the fishes, and of punishing with death the crime of breaking a glass; he who during a feast, to gratify his caprice, can take away the life of one of his brethren; he who can rest upon a voluptuous couch, surrounded by the most sumptuous magnificence, while he knows that hundreds of men, crowded together in dark vaults, work incessantly for his cupidity and his pleasures; he who can hear without emotion the lamentations of a crowd of unhappy beings imploring a morsel of bread to pass through the night's misery which is to unite their labors and fatigues of the evening with those of the morning, such a man may have effeminate, but he cannot have gentle manners; his heart may become enervated, but it will not cease to be cruel. This was precisely the situation of the free man in ancient society: the organization of which we have just stated the results was regarded as indispensable; they could not even conceive the possibility of any other order of things. What removed this obstacle? was it not the Catholic Church, by abolishing slavery, after having ameliorated the cruel lot of slaves? Those who revert to the 15th, 16th, 17th, 18th, and 19th chapters of this work, with the notes appended to them, will find the truth of this demonstrated by incontestable reasons and documents.

In the second place, the right of life and death, given by the laws to the paternal power, introduced into families an element of severity which could not but produce injurious effects. Happily, the hearts of fathers were continually contending against the power thus granted by law: but if this feeling did not prevent some deeds the perusal of which makes us shudder, must we not suppose that, in the ordinary course of life, cruel scenes constantly reminded the members of families of this atrocious right with which the chief was invested? Will not he who is possessed of the power of killing with impunity, be frequently hurried into acts of cruel despotism? Now this tyrannical extension of the rights of paternal authority, carried far beyond the limits pointed out by nature, was taken away by the force of laws and manners which were much aided by the influence of Catholicity (see the 24th chap. of this work). To the two causes which I have just pointed out, may be added another perfectly analogous, viz. the despotism which the husband exercised over his wife, and the little respect which was paid to her. Public spectacles were, among the Romans, another element of severity and cruelty. What could be expected of a people whose principal amusement is to look coolly upon homicide—who took pleasure in witnessing the slaughter in the arena of hundreds of men fighting against each other, or against wild beasts?

As a Spaniard, I feel called upon here to insert a paragraph, in reply to the observations which will be made against me on this point: I allude to the Spanish bull-fights. I shall naturally be asked, Is it not in a Christian and Catholic country that the custom of making men fight against animals is preserved? The objection, however plausible it may seem, can be answered. In the first place, to avoid any misunderstanding, I declare that this popular amusement is, in my opinion, barbarous, and ought, if possible, to be completely extirpated. But after this full and explicit avowal, let me be permitted to make a few observations, to screen the honor of my country. In the first place, it must be remarked, that there is in the human heart a secret taste for risks and dangers; in order to make an adventure interesting, it is necessary that the hero should be encompassed with great and multiplied perils; if a history is to excite curiosity to a high degree, it must not be an uninterrupted chain of peaceful and happy events. We wish to find ourselves frequently in the presence of extraordinary and surprising facts; and, however unpleasant may be the avowal, our hearts, while they feel the tenderest compassion for the unfortunate, seem to require the contemplation of scenes of a more violent and exciting character. Hence the taste for tragedies: hence the love of scenes in which the actors incur great risks, in appearance or in reality. It is not my duty here to explain the origin of this phenomenon; it is enough for me here to point out its existence—to show foreigners who accuse us of being barbarians, that the taste of the Spanish people for bull-fights is only the application to a particular case, of an inclination inherent everywhere in the heart of man. Those who, with respect to this custom of the Spanish people, affect so much humanity, would do well to answer the following questions: To what is owing the pleasure taken by the multitude in every exhibition, when the actors run any risk in one way or another? Whence comes it that all would willingly be present at the bloodiest battle, if they could do so without danger? Whence comes it that everywhere an immense multitude assembles to witness the agonies and the last convulsions of a criminal on the gibbet? Whence comes it, in fine, that foreigners, when at Madrid, render themselves accomplices in the barbarity of Spaniards by assisting at these bull-fights? I say this, not in any degree to excuse a custom which appears to me to be unworthy of a civilized people, but to show that in this point, as well as in almost all that relates to the Spanish people, there are exaggerations which ought to be reduced within reasonable limits. Let us add an important observation, which is the best excuse that can be made for this reprehensible exhibition: instead of fixing our attention on the spectacle itself, let us consider the evils that flow from it. Now, I ask, how many men die in Spain in bull-fights? The number is extremely small, and altogether insignificant in proportion to the frequency of these spectacles; so that if a comparison were made between the accidents which occur in consequence of this amusement and those that happen in other sports, such as horse-races and others of the same kind, we should perhaps find that bull-fights, however barbarous they may be in themselves, still do not deserve all the anathemas with which foreigners have loaded them. To return to our principal object, how, we ask, is it possible to compare an amusement which, perhaps, may not cost the life of one man during many years, to those terrible shows in which death was a necessary condition for the pleasure of the spectators? After the triumph of Trajan over the Dacians, the public games lasted twenty-three days, and the fearful number of six thousand gladiators was slain. Such were the amusements at Rome, not only of the populace, but of the highest classes; such were the horrible spectacles required by a people who added voluptuousness to the most atrocious cruelty. This is a most convincing proof of what I have said, viz.

that manners may be effeminate without being gentle, and that the brutality of unbounded luxury is not inconsistent with the instinct of blood-thirsty ferocity.

It is impossible that such spectacles should be tolerated among modern nations, however corrupt their manners may be. The principle of charity has extended its empire too universally for such excesses to be renewed. This charity, it is true, does not induce men to do all the good to each other that they ought; but, at least, it prevents their coldly perpetrating evil, and assisting quietly at the slaughter of their brethren to gratify the pleasure of the moment. Christianity, at its birth, cast into society the seed of this aversion to homicide. Who is not aware of the repugnance of Christians for the shows of the Gentiles—a repugnance prescribed and kept alive by the admonitions of the early pastors of the Church? It was an acknowledged fact, that Christian charity prohibited the being present at games where homicide formed part of the spectacle. "As for us," said one of the apologists of the early ages, "we make little difference between committing murder and seeing it committed."(21)

CHAPTER XXXII.

THE IMPROVEMENT OF MANNERS BY THE ACTION OF THE CHURCH.

MODERN society ought, it would seem, to be distinguished for severity and cruelty, since it was formed from that of the Romans and barbarians, from both of whom it should have inherited these qualities. Who is not aware of the fierce manners of the northern barbarians? The historians of that time have left us statements that make us shudder when we read them. It was believed that the end of the world was at hand; and, indeed, it was excusable to consider the last catastrophe as near, when so many other melancholy ones had already been heaped upon humanity. The imagination cannot figure to itself what would have happened to the world at this crisis, if Christianity had not existed. Even supposing that society would have been organized anew under one form or another, it is certain that private and public relations would have remained in a state of lamentable disorder, and that legislation would have been unjust and inhuman. Thus the influence of the Church on civil legislation was an inestimable benefit; thus even the power of the clergy in temporal things was one of the greatest safeguards of the highest interests of society.

Attacks are often made upon this temporal power of the clergy and this influence of the Church in worldly affairs. But, in the first place, it should be remembered, that this power and influence were brought about by the very nature of things; that is to say, they were natural, and, consequently, to assail them is to declaim in vain against the force of events, of which no man could hinder the realization. This power and influence, besides, were legitimate; for when society is in danger, nothing can be more legitimate than that that which can save it should save it. Now, at the time we speak of, the Church alone could save society. The Church, which is not an abstract being, but a real and substantial society, acted upon civil society by real and substantial means. If the purely material interests of society were in question, the minister of the Church ought, in some way or other, to take part in the direction of those interests. These reflections are so natural and simple, that their truth must be seen by good sense. All those who know any thing of history are now generally agreed on this point; and if we are not aware how much it generally costs the human mind to enter upon the path of truth, and, above all, how much bad faith there has been in the examination of these questions, we shall have a difficulty in understanding that so much time should have been required to bring the world to agree on a thing which is apparent to those who read history. But let us return to our subject. This extraordinary mixture of the cruelty of a cultivated but corrupted people with the atrocious ferocity of a barbarous one, proud of its triumphs, and intoxicated with blood during long wars, placed in European society a germ of severity and cruelty which fermented there for ages, and the remains of which we find at a late period. The precept of Christian charity was in men's heads, but Roman cruelty and barbarian ferocity still prevailed in their hearts; ideas were pure and beneficent, since they proceeded from a religion of love, but they encountered a terrible resistance in the habits, manners, institutions, and laws, for all these were more or less disfigured by the two mixed principles which I have just pointed out. If we reflect upon the constant and obstinate struggle between the Catholic Church and the elements which contended with her, we shall clearly see that Christian ideas could never have prevailed in legislation and manners, if Christianity had been a religious idea abandoned to human caprice, as Protestants imagine; it was necessary for it to be realized in a powerful institution, in a strongly constituted society, such as we find in the Catholic Church. In order to give an idea of the efforts made by the Church, I will point out some of the regulations which she made for the purpose of improving manners. Private animosities were very violent at the time of which we speak; and right was decided by force, and the world was threatened with becoming the patrimony of the strongest. Public law did not exist, or was hurried away and confounded by outrages which its feeble hand could never prevent or repress; it was altogether powerless in rendering manners pacific, and in subjecting men to reason and justice. Then we see that the Church, besides the instruction and the general admonitions inseparable from her sacred mission, adopted at that time certain measures calculated to restrain the torrent of violence which ravaged and destroyed every thing. The Council of Arles, celebrated in the middle of the fifth century, between 443 and 452, ordains, in its 50th canon, that the Church should be interdicted to those who have public animosities, until they were reconciled. The Council of Angers, celebrated in 453, proscribes, by its 3d canon, acts of violence and mutilation. The Council of Agde, in Languedoc, celebrated in 506, ordains, in its 31st canon, that enemies who would not be reconciled should be admonished by the priests, and excommunicated if they did not follow their apostolical counsels.

The Franks at that time had the custom of going armed, and they always entered the churches with their arms. It will be understood that such a custom must have produced great evils; the house of prayer was often converted into an arena of blood and vengeance. In the middle of the seventh century, the Council of Chalons-sur-Saone, in its 17th canon, pronounces excommunication against all laymen who excite tumults, or draw their swords to strike any one in the churches or in their precincts. Thus, we see the prudence and foresight which dictated the 29th canon of the third Council of Orleans, celebrated in 538, which forbids any one to be present at mass or vespers, armed. It is curious to observe the uniformity of design and plan pursued by the Church. In countries the most distant from each other, and at times when communication could not be frequent, we find regulations analogous to those which we have pointed out. The Council of Lerida, held in 546, ordains, by its 7th canon, that he who shall have sworn not to be reconciled with his enemy, shall be deprived of the participation of the body and blood of Jesus Christ until he has done penance for his oath and been reconciled.

Centuries passed away, acts of violence continued, the precept of fraternal charity, which obliges us to love even our enemies, always met with open resistance in the harsh character and fierce passions of the descendants of the barbarians; but the Church did not cease to preach the divine command; she continually inculcated and labored to render it efficacious by means of spiritual penalties. More than four hundred years had elapsed since the celebration of the Council of Arles, where we have seen the church forbidden to those who were openly at variance; we then see the Council of Worms, held in 868, pronouncing, in its 41st canon, excommunication against enemies who refused to be reconciled. It will suffice to have some idea of the disorders of that time, to know whether it was possible to appease the violence of animosities during this long period. One would fancy that the Church would have been wearied of inculcating a precept which the unhappy state of circumstances so often rendered fruitless; but such was not the case: she continued to speak as she had spoken for ages; she never lost her confidence that her words would produce fruit in the present, and would be productive in the future. Such is her system; one would think that she heard these words constantly repeated, "Cry out, cry out without ceasing; raise thy voice like a trumpet" It is then that she triumphs over all resistance; when she cannot exert her power over the will of a nation, she makes her voice heard with indefatigable diligence in the sanctuary. There she assembles seven thousand who have not bent the knee to Baal; and while she endeavors to confirm them in faith and good works, she protests, in the name of God, against those who resist the Holy Spirit. Let us imagine that, amid the dissipation and distraction of a populous city, we enter a sacred place, where seriousness and moderation reign, in the bosom of silence and religious retirement; there a minister of the sanctuary, surrounded by a chosen number of the faithful, utters from time to time some serious and solemn words. This is the personification of the Church in times disastrous from weakened faith and corrupted morals. One of the rules of conduct of the Catholic Church has been, not to bend before the powerful. When she has proclaimed a law, she has proclaimed it for all, without distinction of rank. In the time of the power of those petty tyrants, who, under different names, persecuted the people, this conduct of the Church contributed in an extraordinary degree to render the ecclesiastical laws popular; for nothing was more likely to make a law tolerable to the people than to show that it applied to nobles, and even to kings. In the times of which we speak, hatred and violence among plebeians were severely proscribed; but the same law extended to great men and to royalty. A short time after the establishment of Christianity in England, we find a very curious example in that country, applicable to this question. It is nothing less than excommunication pronounced against three kings in the same year, and in the same town; all these were compelled by the Councils to do penance for the crimes which they had committed. The town of Llandaff, in Wales, within the metropolitan see of Canterbury, witnessed the celebration of three Councils, in the year 560. In the first, Monric, king of Glamorgan, was excommunicated for having put to death King Cinétha, although he had sworn the peace on the sacred relics; in the second, King Morcant was excommunicated for having put to death Friac, his uncle, in whose favor he had equally sworn the peace; in the third, King Guidnert was excommunicated for having put to death his brother, the competitor for the throne.

Thus, these barbarian chiefs, just changed into kings, and prone to slaughter, are compelled to acknowledge the authority of a superior power, and to expiate by penance the murder of their relatives and the violation of sacred engagements; it is useless to point out how much this must have contributed to the improvement of manners. "It was easy," the enemies of the Church will say —those who endeavor to lower the merit of her acts—"it was easy to preach gentleness of manners, to impose the observance of divine precepts on chiefs whose power was limited, and who had only the name of kings; it was easy to manage those petty barbarian chiefs, who, rendered fanatical by a religion of which they understood nothing, humbly bowed before the first priest who ven tured to menace them on the part of God. But of what importance was that? What influence could it have on the course of great events? The history of European civilization presents a vast theatre, where events must be studied on a large scale, and where none but the most important scenes exercised any influence on the spirit of nations." Let us observe, that these petty barbarian kings were the origin of the principal families which now occupy the most important thrones of the world. To place the germ of real civilization in their hearts, was to graft the tree which was one day to overshadow the earth. But without staying to show the futility of such reasoning, and as our opponents desire great scenes capable of influencing European manners on a large scale, let us open the history of the Church in the first ages, and we shall soon find a page which redounds to the eternal honor of Catholicity. The whole of the known world was subject to an emperor, whose name, then universally venerated, will continue to be respected by the remotest posterity. In an important city, the rebellious inhabitants put to death the commander of the garrison; the emperor, transported with anger, orders them to be exterminated. Returning to himself, he revokes the order; but it was too late, the order was executed, and thousands of victims had been involved in the horrible carnage; at the news of this dreadful catastrophe, a bishop quits the court of the emperor, leaves the city, and writes to him in this grave language: "I dare not offer the sacrifice if you attempt to be present at it; the blood of one innocent person would suffice to forbid me; how much more the massacre of a large number." The emperor, confident in his power, takes no notice of this letter, and goes towards the church. When he arrives at the door, he finds himself in the presence of a venerable man, who, with a grave and stern countenance, stops him and forbids him to enter the church. "Thou hast imitated David in crime," he says, "imitate him also in penance." The emperor yields, humbles himself, and submits to the regulations of the bishop, and religion and humanity gain an immortal triumph. This unhappy city was Thessalonica; the emperor was Theodosius; the prelate was St. Ambrose, Archbishop of Milan.

We find face to face, in this sublime fact, force and justice personified. Justice triumphs over force; but why? Because he who represents justice, represents it in the name of Heaven; because the sacred vestments and the imposing attitude of the man who stops the emperor reminds Theodosius of the divine mission of the holy bishop, and of the office which he holds in the sacred ministry. Put a philosopher in the place of the bishop, and tell him to arrest the proud culprit by an injunction of doing penance, and you will see whether human wisdom can do as much as the Catholic priest speaking in the name of God. Put, if you please, a bishop of the Church, who has acknowledged spiritual supremacy in the civil power, and you will see whether in his mouth words have the same effect in obtaining so glorious a triumph. The spirit of the Church was always the same; her arms were always directed towards the same end; her language was always equally strict, equally strong, whether she spoke to the Roman plebeian or a barbarian, whether she addressed her admonitions to a patrician of the empire or to a noble German. She was no more afraid of the purple of the Cæsars than of the frowns of the long-haired kings. The power which she possessed during the middle ages was not exclusively owing to her having preserved alone the light of science and the principles of government; but it was also owing to the invincible firmness, which no resistance and no attack could destroy. What would Protestantism have effected in such difficult and dangerous circumstances? Without authority, without a centre of action, without security for her own faith, without confidence in her resources, what means would she have had to assist her in restraining the torrent of violence—that impetuous torrent, which, after having inundated the world, was about to destroy the remains of ancient civilization, and opposed to all attempts at social reorganization an obstacle almost insurmountable? Catholicity, with its ardent faith, its powerful authority, its undivided unity, its well-compacted hierarchy, was able to undertake the lofty enterprise of improving manners; and it brought to the undertaking that constancy which is inspired by conscious strength, and that boldness which animates a mind secure of triumph.

We must not, however, imagine that the conduct of the Church, in her mission of improving manners, always brought her into collision with force. We also see her employ indirect means, limit her demands to what she could obtain, and ask for as little, in order to obtain as much as possible. In a capitulary of Charlemagne, given at Aix-la-Chapelle in 813, and consisting of twenty-six articles, which are nothing more than a sort of confirmation and *résumé* of the five Councils held a little before in France, we find in an appendix of two articles the method of proceeding judicially against those who, under pretext of the right called *faida*, excited tumults on Sundays, holidays, and also working days. We have already seen above that they had recourse to the holy relics, to give greater authority to the oaths of peace and friendship taken by kings towards each other—an august act, in which Heaven was invoked to prevent the effusion of blood, and to establish peace on earth. We see in the capitulary which we have just quoted, that the respect for Sundays and holidays was made use of to bring about the abolition of the barbarous custom, which authorized the relations of a murdered man to avenge his death in the blood of the murderer. The deplorable state of European society at that time is vividly painted by the means which the ecclesiastical power was compelled to use, to diminish in some degree the disasters occasioned by the prevailing violence. Not to attack, not to maltreat any one, not to have recourse to force to obtain reparation or to gratify a desire of vengeance, appears to us to be so just, so reasonable, and so natural, that we can hardly imagine another way of acting. If, now, a law were promulgated, to forbid one to attack one's enemy on such or such a day, at such or such an hour, it would appear to us the height of folly and extravagance. But it was not so at that time; such prohibitions were made continually, not in obscure hamlets, but in great towns, in very numerous assemblies, when bishops were present in hundreds, and where counts, dukes, princes, and kings were gathered together. This law, by which authority was glad to make the principles of justice respected, at least on certain days,—principally on the great solemnities,—this law, which now would appear to us so strange, was, in a certain way, and for a long period, one of the chief points of public and private law in Europe. It will be understood that I allude to the truce of God, a privilege of peace very necessary at that time, as we see it very often renewed in various countries. Of all that I might say on this point, I shall content myself with selecting a few of the decisions of Councils at the time. The Council of Tubuza, in the diocese of Elne, in Roussillon, held by Guifred, Archbishop of Narbonne, in 1041, established the truce of God, from the evening of Friday until Monday morning. Nobody during that time could take any thing by force, or revenge any injury, or require any pledge in surety. Those who violated this decree were liable to the same legal composition as if they had merited death; in default of which, they were excommunicated and banished from the country.

The practice of this ecclesiastical regulation was considered so advantageous, that many other Councils were held in France during the same year, on the same subject. Moreover, care was taken frequently to repeat the obligation, as we see by the Council of Saint Gilles, in Languedoc, held in 1042, and by that of Narbonne, held in 1045. In spite of these, repeated efforts did not obtain all the desired fruit; this is indicated by the changes which we observe in the regulations of the law. Thus we see that, in the year 1047, the truce of God was fixed for a less time than in 1041; the Council of Telugis, in the same diocese of Elne, held in 1047, only ordains that it is forbidden to any one in all the *comté* of Roussillon to attack his enemy between the hours of none on Sunday and prime on Monday; the law was then much less extensive than in 1041, when, as we have seen, the truce of God was extended from Friday evening till Monday morning. We find in the same Council a remarkable regulation, the object of which was to preserve from all attack men who were going to church or returning from it, or who were accompanying women. In 1054, the truce of God had gained ground; we see it extended, not only from Friday evening till Monday morning after sunrise, but over considerable periods of the year. Thus we see that the Council of Narbonne, held by Archbishop Guifred, in 1045, after having included in the truce of God the time from Friday evening till Monday morning, declares it obligatory during the following periods: from the first Sunday of Advent till the octave of the Epiphany; from Quinquagesima Sunday till the octave of Easter; from the Sunday preceding the Ascension till the octave of Pentecost; the festival days of Our Lady, of St. Peter, of St. Laurence, of St. Michael, of All Saints, of St. Martin, of St. Just and Pasteur, titularies of the Church of Narbonne, and all fasting days, under pain of anathema and perpetual banishment. The same Council gives some other regulations, so beautiful that we cannot pass them over in silence, when we are engaged in showing the influence of the Catholic Church in improving manners. The 9th canon forbids the cutting of olive-trees; a reason for it is given, which, in the eyes of jurists, will not appear sufficiently general or adequate, but which, in the eyes of the philosophy of history, is a beautiful symbol of the beneficial influence exercised over society by religion. This is the reason given by the Council: "It is," it says, "*that the olive-trees may furnish matter for the holy chrism, and feed the lamps that burn in the churches.*" Such a reason was sure to produce more effect than any that could be drawn from Ulpian and Justinian. It is ordained in the 10th canon that shepherds and their flocks shall enjoy at all times the security of the truce; the same favor is extended by the 11th canon to all houses within thirty paces of the churches. The 18th canon forbids those who have a suit, to take any active steps, to commit the least violence, until the cause has been judged in presence of the bishop and lord of the place. The other canons forbid the robbing of merchants and pilgrims, and the commission of wrong against any one, under pain of being separated from the Church, if the crime be committed during the time of the truce.

In proportion as we advance in the 11th century, we see the salutary practice of the truce of God more and more inculcated; the Popes interpose their authority in its favor. At the Council of Gironne, held by Cardinal Hugues-le-Blanc, in 1068, the truce of God is confirmed by the authority of Alexander II., under pain of excommunication; the Council held in 1080, at Lillebonne, in Normandy, gives us reason to suppose that the truce was then generally established, since it ordains, by its first canon to bishops and lords, to take care that it was observed, and to inflict on offenders against it censures and other penalties. In the year 1093, the Council of Troja, in Apulia, held by Urban II., continues the truce of God. To judge of the extent of this canonical regulation, we should know that this Council consisted of sixty-five bishops. The number was much greater at the Council of Clermont, in Auvergne, held by the same Urban II., in 1095; it reckoned no less than thirteen archbishops, two hundred and twenty bishops, and a great number of abbots. The first canon of this Council confirms the truce for Thursday, Friday, Saturday, and Sunday; it wishes, moreover, that it should be observed on all the days of the week, with respect to monks, clergy, and women. The canons 29 and 30 ordain, that if a man pursued by an enemy take refuge near a cross, he should be in safety, as if he had found asylum in a church. The sublime sign of redemption, after having given salvation to the world, by drinking on Calvary the blood of the Son of God, had already proved a refuge, during the sack of Rome, to those who fled from the fury of the barbarians; centuries later, we find it erected on the roads, to save the unfortunate, who, by embracing it, escaped their enemies, who were thus deterred from vengeance.

The Council of Rouen, held in 1096, extending still further the benefit of the truce, ordains the observance of it from the Sunday before Ash Wednesday till the second feast after the octave of Pentecost, from sunset on Wednesday preceding Advent to the octave of Epiphany, and every week from Friday after sunset till the Monday following at sunrise; in fine, on all the feasts and vigils of the Virgin and the Apostles. The 2d canon of the same Council secures perpetual peace to all clergy, monks, and nuns, to women, to pilgrims, to merchants and their servants, to oxen and horses of labor, to carmen and laborers; it gives the same privileges to all lands that belong to sacred institutions; all such persons, animals, and lands are protected from the attacks of pillage and all kinds of violence. At this time the law felt itself stronger; it could now call for obedience in a firmer tone; we see, indeed, that the third canon of the same Council enjoins upon all who have reached the age of twelve, to engage by oath to observe the truce; in the fourth canon, all who refuse to take this oath are excommunicated. Some years after, in 1115, the truce, instead of comprising certain stated parts of the year, embraces whole years; the Council of Troja in Apulia, held in that year by Pope Pascal, establishes the truce for three years.

The Popes pursued with ardor the work thus commenced; they sanctioned it with their authority, and extended the observance of the truce by means of their influence, then universal and powerful over all Europe. Although the truce was apparently only a testimony of respect paid to religion by the violent passions, which, in her favor, consented to suspend their hostilities, it was, in reality, a triumph of right over might, and one of the most admirable devices ever used to improve the manners of a barbarous people. The man who, during four days of the week, and during long periods of the year, was compelled to suspend the exercise of force, was necessarily led to more gentle manners; he must, in the end, entirely renounce it. The difficulty is not, to convince a man that he does ill, but to make him lose the habit of doing so; and it is well known that habits are engendered by the repetition of acts, and are lost when they cease for a time. Nothing is more pleasing to the Christian soul than to see the Popes laboring to maintain and extend this truce. They renew the command of it with a power the more efficacious and universal according to the number of bishops who assist at the Councils where their supreme authority presides. At the Council of Rheims, opened by Pope Calixtus II. in person, in 1119, a decree confirming the truce is promulgated. Thirteen archbishops, more than two hundred bishops, and a great number of abbots and ecclesiastics, distinguished for their rank, assisted at this Council. The same command is renewed at the General Council of Lateran, held under the care of the same Pontiff, Calixtus II., in 1123. There were assembled more than three hundred archbishops and bishops, and more than six hundred abbots. In 1130, the Council of Clermont, in Auvergne, held by Innocent II., insists on the same point, and repeats the regulations concerning the observance of the truce. The Council of Avignon, held in 1209, by Hugh, Bishop of Riez, and Milon, notary of Pope Innocent III., both legates of the Holy See, confirms the laws before enacted on the subject of the peace and the truce, and condemns the rebellious who dare to infringe them. In the year 1215, at the Council of Montpellier, assembled by Robert de Courçon, and presided over by Cardinal Benavent, in his office as legate of the province, all the regulations established at different times for the public safety, and more recently to secure peace between lord and lord, and town and town, are renewed and confirmed.

Those who have regarded the intervention of the ecclesiastical power in civil affairs as a usurpation of the rights of public authority, should tell us how it is possible to usurp that which does not exist, and how a power which is unable to exercise the authority which ought to belong to it, can reasonably complain when that authority passes into the hands of those who have force and skill to make use of it. At that time, the public authority did not at all complain of these pretended usurpations. Governments and nations looked upon them as just and legitimate; for, as we have said above, they were natural and necessary, they were brought about by the force of events, they were the result of the situation of affairs. Certainly, it would now seem extraordinary to see bishops provide for the security of roads, publish edicts against incendiaries, against robbers, against those who cut down olive-trees and commit other injuries of the kind; but, at the time we are speaking of, this proceeding was very natural, and more, it was necessary. Thanks to the care of the Church, to that incessant solicitude which has been since so inconsiderately blamed, the foundations of the social edifice, in which we now dwell in peace, were laid; an organization was realized which would have been impossible without the influence of religion and the action of ecclesiastical authority. If you wish to know whether any fact of which you have to judge is the result of the nature of things, or the fruit of well contrived combinations, observe the manner in which it appears, the places where it takes its rise, the times which witness its appearance; and if you shall find it reproduced at once in places far distant from each other, by men who can have had no concert, be assured that it is not the result of human contrivance, but of the force of events. These conditions are found united in a palpable manner in the action of the ecclesiastical power on public affairs. Open the Councils of those times, and everywhere the same facts meet your eyes; thus, to quote a few examples, the Council of Palentia, in the kingdom of Leon, held in 1129, decrees, in its 12th canon, exile or seclusion in a monastery, against those who attack the clergy, monks, merchants, pilgrims, and women. Let us pass into France; the Council of Clermont, in Auvergne, held in 1130, pronounces, in its 13th canon, excommunication against incendiaries. In 1157, the Council of Rheims, in the 3d canon, orders to be respected, during war, the persons of the clergy, of monks, women, travellers, laborers, and vine-dressers. Let us pass into Italy; the 11th Council of Lateran, a General Council, convoked in 1179, forbids, in its 22d canon, to maltreat or disturb monks, clergy, pilgrims, merchants, peasants, either travelling or engaged in the labors of agriculture, and animals laboring in the fields. In its 24th canon, the same Council excommunicates those who make slaves of, or rob, Christians on voyages of commerce, or for other lawful purposes; those who plunder the shipwrecked are subjected to the same penalty, unless they make restitution. Let us go to England; there the Council of Oxford, held in 1222, by Stephen Langton, Archbishop of Canterbury, forbids, by its 20th canon, any one to have robbers in their service. In Sweden, the Council of Arbogen, held in 1396, by Henry, Archbishop of Upsala, directs, by its 5th canon, that church-burial shall be refused to pirates, ravishers, incendiaries, highway robbers, oppressors of the poor, and other malefactors; so that in all parts, and at the same periods, we see the same fact appear, viz. the Church struggling against injustice and violence, and endeavoring to substitute in their stead the empire of law and justice.

In what spirit must they read the history of the Church, who do not feel the beauty of the picture presented to us by the multitude of regulations, scarcely indicated here, all tending to protect the weak against the strong? The clergy and monks, on account of the weakness consequent on their peaceful profession, find in the canons which we have just quoted peculiar protection; but the same is granted to females, to pilgrims, to merchants, to villagers, travelling, or engaged in rural labors, and to beasts of labor—in a word, to all that is weak; and observe, that this protection is not a mere passing effort of generosity, but a system practised in widely different places, continued for centuries, developed and applied by all the means that charity suggests—a system inexhaustible in resources and contrivances, both in producing good and in preventing evil. And surely it cannot be said that the Church was influenced in this by views of self-interest: what interested motive could she have in preventing the spoliation of an obscure traveller, the violence inflicted on a poor laborer, or the insult offered to a defenceless woman? The spirit which then animated her, whatever might be the abuses which were introduced during unhappy times, was, as it now is, the spirit of God himself—that spirit which continually communicates to her so marked an inclination towards goodness and justice, and always urges her to realize, by any possible means, her sublime desires. I leave the reader to judge whether or not the constant efforts of the Church to banish the dominion of force from the bosom of society were likely to improve manners. I now speak only of times of peace; for I need not stay to prove that during the time of war that influence must have had the happiest results. The *væ victis* of the ancients has disappeared from modern history, thanks to the divine religion which knew how to inspire man with new ideas and new feelings—thanks to the Catholic Church, whose zeal for the redemption of captives has softened the fierce maxims of the Romans, who, as we have seen, had considered it necessary to take from brave men the hope of being redeemed from servitude, when by the chances of war they had fallen into the hands of their enemies. The reader may revert to the seventh chapter of this work, and the third paragraph of the fifteenth note, where there are, in the original text, numerous documents that may be quoted in support of our assertion; he will thus be better able to judge of the gratitude which is due to the charity, disinterestedness, and indefatigable zeal of the Catholic Church in favor of the unfortunate, who groaned in bondage in the power of their enemies. We must also consider that, slavery once abolished, the system was necessarily improved; for if those who surrendered could no longer be put to death, or be kept in slavery, the only thing to be done was, to retain them for the time necessary to prevent their doing mischief, or until they were ransomed. Now, this is the modern system, which consists in retaining prisoners till the end of the war, or until they are exchanged.

Although the amelioration of manners, as I have said above, consists, properly speaking, in the exclusion of force, we must yet avoid considering this exclusion of force in the abstract, and believing that such an order of things was possible, by virtue of the mere development of mind. All is connected in this world; it is not enough, to constitute the real improvement of manners, that they avoid violence as much as possible; they must also be benevolent. As long as they are not so, they will be less gentle than enervated; the use of force will not be banished from society, but it will remain artificially disguised. It will be understood, then, that we are obliged here to take a survey of the principle whence European civilization has drawn the spirit of benevolence which distinguishes it; we shall thus succeed in showing that the gentleness of our present manners is principally owing to Catholicity. There is, besides, in the examination of the principle of benevolence, so much importance of its own, independently of its connection with the question which now occupies us, that we cannot avoid devoting some pages to it, in the course of an analytical review of the elements of our civilization. (22)

CHAPTER XXXIII.

ON THE DEVELOPMENT OF PUBLIC BENEFICENCE IN EUROPE.

Never will manners be perfectly gentle without the existence of public beneficence; so that gentleness of manners and beneficence, although distinct, are sisters. Public beneficence, properly so called, was unknown among the ancients. Individuals might be beneficent there, but society was without compassion. Thus, the foundation of public establishments of beneficence formed no part of the system of administration among ancient nations. What, then, did they do with the unfortunate? We will answer with the author of the *Génie de Christianisme*, that they had no resources but infanticide and slavery. Christianity having become predominant everywhere, we see the authority of the Church employed in destroying the remains of cruel customs. In the year 442, the Council of Vaison, establishing a regulation for the legitimate possession of foundlings, decrees ecclesiastical censure against those who disturb by importunate reproaches charitable persons who have received children. The Council adopts this measure with the view of protecting a beneficent custom; for, adds the canon, *these children were exposed to be eaten by dogs.* There were still found fathers unnatural enough to kill their children. The Council of Lerida, held in 546, imposes seven years of penance on those who commit such a crime; and that of Toledo, held in 589, forbids, in the 17th canon, parents to commit this crime. Still, the difficulty did not consist in correcting these excesses; crimes thus opposed to the first notions of morality—so much in contradiction to the feelings of nature—tended to their own extirpation. The difficulty consisted in finding proper means to organize a vast system of beneficence, to provide constant succor, not only for children, but for old men, for the sick, for the poor incapable of living by their own labor; in a word, for all the necessitous. Familiarized as we are with such a system universally established, we see nothing in it but what is simple and natural; we can hardly find any merit in it. But let us suppose for a moment that such institutions do not exist; let us transport ourselves to the times when there was not even the first idea of them, what continued efforts would there not be required to establish and organize them!

It is clear that by the mere extension of Christian charity in the world the various wants of humanity must have been more frequently succored, and with more efficacy, than they were before; and this even if we suppose that the exercise of charity was limited to purely individual means. Assuredly, there would always have been a great number of the faithful who would have remembered the doctrines and example of Jesus Christ. Our Saviour did not content Himself with teaching us by his discourses the obligation of loving our neighbor as ourselves, nor with a barren affection, but by giving food to the hungry, drink to the thirsty, clothes to the naked; by visiting the sick and prisoners. He showed us in his own conduct a model of the practice of charity. He could have shown in a thousand ways the power which belonged to Him in heaven and on earth; his voice could have controlled all the elements, stopped the motions of the stars, and suspended all the laws of nature; but He delighted above all in displaying his beneficence; He only attested his divinity by miracles which healed or consoled the unfortunate. His whole life is summed up in the sublime simplicity of these two words of the sacred text: *pertransiit benefaciendo; He went about doing good.*

Whatever good might be expected from Christian charity when left to its own inspiration, and acting in a sphere purely individual, it was not desirable to leave it in this state. It was necessary to realize it in permanent institutions, and not to leave the consolation of the unfortunate to the mercy of man and passing circumstances; this is the reason why there was so much wisdom and foresight in the idea of founding establishments of beneficence. It was the Church that conceived and executed this idea. Therein she only applied to a particular case her general rule of conduct; which is, never to leave to the will of individuals what can be connected with an institution: and observe, that this is one of the causes of the strength inherent in all that belongs to Catholicity. As the principle of authority in matters of faith preserves to her unity and constancy therein, so the rule of intrusting every thing to institutions secures the solidity and duration of all her works. These two principles have an intimate connection; for if you examine them attentively, the one supposes that she distrusts the intellect of man, the other, that she distrusts his individual will and capacity. The one supposes that man is not sufficient of himself to attain to, and preserve the knowledge of, certain truths; the other, that he is so feeble and capricious, that it is unwise to leave to his weakness and inconstancy the care of doing good. Now, neither one nor the other is injurious to man; neither one nor the other lowers his proper dignity. The Church only tells him, that he is, in reality, subject to error, inclined to evil, inconstant in his designs, and very miserable in his resources. These are melancholy truths; but the experience of every day attests them, and the Christian religion explains them, by establishing, as a fundamental dogma, the fall of man in the person of our first parent. Protestantism, following principles diametrically opposite, applies the same spirit of individuality to the will as to the intelligence; it is even the natural enemy of institutions. Without going further than our present subject, we see that its first step, on its appearance, was to destroy what existed, without in any way replacing it. Will it be believed that Montesquieu went so far as to applaud this work of destruction? This is another proof of the fatal influence exerted over minds by the pestilential atmosphere of the last century: "Henri VIII.," says Montesquieu, "voulant réformer l'église d'Angleterre, détruisit les moines: nation paresseuse elle-même, et qui entretenait la paresse des autres, parceque, practiquant l'hospitalité, une infinité de gens oisifs, gentilhommes et bourgeois, passoient leur vie à courir de couvent en couvent. *Il ôta encore les hôpitaux, où le bas peuple trouvait sa subsistence,* comme les gentilhommes trouvaient la leur dans les monastères. Depuis ce changement, l'esprit de commerce et d'industrie s'établit en Angleterre." (*De l'Esprit des Lois*, liv. xxiii. chap. 19.) That Montesquieu should praise this conduct of Henry VIII., and the destruction of monasteries, for the miserable reason, that it was good to deprive the idle of the hospitality of the monks, is a notion which ought not to astonish us, as such vulgar ideas were in accordance with the taste of the philosophy which had then begun to prevail. It attempted to find profound economical and political reasons for all that was in opposition to the institutions of Catholicity; and this was not difficult, for a prejudiced mind always finds in books, as well as in facts, what it seeks. We might inquire of Montesquieu, however, what is become of the property of the monasteries? As these rich spoils were in great part given to the same nobles who found hospitality with the monks, we might observe to him, that it was a singular way of diminishing the idleness of people, to give them as their own the property which they had previously enjoyed as guests. It cannot be denied, that to take to the houses of the nobles the property which had supported the hospitality which the monks showed them, was certainly to save them the trouble of *running from monastery to monastery.* But what we cannot tolerate is, to hear vaunted as a political *chef-d'œuvre*, the *suppression of the hospitals where the poor people found their subsistence.* What! are these your lofty views, and is your philosophy so devoid of compassion, that you think the destruction of the asylums of misfortune proper means for encouraging industry and commerce? The worst of it is, that Montesquieu, seduced by the desire of offering new and piquant obser vations, goes so far as to deny the utility of hospitals, pretending that, in Rome, they make all live in comfort except those who labor. He does not wish to have them in rich nations or in poor ones. He supports this cruel paradox by a reason stated in the following words: "Quand la nation est pauvre," says he, "la pauvreté particulière dérive de la misère générale, et elle est, pour ainsi dire, la misère générale. Tous les hôpitaux du monde ne sauraient guérir cette pauvreté particulière; *au contraire l'esprit de paresse qu'ils inspirent augmente la pauvreté générale, et par conséquent la particulière.*" Thus, hospitals are represented as dangerous to poor nations, and consequently condemned. Let us now listen to what is said of rich ones: "J'ai dit que les nations riches avaient besoin d'hôpitaux, parceque la fortune y était sujette a mille accidents; mais *on sent que les recours passagers vaudraient bien mieux que les établissements perpétuels.* Le mal est momentané; il faut donc des secours de même nature, et qui soient applicables à l'accident particulier." (*De l'Esprit des Lois*, liv. xxiii. chap. 19.) It is difficult to find any thing more empty or more false. Undoubtedly, if we were to judge, by these passages, of the *Esprit des Lois*, the merit of which has been so much exaggerated, we should be compelled to condemn it in terms more severe than those employed by M. de Bonald, when he called it "the most profound of superficial works." Happily for the poor, and for the good order of society, Europe in general has not adopted these maxims; and on this point, as on many others, prejudices against Catholicity have been laid aside, in order to continue, with more or less modification, the system which she taught. We find in England herself a considerable number of establishments of beneficence; and it is not believed in that country that it is necessary, in order to excite the activity of the poor, to expose them to the danger of dying of hunger. We should always remember that the system of public establishments for beneficence, now general in Europe, would not have existed without Catholicity; indeed, we may rest assured, that if the religious schism had taken place before the foundation and organization of this system, European society would not now have enjoyed these establishments which do it so much honor, and are so precious an element of good government and public tranquillity. It is one thing to found and maintain an establishment of this kind, when a great number of similar ones already exist,—when governments possess immense resources, and strength sufficient to protect all interests; but it is a very different thing to establish a multitude of them in all places, when there is no model to be copied, when it is necessary to *improvise* in a thousand ways the indispensable resources,—when public authority has no *prestige* or force to control the violent passions that struggle to gain every thing that they can feed on. Now, in modern times, since the existence of Protestantism, the first only of these things has been done; the second was accomplished centuries before by the Catholic Church; and let it be observed, that what has been done in Protestant countries in favor of public beneficence, has been done by administrative acts of the government, acts which were necessarily inspired by the view of the happy results already obtained from similar institutions. But Protestantism, by itself, considered as a separate Church, has done nothing, and it could do nothing; for in all places where it preserves any thing of hierarchical organization, it is the mere instrument of the civil power; consequently it cannot there act by its own inspirations. Such is the vice of its constitution. Its prejudice against the religious institutions, both of men and women, make it sterile in this respect. Thus, indeed, it is deprived of one of the most powerful elements possessed by Catholicity to accomplish the most arduous and laborious works of charity. For the great works of charity, it is necessary to be free from worldly attachments and self-love; and these qualities are found in an eminent degree in persons who are devoted to charity in religious institutions. There they commence with that freedom which is the root of all the rest—the absence of self-love.

The Catholic Church has not been instigated to this by the civil power; she has considered it as one of her own peculiar duties to provide for the unfortunate. Her bishops have always been looked upon as the protectors and the natural inspectors of beneficent establishments. Therefore there was a law which placed hospitals under the charge of the bishops; and thence it comes that that class of charitable institutions has always occupied a distinguished place in canonical legislation. The Church, from remote times, has made laws concerning hospitals. Thus, we see the Council of Chalcedon place under the authority of the bishop the clergy residing in Ptochüs,—that is, as explained by Zonarus, in the establishments destined to support and provide for the poor: "Such," he says, "as those where orphans and the old and infirm are received and cared for." The Council makes use of this expression, *according to the tradition of the holy Fathers;* thereby indicating that regulations had been made of old by the Church concerning establishments of this kind. The learned also know what the ancient *diaconies* were,—places of charity, where poor widows, orphans, old men, and other unfortunate persons, were received.

When the irruption of the barbarians had introduced everywhere the reign of force, the possessions which hospitals already had, and those which they afterwards gained, were exposed to unbounded rapacity. The Church did all she could to protect them. It was forbidden to take them, under the severest penalties; those who made the attempt were punished as murderers of the poor. The Council of Orleans, held in 549, forbids, in its 13th canon, taking the property of hospitals; the 15th canon of the same Council confirms the foundation of a hospital at Lyons, a foundation due to the charity of King Childebert and Queen Ultrogotha. The Council takes measures to secure the safety and good management of the funds of that hospital; all violating these regulations are anathematized as guilty of homicide of the poor.

We find, with respect to the poor, in very ancient Councils, regulations of charity and police at the same time, quite similar to measures now adopted in certain countries. For example, parishes are enjoined to make a list of their poor, to maintain them, &c. The Council of Tours, held in 566 or 567, by its 5th canon orders every town to maintain its poor; and the priests in the country, as well as the faithful, to maintain their own, in order to prevent mendicants from wandering about the towns and provinces. With respect to lepers, the 21st canon of the Council of Orleans, before quoted, prescribes to bishops to take particular care of these unfortunate beings in all dioceses, and to furnish them with food and clothing out of the Church funds; the Council of Lyons, held in 583, in its 6th canon ordains that the lepers of every town and territory shall be supported at the expense of the Church under the care of the bishop. The Church had a register of the poor, intended to regulate the distribution which was made to them of a portion of the ecclesiastical property; it was expressly forbidden to demand any thing from the poor for being inscribed in this book of charity. The Council of Rheims, held in 874, in the second of its five articles forbids receiving any thing from the poor thus inscribed, and that under pain of deposition. Zeal for improving the condition of prisoners, a kind of charity which has been so much displayed in modern times, is extremely ancient in the Church. We must observe that in the sixth century there was already an inspector of prisons; the archdeacon or the provost of the church was obliged to visit prisoners on all Sundays; no class of criminals was excluded from the benefit of this solicitude. The archdeacon was bound to learn their wants, and to furnish them, by means of a person recommended by the bishop, with food and all they stood in need of. This was ordered by the 20th canon of the Council of Orleans, held in 549. It would be too long to enumerate even a small part of the ordinances which attest the zeal of the Church for the comfort and consolation of the unfortunate; besides, it would be beyond my purpose, for

I have only undertaken to compare the spirit of Protestantism with that of Catholicity with respect to works of charity. Yet, and as the development of this question has naturally led me to state several historical facts, I shall allude to the 141st canon of the Council of Aix-la-Chapelle, enjoining upon prelates to found, according to the example of their predecessors, a hospital to receive all the poor that the revenues of the Church were able to support. Prebendaries were bound to give to the hospital the tenth of their fruits; one of them was appointed to receive the poor and strangers, and to watch over the administration of the hospital. Such was the rule of prebendaries. In the rule destined for the canonesses, the same Council ordains that a hospital shall be established close to the house, and that it shall itself contain a place reserved for poor women. Therefore, were there seen, many centuries later, in various places, hospitals near to prebendal churches. As we approach our own times, we everywhere see innumerable institutions founded for charity. Ought we not to admire the fruitfulness with which there arise, on all sides, as many resources as are necessary to succour all the unfortunate? We cannot calculate with precision what would have happened if Protestantism had not appeared, but at least there is a conjecture authorized by reasons of analogy. If the development of European civilization had been fully carried out under the principle of religious unity, if the so-called Reformation had not plunged Europe into continual revolutions and reactions, there would certainly have been produced in the bosom of the Catholic Church some general system of beneficence, which, organized on a grand scale and in conformity with the new progress of society, would have been able to prevent or effectually to remedy the sore of pauperism, that cancer of modern nations. What was not to be expected from all the intelligence and all the resources of Europe, working in concert to obtain this great result? Unhappily, the unity of faith was broken; authority, the proper centre, past, present, and future, was rejected. From that time Europe, which was destined to become a nation of brothers, was changed into a most fiercely-contested battle-field. Hatred, engendered by religious differences, prevented any united efforts for new arrangements; and the necessities which arose out of the bosom of the social and political organization, which was for Europe the fruit of so many centuries of labor, could not be provided for. Bitter disputes, rebellions, and wars were acclimatized among us.

Let us remember that the Protestant schism not only prevented the union of all the efforts of Europe to attain the end in question, but, moreover, it has been the reason why Catholicism has not been able to act in a regular manner even in those countries where it has preserved its complete empire, or a decided predominance. In these countries it has been compelled to hold itself in an attitude of defence; it has been obliged, by the attacks of its enemies, to employ a great part of its resources in defending its own existence: it is very probably for this reason that the state of things in Europe is entirely different from what it would have been on a contrary supposition; and perhaps in the latter case there would not have existed the sad necessity of exhausting itself in impotent efforts against an evil, which, according to all appearances, and unless hitherto unknown means can be devised, appears without remedy. I shall be told that the Church in this case would have had an excessive authority over all that relates to charity, and would have unjustly usurped the civil power. This is a mistake; the Church has never claimed any thing that is not quite conformable to her indelible character of protector of all the unfortunate. During some centuries, it is true, we hardly hear any other voice or perceive any other action than hers, in all that relates to beneficence; but we must observe that the civil power during that time was very far from possessing a regular and vigorous administration, capable of doing without the aid of the Church The latter was so far from being actuated by any motives of ambition, that her double charge of spiritual and temporal things imposed on her all sorts of sacrifices.

Three centuries have passed away since the event of which we now lament the fatal results. Europe during this period has been submitted in great part to the influence of Protestantism, but it has made no progress thereby. I cannot believe that these three centuries would have passed away under the exclusive influence of Catholicity, without producing in the bosom of Europe a degree of charity sufficient to raise the system of beneficence to the height demanded by the difficulties and new interests of society. If we look at the different systems which ferment in minds devoted to the study of this grave question, we shall always find there *association* under one form or another. Now association has been at all times one of the favorite principles of Catholicity, which, by proclaiming unity in faith, proclaims it also in all things; but there is this difference, that a great number of associations which are conceived and established in our days are nothing but an agglomeration of interests; they want unity of will and of aim, conditions which can be obtained only by means of Christian charity. Yet these two conditions are indispensably necessary to accomplish great works of beneficence, if any thing else is required than a mere measure of public administration. As to the administration itself, it is of little avail when it is not vigorous; and unfortunately, in acquiring the necessary vigor, its action becomes somewhat stiff and harsh. Therefore it is that Christian charity is required, which, penetrating on all sides like a balsam, softens all that is harsh in human action. I pity the unfortunate who in their necessities find only the succor of the civil authorities, without the intervention of Christian charity. In reports presented to the public, philanthropy may and will exaggerate the care which it lavishes on the unfortunate, but things will not be so in reality. The love of our brethren, when it is not founded on religious principle, is as fruitful in words as it is barren in deeds. The sight of the poor, of the sick, of impotent old age, is too disagreeable for us long to bear it, unless we are urged to it by very powerful motives. Even much less can we hope that a vague feeling of humanity will suffice to make us encounter, as we should, the constant cares required to console these unfortunate beings. When Christian charity is wanting, a good administration will no doubt enforce punctuality and exactitude —all that can be demanded of men who receive a salary for their services: but one thing will be wanting, which nothing can replace and money cannot buy, viz. love. But it will be asked, have you no faith in philanthropy? No; for as M. de Chateaubriand says, philanthropy is only the false coin of charity. It was then perfectly reasonable that the Church should have a direct influence in all branches of beneficence, for she knew better than any others how to make Christian charity active, by applying it to all kinds of necessities and miseries. Therein she did not gratify her ambition, but found food for her zeal; she did not claim a privilege, but exerted a right. In fine, if you will persevere in calling such a desire ambition, you cannot deny at least that it was ambition of a new kind. An ambition truly worthy of glory and reward, is that which claims the right of succoring and consoling the unfortunate. (23)

CHAPTER XXXIV.

ON TOLERATION IN RELIGIOUS MATTERS.

THE question of the improvement of manners, treated in the preceding chapters, naturally leads me to another, sufficiently thorny in itself, and rendered still more so by innumerable prejudices. I allude to toleration in matters of religion. The word Catholicity, to certain persons, is the synonyme of intolerance; and the confusion of ideas on this point has become such, that no more laborious task can be undertaken than to clear them up. It is only necessary to pronounce the word intolerance, to raise in the minds of some people all sorts of black and horrible ideas. Legislation, institutions, and men of past times, all are condemned without appeal, the moment there is seen the slightest appearance of intolerance. More than one cause contributes to this universal prejudice. Yet, if called upon to point out the principal one, we would repeat the profound maxim of Cato, who, when accused at the age of eighty-six of certain offences of his past life, committed at times long gone by, said, "It is difficult to render an account of one's own conduct to men belonging to an age different from that in which one has lived." There are some things of which one cannot accurately judge without, not only a knowledge of them, but also a complete appreciation of the times when they occurred. How many men are capable of attaining to this? There are few who are able to succeed in freeing their minds from the influence of the atmosphere which surrounds them; but there are fewer still who can do the same with their hearts. The age in which we live is precisely the reverse of the ages of intolerance; and this is the first difficulty which meets us in discussing questions of this kind. The prejudice and bad faith of some who have applied themselves to this subject, have contributed also in a considerable degree to erroneous opinions. There is nothing in the world which cannot be undervalued by showing only one side of it; for thus considered, all things are false, or rather are not themselves. All bodies have three dimensions; only to look at one is not to form an idea of the body itself, but of a quantity very different from it. Take any institution, the most just and useful that can be imagined, then all the inconveniences and evils which it has caused, taking care to bring together into a few pages what in reality was spread over a great many ages; then your history will be disgusting, hideous, and worthy of execration. Let a partisan of democracy describe to you in a narrow compass, and by means of historical facts, all the inconveniences and evils of monarchy, the vices and the crimes of kings; how will monarchy then appear to you? But let a partisan of monarchy paint to you, in his turn, by the same method of historical facts, democracy and demagogues; and what will you then think of democracy? Assemble in one picture all the evils occasioned to nations by a high degree of development of the social state; civilization and refinement will then appear detestable. By seeking and selecting in the annals of the human mind certain traits, the history of science may be made the history of folly, and even of crime. By heaping together the fatal accidents that have occurred to masters of the healing art, their beneficent profession may be represented as a career of homicide. In a word, every thing may be falsified by proceeding in this way. God himself would appear to us as a monster of cruelty and tyranny, if, taking away his goodness, wisdom, and justice, we only attended to the evils which we see in a world created by his power and governed by his providence.

Having laid down these principles, let us apply them. The spirit of the age, particular circumstances, and an order of things quite different from ours, are all forgotten, and the history of the religious intolerance of Catholics is composed by taking care to condense into a few pages, and paint in the blackest colours, the severity of Ferdinand and Isabella, of Philip II., of Mary of England, of Louis XIV., and every thing of the kind that occurred during three centuries. The reader who receives, almost at the same moment, the impression of events which occurred during a period of three hundred years,—the reader, accustomed to live in society where prisons are being converted into houses of recreation, and where the punishment of death is vigorously opposed, can he behold the appearance of darksome dungeons, the instruments of punishment, the *sanbenitos* and scaffolds, without being deeply moved? He will bewail the unfortunate lot of those who perish; he will be indignant against the authors of what he calls horrible atrocities. Nothing has been said to this candid reader of the principles and conduct of Protestants at the same time; he has not been reminded of the cruelty of Henry VIII. and of Elizabeth of England. Thus all his hatred is directed against Catholics, and he is accustomed to regard Catholicity as a religion of tyranny and blood. But will a judgment thus formed be just? Will this be a sentence passed with a full knowledge of the cause? What would impartiality direct us to do, if we met with a dark picture, painted in the way we have described, of monarchy, democracy, or civilization, of science, or of the healing art? What we should do, or rather what we ought to do, is to extend our view further, to examine the subject in its different phases; to inquire into its good as well as its evil: this would be to look upon these evils as they really are, that is, spread at great distances over the course of centuries; this would weaken the impression they had made upon us: in a word, we should thus be just, we should take the balance in hand to weigh the good and evil, to compare the one with the other, as we ought always to do when we have duly to appreciate things in the history of humanity. In the case in question, we should act in the same way, in order to provide against the error into which we may be led by the false statements and exaggerations of certain men, whose evident intention it has been to falsify facts by representing only one side of them. The Inquisition no longer exists, and assuredly there is no probability of its being re-established; the severe laws in force on this matter in former times no longer exist; they are either abrogated or they are fallen into desuetude: no one, therefore, has an interest in representing this institution in a false point of view. It may be imagined that some men had an interest in this while they were engaged in destroying their ancient laws, but that once attained, the Inquisition and its laws are become a historical fact, which ought to be examined here with attention and impartiality. We have here two questions, that of principle, and that of its application; in other words, that of intolerance, and that of the manner of showing it. We must not confound these two things, which, although very closely connected, are very different. I shall begin with the first.

The principle of universal toleration is now proclaimed, and all kind of intolerance is condemned without appeal. But who takes care to examine the real meaning of these words? who undertakes to analyze the ideas which they contain by the light of reason, and explain them by means of history and experience? Very few. They are pronounced mechanically; they are constantly employed to establish propositions of the highest importance, without even the suspicion that they contain ideas, the right or wrong comprehension and application of which is every thing for the preservation of society. Few persons consider that these words include questions as profound as they are delicate, and the whole of a large portion of history; very few observe that, according to one solution given to the problem of toleration, all the past is condemned, and all the present overturned; nothing is left thereby to build on for the future but a moving bed of sand. Certainly, the most convenient way in such a case is, to adopt and employ these words such as we already find them in circulation, in the same way as we take and circulate the current coin, without considering whether it be composed of alloy or not. But what is the most convenient is not always the most useful; and, as when receiving coins of value, we carefully examine them, so we ought to weigh words the meaning of which is of such paramount importance. Toleration—what is the meaning of this word? It means, properly speaking, the patience with which we suffer a thing which we judge to be bad, but which we think it desirable not to punish. Thus, some kinds of scandals are tolerated; prostitutes are tolerated; such and such abuses are tolerated; so that the idea of toleration is always accompanied by the idea of evil. When toleration is exercised in the order of ideas, it always supposes a misunderstanding, or error. No one will say that he tolerates the truth. We have an observation to make here. The phrase *to tolerate opinions* is commonly used: now, opinion is very different from error. At first sight, the difficulty appears great; but if we examine the thing well, we shall be able to explain it. When we say that we tolerate an opinion, we always mean an opinion contrary to our own. In this case, the opinion of another is, according to us, an error; for it is impossible to have an opinion on any point whatever—that is, to think that a thing is or is not, is in one way or in another—without thinking at the same time that those who judge otherwise are deceived. If our opinion is only an opinion—that is, if our judgment, although based on reasons which appear to us to be good, has not attained to a degree of complete certainty—our judgment of another will be only a mere opinion; but if our conviction has become completely established and confirmed—that is, if it has attained to certainty—we shall be sure that those who form a judgment opposed to ours are deceived. Thence it follows, that the word toleration, applied to opinions, always means the toleration of an error. He who says, yes, thinks no is false; and he who says, no, thinks yes is a mistake. This is only an application of the well-known principle, *that it is impossible for the same thing to be and not to be at the same time.* But, we shall be asked, What do you mean when you use these words, 'to respect opinions?' is it always understood that we respect errors? No; for these words can have two different and equally reasonable meanings. The first is founded on the feebleness of the conviction of the person from whom the respect comes. When on any particular point we have only just formed an opinion, it is understood that we have not reached certainty; consequently, we know that there are reasons on the other side. In this sense, we may well say that we respect the opinions of others: we express thereby our conviction that it is possible that we are deceived—that it is possible the truth is not on our side. In the second meaning, to respect opinions is to respect, sometimes those who profess them, sometimes their good faith, sometimes their intentions. Thus, when we say that we respect prejudices, it is clear that we do not mean a real respect professed in this place. We see thus, that the expression 'to respect the opinions of others' has a very different meaning, according as the person from whom the respect comes has or has not assured convictions in the contrary sense.

In order the better to understand what toleration is, what its origin and its effects, it is necessary, before we examine it in society, to reduce it to its simplest element. Let us analyze toleration considered in the individual. An individual is called tolerant, when he is habitually in a disposition of mind to bear without irritation or disturbance opinions contrary to his own. This toleration will bear different names, according to the different matters to which it relates. In religious matters, tolerance as well as intolerance may be found in those who have religion as well as in those who have none; so that neither of these situations, with respect to religion, necessarily implies the one or the other. Some people imagine that tolerance is peculiar to the incredulous, and intolerance to the religious; but they are mistaken. Who is more tolerant than St. Francis de Sales? who more intolerant than Voltaire?

Tolerance in religious men—that tolerance which does not come from want of faith, and which is not inconsistent with an ardent zeal for the preservation and propagation of the faith—is born of two principles, charity and humility. Charity, which makes us love all men, even our greatest enemies; charity, which inspires us with compassion for their faults and errors, and obliges us to regard them as brothers, to employ all the means in our power to withdraw them from being fatally deceived; charity, which forbids us ever to regard them as deprived of the hope of salvation as long as they live. Rousseau has said, that "it is impossible to live in peace with those that one believes to be damned." We do not, and we cannot, believe in the condemnation of any man as long as he lives; however great may be his iniquity, the mercy of God and the value of the blood of Jesus Christ are still greater. We are so far from thinking with the philosopher of Geneva, "that to love such people would be to hate God," that no one could maintain such a doctrine among us without ceasing to belong to our faith. The other source of tolerance is Christian humility: humility, which inspires us with a profound sense of our weakness, and makes us consider all that we have as given by God; humility, which makes us consider our advantages over our neighbor as so many more powerful motives for acknowledging the liberality of Providence; humility, which, placing before our eyes the spectacle of humanity in its proper light, makes us regard ourselves and all others as members of the great family of the human race, fallen from its ancient dignity by the sin of our first parent; humility, which shows us the perverse inclinations of our hearts, the darkness of our minds, and the claims which man has to pity and indulgence in his faults and errors; humility, that virtue sublime even in its abasement. "If humility is so pleasing to God," is the admirable observation of St. Theresa, "it is because it is the truth." This is the virtue which renders us indulgent towards all men, by never allowing us to forget that we ourselves, perhaps, more than any others, have need of indulgence.

Yet for a man to be tolerant, in the full extent of the word, it is not enough for him to be humble and charitable; this is a truth which experience teaches and reason explains to us. In order perfectly to clear up a point, the obscurity of which produces the confusion which almost always prevails in these questions, let us make a comparison between two men equally religious, whose principles are the same, but whose conduct is very different. Let us suppose two priests both distinguished for learning and eminent virtue. The one has passed his life in retirement, surrounded by pious persons, and having no intercourse with any but Catholics: the other has been a missionary in countries where different religions are established, he has been obliged to live and converse with men of creeds different from his own; he has been under the necessity of witnessing the establishment of temples of a false religion close to those of the true one. The principles of Christian charity will be the same with both these priests; both will look upon faith as a gift of God, which he has received, and must preserve; their conduct, however, will be very different, if they meet with a man of a faith different from their own, or of none at all. The first, who, never having had intercourse with any but the faithful, has always heard religion spoken of with respect, will be horrified, will be indignant, at the first word he shall hear against the faith or ceremonies of the Church; it will be impossible, or nearly so, for him to remain calm during a conversation or discussion on the question: the second, accustomed to such things, to hear his faith impugned, to dispute with men of creeds opposed to his own, will remain tranquil; he will engage in a discussion with coolness, if it be necessary; he will skilfully avoid one, if prudence shall advise such a course. Whence comes this difference? It is not difficult to discover. The second of these priests, by intercourse with men, by experience, by contradiction, has obtained a clear notion of the real condition of men's minds in the world; he is aware of the fatal combination of circumstances which has led a great number of unfortunate persons into error, and keeps them there; he knows how, in some measure, to put himself in their place; and the more lively is his sense of the benefit conferred upon him by Providence, the more mild and indulgent he is towards others. The other may be as virtuous, as charitable, and as humble as you please; but how can you expect of him that he will not be deeply moved, and give utterance to his indignation, the first time that he hears that denied which he has always believed with the most lively faith? He has up to this time met with no opposition in the world, but a few arguments in books. Certainly he was not ignorant that there existed heretics and unbelievers, but he has not frequently met with them, he has not heard them state their hundred different systems, and he has not witnessed the erroneous creeds of men of all sorts, of different characters, and the most varied minds; the lively susceptibility of his mind, which has never met with resistance, has not been blunted; for this reason, although endowed with the same virtues, and, if you will, with the same knowledge as the other, he has not acquired that penetration, that vivacity, so to speak, with which a man of practised intellect enters into the minds of those with whom he has to deal, discerns the reasons, seizes the motives which blind them and hinder them from obtaining a knowledge of the truth.

Thus tolerance, in a person who is religious, supposes a certain degree of gentleness of mind, the fruit of intercourse with men, and the habits thereby engendered; yet this quality is consistent with the deepest conviction, and the purest and most ardent zeal for the propagation of the truth. In the moral, as in the physical world, friction polishes, use wears away, and nothing can remain for a long time in an attitude of violence. A man will be indignant, once, twice, a hundred times, when he hears his manner of thinking attacked; but it is impossible for him to remain so always; he will, in the end, become accustomed to opposition; he will, by habit, bear it calmly. However sacred may be his articles of belief, he will content himself with defending and putting them forward at convenient opportunities; in all other cases, he will keep them in the bottom of his soul, as a treasure which he is desirous to preserve from any thing that may injure them. Tolerance, then, does not suppose any new principles in a man, but rather a quality acquired by practice; a disposition of mind, into which a man finds himself insensibly led; a habit of patience, formed in him by constantly having to bear with what he disapproves of.

Now, if we consider tolerance in men who are not religious, we shall observe that there are two ways of being irreligious. There are men who not only have no religion, but who have an animosity against it, either on account of some fatal error they entertain, or because they find it an obstacle to their designs. These men are extremely intolerant; and their intolerance is the worst of all, because it is not accompanied by any moral principle which can restrain it. A man thus circumstanced feels himself, as it were, continually at war with himself and the human race; with himself, because he must stifle the cries of his own conscience: with the human race, because all protest against the mad doctrine that pretends to banish the worship of God from the earth. Therefore we find among men of this kind much rancor and spleen; therefore their words are full of gall; therefore they have constantly recourse to raillery, insult, and calumny.

But there is another class of men who, although devoid of religion, are not strongly prejudiced against the faith. They live in a kind of skepticism, into which the reading of bad books, or the observations of a superficial and frivolous philosophy, have led them; they are not attached to religion, but they are not its enemies. Many of them acknowledge the importance of religion for the good of society, and some of them even feel within themselves a certain desire to return to the faith; in their moments of recollection and meditation, they remember with pleasure the days when they offered to God an obedient spirit and a pure heart; and at the sight of the rapid course of life, they perhaps love to cherish the hope of becoming reconciled with the God of their fathers, before they descend into the grave. These men are tolerant; but, if carefully examined, their tolerance is not a principle or a virtue, it is only a necessity resulting from their position. It is difficult to be indignant at the opinions of others, when we have none of our own—when, consequently, we do not come into collision with any. It is difficult to be violently opposed to religion, when we consider it as a thing necessary for the welfare of society; there can be no hatred or rancor towards faith in a soul which desires its mercy, and which, perhaps, fixes its eyes upon it as the last beam of hope amid the terrors of an alarming future. Tolerance, in this case, is nothing strange; it is natural and necessary. Intolerance would be inconceivable and extravagant, and could arise only from a bad heart.

In applying these remarks to society instead of individuals, it must be observed that tolerance, as well as intolerance, may be considered in government, or in society. It sometimes happens that government and society are not agreed; while the former maintains one principle, the reverse may prevail in the latter. As governments are composed of a limited number of individuals, all that has been said of tolerance, considered individually, may be applied to them. Let us not forget, however, that men placed in authority are not free to give themselves up without limit to the impulses of their own opinions or feelings; they are often forced to immolate their own feelings on the altar of public opinion. They may, owing to peculiar circumstances, oppose or impede that opinion for a time; but it will soon stop them, and force them to change their course.

As sooner or later government becomes the expression of the ideas and feelings of society, we shall content ourselves with considering tolerance in the latter; we shall observe that society, with respect to tolerance, follows the same path as individuals. This is with it not the effect of a principle, but of a habit Men of different creeds, who live together for a long time in the same society, end by tolerating each other; they are led to this by growing weary of collision with each other, and by the wish for a kind of life more quiet and peaceful But when men, thus divided in creed, find themselves face to face for the first time, a shock more or less rude is the inevitable result. The causes of this phenomenon are to be found in human nature itself; it is one of those necessities against which we struggle in vain.

Some modern philosophers have imagined that society is indebted to them for the spirit of toleration which prevails there; they have not seen that it is much rather a fact slowly brought about by the force of circumstances, than it is the fruit of their doctrines. Indeed, what have they said that is new? They have recommended universal fraternity; but this has always been one of the doctrines of Christianity. They have exhorted men of all the different religions to live in peace together; but before they had opened their mouths to tell them this, men began to adopt this course in many countries of Europe; for, unhappily, religions in many countries were so numerous and different, that none of them could pretend to exclusive dominion. It is true that some infidel philosophers have a claim, and a deplorable one, in support of their pretensions with respect to the development of toleration; it is, that, by their efforts to disseminate infidelity and skepticism, they have succeeded in making general, in nations and governments, that false toleration which has nothing virtuous, but is indifference with respect to all religions. Indeed, why is tolerance so general in our age? or, rather, in what does our tolerance consist? If you observe well, you will find that it is nothing but the result of a social condition perfectly similar to that of the individual who has no creed, but who does not hate creeds, because he considers them as conducive to the public good, and cherishes a vague hope of one day finding a last asylum therein. All that is good in this is in no degree owing to the infidel philosophers, but may rather be said to be a protest against them. Indeed, when they could not obtain the supreme command, they lavished calumnies and sarcasms on all that is most sacred in heaven and on earth; and, when they did raise themselves to power, they overturned with indescribable fury all that existed, and destroyed millions of victims in exile or on the scaffolds. The multitude of religions,—infidelity, indifference, the improvement of manners, the lassitude produced by wars,—industrial and commercial organization, which every day becomes more powerful in society,—communication rendered more frequent among men by means of travelling,—the diffusion of ideas by the press;—such are the causes which have produced in Europe that universal tolerance which has taken possession of all, and has been established in fact when it could not by law. These causes, as it is easy to observe, are of different kinds; no doctrine can pretend to an exclusive influence; they are the result of a thousand different influences, which act simultaneously on the development of civilization. (24)

CHAPTER XXXV.

ON THE RIGHT OF COERCION IN GENERAL.

How much, during the last century, was said against intolerance! A philosophy less superficial than that which then prevailed would have reflected a little more on a fact which may be appreciated in different ways, but the existence of which cannot be denied. In Greece, Socrates died drinking hemlock. Rome, whose tolerance has been so much vaunted, tolerated, indeed, foreign gods; but these were only foreign in name, since they formed a part of that system of pantheism which was the foundation of the Roman religion; gods, who, in order to be declared gods of Rome, only needed the mere formality, as it were, of receiving the name of citizens. But Rome did not admit the gods of Egypt any more than the Jewish or Christian religion. She had, no doubt, many false ideas with respect to these religions; but she was sufficiently acquainted with them to know that they were essentially different from her own. The history of the Pagan emperors is the history of the persecution of the Church; as soon as they became Christians, a system of penal legislation was commenced against those who differed from the religion of the state. In subsequent centuries, intolerance continued under various forms; it has been perpetuated down to our times, and we are not so free from it as some would wish to make us believe. The emancipation of Catholics in England is but of recent date; the violent disputes of the Prussian government with the Pope, on the subject of certain arbitrary acts of that government against the Catholic religion, are of yesterday; the question of Argau, in Switzerland, is still pending; and the persecution of Catholicity by the Russian government is pursued in as scandalous a manner as at any former period. Thus it is with religious sects. As to the toleration of the *humane* philosophers of the 18th century, it was exemplified in Robespierre.

Every government professing a religion is more or less intolerant towards those which it does not profess; and this intolerance is diminished or destroyed, only when the professors of the obnoxious religions are either feared on account of their great power, or despised on account of their weakness. Apply to all times and countries the rule which we have just laid down, you will everywhere find it exact; it is an abridgment of the history of governments in their relations with religions. The Protestant government of England has always been intolerant toward Catholics; and it will continue to be so, more or less, according to circumstances. The governments of Russia and Prussia will continue to act as they have done up to this time, with the exception of modifications required by difference of times; in the same way, in countries where Catholicity prevails, the exercise of the Protestant worship will always be more or less interfered with. I shall be told of the instance of France as a proof of the contrary; in that country, where the immense majority profess the Catholic religion, other worships are allowed, without any disposition on the part of the state to disturb them. This toleration will perhaps be attributed to public opinion; it comes, I think, from this, that no fixed principle prevails there in the government: all the policy of France, internal and external, is a constant compromise to get out of difficulties in the best possible way. This is shown by facts; it appears from the well-known opinions of the small number of men who, for some years, have ruled the destinies of France. It has been attempted to establish in principle universal toleration, and refuse to government the right of violating consciences in religious matters; nevertheless, in spite of all that has been said, philosophers have not been able to make a very clear exposition of their principle, still less have they been able to procure its general adoption as a system in the government of states. In order to show that the thing is not quite so simple as has been supposed, I will beg leave to ask a few questions of these *soi-disant* philosophers. If a religion which required human sacrifices were established in your country, would you tolerate it? No. And why? Because we cannot tolerate such a crime. But then you will be intolerant; you will violate the consciences of others, by proscribing, as a crime, what in their eyes is a homage to the Divinity. Thus thought many nations of old, and so think some now. By what right do you make your conscience prevail over theirs?—It matters not; we shall be intolerant, but our intolerance will be for the good of humanity.—I applaud your conduct; but you cannot deny that it is a case in which intolerance with respect to a religion appears to you a right and a duty. Still further: if you proscribe the exercise of this atrocious worship, would you allow the doctrine to be taught which preaches as holy and salutary the practice of human sacrifices? No; for that would be permitting the teaching of murder. Very well, but you must acknowledge that this is a doctrine with respect to which you have a right to be, and are obliged to be, intolerant. Let us pursue our subject. You are aware, no doubt, of the sacrifices offered in antiquity to the goddess of Love, and the infamous worship which was paid to her in the temples of Babylon and Corinth. If such a worship reappeared among you, would you tolerate it? No; for it is contrary to the sacred laws of modesty. Would you allow the doctrine on which it was based to be taught? No; for the same reason. This, then, is another case in which you believe you have the right and the obligation to violate the consciences of others; and the only reason you can assign for it is, that you are compelled to do so by your own conscience. Moreover, suppose that some men, over-excited by reading the Bible, desired to establish a new Christianity, in imitation of Mathew of Haarlem or John of Leyden; suppose that these sectaries began to propagate their doctrines, to assemble together in bodies, and that their fanatical declamation seduced a portion of the people, would you tolerate this new religion? No; for these men might renew the bloody scenes of Germany in the 16th century, when, in the name of God, and to fulfil, as they said, the order of the Most High, the Anabaptists invaded all property, destroyed all existing power, and spread everywhere desolation and death. This would be to act with as much justice as prudence; but you cannot deny that you would thereby commit an act of intolerance. What, then, becomes of universal toleration, that principle so evident, so predominant, if you are compelled at every step to limit, and I will say more, to lay it aside, and act in a way diametrically opposite to it? You will say that the security of the state, the good order of society, and public morality compel you to act in this way. But then, what sort of a principle is it that, in certain cases, is in opposition to the interests of morality and to society, and to the safety of the state? Do you think that the men against whom you declaim did not intend also to protect these interests, by acting with that intolerance which is so revolting to you?

It has been acknowledged at all times and in all countries, as an incontestable principle, that the public authority has, in certain cases, the right of prohibiting certain acts, in violation of the consciences of individuals who claim the right of performing them. If the constant testimony of history were not enough, at least the dialogue which we have just held ought to convince us of this truth; we have seen that the most ardent advocates of tolerance may well be compelled, in certain cases, to be intolerant. They would be obliged to be so in the name of humanity, of modesty, of public order; universal toleration, then, with respect to doctrines and religions—that toleration which is proclaimed as the duty of every government—is an error; it is a theory which cannot be put in practice. We have clearly shown that intolerance has always been, and still is, a principle recognised by all governments, and the application of which, more or less indulgent or severe, depends on circumstances, and above all, on the particular point of view in which the government considers things.

A great question of right now presents itself—a question which seems, at first sight, to require to be solved by condemning all intolerance, both with respect to doctrines and acts; but which, when thoroughly examined, leads to a very different result. If we grant that the mind is incapable of completely removing the difficulty by means of direct reasoning, it is not the less certain that indirect means, and the reasoning called *ad absurdum*, are here sufficient to show us the truth, at least as far as it is necessary for us to know it as a guide for human prudence, always uncertain. The question is this: "By what right do you hinder a man from professing a doctrine, and acting in conformity with it, if he is convinced that it is true, and that he only fulfils his duty, or exercises a right, by acting as it prescribes?" In order to prevent the prohibition being vain and ridiculous, there must be a penalty attached to it; now, if you inflict this penalty, you punish a man who, according to his own conscience, is innocent. Punishment by the hand of justice supposes culpability; and no one is culpable without being so first in his conscience. Culpability has its root in the conscience; and we cannot be responsible for the violation of a law, unless that law has addressed us through our conscience. If our conscience tells us that an action is bad, we cannot perform it, whatever may be the injunctions of the law which prescribes it; on the contrary, if conscience tells us that an action is a duty, we cannot omit it, whatever may be the prohibitions of the law. This is, in a few words, and in all its force, the whole argument that can be alleged against intolerance in regard to doctrines and facts emanating from them. Let us now see what is the real value of these observations, apparently so conclusive.

It is apparent that the admission of this principle would render impossible the punishment of any political crime. Brutus, when plunging his dagger into the heart of Cæsar; Jacques Clement, when he assassinated Henry III., acted, no doubt, under the influence of an excitement of mind, which made them view their attempts as deeds of heroism; and yet, if they had both been brought before a tribunal, would you have thought them entitled to impunity—the one on account of his love of country, and the other on account of his zeal for religion? Most political crimes are committed under a conviction of doing well; and I do not speak merely of those times of trouble, when men of parties the most opposed are fully persuaded that they have right on their side. Conspiracies contrived against governments in times of peace are generally the work of some individuals who look upon them as illegal and tyrannical; when working to overthrow them, they are acting in conformity with their own principles. Judges punish them justly when they inflict on them the penalties appointed by legislators; and yet, neither legislators when they decree the penalty, nor the judges when they inflict it, are, or can be, ignorant of the condition of mind of the delinquent who has violated the law. It may be said, that compassion and indulgence with respect to political crimes increase every day, for these reasons. I shall reply, that if we lay down the principle that human justice has not the right to punish, when the delinquent acts according to his conviction, we must not only mitigate our punishments, but even abolish them. In this case, capital punishment would be a real murder, a fine a robbery, and other penalties so many acts of violence. I shall remark in passing, that it is not true that severity towards political crimes diminishes as much as it is said to do; the history of Europe of late years affords us some proofs to the contrary. We do not now see those cruel punishments which were in use at other times; but that is not owing to the conscience of the criminal being considered by the judge, but to the improvement of manners, which, being everywhere diffused, has necessarily influenced penal legislation. It is extraordinary that so much severity has been preserved in laws relating to political crimes, when so great a number of legislators among the different nations of Europe knew well that they themselves, at other times, had committed the same crimes. And there is no doubt that more than one man, in the discussion of certain penal laws, has inclined to indulgence, from the presentiment that these very laws might one day apply to himself. The impunity of political crimes would bring about the subversion of social order, by rendering all government impossible. Without dwelling longer on the fatal results which this doctrine would have, let us observe, that the benefit of impunity in favor of the illusions of conscience would not be due to political crimes alone, but would be applicable also to those of an ordinary kind. Offences against property are crimes of this nature; and yet we know that many at former periods regarded, and that unfortunately some still regard, property as a usurpation and an injustice. Offences against the sanctity of marriage are ordinarily considered crimes; and yet have there not been sects in whose sight marriage was unlawful, and others who have desired, and still desire, a community of women? The sacred laws of modesty and respect for innocence have alike been regarded by some sects as an unjust infringement of the liberty of man; to violate these laws, therefore, was a meritorious action. At the time when the mistaken ideas and blind fanaticism of the men who professed these principles were undoubted, would any one have been found to deny the justice of the chastisement which was inflicted on them when, in pursuance of their doctrines, they committed a crime, or even when they had the audacity to diffuse their fatal maxims in society?

If it were unjust to punish the criminal for acting according to his conscience, all imaginable crimes would be permitted to the atheist, the fatalist, the disciple of the doctrine of private interest; for by destroying, as they do, the basis of all morality, these men do not act against their consciences; they have none. If such an argument were to hold good, how often would we have reason to charge tribunals with injustice, when they inflict any punishment on men of this class. By what right, we would say to magistrates, do you punish this man, who, not admitting the existence of God, does not acknowledge himself culpable in his own eyes, or consequently in yours? You have made a law, by virtue of which you punish him; but this law has no power over the conscience of this man, for you are his equals; and he does not acknowledge the existence of any superior, to give you the power of controlling his liberty. By what right do you punish another, who is convinced that all his actions are the effect of necessary causes, that free-will is a chimera, and who, in the action which you charge on him as a crime, believes that he had no more power of restraining himself than the wild beast, when he throws himself upon the prey before his eyes, or upon any other animal that excites his fury? With what justice do you punish him, who is persuaded that all morality is a lie; that there is no other principle than individual interest; that good and evil are nothing but this interest, well or ill understood? If you make him undergo any punishment, it will not be because he is culpable in his own conscience; you will punish him for being deceived in his calculation, for having ill-understood the probable result of the action which he was about to commit. Such are the necessary and inevitable deductions from the doctrine, which refuses to the public authority the power of punishing crimes committed in consequence of an error of the mind.

But I shall be told that the right of punishment only extends to actions, and not to doctrines; that actions ought to be subject to the law, but that doctrines are entitled to unbounded liberty. Do you mean doctrines shut up in the mind and not outwardly manifested? It is clear that not only the right, but also the possibility of punishing them is wanting, for God alone can tell the secrets of the heart of man. If avowed doctrines are meant, then the principle is false; and we have just shown that those who maintain it in theory, find it impossible to reduce it to practice. In fine, we shall be told that, however absurd in its results may be the doctrine which we have been combating, it is still impossible to justify the punishment of an action which was ordered or authorized by the conscience of the man who committed it. How is this difficulty to be solved? How is this great obstacle to be removed? Is it lawful in any case to treat as culpable the man who is not so at the tribunal of his own conscience?

Although this question seems entirely to turn upon some point on which men of all opinions are agreed, there is nevertheless a wide difference in this respect between Catholics on one side and unbelievers and Protestants on the other. The first lay it down as an incontestable principle, *that there are errors of the understanding which are faults;* the others, on the contrary, think, *that all errors of the understanding are innocent.* The first consider error in regard to great moral and religious truths, as one of the gravest offences which man can commit against God; their opponents look upon errors of this kind with great indulgence, and they ought to do so in order to be consistent. Catholics admit the possibility of invincible ignorance with respect to some very important truths; but with them this possibility is limited to certain circumstances, out of which they declare man to be culpable: their opponents constantly extol liberty of thought, without any other restriction than that imposed by the taste of each one in particular; they constantly affirm that man is free to hold the opinions which he thinks proper; they have gone so far as to persuade their followers that there are no culpable errors or opinions, that man is not obliged to search into the secret recesses of his soul, to make sure that there are no secret causes which induce him to reject the truth; they have in the end monstrously confounded physical with moral liberty of thought; they have banished from opinions the ideas of lawful and unlawful, and have given men to understand that such ideas are not applicable to thought. That is to say, in the order of ideas, they have confounded right with fact, declaring, in this respect, the uselessness and incompetency of all laws, divine and human. Senseless men! as if it were possible for that which is most noble and elevated in human nature to be exempt from all rule; as if it were possible for the element which makes man the king of the creation, to be exempted from concurring in the ineffable harmony of all parts of the universe with themselves and with God; as if this harmony could exist, or even be conceived in man, unless it were declared to be the first of human obligations to adhere constantly to truth.

This is one of the profound reasons which justify the Catholic Church, when she considers the sin of heresy as one of the greatest that man can commit. You, who smile, with pity and contempt at these words, *the sin of heresy;* you, who consider this doctrine as the invention of priests to rule over consciences, by retrenching the liberty of thought; by what right do you claim the power of condemning heresies which are opposed to your orthodoxy? By what right do you condemn those societies that profess opinions hostile to property, public order, and the existence of authority? If the thought of man is free, if you cannot attempt to restrain it without violating sacred rights, if it is an absurdity and a contradiction to wish to oblige a man to act against his conscience, or disobey its dictates—why do you interfere with those men who desire to destroy the existing state of society? Why baffle, why oppose those dark conspiracies, which, from time to time, send one of their members to assassinate a king? You invoke your convictions to declare unjust and cruel the intolerance which has been practised at certain times against your enemies; but you must remember that such societies and such men can also invoke their convictions. You say that the doctrines of the Church are human inventions; they say that the doctrines prevailing in society are also human inventions. You say that the ancient social order was a monopoly; they say the present social order is a monopoly. In your eyes, the ancient authorities were tyrannical; in theirs the present ones are so. You pretended to destroy what existed, in order to found new institutions conducive to the good of humanity; to-day these men hold the same language. You have proclaimed holy the war which was waged against ancient power; they proclaim holy the war against present power. When you availed yourselves of the means which offered themselves, you pretended that necessity rendered them legitimate; they declare to be not less legitimate the only means which they possess, that of combinations, of preparing for their opportunity, and of hastening it by assassinating great men. You have pretended to make all opinions respected, even atheism, and you have taught that nobody has a right to prevent your acting in conformity with your principles; but the fanatics in question have also their horrible principles and their dreadful convictions. Do you require a proof of this? See them amid the gayety of public celebrations, glide, pale and gloomy, among the joyful multitude, choose the fitting moment to cast desolation over a royal family, and cover a nation with mourning, while they accumulate on their own heads the public execration, certain, moreover, of finishing their lives on the scaffold. But our adversaries will say, such convictions are inexcusable. Yours are so also. All the difference is, that you have contrived your ambitious and fatal systems amid ease and pleasure, perhaps in opulence, and under the shadow of power, while they have conceived their abominable doctrines in the bosom of obscurity, poverty, misery, and despair.

Indeed, the inconsistency of some men is shocking to the last degree. To ridicule all religions, to decry the spirituality and immortality of the soul, and the existence of God, to overturn all morality, and sap its deepest foundations, all this they have considered excusable, and we may even say, worthy of praise; moreover, the writers who have undertaken this fatal task are worthy of apotheosis; men must expel the Divinity from his temples to place there the names and busts of the leaders of their schools; under the vaults of splendid basilicas, where repose the ashes of Christians awaiting the resurrection, they must raise the mausoleum of Voltaire and Rousseau, in order that future generations, when they descend into their dark and silent abodes, may receive the inspirations of their genius. But have they, then, a right to complain that property, and domestic life, and social order are attacked? Property is sacred; but is it more sacred than God? However great may be the importance of the truths relating to the family and to society, are they of a superior order to the eternal principles of morality, or rather, are they any thing more than the application of these principles?

But let us resume the thread of our discourse. When the principle, that there are culpable errors, is once established (a principle which in practice, if not in theory, must be received by all men, but which Catholicity alone can logically maintain in theory), it is easy to see the reason of the punishments which human power decrees against the propagation and teaching of certain doctrines; and we can understand why it is legitimate to punish, without considering the conviction that animated the culprit, the actions which are the result of his doctrines. The law shows that this mortal error has existed, or can exist; but in this case it declares the error itself to be culpable; and if man adduces the testimony of his own conscience, the law reminds him that it is his duty to rectify his conscience. Such is, in truth, the foundation of a legislation which has appeared so unjust; a foundation which it is necessary to point out, in order to vindicate a great many human laws from a deep disgrace; for it would be a great disgrace to claim the right of punishing a man who was really innocent. Such an absurd right is so far from belonging to human justice, that it does not belong even to God. The infinite justice of God would cease to be what it is, if it could punish the innocent.

Perhaps another origin will be assigned for the right which governments possess, of punishing the propagation of certain doctrines and the actions committed in consequence of them, when the criminal has acted from the deepest conviction. "Governments," it may be said, "act in the name of society, which, like every being, possesses the right of self-defence. There are certain doctrines which menace its existence; it has, therefore, of necessity and right, the power of resisting those who promulgate them." Such a reason, however plausible it may appear, is liable to this grave objection, that it destroys at one blow the idea of punishment and justice. To wound an aggressor in self-defence is not to chastise but to resist him. If we consider society in this point of view, the criminal led to punishment will no longer be a real criminal, but the unfortunate victim of a rash and unequal struggle. The voice of the judge condemning him will no longer be the august voice of justice; his sentence will only be the act of society avenging the attack made upon it. The word punishment will then assume quite a different meaning; the gradations of it will depend entirely upon calculations, and not on justice. We must remember this; if we suppose that society, by virtue of the right of self-defence, inflicts a punishment upon the man whom it considers quite innocent, it no longer judges or condemns, but fights and struggles. That which is perfectly suitable with respect to the relations between one society and another, is in no way suitable to society in its relations with individuals. It then appears like a combat between a giant and a pigmy. The giant takes the pigmy in his hand, and crushes him against a stone.

The doctrine which I have just explained evidently shows the value of the much vaunted principle of universal toleration; it has been demonstrated that that principle is as impracticable in fact as it is unsustainable in theory; consequently all the accusations made against the Catholic Church on the subject of intolerance are overturned. It has been clearly shown that intolerance is in some measure the right of all public power; this has always been acknowledged; it is acknowledged still, generally speaking, when philosophers, the partisans of tolerance, attain to power. No doubt, governments have a thousand times abused this principle; no doubt, more than once the truth has been persecuted in virtue of it; but what do men not abuse? Their duty, then, as good philosophers, was not to establish principles that cannot be sustained, and are extremely dangerous; not to declaim to satiety against the times and institutions which have preceded us; but to endeavor to propagate sentiments of mildness and indulgence, and, above all, not to impugn important truths, without which society cannot be sustained, and which cannot be destroyed without abandoning the world to the empire of force, and, consequently, to despotism and tyranny.

Men have attacked dogmas; but they have not been willing to see that morality was intimately connected with dogmas, and that it was itself a dogma. By proclaiming unbounded liberty of thought, they have asserted the impeccability of the mind; error has ceased to figure among the faults of which men can be guilty. They have forgotten that, in order to *will*, it was necessary to *know;* and that to *will rightly*, it was necessary to *know truly*. If we examine the greater part of the errors of our hearts, we shall see that they have their source in a misunderstanding; is it possible, then, that it should not be the duty of man to preserve his mind from error? But since it has been said that opinions are of little importance, that man is free to choose such as please him, even in matters of religion and morality, truth has lost its value; its intrinsic worth is no longer what it was in the eyes of man; and too many consider themselves exempt from attempting to attain it,—a deplorable condition of mind, which is one of the greatest evils afflicting society. (25)

CHAPTER XXXVI.

ON THE INQUISITION IN SPAIN.

I FIND myself naturally led to make a few observations on the intolerance of certain Catholic princes, on the Inquisition, and in particular on that of Spain. I must make a rapid examination of the charges against Catholicity on account of its conduct during the last centuries. The dungeons, the burnings of the Inquisition, and the intolerance of some Catholic princes, have furnished the enemies of the Church with one of their most effective arguments in depreciating her, and rendering her the object of odium and hatred; and it must be allowed that they have, in attacks of this kind, many advantages, which give them good prospects of success. Indeed (as we have said above, for the generality of readers, who, without undertaking to examine things to the bottom, *naïvely* allow themselves to be led away by a subtle writer; as we have said, for all those who have sensitive hearts, and are prompt to pity the unfortunate), what is more likely to excite indignation than the exhibition of dark dungeons, instruments of torture, *san-benitos*, and burnings? Imagine what effect must be produced, amid our toleration, our gentle manners, our humane penal codes, by the sudden exhibition of the severities, the cruelties of another age; the whole exaggerated and grouped into one picture, where are shown all the melancholy scenes which occurred in different places, and were spread over a long period of time. They take care to remind us that all this was done in the name of the God of peace and love; thereby the contrast is rendered more vivid, the imagination is excited, the heart becomes indignant; and the result is, that the clergy, magistrates, kings, and popes of those remote times, appear like a troop of executioners, whose pleasure consists in tormenting and desolating the human race. Writers, who have ventured to act in this way, have certainly not added to their reputation for delicacy of conscience. There is a rule which orators and writers ought never to forget, viz. that it is not allowable to excite the passions, until they have convinced the reason, unless it had been convinced before. Besides, there is a degree of bad faith in appealing to the feelings with respect to matters which ought to be examined by the light of reason alone, if they are to be examined properly. In such a case we ought not to begin by moving, but by convincing; to do otherwise is to deceive the reader.

I am not going to write the history of the Inquisition, or of the different systems which various countries have adopted with respect to religious intolerance; this would be impossible within my narrow limits; besides, it would lead me away from the object of my work. Ought we to draw from the Inquisition in general, that of Spain in particular, or from the greater or less intolerance of the legislation of some countries, an accusation against Catholicity? Can it, in this respect, be put in comparison with Protestantism? Such are the questions I have to examine.

Three things at first present themselves to the eyes of the observer: 1st, the legislation and institutions proceeding from the principle of intolerance; 2d, the use which has been made of this legislation and these institutions; 3d, the intolerant acts which have been committed illegally. With respect to the latter, I must say at once that they have nothing to do with the question. The Massacre of St. Bartholomew, and other atrocities committed in the name of religion, ought not to trouble the apologists of religion: to render her responsible for all that has been done in her name, would be to act with manifest injustice. Man is endowed with so strong and lively a sense of the excellence of virtue, that he endeavors to cover the greatest crimes with her mantle;—would it be reasonable to banish virtue from the earth on that account? There are, in the history of mankind, terrible periods, where a fatal giddiness seizes upon the mind; rage, inflamed by disorder, blinds the intellect and changes the heart; evil is called good, and good evil; the most horrible attempts are made under the most respectable names. Historians and philosophers, in treating of such periods, should know what ought to be their line of conduct; strictly accurate in the narration of such facts, they ought to beware of drawing from them a judgment as to the prevailing ideas and institutions. Society then resembles a man in a state of delirium; we should ill judge of the ideas, character, and conduct of such a man, from what he says and does in that deplorable condition. What party, in those calamitous times, can boast of not having committed great crimes? If we fix our eyes on the period just mentioned, do we not see the leaders of both parties assassinated by treason? Admiral Coligny died by the hands of the assassins who began the massacre of St. Bartholomew; but the Duke of Guise had been also assassinated by Poltrot, before Orleans. Henry III. was assassinated by Jacques Clement; but this same Henry III. had treacherously murdered the other Duke of Guise in the corridors of his palace, and his brother, the Cardinal, in the tower of Moulins; this same Henry III. had taken part in the massacre of St. Bartholomew. We see atrocities committed by the Catholics; but did not their opponents also commit them? Let us throw a veil over these catastrophes, over these afflicting proofs of the misery and perversity of the human heart. The tribunal of the Inquisition, considered in itself, is only the application to a particular case of that doctrine of intolerance, which, to a greater or less degree, is that of every existing power. Thus, we have only to examine the character of that particular application, and see whether its enemies are correct in their charges against it. In the first place, we must observe that those who extol antiquity, sadly falsify history, if they pretend that intolerance only appeared after the time when, according to them, the Church had degenerated from her primitive purity. As for myself, I see that from the earliest times, when the Church began to exert political influence, heresy began to figure in the codes as a crime; and I have never been able to discover a period of complete tolerance. I must here make an important remark, which shows one of the causes of the rigor displayed in later centuries. The Inquisition was first directed against the Manichean heretics; that is, against the sectaries who at all times were treated with the greatest severity. In the 11th century, when the punishment of fire had not yet been applied to the crime of heresy, the Manicheans were excepted from this rule. Even in the time of the Pagan emperors, these sectaries were treated with extreme rigor. In the year 296, we see Diocletian and Maximilian, by an edict, condemning to different punishments the Manicheans who had not abjured their dogmas, and consigning their leaders to the fire. These sectaries have always been considered as great criminals; and to punish them has always been judged necessary, not only for the interests of religion, but even for the morals and good order of society. This was one of the causes of the rigor of the Inquisition at its commencement: if we add to this, the turbulent character of the sects which, under various names, arose in the 11th, 12th, and 13th centuries, we shall have two of the causes that contributed to produce those scenes which now we can scarcely credit. In studying the history of those centuries, and fixing our attention on the troubles and disasters which ravaged the south of France, we clearly see that it was not a dispute as to a particular dogma, but that the whole social system was compromised. The sectaries of those times were precursors of those of the 16th century; with this difference, that the latter, if we except the frantic Anabaptists, were less democratic, less apt to address the multitude. Amid the cruelties of those times, when long ages of violence and revolution had given an excessive preponderance to brute force, what could be expected from governments incessantly menaced with such imminent danger? It is clear that the laws, and their application, must savour of the times.

As to the Spanish Inquisition, which was only an extension of that which was established in other countries, we must divide it, with respect to its duration, into three great periods;—we omit the time of its existence in the kingdom of Aragon, before its introduction into Castille. The first of these comprehends the time when the Inquisition was principally directed against the relapsed Jews and Moors, from the day of its installation under the Catholic sovereigns, till the middle of the reign of Charles V. The second extends from the time when it began to concentrate its efforts to prevent the introduction of Protestantism into Spain, until that danger entirely ceased; that is, from the middle of the reign of Charles V. till the coming of the Bourbons. The third and last period is that when the Inquisition was limited to repress infamous crimes, and exclude the philosophy of Voltaire; this period was continued until its abolition in the beginning of the present century. It is clear that, the institution being successively modified according to circumstances at these different epochs,—although it always remained fundamentally the same,—the commencement and termination of each of these three periods which we have pointed out cannot be precisely marked; nevertheless, these three periods really existed in its history, and present us with very different characters.

Every one knows the peculiar circumstances in which the Inquisition was established in the time of the Catholic sovereigns; yet it is worthy of remark, that the Bull of establishment was solicited by Queen Isabella; that is, by one of the most distinguished sovereigns in our history,—by that queen who still, after three centuries, preserves the respect and admiration of all Spaniards. Isabella, far from opposing the will of the people in this measure, only realized the national wish. The Inquisition was established chiefly against the Jews; the Papal Bull had been sent in 1478; now, before the Inquisition published its first edict, dated Seville, in 1481, the Cortes of Toledo, in 1480, had adopted severe measures on the subject. To prevent the injury which the intercourse between Jews and Christians might occasion to the Catholic faith, the Cortes had ordered that unbaptized Israelites should be obliged to wear a distinctive mark, dwell in separate quarters, called *Juiveries*, and return there before night. Ancient regulations against them were renewed; the professions of doctor, surgeon, shopkeeper, barber, and tavern-keeper, were forbidden them. Intolerance was, therefore, popular at that time. If the Inquisition be justified in the eyes of friends to monarchy, by conformity with the will of kings, it has an equal claim to be so in the eyes of lovers of democracy.

No doubt the heart is grieved at reading the excessive severities exercised at that time against the Jews; but must there not have been very grave causes to provoke such excesses? The danger which the Spanish monarchy, not yet well established, would have incurred if the Jews, then very powerful on account of their riches and their alliances with the most influential families, had been allowed to act without restraint, has been pointed out as one of the most important of these causes. It was greatly to be feared that they would league with the Moors against the Christians. The respective positions of the three nations rendered this league natural: this is the reason why it was looked upon as necessary to break a power which was capable of compromising anew the independence of the Christians. It is necessary also to observe, that at the time when the Inquisition was established, the war of eight hundred years against the Moors was not yet finished. The Inquisition was projected before 1474; it was established in 1480, and the conquest of Granada did not take place till 1492. Thus it was founded at the time when the obstinate struggle was about to be decided; it was yet to be known whether the Christians would remain masters of the whole peninsula, or whether the Moors should retain possession of one of the most fertile and beautiful provinces; whether these enemies, shut up in Granada, should preserve a position, excellent for their communication with Africa, and a means for all the attempts which, at a later period, the Crescent might be disposed to make against us. Now, the power of the Crescent was very great, as was clearly shown by its enterprises against the rest of Europe in the next century. In such emergencies, after ages of fighting, and at the moment which was to decide the victory for ever, have combatants ever been known to conduct themselves with moderation and mildness? It cannot be denied that the system of repression pursued in Spain, with respect to the Jews and the Moors, was inspired, in great measure, by the instinct of self-preservation: we can easily believe that the Catholic princes had this motive before them when they decided on asking for the establishment of the Inquisition in their dominions. The danger was not imaginary: it was perfectly real. In order to form an idea of the turn which things might have taken if some precaution had not been adopted, it is enough to recollect the insurrections of the last Moors in later times.

Yet it would be wrong, in this affair, to attribute all to the policy of royalty; and it is necessary here to avoid exalting too much the foresight and designs of men; for my part, I am inclined to think that Ferdinand and Isabella naturally followed the generality of the nation, in whose eyes the Jews were odious when they persevered in their creed, and suspected when they embraced the Christian religion. Two causes contributed to this hatred and animadversion. First, the excited state of religious feeling then general in all Europe, and especially in Spain; 2d, the conduct by which the Jews had drawn upon themselves the public indignation.

The necessity of restraining the cupidity of the Jews, for the sake of the independence of the Christians, was of ancient date in Spain: the old assemblies of Toledo had attempted it. In the following centuries the evil reached its height; a great part of the riches of the peninsula had passed into the hands of the Jews, and almost all the Christians found themselves their debtors. Thence the hatred of the people against the Jews; thence the frequent troubles which agitated some towns of the peninsula; thence the tumults which more than once were fatal to the Jews, and in which their blood flowed in abundance. It was difficult for a people accustomed for ages to set themselves free by force of arms, to resign themselves peacefully and tranquilly to the lot prepared for them by the artifices and exactions of a strange race, whose name, moreover, bore the recollection of a terrible malediction.

In later times, an immense number of Jews were converted to the Christian religion; but the hatred of the people was not extinguished thereby, and mistrust followed these converts into their new state. It is very probable that a great number of these conversions were hardly sincere, as they were partly caused by the sad position in which the Jews who continued in Judaism were placed. In default of conjectures founded on reason in this respect, we will regard as a sufficient corroboration of our opinion, the multitude of Judaizing Christians who were discovered as soon as care was taken to find out those who had been guilty of apostacy. However this may be, it is certain that the distinction between *new and old* Christians was introduced; the latter denomination was a title of honor, and the former a mark of ignominy; the converted Jews were contemptuously called *marranos*,—impure men, pigs. With more or less foundation, they were accused of horrible crimes. In their dark assemblies they committed, it was said, atrocities which could hardly be believed, for the honor of humanity. For example, it was said that, to revenge themselves on the Christians and in contempt of religion, they crucified Christian children, taking care to choose for the purpose the greatest day among Christian solemnities. There is the often-repeated history of the knight of the house of Guzman, who, being hidden one night in the house of a Jew whose daughter he loved, saw a child crucified at the time when the Christians celebrated the institution of the sacrifice of the Eucharist. Besides infanticide, there were attributed to the Jews, sacrileges, poisonings, conspiracies, and other crimes. That these rumors were generally believed by the people is proved by the fact, that the Jews were forbidden by law to exercise the professions of doctor, surgeon, barber, and tavern-keeper; this shows what degree of confidence was placed in their morality. It is useless to stay to examine the foundations for these sinister accusations. We are not ignorant how far popular credulity will go, above all when it is under the influence of excited feelings, which makes it view all things in the same light. It is enough for us to know that these rumors circulated everywhere and with credit, to understand what must have been the public indignation against the Jews, and consequently how natural it was that authority, yielding to the impulse of the general mind, should be urged to treat them with excessive rigor.

The situation in which the Jews were placed is sufficient to show, that they might have attempted to act in concert to resist the Christians; what they did after the death of St. Peter Arbues shows what they were capable of doing on other occasions. The funds necessary for the accomplishment of the murder, the pay of the assassins, and the other expenses required for the plot, were collected by means of voluntary contributions imposed on themselves by all the Jews of Aragon. Does not this show an advanced state of organization, which might have become fatal if it had not been watched.

In alluding to the death of St. Peter Arbues, I wish to make an observation on what has been said on this subject, as proving the unpopularity of the establishment of the Inquisition in Spain. What more evident proof, we shall be told, can you have than the assassination of the Inquisitor? Is it not a sure sign that the indignation of the people was at its height, and that they were quite opposed to the Inquisition? Would they otherwise have been hurried into such excesses? If by 'the people' you mean the Jews and their descendants, I will not deny that the establishment of the Inquisition was indeed very odious to them; but it was not so with the rest of the nation. The event we are speaking of gave rise to a circumstance which proves just the reverse. When the report of the death of the Inquisitor was spread through the town, the people made a fearful tumult to avenge his death. They spread through the town, they went in crowds in pursuit of the *new Christians*, so that a bloody catastrophe would have ensued, had not the young Archbishop of Saragossa, Alphonsus of Aragon, presented himself to the people on horseback, and calmed them by the assurance that all the rigor of the laws should fall on the heads of the guilty. Was the Inquisition as unpopular as it has been represented; and will it be said that its adversaries were the majority of the people? Why, then, could not the tumult at Saragossa have been avoided in spite of all the precautions which were no doubt taken by the conspirators, at that time very powerful by their riches and influence?

At the time of the greatest rigor against the Judaizing Christians, there is a fact worthy of attention. Persons accused, or threatened with the pursuit of the Inquisition, took every means to escape the action of that tribunal: they left the soil of Spain and went to Rome. Would those who imagine that Rome has always been the hotbed of intolerance, the firebrand of persecution, have imagined this? The number of causes commenced by the Inquisition, and summoned from Spain to Rome, is countless, during the first fifty years of the existence of that tribunal; and it must be added, that Rome always inclined to the side of indulgence. I do not know that it would be possible to cite one accused person who, by appealing to Rome, did not ameliorate his condition. The history of the Inquisition at that time is full of contests between the Kings and Popes; and we constantly find, on the part of the Holy See, a desire to restrain the Inquisition within the bounds of justice and humanity. The line of conduct prescribed by the court of Rome was not always followed as it ought to have been; thus we see the Popes compelled to receive a multitude of appeals, and mitigate the lot that would have befallen the appellants, if their cause had been definitely decided in Spain. We also see the Pope name the judge of appeal, at the solicitation of the Catholic sovereigns, who desired that causes should be finally decided in Spain: the first of these judges was Dr. Inigo Manrique, Archbishop of Seville. Nevertheless, at the end of a short time, the same Pope, in a Bull of the 2d of August, 1483, said that he had received new appeals, made by a great number of the Spaniards of Seville, who had not dared to address themselves to the judge of appeal for fear of being arrested. Such was then the excitement of the public mind; such was, at that time, the necessity of preventing injustice, or measures of undue severity. The Pope added, that some of those who had had recourse to his justice had already received the absolution of the Apostolical Penitentiary, and that others were about to receive it; he afterwards complained that indulgences granted to divers accused persons had not been sufficiently respected at Seville; in fine, after several other admonitions, he observed to Ferdinand and Isabella, that mercy towards the guilty was more pleasing to God than the severity which it was desired to use; and he gave the example of the good Shepherd following the wandering sheep. He ended by exhorting the sovereigns to treat with mildness those who voluntarily confessed their faults, desiring them to allow them to reside at Seville, or in some other place they might choose; and to allow them the enjoyment of their property, as if they had not been guilty of the crime of heresy.

Moreover, it is not to be supposed that the appeals admitted at Rome, and by virtue of which the lot of the accused was improved, were founded on errors of form and injustice committed in the application of the law. If the accused had recourse to Rome, it was not always to demand reparation for an injustice, but because they were sure of finding indulgence. We have a proof of this in the considerable number of Spanish refugees convicted at Rome of having fallen into Judaism. Two hundred and fifty of them were found at one time; yet there was not one capital execution. Some penances were imposed on them, and when they were absolved, they were free to return home, without the least mark of ignominy. This took place at Rome in 1498.

It is a remarkable thing that the Roman Inquisition was never known to pronounce the execution of capital punishment, although the Apostolic See was occupied during that time by Popes of extreme rigor and severity in all that relates to the civil administration. We find in all parts of Europe scaffolds prepared to punish crimes against religion; scenes which sadden the soul were everywhere witnessed. Rome is an exception to the rule; Rome, which it has been attempted to represent as a monster of intolerance and cruelty. It is true, that the Popes have not preached, like Protestants, universal toleration; but facts show the difference between the Popes and Protestants. The Popes, armed with a tribunal of intolerance, have not spilled a drop of blood; Protestants and philosophers have shed torrents. What advantage is it to the victim to hear his executioners proclaim toleration? It is adding the bitterness of sarcasm to his punishment. The conduct of Rome in the use which she made of the Inquisition, is the best apology of Catholicity against those who attempt to stigmatize her as barbarous and sanguinary. In truth, what is there in common between Catholicity and the excessive severity employed in this place or that, in the extraordinary situation in which many rival races were placed, in the presence of danger which menaced one of them, or in the interest which the kings had in maintaining the tranquillity of their states, and securing their conquests from all danger? I will not enter into a detailed examination of the conduct of the Spanish Inquisition with respect to Judaizing Christians; and I am far from thinking that the rigor which it employed against them was preferable to the mildness recommended and displayed by the Popes. What I wish to show here is, that rigor was the result of extraordinary circumstances,—the effect of the national spirit, and of the severity of customs in Europe at that time. Catholicity cannot be reproached with excesses committed for these different reasons. Still more, if we pay attention to the spirit which prevails in all the instructions of the Popes relating to the Inquisition; if we observe their manifest inclination to range themselves on the side of mildness, and to suppress the marks of ignominy with which the guilty, as well as their families, were stigmatized, we have a right to suppose that, if the Popes had not feared to displease the kings too much, and to excite divisions which might have been fatal, their measures would have been carried still further. If we recollect the negotiations which took place with respect to the noisy affair of the claims of the Cortes of Aragon, we shall see to which side the court of Rome leaned.

As we are speaking of intolerance with regard to the Judaizers, let us say a few words as to the disposition of Luther towards the Jews. Does it not seem that the pretended reformer, the founder of independence of thought, the furious declaimer against the oppression and tyranny of the Popes, should have been animated with the most humane sentiments towards that people? No doubt the eulogists of this chieftain of Protestantism ought to think thus also. I am sorry for them; but history will not allow us to partake of this delusion. According to all appearances, if the apostate monk had found himself in the place of Torquemada, the Judaizers would not have been in a better position. What, then, was the system advised by Luther, according to Seckendorf, one of his apologists? "Their synagogues ought to be destroyed, their houses pulled down, their prayer-books, the Talmud, and even the books of the Old Testament, to be taken from them; their rabbis ought to be forbidden to teach, and be compelled to gain their livelihood by hard labor." The Inquisition, at least, did not proceed against the Jews, but against the Judaizers; that is, against those who, after being converted to Christianity, relapsed into their errors, and added sacrilege to their apostacy, by the external profession of a creed which they detested in secret, and which they profaned by the exercise of their old religion. But Luther extended his severity to the Jews themselves; so that, according to his doctrines, no reproach can be made against the sovereign who expelled the Jews from their dominions.

The Moors and the Mooriscoes no less occupied the attention of the Inquisition at that time; and all that has been said on the subject of the Jews may be applied to them with some modifications. They were also an abhorred race—a race which had been contended with for eight centuries. When they retained their religion, the Moors inspired hatred; when they abjured it, mistrust; the Popes interested themselves in their favor also in a peculiar manner. We ought to remark a Bull issued in 1530, which is expressed in language quite evangelical: it is there said, that the ignorance of these nations is one of the principal causes of their faults and errors; the first thing to be done to render their conversion solid and sincere was, according to the recommendation contained in this Bull, to endeavor to enlighten their minds with sound doctrine.

It will be said that the Pope granted to Charles V. the Bull which released him from the oath taken in the Cortes of Saragossa in the year 1519; an oath, by which he had engaged not to make any change with respect to the Moors; whereby, it is said, the Emperor was enabled to complete their expulsion. But, we must observe, that the Pope for a long time resisted that concession; and, that if he at length complied with the wishes of the Emperor, it was only because he thought that the expulsion of the Moors was indispensable to secure the tranquillity of the kingdom. Whether this was true or not, the Emperor, and not the Pope, was the better judge; the latter, placed at a great distance, could not know the real state of things in detail. Moreover, it was not the Spanish monarch alone who thought so; it is related that Francis I., when a prisoner at Madrid, one day conversing with Charles V., told him that tranquillity would never be established in Spain, if the Moors and Mooriscoes were not expelled.

CHAPTER XXXVII.

SECOND EPOCH OF THE INQUISITION IN SPAIN.

It has been said that Philip II. founded a new Inquisition in Spain, more terrible than that of the Catholic sovereigns; at the same time the Inquisition of Ferdinand and Isabella receives a certain degree of indulgence, which is refused to that of their successors. At the very outset, we find an important historical mistake in this assertion. Philip did not establish a new Inquisition; he maintained that which the Catholic sovereigns had left him, and which Charles V., his father and predecessor, had particularly recommended to him by will. The Committee of the Cortes of Cadiz, in the project for the abolition of the tribunal of the Inquisition, excuses the conduct of the Catholic sovereigns, and blames with severity that of Philip II.; it attempts to make all the fault and odium fall on that prince. An illustrious French writer, very recently treating of this important question, has allowed himself to be led into the same errors, with that candor which sometimes accompanies genius. "There were," says M. Lacordaire, "in the Spanish Inquisition, two solemn periods, which must not be confounded; the one at the end of the fifteenth century, under Ferdinand and Isabella, before the Moors were expelled from Granada, their last asylum; the other, in the middle of the sixteenth, under Philip II., when Protestantism threatened to propagate itself in Spain. The Committee of the Cortes has perfectly distinguished these two epochs; and while it stigmatizes the Inquisition of Philip II., expresses itself with moderation with respect to that of Ferdinand and Isabella." After these words the writer quotes a text, where it is affirmed that Philip II. was the real founder of the Inquisition; if that institution attained in the end to a high degree of power, it was owing, it says, to the refined policy of that prince. We read, a little further on, that Philip II. was the inventor of the *auto-da-fé*, to terrify heretics; and that the first of these bloody spectacles was seen at Seville in 1559. (*Mémoire pour le rétablissement de l'Ordre des Frères Precheurs*, chap. vi.) Setting aside the historical mistake with respect to the *auto-da-fés*, it is well known that neither the *sanbenitos* nor the fagots were the invention of Philip II. Such mistakes easily escape a writer who is satisfied with alluding to a fact incidentally; if we bring forward this one, it is because it contains an accusation against a monarch to whom, for a long time, too little justice has been done. Philip II. continued the work which had been begun by his predecessors; if they are excused, he ought not to be treated with greater severity. Ferdinand and Isabella directed the Inquisition against the apostate Jews; why could not Philip II. avail himself of it against Protestants? But I shall be told he abused his right and carried rigor to excess. Certainly there was not more indulgence in the times of Ferdinand and Isabella. Are the numerous executions at Seville and other places forgotten? Or what Mariana says in his history, and the public measures taken by the Popes for the purpose of checking the excessive severity? The words quoted against Philip II. are taken from the work called *La Inquicitión sin mascura* (the Inquisition unveiled,) published in Spain in 1811. We may judge of the value of this authority, when we know that the author of the book was distinguished till his death by a deep hatred to the Spanish kings. The book bears the name of Nathanael Jomtob; but the real author is a well-known Spaniard, who, in his latter writings, seems to have undertaken to avenge, by his unbounded exaggerations and furious invectives, all that he had previously attacked; a writer who assails, with an intolerable partiality, all that presents itself before him—religion, country, classes of society, individuals, and opinions—insulting and tearing to pieces all, as if he had been seized with a sally of passion, and not even sparing the men of his own party. Is it, then, surprising that this writer regarded Philip II. as Protestants and philosophers do, that is, as a monarch placed on the earth for the disgrace and misfortune of humanity,—a monster of Machiavellianism, anxious to diffuse darkness, in order to maintain himself in safety in his cruelty and perfidy? I will not undertake to justify, on all points, the policy of Philip II.; I will not deny that there are exaggerations in the eulogiums which some Spanish writers have given to that prince. But, on the other hand, it cannot be doubted, that Protestants and the political enemies of Philip II. have ever been careful to denounce him. And do you know why Protestants have done this? It is because it was he who prevented Protestantism from penetrating into Spain; it was he who, at that period of agitation, maintained the cause of Catholicity. Let us set aside the great events of the rest of Europe, of which each one will judge as he pleases; let us limit ourselves to Spain. We do not fear to assert, that the introduction of Protestantism into that country was imminent and inevitable without the system which he pursued. Whether Philip used the Inquisition for political purposes, in certain cases, is not the question we have to examine here; but at least it must be acknowledged that it was not a mere instrument of ambitious projects; it was an institution strengthened and maintained in presence of an imminent danger.

It appears, from the proceedings of the Inquisition at this time, that Protestantism began to spread in an incredible manner in Spain; eminent ecclesiastics, monks, nuns, seculars of distinction, in a word, individuals of the most influential classes, were attached to the new errors. Could the efforts of Protestants to introduce their creed into Spain remain altogether unproductive, when they employed every stratagem in their ardor to introduce their books? They went so far as to place their prohibited writings in casks of Champagne and Burgundy wine, with so much art as to deceive the custom-house men: thus wrote the Spanish Ambassador at Paris.

To perceive the whole danger, it is enough to observe with attention the state of minds in Spain at this time; besides, incontestable facts come in support of conjectures. The Protestants, taking great care to declaim against abuses, represented themselves as reformers, and labored to draw to their side all who were animated by an ardent desire for reform. This desire for reform had existed for a long time in the Church; but with some it was inspired by bad intentions; in other words, the specious name of reform concealed the real intention of many, which was to destroy. At the same time, with some sincere Catholics, this desire, although pure in principle, went to imprudent zeal, and reached an ill-regulated ardor. It is probable that such zeal, carried to too great an extent, was, with many, changed into acrimony; thence a certain facility in receiving the insidious suggestions of the enemies of the Church. Many people who had begun with indiscreet zeal, perhaps fell into exaggeration, then into bitterness, and finally into heresy. Spain was not exempt from this disposition of mind, from whence the course of events might have drawn very bitter results, if Protestantism had obtained any footing on our soil. We know that the Spaniards at the Council of Trent distinguished themselves by their reforming zeal, and their boldness in expressing their opinions. Let us remark, moreover, that religious discord being once introduced into a country, minds are excited by disputes, they are irritated by frequent shocks, and it sometimes happens that respectable men precipitate themselves into excesses which they would have abhorred a short time before. It is difficult to say with precision what would have happened if the rigor had been at all relaxed on this point. Certain it is, that, when reading some passages of Luis Vives, of Arias Montanus, of Carranza, and of the consultation of Melchior Cano, we can fancy we find, at the bottom of their minds, a sort of disquietude and agitation, which may best be compared to those heavy murmurings which announce from afar the commencement of a tempest.

The famous trial of the Archbishop of Toledo, Fray Bartolomé de Carranza, is one of the facts which are most frequently cited to show the arbitrary nature of the proceedings of the Spanish Inquisition. We certainly cannot see without emotion, shut up in prison for many years, one of the most learned men in Europe, the Archbishop of Toledo, honored with the intimate confidence of Philip II. and the Queen of England, allied in friendship with the most distinguished men of the time, and known to all Christendom by the brilliant part which he had played at the Council of Trent. The process lasted seventeen years; and although the cause was carried to Rome, where the Archbishop must have found powerful friends, a declaration of innocence in his favor could not be obtained. Without staying to notice the many incidents of a cause so long and so complicated, without insisting on the more or less reason which the discourses and writings of Carranza may have afforded for suspicions against his faith, I am quite certain, in my own mind, that, in his own conscience and before God, he was perfectly innocent. Here is a proof that places my opinion beyond a doubt. A short time after the judgment was given, he fell ill; his malady was supposed to be mortal, and the sacraments were administered to him. At the moment of receiving the Viaticum, in the presence of a large concourse, he declared, in the most solemn manner, that he had never left the Catholic faith, that his conscience acquitted him of all the accusations made against him; and he confirmed his declaration by calling to witness God, in whose presence he was, whom he was about to receive under the most sacred species, and before whose awful tribunal he was in a few moments to appear This pathetic act drew tears from all present; all suspicions against him were dissipated as by a breath, and a new sympathy was added to that which his continued misfortunes had excited. The Sovereign Pontiff did not doubt the sincerity of the declaration, as a magnificent epitaph was placed upon his tomb, which certainly would not have been allowed if there had been the least doubt of it. It certainly would be rash to refuse to believe a declaration so explicit from the mouth of such a man as Carranza, expiring, and in the presence of Jesus Christ Himself.

After having paid this tribute to the knowledge, virtues, and misfortunes of Carranza, it remains for us to examine whether, whatever may have been the purity of his conscience, it can be justly said that his trial was a perfidious intrigue, carried on by envy and hatred. This is not the place to examine the immense procedure in this case; but since allusion has been made to it to condemn Philip II. and the adversaries of Carranza, I wish, in my turn, to make some observations, to endeavor to place the affair in its proper light. In the first place, is it not astonishing that a trial devoid of all foundation should have had so extraordinary a duration? At least there must have been some appearance of it. Besides, if the cause had been decided in Spain, the length of the trial might not have been so extraordinary. But it was not so; the cause remained pending in Rome many years. Were the judges so blind or so wicked that they could not discover the calumny, or that they wanted the virtue to destroy it, supposing it to have been as clear and evident as it has been pretended? It may be replied to this, that the intrigues of Philip II., who was determined on the destruction of the Archbishop, prevented the truth from appearing; in proof of this assertion, have we not the difficulties which the king made to allow the prisoner to be transferred to Rome? It was necessary, it is said, for Pius V. to effect this by the threat of excommunication. I will not deny that Philip II. attempted to aggravate the situation of the Archbishop, and wished for a sentence little favorable to the illustrious accused. Yet, before deciding that the conduct of the king was criminal, we must know whether he acted thus from personal resentment, from conviction, or from the suspicion that the Archbishop inclined towards Lutheranism. Carranza, before his disgrace, was highly favored and esteemed by Philip, as appears from the missions which were confided to him in England, and from his elevation to the first ecclesiastical dignity in Spain. How, then, can we presume that so much good-will was converted on a sudden into personal and violent hatred? Is it not, at least, necessary that history should afford a fact in support of this conjecture? Now, I find this nowhere in history, nor am I aware that others have done so. If Philip took so decided a part against the Archbishop, it was evidently because he believed, or strongly suspected him of being heretical. In that case, Philip may have been rash, imprudent—all that you please; but it cannot be said that, in the pursuit, he was moved by the spirit of vengeance, or by low animosity.

Other men of the time were equally accused. Among the rest, Melchior Cano. Carranza himself seemed to be suspicious; he bitterly complained that Melchior Cano had ventured to say that the Archbishop was as heretical as Luther. But Salazar de Mendoza, when relating the fact in the life of Carranza, asserts that Cano, hearing this, openly denied it, saying, that he had said nothing of the kind. Indeed, the mind is easily inclined to believe him; men with intellects as favored as his, have, in their own dignity, too powerful a preservative against baseness, to allow them to be suspected of playing the infamous part of calumniators.

I do not believe that it is necessary to seek for the cause of the misfortunes of Carranza in private hatred or jealousy; it is found in the critical circumstances of the time, and in the character of this illustrious man himself. The grave symptoms which produced alarm lest Protestantism might make proselytes in Spain; the efforts of the Protestants to introduce their books and emissaries there; the experience of what happened in other countries, and particularly in the kingdom of France, created so much dread in men's minds, rendered them so fearful and mistrustful, that the least suspicion of error, above all, in persons elevated in dignity or distinguished for their knowledge, occasioned disquietude and apprehension. We are aware of the hot disputes which took place with respect to the Polyglot of Antwerp and Arias Montanus, and we are not ignorant of the sufferings of the famous Fray Luis de Leon, and some other illustrious men of that time. Another conjuncture which contributed to push things to extremes was, the political situation of Spain with respect to strangers. The Spanish monarchy had too many enemies and rivals for her not to have reason to fear that heresy, in the hands of her adversaries, would become a means of introducing discord and civil war into her bosom. These causes united, naturally rendered Philip suspicious and mistrustful; the hatred of heresy combining in his mind with the desire of self-preservation, he showed himself severe and inexorable with respect to all that could affect the purity of the Catholic faith in his empire.

On the other hand, it must be acknowledged that the character of Carranza was not exactly what was required, in such critical times, to avoid all dangerous wanderings. We perceive, in reading his commentaries on the Catechism, that he was a man of acute penetration, of vast erudition, of profound learning, of severe character, and of a heart generous and frank. He spoke his thoughts without circumlocution, without regard to the displeasure which his words might give to this person or that. When he believed that he had discovered an abuse, he pointed it out and condemned it openly, wherein he resembled his supposed adversary, Melchior Cano, in more features than one. The accusations against him in the trial were founded, not only on his writings, but also on some of his sermons and private conversations. I know not to what extent he exceeded the just limits; but I hesitate not to affirm, that a man who wrote in the tone which we find in his works, must have expressed himself *viva voce* with great force, and perhaps with excessive boldness. It must be added, to speak the whole truth, that when treating of justification, in his commentaries on the Catechism, he does not explain himself with all the clearness desirable, and is wanting in the simplicity required by the unhappy circumstances of the times. Men versed in this delicate matter know how delicate certain points are. These points were then the subject of the errors of Germany; and it may be easily imagined how much the attention must have been fixed on the words of Carranza, and how alarming the least shadow of ambiguity must have been. It is certain that, at Rome he was not acquitted of all the accusations; he was compelled to abjure a series of propositions, with respect to which he was judged liable to suspicion; and some penances were imposed on him. Carranza on his death-bed protested his innocence; but he took care to declare that he did not regard the sentence of the Pope as unjust. The explanation of the enigma is this: the innocence of the heart is not always accompanied by the prudence of the lips.

I have dwelt upon this famous cause because it involves considerations which strikingly exhibit the spirit of the age. These considerations have, besides, the advantage of showing the truth in its proper light, and prevent every thing being explained according to the wretched measure of the malice of men. There is unhappily a tendency to explain all in this way; and it may be truly said, that men too often give a just foundation for it; yet, whenever there is no evident necessity to do so, we ought to abstain from condemnation. The picture of the history of humanity is sombre enough in itself; let us not take pleasure in darkening it still more by new stains. We often call crime that which was only ignorance. Man is inclined to evil; but he is not less subject to error, and error is not always culpable.

Moreover, I believe that to Protestants themselves were owing the rigor and anxious mistrust which the Inquisition of Spain displayed at that time. They excited a religious revolution; and it is a constant law, that all revolutions either destroy the power assailed, or render it more harsh and severe. What before was looked upon as indifferent, is now considered as suspected; and what, in all other circumstances, would only have appeared a fault, is now regarded as a crime. Men are in continual dread of seeing liberty converted into licentiousness; and as revolutions destroy all, while they profess to reform, whoever ventures to speak of reform, runs the risk of being blamed as a disturber. Even prudent conduct is stigmatized as hypocritical caution; frank and sincere language is termed insolence and dangerous suggestion; reserve is a concealment full of cunning; even silence itself assumes a meaning—it becomes alarming dissimulation. We have seen so many things come to pass in our days, that we are placed in an incomparable situation easily to understand the various phases of the history of humanity. It is an undoubted fact, that Protestantism produced a reaction in Spain. Its errors and excesses were the reason why the ecclesiastical and civil power infinitely restrained the liberty which had been previously enjoyed in all that related to religion. Spain was preserved from the Protestant doctrines, when all the probabilities were in favor of their being introduced there, in one way or another. It is clear that this could not be obtained without extraordinary efforts. Spain, at that time, appears to me like a place besieged by a powerful enemy, where the leaders continually watched, not only against attacks from without, but also against treason from within. I will confirm these observations by an example, which will serve for many others. Let us remember what took place with respect to Bibles in the vulgar tongue; we shall then have an idea of what passed with relation to all the rest, according to the natural order of things. I have before me a testimony of what I have just said, as respectable as it is worthy of interest—that of Carranza himself. Hear what he says in his prologue to his commentaries on the Christian Catechism: "Before the heresies of Luther had come from the infernal regions to the light of this world, I do not know that the Holy Scriptures in the vulgar tongue were anywhere forbidden. In Spain, Bibles were translated into it by order of the Catholic sovereigns, at the time when the Moors and Jews were allowed to live among the Christians according to their own law. After the expulsion of the Jews from Spain, the judges of religion found that some of those who had been converted to our holy faith instructed their children in Judaism, and taught them the ceremonies of the law of Moses by means of those Bibles in the vulgar tongue, which they took care to have printed in Italy, in the town of Ferrara. This is the real cause why Bibles in the vulgar tongue were forbidden in Spain; but the possession and reading of them were always allowed to colleges and monasteries, as well as to persons of distinction above all suspicion." Carranza continues to give, in a few words, the history of these prohibitions in Germany, France, and other countries; then he adds: "In Spain, which was, and still is, by the grace and goodness of God, pure from the cockle, care was taken to forbid generally all the translations of the Scriptures in the vulgar tongue, in order to prevent strangers having an opportunity of holding controversy with simple and ignorant persons, and also because they had, and still have, experience of certain particular cases, and of the errors which began to arise in Spain from the ill-understood reading of certain passages of the Bible. What I have just stated is the real history of what took place; this is why the Bible in the vulgar tongue was prohibited."

This curious passage of Carranza shows us, in a few words, the progress of things. At first there was no prohibition; but the abuse committed by the Jews provoked one, although still confined, as we have just seen, within certain limits. Afterwards came the Protestants, upsetting all Europe by means of their Bibles; Spain is threatened with the introduction of the new errors; it is discovered that some persons have been misled by the false interpretation of certain passages of the Bible; they are compelled to take away this weapon from these strangers, who attempt to use it to seduce simple people: from that time the prohibition becomes rigorous and general.

To return to Philip II., let us not forget that this monarch was one of the firmest defenders of the Catholic Church; and that in him was personified the policy of the faithful ages, amid the vertigo which, under the impulse of Protestantism, had taken possession of European policy. If the Catholic Church, amid these great perturbations, could reckon on a powerful protection from the princes of the earth, it was in great measure owing to Philip II. This age was critical and decisive in Europe. If it is true that he was unfortunate in Flanders, it is not less undoubted that his power and ability afforded a counterpoise to the Protestant power, which prevented it making itself master of Europe. Even supposing that the efforts of Philip had only the result of gaining time, by breaking the first shock of the Protestant policy, this was not a slight service rendered to the Catholic Church, then attacked on so many sides. What would have happened to Europe, if Protestantism had been introduced into Spain as into France? if the Huguenots had been able to count on the assistance of the Peninsula? And what would have happened in Italy, if she had not been held in respect by the power of Philip? Would not the sectaries of Germany have succeeded in introducing their errors there? Here I appeal to all men who are acquainted with history, whether, if Philip had abandoned his much-decried policy, the Catholic religion would not have run the risk of finding itself, at the beginning of the seventeenth century, under the hard necessity of existing only as a tolerated religion in the generality of the kingdoms of Europe? Now, we know what this toleration is worth to the Catholic Church; England has told us for centuries; Prussia shows us at this moment, and Russia adds her testimony in a manner still more lamentable. Such is the point of view in which we must consider Philip II. One is forced to allow that, considered in this way, that prince is a great historical personage,—one of those who have left the deepest marks on the policy of the age which followed,—one of those who exert the greatest influence after them on the course of events.

Spaniards, who anathematize the founder of the Escurial, have you, then, forgotten our history, or do you esteem it of no value? Do you stigmatize him as an odious tyrant? Do you not know that, in denying his glory, in covering it with ignominy, you efface a feature of your own glory, and throw into the mud the diadem which encircled the brows of Ferdinand and Isabella? If you cannot pardon Philip II for having sustained the Inquisition,—if that reason alone obliges you to load his name with execration, do the same with his illustrious father, Charles V.; and, going back to Isabella of Castille, write also on the list of the tyrants and scourges of humanity that name which was venerated by both worlds, and which is the emblem of the glory and power of the Spanish monarchy. They all took part in the fact which excites your indignation; do not curse some, while you lavish hypocritical indulgence on the others. If that indulgence is found in your words, it is that the feeling of nationality which beats in your bosom compels you to partiality—to inconsistency; you recoil when you are about to efface the glories of Spain with a stroke of the pen—to wither all her laurels—to deny your country. We have nothing left, unfortunately, but great recollections; let us at least avoid despising them: these recollections are, in a nation, like the titles of ancient nobility in a fallen family; they raise the mind, they fortify the soul in adversity; and, nourishing hope in the bottom of the heart, they serve to prepare what is to come.

The immediate effect of the introduction of Protestantism into Spain would have been, as in other countries, civil war; and this war would have been more fatal to us than to other people, because the circumstances were much more critical for us. The unity of the Spanish monarchy could not have resisted the shocks and disturbances of intestine dissension; the different parts were so heterogeneous among themselves, and were so slightly united, that the least blow would have parted them. The laws and manners of the kingdoms of Navarre and Aragon were very different from those of Castille; a lively feeling of independence, supported by frequent meetings of their own Cortes, was kept alive in the hearts of those unconquered nations; they would certainly have availed themselves of the first opportunity to shake off a yoke which was not pleasing to them. Moreover, in the other provinces, factions were not wanting to distract the country. The monarchy would have been miserably divided at a time when it was necessary to make head in the affairs of Europe, Africa, and America. The Moors were still in sight of our coasts; the Jews had not had time to forget Spain: certainly both would have availed themselves of the conjuncture to raise themselves by means of our discords. On the policy of Philip depended not only the tranquillity, but perhaps even the existence of the Spanish monarchy. He is now accused of having been a tyrant; if he had pursued another course, he would have been taxed with incapacity and weakness.

One of the most unjust attacks of the enemies of religion against her friends is, to attribute bad faith to them, to accuse them of having in every thing false intentions, tortuous and interested views. When they speak of the Machiavellianism of Philip II., they suppose that the Inquisition, while apparently only religious in its object, was, in reality, an obedient instrument of policy in the hands of a crafty monarch. Nothing is more specious to the man in whose eyes history is only a matter for piquant and malicious observations; but nothing is more false according to facts. Some people, seeing in the Inquisition an extraordinary tribunal, have not been able to imagine the existence of that exceptional tribunal, without supposing, in the monarch who sustained and encouraged it, profound reasons, and views carried much further than appears on the surface of things. They have not been willing to see that an epoch has its spirit, its own manner of regarding things, its own system of action, both in doing good and in preventing evil. During those times, when all the nations of Europe appealed to fire and sword to decide questions of religion, when Protestants and Catholics burnt their adversaries, when England, France, and Germany assisted at the bloodiest scenes, to bring a heretic to the scaffold was a natural and customary thing, which gave no shock to prevailing ideas. We feel our hair grow stiff on our heads at the mere idea of burning a man alive. Placed in society where the religious sentiment is considerably diminished; accustomed to live among men who have a different religion, and sometimes none at all; we cannot bring ourselves to believe that it could be at that time quite an ordinary thing to see heretics or the impious led to punishment. But, if we read the authors of the time, we shall see the immense difference on this point between their manners and ours; and we shall remark, that our language of moderation and toleration would not even have been understood by the man of the sixteenth century.

Do you know what Carranza himself, who suffered so much from the Inquisition, thought of this matter? Every time that he has occasion to touch on this point in the work which I have quoted, he expresses the ideas of his time, without even staying to prove them; he gives them as undoubted principles. In England, with Queen Mary, he did not fear to express his opinions as to the rigor with which heretics ought to be treated; and he was certainly far from suspecting that his name would one day be made use of to attack this intolerance. Kings and peoples, ecclesiastics and seculars, were all agreed on this point. What would be said now-a-days of a king who would carry with his own hands the wood to burn heretics, and would condemn blasphemers to have their tongues pierced with a hot iron? Now, the first of these things is related of St. Ferdinand, and we know that the second was done by St. Louis. We now exclaim in seeing Philip II. assisting at an *auto-da-fé*; but, if we consider that the court, the great men, all that was most select in society, surrounded the king on these occasions, we shall understand that, if this spectacle is horrible and intolerable to us, it was not so in the eyes of those men, widely different from us in ideas and feelings. And let it not be said that they were forced there by the will of the monarch,—that they were compelled to obey: this was not the effect of the monarch's will; it was only a consequence of the spirit of the age. No monarch would have been sufficiently powerful to perform such a ceremony, if the spirit of the age had been opposed to it; besides, no monarch is so hard and insensible as not to feel the influence of the times in which he lives. Suppose the most absolute despot of our time, Napoleon, at the height of his power, or the present Emperor of Russia, and see whether they could thus violate the manners of the age.

An anecdote is related which is little adapted to confirm the opinion of those who assert that the Inquisition was a political instrument in the hands of Philip. As it paints in a curious and interesting manner the customs and ideas of the age, I will insert it here. Philip II. held his court at Madrid; a certain preacher, in a sermon delivered in presence of the king, advanced, that *sovereigns had an absolute power over the persons as well as over the property of their subjects.* The proposition was not of a nature to displease a king; the preacher at one blow relieved kings from all control over the exercise of their power. Now, it seems that at that time all men were not in such abject subjection to despotic control as we have been led to believe; some one was found to denounce to the Inquisition the words in which the preacher had not been ashamed to flatter the absolute power of kings. Surely the orator had chosen a secure asylum; and our readers may well suppose that this denunciation coming into collision with the power of Philip, the Inquisition would have maintained a prudent silence. Yet it was not so: the Inquisition made an inquiry, found the proposition contrary to sound doctrine, and the preacher, who was perhaps far from expecting such a reward, had divers penances imposed on him, and was condemned to retract publicly his proposition in the same place where he had made it. The retractation took place with all the ceremonies of a juridical proceeding; the preacher declared that he retracted his proposition as erroneous; he explained the reasons by reading, as he had been directed, the following words, well worthy of remark: "*Indeed, messieurs, kings have no other power over their subjects than that which is given to them by the divine and human law; they have none proceeding from their own free and absolute will.*" This is related by D. Antonio Perez, as may be seen at length in the note which corresponds to the present chapter. We know, moreover, that he was not a fanatical partisan of the Inquisition.

This took place at the time which some persons never mention without stigmatizing it with the words obscurantism, tyranny, and superstition. Yet I doubt whether, at a time nearer to us—that, for example, when it is asserted that light and liberty dawned on Spain under the reign of Charles III.—a public and solemn condemnation of despotism would have been carried so far. This condemnation, at the time of Philip II., did as much honor to the tribunal which ordered it as to the monarch who consented to it.

With respect to knowledge, it is a calumny to say that a design was formed to maintain and perpetuate ignorance. Certainly the conduct of Philip does not indicate such a design, when we see this prince, not content with favoring the great enterprise of the Polyglot of Antwerp, recommending to Arias Montanus to devote to the purchase of chosen works, printed or manuscript, the money which would revert to the printer Plantinus, to whom the king had advanced a large sum to aid in the enterprise. This chosen collection was to be placed in the library of the monastery of the Escurial, which was then built. The king had also charged *Don Francis de Alaba, his ambassador in France, to collect in that kingdom the best books which it was possible for him to procure*, as he himself says in his letter to Arias Montanus. No; the history of Spain, with respect to intolerance in religious matters, is not so black as it has been represented. When foreigners reproach us with cruelty, we will reply that, when Europe was stained with blood by civil wars, Spain was at peace. As to the number of persons who perished on the scaffold or died in exile, we challenge the two nations who claim to be at the head of civilization, France and England, to show us their statistics on that subject at the same time, and to compare them with ours: we do not fear the comparison.

In proportion as the danger of the introduction of Protestantism into Spain diminished, so did the rigor of the Inquisition. We may observe, moreover, that the procedure of that tribunal always became milder, in accordance with the spirit of criminal legislation in the other countries of Europe. Thus we see the *auto-da-fé* becoming more rare as we approach our own times, so that, at the end of the last century, the Inquisition was only a shadow of what it had been. It is useless to insist on this point, which nobody denies, and on which we are in unison with the most ardent enemies of that tribunal; and this it is which, in our eyes, proves, in the most convincing manner, that we must seek in the ideas and manners of the time, what people have attempted to find in the cruelty, in the wickedness, or in the ambition of men. If the doctrines of those who plead for the abolition of the punishment of death are carried into effect, posterity, when reading the executions of our time, will be seized with the same horror with which we view the punishment of times past, and the gibbet and the guillotine will figure in the same rank as the ancient Quemaderos. (26)

CHAPTER XXXVIII.

RELIGIOUS INSTITUTIONS IN THEMSELVES.

Religious institutions are another of those points whereon Protestantism and Catholicity are in complete opposition to each other: the first abhors, the second loves them; the one destroys them, the other establishes and encourages them. One of the first acts of Protestantism, whenever it is introduced, is to attack religious institutions by its doctrines and its acts; it labors to destroy them immediately; one would say that the pretended Reformation cannot behold without irritation those holy abodes, which continually remind it of the ignominious apostacy of its founder. Religious vows, especially that of chastity, have been the subject of the most cruel invectives on the part of Protestants; but it must be observed, that what is said now, and what has been repeated for three centuries, is only the echo of the first voice which was raised in Germany; and what was that voice? It was the voice of a monk without modesty, who penetrated into the sanctuary and carried away a victim. All the pomp of learning employed to combat a sacred dogma is insufficient to hide so impure an origin. Through the excitement of the false prophet we perceive the impure flames which devour his heart.

Let us observe in passing, that the same thing took place with respect to the celibacy of the clergy. Protestants, from the beginning, could not endure this; they threw off the mask, and condemned it without disguise; they attempted to combat it with a certain ostentation of learning; but, at the bottom of all their declamation, what do we find? The clamor of a priest who has forgotten his duty; who strives against the remorse of his conscience, and endeavors to hide his shame by diminishing the horror of the scandal by the allegations of falsehood. If such conduct had been pursued by the Catholics, all the arms of ridicule would have been employed to cover them with contempt, to stamp it, as it deserves, with the brand of infamy; but it was a man who declared deadly war against Catholicity: that was enough to turn away the contempt of philosophers, and find indulgence for the declamation of a monk whose first argument against celibacy was, to profane his vows and consummate a sacrilege.

The rest of the disturbers of that age imitated the example of so worthy a master. All demanded and required from Scripture and philosophy a veil to cover their weakness and baseness. Just punishment! blindness of the mind was the result of corruption of the heart; impudence sought and obtained the companionship of error. Never is the mind more vile than when, to excuse a fault, it becomes the accomplice of it; then it is not deceived, but prostituted.

This hatred of religious institutions has been inherited by philosophy from Protestantism. This is the reason why all revolutions, excited and guided by

Protestants or philosophers, have been signalized by their intolerance towards the institutions themselves, and by their cruelty towards those who belonged to them. What the law could not do was completed by the dagger and the torch of the incendiary. What escaped the catastrophe was left to the slow punishment of misery and famine. On this point, as well as on many others, it is manifest that the infidel philosophy is the daughter of the Reformation. It is useless to seek for a more convincing proof of this than the parallel of the histories of both, in all that relates to the destruction of religious institutions; the same flattery of kings, the same exaggeration of the civil power, the same declamation against the pretended evil inflicted on society, the same calumnies; we have only to change the names and the dates. And we must also remark this peculiarity, that, in this matter, the difference which, apparently, ought to have resulted from the progress of toleration and the softening of manners in recent times, has scarcely been felt.

But is it true that religious institutions are as contemptible as they have been represented? is it true that they do not even deserve attention, and that all the questions relating to them can be solved by merely pronouncing the word fanaticism? Does not the man of observation, the real philosopher, find in them any thing worthy of attracting his attention? It is difficult to believe that such was the nullity of these institutions, whose history is so grand, and which still preserve in their existence the promise of a great future. It is difficult to believe that such institutions are not worthy of attention in the highest degree, and that their study is wholly devoid of lively interest and solid profit. We see them appear at every epoch of Church history; their memorials and monuments are found every moment under our feet; they are preserved in the regions of Asia, in the sands of Africa, in the cities and solitudes of America; in fine, when, after so much adversity, we see them more or less prosperous in the various countries of Europe, sending forth again fresh shoots in those lands where their roots had been the most deeply torn up, there naturally arises in the mind a spirit of curiosity to examine this phenomenon, to inquire what is the origin, the genius, and the character of these institutions. Those who love to descend into the heart of philosophical questions discover, at first sight, that there must be there an abundant mine of the most precious information for the science of religion, of society, and of man. He who has read the lives of the ancient fathers of the desert without being touched, without feeling profound admiration, and being filled with grave and lofty thoughts; he who, treading under his feet with indifference the ruins of an ancient abbey, has not called up in fancy the shades of the cenobites who lived and died there; he who passes coldly through the corridors and cells of convents half demolished, and feels no recollections, and not even the curiosity to examine,—he may close the annals of history, and may cease to study the beautiful and the sublime. There exist for him no historical phenomena, no beauty, no sublimity; his mind is in darkness, his heart is in the dust.

With the intention of hiding the intimate connection which subsists between religious institutions and religion herself, it has been said that she can exist without them. This is an incontrovertible truth, but abstract and wholly useless—a barren and isolated assertion, which can throw no light upon science, nor serve as any practical guide—an insidious truth, which only tends entirely to change the whole state of the question, and persuade men that when religious institutions are concerned, religion has nothing to do with the matter. There is here a gross sophism, which is too much employed, not only on this question, but on many others. This consists in replying to all difficulties by a proposition perfectly true in itself, but which has nothing to do with the question. By this means, attention is turned another way; the palpable truth which is presented to the mind makes men wander from the principal object, and induces them to take that for a solution which is only a distraction. With respect, for example, to the support of the clergy and divine worship, it is said, "Temporals are altogether different from spirituals." When the ministers of religion are systematically calumniated, "Religion," they say, "is one thing, and her ministers are another." If it is wished to represent the conduct of Rome for many centuries as an uninterrupted chain of injustice, of corruption, and of invasion of right, all reply is anticipated by saying, "The supremacy of the Sovereign Pontiff has nothing to do with the vices of Popes or their ambition." Reflections perfectly just, and truths palpable, no doubt, which are very useful in certain cases, but which writers of bad faith cunningly employ to conceal from the reader the real object they have in view. Such are the jugglers who attract the attention of the simple multitude on one side, while their companions perform their criminal operations on the other.

Because a thing is not necessary to the existence of another, it does not follow that the first does not originate in the second,—does not find in the spirit of the latter its peculiar and permanent existence, and that a system of intimate and delicate relation does not subsist between them. The tree can subsist without flowers and fruits; these can certainly fall without destroying the trunk; but as long as the tree shall exist, will it ever cease to give proofs of its vigor and its beauty, and to offer its flowers to the eye, and its fruits to the taste? The stream may constantly flow in its crystal bed without the green margin which embellishes its sides; but while its source is not dried up—as long as the fertilizing water penetrates the ground, can its favored banks remain dry, barren, without color and ornament? Let us apply these images to our subject. It is certain that religion can exist without religious communities, and that their ruin does not necessarily entail that of religion herself. More than once it has been seen that in countries where religious institutions have been destroyed, the Catholic faith has been long preserved. But it is not less certain, that there is a necessary dependence between them and religion; that is, that she has given being to them, that she animates them with her spirit, and nourishes them with her substance: this is the reason why they immediately germinate wherever the Catholic faith takes root; and if they have been driven from a country where she continues to exist, they will reappear. Without alluding to the examples of other countries, do we not see this phenomenon take place in France in a remarkable manner? The number of convents of men and women which are again established on the French soil is already very considerable. Who would have told the men of the Constituent Assembly, the Legislative Assembly, the Convention, that half a century should not elapse without seeing religious institutions reappear and flourish in France, in spite of all their efforts to destroy even their memory? "If that happen," they would have said, "it will be because the revolution which we are making will not be allowed to triumph—because Europe will have again imposed despotism upon us; then, and then only, will be witnessed in France—in Paris—in this capital of the Christian world—the re-establishment of religious institutions, that legacy of fanaticism and superstition, transmitted to us by the ideas and manners of an age which has passed away, never to return."

Senseless men! your revolution *has* triumphed; you *have* conquered Europe; the old principles of the French monarchy *have* been erased from legislation, institutions, and manners; the genius of war has led your doctrines in triumph over Europe, and they were gilded by the rays of your glory. Your principles, all your recollections have again triumphed at a recent period; they still live in all their force and pride, personified in some men who glory in being the heirs of what they call the glorious Revolution of '89; and yet, in spite of so many triumphs, although your revolution has only receded as much as was necessary the better to secure its conquests, religious institutions have again arisen—they extend, they are propagated everywhere, and they regain an important place in the annals of our times. To prevent this revival, it would have been necessary to extirpate religion; it was not enough to persecute her; faith remained like a precious germ covered by stones and thorns; Providence sends down a ray of that divine star which softens stones, and gives life and fertility; the tree rises again in all its beauty, in spite of the ruins which hindered its growth and development, and its leaves are immediately covered with charming blossoms:—behold the religious institutions which you thought were for ever annihilated!

The example which we have just mentioned clearly shows the truth of what we wish to establish, with respect to the intimate connection which exists between religion and religious institutions. Church history furnishes proofs in support of this truth. Besides, the mere knowledge of religion, and of the nature of the institutions of which we speak, would suffice to prove it to us, even if we had not history and experience in our favor.

The force of general prejudice on this subject is such, that it is necessary to descend to the root of things, to show the complete mistake of our adversaries. What are religious institutions considered generally? Putting aside the differences, the changes, the alterations necessarily produced by variety of times, countries, and other circumstances, we will say that a religious institute is a society of Christians living together, under certain rules, for the purpose of practising the Gospel precepts. We include, in this definition, even the orders which are not bound by a vow. It will be seen that we have considered the religious institution in its most general sense, laying aside all that theologians and canonists say with respect to the conditions indispensable to constitute or complete its essence. We must, moreover, observe that we ought not to exclude from the honorable denomination of religious institutes, those associations which possess all the conditions except the vows. The Catholic religion is fertile enough to produce good by means and forms widely different. In the generality of religious institutions, she has shown us what man can do by binding himself by a vow, for his whole life, to a holy abnegation of his own will; but she has also wished to show us that, while leaving him at liberty, she could attach him by a variety of ties, and make him persevere until death, as if he had been obliged by a perpetual vow. The congregation of the oratory of St. Philip Neri, which is found in this latter category, is certainly worthy of figuring among religious institutions as one of the finest monuments of the Catholic Church. I am aware that the vow is comprised in the essence of religious institutes, as they are commonly understood; but my only object now is, to vindicate this kind of association against Protestants. Now we know that they condemn indiscriminately, associations bound by vows and those which only consist of the permanent and free adhesion of the persons who compose them. All that has the form of a religious community is regarded by them with a look of anger. When they proscribed the religious orders, they included in the same fate those which had vows and those which had not. Consequently, when defending them, we must class them together. Moreover, this will not prevent our considering the vow in itself, and justifying it before the tribunal of philosophy.

I do not imagine that it is necessary to say more to show that the object of religious institutions—that is, as we have just said, the putting in practice of the Gospel counsels—is in perfect uniformity with the Gospel itself. And let us well observe that, whatever may be the name, whatever may be the form of the institutions, they have always for their object something more than the simple observance of the precepts; the idea of perfection is always included, then, either in the active or the contemplative life. To keep the Divine commandments is indispensable to all Christians who wish to possess eternal life; the religious orders attempt a more difficult path; they aim at perfection. This i the object of the men who, after having heard these words from the mouth o their Divine Master: "If you wish to be perfect, go sell all you have, and give it to the poor," have not departed sorrowful, like the young man in the Gospel, but have embraced with courage the enterprise of quitting all and following Jesus Christ.

We have now inquired whether association is the best means to carry into execution so holy an object. It would be easy for me to show this by adducing various texts of Scripture, where the true spirit of the Christian religion, and the will of our Divine Master, are clearly shown on this point; but the taste of our age, and the self-evidence even of the truths in question, warn us to avoid, as much as possible, all that savors of theological discussion. I will remove the question, then, from this level, to consider it in a light purely historical and philosophical; that is to say, without accumulating citations and texts, I will prove that religious institutes are perfectly conformable to the spirit of the Christian religion; and that consequently that spirit has been deplorably mistaken by Protestants, when they have condemned or destroyed them. If philosophers, while they do not admit the truth of religion, still avow that it is useful and beautiful, I will prove to them that they cannot condemn those institutions which are the necessary result of it. In the cradle of Christianity, when men preserved, in all their energy and purity, the sparks from the tongues of the Holy Spirit; in those times, when the words and examples of its Divine Founder were still fresh, when the number of the faithful who had had the happiness of seeing and hearing Him was still very great in the Church, we see the Christians, under the direction of the Apostles themselves, unite, have all their property in common; thus forming only one family, the Father of which was in heaven, and *which had only one heart and one soul.*

I will not dispute as to the extent of this primitive proceeding; I will abstain from analyzing the various circumstances which accompanied it, and from examining how far it resembled the religious institutions of latter times; it is enough to state its existence, and show therefrom what is the true spirit of religion with respect to the most proper means to realize evangelical perfection. I will only allude to the fact, that Cassian, in the description which he gives of the commencement of religious institutions, assigns as their cradle the proceeding we have just mentioned, and which is reported in the Acts of the Apostles. According to the same author, this kind of life was never wholly interrupted; so that there were always some fervent Christians who continued it; thus attaching, by a continued chain, the existence of the monks to the primitive associations of the apostolical times. After having described the kind of life of the first Christians, and traced the alterations of the times that followed, Cassian continues thus: "Those who preserved the apostolical fervor in this way, recalling primitive perfection, quitted towns, and the society of those who believed that they were allowed to live with less severity; they began to choose secret and retired places, where they could follow in private the rules which they remembered to have been appointed by the Apostles for the whole body of the Church in general. Thus commenced the formation of the discipline of those who had quitted that contagion, as they lived separate from the rest of the faithful; abstaining from marriage, and having no communication with the world, even with their own families. In the progress of time, the name of monks was given to them, in consideration of their singular and solitary life." (*Collat.* 18, cap. 5.)

Times of persecution immediately followed, which, with some interruptions, that may be called moments of repose, lasted till the conversion of Constantine. There were, then, during this time, some Christians who attempted to continue the mode of life of the apostolical years. Cassian clearly indicates this in the passage which we have just read. He omits to say that this primitive life was necessarily modified, in its exterior form, by the calamities with which the

Church was afflicted at that period. In all that time we ought not to look for Christians living in community; we shall find them confessing Jesus Christ, with imperturbable calmness, on the rack, amid all torments, in the circus, where they were torn to pieces by wild beasts, on the scaffold, where they quietly gave up their heads to the axe of the executioner. But observe what happened even during the time of persecution; the Christians, of whom the world was not worthy, pursued in the towns like wild beasts, wandered about in solitude, seeking refuge in the deserts. The solitudes of the East, the sand and rocks of Arabia, the most inaccessible places of the Thebaïd, receive those troops of fugitives, who dwell in the abodes of wild beasts, in abandoned graves, in dried-up cisterns, in the deepest caverns, only asking for an asylum for meditation and prayer. And do you know the result of this? These deserts, in which the Christians wandered, like a few grains of sand driven by the wind, became peopled, as it were by magic, with innumerable religious communities. There they meditated, prayed, and read the Gospel; hardly had the fruitful seed touched the earth, when the precious plant arose in a moment.

Admirable are the designs of Providence! Christianity, persecuted in the towns, fertilizes and embellishes the deserts; the precious grain requires for its development neither the moisture of the earth nor the breeze of a mild atmosphere; when carried through the air on the wings of the storm, the seed loses nothing of its vitality; when thrown on a rock, it does not perish. The fury of the elements avails nothing against the work of God, who has made the north wind His courser: the rock ceases to be barren when He pleases to fertilize it. Did He not make pure water spring forth at the mysterious touch of His Prophet's rod?

When peace was given to the Church by the conqueror of Maxentius, the germs contained in the bosom of Christianity were able to develope themselves everywhere; from that moment the Church was never without religious communities. With history in our hands, we may defy the enemies of religious institutions to point out any period, however short, when these institutions had entirely disappeared. Under some form or in some country, they have always perpetuated the existence which they had received in the early ages of Christianity. The fact is certain and constant, and is found in every page of ecclesiastical history; it plays an important part in all the great events in the annals of the Church. It is found in the west and in the east, in modern and in ancient times, in the prosperity and in the adversity of the Church; when the pursuit of religious perfection was an honor in the eyes of the world, as well as when it was an object of persecution, raillery, and calumny. What clearer proof can there be that there is an intimate connection between religious institutions and religion herself? What more is required to show us that they are her spontaneous fruit? In the moral and in the physical order of things, the constant appearance of the one following the other, is regarded as a proof of the reciprocal dependence of two phenomena. If these phenomena have towards each other the relations of cause and effect—if we find in the essence of the one all the principles that are required in the production of the other, the first is called the cause and the other the effect. Wherever the religion of Jesus Christ is established, religious communities are found under some form or other; they are, therefore, its spontaneous effect. I do not know what reply can be made to so conclusive an argument.

By viewing the question in this way, the favor and protection which religious institutions always found with the Pontiff is naturally explained. It was his duty to act in conformity with the spirit which animates the Church, of which he is the chief ruler upon earth; it is certainly not the Pope who has made the regulation, that one of the means most apt to lead men to perfection is to unite themselves in associations under certain rules, in conformity with the instructions of their Divine Master. The Eternal Lord thus ruled in the secrets of His infinite wisdom, and the conduct of the Popes could not be contrary to the designs of the Most High. It has been said that interested views interposed; it has been said that the policy of the Popes found in these institutions a powerful means of sustaining and aggrandizing itself. But can you not see any thing but the sordid instruments of cunning policy in the societies of the primitive faithful, in the monasteries of the solitudes of the East, in that crowd of institutions which have had for their object only the sanctification of their own members and the amelioration of some of the great evils of humanity? A fact so general, so great, so beneficent, cannot be explained by views of interest and narrow designs; its origin is higher and nobler; and he who will not seek for it in heaven ought at least to seek for it in something greater than the projects of a man or the policy of a court; he ought to seek for lofty ideas, sublime feelings, capable, if they do not mount to heaven, at least of embracing a large part of the earth; nothing less is here required than one of those thoughts which preside over the destinies of the human race.

Some persons may be inclined to imagine private designs on the part of the Popes, because they see their authority interfere in all the foundations of later ages, and their approbation constitute the validity of the rules of religious institutions; but the course pursued in this respect by ecclesiastical discipline shows us that the most active intervention of the Popes, far from emanating from private views, has been called for by a necessity of preventing an excessive multiplication of the religious orders in consequence of an indiscreet zeal. This vigilance in preventing abuses was the origin of this supreme intervention. In the twelfth and thirteenth centuries the tendency to new foundations was so strong that the most serious inconveniences would have resulted from it, without a continual watchfulness on the part of the ecclesiastical authority. Thus we see the Sovereign Pontiff Innocent III. ordain, in the Council of Lateran, that whoever wished to found a new religious house shall be bound to adopt one of the approved rules and institutions.

But let us pursue our design. I can understand how those who deny the truth of the Christian religion, and turn into ridicule the counsels of the Gospel, bring themselves to deny all that is celestial and divine in the spirit of the religious communities; but the truth of religion once established, I cannot conceive how men who boast of following its laws can declare themselves the enemies of these institutions considered in themselves. How can he who admits the principle refuse the consequence? How can he who loves the cause reject the effect? They must either affect a religion hypocritically, or they profess without comprehending it.

In default of any other proof of the anti-evangelical spirit which guided the leaders of the pretended Reformation, their hatred to an institution so evidently founded on the Gospel itself should suffice. Did not these enthusiasts for reading the Bible *without note or comment*—they who pretend to find all its passages so clear—did they not remark the plain and easy sense of that multitude of passages which recommend self-abnegation, the renunciation of all possessions, and the privation of all pleasures? These words are plain—they cannot be taken in any other signification—they do not require for their comprehension a profound study of the sacred sciences, or that of languages; and yet they have not been heard: we should rather say, they have not been listened to. The intellect has understood, but the passions have rejected them.

As to those philosophers who have regarded religious institutions as vain and contemptible, if not dangerous, it is clear that they have meditated but little on the human mind, and on the deep feelings of our hearts, full as they are of mystery. As their hearts have felt nothing at the sight of those numbers of men and women assembled for the purpose of sanctifying themselves or others, or of relieving wants, and consoling the unfortunate, it is but too clear that their souls have been dried up by the breath of skepticism. To renounce for ever all the pleasures of life; to live in solitude, there to offer one's self, in austerity and penance, as a holocaust to the Most High: this, certainly is a matter of horror to those philosophers who have only viewed the world through their own prejudices. But humanity has other thoughts; it feels itself attracted by those objects which philosophers find so vain, so devoid of interest, so worthy of horror.

Wonderful are the secrets of our hearts! Although enervated by pleasure, and involved in the whirlwind of amusement and mirth, we cannot avoid being seized with deep emotion at the sight of austerity and recollection of soul. Solitude, and even sadness itself, exert an inexpressible influence over us. Whence comes that enthusiasm which moves a whole nation, excites and makes it follow, as if by enchantment, the steps of a man whose brow is marked by recollection, whose features display austerity of life, whose clothes and manners show freedom from all that is earthly, and forgetfulness of the world? Now, it is a fact, proved by the history both of true and of false religions; so powerful a means of attracting respect and esteem has not remained unknown to imposture: licentiousness and corruption, desirous of making their fortunes in the world, have more than once felt the imperious necessity of disguising themselves under the mantle of austerity and purity. What at first sight might appear the most opposed to our feelings, the most repugnant to our tastes—this shade of sadness diffused over the recollection and solitude of the religious life—is precisely what enchants and attracts us the most. The religious life is solitary and pensive; therefore it is beautiful, and its beauty is sublime. Nothing is more apt than this sublimity to move our hearts deeply, and make indelible impressions on them. In reality, our soul has the character of an exile; it is affected by melancholy objects only; it has not attained to that noisy joy which requires to borrow a tint of melancholy only for the sake of a happy contrast. In order to clothe beauty with its most seductive charms, it is necessary that a tear of anguish should flow from her eyes, that her forehead should assume an air of sadness, and her cheeks grow pale with a melancholy remembrance. In order that the life of a hero excite a lively interest in us, it is requisite that misfortune be his companion, lamentation his consolation—that disaster and ingratitude be the reward of his virtues. If you wish that a picture of nature or art should strongly attract our attention, take possession of and absorb the powers of our soul, it is necessary that a memorial of the nothingness of man, and an image of death, should be presented to our minds; our hearts should be appealed to by the feelings of a tranquil sadness; we desire to see sombre tints on a monument in ruins—the cross reminding us of the abode of the dead, the massive walls covered with moss, and pointing out the ancient dwelling of some powerful man, who, after having lived on earth for a short time, has disappeared.

Joy does not satisfy us, it does not fill our hearts; it intoxicates and dissipates them for a few moments; but man does not find there his happiness, because the joys of earth are frivolous, and frivolity cannot attach a traveller who, far from his country, walks painfully through the valley of tears. Thence it comes that, while sorrow and tears are accepted—we should rather say, are carefully sought for by art—whenever a deep impression is to be made upon the soul, joy and smiles are inexorably banished. Oratory, poetry, sculpture, painting, music, have all constantly followed the same rule; or, rather, have always been governed by the same instinct. It certainly required a lofty spirit and a heart of fire to declare *that the soul is naturally Christian.* In these few words an illustrious thinker has known how to express all the relations which unite the faith, morality, and counsels of this divine religion, with all that is most intimate, delicate, and noble in our hearts. Do you know Christian pensiveness; that grave and elevated feeling which is painted on the forehead of the Christian, like a memorial of sorrow on that of an illustrious proscribed one; this feeling which moderates the enjoyments of life by the image of the tomb, and lights up the depths of the grave with the rays of hope; that pensiveness so natural and consoling, so grave and noble, which causes diadems and sceptres to be trodden under foot like dust, and the greatness and splendor of the world to be despised as a passing illusion? This melancholy, carried to its perfection, vivified and fertilized by grace, and subjected to a holy rule, is what presides over the foundation of religious institutions, and accompanies them as long as they preserve their primitive fervor, which they received from men who were guided by divine light, and animated by the Spirit of God. This holy melancholy, which carries with it freedom from all earthly things, is the feeling which the Church wishes to instil into and preserve in, the religious orders, when she surrounds their silent abodes with a shade of retirement and meditation.

That amid the fury and the convulsions of parties, a mad and sacrilegious hand, secretly excited by malice, should plunge a fratricidal dagger into an innocent heart, or set fire to a peaceful dwelling, may be conceived; for, unhappily, the history of man abounds in crimes and frenzies; but that the essence of religious institutions should be attacked, that their spirit should be considered narrow and imbecile, that they should be deprived of the noble titles which give honor to their origin, and the beauties which adorn their history, can be allowed neither by the intellect nor by the heart. A false philosophy, which dries up and withers all that it touches, has undertaken so mad a task. But, setting aside religion and reason, literature and the fine arts have rebelled against this attempt; literature and the fine arts, which have need of old recollections, and which are indebted for their wonders to lofty thoughts, to grave and noble scenes, and deep and melancholy feelings; literature and the arts, which delight in transporting the mind of man into regions of light, in guiding the imagination through new and unknown paths, and in ruling the heart by mysterious charms.

No; a thousand times no! As long as the religion of that God made man, who had not where to repose his head, and who sat down by a well on the wayside to rest, like an humble traveller, shall last; of that God-man, whose appearance was announced to the nations by a mysterious voice coming from the desert—by the voice of a man clothed in a goat-skin, whose reins were bound with a leathern girdle, and who lived on nothing but locusts and wild honey: as long as this divine religion shall last, nothing will be more holy or more worthy of our respect than those institutions, the true and original object of which is to realize what Heaven intended to teach man by such eloquent and sublime lessons. Times, vicissitudes, and revolutions, succeed each other; the institution will change its form, will undergo alterations, will be affected more or less by the weakness of men, by the corrosive action of time, and the destructive power of events; but it will live—it will never perish. If one society rejects it, it will seek an asylum in another; driven from towns, it will take refuge in forests; if there pursued, it will flee to the horrors of the desert. There will always be, in some privileged hearts, an echo for the voice of that sublime religion, which, holding in her hand a standard of sorrow and love—the sacred standard of the sufferings and death of the Son of God—the Cross, will proclaim to men: "Watch and pray, that you enter not into temptation; if you assemble to pray, the Lord will be in the midst of you; all flesh is but grass; life is a dream; above your heads is an ocean of light and happiness; under your feet an abyss; your life on earth is a pilgrimage, an exile." Then she marks his forehead with the mysterious ashes, telling him, "Thou art dust, and unto dust thou shalt return."

We shall perhaps be asked why the faithful cannot practise evangelical perfection while living in the bosom of their families, without assembling in communities? We shall reply, that we have no intention of denying the possibility of that practice, even in the midst of the world; and we willingly acknowledge that a great number of Christians have done so at all times, and do so now; but this does not prove that the surest and easiest means is not that of the life in community with others who have the same object in view, and in retirement from all the things of this world. Laying aside for a moment all consideration of religion, are you not aware of the ascendency which the spirit of repeated examples exerts on those with whom we live? Do you not know how easily our spirit fails when we find ourselves alone in a difficult enterprise? Do you not know that, in the greatest misfortunes, it is a consolation to behold others participate in our sorrows? On this point, as well as on all others, religion accords with sound philosophy, and both unite in explaining to us the profound meaning contained in those words of Scripture: "*Væ soli! Wo to him who is alone!*"

Before concluding this chapter, I wish to say a few words on the vows which commonly accompany religious institutes. Perhaps they are one of the principal causes of the violent antipathy of Protestantism against these institutions. Vows render things fixed and stable; and the fundamental principle of Protestantism does not admit of fixity or stability. Essentially separating and anarchical, this principle rejects unity and destroys the hierarchy; dissolving in its nature, it allows the mind neither to remain in a permanent faith nor to be subject to rule. For if virtue itself is only a vague entity, which has no fixed foundation—a being which is fed on illusions, and which cannot endure the application of any certain and constant rule, this holy necessity of doing well, of constantly walking in the path of perfection, must be incomprehensible to it, and in the highest degree repugnant; this necessity must appear to it inconsistent with liberty; as if man, by binding himself by a vow, lost his free will; as if the sanction which a promise given to God imparts to a design, at all diminished the merit of him who has the firmness necessary to accomplish what he had the courage to promise.

Those who, to condemn this necessity which man imposes on himself, invoke the rights of liberty against it, seem to forget that this effort of man to make himself the slave of good, and secure his own future, besides the sublime disinterestedness which it supposes, is the vastest exercise which man can make of his liberty. By one act alone, he disposes of his whole life, and by fulfilling the duties resulting from that act, he continually fulfils his own will. But we shall be told that man is so inconstant: this is the reason why, in order to prevent the effects of this inconstancy, he finds himself penetrating into the vicissitudes of the future, renders himself superior to them, and governs them in advance. But, it will be said, in that case, good is done from necessity: this is true; but do you not know that the necessity of doing good is a happy one, and in some measure assimilates man with God? Do you not know that Infinite Goodness is incapable of doing evil, and Infinite Holiness can do nothing that is not holy? Theologians explain why a created being is capable of sinning by pointing out this profound reason. "It is," they say, "because the creature is made out of nothing." When man forces himself, as far as he can, to do well, when he thus fetters his will, he ennobles it, he renders himself more like to God, he assimilates himself to the state of the blessed, who have no longer the melancholy liberty of doing evil, and who are under the happy necessity of loving God.

The name of liberty, from the time when Protestants and false philosophers took possession of it, seems condemned to be ill understood in all its applications. In the religious, moral, social, and political order, it is enveloped in such obscurity, that we can perceive the many efforts which have been made to darken and misrepresent it. Cicero gives an admirable definition of liberty when he says, that it consists in being the slave of law. In the same way it may be said, that the liberty of the intellect consists in being the slave of truth; and the liberty of the will in being the slave of virtue; if you change this, you destroy liberty. If you take away the law, you admit force; if you take away the truth, you admit error; if you take away virtue, you admit vice. If you venture to exempt the world from the external law, from that law which embraces man and society, which extends to all orders, which is the divine wisdom applied to reasonable creatures; if you venture to seek for an imaginary liberty out of that immense circle, you destroy all; there remains in society nothing but the empire of brute force, and in man that of the passions; with tyranny, and consequently slavery.

CHAPTER XXXIX.

OF RELIGIOUS INSTITUTIONS IN HISTORY.—THE FIRST SOLITARIES.

I HAVE just examined religious institutions in a general point of view, by considering them in their relations with religion and the human mind. I am now going to take a glance at the principal points of their history. This examination, I think, will show us an important truth: viz. that the appearance of these institutions under different forms has been the expression and the fulfilment of great moral necessities, and a powerful means, in the hands of Providence, of promoting not only the spiritual good of the Church, but also the salvation and regeneration of society. It will be understood that it is not possible for me to enter into details, or pass in review the numerous religious institutions which have existed; besides, this is not necessary for my object. I shall limit myself, therefore, to running over the principal phases of religious institutes, and making a few remarks on each of them; I shall act like the traveller who, being unable to make a stay in the country through which he passes, looks at it for a short time from the highest points. I will begin with the solitaries of the East.

The Colossus of the Roman Empire threatened an approaching and stunning fall: the spirit of life was rapidly becoming extinguished, and there was no longer any hope of a breath to reanimate it. The blood circulated slowly in its veins; the evil was incurable: the symptoms of corruption everywhere manifested themselves, and this agony was exactly coincident with the critical and formidable hour when it was necessary to collect all its forces to resist the violent shock which was about to destroy it. The barbarians appeared on the frontiers of the empire, like the carnivorous animals attracted by the exhalations of a dead body; and at this crisis society found itself on the eve of a fearful catastrophe. All the world was about to undergo an alarming change; the next day was not likely to resemble the last; the tree was about to be torn up; but its roots were too deep for it to be extirpated without changing the whole face of the soil where it was planted. The greatest refinement had to contend with barbarian ferocity,—the effeminate luxury of southern nations with the energy of the robust sons of the forest; the result of the struggle could not be doubtful. Laws, customs, manners, monuments, arts and sciences,—all the civilization and refinement acquired during the course of many ages was all in peril, all foreboded approaching ruin, all understood that God had appointed an end to the power, and even the existence of the rulers of the globe. The barbarians were only the instrument of Providence; the hand which had given a mortal blow to the mistress of the world, the queen of nations, was that formidable hand which touches mountains with fire, and reduces them to ashes, which touches the rocks and melts them like metal; it was the hand of

Him who sends forth His fiery breath upon the nations, and burns them up like straw.

The world must be the prey of chaos for a short time; but was not light again to come upon it? Was mankind to be melted, like gold in the furnace, in order to come out more brilliant and more pure? Were ideas respecting God and man to be corrected? Were more delicate and exalted notions of morality to be diffused? Was it reserved for the heart of man to receive more grave and sublime inspirations, to emerge from its corrupt state, and live in an atmosphere higher and more worthy of an immortal being? Yes! Providence thus decreed, and His infinite wisdom has brought about this end by ways which man could not understand.

Christianity was already spread over the face of the world; her holy doctrines, rendered fruitful by grace, prepared the complete regeneration of the world; but it was necessary that mankind should again receive a new impulse from her divine hands, that the mind of man should be moved by a new shock, that it might take its proper flight, and raise itself at once to the exalted position which was intended for it, and from which it was never to descend. History tells us of the obstacles which opposed the establishment and development of Christianity. According to the warlike expression of the Prophet, God was compelled to assume His sword and buckler; by the strength of wonderful prodigies, He broke the resistance of the passions, destroyed every knowledge which raised itself against the knowledge of God, scattered all the powers which rebelled against Him, and extinguished the pride and obstinacy of hell. When, after three centuries of persecution, victory declared itself throughout the world in favor of the true religion; when the temples of the false gods were deserted, and those idols which were not yet overthrown trembled on their pedestals; when the sign of Calvary was inscribed on the Labarum of the Cæsars, and the legions of the empire bowed religiously before the Cross, then had the moment arrived for Christianity to realize, in a permanent manner, in those sublime institutions conceived and established by herself alone, the lofty counsels given three centuries before in Palestine. The wisdom of philosophers had been vain; the time was come to realize the wisdom of the Carpenter of Nazareth, of Him who, without having consulted human learning, had proclaimed and taught truths unknown to the most privileged of mortals.

The virtues of the Christians had already emerged from the obscurity of the catacombs; they were to be resplendent in the light of heaven and amid peace, as they had formerly shone in the depths of dungeons and amid the flames. Christianity had obtained possession of the sceptre of command, as of the domestic hearth; her disciples, who now were multitudinous, no longer lived in a community of goods; it is clear that entire continence, and complete freedom from all earthly things, could no longer be the mode of life of the regenerated families. The world was to continue; the duration of the human race was not to cease at this point of its career; therefore, all Christians were not to observe the lofty counsels which convert the life of man on earth into the angelic. A great number of them were to belong to those who, in order to obtain eternal life, were satisfied with keeping the precepts, without aspiring to the sublime perfection which results from the renouncement of all that is earthly, and the complete abnegation of self. Yet the Founder of the Christian religion was unwilling that the counsels which He had given to men should be for a moment without some disciples amid the coldness and dissipation of the world. He had not given them in vain; and, besides, the practice of them, although confined to a limited number of the faithful, exerted on all sides a beneficent influence which facilitated and secured the observance of the precepts. The force of example exerts so powerful an ascendency over the human heart, that it is often sufficient of itself to triumph over the strongest and most obstinate resistance there is something in our hearts which inclines them to sympathize with all that approaches them, whether good or evil; and there seems to be a secret stimulus urging us to follow others, whatever direction they may take. Therefore it is that there are so many advantages in the establishment of religious institutions, in which the virtues and austerity of life are given as an example to the generality of men, and make an eloquent reproach to the errors of passion.

Providence desired to attain this great end by singular and extraordinary means; the Spirit of God breathed on the earth, and immediately the men and power to commence this great work appeared. The frightful deserts of Thebaïd, the burning solitudes of Arabia, Palestine, and Syria, show us men rudely clad, with a mantle of goat-skin on their shoulders, and a plain cowl on their heads: behold all the luxury with which they confound the vanity and pride of worldlings! Their bodies, exposed to the rays of the most burning sun and the most severe cold, besides being attenuated by long fasts, resemble walking spectres who have arisen from the dust of their sepulchres. The herbs of the earth are their only food, water their only drink; the labor of their hands procures for them the scanty resources they require. Under the direction of a venerable old man, whose claims to rule are a long life passed in the desert, and hairs grown white amid privations and austerities, they constantly keep the profoundest silence; their lips are opened only to pronounce the words of prayer; their voice is only heard to intone a hymn of praise to God. For them the world has ceased to exist; the relations of friendship, the sweet ties of family and relationship, are all broken by a spirit of perfection, carried to an extent which surpasses all earthly considerations. The cares of property do not disturb them; before retiring to the desert, they have abandoned all to him who was to succeed them; or they have sold all they had, and given the price to the poor. The Holy Scriptures are the nourishment of their minds; they learn by heart the words of that divine book; they meditate on them unceasingly, beseeching the Lord to grant that they may understand them aright. In their retired meetings, nothing is heard but the voice of some venerable cenobite, explaining with naïve simplicity and touching unction the sense of the sacred text; but always in such a way as to draw profit for the purification of souls.

The number of these solitaries was so great that we could not credit it, if it were not vouched for by eye-witnesses worthy of the highest respect. As to their sanctity, spirit of penance, and purity of life, we cannot doubt them after the testimonies of Rufinus, Palladius, St. Jerome, St. John Chrysostom, St. Augustine, and all the other illustrious men who distinguished themselves at that time. The fact is singular, extraordinary, prodigious; but no one can question its historical truth; it is attested by all who came to the desert from all parts to seek for light in their doubts, cures for their evils, and pardon for their sins. I could quote a thousand authorities to prove what I have said; but I will content myself with one, which shall suffice for all—that of St. Augustine. Hear how this holy doctor describes the life of these extraordinary men: "These fathers, not only very holy in their manners, but very learned in the Christian doctrine, excellent men in all respects, do not govern with pride those whom they justly call their sons, on account of the high authority of those who command, and the ready will of those who obey. At the decline of day, one of them, still fasting, quits his habitation, and all assemble to hear their master. Each of these fathers *has at least three thousand under his direction; for the number is sometimes much greater*. They listen with incredible attention, in profound silence, manifesting by their groans, or tears, or by their modest and tranquil joy, the various feelings which the discourse excites in their souls." (St. Augustin. lib. 1, *De Moribus Ecclesiæ*, cap. 31.)

But it will be said, Of what use were these men, except for their own sanctification? what good did they do to society? what influence did they exert on ideas? what change did they make in manners? If we admit that this plant of the desert was beautiful and fragrant, yet what did it avail? it remained sterile. It certainly would be an error to think that so many thousands of solitaries did not exercise great influence. In the first place, and to speak only of what relates to ideas, we must observe, that the monasteries of the East arose within reach, and under the eyes of, the schools of philosophy. Egypt was the country where the cenobetic life flourished the most. Now every one is aware of the high renown which the schools of Alexandria enjoyed a short time before. On all sides of the Mediterranean—on that border of land which, beginning in Libya, terminates in the Black Sea—men's minds were at that time in a state of extraordinary motion. Christianity and Judaism, the doctrines of the East and those of the West—all was collected and accumulated in this part of the world; the remains of the ancient schools of Greece were formed of the treasures, which the course of ages and the passage of the most famous nations of the earth had brought to those countries. New and gigantic events were come to throw floods of light upon the character and the value of ideas; minds had felt shocks which did not allow them any longer to be contented with the quiet lessons contained in the dialogues of the ancient masters. From these famous countries came the most eminent men of the early ages of Christianity; and we know from their works the extent and elevation of mind which man had attained at that time. Was it possible that a phenomenon so extraordinary—a girdle of monasteries and hermitages, embracing this zone of the world, and showing themselves in the face of the schools of philosophy—should not exert great influence on men's minds? The ideas of the solitaries passed incessantly from the desert into the towns; since, in spite of all the care which they took to avoid the contact of the world, the world sought and approached them, and continually came to receive their inspirations.

When we see the nations crowd to the solitaries the most eminent for their sanctity, to implore from their wisdom a remedy for suffering and a consolation in misfortunes; when we see these venerable men impart, together with the unction of the Gospel, the sublime lessons which they had learned during long years of meditation and prayer in the silence of solitude, it is impossible not to understand how much these communications must have contributed to correct and elevate ideas relating to religion and morality, and to amend and purify morals. Let us not forget that the human mind was, as it were, materialized by the corruption and grossness of the pagan religion. The worship of nature, of sensible forms, was so deeply rooted that, in order to raise minds to the conception of superior things, a strong and extraordinary reaction was required; it was necessary in some measure to annihilate matter in order to present to man only the mind. The life of the solitaries was the best adapted to produce this effect. In reading the history of these times, we seem to find ourselves transported out of this world; the flesh has disappeared, and there remains nothing but the spirit; and the force which has been employed in order to subdue the flesh is such—they have insisted so much on the vanity of earthly things—that reality itself is changed into illusion, and the physical world vanishes to make way for the moral and intellectual; all the ties of earth have been broken; man puts himself in intimate communication with Heaven. Miracles multiply exceedingly in these lives; apparitions continually appear; the abodes of the solitaries are arenas where earthly means are nothing; good angels struggle against demons, heaven against hell, God against Satan: the earth is there only to serve as a field of battle; the body exists no longer except to be consumed as a holocaust on the altars of virtue, in the presence of the demon who struggles furiously to render it the slave of vice.

What has become of the idolatrous worship which Greece paid to sensible forms, that adoration which it offered to nature by deifying all that was delicious and beautiful, all that could interest the senses and the heart? What a profound change! the same senses are subjected to the most severe privations; they are most strictly circumcised in heart; and man, who then scarcely attempted to raise his mind above the earth, now keeps it constantly fixed on Heaven. It is impossible to form an idea of what we are attempting to describe, without having read the lives of these solitaries; to understand all the effect of their great prodigies, it is necessary to have spent many hours over these pages where, so to speak, nothing is found which follows the natural course of things It is not enough to imagine pure lives, austerities, visions, and miracles; it is necessary to see all this collected together, and carried to the most wonderful extent in the path of perfection.

If you refuse to acknowledge the action of grace in facts so surprising; if you will not see any supernatural effect in this religious movement; I say more, if you go so far as to suppose that the mortification of the flesh and the elevation of the soul are carried to blamable exaggeration, still you cannot help allowing that such a reaction was very likely to spiritualize ideas, to awaken the moral and intellectual forces in man, and to concentrate all within himself, by giving him the sentiment of that interior, intimate, and moral life, with which, until then, he had not been occupied. The forehead which, till then, had been bent towards the earth, was raised towards the Divinity; something nobler than material enjoyments was offered to the mind, and the brutal excesses authorized by the example of the false divinities of paganism, at length appeared an offence against the high dignity of human nature.

In the moral order, the effect must have been immense. Man, until then, had not even imagined that it was possible to resist the impetuosity of his passions. There were found, it is true, in the cold morality of a few philosophers, certain maxims intended to restrain the dangerous passions; but this morality was only in the books, the world did not regard it as practicable, and if some men attempted to realize it, they did so in such a manner that, far from giving it credit, they rendered it contemptible. What did it avail to abandon riches and profess freedom from all earthly things, as some philosophers did, if at the same time they appeared so vain, so full of themselves, that it was evident that they only sacrificed on the altar of pride? It was to overturn all the idols in order to place themselves on the altar, and reign there without rival gods; this was not to direct the passions, to subject them to reason, but to create a monster passion surpassing and devouring all. Humility, the foundation-stone whereon the solitaries raised the edifice of their virtue, placed them immediately in a position infinitely superior to that of the ancient philosophers who were distinguished for a life more or less severe. In fine, men were taught to avoid vice and practise virtue, not for the futile pleasure of being regarded and admired, but for superior motives founded on the relations of man with God, and the destinies of eternity. From that moment man knew that it was not impossible for him to triumph over evil, in the obstinate struggle which he felt continually going on within himself. At the sight of so many thousands of persons of both sexes who followed a rule of life so pure and austere, mankind took fresh courage, and were convinced that the paths of virtue were not impracticable for them.

The generous confidence with which man was inspired by the sight of such sublime examples, lost nothing of its strength in presence of the Christian dogma, which does not allow actions meritorious of eternal life to be attributed to man himself, and teaches him the necessity of divine aid, if he wishes to escape the paths of perdition. This dogma, which, on the other hand, accords so well with the daily lessons of experience as to human frailty, far from destroying the strength of the mind or diminishing its courage, on the contrary, animates it more and more to persevere in spite of all obstacles. When man thinks himself alone, when he does not feel himself supported by the powerful hand of Providence, he walks with the tottering steps of infancy; he wants confidence in himself, in his own strength; the object he has in view seems too distant, the enterprise too arduous, and he is discouraged. The dogma of grace, as it is explained by the Catholic Church, is not that fatalist doctrine, the mother of despair, which has hardened the heart among Protestants, as Grotius laments. It is a doctrine which, leaving man all his free will, teaches him the necessity of superior aid; but that aid will be abundantly furnished him by the infinite goodness of God, who has shed His blood for him in torments and ignominy, and has breathed out for him His last sigh on Mount Calvary.

It seems as if Providence had been pleased to choose a climate where mankind could make a trial of their strength vivified and sustained by grace. It was under a sky apparently the most fatal for the corruption of the soul, in countries where the relaxation of the body naturally leads to relaxation of mind, and where even the air that they breathed inclined to pleasure,—it was there that the greatest energy of mind was displayed, that the greatest austerities were practised, and the pleasures of the senses were proscribed and banished with the greatest severity. The solitaries fixed their abodes in deserts within the influence of the balmy breezes of the neighboring lands; from their mountains and sandy hills their eyes could distinguish the peaceful and smiling countries which invited to pleasure and enjoyment; like the Christian virgin who abandoned her obscure cave to go and place herself in the hollow of a rock, whence she saw the palace of her fathers overflowing with riches, pleasures, and delights, while she herself lamented like a solitary dove in the holes of the rock. From that time all climates were good for virtue; austerity of morals did not at all depend on the proximity of the equatorial line; the morality of man, like man himself, could live in all climates. When the most perfect continence was practised in so wonderful a manner under the sky which we have described, the monogamy of Christianity could well be established and preserved. When, in the secrets of the Eternal, the time had arrived for calling a people to the light of truth, it mattered not whether they lived amid the snows of Scandinavia, or on the burning plains of India. The spirit of the divine laws was not to be confined within the narrow circle which the *Esprit des Loix* of Montesquieu has attempted to assign it.

CHAPTER XL.

ON RELIGIOUS INSTITUTIONS IN THE EAST.

THE influence exercised by the lives of the solitaries of the East over religion and morality is beyond a doubt; in truth it is not easy to appreciate it in all its extent and in all its effects; but it is not the less true and real on that account. It has not marked the doctrines of humanity like those thundering events the effects of which are often inadequate to their promises; but it is like a beneficial rain which, diffusing itself gently over the thirsty earth, fertilizes the meadows and the fields. If it were possible for man to comprehend and distinguish the vast assemblage of causes which have contributed to raise his mind, to give him a lively consciousness of his immortality, and to render a return to his ancient degradation almost impossible, perhaps it would be found that the wonderful phenomenon of the Eastern solitaries had a considerable share in that immense change. Let us not forget that from thence did the great men of the East receive their inspiration; St. Jerome lived in a cave at Bethlehem, and the conversion of St. Augustine was accompanied by a holy emulation excited in his mind by reading the life of St. Anthony the Abbot.

The monasteries which were founded in the East and West in imitation of these early establishments of the solitaries, were a continuation of them, although with many differences, in consequence of times and circumstances. Thence came the Basils, the Gregories, the Chrysostoms, and so many distinguished men, the glory of the Church. If a miserable spirit of dispute, ambition, and pride, sowing the seeds of discord, had not prepared the rupture which was to deprive the East of the vivifying influence of the Roman See, perhaps the ancient monasteries of the East would have served, like those of the West, to prepare a social regeneration, by forming one people out of the conquerors and the conquered.

It is evident that the want of unity was one of the causes of the weakness of the East; I will not deny that their position was very different from ours; the enemy opposed to them did not at all resemble the barbarians of the North; but I am not sure that it was easier to subdue the latter than it was to rule the nations by whom the East was conquered. In the East, the victory remained with the aggressors, as with us; but a conquered nation is not dead; its defeat does not take from it all the great advantages which are able, by giving it a moral ascendency over the conquerors, to prepare, in silence, their transformation, if not their expulsion. The northern barbarians conquered the South of Europe; but the South, in its turn, triumphed over them by the Christian religion; the barbarians were not driven out, but they were transformed. Spain was conquered by the Arabs, and the Arabs could not be transformed; but they were driven out in the end. If the East had preserved unity, if Constantinople and the other episcopal sees had remained subject to Rome like those of the West; in a word, if all the East had been contented to be a member of a great body, instead of having the ambitious pretensions of being a great body itself, I consider it certain that, after the conquest of the Saracens, a struggle, at once intellectual, moral, and physical, would have been engaged in; a profound change would have been worked in the conquered nation, or the struggle would have ended by the conquering barbarians being driven back to their deserts.

It will be said that the transformation of the Arabs was the work of ages. But was not that of the barbarians of the North so likewise? Was this great work finished by their conversion to Christianity? A considerable part of them were Arians; and besides, they understood the Christian ideas so ill, they found the practice of Gospel morality so difficult, that for a long time it was almost as difficult to treat with them as with nations of a different religion. On the other hand, let us not forget that the irruption of the barbarians was not a solitary event; an event which, when once finished, did not recur; it was continued for ages. But the force of the religious principle in the West was such, that all the invading nations were compelled to retire, or were forced to bend to the ideas and manners of the countries they had recently acquired. The defeat of the hordes of Attila, the victories of Charlemagne over the Saxons and the other nations beyond the Rhine, the successive conversion of the various idolatrous nations of the North by means of the missionaries sent from Rome,—in fine, the vicissitudes and the final result of the invasions of the Normans, and the ultimate triumph of the Christians of Spain over the Moors after a war of eight centuries, are so many decisive proofs of what I have just laid down—viz. that the West, vivified and fortified by Catholic unity, had had the secret of assimilating and appropriating to itself all that it was not able to reject, and the force to reject all that it could not make its own.

This is what was wanting in the East: the enterprise was not more difficult there than in the West. If the West alone was able to liberate the Holy Sepulchre, the West and East together would never have lost it; or, at least, after having freed it, they would have kept it for ever. The same cause prevented the monasteries of the East from attaining to the same vitality and energy which distinguished those of the West; therefore, they have always been seen to grow weak with time, without producing any thing great, and capable of preventing social dissolution, of silently preparing and slowly elaborating regeneration for posterity, after the calamities with which it pleased Providence to afflict ancient times. He who has seen in history the brilliant commencement of the Eastern monasteries, cannot behold without pain the decline of their strength and splendor in the course of ages, after the ravages caused by invasion, wars, and finally, the deadly influence of the schism of Constantinople; the ancient abodes of so many men illustrious for science and sanctity gradually disappeared from the page of history like expiring lamps, or the dying fires of an abandoned camp.

Immense injury was done to all the branches of human knowledge by this decline, which, after having rendered the East barren, ended by destroying it. If we pay attention, we shall see that, amid the great shocks and revolutions which disturbed Europe, Africa, and Asia, the natural refuge for the remains of ancient knowledge, was not the West, but the East. It was not in our monasteries that the books, and other intellectual riches, of which quieter and happier generations were one day to enjoy the benefit, should naturally have been preserved; this, it would seem, belonged to the monasteries of the eastern countries; those lands, where the most different civilizations were brought together and commingled as on neutral ground; those regions, where the human mind had displayed the greatest activity, and taken the highest flights; where the most abundant treasures of tradition and sciences, and the beauties of art were accumulated; in a word, it was in this vast mart of all the riches of the civilization and refinement of all nations,—it was in this sanctuary and museum of antiquity, that the intellectual patrimony of future generations ought to have been preserved.

Let it not, however, be supposed that the monasteries of the East were of no service to the human mind; the science and literature of Europe are still mindful of the impulse which was communicated to them, by the arrival of the precious materials thrown upon the coasts of Italy, after the taking of Constantinople: but even these riches, brought to Europe by a few men, driven upon our shores by a tempest, came to us, like the remains of a shipwrecked crew, who, after having with difficulty saved their lives from the fury of the waves, have only preserved in their benumbed hands some gold and a few precious stones.

For this reason, precisely, do we lament, because from the example we have adduced, we are enabled the better to understand the immense riches of the vessel which was lost; this makes us grieve the more bitterly that the early times of the illustrious cenobites of the East have not been brought down to our day by a continued chain. When we see their works overflow with sacred and profane learning, when their labors show us proofs of indefatigable activity, we think with sorrow of the inestimable treasures which their libraries must have contained.

Yet, in spite of the justness of the melancholy reflections we have here made, it must be allowed that the influence of these monasteries never ceased to be extremely useful to the preservation of knowledge. The Arabs, in the times of their success, showed themselves to be intelligent and cultivated; and Europe, in many respects, is indebted to them for much advancement. Bagdad and Grenada, during the middle ages, are two brilliant centres of intellectual movement and art, which serve not a little to diminish the sombre effect of the barbarities of Islamism: they are two tranquil and pleasing features in a frightful picture. If it were possible to follow the history of intellectual development among the Arabs, through the transformations and catastrophes of the East, perhaps we should find in the sciences of the nations which they conquered or destroyed the origin of much of their progress. It is certain that their own civilization did not contain any vital principle favorable to the development of the mind; we have a proof of this in their religious and social organization, and in the small results which they obtained, after having been for so many centuries peacefully established in the conquered countries. Their whole system, with respect to letters and intellectual cultivation, is founded on that stupid maxim, uttered by one of their chiefs, when he condemned an immense library to the flames: "If these books are contrary to the Alcoran, they should be burnt as pernicious; if they are not contrary to it, they should be burnt as useless."

We read in Palladius, that the monks of Egypt did not content themselves with working with rude and simple objects, but that they devoted themselves to labors of all kinds. These thousands of men, who, belonging to all classes and to all countries, embraced the solitary life, must have brought to the desert a large treasure of knowledge. We know how far the human mind can go when left to itself, and applied to a fixed occupation; there is always some reason for thinking that a great part of the valuable ideas on the secrets of nature, the utility and properties of certain ingredients, the principles of some of the arts and sciences, knowledge which formed the rich patrimony of the Arabs at the time when they appeared in Europe, were nothing but the remains of ancient learning, gathered by them in countries which had formerly been inundated by men from all parts. We must remember that at the time of the first invasions of the northern barbarians, when Spain, the south of France, Italy, the north of Africa, and all the islands adjacent to these countries, were ravaged by these terrible men, the East became a refuge, an asylum, for all those who could undertake the voyage. Thus the treasures of Western science accumulated every day in these countries; this emigration from all the Western regions may have contributed, in an extraordinary manner, to convey to the East the remains of ancient knowledge, which afterwards came to us transformed and disfigured by the hands of the Arabs.

Deeply convinced of the nothingness of the world by so long a succession of heavy misfortunes, these unfortunate men felt the religious sentiment strengthened in their hearts; the fugitives assembled in the East listened with lively emotion to the energetic words of the solitary of the cave of Bethlehem. A great many of them retired into the monasteries, where they found relief for their wants, and consolation for their souls; thus did the Eastern monasteries gain a great addition of valuable knowledge and information of all sorts.

If European civilization one day become complete mistress of the countries which now groan under the Mussulman yoke, perhaps it will be given to the history of science to add a noble page to its labors, when, through the obscurities of the times, and by means of manuscripts discovered by curiosity or chance, she shall have found the thread which shall lead to a knowledge of the connection of Arabian science with that of antiquity. The succession of transformations will then be displayed, and we shall understand how the science of the sons of Omar has appeared to have a different origin in our eyes. The archives of Spain contain, in documents relating to the dominion of the Saracens, riches, the examination of which may be said not yet to be commenced; perhaps they will throw some light on this point. There is no doubt that they afford matter for careful investigation, extremely curious for appreciating these two very different civilizations, the Mohammedan and the Christian.

CHAPTER XLI.

OF RELIGIOUS INSTITUTIONS IN THE HISTORY OF THE WEST.

LET us now examine religious institutions, such as they appear in the West, but laying aside those which, although established in various parts of the West, were only a sort of ramification of the Eastern monasteries. We observe that the religious establishments among us added to the Gospel spirit, the principle of their foundation, a new character, that of conservative, restorative, and regenerative associations. The monks of the West were not content with sanctifying themselves; from the first they influenced society. The light and life which their holy abodes contained, labored to enlighten and fertilize the chaos of the world. I do not know in history a nobler or more consoling spectacle than that which is presented to us by the foundation, existence, and development of the religious institutions of Europe. Society had need of strong efforts to preserve its life in the terrible crisis through which it had to pass. The secret of strength is in the union of individual forces, in association; and it is remarkable that this secret has been taught to European society as if by a revelation from heaven. Every thing shakes, falls to pieces, and perishes. Religion, morality, public authority, laws, manners, sciences, and arts—every thing has sustained immense losses, every thing goes to ruin; and judging of the future fate of the world according to human probabilities, the evils are so great and numerous that a remedy appears impossible.

The observer who, fixing his eyes upon those desolate times, finds there St. Bennet giving life to and animating the religious institutions, organizing them, giving them his wise rule and stability, imagines that he sees an angel of light issuing from the bosom of darkness. Nothing can be imagined better calculated to restore to dissolved society a principle of life capable of reorganizing it, than the extraordinary and sublime inspiration which guided this man. Who does not know what at that time was the condition of Italy—I should rather say, of the whole of Europe? What ignorance, what corruption, what elements of social dissolution! What desolation everywhere! and it is amid this deplorable state of things that the holy solitary appears, the child of an illustrious family of Norcia, resolved to combat the evil which threatens to invade the world. His arms are his virtues; the eloquence of his example gives him an irresistible ascendency; elevated above the whole age, burning with zeal, and yet full of prudence and discretion, he founds that institution which is to remain amid the revolution of ages, like the pyramids unmoved by the storms of the desert.

What idea has there been more grand, more beneficent, more full of foresight and wisdom? At a time when knowledge and virtue had no longer an asylum, when ignorance, corruption, and barbarism rapidly extended their conquests, was it not a grand idea to raise a refuge for misfortune, to form a sacred deposit for the precious monuments of antiquity, and to open schools of knowledge and virtue, where men destined one day to figure in the vortex of the world might come for instruction? When the reflecting man fixes his attention on the silent abode of Monte Cassino, where the sons of the most illustrious families of the empire are seen to come from all parts to that monastery; some with the intention of remaining there for ever, others to receive a good education, and soon to carry back to the world a recollection of the serious inspirations which the holy founder had received at Subiaco; when the monasteries of the order are seen to multiply everywhere, to be established as great centres of activity in all places—in the plains, in the forests, in the most uninhabited countries; he cannot help bending, with profound veneration, before the extraordinary man who has conceived such grand designs. If we are unwilling to acknowledge in St. Bennet a man inspired by Heaven, at least we ought to consider him as one of those geniuses who, from time to time, appear on earth to become the tutelary angels of the human race.

Not to acknowledge the powerful effect of such institutions would be to show but little intelligence. When society is dissolved, it requires not words, nor projects, not laws, but strong institutions, to resist the shock of the passions, the inconstancy of the human mind, and the destructive power of events; institutions which raise the mind, pacify and ennoble the heart, and establish in society a deep movement of reaction and resistance to the fatal elements which lead it to destruction. If there exists, then, an active mind, a generous heart, a soul animated by a feeling of virtue, they will all hasten to seek a refuge in the sacred asylums; it is not always granted to them to change the course of the world, but at least, as men of solitude and sacrifice, they labour to instruct and calm their own minds, and they shed a tear of compassion over the senseless generations who are agitated by great disasters. From time to time they succeed in making their voices heard amid the tumult, to alarm the hearts of the wicked by accents which resemble the formidable warnings of Heaven; thus they diminish the force of the evil while it is impossible to prevent it entirely; by constantly protesting against iniquity, they prevent its acquiring prescriptive right; in attesting to future generations, by a solemn testimony, that there were always, amid darkness and corruption, men who made efforts to enlighten the world and to restrain the torrent of vice and crime, they preserve faith in truth and virtue, and they reanimate the hopes of those who are afterwards placed in similar circumstances. Such was the action of the monks in the calamitous times of which we speak; such was their noble and sublime mission to promote the interests of humanity.

Perhaps it will be said that the immense properties acquired by the monasteries were an abundant recompense for their labors, and perhaps also a proof that their exertions were little disinterested. No doubt, if we look at things in the light in which certain writers have represented them, the wealth of the monks will appear as the fruit of unbounded cupidity, of cruelty, and perfidious policy; but we have the whole of history to refute the calumnies of the enemies of religion; and impartial philosophy, while acknowledging that all that is human is liable to abuse, takes care to assume a higher position, to regard things *en masse*, and to consider them in the vast picture where so many centuries have painted their features. It therefore despises the evil, which is only the exception, while it contemplates and admires the good, which is the rule.

Besides the numerous religious motives which brought property into the hands of the monks, there is another very legitimate one, which has always been regarded as one of the justest titles of acquisition. The monks cultivated waste lands, dried up marshes, constructed roads, restrained rivers within their beds, and built bridges over them; that is to say, in countries which had undergone another kind of general deluge, they renewed, in some measure, what the first nations had done to restore the revolutionized globe to its original form. A considerable portion of Europe had never received cultivation from the hands of men; the forests, the rivers, the lakes, the thorny thickets, were as rough as they had been left by the hands of nature. The monasteries which were founded here and there may be regarded as the centres of action, which the civilized nations established in the new countries, the faces of which they proposed to change by their powerful colonies. Did there ever exist a more legitimate title for the possession of large properties? Is not he who reclaims a waste country, cultivates it, and fills it with inhabitants, worthy of preserving large possessions there? Is not this the natural course of things? Who knows how many cities and towns arose and flourished under the shadow of the abbeys?

Monastic properties, besides their substantial utility, had another, which perhaps has not been sufficiently noticed. The situation of a great part of the nations of Europe, at the time we speak of, much resembled the state of fluctuation and inconstancy in which nations are found, who have not yet made any progress in the career of civilization and refinement. The idea of property, one of the most fundamental in all social organization, was but little rooted. Attacks on property at that time were very frequent, as well as attacks on persons. The man who is constantly compelled to defend his own, is also constantly led to usurp the property of others; the first thing to do to remedy so great an evil, was to locate and fix the population by means of the agricultural life, and to accustom them to respect for property, not only by reasons drawn from morality and private interest, but also by the sight of large domains belonging to establishments regarded as inviolable, and against which a hand could not be raised without sacrilege. Thus religious ideas were connected with social ones, and they slowly prepared an organization which was to be completed in more peaceable times.

Add to this a new necessity, the result of the change which took place at that time in the habits of the people. Among the ancients, scarcely any other life than that of cities was known; life in the country, that dispersion of an immense population, which in modern times forms a new nation in the fields, was not known among the ancients; and it is remarkable that this change in the mode of life was realized exactly when the most calamitous circumstances seemed to render it the most dangerous and difficult. It is to the existence of the monasteries in fields and in retired places that we owe the establishment and consolidation of this new kind of life, which, no doubt, would have been impossible without the ascendency and the beneficial influence of the powerful abbeys. These religious foundations joined all the riches and the power of feudal lords with the mild and beneficent influence of religious authority.

How much does not Germany owe to the monks! Did they not bring her lands into cultivation, make her agriculture flourish, and cover her with a numerous population? How much are not France, Spain, and England indebted to them! It is certain that this latter country would never have reached the high degree of civilization of which she now boasts, if the apostolic labors of the missionaries who penetrated thither in the sixth century had not drawn her out of the darkness of gross idolatry. And who were these missionaries? Was not the chief of them Augustine, a monk full of zeal, sent by a Pope who had also been a monk, St. Gregory the Great? Where do you find, amid the confusion of the middle ages, the great writers of knowledge and virtue, except in those solitary abodes whence issue St. Isidore, the Archbishop of Seville; the holy abbot St. Columbanus; St. Aurelian, Bishop of Arles; St. Augustine, the Apostle of England; that of Germany, St. Boniface; Bede, Cuthbert, Auperth, Paul, monks of Monte Cassino; Hincmar of Rheims, brought up at the monastery of St. Denis; St. Peter Damiens, St. Ives, Lanfranc, and so many others, who form a generation of distinguished men, resembling in no respect the other men of their time.

Besides the service rendered to society by the monks in religion and morals, they conferred inestimable benefits on letters and science. It has already been observed more than once, that letters took refuge in the cloisters, and that the monks, by preserving and copying the ancient manuscripts, prepared the materials which were one day to assist in the restoration of human learning. But we must not limit their merit to that of mere copyists. Many of them advanced far in science, many ages in advance of the times in which they lived. Not content with the laborious task of preserving and putting into order the ancient manuscripts, they rendered the most eminent service to history by compiling chronicles. Thereby, while continuing the tradition of the most important branches of study, they collected the contemporary history, which, perhaps, without their labor would have been lost. Adon, Archbishop of Vienne, brought up in the Abbey of Ferrière, writes a universal history, from the beginning of the world to his own time; Abbon, monk of St. Germain-des-Prés, composes a Latin poem, in which he relates the siege of Paris by the Normans; Aymon of Aquitaine writes the history of the French in four books; St. Ives publishes a chronicle of their kings; the German monk Witmar leaves us the chronicle of Henry I., of the Kings Otho and Henry II., which is much esteemed for its candor, and has been published many times; Leibnitz has used it to throw light on the history of Brunswick. Adhemar is the author of a chronicle, which embraces the whole time from 829 to 1029. Glaber, monk of Cluny, has composed a much-esteemed history of the events which happened in France from 980 to his own time; Herman, a chronicle which embraces the six ages of the world down to the year 1054. In fine, we should never finish if we were to mention the historical labors of Sigebert, Guibert, Hugh, Prior of St. Victor, and so many other illustrious men, who, rising above their times, applied themselves to labors of this kind; of which we cannot easily appreciate the difficulty and the high degree of merit, we who live in an age when the means of knowledge are become so easy, when the accumulated riches of so many ages are inherited, and when we find on all sides wide and well-beaten paths. Without the existence of religious institutions, without the asylum of the cloisters, these eminent men would never have been formed. Not only had the sciences and letters been lost sight of, but ignorance was so great, that seculars who knew how to read and write were very rare. Surely such circumstances were not well adapted to form men of merit enough to do honor to advanced ages. Who has not often paused to contemplate the distinguished triumvirate, Peter the Venerable, St. Bernard, and the Abbot Suger? May it not be said that the twelfth century is elevated above its rank in history, by producing a writer like Peter the Venerable, an orator like St. Bernard, and a statesman like Suger?

These ages show us another celebrated monk, whose influence on the progress of knowledge has not been rated at its just value by many critics who love only to point out defects: I mean Gratian. Those who have declaimed against him, eager to look for his mistakes, should have placed themselves in the position of a compiler in the thirteenth century, at a time when all resources were wanting, when the lights of criticism were yet to be created; they would then have seen whether the bold enterprise of the monk was not attended with more success than there was reason to hope for. The profit which was drawn from the collection of Gratian is incalculable. By giving in a small compass a great part of what was most precious in antiquity with respect to civil and canon law; by making an abundant collection of texts from the holy fathers, applied to all kinds of subjects, he awakened a taste for that species of research; he created the study of them; he made an immense step towards satisfying one of the first necessities of modern nations, the formation of civil and ecclesiastical codes. It will be said that the errors of Gratian were contagious, and that it would have been better to have recourse directly to the originals; but to read the originals it was necessary to know them; it was necessary to be informed of their existence, to be excited by the desire of explaining a proposed difficulty, to have acquired a taste for researches of that kind; all this was wanting before Gratian; all this was brought out by his enterprise. The general favor with which his labors were received is the most convincing proof of their merit; and if it be objected that this favor was owing to the ignorance of the time, I will reply, that we owe a tribute of gratitude to any one who throws a ray of light on the darkness, however feeble and wavering this ray may be.

CHAPTER XLII.

OF RELIGIOUS INSTITUTIONS DURING THE SECOND HALF OF THE MIDDLE AGES. THE MILITARY ORDERS.

THE rapid view which we have just taken of religious institutions from the irruption of the barbarians to the twelfth century, has shown us that the monastic foundations, during that time, were a powerful support for that remaining portion of society which was ready to fall to pieces in the universal ruin; an asylum for misfortune, for virtue, and for knowledge; a storehouse for the precious monuments of antiquity, and in some measure an assemblage of civilizing associations, which labored in silence at the reconstruction of the social edifice, by neutralizing the force of the dissolving principles which had ruined its basis; they were, besides, a nursery for forming the men who were required for the elevated posts in Church and State. In the twelfth and the following centuries, these institutions take a new form, and assume a character very different from that which we have just pointed out. Their aim remains not less highly religious and social; but the times are changed, and we must remember the words of the Apostle, *omnia omnibus.* Let us examine the causes and the results of these novelties.

Before going further, I will say a few words on the religious military orders, the name of which sufficiently indicates their double character of monk and soldier. The union of the monastic state with war: what a monstrous mixture! will be the cry. In spite of the supposed monstrosity, this union was in conformity with the natural and regular order of things; it was a strong remedy applied to very great evils; a rampart against imminent dangers; in a word, the expression of a great European necessity. This is not the place to relate the annals of the military orders, annals which, like the most illustrious history, afford wonderful and interesting pictures, with that mixture of heroism and religious inspiration which assimilates history with poetry. It is enough to pronounce the names of the knights of the Temple, of St. John of Jerusalem, of the Teutonic order, of St. Raymond, of the Abbot of Fitero, of Calatrava, instantly to remind the reader of a long series of marvellous events, forming one of the noblest pages in the history of that time. Let us omit these narrations, which do not regard us; but let us pause for a moment to examine the origin and spirit of these famous institutions.

The Cross and the Crescent were enemies irreconcilable by nature, and urged to the greatest fury by a long and bloody struggle. Both had great power and vast designs; both were supported by brave nations, full of enthusiasm and ready to throw themselves on each other; both had great hopes of success founded on former achievements; on which side will the victory remain? What course ought the Christians to pursue in order to avoid the dangers which threaten them? Is it better quietly to await the attack of the Mussulmen in Europe, or make a levy *en masse* to invade Asia and seek the enemy in his own country, where he believes himself to be invincible? The problem was solved in the latter way; the Crusades took place, and centuries have given their suffrage as to the wisdom of that resolution. What avails a little declamation affecting to favor the cause of justice and humanity? Let no one allow himself to be dazzled; the philosophy of history taught by the lessons of experience, enriched with a more abundant treasure of knowledge, the fruit of a more attentive study of the facts, has given a decisive judgment in this case; in this, as in other cases, religion has retired in triumph from the tribunal of philosophy. The Crusades, far from being considered as an act of barbarism and rashness, are justly regarded as a *chef-d'œuvre* of policy, which, after having secured the independence of Europe, gave to the Christian nations a decided preponderance over the Mussulmen. The military spirit was thereby increased and strengthened among European nations; they all received a feeling of fraternity, which transformed them into one people; the human mind was developed in many ways; the state of feudal vassals was improved, and feudality was urged towards its entire ruin; navies were created, commerce and manufactures were encouraged; thus society received from the Crusades a most powerful impulse in the career of civilization. We do not mean to say, that the men who conceived them, the Popes who excited, the nations who undertook, the princes and lords who promoted them with their power, were aware of the whole extent of their own works, or even had a glimpse of the immensity of their results; it is enough that they settled the existing question in the way the most favorable to the independence and prosperity of Europe; this, I repeat, is enough. I would observe, moreover, that we should attribute so much the more importance to things as human foresight has had little share in the events; now these things are nothing less than the principles and feelings of religion in connection with the preservation and happiness of society, Catholicity covering with her ægis and animating with her breath the civilization of Europe.

Such were the Crusades. Now, remember that this idea, so great and generous, was conceived with a degree of vagueness, and executed with that precipitation which is the fruit of the impatience of ardent zeal; remember that this idea—the offspring of Catholicity, which always converts its ideas into institutions—was to be realized in an institution, which faithfully represented it, and served, as it were, as its organ, in order that it might render itself felt, and gain strength and fruitfulness for its support. After this, you will look for some means of uniting religion and arms; and you will be filled with joy when, under a cuirass of steel, you shall find hearts zealous for the religion of Jesus Christ—when you shall see this new kind of men, who devote themselves without reserve to the defence of religion, while they renounce all that the world can offer—gentler than lambs, bolder than lions, in the words of St. Bernard. Sometimes they assembled in community, to raise their voices to Heaven in fervent prayer; sometimes they boldly marched to battle, brandishing their formidable lances, the terror of the Saracens. No; there does not exist in the annals of history an event so colossal as the Crusades, and you might search there in vain for an institution more generous than the military orders. In the Crusades we see numberless nations arise, march across deserts, bury themselves in countries with which they are unacquainted, and expose themselves to all the rigors of climates and seasons; and for what purpose? To deliver a tomb! Grand and immortal movement, where hundreds of nations advance to certain death—not in pursuit of a miserable self-interest—not to find an abode in milder and more fertile countries—not from an ardent desire to obtain for themselves earthly advantages—but inspired only by a religious idea, by a jealous desire to possess the tomb of Him who expired on the cross for the salvation of the human race! When compared with this, what becomes of the lofty deeds of the Greeks, chanted by Homer? Greece arises to avenge an injured husband; Europe to redeem the sepulchre of a God.

When, after the disasters and the triumphs of the Crusades, we see the military orders appear, sometimes fighting in the oriental regions, sometimes in the islands of the Mediterranean, sustaining and repelling the rude assaults of Islamism, which, emboldened by its victories, again longs to throw itself on Europe, we imagine that we behold those brave men, who, on the day of a great battle, remain alone upon the field, one against a hundred, securing by their heroism, and at the hazard of their lives, the safety of their companions in arms who retire behind them. Honor and glory to the religion which has been capable of inspiring such lofty thoughts, and has been able to realize such great and generous enterprises!

CHAPTER XLIII.

CONTINUATION OF THE SAME SUBJECT—EUROPE IN THE THIRTEENTH CENTURY.

PERHAPS they who are the most opposed to religious communities may be reconciled to the solitaries of the East, when they perceive in them a class of men who, by practising the most sublime and austere counsels of religion, have communicated a generous impulse to humanity, have raised it from the dust where Paganism had held it, and made it wing its flight towards purer regions. To accustom man to grave and strict morality; to bring back the soul within itself; to give a lively feeling of the dignity of his nature, of the loftiness of his origin and his destiny; to inspire him, by means of extraordinary examples, with confidence that the mind, aided by divine grace, can triumph over the animal passions, and make man lead an angelic life upon earth: these are benefits so signal, that a noble heart must show itself grateful and full of lively interest for the men who have given them to the world. As to the monasteries of the West, the benefits of their civilizing influence are so visible, that no man who loves humanity can regard them with animadversion; in fine, the military orders present us with an idea so noble, so poetical, and realize in so admirable a manner one of those golden dreams which cross the human mind in moments of enthusiasm, that they must certainly find respectful homage in every heart which beats at a noble and sublime spectacle.

There yet remains a more difficult task, that of presenting at the tribunal of philosophy—that philosophy so indifferent in religious matters—the other religious communities which are not comprised in the sketch which I have just made. Judgments of great severity have been passed upon those institutions which I have now to speak of; but in such things justice cannot be prescriptive. Neither the applause of irreligious men, nor the revolutions which upset all that stand in their way, can prevent the truth being placed in its true light, and folly and crime being stigmatized with disgrace.

The thirteenth century has just commenced; there appears a new kind of men, who, under different titles, denominations, and forms, profess a singular and extraordinary way of life. Some put on clothing of coarse cloth; they renounce all wealth and property; they condemn themselves to perpetual mendicity, spreading themselves over the country and the towns for the sake of gaining souls for Jesus Christ. Others bear on their dress the distinctive mark of the redemption of man, and undertake the mission of releasing from servitude the numberless captives who, from the misfortune of the times, have fallen into the hands of the Mussulmen. Some erect the cross in the midst of a people who eagerly follow them, and they institute a new devotion—a constant hymn of praise to Jesus and to Mary; at the same time they indefatigably preach the faith of the Crucified. Others go in search of all the miseries of man, bury themselves in hospitals, in all the asylums of misfortune, to succour and console. They all bear new standards; all show equal contempt for the world; they all form a portion separate from the rest of mankind; but they resemble neither the solitaries of the East, nor the sons of St. Bennet. The new monks arise not in the desert, but in the midst of society: their object is not to live shut up in monasteries, but to spread themselves over the fields and hamlets, to penetrate to the heart of the great masses of the population, and to make their voices heard both in the cottage of the shepherd and in the palace of the monarch. They increase on all sides in a prodigious manner. Italy, Germany, France, Spain, England, receive them; numerous convents arise as if by enchantment in the villages and towns; the Popes protect them and enrich them with many privileges; kings grant them the highest favors, and suppor them in their enterprises; the people regard them with veneration, and listen to them with respectful docility. A religious movement appears on all sides; religious institutions, more or less resembling each other, arise like the branches from the same trunk. The observer, when he sees this immense and astonishing picture, asks himself, What are the causes of so extraordinary a phenomenon? whence this singular movement? what is its tendency? what will be its effects on society?

When a fact of such high importance is realized all at once in many different countries, and lasts for centuries, it is a proof that there existed very powerful means to produce it. It is vain to be entirely forgetful of the views of Providence: no one can deny that such a fact must have had its root in the essence of things; consequently it is useless to declaim against the men and the institutions. Acknowledging this, the true philosopher will not lose his time in anathematizing the fact, but he will examine and analyze it. No declamation or invectives against the monks can efface their history; they have existed for many centuries, and centuries do not retrace their steps.

We will not inquire if there was here some extraordinary design of Providence, and we will lay aside the reflections which religion suggests to every true Catholic; we will confine ourselves to considering the religious institutions of modern times in a purely philosophical point of view; we can show that they were not only very conformable to the well-being of society, but also perfectly adapted to the situation in which it was placed; we can show that they displayed neither cunning, malice, nor vile self-interest; that their object was highly advantageous, and that they were at the same time the expression and the fulfilment of great social necessities.

The question of its own accord assumes the position in which we have just regarded it; and it is strange that men have not acknowledged all the importance of the magnificent points of view which here present themselves.

In order the better to clear up this important matter, I will enter upon an examination of the social condition of Europe at the time of which we speak. As soon as we take the first glance at this epoch, we observe that, in spite of the intellectual rudeness which one would imagine must have kept nations in abject silence, there was at the bottom of men's minds an anxiety which deeply moved and agitated them. These times are ignorant; but it is an ignorance which is conscious of itself and which longs for knowledge. There is felt a want of harmony in the relations and institutions of society; but that want is everywhere felt and acknowledged, and a continual agitation indicates that this harmony is anxiously desired and ardently sought for. I know not what singular character is stamped upon the nations of Europe, but we do not find there the symptoms of death; they are barbarous, ignorant, corrupt, any thing you please; but, as if they constantly heard a voice calling them to light, to civilization, to a new life, they incessantly labor to leave the fatal condition into which unhappy circumstances have plunged them. They never sleep in tranquillity amid the darkness; they never live without remorse amid the corruption of manners. The echo of virtue continually resounds in their ears; flashes of light appear in the darkness; a thousand efforts are made to advance a step in the career of civilization; a thousand times they are vain; but they are renewed as often as they are repulsed; the generous attempt is never abandoned; they fail a thousand times; but they never lose courage. Courage and ardour are never wanting. There is this remarkable difference between the nations of Europe, and those nations among whom the Christian religion has not yet penetrated, or from whose bosom it has been banished. Ancient Greece falls, never to rise again; the Republics of the shore of Asia disappear, and do not rise out of their ruins. The ancient civilization of Egypt is broken to pieces by the conquerors, and posterity has scarcely preserved a remembrance of them. Certainly none of the nations on the coast of Africa can show us signs which reveal the ancient country of St. Cyprian, of Tertullian and St. Augustine. Still more; a considerable portion of Asia has preserved Christianity, but a Christianity separated from Rome; and this has been unable to establish or regenerate any thing. Political power has aided and protected it, but the nation remains feeble; it cannot stand erect; it is a dead body, incapable of advancing; it is not like Lazarus, who has just heard the all-powerful voice: "Lazarus, come forth; *Lazare veni foras.*"

This anxiety, this agitation, this extreme eagerness towards a greater and happier future, this desire for reformation in manners, for enlargement and correction in ideas, for amelioration in institutions—the distinctive characteristics of modern nations—made themselves felt in a fearful manner at the time to which we allude. I will say nothing of the military history of those times, which would furnish us with abundant proofs of our assertion; I will confine myself to facts which, owing to their religious and social character, have the greatest analogy with the subject which now occupies us. A formidable energy of mind, a great fund of activity, a simultaneous development of the most ardent passions, an enterprising spirit, a lively desire of independence, a decided inclination to employ violent means, an extraordinary zeal for proselytism, ignorance combined with a thirst for knowledge, even combined with enthusiasm and fanaticism for all that bears the name of science; a high esteem for the titles of nobility, and of illustrious blood, united with the spirit of democracy, and a profound respect for merit, wherever it may be found; a childlike candor, an excessive credulity, and, at the same time, the most obstinate indocility; a tenacious spirit of resistance, fearful stubbornness, corruption, and licentiousness of manners, allied with admiration for virtue; a taste for the most austere practices, combined with an inclination for the most extravagant habits and manners; such are the traits which history exhibits among these nations.

So singular a mixture appears strange at first sight; and yet nothing was more natural. Things could not be otherwise: societies are formed under the influence of certain principles, and of certain particular circumstances, which impart to them their genius, character, and countenance. It is the same with society as with individuals; education, instruction, temperament, and a thousand other physical and moral circumstances, concur in forming a collection of influences which produce qualities the most different, and sometimes the most contradictory. This concurrence of different causes was shown in a singular and extraordinary manner among the nations of Europe; it is on this account that we observe there the most extravagant and discordant effects. Let us recollect the history of those nations since the fall of the Roman empire to the end of the Crusades; never did an assemblage of nations present a combination of more varied elements, and a spectacle of greater events. The moral principles which preside over the development of these nations were in direct opposition to their genius and situation. These principles were essentially pure, unchangeable as the God who had established them; radiant with light, because they emanated from the source of all light and life: the nations, on the contrary, were ignorant, rude, fluctuating, like the waves of the sea, and corrupted, as was to be expected of every thing which was the result of an impure mixture. Wherefore a terrible struggle took place between principles and facts; wherefore there were witnessed the most extraordinary contradictions, according as good and evil alternately preponderated. Never was the struggle between elements which could not remain at peace, more clearly seen; the genii of good and of evil seemed to descend into the arena, and to fight hand to hand.

The nations of Europe were not in their infancy, for they were surrounded by old institutions. Full of the recollections of ancient civilization, they preserved various remains of it. They were themselves produced by the mixture of a hundred nations, differing in laws, customs, and manners. They were not yet adult nations; as this denomination cannot be applied either to individuals or to society before they have reached a certain development, from which the nations of Europe were still far removed. It is very difficult to find a word to express this social state; it was neither a state of civilization, nor that of barbarism; for a number of laws and institutions existed there, which certainly did not deserve the epithet of barbarous. If we call these nations semi-barbarous, perhaps we shall approach the truth. Words are of little importance, if we have a clear idea of the things.

It cannot be denied that the European nations, owing to a long series of revolutions, and the extraordinary mixture of races, of ideas, and manners, of the conquerors with each other, and of the conquerors with the nations conquered, had a large portion of barbarism, and a fruitful germ of agitation and disorder. But the malignant influence of these elements was combated by the action of Christianity, which had obtained a decided preponderance over minds, and which, besides, was supported by powerful institutions. Christianity, to accomplish this difficult work, had the assistance of great material force. The Christian doctrines, which penetrated on all sides, tended, like a sweetening liquid, to soften and improve every thing; but, at every step, the mind comes into collision with the senses, morality with the passions, order with anarchy, charity with ferocity, and law with fact. Thence a struggle, which, although general to a certain extent in all times and countries, since it is founded on the nature of man, was then more rude, violent, and clamorous. The two most opposite principles, barbarism and Christianity, were then face to face in the same arena, with no one between them. Observe these nations with attention, read their history with reflection, and you will see that those two principles are constantly struggling, and constantly contending for influence and preponderance; thence the most strange situations, and the most singular contrasts. Study the character of the wars of that time, and you will hear the holiest maxims constantly proclaimed; legitimacy, law, reason, and justice are invoked; the tribunal of God is incessantly appealed to: this is the influence of Christianity. But, at the same time, you will be afflicted at the sight of numberless acts of violence, of cruelties, atrocities, pillages, rapines, murders, fires, and disasters without end: this is barbarism. If you look at the Crusades, you will observe that grand ideas, vast plans, noble inspirations, social and political views of the highest importance, fermented in men's heads; that all hearts overflowed with noble and generous feelings, and that a holy enthusiasm, transporting men out of themselves, rendered them capable of heroic actions: this is the influence of Christianity. But, if you examine the execution, you will see disorder, improvidence, want of discipline in the armies, injuries, and acts of violence; you will seek in vain for concert and harmony among those who take part in the gigantic and perilous enterprise: there is barbarism. Youths, thirsting for knowledge, crowd to the lectures of the famous masters, from the most distant countries; Italians, Germans, English, Spanish, and French are mingled and confounded around the chairs of Abelard, Peter Lombard, Albertus Magnus, and St. Thomas of Aquin; a powerful voice resounds in their ears, calling them to leave the shades of ignorance and raise themselves to the regions of science; the love of knowledge animates them; the longest journeys cannot stop them; the enthusiasm for illustrious masters is carried to an indescribable extent. behold the influence of Christianity; behold her constantly stirring and illuminating the mind of man, never allowing him to repose tranquilly in obscurity, and continually exciting him to new intellectual labors and researches after truth! But behold these same youths, who exhibit such noble dispositions, and inspire such legitimate and consoling hopes; are they not also those licentious, restless, and turbulent young men, giving way to the most deplorable acts of violence, continually fighting in the streets, and forming in the midst of great cities a small republic, an unruly democracy, where there is much difficulty in maintaining law and good order? Behold here barbarism!

It is good, it is perfectly conformable to the spirit of religion, that the guilty man who raises a repentant and humiliated heart to God, should manifest his feeling and the affliction of his soul by external acts; that he should labor to fortify his mind, and restrain his evil inclinations, by employing the rigors of gospel austerity against his flesh: all this is sovereignly reasonable, just, holy, and conformable to the maxims of the Christian religion, which thus ordains for the justification and sanctification of the sinner, to repair the injury done to the souls of others by the scandal of a bad life. But that penitents, half naked, should wander about loaded with chains, carrying horror and alarm everywhere, as happened at this time, when we see ecclesiastical authority compelled to repress the abuse: this marks the spirit of rudeness and ferocity which always accompany the state of barbarism. Nothing is more true, noble, and salutary for society, than to imagine God always ready to defend innocence, to protect it against injustice and calumny, and to raise it above humiliation and disgrace, by restoring to it, sooner or later, the purity and lustre of which they have attempted to deprive it. This supposition is an effect of faith in Providence—that faith emanating from Christian ideas, which represent to us God as embracing the whole world in his view, reaching with his penetrating eye the deepest recesses of the heart, and not even excluding the meanest of his creatures from his paternal love. But who does not perceive the infinite distance which separates this pure faith from the trials by fire, water, and single combat? Who does not here discover rudeness confounding all things—the spirit of violence laboring to subject every thing to a rigorous law—attempting, in some measure, to oblige God himself to comply with our wants and caprices, in order to interpose the testimony of his solemn miracles, whenever it suits our pleasure or convenience to find out the truth?

I introduce these contrasts here in order to awaken the recollections of those who have read history, and to enable me to establish, in a few words, the simple and general formula which sums up all those periods: "Barbarism tempered by religion; religion disfigured by barbarism."

In the study of history we constantly encounter a serious obstacle, which renders it always difficult, and sometimes impossible, to understand it perfectly. We make the mistake of referring every thing to ourselves, and to the objects which surround us—a mistake which is excusable, no doubt, since it has its root in our own nature, but against which we must be carefully on our guard, if we wish to avoid deplorable errors. We imagine the men of other times to be like ourselves; without thinking of it, we communicate to them our own ideas, manners, inclinations, and even temperaments; and, after having fashioned men who exist only in our own imaginations, we desire and demand that the real men should act in the same manner as these imaginary men; and at the slightest discord between the historical facts and our unreasonable suppositions, we cry out that it is strange and monstrous, taxing with being strange and monstrous what was perfectly regular and ordinary according to the epoch.

It is the same with respect to laws and institutions: when we do not find them according to the types which we have under our eyes, we declaim against the ignorance, iniquity, and cruelty of the men who have conceived and established them. If we wish to form an exact idea of an epoch, it is necessary to transport ourselves there—to make an effort of imagination, in order, as it were, to live and converse with its men; it is not enough to hear the recital of the events, it is necessary to witness them, to become one of the spectators, one of the actors, if possible; it is necessary to call forth generations from the tomb, and make them act under our eyes. I shall be told that this is very difficult. I grant it; but it is necessary, if we wish that our knowledge of history should be something more than a mere notion of names and dates. It is quite sure that we do not know an individual well, unless acquainted with his ideas, character, and conduct. It is the same with a society: if we are ignorant by what doctrines it was guided, what was its manner of considering and feeling things, we shall see the events only superficially—we shall know the words of the law, but we shall not penetrate its spirit or genius; when contemplating an institution, we shall see only the external frame-work, without reaching the mechanism, or guessing the moving machinery. If we attempt to avoid these defects, it is certain that the study of history becomes the most difficult of all; but this knowledge has been wanting for a long time. The secrets of man and the mysteries of society are, at the same time, the most important subject which can be proposed to the human mind, and the most arduous, the most difficult, and the least accessible to the generality of intellects.

The individual in the times to which we allude was not the individual of to-day; his ideas were very different, his manner of seeing and feeling was not ours, his soul was of quite another temper from our own; what is inconceivable to us, was perfectly natural to men of those times; they took pleasure in what is now repugnant to us.

At the beginning of the thirteenth century, Europe had already experienced the powerful shock of the Crusades; the sciences began to germinate; the spirit of commerce was in some degree developed; the taste for industry made itself felt; and the inclination of men to enter into communication with other men, and of nations to mingle with other nations, was every day extended and increased. The feudal system, already shaken, was about to fall to pieces; the power of the commonalty rapidly increased; the spirit of enfranchisement showed itself everywhere; in fine, owing to the almost complete abolition of slavery, and to the change effected by the Crusades in the condition of vassals and serfs, Europe was covered with a numerous population who knew not slavery, and who bore with difficulty the feudal yoke. Yet this population was still far from possessing all that is necessary to rise to the rank of free citizens. Modern democracy already offered itself to the view, with its great advantages, its numerous difficulties, its immense problems, which still embarrass and disconcert us, after so many centuries of trial and experience. The lords preserved in great measure their habits of barbarism and ferocity, by which they had been unfortunately distinguished at former periods; the royal power was far from having acquired that force and *prestige* necessary for ruling such opposite elements, and to raise itself in the midst of society as a symbol of respect for all interests—a centre of reunion for all forces, and a sublime personification of reason and justice.

In the same century, wars began to assume a character more popular, and consequently more vast and important; the agitations of the people began to wear the aspect of political commotions. Already we discover something more than the ambition of emperors attempting to impose their yoke on Italy; we have no longer petty kings who contend for a crown or a province, or counts or barons who, followed by their serfs, fight with each other or with the neighboring municipalities, covering the land with blood and rapine. We observe in the movements of that period something more important and alarming. Numerous nations arise and crowd around a banner on which, instead of the ensigns of a baron or of a monarch, appears the name of a system of doctrines. No doubt, the lords take part in the struggle, and their power raises them still far above the crowd which surrounds and follows them; but the cause in question is not that of these men; they are accounted something in the problems of the times; but mankind looks beyond the horizon of castles. This agitation and movement, produced by the appearance of new religious and social doctrines, is the announcement and the beginning of that chain of revolutions which Europe has to undergo.

The evil did not consist in the disposition of nations to carry out their ideas, and refuse to take as their only guide the interests and doctrines of a few tyrants. On the contrary, this was a great step gained in the path of civilization; men thus showed that they felt and understood their own dignity better, that they took a more extended view, and had a better understanding of their own situation and interests. This progress was the natural result of the higher flight which was every day taken by the faculties of the mind. The Crusades had greatly contributed to this new movement; from that great epoch the different nations of Europe were accustomed no longer to fight for the possession of a small territory, or to gratify private ambition or revenge. The nations fought in support of a principle by laboring to avenge the outrage offered to the true religion; in a word, they became accustomed to be moved, to contend, to die, for an idea which, far from being limited to a small territory, embraced heaven and earth. Thus, we will observe in passing, that the popular movement, the movement in ideas, began in Spain much sooner than in the rest of Europe, because the war against the Moors had advanced the period of the Crusades for that country. The evil, I repeat it, was not in the interest which the people took in ideas, but in the imminent danger of seeing those nations, on account of their rudeness and ignorance, allow themselves to be abused and deceived by the first fanatic who came. At a moment when the movement was so vast, the fate of Europe depended on the direction which was about to be given to the universal activity: unless I am deceived, the twelfth and thirteenth centuries were the critical epochs, when, in the face of great probabilities on both sides, there was decided the great question of knowing whether Europe, in its twofold social and political relations, was to take advantage of the benefits of Christianity, or permit all the promise of a better future to be lost and annihilated.

When we fix our eyes on this period, we find, in different parts of Europe, a certain germ and index of the greatest disasters; the most horrible doctrines arise among the masses who begin to be agitated; the most fearful disorders signalize the first step of these nations in the career of life. Before this, we have discovered only kings and lords, but now the people appear on the scene. Thus we see that some rays of light and heat have penetrated this shapeless mass. At this sight the heart is dilated and encouraged, presaging the new future which is reserved for humanity. But, at the same time, the observer is alarmed, for he is aware that this heat may produce excessive fermentation, engender corruption, and multiply impure insects in the field which promises soon to become an enchanting garden.

The extravagances of the human mind at this time appear under so alarming an aspect, and with a turbulence of character so fearful, that apprehensions apparently the most exaggerated are supported by facts, and become terrible probabilities. Let me recall some of those facts which so vividly paint the condition of minds at that time; facts which besides are connected with the principal point which we are examining. At the beginning of the twelfth century, we find the famous Tanchème, or Tanquelin, teaching the maddest theories and committing the greatest crimes; yet at Antwerp, in Zealand, in the country of Utrecht, and in many other towns in the same countries, he draws after him a numerous crowd. This wretched man advanced that he was more worthy of supreme worship than Jesus Christ himself, "for," said he, "if Jesus Christ had received the Holy Spirit, he (Tanchème) had received the plenitude of that Holy Spirit." He added that the whole Church was comprised in his own person and in his disciples. The pontificate, episcopate, and priesthood were, according to him, mere chimeras. His instructions and discourses were particularly addressed to women; the result of his doctrines and proceedings was the most revolting corruption. Yet the fanaticism which was excited by this abominable man went so far that the sick eagerly drank the water in which he had bathed, believing it to be the most salutary remedy for body and soul. Women thought themselves happy to have obtained the favors of the monster; mothers considered it an honor for their daughters to be selected as the victims of his profligacy, and husbands were offended when their wives were not stained with this disgrace. Tanchème, knowing all the ascendency which he was able to exert over minds, was not backward in making use of the fanaticism of his followers; one of the principal virtues with which he labored to inspire them was liberality in favor of his own interest.

One day when he was surrounded with a large concourse of people, he had a picture of the Virgin brought to him; touching it with his sacrilegious hand, he said that he took the Virgin as his wife. Then, turning toward the spectators, he added, that as he had contracted marriage with the Queen of Heaven, as they had just seen, it was their duty to make the wedding presents. He immediately placed two boxes, one on the right and the other on the left of the picture, to receive on one side the offerings of the men, and on the other those of the women; for the purpose of learning, as he said, which of the two sexes had the greater affection for him. This artifice, as low and gross as it was sacrilegious, seemed only calculated to excite the indignation of those who were present; yet the results corresponded with the expectations of the artful impostor. The women, always jealous of the affection of Tanchème, surpassed in liberality; in a perfect frenzy, they stripped themselves of their necklaces, golden rings, and most precious jewels.*

When he felt himself strong enough, Tanchème did not content himself with preaching; he was desirous of surrounding himself with an armed troop, in order to give him in the eyes of the world a far different appearance from that of an apostle. Three thousand men accompanied him everywhere. Surrounded by this respectable escort, clothed in magnificent apparel, and preceded by his standard, he moved with all the pomp of a king. When he stopped to preach, the three thousand satellites stood armed around him with drawn swords. It is evident, the aggressive character of the heretical sects of succeeding ages was already traced out.

Every one knows how numerous were the partisans of Eon. This unhappy man was excited by hearing the frequent repetition of the words: "Per eum qui judicaturus est vivos et mortuos:" and he became persuaded and he asserted, that he himself was the judge who was to judge the living and the dead. We are also aware of the troubles excited by the seditious speeches of Arnauld of Brescia, the iconoclastic fanaticism of Pierre de Bruis and Henri. If I did not fear to fatigue the attention of my readers, it would be easy for me to relate here the most revolting scenes which represent to the life the spirit of the sects of those times, and the unfortunate predisposition which led men's minds to novelty, to extravagant spectacles, and I know not what fatal giddiness, whereby they were precipitated into the most strange errors and the most deplorable excesses. At all events, I must say a few words of the Cathari, Vaudois, Paterins of Arras, Albigenses, and poor men of Lyons. These sects, besides the influence which they had on the times of which we speak and on the later events of European history, will be of great use in making us fathom more deeply the question now before us. From the first ages of the Church, the sect of the Manichees was remarkable for errors and extravagances. Under different names, with more or less of followers, and with doctrines more or less various, it continued from age to age until the eleventh century, when it excited disturbances in France. From that time, Heribert and Lisoy acquired an unhappy celebrity by their obstinacy and fanaticism. In the time of St. Bernard, the sects called apostolical were distinguished by their dislike to marriage; while, on the other hand, they gave themselves up to the basest and most un bridled licentiousness. Nevertheless, all these irregularities were favorably received by the ignorance or the corruption of the people. This is proved by the rapidity with which they gained the masses and spread like a pestilence wherever they appeared. Besides the hypocrisy, which is common to all the sects, that of the Manichees imagined an artifice the most apt to seduce rude and ignorant people: they appeared with the most rigid austerity and the most miserable clothes. Before the year 1181, we see the Manichees bold enough to venture out of their conventicles and openly teach their doctrines in the light of day. They associated with the celebrated bandits called *Cottereaux*, and feared not to commit all sorts of excesses, as they had seduced some knights and had secured the protection of some seigneurs of the country of Toulouse; they succeeded in exciting a formidable insurrection, which could be repressed only by force of arms. An eye-witness, Stephen, Abbot of St. Genevieve, at that time sent to Toulouse by the king, describes to us in a few words the acts of violence committed by these sectaries: "I have seen on all sides," he says, "churches burnt and ruined to their foundations: I have seen the dwellings of men changed into the dens of beasts."

About the same time, the Vaudois, or poor men of Lyons, became famous. This last name was given to them on account of their extreme poverty, their contempt for all riches, and the rags with which they were covered. Their shoes also gave them the name of Sabatathes. They were perverse imitators of another kind of poor, celebrated at that time, and who were distinguished by their virtues, and particularly by their spirit of humility and disinterestedness. These latter, who formed a kind of association, comprising priests and laymen, attracted the respect and esteem of real Christians, and obtained the Pope's permission to teach publicly. The disciples showed a profound contempt for Church authority; they afterwards entertained monstrous errors, and in the end became a sect in opposition to religion, injurious to good morals, and incompatible with public tranquillity.

These errors, which were the germs of so many calamities and troubles, could not be extirpated; with time they became more and more rooted in various countries, and the progress of things was so fatal, that at the beginning of the thirteenth century the period of short-lived seditions and isolated troubles was already long gone by, the errors had already spread on a large scale, and appeared with formidable resources for the contest. Already the south of France, agitated by civil discord, and precipitated into a fearful war, was in a state of terrible conflict. In the political organization of that time, the throne had not strength enough to exercise a controlling power, the lords had still the means of resisting kings and doing violence to the people. When a spirit of disobedience, agitation, and movement is spread throughout the masses, there is only one means of restraining them, that of religion; and this very ascendency of religious ideas was taken advantage of by the wicked and the fanatical; and to mislead the multitude they availed themselves of violent declamation, where religion and politics formed a confused mixture, and where the spirit of austerity and disinterestedness was the subject of hypocritical affectation. The new errors were no longer confined to subtile attacks on particular dogmas, they assailed the fundamental ideas of religion, penetrated to the sanctuary of the family, on the one side condemning marriage, and on the other promoting infamous abominations: in fine, the evil was not limited to countries which by a tardy and incomplete initiation into the doctrines of Christianity, or for any other reason, had not fully participated in the European movement. The arena principally chosen was the south; that is, the country where the human mind was developed in the most prompt and lively manner.

In the midst of such a concourse of unfortunate circumstances, all attested and placed beyond a doubt by history, was not the future of Europe very dark and tempestuous? Ideas and manners were in imminent danger of taking a wrong direction; the bands of authority, the ties of family, seemed ready to break asunder; the nations might be led away by fanaticism or superstition; Europe was in danger of being replunged into the chaos whence it had emerged with so much difficulty. At that time the Crescent shone in Spain, it reigned in Africa, it triumphed in Asia. Was Europe at such a moment to lose her religious unity, and see new errors penetrate everywhere, sowing schism in all countries, and with it discord and war? Were all the elements of civilization and refinement created by Christianity to be dispersed and stricken with sterility for ever? Were the great nations formed under the influence of Catholicity, the laws and institutions impregnated with that divine religion, to be corrupted, falsified, and destroyed by changes in the ancient faith? In fine, was the course of European civilization to be violently diverted, and were the nations who were already advancing towards a peaceful, prosperous, and glorious future, to be condemned to see their most flattering hopes dissipated in a moment, and miserably to retrograde towards barbarism? Such was then the vast problem placed before society; and I fear not to assert that the religious movement which at that time displayed itself in so extraordinary a manner, and the new religious institutions, so inconsiderately accused of folly and extravagance, were a powerful means employed by Providence to save religion and society. If the illustrious Spaniard, St. Dominic de Guzman, and the wonderful man of Assisi, did not occupy a place on our altars, there to receive the veneration of the faithful for their eminent sanctity, they would deserve to have statues raised to them by the gratitude of society and humanity. But what! are our words an object of scandal to you, who have only read and considered history through the deceitful medium of Protestant and philosophical prejudices? Tell us, then, what you find reprehensible in these men, whose establishments have been the subject of your endless diatribes, as if they had been the greatest calamities of the human race? Their doctrines are those of the Gospel; they are the same doctrines, to the loftiness and sanctity whereof you have been compelled to render solemn homage, and their lives are pure, holy, heroic, and conformable in every thing to their teachings. Ask them what is the object they have in view; that of preaching the Catholic truth to all men, they will tell you; of making every effort, of exerting every energy to destroy error and reform morals; of inspiring nations with the respect which is due to all legitimate authorities, civil and ecclesiastical. That is to say, you will find among them a firm resolution to devote their lives to remedy the evils of Church and State.

They do not content themselves with barren wishes; they are not satisfied with a few discourses and transitory efforts; they do not confine their plans to their mere personal sphere, but, extending their views to all countries and future times, they found institutions whereof the members may spread themselves over the whole surface of the world, and transmit to future generations the apostolical spirit which has inspired them with their grand ideas. The poverty to which they condemn themselves is extreme; the dress they wear is rude and miserable; but do you not see the profound reasons for this conduct? Remember that they propose to renew the gospel spirit, so much forgotten in their time; that they frequently happen to meet face to face the emissaries of the corrupt sects, who, endeavoring to imitate Christian humility, and affecting an absolute disinterestedness, make a parade of presenting themselves in public in the garb of beggars; remember, in fine, that they go to preach to semi-barbarous nations, and that to preserve them from the giddiness of error which has begun to take possession of their heads, words are not enough, even accompanied by a regular and uniform conduct; extraordinary examples, a mode of life which bears with it the most powerful edification, and sanctity clothed with an exterior adapted to make a lively impression on the imagination, are required.

The number of the new religious is very considerable; they increase without measure in all the countries where they are established; they are found, not only in the country and in the hamlets, but they penetrate into the midst of the most populous cities. Observe, that Europe is no longer composed of a collection of small towns and wretched cottages erected round feudal castles, and humbly obedient to the authority or the influence of a proud baron; Europe no longer consists of villages grouped round rich abbeys, listening with docility to the instructions of the monks, and receiving with gratitude the benefits conferred on them. A great number of vassals have already thrown off the yoke of their lords; powerful municipalities arise on all sides, and in their presence the feudal system is frequently compelled to humble itself in alarm. Towns become every day more populous—every day, from the effects of the emancipation which takes place in the country, they receive new families. Reviving industry and commerce display new means of subsistence, and excite an increase of population. It results from all this that religion and morality must act upon the nations of Europe on a larger scale; more general means, issuing from a common centre, and freed from ordinary fetters, are necessary to satisfy the new necessities of the time. Such are the religious institutions of the time of which we speak; this is the explanation of their astonishing number, of their numerous privileges, and of that remarkable regulation which places them under the immediate control of the Pope.

Even the character which marked these institutions—a character in some degree democratic, not only because men of all classes are there united, but also because of the special organization of their government—was eminently calculated to give efficacy to their influence over a democracy, fierce, turbulent, and proud of its recent liberty, and consequently little disposed to sympathize with any thing which might have been presented to it under aristocratic or exclusive forms. This democracy found in these new religious institutions a certain analogy with its own existence and origin. These men come from the people, they live in constant communication with them, and, like them, they are poor and meanly clad; and as the people have their assemblies where they choose their municipal officers and bailiffs, so do the religious hold their chapters, where they name their priors and provincials. They are not anchorites living in remote deserts, nor monks sheltered in rich abbeys, nor clergy whose functions and duties are confined to any particular country. They are men without fixed abodes, and who are found sometimes in populous cities and sometimes in miserable hamlets—to-day in the midst of the old continent, to-morrow on a vessel which bears them to perilous missions in the remotest countries of the globe; sometimes they are seen in the palaces of kings, enlightening their councils, and taking part in the highest affairs of state; sometimes in the dwellings of obscure families, consoling them in misfortune, making up their quarrels, and giving them advice on their domestic affairs. These same men, who are covered with glory in the chairs of the universities, teach catechism to children in the humblest boroughs; illustrious orators who have preached in courts, before kings and great men, go to explain the Gospel in obscure villages. The people find them everywhere, meet them at every step, in joy and in sorrow; these men are constantly ready to take part in the happy festivities of a baptism which fills the house with joy, or to lament a misfortune which has just covered it with mourning.

We can imagine without difficulty the force and ascendency of such institutions. This influence on the minds of nations must have been incalculable; the new sects which tended to mislead the multitude by their pestilential doctrines, found themselves face to face with an adversary who completely conquered them. They wished to seduce the simple by the ostentation of great austerity and wonderful disinterestedness; they desired to deceive the imagination, by striking it with the sight of exterior mortification, of poor and mean clothing. The new institutions united these qualities in an extraordinary manner. Thus the true doctrine had the same attributes which error had assumed. From among the classes of the people there come forth violent declaimers, who captivate the attention and take possession of the minds of the multitude by fiery eloquence. In all parts of Europe we meet with burning orators, pleading the cause of truth, who, well versed in the passions, ideas, and tastes of the multitude, know how to interest, move, and direct them, making use, in defence of religion, of what others attempt to avail themselves of in attacking her. They are found wheresoever they are wanted to combat the efforts of sects. Free from all worldly ties, and belonging to no particular church, province, or kingdom, they have all the means of passing rapidly from one place to another, and are found at the proper time wherever their presence is urgently required.

The strength of association, known to the sectaries, and used by them with so much success, is found in a remarkable degree in these new religious institutions. The individual has no will of his own: a vow of perpetual obedience has placed him at the disposal of another's will; and this latter is in his turn subject to a third; thus there is formed a chain, whereof the first link is in the hands of the Pope; the strength of association, and that of unity, are thus united in authority. There is all the motion, all the warmth of a democracy; all the vigor, all the promptitude of monarchy.

It has been said that these institutions were a powerful support to the authority of the Popes; this is certain: we may even add, that if these institutions had not existed, the fatal schism of Luther would perhaps have taken place centuries earlier. But, on the other hand, we must allow that the establishment of them was not due to projects of the papacy; the Sovereign Pontiffs did not conceive the idea of them; isolated individuals, guided by superior inspiration, formed the design, traced out the plan, and submitting that plan to the judgment of the Holy See, asked for authority to realize their enterprise. Civil institutions, intended to consolidate and aggrandize the power of kings, emanate sometimes from monarchs themselves, sometimes from some of their ministers, who, identifying themselves with their views and interests, have formed and executed the idea of the throne. It is not thus with the power of the Popes; the support of new institutions contributes to sustain that power against the attacks of dissenting sects; but the idea of founding the institutions themselves comes neither from the Popes nor their ministers. Unknown men suddenly arise among the people; nothing which has taken place affords reason to suspect them of having any previous understanding with Rome; their entire lives attest that they have acted by virtue of inspiration, communicated to themselves, an inspiration which does not allow them any repose, until they have executed what was prescribed to them. There are not, there cannot be, any private designs of Rome; ambition has no share. From this, all sensible men should draw one of these two consequences: either the appearance of these new institutions was the work of God, who was desirous of saving His Church by sustaining her against new attacks, and protecting the authority of the Roman Pontiff; or, Catholicity herself contained within her breast a saving instinct which led her to create these institutions, which were required to enable her to come triumphant out of the fearful crisis in which she was engaged. To Catholics, these two propositions are identical: in both we see only the fulfilment of the promise, "*On this rock I will build my Church, and the gates of hell shall never prevail against her.*" Philosophers who do not regard things by the light of faith, in order to explain this phenomenon, may make use of what terms they please; but they will be compelled to acknowledge that wonderful wisdom and the highest degree of foresight appear at the bottom of these facts. If they persist in not acknowledging the finger of God, and in seeing in the course of events only the fruit of well-concerted plans, or the result of organization combined with art, at least they cannot refuse a sort of homage to these plans and that organization. Indeed, as they confess that the power of the Roman Pontiff, considered in relations merely philosophical, is the most wonderful of all the powers which have appeared on earth, is it not evident that the society called the Catholic Church shows in her conduct, in the spirit of life which animates her, and in the instinct which makes her resist her greatest enemies, the most incomprehensible combination of phenomena which have ever been witnessed in society? It is of little importance to the truth, whether you call this instinct, mystery, spirit, or whatever name you please. Catholicity defies all societies, all sects, and all schools, to realize what she has realized, to triumph over what she has triumphed over, and to pass through, without perishing, the crises through which she has passed. A few examples, where the work of God was more or less imitated, may be alleged against us; but the magicians of Egypt, placed in the presence of Moses, came to an end of their artifices; the envoy of God performed wonders which they could not; and they were compelled to exclaim, "*The finger of God is here—the finger of God is here!*"

CHAPTER XLIV.

THE RELIGIOUS ORDERS FOR THE REDEMPTION OF CAPTIVES.

WHEN viewing the religious institutions produced by the Church during the thirteenth century, we did not pause to consider one among them, which, to the merit of participating in the glory of the others, adds a peculiar character of beauty and sublimity, and which is inexpressibly worthy of our attention: I speak of that institution, the object of which was to redeem captives from the hands of the Infidels. If I make use of this general designation, it is because I do not intend to enter into a particular examination of the various branches which compose it. I consider the unity of the object, and, on account of that unity, I attribute unity to the institution itself. Thanks to the happy change which has taken place in the circumstances which occasioned its foundation, we can now scarcely estimate the institution at its just value, and appreciate in a proper manner the beneficent influence and the holy enthusiasm which it must have produced in all Christian countries.

In consequence of the long wars with the Infidels, a very great number of the faithful groaned in fetters, deprived of their liberty and country, and often in danger of apostatizing from the faith of their fathers. The Moors still occupied a considerable part of Spain; they reigned exclusively on the coasts of Africa, and proudly triumphed in the East, where the Crusaders had been vanquished. The Infidels thus held the south of Europe closely confined, and were constantly able to seize favorable moments, and procure multitudes of Christian slaves. The revolutions and disorders of those times continually offered favorable opportunities; both hatred and cupidity urged them to gratify their revenge on the Christians taken unawares. We may be sure that this was one of the severest scourges which the human race had to endure at that time in Europe. If the word charity was to be any thing more than a mere name, if the nations of Europe were not to allow their bonds of fraternity and the ties which connected their common interests to be destroyed, there was an urgent necessity for them to come to an understanding, in order to remedy this evil. The veteran who, instead of a reward for his long services to religion and his country, had found slavery in the depths of a dungeon; the merchant who, ploughing the seas to carry provisions to the Christian armies, had fallen into the power of an implacable enemy, and paid by heavy chains for the boldness of his enterprise; the timid virgin who, playing upon the sea-shore, had been perfidiously carried away by the merciless pirates, like a dove borne away by a hawk:—all these unfortunate beings had undoubtedly some right to be looked at with compassion by their brethren in Europe, and to have an effort made to restore them to liberty.

How shall this charitable end be attained? Can means be employed to accomplish an enterprise which cannot be confided either to force or stratagem? Nothing is more fertile in resources than Catholicity. Whatever may be the necessity which presents itself, she immediately finds proper means of succor and remedy, if allowed to act with freedom. The remonstrances and negotiations of Christian princes could obtain nothing in favor of the captives; new wars undertaken for this purpose only served to increase the public calamities—they deteriorated the lot of those who groaned in slavery, and perhaps increased their number, by sending them fresh companions in misfortune; pecuniary means, without a central point of action and direction, produced but little fruit, and were lost in the hands of agents. What resource, then, does there remain? The powerful resource which is always found in the hands of the Catholic religion—the secret whereby she accomplishes her greatest enterprises, viz. *charity*.

But how ought this charity to act? In the same way as all the virtues of Catholicity. This divine religion, which has come down from the loftiest regions, and constantly raises the human mind to sublime meditations, presents at the same time a singular characteristic, whereby she is distinguished from all the schools and sects who have attempted to imitate her. In spite of the spirit of abstraction, if I may so speak, which holds her continually detached from earthly things, she has nothing vague, unsubstantial, or merely theoretical. With her, all is speculative and practical, sublime and simple; she adapts and accommodates herself to all that is compatible with the truth of her dogmas and the severity of her maxims. While her eyes are fixed on heaven, she forgets not that she is on earth, and that she has to deal with mortal men, subject to miseries and calamities. With one hand she shows them eternity, with the other she succors their misfortunes, solaces their pains, and dries up their tears. She does not content herself with barren words; the love of our neighbor is to her nothing, if that love does not manifest itself in giving bread to him who is hungry, drink to him who is thirsty; in clothing the naked, consoling the afflicted, visiting the sick, solacing the prisoner, and redeeming the captive. To make use of an expression of this age, I will say that religion is eminently *positive*. Wherefore she labors to realize her ideas by means of beneficent and fruitful institutions, thereby distinguishing herself from human philosophy, the pompous language and gigantic projects of which form so miserable a contrast with the littleness and nothingness of its works. Religion speaks little, but she meditates and executes as the worthy daughter of that infinite Being who, although absorbed in the contemplation of an ocean of light, His own essence and His impenetrable nature, has not the less created the universe the object of our admiration, and ceases not to preserve it with ineffable goodness, while governing it with incomprehensible wisdom.

It was necessary to go to the succor of the unhappy captives; assuredly, therefore, we should applaud the idea of a vast association, which, extending over all the countries of Europe, and placing itself in connection with all the Christians who would give alms in favor of so holy a work, would have in its service a certain number of individuals always ready to traverse the seas, and resolved to brave slavery and death for the redemption of their brethren. Numerous means would be thus combined, and the good employment of the funds would be secured. There was a certainty that the negotiations for the redemption of captives would be conducted by men of zeal and experience; in a word, such an association would completely fulfil its object; and when it was established, the Christians might hope for the most prompt and efficacious succor. Now, this was precisely the idea realized in the foundation of the religious orders for the redemption of captives.

The religious who embraced these orders bound themselves by vow to the accomplishment of this work of charity. Free from the embarrassments of family relations and worldly interests, they could devote themselves to their task with all the ardor of their zeal. Long voyages, the perils of the sea, the danger of unhealthy climates, or the ferocity of the Infidels—nothing stopped them. In their dress, in the prayers of their institution, they found a constant remembrance of the vow which they had taken in the Divine presence. Neither repose, comfort, nor even their very lives, any longer belong to them; all are become the property of the unhappy captives, who groan in the dungeons or wear heavy chains in presence of their masters, on the other side of the Mediterranean. The families of the unhappy victims, fixing their eyes on the religious, required of him the accomplishment of his promise; their groans and lamentations continually urge him to find means, and to expose his life, if necessary, to restore the father to the son, the son to the father, the husband to the wife, the innocent young girl to her desolate mother.

From the earliest ages of Christianity we see great zeal displayed for the redemption of captives, which has always been preserved, and the inspiration of which from that time has called forth the greatest sacrifices. The seventeenth chapter of this work, and the notes attached to it, have incontestably proved this truth; and it is not necessary that I should stay to confirm it here. Yet I will not lose the opportunity of observing that the Church, in the present case, as in all circumstances, has adopted her constant rule, viz. to realize her ideas by means of institutions. If you observe her conduct attentively, you will find that she begins by teaching and highly extolling a virtue; then she mildly persuades men to put it in practice; the practice extends and gains strength, and what was merely a good work becomes for some a work of obligation; what was a simple wise act is converted into a strict duty for some select men. At all times has the Church been engaged in the redemption of captives; at all times some Christians of heroic charity have stripped themselves of their property, of their liberty, to accomplish this work of mercy; but this care was still left to the discretion of the faithful, and no bodies of men existed to represent this charitable idea. New necessities arise; the ordinary means do not suffice; it is necessary that aid should be collected with promptitude, and employed with discernment; charity, as it were, requires an arm always ready to execute her orders; a permanent institution becomes necessary; the institution appears, and the want is satisfied.

We are so accustomed to see the beautiful and the sublime in the work of religion, that we scarcely observe the greatest prodigies there, in the same way as, while profiting by the benefits of nature, we look upon her most wonderful works and productions with an eye of indifference. The different religious institutions which, under various forms, have appeared since the beginning of Christianity, are worthy of exciting in the highest degree the astonishment of the philosopher and the Christian; but I doubt whether it be possible to find in the whole history of these institutions any thing more beautiful, interesting, and touching, than the picture of the orders for the redemption of captives. Does there exist a more admirable symbol of religion protecting the unfortunate? Which is the most sublime emblem of the redemption consummated on Calvary and extending itself to earthly captivity? Is it not the celebrated vision which preceded the establishment of the holy institutes of Mercy and the Trinity?

Some will say that these apparitions were only chimeras and mere illusions! Happy are those illusions, we will reply, which produce the consolation of the human race! However this may be, we will here recall these visions, braving, if necessary, the smiles of the incredulous. If they have preserved in their hearts any generous feelings, they will be compelled to allow that if these visions appear to them devoid of all historical truth, there is at least in the sublime sacrifice which is made by the man who devotes himself to slavery for the ransom of his brethren, a lofty poetry, a sincere love of the human race, an ardent desire to succor them, and an heroic disinterestedness.

A doctor of the University of Paris, known by his virtues and his wisdom, had just been raised to the priesthood, and celebrated for the first time the holy sacrifice of the altar. In consideration of these exalted favors of the Most High, he redoubles his ardor, he excites his faith, and endeavors to offer to the Lamb without spot, with all the recollection, purity, and fervor of which he is capable, his heart inundated with favors and inflamed by charity. He knows not how to manifest to God his profound gratitude for so great a benefit; his lively desire is to be able to prove to Him in some way his gratitude and his love. He who had said, "What you have done to one of my little children you have done to myself," immediately showed him a way to exhibit the fire of his charity. The vision begins: the priest sees an angel whose dress is white as snow and as brilliant as light; the angel wears on his breast a red and blue cross; at his sides are two captives, the one a Christian, the other a Moor; he places his hands over the heads of each. At this sight, the priest, ravished into ecstasy, understands that God calls him to the holy work of the redemption of captives; but before going any further, he retires into solitude, and devotes himself for three years to prayer and penance, humbly begging of the Lord that He would make known to him His sovereign will. In the desert he met with a pious hermit; the two solitaries aid each other by their prayers and examples. One day, when they were absorbed in pious communication by the side of a fountain, a stag suddenly appears to them bearing on his horns the mysterious cross of two colors. The priest relates to his astonished companion the first vision which he has had; both redouble their prayers and penances; both receive the celestial admonition for the third time. Then, unwilling any longer to defer the accomplishment of the Divine pleasure, they hasten to Rome, and ask of the Sovereign Pontiff his counsels and permission. The Pope, who at the same time had had a similar vision, joyfully accedes to the request of the two pious solitaries; the order of the Most Holy Trinity for the Redemption of Captives is thus established. The priest was called John of Matha; the hermit, Felix of Valois. They apply with ardent zeal to their work of charity; after having dried up the tears of numbers of unhappy beings, they now receive in heaven the reward of their labors. The Church, wishing to celebrate their memories, has placed them on her altars.

The foundation of the order of Mercy had a similar origin. St. Peter Nolasco, having spent all he possessed in the redemption of captives, had sought in vain for new resources to continue his pious undertaking. He had set himself to pray, in order to strengthen himself in his holy resolution of selling his own liberty, or remaining himself a captive in the place of some of his brethren. During his prayer the Blessed Virgin appeared to him; she gave him to understand how pleasing the foundation of an order for the redemption of captives would be to herself and her Divine Son. The saint, after consulting the King of Aragon and St. Raymond of Penafort, proceeded to the establishment of the order. He converted into a vow, not only for himself but for all those who embraced the institute, the holy desire which he had previously had to devote himself to slavery for the ransom of his brethren.

I repeat what I have already said: in whatever manner you judge of these apparitions, and if even you attempt to lay them aside altogether as mere illusions, it is not the less proved that the Catholic religion has labored with immense power to relieve a great misfortune, and that no one can call in question the utility of the holy institution in which the heroism of charity is so wonderfully personified. Indeed, supposing that the founder, the dupe of illusions, took for a revelation from heaven what was only the inspiration of ardent zeal, do not the benefits lavished on the unhappy captives remain the same? We hear much of illusions; but certain it is that these illusions produced a reality When St. Peter Armengol, wanting all resources to deliver some unfortunates, remained as a hostage in their place, and when the day of ransom had expired, resigned himself to be hung because the money had not arrived from Europe, the illusions certainly did not remain sterile. What reality could produce greater prodigies of zeal and heroism? Long ago have the things of religion been condemned as illusions and madness; from the earliest times of Christianity the mystery of the cross was treated as folly; but we do not see that this prevented the pretended folly from changing the face of the world.

CHAPTER XLV.

THE UNIVERSAL PROGRESS OF CIVILIZATION IMPEDED BY PROTESTANTISM.

In the rapid sketch which I have just given, my intention has not been to write the history of the religious orders; this did not form part of my design. I am satisfied with having offered a series of remarks which, by showing the importance of these institutions, were calculated to vindicate Catholicity from the accusations made against her on account of the protection which she has at all times afforded them. How could a comparison be made between Catholicity and Protestantism in their relations with the civilization of Europe, without devoting a few pages to the examination of the influence which these institutions have exercised on civilization? Now, if it is once shown that this influence was salutary, Protestantism, which has persecuted and calumniated these religious institutions with so much hatred and rancor, remains convicted of having done violence to the history of our civilization, of having mistaken its spirit, and still more of having aimed a blow at the legitimate development of that civilization itself.

These reflections naturally lead me to point out another fault which Protestantism has committed. When breaking the unity of European civilization, it introduced discord into the bosom of that civilization, and weakened the physical and moral action which it exercised on the rest of the world. Europe was apparently destined to civilize the whole world. The superiority of her intelligence, the preponderance of her strength, the superabundance of her population, her enterprising and valiant character, her transports of generosity and heroism, her communicating and propagating spirit, seemed to call her to diffuse her ideas, feelings, laws, manners, and institutions to the four quarters of the universe. How does it happen that she has not realized this destiny? How does it happen that barbarism is still found at her gates, and that Islamism still maintains itself in one of the finest climates and countries of Europe? Asia, with her want of moving power, weakness, despotism, and degradation of women; Asia, with all the disgraces of humanity, lies under our eyes; and scarcely have we done any thing which gives reason to hope that she will emerge from her degraded state. Asia Minor, the coasts of Palestine, Egypt, and the whole of Africa, are before us in a deplorable condition—a degradation which excites pity, and forms a melancholy contrast with the great recollections of history. America, after four centuries of incessant communication with us, is still so much behindhand that a great part of her intellectual powers and the resources with which nature has furnished her, remain until this day to be improved. How does it happen that Europe, full of life, rich in means of all kinds, overflowing with vigor and energy, has remained within the narrow limits in which she still is? If we pay deep attention to this melancholy phenomenon, a phenomenon with which it is very strange that the philosophy of history has not occupied itself, we shall find the cause. The entire cause thereof is the want of unity; her external action has been without concert, and consequently without efficacy. Men constantly vaunt the utility of association; they point out how necessary it is to obtain grand results, and they do not dream that because this principle applies to nations as well as to individuals, nations, like individuals, cannot accomplish great works, without conforming to this general law. When an assemblage of nations of the same origin, and subject for many ages to the same influence, have reached the development of their civilization under the guidance and control of a common idea, among them association becomes a real necessity; they form a family of brothers; now, among brothers, division and discord have worse results than among strangers.

I do not pretend to say that the nations of Europe could have attained to so perfect a concord, that perpetual peace would have been established among them, and that perfect harmony would have eventually presided over all their undertakings with respect to the other countries of the globe; but without giving way to beautiful illusions, the reality whereof is beyond the bounds of possibility, we may nevertheless, and without hazard of contradiction, say, that, in spite of particular differences between nation and nation, in spite of the greater or less degree of opposition between external and internal interests, Europe could have kept and perpetuated in her own breast a civilizing idea which, raising itself above all the misery and littleness of human passions, would have placed her in a condition to acquire a greater ascendency and a stronger and more useful influence over the other nations of the world. Amid the interminable series of wars and calamities which afflicted Europe during the fluctuations of the barbarous nations, this unity of thought existed; and it was owing to it that order in the end came out of confusion, and that light conquered darkness. In the long struggle of Christianity against Islamism, whether in Europe, Asia, or Africa, this same unity of thought enabled Christian civilization to triumph, in spite of the rivalries of kings and the excesses of the people. While this unity existed, Europe preserved a transforming power which made all that it touched become European sooner or later.

The heart is grieved at the sight of the disastrous event which broke this precious unity, by diverting the course of our civilization and destroying its fertilizing power. One can hardly observe without pain, not to say without anger, that the appearance of Protestantism was exactly coincident with the critical moment when the nations of Europe, about at length to reap the fruits of long ages of continued labor and unheard-of efforts, appeared to the world full of vigor, energy, and splendor. Putting forth gigantic strength, they discovered new worlds, and placed one hand on the East and the other on the West. Vasco de Gama had doubled the Cape of Good Hope, he had showed the way to the East Indies, and opened communication with unknown nations. Christopher Columbus, with the fleet of Isabella, ploughed the Western seas, discovered a new world, and planted the standard of Castile in unheard-of lands. Ferdinand Cortez, at the head of a handful of brave men, penetrated to the heart of the new continent, and took possession of its capital; his arms, which the natives had not yet seen, made him appear like a God launching his lightnings. Europe everywhere displayed extreme activity; a spirit of enterprise was developed in all hearts; the hour had come when the nations of Europe were about to see open before them a new horizon of power and grandeur, the limits whereof were invisible to the eye. Magellan discovered the strait which united the east and west; and Sebastian d'Elcano, returning to the Spanish coasts, after having made the tour of the world, seemed to be the sublime personification of European civilization taking possession of the universe. At one extremity of Europe, the crescent still shows itself powerful and threatening, like a dark figure appearing in the corner of a splendid picture: but fear nothing; its armies have been driven from Granadà, the Christian host is encamped on the coast of Africa, the standard of Castile floats on the walls of Oran, and in the heart of Spain grows up in silence the wonderful child, who, when he has but just laid aside the playthings of his age, will frustrate the last efforts of the Moors of that country by the triumphs of Alpujarres, and shortly after will break the Mussulman power for ever on the waves of Lepanto.

The development of mind kept pace with the increase of power. Erasmus examined all the sources of knowledge, astonished the world by his talents and his learning, and spread his fame in triumph from one end of Europe to the other. The distinguished Spaniard, Louis Vives, rivalled the *savant* of Rotterdam, and undertook nothing less than to regenerate the sciences, and give a new direction to the human mind. In Italy, the schools of philosophy were in a state of fermentation, and they seized with avidity the new lights brought from Constantinople. In the same country, the genius of Dante and Petrarch was continued in their illustrious successors; the land of Tasso resounded with his accents like the nightingale announcing the coming of the dawn; while Spain, intoxicated with her triumphs, and transported with pride at the sight of her conquests, sang like a soldier who, after victory, reposes on a heap of trophies. What could resist such superiority, such brilliant display, such great power? Europe, already secure against all her enemies, enjoying a prosperity which must every day increase, put in possession of laws and institutions better than any which had before been seen, and whereof the completion and perfection could not fail to come with the slow progress of time: Europe, we say, in a condition so prosperous, replete with noble hopes, was about to commence the work of civilizing the world. Even the discoveries which were every day made, indicated that the happy moment had arrived. Fleets transported, together with warriors, apostolic missionaries, whose hands were about to scatter in the new countries the precious seed, whence, in the progress of time, was to grow up the tree under whose shadow new nations were to find shelter. Thus was the noble work begun, which, favored by Providence, was about to civilize America, Africa, and Asia.

But the voice of the apostate who was about to cast discord into the bosoms of fraternal nations already resounded in the heart of Germany. The dispute begins, minds are excited, the irritation reaches its height, an appeal is made to arms, blood flows in torrents, and the man who had been commisioned by hell to scatter this cloud of calamities over the earth, contemplating before his death the dreadful fruit of his labors, can insult the sorrows of the human race with a cruel and impudent smile. Such do we figure to ourselves the genius of evil leaving his dark abode and his throne in the midst of horrors. He suddenly appears on the face of the globe, his hand sheds desolation and tears on all sides; he casts a look over the devastation which he has made, and then buries himself in eternal darkness.

By extending itself over Europe, the schism of Luther weakened in a deplorable manner the action of Europeans on the other nations of the world; the flattering hopes which had been conceived were dissipated in a moment, and became no more than a golden dream. Henceforth, the largest part of our intellectual, moral, and physical powers was condemned to be employed and sadly wasted in a struggle which armed brethren against brethren. The nations which had preserved Catholicity were compelled to concentrate all their resources, power, and energy, in order to make head against the impious attacks which the new sectaries made upon them by the press or by force of arms. The nations among whom the contagion of the new errors had been propagated were thrown into a sort of giddiness; they had no other enemies but the Catholics, and they considered only one enterprise worthy of their efforts—the degradation and destruction of the Roman See. Their thoughts no longer tended towards the invention of means for improving the lot of the human race; the immense field which had been thrown open to noble ambition by the recent discoveries, no longer merited attention; for them there was only one holy work—that of destroying the authority of the Roman Pontiff.

This condition of men's minds struck with sterility the ascendency over nations recently discovered or conquered, which naturally belonged to Europeans. When the nations of Europe simultaneously approached new regions, they no longer met as brothers or generous rivals, stimulated by noble ambition; they were exasperated and implacable enemies, men who differed in religion, and who fought battles against each other as bloody as those which had formerly been witnessed between the Christians and the Moors. The name of the Christian religion, which had been the symbol of peace for so many ages—a name which on the eve of battle was able to compel adversaries to lay aside their hatred, and embrace like brothers, instead of tearing each other in pieces like lions; a name which had served as an ensign to secure their triumph over Mohammedan legions: this name, now disfigured by sacrilegious hands, became a type of discord; and after Europe had been covered with blood and mourning, the scandal was transported to the nations of the New World. These simple and confiding nations were stricken with stupefaction on seeing the miseries, the spirit of division, hatred, and revenge which reigned among the same men upon whom they had just looked as demigods.

From that time forward, the forces of Europe were not united in any of those great enterprises which had shed so much glory on previous ages. The Catholic missionary, watering the Indian or American forests with his sweat and blood, could reckon on the assistance of the nation to which he belonged, if that nation remained Catholic; but he could not hope that all Europe, uniting in the work of God, would come to sustain the distant missions with her resources; he knew, on the contrary, that a great many Europeans would calumniate and insult him, and use all imaginable means to prevent the seed of the gospel from taking root on the new soil, and increasing the power of the Popes, by adding to the renown of the Catholic Church.

There was a time when the profanations of the Mussulmen in Jerusalem, and the injuries inflicted on the pilgrims who visited the Holy Sepulchre, were sufficient to arouse the indignation of all Christian nations. They all uttered the cry, *To arms!* and in crowds they followed the monk who led them to avenge the outrages against religion and the pious pilgrims. After the heresy of Luther, all was changed: the death of a missionary sacrificed in a foreign land, his torments and martyrdom, sublime scenes in which the zeal and charity of the first ages of the Church reappeared with all their energy: all this was devoted to contempt and ridicule by men who called themselves Christians—the unworthy posterity of the heroes whose blood had flowed under the walls of Jerusalem.

In order to conceive in its full extent the evil caused by Protestantism in this respect, let us imagine for a moment that Protestantism had not appeared; and in this hypothesis, let us make a few reflections on the probable course of events. In the first place, all the strength, genius, and resources which Spain employed to make head in the religious wars excited on the continent, would have been able to exert themselves in the New World. The same would have been the case with France, the Low Countries, and England. These nations, although divided, have been able to furnish brilliant and glorious pages in history; if their action on the new countries had been united and concentrated, would they not have exerted a vigor and energy which would have been irresistible? Imagine all the ports from the Baltic to the Adriatic sending their missionaries to the East and to the West, as did France, Spain, Portugal, and Italy; imagine all the great cities of Europe as so many centres where means for this great object are collected; imagine all the missionaries guided by the same views, under the influence of the same thought, and burning with the same zeal for the propagation of the same faith; wherever they meet, they meet as brothers, and co-operate in the common cause; all are under the same authority: do you not imagine that you see the Christian religion exerting herself on an immense scale, and everywhere gaining the most signal triumphs? The vessel which bears the apostolic men to distant regions may fearlessly unfurl her sails; when she discovers the flag of another country on the horizon, she is under no apprehension of meeting with enemies; she is sure of finding friends and brothers wherever there are Europeans.

The Catholic missions, in spite of the obstacles which have been opposed to them by the turbulent spirit of Protestantism, have accomplished the most difficult enterprises, and realized prodigies which form a brilliant page in modern history; but how much nobler would have been their results, if Italy, Spain, Portugal, and France had been supported by the whole of Germany, the United Provinces, England, and other northern nations? This association was natural, and must have been realized, had not the schism of Luther destroyed it. It may be observed, moreover, that this fatal event not only placed an obstacle in the way of universal association, but hindered the Catholic nations themselves from devoting the greatest part of their resources to the great work of converting and regenerating the world: they were compelled to remain continually under arms, on account of religious wars and civil discords. At this epoch the religious orders were apparently called to be the arm of religion; by their means religion, consolidated in Europe and satisfied with the social regeneration which she had just worked, would have extended her action to the infidel nations.

When we glance over the course of events during the earliest ages of the Church, and compare them with those of modern times, we clearly see that some powerful cause must have interfered in modern times to oppose the propagation of the faith. Christianity appears, and she extends herself immediately with rapidity, without any aid on the part of men, and in spite of all the efforts of princes, sages, priests, the passions, and of all the stratagems of hell. She is but of yesterday, and already she is powerful, and prevails in all parts of the empire; nations differing in language and manners, nations of various degrees of civilization, abandon the worship of their false gods, and embrace the religion of Jesus Christ. The barbarians themselves, as intractable and indomitable as wild horses, listen to the missionaries who are sent to them, and bow their heads; in the midst of conquest and victory, they are seen to embrace the religion of those whom they have just conquered. Christianity in modern times has been in possession of the exclusive empire of Europe; and yet she has not been able to succeed in introducing herself again on the coasts of Africa and Asia, which lie under her eye. It is true, that the greatest part of America is become Christian; but observe, that the nations of those countries have been conquered; there the conquering nations have established those governments which have lasted for ages; the European nations have inundated the New World with their soldiers and colonies, so that a considerable portion of America is a kind of importation from Europe; consequently, the religious transformation of that country does not resemble that which took place in the early ages of the Church. Turn towards the West, where European arms have not obtained a decided preponderance; see what takes place there: the nations are still under the yoke of false religions. Christianity has not been able to enlighten them; although the Catholic missions have obtained the means of founding a few establishments more or less considerable, the precious seed has not been able to take sufficient root in the soil, in order to bear the fruits which ardent charity hoped for, and heroic zeal labored to produce. From time to time, the rays of divine light have penetrated to the heart of the great empires of Japan and China; at certain moments flattering hopes might be conceived; but these hopes have been dissipated, these rays of light have disappeared like a brilliant meteor amidst the darkness of midnight.

What is the cause of this impotence? whence comes it that the fertilizing power, after having been so great in the first ages, had proved so vain in the last? Let us not examine the profound secrets of Providence, or seek to inquire into the incomprehensible mysteries of the Divine ways; but as far as it is given to a feeble spirit to learn the truth by the evidences contained in the history of the Church, as far as it is allowed us to carry our conjectures on the designs of the Most High, according to the indications which the Lord himself has been pleased to communicate to us, let us hazard an opinion on the facts: although dependent on a superior order, they yet have an ordinary course, which is regulated by God himself. The apostle St. Paul says that faith comes from hearing. He asks, how it is possible to hear, if there is no one who preaches, and how can there be preaching, if there is no one who sends? Hence, we must conclude that missions are necessary for the conversion of nations, since God has not thought fit by constant miracles to send legions of angels from heaven to teach the nations who are deprived of the light of the earth.

Having laid down this principle, I will say that what was required for the conversion of infidel nations was the organization of missions on a large scale. There were required missions which, by the abundance of their resources and the number of their laborers, might be in proportion to the greatness of the object. Observe that the distances are immense, that the nations to whom the divine word is to be announced are dispersed in many countries, and live under the influence of laws, prejudices, and climates the most opposite to the spirit of the Gospel. To make head against such vast wants, and surmount such great difficulties, there was required a perfect inundation of missionaries; without whom the result would remain doubtful, the existence of religious establishments very precarious, and the conversion of great nations little probable, unless Providence interfered by one of those prodigies which change the face of the world in an instant. Now Providence does not renew these prodigies every moment; sometimes he does not even accord them to the most ardent supplications of the Saints.

In order to form a complete idea of what took place in the latter ages, let us pay attention to what exists. What is wanting to infidel nations? What is the incessant cry of the zealous men who devote themselves to the propagation of the Gospel? Do we not constantly hear lamentations on the small number of laborers, and on the scanty resources which are devoted to the subsistence of the missionaries? Is not this penury of resources the cause of the associations now formed among the Catholics of Europe?

The organization of missions on a large scale would have been realized if Protestantism had not come to prevent it. The nations of Europe, the privileged children of Providence, had the obligation and showed a decided will to procure for the other nations of the world, by all the means in their power, a participation in the benefits of the faith. Unhappily this faith was weakened in Europe, it was given up to the caprices of human reason, and henceforth what had before been of easy execution became impossible. Providence, which had permitted the deplorable disaster of the schism, permits also to be deferred to a more remote period the happy day when the benighted nations shall enter in great numbers into the fold of the Church.

But perhaps I shall be told that the zeal of modern Catholicity is not that of the early ages of Christianity, and this is one of the reasons which have prevented the conversion of infidel nations. I will not make a long comparison on this point; I will not say all that might be said; I will content myself with making an observation which will remove the difficulty at once. Our Divine Saviour, in order to send His disciples to preach the Gospel, wished that they should abandon all they had and follow Him. The same Saviour, revealing to us the infallible sign of true charity, tells us that there is nothing greater than to give one's life for one's brethren. The Catholic missionaries of the three last centuries have renounced all, have abandoned their country, their families, all the comforts of life, all that can engage the heart of man on earth; they have gone to seek the infidels amid the most imminent dangers, and they have sealed with their blood, in all parts of the world, their ardor for the conversion of their brethren, and for the salvation of souls. I believe that such missionaries are worthy of succeeding to those of the first ages of the Church; all declamations and calumnies are impotent before the triumphant evidence of facts. The Church of the early ages would be honored, like that of our times, by a St. Francis Xavier and the martyrs of Japan.

We have spoken, also, of the abundance of the missionaries. The Church had a wonderful fecundity for the conversion of the ancient and barbarian world. At her first appearance, the fiery tongues of the Cenacle and the multitude of prodigies made up for numbers, and multiplied the servants of God. Nations of different languages, listening to the same discourse, heard it at the same time each one in his own tongue; but after this first impulse, by which the Almighty was pleased to confound the powers of hell, things followed the ordinary course, and a greater number of missionaries was required for a greater number of conversions. The great centres of faith and charity, the numerous churches of the East and West, furnished in abundance the apostolic men necessary for the propagation of the faith; and this sacred army had a powerful reserve at hand ready to make up its deficiencies when sickness, fatigues, and martyrdom had thinned its ranks. Rome was the centre of this great movement; but Rome, in order to give the impulse, had no need either of fleets ready to transport the holy colonies to many thousand places, or of great treasures to support missionaries in desert regions and countries altogether unknown. When the missionary, prostrate at the feet of the Sovereign Pontiff, asked his apostolical benediction, the holy father could send him in peace with his pastoral staff alone; he knew that the Gospel envoy was about to traverse Christian countries, and that even in idolatrous lands he would not be far from princes already converted, from bishops, priests, and faithful nations; none of whom would refuse succor to him who went to sow the divine word in the neighboring countries.

I leave the reflections which I have just made, on the injury done to the influence of Europe by the schism of Protestantism, with confidence to the judgment of thinking men. I am deeply convinced that this influence thereby received a terrible blow. Without the fatal event of the sixteenth century, the condition of the world would now be very different from what it is. I may, no doubt, delude myself in some degree on this point; but I will appeal to simple good sense whether it is not true, that unity of action, of principles, and of views, the combination of resources, and the association of agents, are not in all things the secret of success, and the surest guarantee for a happy result. I will then ask whether Protestantism did not break this unity, render this combination impossible, and this association impracticable? Are not these facts indisputable, as clear as the light of day? These facts are recent—they are of yesterday; what is their consequence? what deduction should be drawn from them? Let impartiality, good sense, and mere common sense, answer me, if they be only accompanied by good faith.

To every thinking man, it is evident that Europe is not what she would have been without the appearance of Protestantism; and certainly it is not less evident, that the results of its civilizing influence on the world have not answered the promises of the early years of the sixteenth century. Let Protestants boast of having given a new direction to European civilization; let them vaunt of having enfeebled the spiritual power of the Popes, by removing millions of souls from the sacred fold; let them glory in having destroyed the religious orders in countries subject to their dominion—of having broken in pieces the ecclesiastical hierarchy, and thrown the Bible in the midst of ignorant crowds, with the assurance that, to understand the sacred volume, private inspiration or the judgment of natural reason was enough; yet it is not the less certain that the unity of the Christian religion has disappeared among them, that they want a centre whence great efforts may proceed, that they are without a guide, wandering like a flock without a shepherd, blown about by every wind of doctrine, and unable to bring forth the least of those great works which Catholicity has produced, and still produces, in such abundance; it is not the less certain that, by their eternal disputes, their calumnies, their attacks upon the dogmas and the discipline of the Church, they have compelled the latter to hold herself in an attitude of defence—to contend for three centuries, depriving her of the precious time and means which she would have used to complete the great projects intended by her, and already so happily begun. Is it a merit to divide men, to provoke discord, to excite wars, to change brother nations into enemies, to convert the great family-party of nations into an arena for rancorous strife? Is it a merit to throw discredit on the missionaries who go to preach the Gospel to infidel nations—to place all imaginable obstacles in their way—to employ every means to render their zeal useless, and their charity without result? If, indeed, all this be a merit, then I acknowledge that this merit belongs to Protestantism; but if all this be disastrous, and injurious to humanity, it is Protestantism which must be responsible for it.

When Luther said that he was charged with a high mission, he spoke the truth, but a fearful and alarming truth, and one which he did not understand. The sins of nations sometimes fill up the measure of the patience of the Most High. The sound of human offences mounts to heaven, and calls for vengeance; the Eternal, in His fearful anger, sends down a look of fire upon the earth; then strikes the fatal hour in His secret and infinite resolves, and the son of perdition, who is to cover the world with mourning and desolation, appears. As the cataracts of heaven were formerly opened to sweep the human race from the face of the earth, so are the calamities which the God of vengeance holds in reserve for the day of His anger, poured forth from their urn and scattered over the world. The son of perdition raises his voice; that moment is marked by the beginning of the catastrophe. The spirit of evil moves over the whole face of the globe, bearing on his sable pinions the echo of that ominous voice. An incomprehensible giddiness takes possession of men's heads; the nations have eyes, and see not; they have ears, and hear not; in their delirium, the most frightful precipices appear to them smooth, peaceful, and flowery paths; they call good evil, and evil good; they drink with feverish eagerness of the poisoned cup; forgetfulness of all the past, ingratitude for all benefits, seize all minds; the work of the genius of evil is consummated; the prince of the rebellious spirits may again bury himself in his empire of darkness; and the human race has learned, by a terrible lesson, that the indignation of the Most High is not to be provoked with impunity

CHAPTER XLVI.

THE JESUITS.

As I am treating of religious institutions, I must not pass over in silence that celebrated order, which, from the first years of its existence, assumed the stature of a colossus, and employed all a giant's strength; that order which perished without having felt decay; which did not follow the common course of others, either in its foundation, in its development, or even in its fall; that order of which it is truly and correctly said, that it had neither infancy nor old age. It is clear that I speak of the society of Jesus, the Jesuits. The name alone will be enough to alarm a certain class of readers; and, therefore, in order to tranquillize them, I will say that I do not here undertake to write an apology for the Jesuits; this task does not belong to the character of my work; moreover, others have undertaken it, and it is not necessary for me to repeat what is well known. But it is impossible to call to mind the religious institutions, the religious, political, and literary history of Europe, during the last three centuries, without meeting the Jesuits at every step: we cannot travel in the most distant countries, traverse unknown seas, visit the most remote lands, or penetrate the most frightful deserts, without finding everywhere under our feet some memorials of the Jesuits. On the other hand, we cannot look at our libraries without immediately remarking the writings of some Jesuits. Since this is the case, even those among our readers who have the greatest horror of them, ought to pardon us for fixing our attention for a moment on this institute which has filled the world with its name. Even if we were to attach no importance to their modern revival, and to regard their present existence and their probable future as unworthy of examination, it would still be altogether inexcusable not to speak of them, at least as a historical fact. To pass them over in silence, would be to imitate those ignorant and heartless travellers, who, with stupid indifference, tread under foot the most interesting ruins and the most valuable remains.

When we study the history of the Jesuits, this very extraordinary circumstance is apparent: they have existed only for a few years, if compared with the duration of other religious bodies, and yet there is no religious order which has been the object of such keen animosity. From their origin, they have had numerous enemies; never have they been free from them, either in their prosperity and greatness, or in their fall, or even after it; never has their persecution ceased; we should rather say, never has the animosity with which they have been pursued ceased. Since their reappearance, men have constantly fixed their eyes upon them; they tremble lest they should resume their ancient power; the splendor which is reflected on them by the recollections of their brilliant history renders them visible everywhere, and augments the fears of their enemies. How many men among us are more alarmed at the foundation of a Jesuits' college than at an irruption of Cossacks! There is, therefore, something very singular and extraordinary in this institute, since it excites the public attention in so high a degree, and its mere name disconcerts its enemies. Men do not despise the Jesuits, but they fear them; sometimes they attempt to throw ridicule on them; but when that weapon is employed against them, it is felt that he who wields it is not sufficiently calm to use it with success. In vain does he attempt to affect contempt; through the affectation every one can perceive disquietude and anxiety. It is immediately seen that he who attacks does not believe himself opposed to insignificant adversaries. His bile is excited, his sallies become checked, his words, steeped in a fearful bitterness, fall from his mouth like drops from a poisoned cup; it is clear that he takes the affair to heart, and does not look upon it as a mere joke. We fancy we hear him say to himself, "Every thing affecting the Jesuits is extremely grave; there is no playing with these men—no regard, no indulgence, no moderation of any kind; it is necessary always to treat them with rigor, harshness, and detestation; with them, the least negligence may become fatal."

Unless I am much deceived, this is the best demonstration that can be given of the eminent merit of the Jesuits. It must be the same with classes and corporations as with individuals—very extraordinary merit necessarily excites numerous enemies, for the simple reason that such merit is always envied, and very often dreaded. In order to know the real cause of this implacable hatred against them, it is enough to consider who are their principal enemies. We know that Protestants and infidels figure there in the first rank; in the second, we remark the men who, with more or less clearness and resolution, show themselves but little attached to the authority of the Roman Church. Both, in their hatred against the Jesuits, are guided by a very rare instinct, for truly they have never met with a more redoubtable adversary. This reflection is worthy of the attention of sincere Catholics, who, for one cause or another, entertain unjust prejudices. When we have to form a judgment on the merit and conduct of a man, it is very often a sure means of deciding between contrary opinions to inquire who are his enemies.

When we fix our attention on the institute of the Jesuits, on the time of its foundation, on the rapidity and greatness of its progress, we find the important truth which I have before pointed out more and more confirmed, viz., that the Catholic Church, with wonderful fruitfulness, always furnishes an idea worthy of her to meet all the necessities which arise. Protestantism opposed the Catholic doctrines with the pomp and parade of knowledge and learning; the *éclat* of human literature, the knowledge of languages, the taste for the models of antiquity, were all employed against religion with a constancy and ardour worthy of a better cause. Incredible efforts were made to destroy the pontifical authority; when they could not destroy it, they attempted at least to weaken and discredit it. The evil spread with fearful rapidity; the mortal poison already circulated in the veins of a considerable portion of the European nations: the contagion began to be propagated even in countries which had remained faithful to the truth. To complete the misfortune, schism and heresy, traversing the seas, corrupted the faith of the simple neophytes of the New World. What was to be done in such a crisis? Could such great evils be remedied by ordinary means? Was it possible to make head against such great and imminent perils by employing common arms? Was it not proper to make some on purpose for such a struggle, to temper the cuirass and shield, to fit them for this new kind of warfare, in order that the cause of truth might not appear in the new arena under fatal disadvantages? Who can doubt that the appearance of the Jesuits was the answer to these questions, that their institute was the solution of the problem?

The spirit of the coming ages was essentially one of scientific and literary progress. The Jesuits were aware of this truth; they perfectly understood it.

It was necessary to advance with rapidity and never to remain behind: this the new institute does; it takes the lead in all sciences; it allows none to anticipate it. Men study the oriental languages; they produce great works on the Bible; they search the books of the ancient Fathers, the monuments of tradition and of ecclesiastical decisions: in the midst of this great activity, the Jesuits are at their posts; many supereminent works issue from their colleges. The taste for dogmatical controversy is spread over all Europe: many schools preserve and love the scholastic discussions: immortal works of controversy come from the hands of the Jesuits, at the same time that they yield to none in skill and penetration in the schools. The mathematics, astronomy, all the natural sciences, make great progress; learned societies are formed in the capitals of

Europe to cultivate and encourage them: in these societies the Jesuits figure in the first rank. The spirit of time is naturally dissolvent: the institute of the Jesuits is interiorly armed against dissolution; in spite of the rapidity of its course, it advances in a compact order, like the mass of a powerful army. The errors, the eternal disputes, the multitude of the new opinions, even the progress of the sciences, by exciting men's minds, give a fatal inconstancy to the human intellect—an impetuous whirlwind, agitating and stirring up all things, carries them away. The order of the Jesuits appears in the midst of this whirlwind, but it partakes neither of its inconstancy nor of its variability; it pursues its career without losing itself; and while only irregularity and vacillation are seen among its adversaries, it advances with a sure step, tending towards its object, like a planet which performs its orbit according to fixed laws. The authority of the Pope, assailed with animosity by Protestants, was indirectly attacked by others with stratagem and dissimulation; the Jesuits showed themselves faithfully attached to that authority; they defend it wherever it is threatened; like vigilant sentinels, they constantly watch over the preservation of Catholic unity. Their knowledge, influence, and riches never affect their profound submission to the authority of the Popes—a submission which was ever their distinctive characteristic. In consequence of the discovery of the new countries in the east and west, a taste for travelling, for observing distant countries, for the knowledge of the language, manners, and customs of the recently discovered nations, was developed in Europe. The Jesuits, spread over the face of the globe, while preaching the Gospel to the nations, do not forget the study of the thousand things which may interest cultivated Europe; and at their return from their gigantic expeditions, they are seen adding their valuable treasures to the common fund of modern science.

How, then, can we be surprised that Protestants have been so violent against an institute in which they found so terrible an enemy; and, on the other hand, was there any thing more natural than to see all the other enemies of religion, enemies some of whom were wholly unmasked and some partially disguised, make common cause with Protestants on this point? The Jesuits were a wall of brass against the assaults upon the Catholic faith; it was resolved to undermine and overturn this rampart; which in the end was accomplished. Very few years had elapsed since the suppression of the Jesuits, and already the memory of the great crimes which were imputed to them was effaced by the ravages of an unexampled revolution. Men of good faith, whose excessive confidence had believed perfidious calumnies, could convince themselves that the riches, knowledge, influence, and the pretended ambition of the Jesuits, would never have been as fatal as the triumph of their enemies; these religious men would never have upset a throne or cut off the head of a king on the scaffold.

M. Guizot, in glancing at European civilization, necessarily encountered the Jesuits; and it must be acknowledged that he has not done them the justice to which they are entitled. After having lamented the inconsistency of the Protestant Reformation, and the narrow spirit which guided it, after having confessed that Catholics knew very well what they did and what they wished, and that they acted up to the principles of their conduct and avowed all their consequences, M. Guizot declares that there never was a more consistent government than that of Rome, and that the court of Rome, always having a fixed idea, has known how to pursue a consistent and regular line of conduct; he extols the strength which results from a full knowledge of what one does and what one wishes; he shows the advantage of a settled design, and of the complete and absolute adoption of a principle and system; that is to say, he makes a brilliant panegyric on, and a powerful apology for, the Catholic Church. Nevertheless, M. Guizot finds the Jesuits in his way, and unworthy as it is of such a mind as his, which, in order to require just renown, has no need of burning incense before vulgar prejudices or mean passions, he attempts, in passing, to throw a reproach upon them. "Every one knows," says M. Guizot, "that the principal power instituted to contend against the religious revolution, was the order of the Jesuits. Throw a glance over their history; they have failed everywhere; wherever they have interfered to any extent, they have brought misfortune to the cause in which they have engaged. In England they have destroyed kings, in Spain nations." M. Guizot had just told us of the superiority which is obtained over an adversary by regular and consistent conduct, by the complete and absolute adoption of a system, and by a fixed idea; as a proof of all this he showed us the Jesuits, he exhibited to us in them the expression of the system of the Church; and behold, without any explanation, if not without a motive, the writer suddenly changes his course; the advantages of the system which he has just praised disappear from his eyes; for those who follow this system, that is the Jesuits themselves, fail everywhere, and everywhere bring misfortunes on the cause which they embrace. How can such assertions be reconciled? The credit, influence, and sagacity of the Jesuits have passed into a proverb. The reproach against them was, of having extended their views too far, of having conceived ambitious plans, and obtained by their skill a decided ascendency in all the places where they succeeded in gaining entrance; Protestants themselves have openly confessed that the Jesuits were their most redoubtable adversaries; it was always thought that the foundation of the order had an immense result, and now we learn from M. Guizot, that the Jesuits have everywhere failed; that their support, far from being a great succour, always brought fatality and misfortune to the cause of which they declared themselves the advocates. If they were such fatal servants, why were their services sought with so much eagerness? If they always conducted affairs so ill, why have the most important ones in the end fallen into their hands? Adversaries so foolish or so unfortunate certainly ought not to have excited in the enemies' camp so much clamor as was raised at their approach.

"In England the Jesuits have destroyed kings, in Spain nations." Nothing is easier than these bold strokes of the pen; the whole of a great history is traced in a single line, and an infinity of facts, grouped and confounded, are made to pass under the eye of the reader with the rapidity of lightning; the eye has not even time to look at them, still less to analyze them as would be necessary. M. Guizot should have devoted some sentences to prove his assertion; he should have stated the facts and pointed out the reasons on which he builds, when he affirms that the influence of the Jesuits has had so fatal an effect. With respect to the kings of England here so boldly sacrificed, I cannot enter into an examination of the religious and political revolutions which agitated and desolated the three kingdoms for two centuries after the schism of Henry VIII. These revolutions, in their immense circle, have presented very different phases; disfigured and perverted by the Protestants, who have success in their favor, that decisive, if not convincing argument, they have made some men of little reflection believe that the disasters of England were in great part due to the imprudence of the Catholics, and, as an indispensable corollary, to the pretended intrigues of the Jesuits. In spite of this, the Catholic movement which England has witnessed for half a century, and the great works which every day carry on the restoration of Catholicity, will at last disperse the calumnies by which our faith has been stigmatized. Before long, the history of the last three centuries will be restored as it ought, and the truth will appear in its proper light. This observation relieves me from the necessity of entering into details on the subject of the first assertion of M. Guizot; but I must not leave without reply what he so gratuitously affirms on the subject of Spain.

"The Jesuits have destroyed nations in Spain," says M. Guizot; I wish that the publicist had explained to us to what great disaster he alluded. To what period does he refer? I have examined our history, and I do not find this destruction which was caused by the Jesuits; I cannot imagine whereon the historian fixed his eyes when he pronounced these words. Nevertheless, the antithesis between Spain and England, between nations and kings, leads us to suspect that M. Guizot alluded to the shipwreck of political liberty; we are not aware that there is any other better-founded or more legitimate interpretation. But then a new difficulty presents itself: how can we believe that a man so versed in the knowledge of history, composing a course of lectures which is particularly devoted to the general history of European civilization, should fall into a palpable error,—should commit an unpardonable anachronism? Indeed, whatever may be the judgments of publicists on the causes which have produced the loss of liberty in Spain, and on the important events of the days of the Catholic sovereigns, of Philippe le Beau, of Jeanne-la-Folle, and the regency of Cisneros, all are unanimous in saying that the war of the Commons was the critical moment, decisive of the liberty of Spain; all are agreed that the two parties played their last stake at that time, and that the battle of Villalar and the punishment of Padilla, by confirming and increasing the royal power, destroyed the last hopes of the partisans of the ancient liberties. Well, the battle of Villalar was fought in 1521; at that time the Jesuits did not exist, and St. Ignatius, their founder, was still a brilliant knight, battling like a hero under the walls of Pampeluna. To this there is no reply; all philosophy and eloquence are unable to efface these dates.

During the sixteenth century, the Cortes met more or less often, and with more or less influence, above all in the kingdom of Aragon; but it is as clear as daylight that the royal power had every thing under its domination, that nothing could resist it, and the unfortunate attempt of the Aragonese, at the time of the affair of Don Antonio Perez, sufficiently shows that there existed then no remains of ancient liberty which could oppose the will of kings. Some years after the war of the Commons, Charles V. gave the *coup de grace* to the Cortes of Castile, by excluding from it the clergy and the nobles, to leave only the *Estamento de Procuradores*, a feeble rampart against the exigencies, against the all-powerful attempts of a monarch on whose dominions the sun never set. This exclusion took place in 1538, at the time when St. Ignatius was still occupied with the foundation of his order; the Jesuits, therefore, could have had no influence therein.

Still more, the Jesuits, after their establishment in Spain, never employed their influence against the liberty of the people. From their pulpits they did not teach doctrines favorable to despotism; if they reminded the people of their duties, they also reminded kings of theirs; if they wished the rights of monarchs to be respected, they would not allow those of the people to be trodden under foot. To prove the truth of this, I appeal to the testimony of those who have read the writings of the Jesuits of that time on questions of public law. "The Jesuits," says M. Guizot, "were called to contend against the general course of events, against the development of modern civilization, against the liberty of the human mind." If the general course of events is nothing but the course of Protestantism, if the development of Protestantism is the development of modern civilization, if the liberty of the human mind consists only in the fatal pride, in the mad independence which the pretended reformers communicated to it, then nothing is more true than the assertion of the publicist; but if the preservation of Catholicity is a fact of any weight in the history of Europe, if her influence during the last three centuries has amounted to any thing, if the reigns of Charles V., Philip II., Louis XIV., do not deserve to be effaced from modern history, and if regard ought to be had to that immense counterpoise to which was owing the equilibrium of the two religions; in fine, if the faith of Descartes, Malebranche, Bossuet, and Fénélon, can make a dignified appearance in the picture of modern civilization, it is impossible to understand how the Jesuits, when intrepidly defending Catholicity, could be struggling against the general course of events, against the development of modern civilization, and against the freedom of human thought.

After having made this first false step, M. Guizot continues to slip in a deplorable manner. I particularly call the attention of my readers to the following evident contradictions: "With the Jesuits, there is no *éclat*, no grandeur. They have performed no brilliant exploits." The publicist entirely forgets what he has just advanced, or rather he directly retracts it, when he adds, a few lines further, "and yet, nothing is more certain than that they have had grandeur; a grand idea belongs to their names, to their influence, and to their history. It is because they knew what they did, and what they wished; it is because they had a clear and full knowledge of the principles on which they acted, and of the end towards which they tended; that is to say, because they have had grandeur of thought and of will." Is genius in its vastest enterprises, in the realization of its most gigantic projects, any thing more than a grand idea and a grand intention? The mind conceives, the will executes; this fashions the model, that makes the application; if there be grandeur in the model and in the application, how can the whole work fail to be grand?

Pursuing the task of lowering the Jesuits, M. Guizot makes a parallel between them and the Protestants; he confounds ideas in such a way, and so far forgets the nature of things, that one would hardly believe it, if the words themselves did not prove it beyond a doubt. Forgetting that it is necessary for the terms of a comparison not to be of a totally different kind, which renders all comparison impossible, M. Guizot compares a religious institute with whole nations; he goes so far as to reproach the Jesuits with not having raised the people *en masse*, and with not having changed the form and condition of states. Here is the passage: "They have acted in subterraneous, dark, and inferior ways; in ways which were not at all apt to strike the imagination, or to conciliate for them that public interest which attaches itself to great things, whatever may be their principle and end. The party against which they contended, on the contrary, not only conquered, but conquered with *éclat;* it has done great things and by great means; it has aroused nations; it has filled Europe with great men; it has changed the form and the lot of nations in the face of day. In a word, all has been against the Jesuits, both fortune and appearances." Without intending to offend M. Guizot, let us avow, that for the honor of his logic, one would desire to efface from his writings such phrases as we have just read. What! ought the Jesuits to have put the nations in motion, made them arise *en masse*, and changed the form and condition of states? Would they not have been extraordinary religious men, if they had been allowed to do such things? It was said of the Jesuits that they had unbounded ambition, and that they attempted to rule the world; and now they are compared with their adversaries in order to throw it in their faces that the latter have overturned the world; a distinguished merit, which must have been a disgrace to the Jesuits themselves. Indeed, the Jesuits have never attempted to imitate their adversaries on this point; with respect to the spirit of confusion and perturbation, they joyfully yield the palm to those to whom it rightly belongs.

As far as great men are concerned, if the question be with respect to the greatness of the enterprises which are becoming in a minister of the God of peace, then have the Jesuits had this kind of grandeur in an eminent degree. Whether it be in the most arduous affairs, or in the vastest projects in science and literature, whether it be in the most distant missions, or in the most redoubtable perils, the Jesuits have never remained behind; on the contrary, they have been seen to display a spirit so bold and enterprising, that they have thereby obtained the most distinguished renown. If the great men of whom

M. Guizot speaks are restless tribunes, who, putting themselves at the head of an ungovernable people, violated the public peace, if they are the Protestant warriors whose names have shone in the wars of Germany, France, and England, the comparison is foolish, and has no meaning; for priests and warriors, religious and tribunes, are so distinct, so different in actions and character, that to compare them is impossible.

Justice required that in such a parallel, where the Jesuits are taken as one of the terms of the comparison, Protestants should not be placed on the other, unless by them the reformed ministers are meant. Even in this later case the comparison would not have been absolutely exact, since, in the midst of the great differences between the two religions, the Jesuits are not found alone in defending Catholicity. The Church, during the last three centuries, has had great prelates, holy priests, eminent *savants*, and writers of the first order, who did not belong to the company of Jesus; the Jesuits were reckoned among the principal champions, but they were not the only ones. Had it been wished fairly to compare Protestantism with Catholicity, it would have been requisite to oppose Protestant to Catholic nations, to compare priests with priests, *savants* with *savants*, politicians with politicians, warriors with warriors; to do otherwise is monstrously to confound names and things, and to reckon too much on the limited understandings and excessive simplicity of hearers and readers. It is certain that if the method we have pointed out were adopted, Protestantism would not appear so brilliant and superior as the publicist has exhibited it to us. Catholics, as M. Guizot well knows, do not yield to Protestants in letters, in war, or in political ability. History is there; let it be consulted.

CHAPTER XLVII.

THE FUTURE OF RELIGIOUS INSTITUTIONS.—THEIR PRESENT NECESSITY.

When, after having fixed our eyes on the vast and interesting picture which religious communities present to us, after having called to mind their origin, their varied forms, their vicissitudes of poverty and riches, of depression and prosperity, of coldness and of fervor, of relaxation and strict reform, we see them still subsist and arise anew on all sides, in spite of the efforts of their enemies, we naturally ask what will be their future? their past is full of glory; what influence have they not exerted in society, under a thousand different aspects, and in the thousand phases of society itself? Yet what spectacle do they show us in modern times? On one hand they have been weakened, like an old wall which we see ruined by the effect of time; on the other we have seen them suddenly disappear, like weak trees overthrown by the whirlwind. Moreover, they seemed to be condemned by the spirit of the age without appeal. Matter having become supreme, extended its empire on all sides, scarcely allowing the mind a moment for reflection and meditation; industry and commerce, carrying their turmoil to the remotest parts of the earth, confirmed the judgment of an irreligious philosophy against a class of men devoted to prayer, silence, and solitude. Nevertheless, facts every day belie their conjectures; the hearts of Christiaus still preserve the most flattering hopes, and these hopes are strengthened and animated more and more. The hand of God, who carries out His high designs and laughs at the vain thoughts of man, shows it more and more wonderful. Philosophy sees a wide field for meditation open before it; it anticipates the probable future of religious communities; it may make conjectures on the influence which is reserved for them in society for the future.

We have already seen what is the real origin of religious institutions; we have found that origin in the spirit of the Catholic religion, and history has told us that they have arisen wherever she is established. They have varied in form, in rule, in object, but the fact has been always the same. Thence we have inferred that wherever the Catholic faith shall be maintained, religious institutions will appear anew under some form or other. This prognostic may be made with complete certainty; we do not fear that time will belie it. We live in an age steeped in voluptuous materialism; interests which are called positive, or, in plainer terms, gold and pleasure, have acquired such an ascendency that we might apparently fear to see some societies lamentably retrograde towards the manners of paganism, towards that period of disgrace when religion might be summed up in the deification of matter. But in the midst of this afflicting picture, when the mind, full of anguish, feels itself on the point of swooning away, the observer sees that the soul of man is not yet dead, and that lofty ideas, noble and dignified feelings, are not entirely banished from the earth. The human mind feels itself too great to be limited to wretched objects; it comprehends that it is given it to rise higher than an air-balloon.

Observe what happens with respect to industrial progress. Those steam-vessels which leave our ports with the rapidity of an arrow to traverse the immensity of ocean, those burning vehicles which skim along our plains, and penetrate into the heart of mountains, realizing under our eyes what would have seemed a dream to our fathers; those other machines which give movement to gigantic workshops, and as if by magic set in motion innumerable instruments, and elaborate with the most wonderful precision the most delicate productions: all this is great and wonderful. But however great, however wonderful it may be, it no longer astonishes; these wonders no longer captivate our attention in a more lively manner than the generality of the objects which surround us. Man feels that he is still greater than these machines and masterpieces of art; his heart is an abyss which nothing can fill; give him the whole world, and the void will be the same. The depth is immeasurable; the soul, created in the image and likeness of God, cannot be satisfied without the possession of Him.

The Catholic religion constantly revives these lofty thoughts, and points out this immense void. In barbarous times she placed herself among rude and ignorant nations to lead them to civilization; she now remains among civilized nations to provide against the dissolution which threatens them. She disregards the coldness and neglect with which indifference and ingratitude reply to her; she cries out without ceasing, addresses her warnings to the faithful with indefatigable constancy, makes her voice resound in the ears of the incredulous, and remains intact and immovable in the midst of the agitation and instability of human things. Thus do those wonderful temples which have been left to us by the remotest antiquity, remain entire amid the action of time, of revolutions, and of convulsions; around them arise and disappear the habitations of men, the palaces of the great and the cottages of the poor, but the time-stained edifice stands like a solemn and mysterious object in the midst of the smiling fields and showy structures which surround it; its vast cupola annihilates all that is near; its summit boldly rises towards the heavens.

The labors of religion do not remain without fruit; penetrating minds acknowledge her truths; even those who refuse their submission to the faith confess the beauty, utility, and necessity of this divine religion; they regard it as an historical fact of the highest importance, and agree that the good order and prosperity of families and states depend upon it. But God, who watches over the safety of the church, is not content with these avowals of philosophy; torrents of all-powerful grace descend from on high, and the Divine Spirit is diffused and renewed on the face of the earth. Even from the whirlwind of the world, corrupt and indifferent as it is, privileged men frequently come forth, whose foreheads have been touched with the flame of inspiration, and whose hearts are on fire with heavenly love. In retreat, in solitude, in meditation on the eternal truths, they have acquired that disposition of mind which is necessary to perform arduous tasks; in spite of raillery and ingratitude, they devote themselves to console the unfortunate, to educate the young, and to convert idolatrous nations. The Catholic religion will last till the end of time, and so long will there be these privileged men separated by God from the rest, to be called to extraordinary sanctity, or to console their brethren in their misfortunes. Now these men will seek each other, will unite to pray, will associate to aid each other in their enterprise, will ask for the apostolical benediction of the Vicar of Jesus Christ, and will found religious institutions. Whether they be old orders only modified, or entirely new ones; whatever be their forms, rules of life or dress, all this is of little importance; the origin, the nature, and the object will be the same. It is vain for men to oppose the miracles of grace.

Even the present condition of society will require the existence of religious institutions. When the organization of modern nations shall have been more profoundly examined, when time by its bitter lessons and terrible experience shall have thrown more light on the real state of things, it will be evident that errors greater than men have imagined, have been committed in the social as well as in the political order. Sad experience has corrected ideas to a great extent, but this does not suffice.

It is evident that present societies want the necessary means to supply the necessities which press upon them. Property is divided and subdivided more and more; every day it becomes more feeble and inconstant, industry multiplies productions in an alarming manner, commerce extends itself indefinitely; that is to say, society, approaching the term of pretended social perfection, is on the point of attaining the wishes of that materialistic school, in whose eyes men are only machines, and which has not imagined that society can undertake any grander or more useful object than the immense development of material interests. Misery has increased in proportion to the augmentation of production; to the eyes of all provident men it is as clear as the light of day that things are pursuing a wrong course, and that if a remedy cannot be applied in time, the *dénouement* will be fatal; the vessel which we see advancing so rapidly, with all her sails set and a favorable wind, is about to strike upon a rock. The accumulation of riches, brought about by the rapidity of the industrial and commercial movement, tends towards the establishment of a system which would devote the sweat and the lives of all to the profit of the few; but this tendency finds its counterpoise in levelling ideas which agitate very many heads, and which, moulded into different theories, more or less openly attack property, the present organization of labor, and the distribution of productions. Immense multitudes, overwhelmed with misery and in want of moral instruction and education, are disposed to promote the realization of projects not less criminal than foolish, whenever an unhappy concurrence of circumstances shall render the attempt possible. It is superfluous to support the melancholy assertions which we have just made with facts; the experience of every day confirms them but too much.

Such being the case, may we be allowed to inquire of society, what means there are, either of improving the state of the masses, or of guiding and restraining them? It is clear that, for the first of these, neither the inspirations of private interests, nor the instinct of preservation which animates the favored classes, are sufficient. These classes, properly speaking, as they exist, have not the character which constitutes a class: they are only a collection of families just emerged from poverty and obscurity, and who rapidly advance towards the abyss whence they came, leaving their place to other families who will run the same course. We find nothing fixed or stable about them. They live from day to day, without thinking of the morrow: far different fiom the old nobility, whose origin was lost in the obscurity of the remotest antiquity, and whose strength and organization promised long centuries of existence. These men could and did follow a system; for what existed to-day was sure of existence to-morrow; now all is changeable and inconstant. Individuals, like families, labor to accumulate, to lay by riches, not in order to sustain for ages the power and splendor of an illustrious house, but to enjoy to-day what has been but just acquired. The presentiment of the short duration which things must have, augments still more the giddiness and frenzy of dissipation. The times are past when opulent families were desirous of founding some enduring establishment to evince their generosity and perpetuate the splendor of their names: hospitals, and other houses of beneficence, do not come from the coffers of the bankers, as they did from those of the old castles. We must acknowledge, however painful may be the avowal, that the opulent classes of society do not fulfil the duty which belongs to them: the poor should respect the property of the rich; but the rich should, in their turn, respect the condition of the poor: such is the will of God.

It follows from what I have stated, that the resource of beneficence is wanting in the social organization; and observe well, that administration does not constitute society. Administration supposes society to be already existing and entirely formed; when we expect the salvation of society from means purely administrative, we attempt a thing which is out of the laws of nature. In vain shall we imagine new expedients; in vain shall we form ingenious plans, and make new experiments; society has need of a more powerful agent. It is essential that the world should submit to the law of love or that of force, to charity or servitude. All the nations who have not had charity, have found no other means of solving the social problem, than that of subjecting the greatest number to slavery. Reason teaches, and history proves, that neither public order, property, nor even society itself, can exist, unless one of these is chosen; modern society will not be exempted from the general law; the symptoms which now present themselves to our eyes clearly indicate the events whereof the generations which are to succeed us will be the witnesses.

Happily, the fire of charity still burns on the earth; but the indifference and prejudices of the wicked compel it to remain under the embers. They are alarmed at the least spark of it which escapes, as if it would enkindle a fatal conflagration. If the development of institutions which are exclusively based upon the principle of charity was favored, their salutary results and the superiority which they possess over all that are founded on other principles would soon be evident. It is impossible to supply the wants which I have just pointed out, without organizing, on a vast scale, systems of beneficence directed by charity: now this organization cannot be made without religious institutions. It cannot be denied that Christians who live in the world may form associations by which this object will be accomplished more or less completely; but there are always a multitude of cases which absolutely require the co-operation of men exclusively devoted to them. It is necessary, moreover, to have a nucleus to serve as the centre of all efforts, which presents, by its own nature, a guarantee for preservation, and which provides against the interruptions and oscillations which are inevitable in a large concourse of agents, who are not bound together by any tie strong enough to preserve them from differences, from separation, and even from intestine contests.

This vast system which we speak of ought to extend not only to beneficence, but also to the education and instruction of the many. The establishment of schools will remain sterile, if not mischievous, as long as they are not founded upon religion; and they will be thus founded only in appearance and name, while the direction of these schools does not belong to the ministers of religion.

The secular clergy may fulfil a portion of this charge, but they are not enough for the task; on the one hand, their limited number, and on the other, their other duties, prevent their acting on a scale sufficiently large to supply all the necessities of the times: hence it follows, that the propagation of religious institutions in our days has a social importance, which cannot be mistaken without shutting one's eyes to the evidence of facts.

If you reflect on the organization of European nations, you will understand that their real advance has been prevented by some fatal cause. Indeed, their situation is so singular, that it cannot be the result of the principles whence these nations have drawn their origin, and which have given them their increase. It is evident that the countless multitude which one sees in society, making use of all its faculties with complete liberty, could not, in the state in which it now is, have been comprised in the primitive design—in the plan of true civilization. When we create forces, we should know what we shall do with them, by what means we shall move and direct them; without this we only prepare violent shocks, endless agitation, disorder, and destruction. The mechanician who cannot introduce a force into his machine without breaking the harmony of the other movers, takes care not to introduce it; and he sacrifices acceleration of movement and the greatest strength of impulse to the fundamental necessity of the preservation of the machine and the order and utility of its functions. In the present state of society, we observe that power which is not in harmony with the others; and the men who are charged with directing the machine pay but little attention to gaining the required harmony. Nothing acts upon the mass of the people but the ardent desire of ameliorating their condition, of placing themselves in comfort, and of obtaining the enjoyments of which the rich are in possession; nothing to induce them to be resigned to the rigors of their lot; nothing to console them in their misfortunes; nothing to render the present evils more supportable by the hopes of a better future; nothing to inspire them with respect for property, obedience to the laws, submission to government; nothing to produce in their minds gratitude towards the powerful classes; nothing to temper their hatreds, diminish their envy, and mollify their anger; nothing to raise their ideas above earthly things, their desires from sensual pleasures; nothing to form in their hearts a solid morality capable of restraining them from vice and crime.

If we pay attention, we shall see that the men of this age have only three means of restraining the masses, and they regard these as enough; but reason and experience show that these expedients are not only not efficacious, but even dangerous; they are these,—private interests well understood, public force well employed, and enervation of body, followed by feebleness of mind, which restrains the populace from violent means.

"Let us make the poor man understand," says the philosopher, "that he has an interest in respecting the property of the rich; that his powers and his labor are also real property, which require to be respected in their turn; let us maintain an imposing public force, always ready to act on the menaced point, in order to stifle any attempts at disorder at their birth; let us organize a police, extending over society like an immense net, and allowing nothing to escape its sight; let us satisfy the people with cheap enjoyments of all kinds; let us furnish them with the means of imitating, in their grosser orgies, the refined pleasures of our saloons and theatres, thereby their manners will be softened—that is to say, they will be enervated; the people will become impotent to make great revolutions, their arms being weak, and their hearts cowardly." This is the sytem of those who attempt to govern society and control disturbing passions without the aid of religion.

Let us pause for a moment to examine these means. It is, no doubt, easy to say, in fine language, that the poor man is interested in respecting the property of the rich; and that from this consideration alone he ought to submit to the established order of things; and this without even saying a word of the principles of morality, and leaving out all that is removed from mere material interests. It is easy to write books to explain such doctrines; but the difficulty consists in making them understood in the same way by the wretched father of a family, who, confined all the day to hard labor, plunged into an unwholesome atmosphere, or buried in the bowels of the earth to work in a coal-mine, can scarcely earn the subsistence of himself and his family; and who, returning in the evening to his squalid abode, instead of repose and consolation, finds only the complaints of his wife and the tears of his children, asking him for a mouthful of bread. In truth, is it strange that such a doctrine should not be graciously received by those wretched beings, whose minds cannot perfectly understand the parity between the poor and the rich with respect to the interests of all, and the respect due to property? We will say plainly, that if you banish from the world the moral principles, and desire to found the respect due to property exclusively on private interest, the words here addressed to the poor man are only a solemn imposture: it is false that his private interest is in accordance with the interests of the rich.

Let us suppose the most fearful revolution, let us imagine that the established order is radically upset, that authority gives way, that all institutions are swallowed up, that laws disappear, that properties are divided, or remain abandoned to the first who shall seize them, there is no doubt that the rich man loses; let us see what can happen to the poor. Will he be robbed of his wretched possessions? no one will dream of doing so; misery tempts not cupidity. You will tell me that he will find no work, and that hunger will therefore be his lot. That is true; but do you not see that in this case the poor man is a gambler at a high stake, for whom the chance of loss, arising from the want of work, is compensated by the probabilities of obtaining a share of the rich booty? You add that he will not be allowed to keep that part; but observe that, if his poverty becomes changed into riches, he will soon imagine a new order of things, a new arrangement, a government which will guarantee acquired rights, and prevent the destruction of established things. Will he be without an example to follow in such circumstances? Have recent examples been so easily forgotten? The poor man sees clearly that a great number of his fellows will suffer evils without end or compensation; he is not ignorant that he himself may, perhaps, be of the number of the unfortunate; but, supposing that he has no other guide than interest, supposing that new misfortunes, in the last excess, can bring him only hunger and nakedness—things to which he is so well accustomed, whether owing to the small return for his labor, or to the frequent interruptions of work and the vicissitudes of industry—you cannot charge with rashness the boldness with which he comes forward, at the risk of increasing his privations in some degree, and with the hope of being delivered from them, perhaps for ever. This is a matter of calculation; and when private interest is in question, we cannot grant to philosophy the right of regulating the calculations of the poor.

The public power, and the vigilance of the police, are the two resources in which the best hopes are founded; and certainly not without reason; for, at the present time, if the world is not revolutionized, it is owing to them. We no longer see, as in ancient times, troops of slaves bound together with chains, but we see whole armies, with arms in their hands, guarding capitals. If you observe closely, after so many discussions, so many trials, so many reforms, so many changes, questions of government and public order have, in the end, resolved themselves into questions of force. The rich class is armed against the poor; and above both, there are armies to maintain tranquillity with cannon, if necessary. Assuredly, the picture which is exhibited to us in this respect, among modern nations, is worthy of our attention. Since the fall of Napoleon, the great powers have enjoyed an Augustan peace; for it is not worth while to speak of the small events which, from time to time, have disturbed this universal peace; neither the occupation of Ancona, nor the siege of Antwerp, nor the war in Poland, can be considered as European wars; as to Spain, limited, as she is by nature, to a narrow theatre, she can neither traverse the seas, nor pass the Pyrenean mountains. Well, in spite of this, the statistics of Europe show us enormous armies; the budgets which are necessary to support them exhaust and overwhelm the nations. What is the use of this military preparation? Do you believe that such gigantic forces are kept on foot only that governments may not be taken unawares by a general war; that war, which always threatens and never breaks out; that war, which is feared neither by the government nor by the people? No! they have another object: these armies are intended to compensate for the moral means, the want of which is deplorably felt on all sides, and nowhere more keenly than where the words justice and liberty have been proclaimed with the most ostentation.

The enervation of the numerous classes, by means of monotonous, effortless labor, and a complete abandonment to pleasure, may be considered by some as an element of order; as their power of striking is thereby taken away, or at least diminished. We allow that the workmen of our age are not capable of displaying the terrible energy of ancient champions of the Commons; of those men who, throwing off the yoke of the feudal lords, struggled hand to hand with formidable warriors, whose names were immortalized on the plains of Palestine. The new revolutionists want, also, that courage and that enthusiasm which are communicated to the soul by great and generous ideas. The man who fights only to procure enjoyments will never be capable of making heroic sacrifices. Sacrifices demand self-denial; they are incompatible with egotism: now the thirst for pleasure is egotism, carried to the last degree of refinement. Nevertheless, it must be observed that a mode of life purely material, and deprived of the stimulus of the moral principles, ends by extinguishing the feelings, and plunges the soul into a sort of stupidity, into a forgetfulness of self, which may, in certain cases, supply the place of valor. The soldier who marches with tranquillity to death, when leaving a brutal *orgie*, and the man who commits suicide with imperturbable calmness, without anxiety for the future, are precisely in the same position. The boldness of the one, and the firmness of the other, show contempt of life. So, if we suppose their passions to be excited by the trouble of the times, the numerous class may display an energy of which they are supposed to be incapable; the sight of their numbers may raise their courage; bold and cunning leaders, putting themselves at their head, may succeed in rendering them terrible.

However this may be, it is at least certain that society cannot continue its career without the aid and influence of moral means; these means cannot suffice, shut up within the narrow circle in which they are confined; consequently, it is indispensable to encourage the development of institutions adapted to exercise moral influence in a practical and efficacious manner. Books are not enough; the extension of instruction is but an inefficient means, which may even become fatal, unless based upon solid religious ideas. The propagation of a vague religious feeling, undefined, without rules, without dogmas or worship, will only serve to propagate gross superstitions among the masses, and to form a religion of poetry and romance among the cultivated classes; they are vain remedies, which do not stop the progress of the disease; but, by augmenting the delirium of the patient, precipitate his death.

The education, the instruction, the improvement of the moral condition of the people, these words, which are in the mouth of everybody, prove how keenly and generally the wound in the social body is felt, and how urgent is the necessity of the timely application of a remedy, in order to prevent incalculable evils.

This is the reason why projects of beneficence ferment in so many minds; why it is attempted, under so many different forms, to establish schools for children and adults, and other similar institutions; but all will be useless, unless the work be confided to Christian charity. Let us profit by the knowledge acquired by experience in this matter; let us take advantage of administrative improvements, the better to attain our end; let the establishments be accommodated to present wants and exigences; let charity never embarrass the action of power, and power, on its side, never oppose the action of charity: all this will be well; but nothing of all this is inconsistent with a system, in which the Catholic religion will recover the influence which belongs to her; of her it may be said, with perfect truth, *that she makes herself all to all, to gain the whole world.*

The little minds which do not carry their views beyond a limited horizon; bad hearts, which nourish only hatred, and delight only in exciting rancor and in calling forth the evil passions; the fanatics of a mechanical civilization, who see no other agent than steam, no other power than gold and silver, no other object than production, no other end than pleasure; all these men, assuredly, will attach but little importance to the observations which I have made; for them, the moral development of individuals and society is of little importance; they do not even perceive what passes under their eyes; for them, history is mute, experience barren, and the future a mere nothing. Happily there is a great number of men who believe that their minds are nobler than metal, more powerful than steam, and too grand and too sublime to be satisfied with momentary pleasure.

Man, in their eyes, is not a being who lives by chance, given up to the current of time and the mercy of circumstances, who is not called upon to think of the destinies which attend him, or to prepare for them, by making a worthy use of the moral and intellectual qualifications wherewith the Author of nature has favored him. If the physical world is subject to the laws of the Creator, the moral world is not less so; if matter can be used in a thousand ways for the profit of man, the mind, created to the image and likeness of God, is also endowed with valuable powers; a vast sphere opens before him; he feels himself called to work for the good of humanity, without confining himself to combinations and modifications of matter, like an instrument or a slave of the material element, whereof the empire and control have been granted to him by God. Let faith in another life, and charity, which have come down from God, fertilize these noble feelings, and enlighten and direct these sublime thoughts; you will then clearly see that matter has no claim to be the ruler of the world; and that the King of the creation has not yet abdicated his rights. But if you attempt to build on any other foundation than that which has been established by God, do not indulge flattering hopes, your edifice will be like the house built upon sand; the rain came, the wind blew, and the edifice was overturned with violence. (27)

CHAPTER XLVIII.

RELIGION AND LIBERTY.

In the thirteenth chapter of this work we said, "The heart is filled with generous indignation when we hear the religion of Jesus Christ reproached with a tendency towards oppression. It is true, that if we confound the spirit of real liberty with that of demagogues, we shall not find it in Catholicity. But if we abstain from a monstrous abuse of the name, if we give to the word liberty its reasonable, just, useful, and pleasant meaning, then the Catholic religion may fearlessly claim the gratitude of the human race, for she has civilized the nations who have professed her, and civilization is true liberty." From what we have already shown, the reader may judge whether Catholicity has been favorable, or otherwise, to European civilization, and, consequently, whether she has done any injury to real liberty. On the various points on which we have compared her with Protestantism, we have seen the injurious tendencies of the one and the advantages of the other; the judgment of clear and enlightened reason cannot be doubtful.

As the real liberty of nations does not consist in appearances, but resides in their intimate organization, in the same way as the life does in the heart, I might dispense with entering into a comparison of the two religions with respect to civil liberty; but I do not wish to be accused of having avoided a delicate question, from a fear that Catholicity would not come out of it with honor, or to allow it to be suspected that my faith has any difficulty in sustaining a parallel as advantageously on this ground as on others.

In order to clear up this question completely, it is necessary to examine thoroughly the vague accusations which have been made on this matter against Catholicity, and the eulogiums lavished on the pretended Reformation. It is necessary to show that only gratuitous calumny has been able to reproach the Catholic religion with favoring servitude and oppression; it is necessary to dissipate, by the light of philosophy and history, that deceitful prejudice, by the aid of which free-thinkers and Protestants have labored to persuade the people that Catholicity is favorable to servitude, that the Church is the bulwark of tyrants, that the name of Pope is synonymous with that of friend and natural protector of whoever desires to debase men and reduce them to servitude.

There are two ways in which this question may be decided; by doctrines and by facts.

Those who have said that the human race had lost its rights, and that they were revived by Rousseau, certainly have not given themselves much trouble in examining what are the real rights of the human race, and what are the apocryphal rights advanced by the philosopher of Geneva in his *Contrat Social.* Indeed, it may be said with more truth, that the human race had very valuable rights, acknowledged as such, and which Rousseau lost sight of. He undertook to examine thoroughly the origin of the civil power, and his wild notions, instead of explaining the matter, have only served to confuse it. I believe that on this important point men have never had ideas less clear and distinct than now. Revolutions have upset every thing in theory and in fact; governments have been sometimes revolutionary, sometimes reactionary; and sometimes revolution, and sometimes reaction, has been predominant. It is extremely difficult to obtain from modern books a clear, accurate, and exact knowledge of the nature of the civil power, of its origin, and of its relations with subjects; in some of these you will find the doctrines of Rousseau, in others those of Bonald: Rousseau is a miner who saps in order to overturn; Bonald is the hero who saves in his arms the tutelary deities of the city delivered to the flames; but in his fear of profanation, he carries them covered with a veil. However, it would not be just to attribute to Rousseau the melancholy honor of having begun the confusion of ideas on this point; at various times there have been found misguided men, who have labored to disturb society by anarchical doctrines; but the embodiment of these doctrines, and the forming of them into seductive theories, dates chiefly from the birth of Protestantism. Luther, in his book *De Libertate Christiana*, sowed the seeds of endless troubles by the extravagant doctrine, that a Christian is subject to no one. In vain did he have recourse to the evasive declaration, that he did not speak of magistrates or civil laws; the peasants of Germany drew their own consequences; they rose up against their lords, and enkindled a dreadful war. The divine right held by Catholics has been accused of favoring despotism; and it has been considered as so much opposed to the rights of the people, that the two expressions are often antithetically employed. Divine right, well understood, is not opposed to the rights, but to the excesses of the people; so far from giving unlimited extent to power, it confines it within the limits of reason, justice, and public advantage. In his lectures on the general history of civilization in Europe, M. Guizot, speaking of this right as proclaimed by the Church, says: "The rights of liberty and political guarantees are combined with difficulty with the principle of religious royalty; but that principle in itself is elevated, moral, and salutary." (Lecture ix.) When men like M. Guizot, who have made these questions their special study, are so lamentably deceived on this point, who can be astonished that the same thing occurs to the generality of writers!

Before I go further, I will make one observation, which we ought always to have present to our minds. On these questions we continually hear mention made of the schools of Bossuet and of Bonald; private names are put forward, sometimes in one way and sometimes in another. Much as I respect the merits of these men, and of others not less illustrious produced by the Catholic Church, yet I must observe that she is not responsible for any doctrines but those which she herself teaches; that she is not personified in any doctor in particular; and that being herself appointed by God himself to be the oracle of infallible truth in faith and morality, she does not permit the faithful to defer blindly to the mere word of any private man, however great may be his merit in science and in sanctity. If you wish to know what the Catholic Church teaches, consult the decisions of her Councils and her Pontiffs; consult also her doctors of distinguished and unsullied reputation; but beware of confounding the opinions of an author, however respectable he may be, with the doctrines of the Church and the voice of the Vicar of Jesus Christ. By this warning I do not mean to prematurely condemn the opinions of any one, but simply to put those on their guard who, little versed in ecclesiastical studies, might, in certain cases, confound revealed dogmas with what is mere human thought. Having premised this much, let us enter freely into the question.

Wherein does this divine right, of which we hear so much, consist? In order to explain this matter completely, we must state the objects over which this right extends; for these objects being widely different, there will also be a great difference in the application made to them of the principle. A great number of questions present themselves in this very important matter; but it appears to me that they may all be reduced to these, which embrace the rest, viz. What is the origin of the civil power? How far does it extend? Is it lawful to resist it in any case?

The first question is, *What is the origin of the civil power? How do we know that this power is from God?* There is much confusion prevailing on these points; and certainly it is to be lamented, that at a time so disturbed as the present they should be misunderstood; for whatever may be said to the contrary, doctrines are never wholly laid aside, either in revolutions or in restorations; men's interests, no doubt, have great weight therein, but they are not left alone in the arena. The best way of forming clear ideas on these points is to have recourse to ancient authors, especially those whose doctrines have been respected for a long period of time, who continue to be respected down to this day, and who are looked upon as safe guides in the right interpretation of ecclesiastical doctrines. This way of studying the question which now occupies us ought to be acceptable to those even who entertain contempt for the writers of whom we speak; for we are now engaged more in seeking in what the doctrine consists, than in examining into its truth. Now for this purpose we cannot find witnesses better informed, or interpreters more competent, than men who have devoted their whole lives to the study of the doctrine.

This last reflection is in no way contradictory to what we have said above, on the care which we ought to take not to confound the mere opinions of men with the doctrines of the Church; it only tends to remind us of the necessity which exists of perusing a certain class of authors, who are certainly not worthy of the ungrateful neglect with which they are treated; indeed, it is impossible that their important labors, conscientiously pursued for so long a time, should produce no fruit. In order to understand the better the opinion of these writers on the matter which now occupies us, we ought to observe the difference which they make in the application of the general principle of divine right to the origin of the civil or to that of the ecclesiastical power. From this comparison there arises a bright light, which resolves and clears up all difficulties. Open the works of the most distinguished theologians, consult their treatises on the origin of the power of the Pope, and you will see that in establishing this power on divine right, they mean that it emanates from God, not only in a general sense, that is, inasmuch as all being comes from God; not only in a social sense, that is, inasmuch as the Church being a society, God has willed the existence of a power to govern it; but in a most special manner that God has Himself instituted this power, that He has Himself established its form, that He has Himself pointed out the person, and that consequently the successor to the chair of St. Peter is of divine right the supreme pastor of the universal Church, having over the whole of this Church supreme honor and jurisdiction.

With respect to the civil power, these authors speak thus. In the first place, all power comes from God; for power exists, and all existence comes from God; power is sovereignty, and God is the lord, the supreme master of all things; power is a right, and in God is found the source of all right; power is a moral movement, and God is the universal cause of all sorts of movements; power tends towards an exalted end, and God is the end of all creatures; His Providence ordains and directs all things with mercy and efficacy. Thus we see that St. Thomas, in his work *De Regimine Principum*, affirms that all power comes from God as supreme master, as may be shown in three ways: as it is a being, as it is a mover, and as it is an end. (Lib. 3, cap. 1.)

As I am treating of this method of explaining the origin of power, I must pause for a moment to refute Rousseau, who, in the allusion which he made to this doctrine, showed that he did not understand it. He says, "All power comes from God, I allow; but all diseases also come from Him. Are we, therefore, to say that it is forbidden to call in a physician?" (*Contrat Social*, liv. i. c. 3.) It is true that one of the senses in which the divine origin of power is affirmed is, that all finite beings emanate from an infinite being; but this sense is not the only one. Indeed, theologians knew very well that this idea, by itself, did not imply its legitimacy, and that it extended as well to physical force; for as the author of the *Contrat Social* adds: "the pistol held by a robber in a wood is also a power." Rousseau, in this passage, has sacrificed the sense to show his ingenuity; the love of making a brilliant sally has seduced him into removing the question from its proper ground. It was easy, indeed, to see that, with respect to the civil power, men do not speak of a physical, but of a moral, a legitimate power; in any other way it would be in vain to seek for its origin: as well might they seek the source of riches, health, strength, courage, subtilty, or the other qualities which contribute to form the material force of all power. The question is with regard to the moral being which is called power; and in the moral order, illegitimate power is not power, it is not a being, it is nothing. Consequently, there is no need of seeking its origin in God, or in any thing else. Therefore, power emanates from God as the source of all right, justice, and legitimacy; and in considering power, not as a mere physical, but as a moral being, it is affirmed that it can come from God alone, who is the plenitude of all being. Not only is this doctrine, taken generally, above all difficulty, but it must be admitted by all who do not profess themselves atheists; they alone can call it in question. Let us now descend to particulars, and see whether Catholic doctors teach any thing which is not perfectly reasonable even in the eyes of philosophers.

Man, they say, was not created to live alone; his existence supposes a family; his inclinations urge him to form an alliance, without which the human race could not be perpetuated. Families are connected with each other by intimate and indestructible ties; they have common wants; none can insure happiness, or even preservation, without the aid of others. Therefore they are bound to enter into society. Society cannot exist without order, or order without justice; and both require a guardian, an interpreter, an executor. This is the civil power. God, who created man, and willed also his preservation, consequently willed the existence of society, and the power which it requires. Now the existence of the civil power is as conformable to the will of God as the existence of the paternal; if families have need of the paternal, society has no less need of the civil power. Our Lord has condescended to secure us from mistakes on this important point by telling us in the Scriptures, that all power emanates from Him, that we are obliged to obey it, that whoever resists it resists the Divine command. I seek in vain for an objection to this way of explaining the origin of society, and of the power which governs it. This doctrine preserves natural, human, and divine right; all these rights are connected, and support each other. The sublimity of the theory rivals its simplicity; revelation sanctions what was shown by the light of reason, and grace fortifies nature. Such, then, is the famous divine right, presented as a bugbear to the ignorant and unsuspecting, in order to make them believe that the Catholic Church, when she teaches the obligation of obeying the legitimate power, and founds this obligation on the law of God, proposes a dogma injurious to true human liberty.

To hear some men ridicule the divine right of kings, one would say that we Catholics believed that certain individuals and families have received bulls of institution from Heaven, and that we are grossly ignorant of the history of the changes of the civil power. If they had examined the matter more deeply, they would have found that, far from being liable to the reproach of such folly, we have only established a principle the necessity of which was acknowledged by all the legislators of antiquity, and that our belief is quite reconcilable with true philosophical doctrines and the events recorded by history. In support of what I have said, see with what admirable clearness St. Chrysostom explains this point in his 23d homily on the Epistle to the Romans: "There is no power that does not come from God." What do you say? Is every prince, then, appointed by God? I do not say that; for I do not speak of any prince in particular, but of the thing itself, that is, of the power itself: I affirm that the existence of principalities is the work of the divine wisdom, and that to it it is owing that all things are not given up to blind chance. Therefore it is that the Apostle does not say, "That there is no prince who does not come from God;" but he says, speaking of the thing in itself, "There is no power which does not come from God." "Non est potestas, nisi a Deo. Quid dicis? Ergo omnis princeps a Deo constitutus? Istud non dico. Non enim de quovis principe mihi sermo est, sed de re ipsa, id est de ipsa potestate. Quod enim principatus sint, quodque non simpliciter et temere cuncta ferantur, divinæ sapientiæ opus esse dico. Propterea non dicit: non enim princeps est nisi a Deo. Sed de re ipsa disserit dicens: non est potestas nisi a Deo." (*Hom.* 23, *in Epist. ad Rom.*) It appears, from the words of St. John Chrysostom, that the meaning of divine right, according to Catholics, is, that there exists a power for the government of society, and that it is not abandoned to the mercy of passion and imagination. This doctrine, which insures public order, by establishing the obligation of obedience on motives of conscience, does not descend to the inferior questions, which do not affect the fundamental principle.

It may perhaps be objected, that if we admit the interpretation of St John

Chrysostom, it was not necessary for the sacred text to teach that which reason so clearly dictated. To this our reply is two-fold: 1st, that the sacred Scripture expressly prescribes to us several obligations which nature imposes on us independently of all divine right, as to honor parents, not to kill, not to rob, and other things of the kind; 2d, that in the present case the Apostles had very good reason to recommend particularly obedience to legitimate power, and to sanction in a clear and conclusive manner this obligation, founded on the natural law itself. Indeed, the same St. Chrysostom tells us, "that at that time a very widely-spread opinion represented the Apostles as seditious men and innovators, laboring by their speeches and acts to bring about the downfall of laws." "Plurima tunc temporis circumferebatur fama, traducens Apostolos veluti seditiosos rerumque novatores; qui omnia ad evertendum leges communes et facerent et dicerent." (*Hom.* 23, *in Epist. ad Tim.*)

It was no doubt to this that St. Paul alluded when, admonishing the faithful of the obligation of obeying authority, he told them that "such was the will of God, that by acting thus they might put to silence the imprudence of foolish men." (Epist. i. c. 2.) We also know from St. Jerome, that in the beginning of the Church, some, hearing the Gospel liberty preached, imagined that universal liberty also was meant. The necessity of inculcating a duty, the fulfilment of which is indispensable for the preservation of society, will be clearly perceived if we consider with what ease an error so flattering to proud and rebellious minds might take root. After fourteen centuries had passed away, we see the error reproduced in the time of Wickliff and John Huss. The Anabaptists made a dreadful application of it when they inundated Germany with blood. At a later period, the fanatical sectaries of England raised the greatest disorders and brought about fearful catastrophes by a similar doctrine, condemning alike the civil and ecclesiastical power.

The religion of Jesus Christ, the law of peace and love, when preaching liberty, spoke of that liberty which draws us from the slavery of sin and the power of the devil, renders us co-heirs of Jesus Christ, and participators of grace and glory. But she was very far from propagating doctrines which could favor disorder, or subvert law and authority. It was, then, of the greatest importance to her to disprove the calumnies by which her enemies attempted to injure her; it was necessary for her to proclaim, by her words and acts, that the public interest had nothing to fear from her doctrines. We also see that after the Apostles had inculcated this sacred obligation on several occasions, the Fathers of the earliest times insist again and frequently on the same point. St. Polycarp, quoted by Eusebius, (lib. iv. *Hist.* cap. 15,) says, when speaking to the proconsul: "It is ordained to render to the magistrates and powers appointed by God the honor which we owe them." St. Justin, in his *Apology for the Christians*, also recalls the precept of Jesus Christ touching the payment of tributes: Tertullian, in his *Apology*, chapter third, reproaches the Gentiles with the persecution they directed against the Christians, even at the time when the latter, with their hands raised to heaven, were praying for the safety of the emperors. The zeal of the saints who were charged with the instruction and direction of the faithful succeeded in inculcating this precept so well, that the Christians were everywhere a model of submission and obedience Thus Pliny, writing to the Emperor Trajan, avowed that, religion excepted, he could not accuse them of being at all wanting in the fulfilment of the laws and imperial edicts.

Nature herself has pointed out the persons in whom resides the paternal power; the wants of the family mark the limits of this power; the feelings of the heart prescribe its object and regulate its conduct. In society it is otherwise: the rights of the civil power are tossed about by the storms of human events; here this right resides in one person, there in several; to-day it belongs to one family, to-morrow to another; one day it is exercised under one form, the next under another very different. The infant who weeps at his mother's bosom reminds her of the obligation of nourishing and watching over it; woman, weak and unsupported, calls unmistakably on man to protect her and her child; youth, without strength to sustain or knowledge to direct itself, shows parents their obligation of care and guardianship. We see clearly the will of God; the order of nature forcibly expresses it; the tenderest feelings are its echo and interpreter; we do not require any thing else to show us what is the will of God; we do not need any refinement to convince us that the parental power is from above. The rights and duties of parents and children are written in characters as distinct as they are beautiful. But where shall we find, with respect to the civil power, an expression as unequivocal? If power comes from God, by what means does he communicate it? In what channel is it conveyed? This leads us to other secondary questions, which all conduce to the explanation and solution of the principal question.

Was there ever a man who by natural right found himself invested with civil power? It is clear that in this case power would have no other origin than paternal authority; that is to say, in that case, the civil power ought to be considered as an amplification of that authority, as a transformation of domestic into civil power. We immediately see the difference between the domestic and the social order, their separate objects, the diversity of rules by which they must be regulated, and we see how different are the means which they both use for their government. I do not deny that the type of society is found in the family, and that society is in the most desirable condition when it most resembles the family in command and in obedience; but mere analogies do not suffice to establish rights, and it always remains indubitable that those of the civil power must not be confounded with those of the paternal.

On the other hand, the nature of things shows that Providence, in ordaining the destinies of the world, did not establish the paternal as the source of the civil. Indeed, we do not see how such a power could have been transmitted, and the legitimacy of its claims have been justified. We can easily understand the limited rule of an old man, governing a society, composed of two or three generations only, who were descended from him; but as soon as this society increased, extended to several countries, and consequently was divided and subdivided, the patriarchal power must have disappeared, its exercise must have become impossible, and we can no longer understand how the pretenders to the throne could come to an understanding with each other and the rest of the people, to justify and legitimize their rule. The theory which acknowledges the paternal as the origin of the civil power may be as promising as you please; it may sustain itself on the example of the patriarchal government, which we observe in the cradle of society; but there are two things against it. First, it asserts, but does not prove; second, it has no means of attaining the end for which it was intended, viz. the consolidation of government, for it cannot establish itself by proving its legitimacy. The greatest of kings and the humblest of subjects equally know that they are the sons of Noe; nothing more I have not been able to find this theory either in St. Thomas, or in any of the other principal theologians; and to go still higher, I do not know that it can find any authority in the doctrines of the Fathers, in the tradition of the Church, or in Scripture itself. It is consequently a mere philosophical opinion, of which the explanation and proof belong to those who advance it. Catholicity says nothing either for or against it.

It is then demonstrated that the civil power does not reside in any man of natural right, and on the other hand, we know that power comes from God. Who receives this power from God, and how does he receive it? It is necessary first to observe, that the Catholic Church, while acknowledging the divine origin of the civil power, an origin which is expressly stated in Scripture, does not define any thing either as to the form of this power, or the means which God employs in communicating it. So that after the Catholic doctrine is established, there still remains to be examined and discussed, who *immediately* receives the power, and how it is transmitted? This is acknowledged by theologians when they have treated of this matter; this should be enough to remove the prejudices of those who consider the doctrine of the Church on this point as conducive to popular degradation. The Church teaches the obligation of obeying legitimate authority, and adds that the power which it exercises emanates from God; this doctrine is as applicable to republics as to absolute monarchies, and does not prejudge either the forms of government or the particular claims of legitimacy. As to these latter questions they cannot be answered in general terms; they depend upon a variety of circumstances into which the general principles which are the foundation of the good order and peace of society cannot enter. I think it is so important to give clear ideas on this point, and to state the doctrines of the most distinguished Catholic divines, that I consider it necessary to devote an entire chapter to this subject.

CHAPTER XLIX.

THE ORIGIN OF SOCIETY, ACCORDING TO CATHOLIC DIVINES.

THERE is nothing more instructive or more interesting, than the study of public law in those writers who, pretending not to pass for statesmen, and entertaining no views of ambition, express themselves without flattery and without bitterness; and explain these matters with as much calmness and tranquillity as they would theories of rare application and limited extent. At the present time it is almost impossible to open a book without immediately perceiving to which of the two contending parties the author belongs; it seldom happens that his ideas are not affected by passion, or adapted to serve particular designs; and it not unfrequently happens that, without conviction, he speaks according to the dictates of his interest.

It is not so with the old writers, of whom we are speaking. Let us render them at least this justice; that their opinions are conscientious, their language loyal and sincere; and whatever may be the judgment with respect to them, whether we consider them as real sages, or as ignorant men and fanatics, we cannot call in question their sincerity; that they are animated by a religious idea, that they develop a philosophical system, that their pens are the faithful interpreters of their thoughts.

Rousseau attempts to seek the origin of society, and of the civil power; and begins the first chapter of his work with these words: "Man is born free, and he is everywhere in fetters." Do you not immediately perceive the tribune under the mantle of the philosopher? Do you not observe that, instead of addressing himself to the reason, the writer appeals to the passions; and wounds the most susceptible of them—viz. pride. It is in vain for the philosopher to endeavor to make us believe that he does not intend to reduce his doctrines to practice; his language betrays his design. In another place, where he attempts nothing less than to give advice to a great nation, he has hardly begun when he holds over Europe the torch of an incendiary.

"When we read ancient history, we fancy ourselves transported to another world, and among other beings. What have the French, the English, the Russians, in common with the Greeks and Romans? Hardly any thing but the form. The great souls of the latter appear to the others as exaggerations of history. How can they, who feel themselves to be so little, imagine that such great men ever existed? They did exist, however; and they were human like ourselves. What hinders our being men like them? Our prejudices, our low philosophy, and grovelling passions, combined with the egotism of men's hearts, by absurd institutions, directed by men of little minds." (*Considerations on the Government of Poland, &c.*, Chap. 2.) Do you not observe the poison conveyed in these words of the publicist? And is it not palpable that he had something more in view than enlightening the mind? See with what address he attempts to produce a feeling of irritation, by harsh and indecent reproaches.

Let us take the opposite extreme of the comparison, and see in how different a tone St. Thomas of Aquin, in his work *De Regimine Principum*, begins his explanation on the same subject, and gives directions for good government.(*a*)[1]

"If man," he says, "was intended to live alone, like many animals, he would not require any one to govern him; every man would be his own king, under the supreme command of God; inasmuch as he would govern himself by the light of reason given him by the Creator. But it is in the nature of man to be a social and political animal, living in community, differently from all other animals; a thing which is clearly shown by the necessities of his nature. Nature has provided for other animals food; skins for a covering, means of defence,—as teeth, horns, claws,—or, at least, speed in flight; but she has not endowed man with any of those qualities; and instead she has given him reason, by which, with the assistance of his hands, he can procure what he wants. But to procure this, one man alone is not enough; for he is not in a condition to preserve his own life; it is, therefore, in man's nature to live in society. Moreover, nature has granted to other animals the power of discerning what is useful or injurious to them: thus the sheep has a natural horror of his enemy the wolf. There are also certain animals who know by nature the herbs which are medicinal to them, and other things which are necessary for their preservation. But man has not naturally the knowledge which is requisite for the support of life, except in society; inasmuch as the aid of reason is capable of leading from universal principles to the knowledge of particular things, which are necessary for life. Thus, then, since it is impossible for man alone to obtain all this knowledge, it is necessary that he should live in society, one aiding another; each one applying to his own task; for example, some in medicine; some in one way, and some in another. This is shown with great clearness in that faculty peculiar to man, language—which enables him to communicate his thoughts to others. Indeed, brute animals mutually communicate their feelings; as the dog communicates his anger by barking, and other animals their passions by various ways. But man, with respect to his fellows, is more communicative than any other animal; even than those who are the most inclined to live in union, as cranes, ants, and bees. In this sense, Solomon says, in Ecclesiastes: 'It is better, therefore, that two should be together than one; for they have the advantage of their society.' Thus, if it be natural for man to live in society, it is necessary that some one should direct the multitude; for if many were united, and each one did as he thought proper, they would fall to pieces, unless somebody looked after the public good, as would be the case with the human body, and that of any other animal, if there did not exist a power to watch over the welfare of all the members. Thus Solomon says: 'Thus, where there is no one to govern, the people will be dispersed.' In man himself the soul directs the body; and in the soul, the feelings of anger and concupiscence are governed by the reason. Among the members of the body, there is one

[1] This subject is so important, so delicate, that I shall not be satisfied with giving a translation of the passages which I quote, however careful I may be to render them exact and literal, at the risk of irregularity of style and violation of the idiom of our language. I wish, therefore, to set before the reader the original texts themselves, desiring him to judge from them and not from my version. [They will be found in the Appendix.]

principal one, which directs all; as the heart or the head. There ought, then, to be in every multitude some governing power." (St. Thomas, *De Regimine Principum*, lib. i. cap. 1.)

This passage, so remarkable for profound wisdom, clearness of ideas, solidity of principles, vigor and exactness of deductions, contains, in a few words, all that can be said with respect to the origin of society, and of power; to the rights enjoyed by the latter, and the obligations incumbent upon it: the matter being considered in general, and by the light of reason alone. In the first place, it was required to show, with clearness, the necessity of the existence of society; and this the holy doctor does by this very simple reasoning—man is of such a nature that he cannot live alone, and then he has need of being united to his fellows. If a proof of this fundamental truth be required, it is found in the fact that he is endowed with speech; this is a sign that by nature he is destined to communicate with other men, and consequently to live in society. After having proved this invincible necessity, it remained to demonstrate a necessity not less absolute—viz. the necessity of a power to govern society. In order to make this demonstration, St. Thomas does not invent extravagant systems, or unfounded theories; he does not appeal to absurd suppositions; he is satisfied with a reason founded on the nature of things, dictated by common sense, and supported by daily experience—viz. that in all bodies of men, there is a director requisite; since, without him, disorder, and even dispersion, are inevitable; for in all societies there must be a chief.

It must be allowed that this clear and simple explanation enables us to understand the theory of the origin of society much better than all the subtilties of explicit and implicit pacts; it is enough for a thing to be founded on nature itself, for it to be viewed as demonstrated as a real necessity, in order that its existence may be easily conceived; why then seek, by subtilties and suppositions, what is apparent at the first view?

Let us not, however, suppose that St. Thomas does not acknowledge divine right, or is ignorant that the obligation of obedience to power may be founded on it: far from it; this truth he establishes in many places in his works; but he does not forget the natural and the human law, which, on this point, are combined and allied with the divine, in such a way, that the latter is only a confirmation of, and gives a sanction to, the others. We ought thus to interpret the passages in which the holy doctor attributes the civil power to human law, considering this law with that of grace. For example, when examining whether infidels can have dominion or supremacy over the faithful, he says: *(b)* "It is necessary here to consider that dominion or supremacy is introduced by virtue of human law; the distinction between the faithful and infidels, is by divine law. Divine law, which emanates from grace, does not take away human law, which is founded on the law of natural reason; therefore the distinction between the faithful and infidels, considered in itself, does not take away the dominion or supremacy of infidels over the faithful."

When inquiring, in another place, if the prince who has apostatized from the faith by this fact loses dominion over his subjects, so that they are no longer called upon to obey him, he expresses himself thus: *(c)* "As has been said before, infidelity does not destroy dominion itself; for dominion was introduced by the law of nations, which is human right; while the distinction between the faithful and infidels is by a divine, which does not take away the human right." Again; when examining if man is obliged to obey another man, he says: *(d)* "As natural actions proceed from natural powers, so human operations proceed from the human will. In natural things, it was necessary that inferior things should be brought into their respective operations by the excellence of the natural virtue which God has given to superior things. In the same way, also, it is necessary that in human things, those which are superior should urge on the inferior, by the force of authority ordained by God. To move, by means of reason and the will, is to command; and as, by virtue of the natural order instituted by God, inferior things in nature are necessarily subject to the motion of superior things, so also, in human things, those which are inferior ought, by natural and divine right, to obey those which are superior."

On the same question, St. Thomas examines whether obedience is a special virtue, and he answers, (*e*) "That to obey a superior is a duty conformable to the divine order communicated to things." In the 6th article, he states the question whether Christians are obliged to obey the secular powers, and says: (*f*). "The faith of Christ is the principle and cause of justice, according to what is said in the Epistle to the Romans, chap. iii. 'the justice of God by the faith of Jesus Christ.' Thus the faith of Christ does not take away the law of justice, but rather confirms it. This law wills that inferiors should obey their superiors; for without that, human society could not be preserved; and thus the faith of Christ does not exempt the faithful from the obligation of obeying the secular powers." I have quoted at some length these passages from St. Thomas, in order to show that he does not understand the divine right in the sense in which the enemies of Catholicity have made it a reproach to us; but that, properly speaking, while he adheres to a dogma so expressly taught in the sacred text, he considers the Divine law as a confirmation and sanction of the natural and human law. We know that for six centuries Catholic doctors have regarded the authority of St. Thomas as worthy of the highest respect in all that concerns faith and morality.

We have just seen that this angel of the schools establishes, as founded on the natural, human, and divine law, the duty of obeying authority, affirming that the source of all power is found in God, without entering into the question whether God communicates this power *directly* or *indirectly* to those who exercise it, and leaving a vast field where human opinions may debate without violating the purity of faith. In the same way, the most eminent doctors who have succeeded him in the Catholic pulpits have contented themselves with establishing and enforcing the doctrine, without rashly making use of the authority of the Church in its application. To prove this I will here insert some passages from distinguished theologians. Cardinal Bellarmin expresses himself in these words: (*g*) "It is certain that public authority comes from God, from whom alone emanate all things good and lawful, as is proved by St. Augustin throughout almost all the forty-five books of the *City of God*. Indeed, the Wisdom of God, in the Book of Proverbs, chap. viii., cries out, 'It is by Me that kings reign;' and further on, 'It is by Me that princes rule.' The prophet Daniel, in the second chapter, 'The God of heaven has given thee the kingdom and the empire;' and the same prophet, in the fourth chapter, 'Thy dwelling shall be with cattle and with wild beasts, and thou shalt eat grass as an ox, and shalt be wet with the dew of heaven, and seven years shall pass over thee, till thou know that the Most High ruleth over the kingdom of men, and giveth it to whomsoever He will.'" After having proved, by the authority of the Holy Scriptures, this dogma, viz. that the civil power comes from God, the illustrious writer explains the sense in which it ought to be understood: (*h*) "But," he says, "it is necessary to make some observations here. In the first place, political power, considered in general, and without descending in particular to monarchy, aristocracy, or democracy, emanates immediately from God alone; for being necessarily annexed to the nature of man, it proceeds from Him who has made that nature. Besides, that power is by natural law, since it does not depend upon men's consent, since they must have a government whether they wish it or not, under pain of desiring the destruction of the human race, which is against the inclination of nature. It is thus that the law of nature is divine law, and government is introduced by divine law; and it is particularly this which the

Apostle seems to have had in view when he says to the Romans, chap. xiii., 'He who resists authority, resists the ordinance of God.'"

This doctrine destroys all the theory of Rousseau, who makes the existence of society and the right of the civil power depend on human conventions; it also overturns the absurd systems of some Protestants, and other heretics, their predecessors, who, in the name of Christian liberty, pretended to condemn all authority. No! the existence of society does not depend on the consent of man; society is not his work; it satisfies an imperious necessity, which, if it were not satisfied, would entail the destruction of the human race. God, when he created man, did not deliver him to the mercy of chance; He has given him the right of fulfilling his necessities, and has imposed on him the care of his own preservation as a duty; therefore the existence of the human race includes also the existence of government, and the obligations of obedience. There is no theory so clear, simple, and solid. Shall it be called the enemy and oppressor of human freedom? Is it any disgrace to man to acknowledge himself the creature of God? to confess that he has received from Him what is necessary for his preservation? Is the intervention of God any infringement of human liberty, and cannot man be free without being an Atheist? It is absurd to say there is any thing favorable to servitude in a doctrine which tells us "God wills not that you should live like wild beasts: He commands you to be united in society, and for this purpose He orders you to live in submission to an authority legitimately established." If this be called servitude and oppression, we desire this servitude, we willingly give up the right which is pretended to be granted to us of wandering in the woods like wild beasts: true liberty does not exist in man when he is stripped of the finest attribute of his nature, that of acting in conformity with reason.

Such is the explanation of divine right according to the illustrious commentator whom we have just quoted; let us now see the applications which he makes of it, and learn in what way, according to him, God communicates the civil power to those who are charged with its exercise. After the words quoted above, Bellarmin continues: (*i*) "In the second place, observe, that this power resides *immediately*, as in its subject, in all the multitude, for it is by divine right. The divine right has not given this power to any man in particular, for it has given it to the multitude; besides, the positive law being taken away, there is no reason why one should rule rather than another, among a great number of equal men; therefore power belongs to the whole multitude. In fine, society should be a perfect state; it should have the power of self-preservation, and, consequently, that of chastising the disturbers of the peace."

This doctrine has nothing in common with the foolish assertions of Rousseau and his followers; no one who has studied public law will confound things so different. Indeed, what the Cardinal establishes in the passage quoted, viz. that power resides immediately in the multitude, is not in opposition to what he himself taught a little before, when he said that it comes from God, and is not owing to human conventions. His doctrine may be conveyed in this form. Suppose a number of men without any positive law; there is then no reason why any one of them should have a right to rule the rest. Nevertheless, this law exists, nature itself indicates its necessity, God ordains a government; therefore there exists among this number of men the legitimate power of instituting one. To explain more clearly the ideas of this illustrious theologian, let us suppose that a considerable number of families, perfectly equal among themselves and absolutely independent of each other, were thrown by a tempest on a desert island. The vessel being destroyed, they have no hope either of returning home or of pursuing their journey. All communication with the rest of mankind is become impossible: we ask, whether these families could live without government? No. Has any one among them a right of governing the rest? Clearly not. Can any individual among them pretend to such a right? Certainly not. Have they a right to appoint the government of which they stand in need? Certainly they have. Therefore in this multitude, represented by the fathers of families or in some other way, resides the civil power, together with the right of transmitting it to one or more persons, according as they shall judge proper. It is difficult to make any valid objection to the doctrine placed in this point of view. That this is the real meaning of his words is clearly shown by the observations which follow: (*k*) "In the third place," he says, "observe that the multitude transfers this power to one person or more by natural right; for the republic not being able to exercise it by itself, is obliged to communicate it to one or to a limited number; and it is thus that the power of princes, considered in general, is by natural and divine law; and the whole human race, if assembled together, could not establish the contrary, viz. that princes or governors did not exist."

But the fundamental principle being once established, Bellarmin allows to society an ample right of appointing the form of government which they think proper. This ought to refute the accusations made against the Catholic doctrine, of favoring servitude; for if all forms of government are reconcilable with this doctrine, it is evident that it cannot justly be accused of being incompatible with liberty. Hear how the same author continues on this point: (*l*) "Observe, in the fourth place," he says, "that particular forms of government are by the law of nations, and not by divine law, since it depends upon the consent of the multitude to place over themselves a king, consuls, or other magistrates, as is clear; and, for a legitimate reason, they can change royalty into aristocracy, or into democracy, or *vice versâ*, as it was done in Rome.

"Observe, in the fifth place, that it follows, from what we have said, that this power in particular comes from God, but by means of the counsel and election of man, like all other things which belong to the law of nations; for the law of nations is, as it were, a conclusion drawn from the natural law by human reasoning. Thence follows a two-fold difference between the political and the ecclesiastical power: first, difference with regard to the subject, since political power is in the multitude, and ecclesiastical in a man *immediately*, as in its subject; second, difference with respect to the cause, since political power, considered generally, is by divine law, and in particular by the law of nations, while the ecclesiastical power is in every way by divine law, and emanates immediately from God."

These last words show clearly how correct I was in saying that theologians understand the divine law in a very different manner, according as it is applied to the civil or to the ecclesiastical power. It must not be supposed that the doctrine now stated is peculiar to Cardinal Bellarmin; the generality of theologians follow him on this point; but I have preferred quoting his authority, because he, being so strongly attached to the See of Rome, if the latter were imbued with the principles of despotism, as it has been charged with being, no doubt, something of them would appear in the writings of this theologian. It is easy to anticipate the objection that will be made to this explanation; we shall be told that Bellarmin, having for his object the exaltation of the authority of the Sovereign Pontiff, with this view attempted to lower the power of kings, in order to take away or diminish all opposition to the authority of the Popes. I will not now enter into an examination of the opinions of Bellarmin with respect to the two powers—this would be foreign to my design; besides, such points of civil and ecclesiastical law excited at that time great interest, on account of circumstances at that period, but now very little, on account of the new course which events have taken, and the great change which has been brought about in ideas. I shall, nevertheless, reply to this supposed difficulty by two very simple observations. The first is, that we have not to inquire the intentions of Bellarmin in explaining his doctrine, but in what that doctrine consists. Whatever his motive may have been, we see an author of vast renown, whose opinion has great weight in Catholic schools, and who wrote at Rome, where, so far from his writings being condemned, he was surrounded with respect and honor: this theologian, I say, explaining the doctrine of the Church on the Divine origin of the civil power, does it in such terms that, while giving sacred guarantees for the good order of society, he does not infringe on the liberty of the people; this is the vindication of Rome against the attacks made upon her. The second is, that Cardinal Bellarmin does not here profess an isolated opinion—the generality of theologians are on his side; therefore, all that can be said against him personally proves nothing against his doctrines. Among the many authors that I could quote, I will select some who will represent many different periods: and as the obligation of being brief confines me within narrow limits, I beg the reader himself to examine the works of Catholic theologians and moralists; he will thus make sure of becoming acquainted with their thoughts on this subject. Hear how Suarez explains the origin of power: (*m*) "Herein," he says, "the common opinion seems to be, that God, inasmuch as He is the author of nature, gives the power; so that men are, so to speak, the matter and subject capable of this power; while God gives the form by giving the power." (*De Leg.* lib. iii. c. 3.)

He goes on to develop his doctrine, relying on the reason usually made use of in this matter; and when he comes to draw the conclusions, he explains how society, which, according to him, receives the power immediately from God, communicates it to certain persons. He adds: (*n*) "In the second place, it follows from what has been said, that the civil power, whenever it is found in a man or a prince, has emanated according to usual and legitimate law, from the people and the community, either directly or remotely, and that it cannot otherwise be justly possessed." (*Ibid.* cap. 4.)

Perhaps some of my readers may not know that a Spanish Jesuit maintained against the King of England in person, the doctrine that princes receive power *mediately* from God, and *immediately* from the people. This Jesuit is Suarez himself, and the book to which I allude is called, (*o*) "*Defence of the Catholic and Apostolic Faith against the errors of the Anglican sect; accompanied by a Reply to the Apology for the Oath of Fidelity, and to the monitary Preface published by the most serene James, King of England.* By P. D. François Suarez, Professor at the University of Coimbra; addressed to the most serene Kings and Princes of the Christian world."

In the third book, chapter second, where he discusses the question, Whether the political sovereignty comes *immediately* from God or from divine institution, Suarez says: "Here the most serene King not only gives a new and singular opinion, but also acrimoniously attacks Cardinal Bellarmin, for having affirmed that Kings have not received authority *immediately* from God like the Popes. He himself affirms that Kings hold their power not from the people, but *immediately* from God; and he attempts to support his opinion by arguments and examples the value of which I shall examine in the next chapter.

"Although *this controversy does not immediately concern the dogmas of faith (for we have nothing in reference to it either in the Scriptures or in the Fathers)*, it may nevertheless be well to discuss and explain it carefully; 1. because it might possibly lead to error in other dogmas; 2. because the above opinion of the King, as he maintains and explains it, is new, singular, and apparently invented to exalt the temporal at the expense of the spiritual power; and 3. because we consider the opinion of the illustrious Bellarmin *ancient, received, true,* and *necessary.*" But we must not attribute these opinions to the circumstances of the times, nor suppose that they disappeared from the schools of theologians as soon as they were advanced. In support of them, a multitude of authors might very easily be cited, who would show that Suarez was correct in saying that the opinion of Bellarmin was received and ancient; they would, moreover, show that this doctrine continued to be admitted as a matter of course, without any doubt of its orthodoxy, or of its containing any thing dangerous to the stability of monarchies. In proof of what is here adduced, I will cite passages from distinguished authors, proving that at Rome this mode of explaining the right divine has never been called in question; and that in France and Spain, where absolute monarchy had taken so deep root, this opinion was no longer regarded as dangerous to the stability of thrones. A long period had already elapsed—the critical position which might more or less influence the direction of ideas had consequently disappeared, yet theologians still maintained the same doctrines. Cardinal Gotti, who wrote in the early part of the last century, gives, in his Treatise upon Laws, the above opinion as previously admitted, without even attempting to confirm it. *(p)* In the Moral Theology of Herman Busenbaum, enlarged by St. Alphonsus Liguori, book 1st, second Treatise upon Laws, (chap. i. dub. 2, § 104,) it is expressly said: "It is certain that the power of making laws exists among men, but as far as civil laws are concerned, this power belongs naturally to no individual. It belongs to the community, who transfer it to one or to more, that by them the community itself may be governed."

Should any one say that I quote the Jesuits only, or suspect that these doctrines are mere casuistry, I will cite remarkable passages from other theologians, who are neither casuists nor prepossessed in favor of the Jesuits. Father Daniel Concina, who wrote at Rome about the middle of the last century, supports the same doctrine as generally admitted; in his *Théologie chrétienne dogmatico-morale*, Roman edition, 1768, he expresses himself as follows: *(q)* "All writers generally assert that the origin of supreme power is of God, as Solomon declares in the Book of Proverbs, c. viii., saying, 'By Me kings reign, and lawgivers decree just things:' as truly as subordinate princes are dependent upon the supreme temporal majesty, so, in like manner, this majesty itself must depend upon the supreme King and Lord of lords. Theologians and jurists dispute whether this supreme power comes *immediately* from God, or merely in an *indirect manner*. Many affirm that it emanates *immediately* from God, because it cannot emanate from men, whether we consider them collectively or individually; for all fathers of families are equal, and each possesses, with regard to his own family, a power merely economical; from which it follows, that they cannot confer upon others that civil and political power which they themselves do not possess. Moreover, if the community, in its superiority, had delegated to one or to more the power here under discussion, it could revoke it at pleasure, for the superior is always at liberty to withdraw the facilities he has delegated to another, and this would be very injurious to society.

"In support of the opposite opinion, many answer, and *certainly with more probability and truth*, that, in reality, all power proceeds from God, but that it is not delegated to any particular individual *directly*, unless by consent of civil society. That this power is not vested *directly* in any individual, but in the entire collection of men, is what St. Thomas expressly teaches (1, 2, qu. 90, art. 3, ad 2, et qu. 97, art. 3, ad 3), followed by Dominic Soto (lib. i. qu. 1, art. 3); by Ledesma (2 part. qu. 18, art. 3); and by Covarruvias (in Pract. cap. i.). The reason of this is evident; for as all men are born free with regard to civil society, no one has any civil power over another, since this power exists not in each, nor in any of them in a fixed manner; it follows, therefore, that it is vested in the whole collection of men. *God does not confer this power by any special act distinct from creation, but it is a property of right reason, inasmuch as right reason dictates that men, united in one moral whole, shall prescribe, by express or tacit consent, in what manner society shall be governed, preserved, and upheld.*"

It is proper to remark, that Father Concina, speaking here of *tacit or express consent*, has not in view the actual existence of society, nor the authority by which it is governed, but merely the mode of exercising this authority for the direction, preservation, and defence of society. Hence, his opinion coincides with that of Bellarmin; society and power are of right divine and natural, but the *mode* of organizing society, and of transmitting and exercising authority, is human. After having shown in what sense we are to understand that civil power comes from God, Concina resumes the question which he had proposed, viz. in what manner authority exists in kings, princes, and other supreme heads of government. He proceeds as follows: (*r*) "It is evident, therefore, that the power existing in the prince, the king, or in many persons whether nobles or plebeians, emanates from the community itself, directly or indirectly; for, if it came immediately from God, it would be manifested to us in a particular manner, as in the instances of Saul and David, who were chosen by God. We consider, therefore, erroneous, the doctrine that God confers this power immediately and directly upon the king, the prince, or any other head of supreme government whatever, to the exclusion of the tacit or express consent of the public. This discussion, it is true, is one of words rather than of things, for this power comes from God, the author of nature, inasmuch as He has ordained and appointed that the public itself shall confer upon one or more the power of supreme government, for the preservation and defence of society. The nomination of the person or persons appointed to command being once made, their power is said to come from God, because society itself is bound by natural and divine right to obey him who commands. In fact, it is the will of God that society shall be governed, whether by one individual or by several. In this manner the several opinions of theologians are reconciled with each other, and the oracles of Scripture appear in their true sense: 'He that resisteth the power, resisteth the ordinance of God.' 'There is no power but from God.' 'Be subject, therefore, to every human creature for God's sake, whether to the king,' &c. 'Thou wouldst not have any power against Me, unless it were given thee from above.' These testimonies, and others of a like nature, ought to convince us that all is ordained and directed by God, the supreme Mediator. This, however, does not exclude the operations of human institutions, as is very justly interpreted by St. Augustin and St. John Chrysostom."

Father Billuart, who lived in the early part of last century, and, consequently, at the same epoch when the highly monarchical traditions of Louis XIV. were in all their vigor, expressed the same ideas on this subject as the theologians above cited. In his work on Moral Theology, which, for almost a century, has been widely circulated, he thus expresses himself: (*s*) "I maintain, in the first place, that legislative power belongs to the community, or to its representative." After quoting St. Thomas and St. Isidore, he continues: "Reason proves, that to make laws belongs of right to him who is appointed to watch over the public good; for the maintenance of the public good, as has been already said, is the end and aim of the laws. It is the duty of the community, or of its ruler, to watch over the public good; for as the welfare of an individual is a fit object for individual agency, so is the public good for the agency of the community, or of him to whom its functions have been delegated; the power of legislation, therefore, is vested in the community, or in its representative. I will confirm what is here advanced. The law has the power of commanding and of coercing in such a manner that no individual has any authority to command or restrain the multitude. This authority belongs exclusively to the community, or to its representative; to these, therefore, legislative power belongs." Having made these reflections, Billuart starts another difficulty with regard to the extreme extension which he appears to have given to the rights of the multitude. On this occasion he developes his system still further. (*t*)

"It will be objected," says he, "that the right of commanding and compelling is vested in the superior, and cannot belong to the community, since it is not superior to itself. To this I reply: Society, in one sense, is not superior to itself, but in another it is. The community may be considered collectively as one moral body, and in this sense it is superior to itself as considered distributively in each of its members. Again; it may be considered as acting in the place of God, from whom emanates all legislative power, as it is said in Proverbs: 'By Me kings reign and the lawgivers decree just things;' or as capable of being governed conformably to the public good. In the former case, it is superior and legislative; in the latter, inferior and subject to the law."

As this explanation might appear somewhat obscure, Billuart proceeds to investigate more profoundly the origin of society and of civil power. He endeavors to show how the natural, the divine, and the human laws agree on this point, defining what belongs to each. He then continues as follows: (*u*) "To render this more clear, it must be observed, that man, unlike other animals, is born destitute of many things necessary both for body and soul, and that for these he is indebted to society and the assistance of his fellow-mortals; consequently he is, by his very nature, a social animal. This society, which nature and reason prescribe to him as indispensable, cannot long exist without some power to direct it, according to what is said in Proverbs: 'Where there is no governor, the people will come to ruin.' Whence it follows, that God, who has given this nature, has also given the power of governing and of legislating. He, in fact, who gives the form, gives, at the same time, all that such form necessarily requires. But as it is not possible for this executive and legislative power to be exercised by the entire multitude, since it would be difficult for all and each forming this multitude to assemble on all occasions when the affairs of the commonweal are to be discussed, or laws to be established, it is usual for the multitude to transfer its right or governing power, either to a number of people selected from all classes, and bearing the name of a democracy; or to a select number of the nobles, which takes the name of an aristocracy; or to one alone, for himself only, or for his successors, by virtue of the right of hereditary succession, which is styled a monarchy. From which it is evident that all power comes from God, as the Apostle says, in his Epistle to the Romans, chap. xiii. This power resides in the community, *directly and by natural right*, but in kings and other rulers merely *indirectly and by human right*, unless God confers it directly upon certain individuals, as He did upon Moses over the Jews, and as Christ has conferred it upon the Supreme Pontiff over the whole Church." What is still more remarkable, our absolute monarchies were never alarmed at these theological doctrines, not only previous to the French Revolution, but since that Revolution, and up to the time commonly styled with us the *fatal decade*, (from 1823 to 1833, the latter part of the reign of Ferdinand VII.) It is well known that during that period the *Compendium Salmaticense* (Compendium of Salamanca) had a most favorable reception in this country, and served as a text-book among the professors of ethics in the colleges and universities. Ye who are continually declaiming against this epoch, imagining, without doubt, that in those days no other doctrines than those in favor of the most arrant despotism could be circulated, listen to what is said in the above book, which was then placed in the hands of every youth destined to the ecclesiastical state. After having established the existence of a civil legislative power, the author thus proceeds: (*x*) "You will ask me, in the second place, whether the prince receives this civil legislative power *immediately* from God. I reply, It is universally admitted that princes receive this power from God; but, at the same time, it is maintained with more truth, that they do not receive it *directly*, but *through the medium* of the people's consent; for all men are naturally equal, and there is no natural distinction of superiority or inferiority. Since nature has not given any individual power over another, God has conferred this power upon the community; which, as it may think it more proper to be ruled by one or by many appointed persons, transfers it to one or to many, that by them it may be ruled; according to St. Thomas (1, 2, qu. 90, art. 3, ad 2). From this natural principle arises the variety in the forms of civil government; for if a state transfers all its power to a single individual, this government is termed monarchical; if it confers it upon the nobles of the nation, it takes the name of an aristocracy; if the people or the state retain this power in their own hands, the civil government is styled a democracy. Princes, therefore, receive from God the power of commanding; for supposing the election made by the whole state, God confers upon the prince the power which was vested in the community. Whence it follows, that the prince rules and governs in the name of God, and whoever resists him resists the ordinance of God, according to the words of the Apostle above cited."

CHAPTER L.

ON THE RIGHT DIVINE, ACCORDING TO THE CATHOLIC DOCTORS.

THE doctrine of the right divine, considered in its relation to society, presents to our notice two particular points which this doctrine contains: 1. The origin of civil power; 2. The mode in which God communicates this power.

The former point is a question of doctrine. No Catholic can entertain any doubt upon it. The second is open to discussion; and various opinions may be formed upon it, without interfering with faith. With regard to the right divine, considered in itself, true philosophy agrees with Catholicity. In fact, if civil power comes not from God, to what source can we trace its origin? Upon what solid principle can we support it? If the man who exercises it does not rest upon God the legitimacy of his power, no title will avail to uphold his right. It will be radically and irretrievably null. On the contrary, supposing authority to come from God, our duty to submit to it becomes evident, and our dignity is not in the least hurt by the submission; but, in the other supposition, we see only force, craft, tyranny, but no reason or justice; perhaps a necessity for submission, but no obligation. By what title does any man pretend to command us? Because he is possessed of superior intellect? Who had the right of adjudging to him the palm? Besides, this superiority does not constitute a right; in some instances its direction might be useful to us, but it will not be obligatory. Is it because he is stronger than we? In that case the elephant ought to be king of the entire world. Is it because he is more wealthy than we? Reason and justice exist not in metal. The rich man is born naked, and his riches will not descend with him into the tomb. Upon earth they have enabled him to acquire power; but they do not confer upon him any right to exercise it over others. Shall it consist in certain faculties conferred on him by others? who has constituted other men our proxies? where is their consent? who has collected their votes? and how can either we or they flatter ourselves that we possess faculties equal to the exercise of civil power? and if we do not possess them, how can we delegate them?

We must here consider the doctrine which places the origin of civil power in the will of men, supposing that this power is the result of a pact, by which individuals have agreed to submit to the retrenchment of a part of their natural liberty, in order to enjoy the benefits of society. According to this system, the rights of the civil power, as well as the duties of the subject, are alike founded on a pact, differing from other contracts only in the nature and extent of its object; so that, in this case, power would emanate from God merely in a general sense, just as all rights and duties emanate from Him. Those writers who thus explain the origin of power, do not always agree with Rousseau. The

Contrat of the philosopher of Geneva has nothing to do with the pact spoken of in other authors. This is not the place to compare the doctrines of Rousseau with those of other writers; suffice it to say, that although they rely upon the pact, they wish, nevertheless, to establish the rights of civil power as they have been hitherto understood by the common consent of mankind, whilst the author of the *Contrat Social* proposes in his book the following problem, which he considers fundamental. I quote his own words: "*To find a form of association which shall defend and protect with all the common strength the person and property of each associate, and by which each one, being united to all, shall nevertheless obey only himself, and remain as free as before.*"

Such is the fundamental problem, the solution of which is given in the *Contrat Social.* This nonsense of having none but one's self to obey, making a *contract, and remaining as free as before,* needs no comment, after what the author himself says in the following line: "The clauses of this contract are so fixed by the very nature of the act, that the least modification would render them vain and of no effect." (Book i. chap. 6.) Rousseau's ideas on this subject do not, therefore, agree with those of many other writers, who also have spoken of pacts, in their explanation of the origin of power; the latter sought a theory in support of power, the former wished to destroy that which existed, and to throw society into a state of excitement. Through a singular idea, Rousseau, in his vault at the Pantheon, is represented to us with the door half open, and a lighted torch in his hand—an emblem, perhaps, more significant than has been imagined. The artist's intention was, to express the idea of Rousseau's enlightening the world even after his death; but it should be remembered, that the torch is also an emblem of the incendiary. La Harpe said of him:

"Sa parole est un feu, mais un feu qui ravage."

To return to the question, I will observe, that the doctrine of a pact is of no avail in accounting for the establishment of power; for it cannot even render legitimate either its origin or its exercise. First, an explicit pact has evidently never existed; and secondly, in the formation of even the most limited society, such a pact never *could* obtain the consent of every individual member. In any convention for such an object, only the heads of families could take part; and hence, women, children, and servants might protest against it. In assenting to such a pact, what right would fathers have to represent the whole of their families? The will of the latter, it will be said, was virtually included in that of their chief; but this is the very point that wants proof. Supposition here is easy enough; proof is not so easy. When you seek the origin of power in principles of strict right, and attempt to maintain that this is only one of those cases to which ordinary conditions of contracts are applicable, you are met at once by a very serious difficulty; for you are obliged to have recourse to a fiction:—the words "*implicit consent*" are a mere fiction, and nothing more. Is it not evident, that the consent of families must have been implicit, even supposing that of their heads to be explicit? This explicit consent would, in fact, be impossible in the formation of any society, however limited in extent. And moreover, the consent of succeeding generations will be equally implicit, since it is impossible to be continually renewing the contract, for the purpose of consulting the wishes of the parties interested in its effects. Reason and history teach that society has never been thus organized; our own experience tells us that it is not now upheld or governed by any such principles. Of what use, then, is this inexplicable theory? When a theory has a practical object, the best way of proving its fallacy is, to prove its impracticability.

The faculties with which civil power is, and always has been, considered to be invested, are of such a nature, that they cannot have proceeded from a pact.

The right of life and death can have come only from God. Man is not in possession of this right. No pact merely human could invest him with a power which he has not, either in relation to himself or to others. I will endeavor to demonstrate this point with all possible precision. If the right of taking away life emanates not from God, but from a pact, it must have originated in the following manner: every member of society must have said, expressly or tacitly, "I consent to the establishment of laws to decree punishment of death for certain crimes; and if I should at any time transgress them, I am willing from that moment to forfeit my life." In this manner, every individual will have given up his life, supposing that the conditions specified are realized; but no individual having a right over his own life, the resigning of it becomes radically null. The joint consent of all the members of society does not obviate the radical and essential nullity of each one's right to give up his life; the sum of their resignations is therefore equally null, and consequently incapable of producing any right whatever. It will be said, perhaps, that man, properly speaking, has no right over his own life, when an arbitrary right is implied, but that when he chooses to dispose of it for his own advantage, the general principle should be restricted. This reflection, at first sight plausible, would lead to the terrible consequence of authorizing suicide. In reply, it will be said, that suicide is no advantage to him who commits it; but if you once grant to the individual the right of disposing of his life, provided he reap an advantage from so doing, you cannot constitute yourselves judges to decide whether or not this advantage exists in any particular case. According to you, he had a right to sacrifice his life when, for example, to satisfy his wants or his taste, he had stolen the property of another. That is to say, that he had a right of choice between the advantages of life and those of satisfying a desire: what will you answer, if he tell you that he prefers death to misery, to ennui, to grief, or to such and such misfortunes which torment him?

The right of life and death cannot consequently emanate from a pact. Man's life is not his own; he has only the use of it so long as it pleases the Creator to grant it him. He has not, therefore, the right of disposing of it, and all conventions he may make for that purpose are null. In some instances, it is lawful, glorious, it may be even obligatory, to deliver one's self up to certain death; but let us not confound ideas: man does not in that case sacrifice his life as being the master of it, he is a voluntary victim to the salvation of his country, or to the good of mankind. The warrior who scales a wall, the charitable man who confronts the most dangerous contagion in visiting the sick, the missionary who resorts to unknown countries, who resigns himself to live in unhealthy climates, and who penetrates into inaccessible forests, seeking ferocious hordes, do not dispose of their lives as being their own; they sacrifice them to a purpose great, sublime, just, and pleasing to God; for God loves virtue, especially heroic virtue; and it is a heroic virtue to die for one's country, to die in visiting the sick, or in carrying the light of truth to those seated in darkness and in the shadow of death. This right of life and death, with which civil power has ever been considered invested, may by some be considered as founded upon the natural right of self-defence vested in society. Every individual, they will say, has the right of taking away the life of another in self-defence; therefore society also has this right. In the chapter on *Intolerance*, I have touched slightly upon this point, and made some reflections which may be repeated here. I will endeavor, nevertheless, to extend them and confirm them by arguments of another kind. In the first place, I maintain that the right of self-defence may confer upon society that of taking away life. If one individual attacked by another may lawfully repel him—kill him even, if necessary to save his own life, it is evident that an assemblage of men have the same right. This appears so evident, that demonstration is superfluous. One society attacked by another has incontestably the right of resisting and repelling the attack—it is justified in making war. With more reason, therefore, might it resist an individual, to make war on him, or kill him. This is all perfectly true and obvious; and I grant that there thus exists, from the very nature of things, a title upon which we may found the right of inflicting capital punishment.

These ideas are plausible, and seem at first sight to nullify the reasons on which we have supported the necessity of having recourse to God for the origin of this formidable right. Nevertheless, when we come to examine them thoroughly, they are far from satisfactory; and it may be even said, that in the sense in which they are understood and applied, they are subversive of the acknowledged principles of society. In fact, if such a theory be admitted, if the right of inflicting capital punishment be made to rest exclusively on this principle, the ideas of penalty, chastisement, and of human justice disappear at once. It has always been thought that the criminal dying upon a gibbet suffers a penalty; and although this terrible act is certainly a satisfaction to society, a means of preservation, yet the principal and predominant idea, that which surpasses all others, which best justifies and exculpates society, which gives to the judge his august character, and stamps disgrace upon the criminal, is the idea of chastisement, of penalty, and of justice. All this disappears when once we can assert that society, in taking away life, only acts in self-defence. Such an act is conformable to reason, it is just, but it no longer merits the honorable title of an executive act of justice. A man is justified in killing an assassin; but in so doing he does not administer justice, he does not execute justice, nor inflict a penalty. These things are very different, and of a distinct order; we cannot confound them without shocking the good sense of mankind.

We will render this distinction more apparent by putting the two theories into the mouth of the judge: the contrast is striking. In the former case, the judge says to the criminal: "You are guilty; the law decrees against you the penalty of death; I, the minister of justice, apply it; the executioner is ordered to inflict it." In the second, he says to him: "You have attacked society, which cannot exist if such attacks are tolerated. It defends itself, and for this reason puts you to death; I, its agent, declare, that the time for its defending itself is come, and hence I give you up to the executioner." In the former supposition, the judge is a minister of justice, and the culprit a criminal who undergoes a just penalty; in the latter, the judge is an instrument of force, the culprit a victim. But, it will be said, the criminal is not on this account less criminal, and still merits the penalty which he undergoes. This is true with respect to the *guilt*, but not with respect to the *penalty*. The fault exists in the eyes of God, and also in the eyes of man, inasmuch as he possesses a conscience capable of judging of the morality of actions; but it does not exist in the eyes of man, considered as a judge. According to you, the judge does not *punish* a crime; he restrains an act injurious to society: but if you say that the judge *inflicts a penalty*, you change the nature of the question, for he then does something more than protect society. It follows from what we have just established, that the right of inflicting capital punishment can only emanate from God, and, consequently, if there existed no other reason for referring to God the origin of power, this alone would suffice. War against an invading nation may be explained by the right of self-defence; invasion also comes under the same principle; for if it be just, it can be entered upon only with a view to enforce some reparation or compensation refused by the enemy. War for the sake of alliance enters into that class of actions which are performed for the assistance of a friend; so that this phenomenon of war, with all its glory, and all its ravages, does not so forcibly oblige us to have recourse to a divine origin as this simple right of condemning a man to the gibbet. The sanction of law,

ful wars also undoubtedly belongs to God, for in Him exists the sanction of all rights and of all duties; but there is not, in this case at least, any need of particular authorization, as in the case of inflicting capital punishment. It is sufficient to have the general sanction which God, as the author of nature, has given to all natural rights and duties.

How do we know that God has granted such an authorization to man? There are three ways of answering this question. 1. The testimony of the Scriptures is sufficient for all Christians. 2. The right of life and death is a universal tradition of the human race, and does, therefore, exist in reality; and as we have shown that it can have its origin only in God, it is right to suppose that He has communicated it to man in one way or another. 3. This right is essential to the preservation of society; God must, therefore, have granted it; for if He wills the preservation of a being, it is evident that He will have bestowed upon it all things necessary for such preservation. To recapitulate what we have hitherto advanced: the Church teaches that civil power comes from God, and this doctrine, which agrees with the formal texts of Scripture, agrees also with natural reason. The Church contents herself with establishing this dogma, and deducing from it the immediate consequence resulting from it, viz. that obedience to the lawful authorities is of right divine. With regard to the mode in which this right divine is communicated, the Church has not determined any thing: the general opinion of theologians is, that society receives it from God, and that, from society, it is transferred, by lawful means, to the person or persons appointed to exercise it. In order that civil power may exact obedience, and be considered invested with this right divine, it must be legitimate; that is to say, the person or persons in possession of it must have acquired it by lawful means, or this power must have become legitimate in their possession, by means acknowledged to be in accordance with right. With respect to political forms, the Church does not determine any thing; but whatever be the form of government, the civil power must be confined within legitimate bounds, while the subject, on his side, is bound to obey. The fitness and legitimacy of such or such persons, and of such and such forms, are subjects not appertaining to right divine. They are particular questions, depending upon a variety of circumstances, and to which no general theory is applicable.

One example of private right will serve to illustrate what we have just explained. Respect for property is of natural and divine right; but the ownership of property, the respective rights of individuals to the same thing, the restrictions to which property should be subject, are questions appertaining to civil right, which have always been resolved, and are still resolved, in various ways. The main object is to adhere to the protective principle of property, the indispensable basis of all social organization; but the application of this principle is, and must be, subject to a variety of circumstances and events, a variety arising from the course of human affairs. It is the same with power. The Church, intrusted with the great deposit of the most important truths, keeps in this deposit the truth which guaranties a divine origin to civil power, and makes the existence of the law an affair of right divine; but she does not interfere in particular cases, which are always controlled more or less by the fluctuation and uncertainty with which the world is agitated. When thus explained, the Catholic doctrine is not in the least opposed to true liberty; it consolidates power, and does not prejudice the questions that may arise between the governors and the governed. No unlawful power can lay claim to the right divine; for it must be legitimate to merit the application of this right. This legitimacy is determined and declared by the laws of each country, from which it follows that the law is the organ of the right divine. This right, therefore, only consolidates what is just; and certainly that which insures justice in the world cannot be said to lead to despotism, for nothing can be more opposed to the liberty and happiness of the people than the absence of justice and legitimacy.

Popular liberties are not endangered by the strong safeguards surrounding the legitimacy of the governing power. On the contrary, reason, history, and experience teach that all illegitimate powers are tyrannical. Their illegitimacy necessarily carries weakness along with it; and it is not the strong, but the weak powers that oppress the people. Real tyranny consists in the person governing taking care of his own instead of the public interest. Now this is precisely what takes place when, feeling himself weak and tottering, he is forced to guard and protect himself. His object is then, no longer society, but himself. Instead of thinking how he may benefit those over whom he rules, he only studies and calculates beforehand the utility he may derive from his own measures. I have said in another place, and I repeat, that, in looking over history, we find continually this important truth written in letters of blood: *Wo to the people governed by a power which is obliged to think of its own preservation!* A fundamental truth in political science, and which has, nevertheless, been lamentably overlooked in modern times. Much labor has been and is still spent to produce guarantees for liberty. To this end a multitude of governments have been overturned, and attempts have been made to weaken them all, without thinking that this was the most certain means of introducing oppression. What signify the veils under which despotism is concealed, and the forms by which it seeks to disguise its existence? History, which has recorded the outrages committed in Europe during the last century; true history, not that written by the authors of those outrages, by their accomplices, or by interested parties, will relate to posterity the injustices and crimes committed in the midst of civil discord by governments foreseeing their end, and feeling in themselves extreme weakness caused by their tyrannical conduct and the illegality of their origin.

How is it, then, that such a violent warfare has been declared against doctrines tending to consolidate civil authority by rendering it legitimate, and to prove this legitimacy by declaring that power descends from Heaven? How has it been overlooked that the legitimacy of power is an essential element of its strength, and that this strength is the safest guarantee of true liberty? Let it not be said that these are paradoxes. What is the object of societies and governments? Is it not the substitution of public for private force, of the rule of right for the rule of the strong? But when once you begin to undermine power, to make it an object of popular aversion or defiance; when once you represent it to the people as their natural enemy, and vilify the sacred titles on which obedience due to it is founded, you attack at once the very object of the institution of society; and by weakening the action of public force, you provoke a development of private force, which is the very thing that governments were instituted to prevent. The secret of that mildness for which European monarchies were remarkable, consisted chiefly in their security and strength, founded upon the loftiness and legality of the titles of their power; whilst you will find in the perils with which the thrones of the Roman emperors and Eastern monarchs were beset, one reason for their monstrous despotism. I do not hesitate to assert, and in the course of this work I shall prove more and more, that one cause of the evils to which Europe has been exposed during the laborious solution of the problem of the alliance between order and liberty, is the oblivion of Catholic doctrines on this point. These doctrines have been condemned without being heard or examined into, and the enemies of the Church have copied each other without ever having recourse to the real sources, where they might easily have found out the truth.

Protestantism, departing from the teaching of Catholicity, has been thrown alternately upon two opposite rocks; wishing to establish order, it has done so to the prejudice of true liberty; and in its desire to maintain liberty, it has become an enemy to order. From the bosom of false reform have arisen the insane doctrines, which, preaching up Christian liberty, discharged the subject from his obedience to the lawful authorities; from the bosom of the same reform has likewise arisen the theory of Hobbes, which sets up despotism in the midst of society as a monstrous idol, to which all should be sacrificed, without regard for the eternal principles of morality, with no other rule than the caprice of him who rules, with no other bounds to his power than those marked out by the extent of his strength. Such is the necessary result of banishing from the world the authority of God. Man, left to himself, can only succeed in producing slavery or anarchy; the same thing under two forms; *the reign of force.*

In explaining the origin of society and power, divers modern writers have said a great deal about a certain state of nature anterior to all societies, and have supposed that these societies were formed by a gradual transition from a barbarous to a civilized state. This erroneous doctrine lies deeper than some persons imagine. If we pay particular attention to the subject, we shall find that the erroneous ideas entertained on this subject may be traced to the forgetfulness of Christian teaching. Hobbes derives every kind of right from a pact. According to him, when men live in a state of nature, they have a right to every thing; which means, in other terms, that there is no difference between good and evil. From which it follows that society was organized without any regard to morality, and ought to be considered merely as a means to an end. Puffendorf and some others, admitting the principle of *sociality,* that is, deriving from society the rules of morality, arrive at last at the principle of Hobbes, and trample under foot both the natural and eternal laws. Investigating the causes of these grave errors, I find them in the deplorable contempt which writers on philosophy and morality in modern times have so eagerly evinced for the treasures of light afforded us by religion. This light, religion affords us on all questions, fixing by its dogmas the cardinal points of all true philosophy, and offering us in its narrations the only thread that can guide us through the labyrinth of the first ages. Read the Protestant writers, compare them with the Catholic, and you will find a remarkable difference between them. The latter reason, give their minds free scope, and allow them a wide range; but they ever leave untouched certain fundamental principles, and every theory which they cannot reconcile with these principles is inexorably rejected by them as erroneous. The former roam without guide or compass in the boundless space of human opinions, presenting to us a lively image of that pagan philosophy which had not the light of faith to guide its inquiries into the principles of things. Instead of finding a God, the Creator and Director, occupied without ceasing, like a tender father, with the happiness of beings whom He has drawn from nothing, this philosophy never discovered any thing but chaos, either in the physical or in the social world. This degraded and brutalized state, disguised under the name of *nature,* is in reality nothing but the chaos of society. This chaos will be found in a great number of modern writers who are not Catholics; and by a surprising coincidence, worthy of the most serious reflection, it will also be found in the principal writers on pagan science.

From the moment that we lose sight of the great traditions of mankind, traditions in which man is represented to us receiving from God himself intelligence, speech, and rules for his conduct in this life; from the moment that we forget the narration of Moses, that simple, sublime, and only true explanation of the origin of man and of society; our ideas become confused, the facts are jumbled, one absurdity creates another, and, like the builders of the tower of Babel, we suffer the just punishment of our pride. How wonderful! that antiquity, which, deprived of the light of Christianity, and lost in the labyrinth of human inventions, had almost forgotten the primitive tradition of the origin of society, and had recourse to the absurd transition from the barbarous to the civilized state, should nevertheless, whenever a society was to be formed, have invoked this right divine, which certain philosophers have treated with so much disdain. The most renowned legislators sought to establish upon Divine authority, the laws they were giving to the people, thus rendering a solemn homage to that truth logically established by Catholics, viz. that all power, to be regarded as legitimate and to exercise its due ascendency, must receive its titles from God. If you desire that the legislator should not be placed under the sad necessity of feigning revelations which he has never received, or bringing forward the intervention of God at every moment in an extraordinary manner in human affairs, establish the general principle that all power proceeds from God, that the author of nature is likewise the author of society, that the existence of society is a precept imposed upon mankind for their own preservation. Let submission and obedience be so regulated as not to wound man's pride; let those who rule over him be invested with superior authority, to which he can submit without a shadow of self-abasement. In short, establish the Catholic doctrine. Whatever be the form of government, you will then have found a solid basis on which to support the respect due to the authorities; you will have placed the social edifice upon a foundation far more secure than human conventions.

Examine the right divine such as I have represented it, supported by the interpretations of illustrious doctors, and I am certain that you cannot refuse to admit its perfect conformity to the lights of true philosophy; but if you persist in giving to this right a strange sense which it does not possess, pretending that it ought to have a different explanation, I shall insist upon one thing which you cannot refuse me: produce me a text of Scripture, a monument of the traditions acknowledged as articles of faith in the Catholic Church, a decision of the Councils or of the Pontiffs, showing your interpretation to be well founded. Until you have done this, I have a right to tell you, that, possessed with the desire of rendering Catholicity odious, you impute to it doctrines which it does not profess, you attribute to it dogmas which it does not acknowledge; that you are adversaries without candor or honesty, and employ weapons disallowed by the laws of combat. (28)

CHAPTER LI.

TRANSMISSION OF POWER, ACCORDING TO THE CATHOLIC DOCTORS.

THE difference of opinion concerning the mode in which God communicates civil power, however grave in theory, does not appear to be of great importance in practice. We have already observed, that, among those who assert that this power comes from God, some maintain that it proceeds from Him *directly*, others *indirectly*. In the opinion of the former, when once the nomination of the persons appointed to exercise authority is made, society not only lays down the necessary conditions for the communication of power, but actually communicates it, having first received it from God. The latter maintain that society merely makes the appointment, and, by means of this act, God confers the power upon the person appointed. I repeat, that, in practice, the result is the same, and the difference therefore vanishes. Nay, even in *theory*, the divergence may not be so great as it appears at first sight. I shall endeavor to demonstrate this by submitting the two opinions to rigorous investigation.

The explanation given of the origin of power by both parties may be set forth in the following terms: In the opinion of some, God says, "Society, for thy preservation and well-being, thou requirest a government; choose, therefore, under what form this government shall be exercised, and appoint the persons who are to take charge of it; I, on my part, will confer upon them the faculties necessary for the fulfilment of their mission." In the opinion of others, God says, "Society, for thy preservation and well-being, thou requirest a government: I confer upon thee the faculties necessary for the fulfilment of this object; choose thyself the form under which this government shall be exercised, and, appointing the persons who are to take charge of it, transmit to them the faculties which I have communicated to thee."

In order to be convinced of the identity of the results of these two formulas, we must examine them in their relations: 1. to the sanctity of their origin; 2. to the rights and duties of power; 3. to the rights and duties of the subject. Whether God has communicated power to society, to be transmitted by it to the persons appointed to exercise it, or has merely conferred upon it the right of determining the form and appointing such persons, that, by means of this determination and appointment, the rights annexed to supreme power may be directly communicated to the persons intrusted with the exercise of it, it follows, in either case, that this supreme power, wherever it exists, emanates from God; and is not less sacred because it passes through an intermediate means appointed by Him. I will illustrate these ideas by a very simple and obvious example. Suppose there exists in a state some particular community, instituted by the sovereign, and having no rights but those granted by him; no duties but those which he imposes upon it; in fine, a community indebted to the sovereign for all that it is and has. This community, however small it may be, will require a government: this government may be formed in two ways; either the sovereign who has given it its laws has conferred upon it the right of governing itself, and of transmitting this right to the person or persons whom it may think proper to elect; or he has left to the community itself the determination of the form and the appointment of the persons, adding that such determination and appointment being once made, it shall be understood that, by this simple act, the sovereign grants to the persons appointed the right of exercising their functions within lawful bounds. It is evident that the parity is complete; and now I ask, Is it not true that, in this case, as in the other, the faculties of him who governs should be considered and respected as an emanation from the sovereign? Is it not true that it would be difficult to discover any difference between these two kinds of investiture? In both suppositions, the community would have the right of determining the form and appointing the person; in both cases, he who governs could only obtain his powers by virtue of the previous determination and appointment; in neither case would there need any new manifestation on the part of the sovereign, that the person nominated might be understood to be invested with faculties corresponding to the exercise of his functions. In practice, therefore, there would be no difference; further, I will assert that, in theory even, it would be difficult to trace the point of separation between the two cases.

Certainly, if we view the matter with the eye of an acute metaphysician, we may very easily discover this difference, by considering the moral entity which we call *power;* not as it is in itself, and in its effects, but as an abstract being, passing from one hand to another, in the manner of corporeal objects. But, instead of examining the question for the curiosity of knowing whether this moral entity, before arriving at one person, has not first passed through another, let us first seek to verify from whence it emanates, and what are the faculties it confers, the rights it imposes: we shall then find that, in saying, "I confer this faculty upon you, transmit it to whomsoever you think proper, and in whatever way you think proper," the sovereign expresses no more than if he should say: "Such or such a faculty shall be conferred by me upon the person you wish, and in the manner you wish, by the simple fact of the election you have made." It follows hence, that whether we adopt the opinion of direct communication, or the contrary one, the supreme rights of hereditary monarchies, of elective monarchies, and in general of all supreme powers, whatever be their forms of government, will not on this account be less sacred, less certainly sealed with divine authority. Difference in the forms of government does not in the least diminish the obligations of submitting to civil power, lawfully established; so that the refusing of obedience to the president of a republic, in a country in which republicanism is the legal form of government, is no less a criminal resistance to the ordinance of God, than the refusing of the same obedience to the most absolute monarch. Bossuet, so strongly attached to monarchy, and writing in a country and at a period in which the king might exclaim, "*I am the state;*" and in a work, in which he proposed nothing less than to offer a complete treatise on Politics, taken from the words of Holy Scripture; established, nevertheless, in a manner the most explicit and conclusive, the truth which I have just pointed out. "We ought to be subject," says he, "to the form of government established in our country." And he afterwards quotes these words of St. Paul in his Epistle to the Romans, chap. xiii.: "Let every soul be subject to higher powers; for there is no power but from God; and those that are, are ordained of God; therefore he that resisteth the power, resisteth the ordinance of God." "There is no form of government," continues Bossuet, "nor any human institution, without its inconveniences; so that it is necessary to remain in the state to which length of time has inured the people. For this reason, God *takes under His protection all legitimate governments, in whatever form they may be established;* whoever undertakes to overturn them, is not only an enemy to the public, but also to God." (Liv. ii. prop. 12.)

It is of little consequence whether power be communicated directly or indirectly; the respect and obedience due to it are not in the least changed, and consequently the sacredness of the origin of power remains the same, whichever opinion be adopted; neither do the rights and duties of government, and those of the subject, remain less sacred. These rights and duties suffer no change, whether there be or not an intermediate means for the communication of power; their nature and limits are founded upon the very object of the institution of society; but this object is totally independent of the mode in which God communicates power to man. Against what I have advanced upon the small amount of difference existing between these various opinions, the authority of the theologians, whose texts I have cited in the preceding chapter, will be objected. "These theologians," it will be said, "certainly understood these affairs; and as they placed so much importance upon the distinction here under discussion, they undoubtedly saw in it some great truth proper to be taken into account." This objection acquires the more force, when we consider that the distinction made upon this point by these theologians does not proceed from a spirit of subtilty, as it might be suspected in the case of those scholastic theologians, whose writings are replete with dialectic arguments, rather than with reasoning founded upon Scripture, upon the apostolical traditions and other theological resources, from which we ought principally to take our arguments in controversies of this nature; but the theologians whom I have quoted are certainly not of this class. We need only name Bellarmin, to recognise a grave and extremely solid author, who opposed the Protestants with Scripture, with traditions, with the authority of the holy Fathers, the decisions of the universal Church and of the Sovereign Pontiffs: Bellarmin was not one of those theologians who excited the lamentations of Melchior Cano, and of whom he said, that in the hour of combat against heresy, instead of wielding well-tempered weapons, they wielded only long reeds: *arundines longas.* Such was the importance given to this distinction, that James, King of England, complained loudly that Cardinal Bellarmin taught that the power of kings came from God only indirectly; and the Catholic schools were so far from looking upon this distinction as insignificant, that they defended it against the attacks of King James; and that one of their most illustrious doctors, Suarez, entered the lists to contend for the doctrines of Bellarmin.

It appears, then, at first sight, that I am wrong in what I have said upon the slight importance of the distinction here mentioned. I believe, nevertheless, that the difficulty may be easily removed, and that it will suffice for this purpose to distinguish the different aspects under which the question presents itself. First of all, I will observe, that the Catholic theologians proceeded upon this point with admirable prudence and foresight; and truly the question, such as it was then proposed, comprehended more than a subtilty; I am inclined to think that it included one of the most serious points of public right. In order to examine deeply these doctrines of Catholic theologians, and to lay hold of their true sense, we must fix our attention upon the tendencies which the religious reform of the sixteenth century communicated to European monarchy. Even before this reform, thrones had acquired a great deal of force and solidity, through the decline in the power of the feudal lords, and the development of the democratic element. That element, which in due time was destined to acquire the power of which it is now possessed, was not then in sufficiently favorable circumstances to exert its action on the vast scale which it embraces in our days. On this account, it was obliged to take refuge under the shadow of the throne—an emblem of order and justice elevated in the midst of society—a sort of universal regulator and leveller, destined gradually to destroy the extreme inequalities so harassing and obnoxious to the people. Thus, democracy itself, which, in after ages, was to overturn so many thrones, served them, at that time, as a firm support, sheltering them from the attacks of a turbulent and formidable aristocracy, unwilling to be transformed into mere courtiers. There was nothing in this state of things very mischievous, so long as matters remained within the limits prescribed by reason and justice; but, unfortunately, good principles were exaggerated, regal authority was gradually converted into an absorbent force, which would have concentrated in itself all other forces. European monarchy lost thus its true character, which consists in monarchy having just limits, even when these limits are not marked out and guarded by political institutions.

Protestantism exalts to an incredible degree the pretensions of kings, by attacking the spiritual power of the Pope, by painting in the darkest colors the dangers of his temporal power, and especially by establishing the fatal doctrine, that the supreme civil power has ecclesiastical affairs totally under its direction; and by accusing of abuse, of usurpation, of unbounded ambition, the independence which the Church claims by virtue of the sacred canons, of the guarantee afforded by the civil law, of the traditions of fifteen centuries, and above all, of the institution of her Divine Founder. He had no need of the permission of any civil power to send His apostles to preach the Gospel, and to baptize in the name of the Father, of the Son, and of the Holy Ghost. A glance at the history of Europe at the epoch here mentioned will convince us of the evil consequences of such a doctrine, and show us how agreeable it must have been to the ears of power, which it invested with unbounded faculties, even in matters purely religious. This exaggeration of the rights of civil power, coinciding with the efforts made on the other hand to repress the pontifical authority, must have favored the doctrine which attempted to place the power of kings upon a level, in every respect, with that of Popes; and consequently, it was very natural that its authors should wish to establish, that sovereigns received their power from God, in the same manner as the Popes, without any difference whatever. The doctrine of *direct* communication, although very susceptible, as we have seen, of a reasonable explanation, might involve a more extensive meaning, which would have made the people oblivious of the special and characteristic manner in which the supreme power of the Church was instituted by God himself. What I have just advanced cannot be considered as merely conjectural; the whole is supported by facts which cannot have been forgotten. The reigns of Henry VIII. and of Elizabeth of England, and the usurpations and violence in which Protestant powers indulged against the Catholic Church, are a sufficient confirmation of these sad truths. But, unfortunately, even in countries where Catholicity remained triumphant, attempts were then, have since been, and still are witnessed, that show clearly enough how strong was the impulse given in this sense to the civil power; for even now it is but too prone to transgress its legitimate bounds.

The circumstances under which the two illustrious theologians above cited, Bellarmin and Suarez, wrote, are another reason in support of what I have just adduced. I have quoted remarkable passages from a work by Suarez, written in refutation of a publication of King James of England. This King could not bear the idea of Cardinal Bellarmin's having established that the power of kings does not emanate directly from God, but is communicated through the medium of society, which receives it in a direct manner. Possessed, as is well known, with the mania for theological debates and decisions, King James did not confine himself to simple theory; he reduced his theory to practice, and said to his Parliament: "that God had appointed him absolute master; and that all privileges which co-legislative bodies enjoyed were pure concessions proceeding from the bounty of kings." His courtiers, in their adulations, decreed him the title of the modern Solomon; he might well, therefore, feel displeased with the Italian and Spanish theologians for endeavoring to humble the pride of his presumptuous wisdom, and restrain his despotism. If we reflect upon the words of Bellarmin, and especially on those of Suarez, we shall find that the aim of these eminent theologians was to point out the difference between the civil and ecclesiastical powers, with respect to the mode of their origin. They admit that both powers come from God; that it is an indispensable duty to be subject to them; and that to resist them is to resist the ordinance of God; but not finding, either in the Scripture or in tradition, the least foundation for establishing that civil power, like that of the Sovereign Pontiffs, has been instituted in a special and extraordinary manner, they are anxious that this difference should remain obvious, and seek to avoid the introduction, in a point of such import, of a confusion of ideas, from which dangerous errors might arise. "This opinion," says Suarez, "is new, singular, and apparently invented to exalt the temporal over the spiritual power." (See above.) Hence, in discussing the question of the origin of civil power, they require you to bear in mind the influence of society. "*By means of man's counsel and election,*" says Bellarmin; thus reminding the King, that how sacred soever his authority might be, it had been very differently instituted from that of the Sovereign Pontiff. The distinction between direct and indirect communication served, in a particular manner, to prove the difference in question; for this very distinction recalled to mind that civil power, although established by God, owed its existence to no extraordinary measure, and could not be considered as supernatural, but was to be looked upon as dependent upon human and natural right, sanctioned, nevertheless, in an express manner, by right divine.

These theologians would not, perhaps, have forcibly insisted upon this distinction, had it not been for the efforts made by others to efface it. It was a matter of consequence with them to humble the pride of power, to prevent it from assuming, whether in respect to its origin or its rights, titles not appertaining to it; to prevent its ascribing to itself an unlawful supremacy, even in religious affairs, and thus causing monarchy to degenerate into a sort of Oriental despotism, in which the governing power is every thing, the people and their affairs nothing. If we weigh their words attentively, we shall find that the predominating idea with them was that which I have just stated. At first sight, their language appears exceedingly democratical, from their frequent use of the words *community, state, society, people;* but on examining closely their system of doctrine, and paying attention to the expressions they use, we perceive that they had no subversive design, and that anarchical theories never once entered their minds. They advocated on the one hand the rights of authority, whilst they protected on the other those of the subject, thus endeavoring to resolve the problem which formed the continual occupation of all honest political writers; to limit power without destroying it, or placing it under too great restraint; to protect society against the disorder of despotism, without rendering it at the same time refractory or turbulent. From the above reasoning we see that the distinction between direct and indirect communication may be of great or of little importance, according to the view we take of it. It is of great importance when serving to remind the civil power that the establishment of governments and the regulation of their forms has in some way been dependent upon society itself, and that no individual, no family, can presume upon having received from God the government of the people without regard to the laws of the country, as if those laws, in whatever form, were a free offering made by them to the people. This same distinction serves, in short, to establish the origin of civil power as an emanation from the Deity, the Author of nature, but not as instituted in an extraordinary manner, as something supernatural, as in the case of the supreme ecclesiastical power. From this latter consideration two consequences follow, one of which is of more importance than the other to the legitimate liberties of mankind and the independence of the Church. To call in the intervention, express or tacit, of society for the establishment of governments and the regulation of their forms, is to prevent the concealment of their origin under any veil of mystery; it is simply and plainly to define their object, consequently to explain their duties, as well as to point out their faculties. By these means a restraint is put upon the disorders and abuses of authority, which it is thenceforth clearly seen are not to find support in enigmatical theories.

The independence of the Church is thus established upon a solid basis. Whenever the civil power attempts to offer it violence, the Church may say: "My authority is established directly and immediately by God in a special, extraordinary, and miraculous manner; yours likewise emanates from God, but through the intervention of man, through the intermediary of the laws, in the ordinary course pointed out by nature and determined by human prudence; but neither man nor the civil power has a right to destroy or change what God Himself, deviating from the course of nature and making use of ineffable prodigies, has thought proper to institute." So long as the ideas here set forth are respected, so long as *direct* communication is not received in too extensive a sense, and care taken not to confound things whose limits so gravely affect religion and society, the distinction here spoken of is of little importance. We have seen, even, that the two opinions may be reconciled with each other. At all events, this distinction will have served to illustrate with what exalted views Catholic theologians have discussed the grave questions of public right. Guided by sound philosophy, and without ever losing sight of the beacon of revelation, they have given equal satisfaction to the desires of both schools. They have not fallen into the errors of either; democratical without being anarchists, monarchical without being base adulators. In establishing the rights of the people, they were not, like modern demagogues, under the necessity of destroying religion, but made her the guardian of the rights of the people, as well as of those of kings. Liberty was not with them a synonyme for license and irreligion; in their opinion, men might be free without being rebellious or impious; liberty consisted in being subject to the law; and, as they could not conceive that law was possible without religion and without God, in like manner also they believed that liberty was not possible without God and religion. What reason, revelation, and history taught them has become evident to us by experience. Shall we be told of the dangers, grave or slight, in which theologians could involve governments? But people now-a-days are not led astray by affected and insidious declamations; and kings well know whether the schools of theologians have exiled royalty, and led it to the scaffold. (29)

CHAPTER LII.

FREEDOM OF SPEECH UNDER THE SPANISH MONARCHY.

EXTREME doctrines neither insure the liberty of the people, nor the force and stability of governments; both require truth and justice, the only foundations upon which we can build with any hope of the durability of the edifice. In general, maxims favorable to liberty are never carried to a higher pitch than on the eve of the establishment of despotism; and it is to be feared that the overthrow and ruin of governments are very near when undue adulations are lavished upon their power. When was the power of kings more extolled than about the middle of last century? Who is not aware of the exaggerations given to the prerogatives of royal power, when the Jesuits were to be expelled, and the authority of the Sovereign Pontiff impugned? In Portugal, Spain, Italy, Austria, and in France, the unanimous voice of the purest and most fervent royalism was heard; and yet what became of this great love, this lively zeal for monarchy, from the moment that the revolutionary storm had placed it in danger? Observe what, generally speaking, has been the conduct of men opposed to the ecclesiastical authority; they have united themselves to demagogues for destroying, at the same time, the authority of the Church and that of kings; they have forgotten their base adulations, and abandoned themselves to insults and violence. People and governments should never lose sight of this rule of conduct, so useful to men of sense, to mistrust flatterers, and to confide in those who warn and correct them. Let them beware whenever they are caressed with an affected tenderness, and their cause is maintained with especial warmth; it is a sure sign of an attempt to make use of them as tools for the furtherance of interests very different from their own. In France, at certain times, monarchical zeal was carried to such an extent as to call forth, in the assembly of the States-General, a motion for establishing, as a sacred principle, that kings receive their supreme authority immediately from God: this was not carried into effect, but the proposal shows how ardently the cause of the throne was then maintained. Now, what did all this ardor mean? Simply an antipathy against the Court of Rome, a dread of the extension of papal power; it was an obstacle to be opposed to the phantom of a *universal monarchy*. Louis XIV., so tenacious of the royal prerogative, assuredly did not foresee the misfortunes of Louis XVI.; and Charles III., in listening to the Count of Aranda and Campomanes, little thought that the constituent Cortes of Cadiz was so near.

In the midst of their splendor, monarchs forgot one principle predominating in the whole modern history of Europe, viz. that social organization is an emanation of religion, and, consequently, that the two powers to which the defence and preservation of society appertain ought to co-exist in perfect harmony.

The power of the Church cannot be diminished without injury to the civil power; he who sows schism will reap rebellion. During the last three centuries the most liberal and popular doctrines upon the origin of power have been circulated amongst us. What did it matter to the Spanish monarchy, since those very persons who advocated these doctrines were the first to condemn resistance to the lawful authorities, to inculcate the obligation of obedience to them, and to establish in all hearts, respect, love, and veneration for the sovereign? The disturbances of our epoch, and the dangers constantly besetting thrones, are not exactly attributable to the propagation of doctrines more or less democratical, but to the absence of moral and religious principles. What will be gained by asserting that power comes from God, if people believe not in God? Point out the sacred character of the duty of obedience, and what effect will it produce upon those who admit not the existence of moral order, and to whom duty is merely a chimerical idea? Suppose, on the contrary, that you have to deal with men penetrated with moral and religious principles, who bow to the will of God, and believe themselves bound to submit to it, so soon as it is manifested to them. What does it matter then whether civil power proceeds from God directly or indirectly? it is enough to convince them, in one way or another, that, whatever be its origin, God approves of it, and wills that it should be obeyed; they will immediately submit with pleasure, for they will see in this submission the accomplishment of a duty.

These considerations serve to explain the reason why certain doctrines appear more dangerous now than formerly: incredulity and immorality give them perverse interpretations, and apply them so as to create nothing but excesses and disorders. From the manner in which the despotism of Philip II. and his successors is now spoken of, we might be led to suppose that in their time no other doctrines than those in favor of the most rigid absolutism could be circulated; and yet we find that there were circulated, without the least apprehension on the part of power, works maintaining theories which, even in our days, would be esteemed too bold. Is it not, therefore, remarkable, that the famous book of Father Mariana, intituled *De Rege et Regis institutione*, which was burned at Paris by the hand of the public executioner, had been published in Spain eleven years before, without the least obstacle to its publication, either on the part of the ecclesiastical or civil authority? Mariana undertook his task at the instigation and request of D. Garcia de Loaisa, tutor to Philip III., and subsequently Bishop of Toledo; so that the work, strange to say, was intended for the instruction of the heir-apparent. Never was more freedom used in speaking to kings; never was tyranny condemned in a louder voice; never were more popular doctrines proclaimed; and the work was, nevertheless, published at Toledo, in 1599, in the printing-office of Pedro Rodrigo, printer to the king, with the approbation of P. Fr. Pedro de Ona, provincial of the Mercenaries of Madrid, with the permission of Stephen Hojeda, visitor of the Society of Jesus in the province of Toledo, under the generalship of Claude Aquaviva; and, what is still more forcible, with the royal sanction, and a dedication to the king himself. We should also observe, that Mariana was not satisfied with this dedication placed at the commencement of the book, but he makes the very title itself serve to show to whom it was addressed: *De Rege et Regis institutione. Libri* 3, *ad Philippum* 3, *Hispaniæ Regem Catholicum;* and, as if this were not sufficient, in dedicating his Spanish version of the History of Spain to Philip III., he says to him: "I last year dedicated to your majesty a work of my own composition, upon the virtues which ought to exist in a good king, my desire being that all princes should read it carefully and understand it." "El ano pasado presenté á V. M. un libro que compuse de las virtudes que debe tener un buen Rey, que deseo lean y entiendan todos los principes con cuidado."

We will pass over his doctrine upon tyrannicide, which was the principal cause of its condemnation in France, where there existed, without doubt, motives of alarm, since kings were perishing there by the hand of the assassin. On examining his theory upon power, we find it as popular and liberal as those of modern democrats could be. Mariana ventures to express his opinions without evasion or disguise. For example, drawing a parallel between the king and the tyrant, he says: "The king exercises with great moderation the power which he has received from his subjects. . . . . . . Hence, he does not, like the tyrant, oppress his subjects as slaves, but governs them as free men; and having received his power from the people, he takes particular care that during his life, the people shall voluntarily yield him submission." "Rex quam a subditis accepit potestatem singulari modestia exercet. . . . . . Sic fit, ut subditis non tanquam servis dominetur, quod faciunt tyranni, sed tanquam liberis præsit, et qui a populo potestatem accepit, id in primis curæ habet ut per totam vitam volentibus imperet." (Lib. 1, cap. 4, p. 57.) This was said in Spain by a simple religious, was sanctioned by his superiors, and attentively listened to by kings. To what grave reflections does this simple fact lead us! Where is that strict and indissoluble alliance which the enemies of the Church have imagined to exist between her dogmas and those of slavery? If such expressions as the above were tolerated in a country in which Catholicity predominated so extensively, how can it be maintained that such a religion tends to enslave the human race, and that its doctrines are favorable to despotism? Nothing would be easier than to fill whole volumes with remarkable passages of our writers, both lay and clerical, showing the extreme liberty granted upon this point, as well by the Church as by the civil government. What absolute monarch in Europe would approve of one of his high functionaries expressing the origin of power after the manner of our immortal Saavedra? "It is from the centre of justice," says he, "that the circumference of the crown has been drawn. The latter would not be necessary, if we could dispense with the former.

Hac una reges olim sunt fine creati,
Dicere jus populis, injustaque tollere facta.

In the first age, there was no necessity for penalties, because the law did not take cognisance of transgressions; rewards were equally unnecessary, because integrity and honor were loved for their own sakes. But vice, growing with the age of the world, intimidated virtue; simple and confiding, the latter, till then, dwelt in the country. Equality was despised, modesty and chastity lost, ambition and force introduced, and after them domination. Prudence, forced by necessity, and aroused by the light of nature, reduced men to a state of civil society, to exercise therein those virtues to which reason inclines them. By means of the articulate voice with which nature had gifted them, they could explain to each other their mutual thoughts, manifest to each other their sentiments, and explain their wants, instruct, counsel, and protect each other. Society once formed, a power was created *by common consent, in the whole of this community, enlightened by the law of nature*, for preserving its different parts, for maintaining them in justice and peace, by punishing vice and rewarding virtue. *As this power could not remain spread through the whole body of the people, on account of the confusion which would have arisen from the resolutions and their execution*, and as it was absolutely necessary that there should be some to command, and others to obey, *one portion divested itself of this power, and vested it in one member, or in a small, or in a great, number of members, that is to say, in one of the three forms of every state government—monarchy, aristocracy, or democracy.* Monarchy was the first; because men selected for their government, out of their families, and afterwards even from among the whole people, some one who excelled the rest in goodness: his greatness increasing, they honored his hand with the sceptre, and encircled his head with a crown as an emblem of majesty, and as a badge of the supreme power which they had conferred upon him. This power, however, consists chiefly in that justice which ought to maintain the people in peace; *this justice failing, the order of the state fails, and the office of king ceases*, as was the case in Castile, when the government by judges was substituted for that by kings, on account of the injustice of D. Ordona and of D. Fruela." (*Character of a Christian Prince's Policy, set forth in a hundred Devices*, by D. Diego de Saavedra Fajardo, Knight of the Order of St. James, Member of his Majesty's Supreme Council for the Indies, *device* 22.)

The words *people, pact, consent*, have ended in becoming the dread of men of sound ideas and upright intentions, on account of the deplorable abuses which have been made of them in those immoral schools which ought rather to be qualified with the epithet of irreligious than with that of democratical. No, it was not the desire of ameliorating the condition of the people which led them to overthrow the world, by overturning thrones and shedding torrents of blood in civil discord; the real cause was a blind rage for reducing to ashes the work of ages, by especially attacking religion, the main support of every thing wise, just, and salutary, that European civilization had acquired. And, in fact, have we not seen impious schools, whilst boasting of their liberty, bend under the hand of despotism, whenever they thought it useful to their designs? Previous to the French Revolution, were they not the basest adulators of kings, whose prerogatives they extended immeasurably, with the intention of making regal power the means of oppressing the Church? After the revolutionary epoch, did we not see them assembled round Napoleon; and even yet, do they not almost deify him? And why? Because Napoleon was revolution personified, the representative and executor of the new ideas sought to be substituted for the old ones. In the same manner Protestantism extols its Queen Elizabeth; because it was she who placed the Establishment upon a solid foundation. Revolutionary doctrines, besides the evils they inflict upon society, produce indirectly another effect, which may, at first sight, appear salutary, but which, in reality, is not so. They occasion dangerous reactions in the order of events, and check the progress of knowledge, by narrowing and debasing men's ideas, leading them to condemn as erroneous and pernicious, or to view with mistrust, principles which would previously have been looked upon as sound, or that would, at all events, have been regarded as mere harmless errors. The reason of all this is, simply, that liberty has no worse enemy than licentiousness.

In support of this last observation, it may be well to show, that the most rigorous doctrines in political matters have originated in countries in which anarchy had made the greatest ravages, and precisely at the time when the evil, still present, or very recent, was most keenly felt. The religious revolution of the sixteenth century, and the political commotions consequent upon it, were principally felt in the north of Europe; the south, and especially Italy and Spain, were almost entirely preserved from them. Now, these last two countries are precisely those in which the dignities and prerogatives of civil power have been the least exaggerated, as well as those in which they were not disparaged in theory, and were respected in practice. Of all modern nations, England was the first in which a revolution, properly so called, was realized; for I do not consider as such the insurrection of the German peasantry, which, in spite of the terrible catastrophe which it caused, never effected any change in the state of society; or that of the United Provinces, which may be considered a war of independence. Now, it was precisely in England that the most erroneous doctrines in favor of the supreme authority of civil power appeared. Hobbes, who, whilst he refused to allow the rights of the Creator, attributed unbounded authority to the monarchs of the earth, lived at the most agitated and turbulent epoch in the annals of Great Britain. He was born in 1588, and died in 1679.

In Spain, where the impious and anarchical doctrines, which had troubled Europe since the schism of Luther, did not penetrate until the latter part of the eighteenth century, we have seen that the greatest license of expression was permitted upon the most important points of public right, and that doctrines were maintained which, in any other country, would have been looked upon as dangerous. Error gave rise to exaggeration; the rights of monarchs were never so much extolled as under the reign of Charles III.; that is, at the time when the modern epoch was inaugurated among us.

Religion, which predominated in all consciences, maintained them in the obedience due to the sovereign, without there being any need of giving this obedience any extraordinary titles, when its real ones were sufficient, as they certainly were. For him who knows that God has prescribed obedience to lawful authority, it matters little whether this authority emanate from Heaven directly or indirectly, or whether society has more or less taken part in the determination of political forms, or in the election of the persons or families who are to exercise the supreme command. Hence we find that in Spain, although the words *people, consent, pacts,* were spoken of, monarchs were held in the most profound veneration, so much so that modern history does not mention a single attempt upon their persons. Popular tumults were also of rare occurrence; and those which did happen are not attributable to either of the two above-mentioned doctrines. How does it happen that, at the end of the sixteenth century, the Council of Castile was not alarmed at the bold principles of Mariana, in his book *De Rege et Regis institutione,* whilst those of the Abbé Spedalieri, at the end of the eighteenth century, were such a terror to it? The reason of this lies not so much in the contents of the works, as in the epoch of their publication. The former appeared at a time when the Spanish nation, confirmed in religious and moral principles, might be compared to those robust constitutions capable of bearing food difficult of digestion. The latter was introduced among us when the doctrines and deeds of the French Revolution were shaking all the thrones of Europe, and when the propagandism of Paris was beginning to pervert us by its emissaries and books. In a nation in which reason and virtue prevail, in which evil passions are never excited, in which the well-being and prosperity of the country are the only aim of every citizen, the most popular and liberal forms of government may exist without danger; for in such a nation numerous assemblies produce no disorder, merit is not obscured by intrigue, nor are worthless persons raised to the government, and the names of public liberty and felicity do not serve as means to raise the fortunes or satisfy the ambition of individuals. So also in a country in which religion and morality rule in every breast, in which duty is not looked upon as an empty word, in which it is considered really criminal to disturb the tranquillity of the state, to revolt against the lawful authorities: in such a country, I say, it is less dangerous to discuss, with more or less freedom, questions arising from theories on the formation of society and the origin of the civil power, and to establish principles favorable to popular rights. But when these conditions do not exist, it is of little use to proclaim rigorous doctrines. To abstain from pronouncing the name of people, as a sacrilegious word, is a useless precaution. How can it be expected, that he who respects not Divine Majesty, should respect human? The conservative schools of our age, proposing to place a restraint upon the revolutionary torrent, and to tranquillize agitated nations, have almost always been infected with a certain failing, which consists in forgetting the truth which I have just noticed: *royal majesty, authority of the government, supremacy of the law, parliamentary sovereignty, respect for established forms, and order:* such are the terms they are constantly making use of. This is their palladium of society; and they condemn with all their might *the state, insubordination, disobedience to the laws, insurrection, riot, anarchy;* but they forget that these doctrines will not suffice, unless there be some fixed point to which the first link of the chain may be riveted. These schools, generally speaking, originate in the bosom of revolu-

.ion; tLey are directed by men who have figured in revolutions, who have con tributed to prepare them, who have given them their force, and who, in order to attain the object of their ardent desires, feared not to ruin the edifice at its foundation, by diminishing the ascendency of religion and opening the way to moral relaxation. Hence they become powerless when prudence, or their own interests, bid them say, "*We have gone far enough;*" and, hurried on like the rest by the furious whirlwind, they have neither the means of stopping the movement nor of giving it a proper direction.

We are continually hearing the *Contrat Social* of Rousseau condemned on account of its anarchical doctrines, whilst at the same time doctrines are circulated tending visibly to weaken religion. Can we possibly believe that the *Contrat Social* has alone caused all the commotions of Europe? It has doubtless produced serious evils, but still more serious ones have been caused by that irreligion which so deeply undermines the foundations of society, which loosens family bonds, and delivers up the individual to the caprice of his passions, with no other restraint or guide than the promptings of his own low egotism. Men of upright and reflecting minds begin to penetrate these truths. We find, nevertheless, in the political sphere, this error, which attributes to the action of civil government sufficient creative power to form, organize, and preserve society, independently of all moral and religious influences. It is of little consequence what be maintained in theory, if this error be acted upon in practice; and what avails the proclaiming of certain sound principles, if our conduct is not guided by them? These philosophico-political schools, which are desirous of ruling the destinies of the world, proceed in a way diametrically opposite to that of Christianity. The latter, whose principal object was heaven, did not, however, neglect the happiness of man upon earth; it addressed itself directly to the understanding and the heart, considering that the community is regulated by the conduct of individuals, and that, in order to have a well-regulated society, it was necessary to have good citizens. To proclaim certain political principles, to institute particular forms—such is the panacea of some schools, who deem it possible to govern society without exercising a due influence over the intelligence and heart of man; reason and experience agree in teaching us what we may expect from such a system.

Profoundly to impress the minds of men with religion and morality,—this is the first step towards the prevention of revolutions and disorganization. When these sacred objects have acquired their full influence over the hearts of men, there is no longer any thing to be apprehended from a greater or less latitude in political opinions. What confidence can a government repose in a man professing highly monarchical opinions, if he join impiety to them? Will he who refuses to give to God his rights, respect those of temporal kings? "The first thing," says Seneca, "is the worship of the gods, and faith in their existence; we are next to acknowledge their majesty, and bounty, without which there is no majesty." "Primum est Deorum cultus, Deos credere; deinde reddere illis majestatem suam, reddere bonitatem, sine qua nulla majestas est." (Seneca, *Epist.* 95.) Observe how Cicero, the first orator and perhaps the greatest philosopher of Rome, expresses himself: "It is necessary," says he, "that the citizens should be first persuaded of the existence of gods, the directors and rulers of all things, in whose hands are all events, who are ever conferring on mankind immense benefits, who search the heart of man, who see his actions, the spirit of piety which he carries into the practice of religion, and who distinguish the life of the pious from that of the ungodly man." "Sit igitur jam hoc a principio persuasum civibus, dominos esse omnium rerum, ac moderatores deos; eaque quæ gerantur, eorum geri ditione ac numine, eosdemque optime de genere hominum mereri, et qualis quisque sit, quid agat, quid inde admittat, qua mente, qua pietate colat religiones intueri: piorumque et impiorum habere rationem." (Cic. *de Nat Deor*. 2.)

These truths should be profoundly impressed upon the mind: the evils of society do not principally emanate from political ideas or systems; the root of the evil lies in religion; and if a check is not put upon irreligion, it is vain to proclaim the most rigid monarchical principles. Hobbes did certainly flatter kings a little more than Bellarmin; and yet, when these two writers are compared, what sensible monarch would not prefer as a subject the learned and pious controvertist? (30)

CHAPTER LIII.

ON THE FACULTIES OF THE CIVIL POWER.

HAVING shown that the Catholic doctrine upon the origin of the civil power does not include any thing but what is perfectly reasonable and reconcilable with the true interests of the people, let us discuss the second of the proposed questions. Let us inquire into the nature of the faculties of this power, and see whether under this aspect the Church teaches any thing favorable to despotism—to that oppression of which she is so calumniously accused of being a supporter. We invite our opponents to demonstrate the contrary, fully confident that they will find it more difficult to succeed in so doing, than to accumulate vague accusations, which serve only to lead too confiding minds astray. To sustain these charges properly, recourse should be had to texts of Scripture, to tradition, to the decisions of Councils, or to those of Supreme Pontiffs, to passages of the Fathers; and it should be shown that these immoderately extend the bounds of power, with the design of placing undue restraint upon the liberty of the people, or of destroying it. But it will be said, if the sources retained their purity, the streams have been polluted by commentators; in other terms, theologians of latter ages, becoming the adulators of civil power, have powerfully labored to extend its faculties, and, consequently, to establish despotism. As many persons too readily claim the right of criticizing the doctors of what is termed the period of decline, flippantly censuring those illustrious men, without having ever taken the trouble to open their works, it is necessary for us to enter into some details on this subject, and to dispel prejudices and errors which are seriously injurious to religion, and not less so to science.

The declamations and invectives of Protestants have induced certain minds to imagine that every idea of liberty would have disappeared from the heart of Europe, had it not been for the timely intervention of the pretended Reformation of the sixteenth century. According to this idea, Catholic theologians are represented as a crowd of ignorant monks, capable only of writing, in bad language and in still worse style, a heap of nonsense, the ultimate and only aim of which was to exalt the authority of Popes and kings, and to support intellectual and political oppression, obscurantism, and tyranny. That a portion should become the victim of illusion in matters the investigation of which is difficult and arduous; that the reader should suffer himself to be deceived by a writer on whose word he must either rely or remain in complete ignorance,—as, for example, in the description of a country or a phenomenon examined only by the narrator,—is nothing strange; but that any one should adhere to errors which a few moments spent in the most obscure library would eradicate, that the authors of the brilliant volumes of Paris should have the privilege of disfiguring with impunity the opinions of a writer lying covered with dust and forgotten in the same library, and perhaps on the same shelf upon which the former glitter; that the reader should peruse with avidity the glossy pages of the newly-published work, filling his mind with the writer's notions, without even so much as putting forth his hand to the voluminous tome within his reach, and which needs only to be opened to furnish at every page a refutation of the censures in which levity, if not bad faith, is so ready to indulge; is difficult to be conceived or excused in any man professing to be a lover of science, and a conscientious investigator of truth. A great number of writers would assuredly not be so ready and free to speak of what they have never studied, to analyze books which they have never read, if they did not reckon upon the docility and levity of their readers; they would certainly refrain from pronouncing magisterially upon an opinion, a system, or a school, in fine, upon the labors of many ages, from deciding the gravest questions by a sally of wit, if they found that the reader, seized in his turn with distrust, and particularly with the skepticism of the period, would not place implicit faith in their assertions, but would take the trouble to confront them with the facts to which they relate.

Our ancestors did not consider themselves justified, I will not say in making an assertion, but even a single allusion, without giving careful references to the source of their information. Their delicacy on this point was carried to excess; but we have done wrong by going to the opposite extreme, and judging that we might dispense with all formality, even in the most important matters which imperiously demand the testimony of facts. But the opinions of ancient writers are facts, facts averred in their writings. By judging them hastily, without entering into details, without imposing upon ourselves the obligation of quoting authorities, we incur the suspicion of falsifying history, and history, I repeat, the most precious, that of the human mind. The levity observable in certain writers proceeds, in a great measure, from the character which science has assumed in our days. There is no longer any particular science, but only a general one, embracing them all, and including in its immense circle all branches of knowledge. Consequently, minds of ordinary capacity are obliged to remain satisfied with vague notions, unfortunately only serving to stimulate abstraction and universality. Never was knowledge so much generalized as now, and never was it more difficult to obtain deserved renown for wisdom. In every aspirant to scientific excellence the state of science requires a laborious activity in the acquisition of knowledge, profound reflection to regulate and direct it, a comprehensive and penetrating view to simplify and concentrate it, an intellect of a high order, elevating him to the regions in which science has established her abode. How many men are endowed with these qualifications? But let us revert to the subject.

Catholic theologians are so far from favoring despotism, that I doubt much whether it would be possible to find better books than theirs for enabling us to form clear and just ideas of the faculties of power. I will even add that, generally speaking, they incline, in a very remarkable manner, to the development of true liberty. The great type of theological schools, the model to the contemplation of which they have constantly turned during several centuries, are the works of St. Thomas of Aquin; and we may with full confidence defy our opponents to find us a jurist or philosopher who expounds with more lucidity, wisdom, noble independence, and generous dignity, the principles to which civil power ought to adhere. His *Treatise upon Laws* is immortal, and whoever has fully comprehended it has no further information to acquire respecting the great principles which ought to guide the legislator. You think lightly of past times, imagining that till now nothing was known of politics or public right; and in your imagination you invent an incestuous alliance between religion and despotism, fancying you have discovered in the distant obscurity of the cloister, the plot contrived by this infamous pact. But have you heard the opinion of a religious of the thirteenth century upon the nature of law? You already imagine that you see in his ideas force dominating over all, and constantly invoking religion the better to disguise his rude snares with a few falsehoods. Learn, then, that you could not yourself have given a milder definition of law. You would never have thought, as he has done, of excluding from it the idea of force; you could never have conceived how, in so few words, he has managed to say all, and with such exactitude, such lucidity, in terms so favorable to the true liberty of the people and to the dignity of man. The definition here spoken of being the summary of his entire doctrine, and at the same time the guide which has directed theologians, may be considered as an abridgment of theological doctrines in their relation to the faculties of civil power. It presents to us at a single glance what were, in this point of view, the predominating principles among Catholics.

Civil power acts upon society through the medium of the law; and, according to St. Thomas, the law is, "*a rule dictated by reason, the aim of which is the public good, and promulgated by him who has the care of society.*" "Quædam rationis ordinatio ad bonum commune, et ab eo qui curam communitatis habet promulgata." (1, 2, quæst. 90, art. 4.) A rule dictated by reason, *rationis ordinatio.* Here by one word despotism and force are banished; here is the principle that the law is not a pure effect of the will. The celebrated maxim, *Quod principi placuit legis habet vigorem*, is here corrected. Although capable of a reasonable and just interpretation, this maxim was, nevertheless, incorrect, and inclined to flattery. A celebrated writer of our days has devoted numerous pages to proving that legitimacy has not its origin in the will of man, but in reason, inferring from this that what ought to command men is not in the will of another man, but reason. With much less pomp, but not less solidity and conciseness, the holy Doctor expresses this idea in the words above quoted, *rationis ordinatio.* On reflection we find that despotism, arbitrary power, and tyranny are nothing else than the absence of reason in power, the domination of the will. When reason commands, there is legitimacy, justice, liberty; when the will alone commands, there is illegitimacy, injustice, despotism. Hence the fundamental idea of all law is, that it be in accordance with reason, that it be an emanation from reason, an application of reason to society; and the will, in giving its sanction to law and carrying it into execution, should be merely auxiliary to reason, its instrument, its arm.

It is evident that, without the action of the will, there is no law; for acts of pure reason, without the co-operation of the will, are thoughts and not commands. They enlighten the mind, but do not produce action. It is, therefore, impossible to conceive the existence of law without the combined operation of the will and of reason. But this is no reason why we should not consider all law to have a rational foundation and to be conformable to reason, that it may merit the name of law. These observations have not escaped the penetration of the holy Doctor; he examines them, and dispels the error of believing that the law consists in the mere will of the prince. He expresses himself as follows: "Reason receives its motive power from the will, as we have observed above (quæst. 17, art. 1;) for whilst the will seeks the end, reason enjoins the means of its attainment; but the will, to have the force of law, must be guided by reason. In this sense only can the will of a sovereign be said to have the force of law; in any other sense it would not be law, but injustice." "Ratio habet vim movendi a voluntate, ut supra dictum est. (Quæst. 17, art. 1.) Ex hoc enim quod aliquis vult finem, ratio imperat de his quæ sunt ad finem, sed voluntas de his quæ imperantur, ad hoc quod legis rationem habeat, oportet quod sit aliqua ratione regulata; et hoc modo intelligitur quod voluntas principis habet vigorem legis; *alioquin voluntas principis magis esset iniquitas quam lex.*" (Quæst. 90, art. 1.)

These doctrines of St. Thomas are the same as those of all theologians. Impartiality and good sense will tell us whether they are favorable to absolutism and despotism, whether they are in any way opposed to true liberty, whether they are not eminently conformable to the dignity of man. These doctrines form the most explicit and conclusive proclamation of the limits of civil power, and they certainly have in this respect more weight than the declarations of imprescriptible rights. That which humbles man, wounds in him the feeling of a just independence, and introduces despotism into the world, is the will of man commanding and exacting submission merely because it is his will; but by submitting to reason, being guided by her dictates, we are not degraded; on the contrary, we are elevated, we are dignified, for we live conformably to eternal order and to the divine will. The obligation of being subject to the law does not originate in the will of another, but in reason. Theologians, however, have not considered the latter of itself sufficient to command. They derive the sanction of the law from a higher source; when the conscience of man was to be acted upon, to be bound by duty, they could find nothing in the sphere of created things capable of attaining so high an object. "Human laws, if they are just," says the holy Doctor, "are binding in conscience, and they derive their power from the eternal law, from which they are formed, according to what is said in Proverbs, chap. viii., 'By Me kings reign, and the lawgivers decree just things.'" "Si quidem justæ sunt, habent vim obligandi in foro conscientiæ a lege eterna, a qua derivantur, secundum illud Proverb. cap. 8, per me reges regnant, et legum conditores justa decernunt." (1, 2, quæst. 96, art. 3.) This proves, according to St. Thomas, that just law is derived not exactly from human reason, but from the eternal law; and that this is what makes it binding upon conscience.

This is doubtless more philosophical than to seek the obligatory force of laws in private reason, in pacts, or in the general will. In this manner the titles, the true titles of humanity are explained, a reasonabie limit is placed upon civil power, and obedience is easily obtained; the rights and duties of governments, as well as those of subjects, are established upon solid and indestructible foundations; the nature of power, society, command, and obedience become perfectly comprehensible. It is no longer the will of one man predominating over that of his fellow-man; it is not his reason, but reason emanating from God, or more properly speaking the reason of God, the eternal law, God Himself. A sublime theory, in which power finds its rights, its duties, its force, its authority, its prestige, and in which society possesses its safest guarantee of order, well-being, and true liberty; a theory which divests authority of the will of man, since it changes this will into an instrument of the eternal law, into a divine ministry, *whose aim is the public good, ad bonum commune.* This, according to St. Thomas, is also one of the essential conditions of law. It has been asked, Whether kings are made for the people, or the people for kings? Such a question could only arise from a want of due reflection upon the nature of society, its object, and its origin, and upon the intent of power. The concise expression above cited, *ad bonum commune,* is a fitting answer to this question. "Laws," says the holy Doctor, "may be unjust in two ways; either by being opposed to the commonweal, or by having an improper aim, as when a government imposes upon its subjects onerous laws, which do not serve the common interest, but rather cupidity and ambition. Such laws are rather injustices than laws." "Injustæ autem sunt leges dupliciter; uno modo per contrarietatem ad bonum commune, e contrario prædictis; vel ex fine, sicut cum aliquis præsidens leges imponit, onerosas subditis non pertinentes ad utilitatem communem, sed magis ad propriam cupiditatem vel gloriam: . . . . Et hujusmodi magis sunt violentiæ quam leges." (1, 2, q. 96, art. 4.) From this doctrine it follows, that command must be exercised for the well-being of all; and, failing in this condition, it is unjust: governors are invested with it only for the advantage of the governed. Kings are not, as some philosophers, regardless of the most palpable inconsistencies, have absurdly maintained, the slaves of their people; neither is their power a simple commission without any real authority, and continually subject to the caprice of their people; but, at the same time, the people are not the property of their kings. The latter can, by no means, consider their subjects as slaves, to be disposed of at their free-will: governments are not, by any means, the absolute arbiters of the lives and fortunes of the governed; they are bound to watch over them, not as a master over slaves from whom he derives profit, but as a father over the son whom he loves and whose happiness he has at heart.

"The kingdom is not made for the king, but the king for the kingdom," says the holy Doctor, from whom I continue to quote; and, in a style remarkable for its force and freedom, he continues as follows: "for God has constituted kings to rule and govern, and to secure to every one the possession of his rights; such is the aim of their institution; but if kings, turning things to their own profit, should act otherwise, they are no longer kings, but tyrants." (*D. Th. de Reg. Princ.* cap. 11.) From this doctrine it is evident, that the people are not made for kings; that the subject is not made for the ruler; but that all governments have been established for the good of society, and that this alone should be the compass to guide those who are in command, whatever be the form of government From the president of the most insignificant republic to the most powerful monarch, none are exempt from this law; for it is a law anterior to society,—a law which presided at the formation of society, and which is superior to human law, inasmuch as it emanates from the Author of all society, from the source of all law.

No, the people are not made for kings; kings are all appointed for the good of the people: and if this object is not accomplished, the government is useless; and this affects the republic as well as the monarchy. To flatter kings with opposite maxims is to ruin them. Religion has not, at any time, done this; this was not the language of those illustrious men who, clothed in the sacerdotal habit, delivered to the powerful ones of the earth the messages of Heaven. "Kings, princes, magistrates," cries out the venerable Palafox, "all jurisdiction is ordained by God for the preservation of His people, not for their destruction; for defence, not for offence; for man's right, and not for his injury. They who maintain that kings can do as they please, and who establish their power upon their will, open the way to tyranny. Those who maintain that kings have power to do as they ought, and what is necessary for the preservation of their subjects and of their crowns, for the exaltation of faith and religion, for the just and right administration of justice, the preservation of peace and the support of just war, for the due and becoming *éclat* of regal dignity, the honorable maintenance of their houses and families, speak the truth without flattery, throw open the gates to justice, and to magnanimous and royal virtues." (*Hist. Real. Sagrada,* lib. i. cap. 11.) When Louis XIV. said, "I am the state," he had not learned this maxim either from Bossuet, Bourdaloue, or Masillon. Pride, exalted by so much grandeur and power, and infatuated by base adulators, was here speaking by his mouth. How unsearchable are the ways of Providence! The corpse of this man, who said he was the *state,* was insulted at his funeral; and, before the lapse of a century, his grandson suffered death on the scaffold! Thus the crimes of families are expiated, as well as those of nations. When the measure of His indignation is filled up, the Lord reminds terrified man that the God of mercy is likewise a God of vengeance, and that, as He opened upon the world the floodgates of heaven, so also He lets loose upon kings and nations the tempests of revolution. When once the rights and duties of power are founded upon a base as solid as that of their divine origin, when once they become established by a rule as exalted as that of the eternal law, there is no longer any necessity for extolling or exaggerating power, nor of attributing to it faculties to which it has no claim; and, on the other hand, it is no longer necessary to exact from it the fulfilment of its obligations with that imperious haughtiness which enervates by humiliating it. Flattery and menace become alike needless when there are other resources for exciting it to action, and other barriers for restraining it within due bounds. The statue of the king, it is true, is not set up in the public squares as an object for the people's adoration; but, on the other hand, the king is no longer placed at the mercy of democrats, soon to become an object of mockery and derision, the contemptible laughing-stock of demagogues.

Observe the moderation and mildness of the definition we have just analysed! It does not contain a single word which can wound the most delicate susceptibility of the most ardent partisans of public liberty. The law, according to this definition, consists in the rule of reason; the common weal is its only aim; and when the authority of him who promulgates and executes it is spoken of, there is no mention made of any sovereignty, no expression is used indicative of slavish subjection, the most measured term which it was possible to select is made use of—*care: Qui* CURAM *communitatis habet.* Bear in mind, that the author here quoted is accustomed to weigh his words like precious metal, and to employ them with the most scrupulous delicacy, pausing a long time, when necessary, to explain any that may present the least ambiguity, and you will then understand what ideas this great man entertained upon power; you will discover whether the spirit of oppressive doctrines could have prevailed in the Catholic schools, in which this Doctor was, and is still, acknowledged as an almost infallible oracle.

Compare the definition given by St. Thomas, and adopted by all theologians, with that which Rousseau has given. In that of St. Thomas, law is the expression of reason; in that of Rousseau, the expression of will: in the former, it is an application of the eternal law; in the latter, the product of general will. On which side are wisdom and good sense? Law was understood among the nations of Europe as it is explained by St. Thomas and all the Catholic schools; and tyranny was banished from Europe, Asiatic despotism was impossible, the admirable institution of European monarchy was established. At a later period, Rousseau's explanation was adopted, and then came the Convention, with its scaffolds and its horrors.

Publicists have already nearly abandoned the theory of "a general will;" and even those who contend for the sovereignty of the people, do not maintain that the will of all the citizens should constitute the law. The law, say they, is not the expression of general will, but of general reason. The philosopher of Geneva would have the will of individuals collected, the aggregate of which he termed the general will. In like manner, the publicists of whom we are speaking are of opinion that it is necessary to collect, amongst the governed, the greatest amount of reason, and to give this to the government for its guidance, the governing body being merely an instrument for the application of it. It is not men who command, say they, but the law; and the law is nothing else than reason and justice.

This theory, so far as it is correct, and apart from the applications which might be made of it, is not a discovery of modern science; it is a traditional principle of all Europe, which presided at the formation of society, and has given to civil power an organisation differing widely from those of antiquity, and equally so from those of modern times that have not participated in our civilisation. This, on close examination, appears to be the reason why European monarchies, even the most absolute, have been so very different from the Asiatic. A singular phenomenon: at the very time when society among us had no legal guarantees against the power of kings, it still had other very forcible ones which were purely moral. Modern science cannot, therefore, claim the discovery of a new principle of government; it has unknowingly resuscitated the ancient one. By rejecting the doctrine of Rousseau, instead of making, according to the vulgar expression, a step in advance, it retrograded; but to retrograde is not always to lose an advantage. What is or can be lost by receding from the brink of a precipice to enter upon a safe road? Rousseau complains, and with reason, that certain writers have so far exaggerated the prerogatives of civil power, as to convert mankind into a common herd, of which rulers could dispose to serve their interest or caprice. Such reproaches, however, cannot be applied to the Catholic Church, nor to any of the illustrious schools sheltered in her bosom. The philosopher of Geneva makes a severe attack upon Hobbes and Grotius for having maintained this servile doctrine. Catholics have nothing to do with the cause of these two writers. I will observe, however, that it would not be just to place the latter upon a parallel with the former. Grotius has certainly afforded reason for the accusation. He maintains that there are cases in which governments are not for the benefit of the governed, but for that of the governing powers. "Sic imperia quædam esse possunt comparata ad regum utilitatem." (*De Jure Belli et Pacis*, lib. i. cap. 3.) But, whilst we acknowledge that this principle has a dangerous tendency, we grant that the doctrines of the Dutch writer do not upon the whole tend to the total ruin of morality.

By rendering Grotius his due share of justice, we prevent any exaggeration of the evil which may exist on the side of our opponents; it must now be permitted to Catholic hearts to remark with noble satisfaction, that such doctrines could never be established amongst the professors of the true faith, and that the fatal maxims which lead to oppression have originated precisely among those who have deviated from the teaching of the Chair of St. Peter. No; Catholics have never brought under discussion whether kings have an unlimited power over the lives and fortunes of their subjects, to such a degree as to admit of no opposition, whatever be the excess of the absolutism and despotism exercised over them. Whenever flattery raised its voice to exaggerate the royal prerogative, this voice was immediately silenced by the unanimous outcry of the supporters of sound doctrine. Witness the remarkable example of a solemn retractation imposed by the tribunal of the Inquisition upon a preacher who had exceeded his bounds. Not so in England, a country proverbial for its hatred of Catholicity. Whilst here, in Spain, it was forbidden under a severe penalty to circulate maxims so degrading, in England the question was proposed with the greatest gravity, and writers upon law were divided in their sentiments. (See end of chapter 39.)

Every impartial reader has already been able to form an opinion on the value of declamations against the right divine, and on that pretended affinity of Catholic doctrines with despotism and slavery. The exposition of these doctrines which I have just given is certainly not founded upon vain reasoning, sought out on purpose to darken the question. I have not in any way shunned the difficulty.

The question was, to know in what these doctrines consisted. I have shown clearly, that those who calumniate them do not understand them, and that we may even be allowed to suppose that they have never taken the trouble to examine them, such is the levity and ignorance with which they express themselves. Perhaps I have adduced too many facts and quotations; but let the reader bear in mind, that my object is not to present him with a code of doctrines, but to give to this point of doctrine an historical investigation. Now, history does not call for discourses, but facts; and in matters of doctrine, the sentiments of authors are facts. Whilst beholding the salutary reaction now taking place in favour of sound principles, let us avoid giving an incomplete statement of the truth. For the cause of religion it is highly important that its advocates should be free from even the most remote suspicion of dishonesty or dissimulation. On this account, I have, without hesitation, given in their integrity the doctrines laid down by Catholic writers, just as I find them in their works. By misrepresenting and confounding facts, Protestants and unbelievers have succeeded in deceiving; let me hope that, by explaining and elucidating them, I shall not be unsuccessful in removing the deception.

I purpose examining, in the remaining part of this work, some other questions relating to the same subject—questions perhaps not more important, but certainly more delicate. And for this reason, I was obliged to smooth the way, that I might proceed with more liberty and ease. I have hitherto made the cause of religion defend itself with its own weapons, without borrowing the support of auxiliaries which were superfluous. I shall proceed in the same course, fully convinced that Catholicity can only lose by any line of vindication that identifies it with political interests, and confines it within a circle too limited for its immensity. Empires appear and disappear; the Church of Christ will last till the end of time. Political opinions undergo changes and modifications; the august dogmas of our religion remain immutable. Thrones rise and fall; and the rock upon which Jesus Christ has built His Church stands unshaken throughout the course of time, ever defying the powers of hell. When we take up arms in her defence, let us be impressed with the importance of our mission; let there be no exaggeration, no flattery—the pure truth in measured, but accurate and firm language. In addressing ourselves to the people, in proclaiming the truth to kings, let us bear in mind that religion is above politics, and God above kings and people.

CHAPTER LIV.

ON RESISTANCE TO THE CIVIL POWER.

THE doctrines of Catholicity, therefore, in reference both to the origin and the exercise of civil power, are unobjectionable. Let us now proceed to another point—one of greater delicacy and difficulty, if not of more importance. To state the question frankly, without any subterfuge or evasion: "*Is it allowable in any case to resist the civil power?*" It is impossible to speak more distinctly, or to employ more precise and simple terms in stating this question, which is the most important, the most difficult, and the most startling of any that the subject we have in hand presents for our investigation. We know that Protestantism from its commencement proclaimed the right of insurrection against civil power; and no one is ignorant of the fact that Catholicity has ever preached up obedience to this power; so that if the former has been from its infancy an element of revolution and of overthrow, the latter has been an element of tranquillity and good order. This distinction might induce us to believe that Catholicity favors oppression, since it leaves the people without arms to defend their liberty. "You preach up obedience to the civil powers," our adversaries will say; "you pronounce, in all cases, an anathema upon any insurrection which attacks them; should tyranny prevail, therefore, you become its most powerful auxiliaries; for, by your doctrine, you arrest the arm ready to be raised in defence of liberty; you stifle with the cry of conscience the indignation awakened in generous hearts." This is a serious charge, which compels us to elucidate, as far as possible, this important point, and to distinguish in it truth from error, certainty from doubt.

Some men would shrink from the investigation of such questions, and prefer drawing a veil over them—a veil which they venture not to raise, lest they should find an abyss. And assuredly their timidity is not inexcusable; for there are abysses unfathomable, and dangers that strike the mind with awe One false step may lead to destruction; one move in a wrong direction may let loose tempests that would lay society in ruins. Whilst, however, I willingly admit the pure intentions of such persons, I may be permitted to observe, that their prudence is quite thrown away, that their foresight and precaution are of no avail. Whether they investigate these questions or not, they *are* investigated, agitated, and decided, in a manner that we must deplore; and, worse still, the theories thence arising have been reduced to practice. Revolutions are no longer confined to books, they have become realities; quitting the quiet path of mere speculative philosophy, they are to be seen in the streets and in the public squares. Since, then, things have come to such a pass, why seek palliatives, make use of restrictions, or invoke silence? Let us tell the truth, just as it is, without concealment; since it is the truth, it will neither shrink before abundance of knowledge, nor the attacks of error. It is truth; its manifestation, its diffusion can have no injurious effect. In a word, God, who is the Author of societies, had no need of establishing them upon falsehood. This candor is the more necessary, because political changes may have led some persons to disavow the truths we are discussing, or no longer to understand them aright; whilst others imagine that obedience to legitimate authority has been taught only by a party anxious to make this doctrine the foundation of their tyranny. Men of erroneous opinions and evil intentions have their own codes, to which they have recourse whenever it will forward their designs: their fatal errors or their sordid interests form the rule of their conduct; this is the source of their knowledge and of their inspirations. Men, therefore, endowed with a pure heart and with upright intentions, should know what to hold by in political oscillations; it is no longer sufficient for them to have a general knowledge of the principle of obedience to the legitimate authorities; they must also be acquainted with their applications.

It is true that, in conflicts arising from civil discord, many men throw aside their own convictions to accommodate themselves to the exigencies of their interests; but it is no less certain, that there is still to be found a great number of conscientious men who adhere to them. We may also add, that the generality of the individuals composing a nation, not being usually in the urgent necessity of choosing between the sacrifice of their convictions and the risk of grave and imminent peril, those who entertain them usually find means to make their influence felt in preventing great evils or in remedying them. According to certain *pessimistes*, reason and justice are for ever banished from the earth, leaving it a prey to self-interest, and substituting for the dictates of conscience the designs of egotism. In their estimation, it is labor in vain to discuss and decide questions which may guide us in practice; for, according to them, whatever a man's conviction may be in theory, his practical decision will always be the same. It is my happiness, or misfortune, to take a different view of the case, and to believe that there still exist in the world, and particularly in Spain, men of profound convictions, and possessed of sufficient strength of mind to regulate their conduct by those convictions. The strongest proof that the inutility of doctrines is exaggerated, is the zeal evinced by all parties to lay hold of them. Whether from interest or from delicacy, all appeal to doctrines; and this interest or delicacy would not exist, if doctrines did not possess a powerful ascendency in society. Nothing, in discussion, is more perplexing than the introduction of several questions at the same time; and for this reason, I shall proceed in such a manner as to distinguish those which present themselves here. I will resolve, one by one, those which relate to our object, and pass over those which are foreign to it. Above all, we must bear in mind the general principle at all times inculcated by Catholicity, viz. *the obligation of obeying legitimate authority*. Let us now see how this principle is to be applied. In the first place, *Are we to obey the civil power when it commands something that is evil in itself?* No, we are not; for the simple reason that what is evil in itself is forbidden by God; now, *we must obey God rather than men.*

In the second place, *Are we to obey the civil power when it interferes in matters not included in the circle of its faculties?* No; for, with regard to these matters, it is not a power. From the very supposition that its faculties do not extend so far, we affirm that, in this point of view, it is not a real power. Besides, what I have advanced does not exactly and exclusively concern spiritual matters, to which I appear to allude. I apply this restriction of civil power also to matters purely temporal. It is necessary to refer here to what I have said in another part of this work, viz., that whilst we grant to civil power sufficient force and attributes for the maintenance of order and unity in the social body, it is just nevertheless, that we should not allow it to absorb the individual and the family, so as to destroy their individuality, to deprive them of their own sphere, and leave them only the means of acting as an integral part of society. This is one of the distinguishing features between Christian and pagan civilisation: the latter, in its zeal for the preservation of social unity, excluded every individual and family right; the former, on the contrary, has amalgamated the interests of the individual with those of families and society, so that they neither destroy nor embarrass each other. Thus, besides the sphere within which the action of the civil power is properly confined, there are others into which it has no right to enter, and in which individuals and families live without clashing with the colossal force of the government.

It is just to observe here, that Catholicity has done much for the maintenance of this principle, which is a strong guarantee of the liberty of the people. The separation of the two powers temporal and spiritual, the independence of the latter with respect to the former, the distinction of the persons in whom it is vested: such has been one of the principal causes of this liberty, which, under different forms of government, is the common inheritance of European nations. Ever since the foundation of the Church, this principle of the independence of the spiritual power has at all times served, by the mere fact of its existence, to remind men that the rights of civil power are limited, that there are things beyond its province, cases in which a man may say, and ought to say, *I will not obey.*

This is another of those cases in which Protestantism has given a wrong direction to the civilisation of Europe, and in which, far from opening the way to liberty, it has riveted the chains of slavery. Its first step was the abolition of the Pontifical authority, the overthrow of the hierarchy, the refusal to grant to the Church any kind of power whatever, and the placing of spiritual supremacy in the hands of princes; that is to say, it has retrograded towards pagan civilisation, in which we find the sceptre united with the pontificate. The grand political problem was precisely the separation of these two powers, in order to save society from subjection to one sole unlimited authority, exercising its faculties without restraint, and from which might consequently be expected vexation and oppression. This separation was effected without any political views, any fixed design on the part of men, wherever Catholicity was established; for her discipline required and her dogmas inculcated it. Is it not strange that the advocates of theories of equilibrium and counterpoise, who have so loudly extolled the utility of separating powers, and of dividing authority among them with a view to prevent it from being converted into tyranny, should not have noticed the profound wisdom of this Catholic doctrine, even when considered merely in a social and political point of view? But no; it is remarkable, on the contrary, that all modern revolutions have manifested a decided tendency towards the amalgamation of the civil and ecclesiastical powers—a convincing proof that these revolutions have proceeded from an origin contrary to the generative principle of European civilisation, and that instead of guiding it towards perfection, they have rather served to lead it astray. The union of Church and State in England, under the reigns of Henry VIII. and Elizabeth, produced the most cruel despotism; and if that country at a later period acquired a higher degree of liberty, it was not assuredly owing to that religious authority given by Protestantism to the head of the state, but in spite of it. It is worthy of remark, that in later times, when England entered upon a more extensive sphere of liberty, it was owing to the diminution of the civil power on all matters appertaining to religion, and to a greater development of Catholicity, opposed in its very principles to this monstrous supremacy. In the North of Europe, where the Protestant system has also prevailed, civil authority has been unlimited; and even at the present time, we find the Emperor of Russia indulging in the most barbarous persecutions against Catholics; more distrustful of those who defend the independence of spiritual power, than of the revolutionary clubs. The autocrat is devoured with a thirst for unlimited authority, and a decided instinct urges him to attack in particular the Catholic religion, which forms his principal obstacle.

It is remarkable with what uniformity all power, in this respect, tends to despotism, whether under a revolutionary or monarchical form. Impatient of the restraint laid upon him by the spiritual power, Louis XIV. attempted to crush the power of Rome. He was urged to it by the same motives as the Constituent Assembly; the monarch rested his cause upon the rights of royalty, and the liberties of the Gallican Church—the Constituent Assembly invoked the rights of the nation, and the principles of philosophy; but in the main they were actuated by one and the same motive, that of ascertaining whether or not civil power should be restricted: in the former case, it was monarchy tending to despotism; in the latter, democracy advancing to the terrors of the Convention. When Napoleon wished to bruise the head of the revolutionary hydra, to reorganize society, to create a power, he made use of religion as the most potent element. Catholicity was the only predominating religion in France; to this he had recourse, and signed the *Concordat.* But, observe, that no sooner did he imagine his work of reparation complete, and the critical moment of the establishment of his power passed, than he began to think of extending it, of freeing himself from all restraint. He began to look upon that pontiff, whose presence at his coronation had so much gratified him, with a more supercilious eye. At first he had some serious disputes with him, and ended by becoming his most inveterate enemy.

These observations, to which I invite the attention of every reflecting mind, acquire more importance from the consideration of what has taken place in our own religious and most Catholic monarchy. In spite of the preponderating influence of the Catholic religion in Spain, the principle of resistance to the court of Rome has ever been preserved in a particular and remarkable manner; thus, whilst the Austrian dynasty and the Bourbons endeavoured to lay aside our old laws, so far as they were favourable to political liberty, they preserved as a sacred deposit the traditional resistance of Ferdinand the Catholic, of Charles V., and of Philip II. The deep root which Catholicity had taken in Spain doubtless prevented matters from being carried to extremes; but it is no less true that the germ existed, and was handed down from generation to generation, as if its complete development was expected at some more favourable period. This fact was placed in peculiarly strong relief at the time of the Bourbon accession, when the monarchy of Louis XIV. was introduced amongst us, and the last vestiges of the ancient liberties of Castile, Aragon, Valencia, and Catalonia disappeared; the mania for kingly rights was at its height in the reigns of Charles III. and Charles IV. Strange coincidence! The epoch in which the greatest jealousy was entertained against the Court of Rome and the independence of Church authority, was exactly that in which ministerial despotism was in its greatest force, and in which there was seen something still worse—the despotism of a favorite, with all its pitiful show. True, the ideas of the French schools were at that time influencing Spain; and of this neither the King, nor, probably, some of his ministers, were aware: but this does not militate against the reflections we are making; on the contrary, it comes in support of them, by showing their applicability to circumstances quite dissimilar, and consequently their soundness and importance. The object here aimed at was the overthrow of the established authority, to make way for another equally unlimited; to effect this, it was necessary to urge on the former to abuse its prerogatives, and, at the same time, to establish precedents to fall back upon, so soon as the revolution should have displaced the absolute monarchy. What important reflections are here presented to us! What strange analogies rise to view between circumstances apparently most antagonistic! In our times, we have seen bishops brought to trial from the same motives that were alleged in a celebrated cause in the reign of Charles III.; and the *Supreme Tribunals* of our own days have heard from the lips of their *fiscals** the same doctrines formerly propounded by those of the *Council*. Thus do doctrines meet, and thus, by different ways, do we arrive at the same end. According to the ancient *fiscals*, the authority of the king was every thing; the rights of the crown, like the ark of old, were held so sacred, that to touch, or even to look upon them, was accounted a sacrilege. Well, the ancient monarchy has disappeared—the throne is no longer any thing more than a shadow of what it once was—the Revolution has triumphed over it; and yet, despite a change so profound, it is not long since a *fiscal* of the Supreme Tribunal, charging a bishop with an offence against the rights of the civil power, made use of these words: "In the state, a leaf cannot be plucked without the permission of government." These words need no comment; the writer of these lines heard them uttered; and this plain, unequivocal declaration of arbitrary power seemed to him to throw a new ray of light upon history.

The gravity and importance of this subject required this digression; it was incumbent on me to show how far the Catholic principle of the independence of spiritual power may serve the cause of true liberty. This principle, in fact, eminently teaches that the faculties of civil power are limited, and it is, consequently, a perpetual condemnation of despotism. To revert to the original question. It remains, then, established, that we are to be subject to the civil power so long as it does not go beyond its proper limits; but that the Catholic doctrine never enjoins obedience when civil power oversteps the limits of its faculties.

It will not be uninteresting to the reader to learn how the principle of obedience was understood by one of the most illustrious interpreters of Catholic doctrine—by the holy Doctor so often cited. According to him, whenever laws are unjust (and observe, that, in his opinion, they may be so in many ways), they are not binding on conscience, unless for fear of creating scandal, or causing greater evils; that is to say, that, in certain cases, an unjust law may become obligatory, not by virtue of any duty which it imposes, but from motives of prudence. These are his words, to which I crave the reader's particular attention: "Laws are unjust in two ways; either because they are opposed to the common weal; or on account of their aim, as is the case when a government imposes upon its subjects onerous laws, not for the good of the commonweal, but for the sake of self-interest or ambition; or on account of

* Crown attorneys, charged with the prosecution of criminal and other causes.

their author, as when any one makes a law without being invested with proper faculties; again, they may be unjust in form, as when the taxes are unequally divided among the multitude, although in other respects tending to the public good. Such laws are rather outrages than laws; since, as St. Augustin observes (lib. i. *de Lib. Arb* cap. 5), 'An unjust law does not appear to be a law.' Such laws, therefore, are not binding in conscience, unless, perhaps, for the avoiding of scandal and trouble—a motive which ought to induce man to give up his right, as St. Matthew observes: 'And whosoever shall force thee to go one mile, go with him other two; and if any man will go to law with thee, and take away thy coat, let him have thy cloak also.' Laws may also be unjust in another point of view, when they are contrary to the will of God; as the laws of tyrants enforcing idolatry, or anything else contrary to divine law. With respect to such laws, it is not allowable, under any circumstances, to obey them; for, as it is said in the Acts of the Apostles, 'We must obey God rather than man.'" "Injustæ autem sunt leges dupliciter; uno modo per contrarietatem ad bonum commune e contrario prædictis, vel ex fine, sicut cum aliquis præsidens leges imponit onerosas subditis non pertinentes ad utilitatem communem, sed magis ad propriam cupiditatem vel gloriam; vel etiam ex auctore, sicut cum aliquis legem fert ultra sibi commissam potestatem; vel etiam ex forma cum inæqualiter onera multitudinis dispensantur, etiamsi ordinentur ad bonum commune; et hujusmodi magis sunt violentiæ quam leges, quia sicut Augustinus dicit (lib. i. *de Lib. Arb.* cap. 5, parum a princ.) lex esse non videtur quæ justa non fuerit, unde tales leges in foro conscientiæ non obligant, nisi forte propter vitandum scandalum vel turbationem, propter quod etiam homo juri suo cedere debet secundum illud Math. cap. v. 'Qui te angariaverit mille passus, vade cum eo alia duo, et qui abstulerit tibi tunicam da ei et pallium.' Alio modo leges possunt esse injustæ per contrarietatem ad bonum divinum, sicut leges tyrannorum inducentes ad idololatriam, vel ad quodcumque aliud quod sit contra legem divinam, et tales leges nullo modo licet observare, quia sicut dicitur Act. cap. v.: 'Obedire oportet Deo magis quam hominibus.'" (*D. Th.* 1, 2, quæst. 90, art. 1.)

This doctrine furnishes us with the following rules:

1. We cannot, under any circumstances, obey the civil power when its commands are opposed to the divine law.
2. When laws are unjust, they are not binding in conscience.
3. It may become necessary to obey these laws from motives of prudence; that is, in order to avoid scandal and commotions.
4. Laws are unjust from some one of the following causes:

When they are opposed to the common weal—when their aim is not the good of the commonweal—when the legislator outsteps the limits of his faculties—when, although in other respects tending to the good of the commonweal, and proceeding from competent authority, they do not observe suitable equity; for instance, when they divide unequally the public imposts.

We have quoted and copied the venerable text whence these rules are derived: their illustrious author has been the guide of all the theological schools during the last six centuries; his authority has never been called in question in these schools on points of dogma or morality; these rules may, therefore, be regarded as the recapitulation of the doctrines of Catholic theologians with reference to the obedience due to authority. We may now, without doubt, appeal with entire confidence to every man of good sense. Let him judge whether these doctrines are in the least inclined to despotism, whether they have the least tendency to tyranny, in fine, whether they aim the slightest blow at liberty. It is vain to seek in them the slightest appearance of flattery to the civil power, whose limits are marked out with rigorous severity; if it outsteps them, it is openly told, "Thy laws are not laws, but outrages; they are not binding in conscience; and if, in some instances, thou art obeyed, it is not owing to any obligation, but to prudence, in order to avoid scandal and commotion; it is thenceforth such a dishonor to thee, that thy triumph, far from entitling thee to renown, assimilates thee to the robber who despoils the peaceable man of his garment, and to whom the latter, for the sake of peace, gives up his cloak also." If these are doctrines of oppression and despotism, we also are advocates for such oppression and despotism; for we cannot conceive doctrines more favorable to liberty.

Upon these principles the admirable institution of European monarchy was founded. This teaching has created the moral defences by which that monarchy is surrounded; defences restraining it within the limits of its duties, even where political guarantees do not exist. The mind, wearied with foolish declamations against the *tyranny of kings*, and, on the other hand, not less tired of the boisterous adulations lavished upon power in modern times, expands and rejoices on meeting with this pure, disinterested, and sincere expression of the rights and duties of governments and of people, on hearing this language, impressed with as much of wisdom as of upright intention and generous freedom. What books were consulted by men making use of such language? The Scriptures, the Fathers, the collections of ecclesiastical documents. Could they have received their inspirations from the society which surrounded them? No; for in that same society disorder and confusion prevailed; sometimes a turbulent disobedience, at others despotism was predominant. And yet they speak with as much discretion, tact, and calmness as if they were living in the midst of well-regulated society. They were guided by divine revelation, which taught them truth. How often did they see it forgotten and trampled under foot! But uninfluenced by circumstances, however unfavorable, they wrote in a region far above the atmosphere of human passions. Truth is of all times; proclaim it ever, and God will effect the rest. (31)

CHAPTER LV.

ON RESISTANCE TO DE FACTO GOVERNMENTS.

THE questions hitherto discussed relating to the obedience due to power are very grave; but those of resistance to it are still more important.

Is it allowable, under any circumstances, in any supposition, to resist the civil power *by physical force?* Does there nowhere exist a deposing power? How far do Catholic doctrines extend on this subject? Such are the extreme points we purpose to discuss. According to one system, obedience is due to a government from the very fact of its existence, even on the supposition that its existence is illegitimate. Now, it is important to demonstrate, at the very outset, the unsoundness of this doctrine, which is contrary to right reason, and has never been taught by Catholicity. In preaching obedience "to the powers that be," the Church speaks of powers that have a legitimate existence. The absurdity, that a simple fact can create right, can never become a dogma of Catholicity. Were it true that resistance would be unlawful, it would be equally true that an illegitimate government has a right to command; for the obligation to obey is correlative with the right to command; and an illegitimate government would, consequently, become legitimatised by the simple fact of its existence. This would legitimatise all usurpations; the most heroic resistance on the part of the people would be condemned; the world would be abandoned to the mere rule of force. No; that degrading doctrine is not true which derives legitimacy from usurpation; which says to a people conquered and subjugated by any usurper whatever, "Obey your tyrant; his rights are founded on force, and your obligation to him on your weakness." No; there cannot be truth in a doctrine that would efface from our history one of its brightest pages, that would entail disgrace upon a nation taking up arms to expel an usurper, struggling for its independence during a period of six years, and finally overthrowing the conqueror of Europe. If Napoleon had succeeded in establishing his power amongst us, the Spanish nation would still have maintained the right on account of which it revolted in 1808; victory could not have rendered usurpation legitimate. The victims of the second of May did not legalise the command of Murat; and had even every corner of the peninsula been made a theatre of horrors similar to those witnessed on the Prado, the blood of martyred patriots, covering the usurper and his satellites with everlasting infamy, would only have confirmed the sacred right of revolting in defence of the throne, of national independence. We must repeat it: the simple fact does not create a right, either in private or public affairs; and so soon as such a principle is acknowledged, every idea of reason and justice disappears from the world. Those who may have wished to flatter governments with so fatal a doctrine, were not aware that this was the very way to ruin them, and to sow the seeds of usurpation and insurrection. What will be safe here below if we admit the principle, that success insures justice, and that the conqueror is always the rightful ruler? Is not this throwing open a wide gate to ambition, and to every crime? Is it not exciting men to forget every idea of right, reason, and justice, to acknowledge no other rule than brute force? Governments protected by so strange a doctrine would assuredly owe little gratitude to their protectors: this, in fact, is no defence; it is an insult; it is more of a cruel sarcasm than an apology. To what, indeed, does it amount, and how would this doctrine sound? Why, as follows: "People, obey him who commands you; you say his authority is usurped; we do not deny it; but, by the very fact of his having attained his end, the usurper has acquired a right. He is, indeed, a robber who has attacked you on the highway; he has stolen your money; but, by the mere fact of your not being able to resist him, and being forced to deliver to him your purse, now that he is possessed of it, you ought to respect this money as an inviolable property: such is your duty. It is a robbery; but this robbery being a *consummated act*, you cannot now obtain redress for it."

In this point of view the doctrine of *consummated facts* appears so much opposed to generally received ideas, that no reasonable man can seriously accept it. I do not deny that there are cases in which obedience, even to an illegitimate government, is to be recommended; when, for instance, we foresee that resistance would be useless, that it would only lead to new disorders, and to a greater effusion of blood: but in recommending prudence to the people, let us not disguise it under false doctrines—let us beware of calming the exasperation of misfortune by circulating errors subversive of all governments, of all society. It is worthy of remark, that all powers, even the most illegitimate, have a truer instinct than that manifested by the maintenance of such maxims. All powers in the first moment of their existence, before commencing their operations, before proceeding to one single act, proclaim their legitimacy. They seek it in right divine and human, they establish it upon birth or election, they derive it from historical titles, or the sudden development of extraordinary events; but all tends to the same point, the pretension to legitimacy. They never speak of the mere fact of their existence; from the instinct that prompts their own preservation they learn better than to rely upon such grounds, since to do so would be to annihilate their authority, to destroy their prestige, to encourage revolt; in a word, to commit self-destruction. We have here the most explicit condemnation of the doctrine we are combating, for the most shameless usurpers have more respect for good sense and the public conscience.

It sometimes happens that doctrines the most erroneous assume a veil of gentleness and Christian meekness. We must overthrow the arguments that might be employed against us, by the advocates of blind submission to any power that happens to be established. "The Scriptures," they will say, "prescribe to us obedience to the authorities, without any distinction; the Christian, therefore, ought not to make any distinction, but submit with resignation to such as he finds established." In reply to this objection, I see the following very decisive answers. 1. Illegitimate authority is no authority at all; the idea of power involves the idea of right, without which it is mere physical power, that is, *force*. When, therefore, the Scriptures prescribe obedience to the authorities, it is the lawful authorities that are implied. 2. The sacred text, in enjoining us obedience to the civil power, tells us that it is ordained by God Himself, that it is the minister of God Himself; and it is evident that usurpation is never invested with so high a character. The usurper is perhaps the instrument of Providence, *the scourge of Heaven*, as Attila designated himself, but not the minister of God. 3. The sacred Scriptures prescribe obedience to the subject in relation to the civil power, in the same way as they prescribe it to the slave in relation to his master. But what sort of masters are here implied? Evidently such as exercised a legitimate dominion, as it was understood at the time, conformable to the prevailing laws and customs; otherwise the Scriptures would require obedience from such slaves as were reduced to slavery by an abuse of power. Hence, as the obedience to masters prescribed by the Scriptures does not deprive the slave unjustly retained in servitude of his right, so also the obedience due to the established authorities should be restricted to the lawful authorities, and to cases in which prudence would dictate it in order to avoid commotion and scandal.

In confirmation of the doctrine of mere *de facto* government, the conduct of the first Christians has been sometimes alleged. "They submitted," it is said, "to the constituted authorities without even inquiring whether they were legitimate or not. At this epoch usurpations were frequent, the imperial throne was established by force, its occupants one after another owed their elevation to military insurrection, and to the assassination of their predecessors. We find, nevertheless, that Christians never meddled with the question of legitimacy; they respected the established power, and this power failing, they submitted without murmuring to the new tyrant who had usurped the throne." This argument, it cannot be denied, is very plausible, and presents at first sight a serious difficulty; a few reflections, however, suffice to show its extreme futility. In order that an insurrection against an unlawful power may be legitimate and prudent, those who undertake to overturn it should be sure of its illegitimacy, should have in view the substitution of a lawful power, and should count besides on the probability of the success of their enterprise. If these conditions are not fulfilled, the insurrection has no object; it is a mere fruitless attempt, an impotent revenge, which, instead of being useful to society, only causes bloodshed, only irritates the power attacked, and can have in consequence no other effect than to increase oppression and tyranny.

None of the conditions here mentioned were in existence at the time we are speaking of; all that upright men could do was quietly to resign themselves to the calamitous circumstances of the times, and by fervent prayer to implore the Almighty to take compassion on mankind.

When every thing was decided by force of arms, who could say whether such or such an emperor was lawfully established? Upon what rules was the imperial succession established? Where was legitimacy to be substituted for illegitimacy? Amongst the Romans—those vile, degraded beings, kissing the chains of the first tyrant who offered them *food* and *games?* In the worthless posterity of those illustrious patricians who formerly gave laws to the universe? Was it vested in the sons or in the family of some assassinated emperor, when the laws had not established hereditary succession, when the sceptre of the empire was at the disposal of the legions, when it frequently happened that the emperor, the victim of usurpation, had been himself merely a usurper, who had mounted to the throne over the corpse of his rival? Did it exist in the ancient rights of those conquered nations now reduced to simple dependencies of the empire, divested of all national spirit, having even lost the recollection of their former condition, without a thought capable of conducting them in the work of their emancipation, and destitute of resources against the colossal force of their masters? What object could any one have, under such circumstances, in making attempts against the established government? When the legions decided the fate of the world, alternately elevating and assassinating their masters, what could or what ought the Christian to do? The disciple of a God of peace and love, he could not take part in criminal scenes of bloodshed and tumult; authority was tottering and uncertain; it was not for him to decide whether it was legitimate or not; it only remained for him to submit to the power generally acknowledged, and at the arrival of one of those changes, at that time of so frequent occurrence, to yield the same obedience to the newly-established government.

The interference of Christians in political disputes would only have served to bring into disrepute the holy religion they professed; it would have given to philosophers and idolaters a pretext for increasing the catalogue of black calumnies which they everywhere brought against the faith. Public report accused Catholicity of being subversive of governments; Christians would have furnished a pretext for extending and accrediting this unfounded report, the hatred of governments would have been redoubled, and the rigors of persecution so cruelly exercised against the disciples of the cross would have been increased. Has this state of things ever existed but once, either in ancient or modern times? And could the conduct of the first Christians in this respect be made a rule for the Spaniards, for instance, at the time they resisted the usurpation of Bonaparte? Or could it be imitated by any other people in similar circumstances? Or will it be received as an argument in favor of every kind of usurpation? No; man, in becoming a Christian, does not cease to be a citizen, to be a man, to have his rights, and he acts in a praiseworthy manner whenever, within the bounds of reason and justice, he attempts to maintain these rights with fearless intrepidity.

Don Felix Amat, Archbishop of Palmyra, in his posthumous work entitled *Idea of the Church Militant*, makes use of these words: "Jesus Christ, by his plain and expressive answer, *Render to Cæsar the things that are Cæsar's*, has sufficiently established, that the mere fact of a government's existence is sufficient for enforcing the obedience of subjects to it." What I have already advanced is enough, in my opinion, to show the fallacy of such an assertion; and, as I intend to revert to this subject, and investigate more attentively this author's opinion, and the reasons upon which he supports it, I shall not now attempt to enter upon its refutation. I will, nevertheless, make one observation, which occurred to me on reading the passages in which the Archbishop of Palmyra developes it. His work was forbidden at Rome; and whatever may have been the motives for such a prohibition, we may rest assured that, in the case of a book advocating such doctrines, every man who is jealous of his rights might acquiesce in the decree of the Sacred Congregation.

As the opportunity is favorable, we may make a few remarks upon *consummated facts*, which are so closely connected with the doctrine under discussion. *Consummated* implies something perfect in its kind; hence an act is consummated when it has attained its completion. This word, applied to crimes, is opposed to mere attempt. We say an attempt at robbery, murder, or arson, when the undertaking to commit these crimes has been manifested by some act; for instance, the lock of a door has been broken, an attack has been made with a murderous weapon, combustible matter has been ignited—but the crime is not said to be consummated till the robbery, murder, or arson has actually been committed. Hence, in a political and social sense, we designate *consummated facts* an usurpation, completely overthrowing the legitimate power, and by means of which the usurper is already substituted in its place; a measure executed in all its points; such as the suppression of the regular clergy in Spain, and the confiscation of their property to the treasury; a revolution which has been triumphant, and which has entirely disposed of a country, as was the case with our American possessions.

From this explanation, we see clearly that a fact does not, by being *consummated*, change its nature; it still remains a simple fact—just or unjust, legal or illegal—as it was before. The most horrible outrages may also be termed *consummated* facts; yet, for all that, they do not cease to deserve disgrace and punishment.

What, then, is the meaning of certain phrases continually uttered by some men? "We must respect consummated facts; we must always accept consummated facts; it is folly to resist consummated facts; it is a wise policy that yields to consummated facts." Far be it from me to assert that all those who establish these maxims, profess the fatal doctrines to which they give rise. We often admit principles, the consequences of which we reject; and point out a certain line of conduct as right, without attending to the abominable maxims in which it originates. In human affairs, good and evil, error and truth are so narrowly separated, and prudence so closely borders on culpable timidity, that in theory, as well as in practice, it is not always easy to remain within the bounds prescribed by reason and the eternal principles of sound morality. If respect for consummated facts is mentioned, perverse men immediately include in it the sanctioning of crime, the spoils of plunder secured to the robber, no hope of restitution left to the victims, and a gag put upon their mouths, to stifle their complaints. Others, I am aware, have no such design in making use of these words, but are the dupes of a confusion of ideas, arising from their not having distinguished between moral principles and public expediency. On this point, therefore, we must distinguish and define, which I will do in a few words.

The simple consummation of a fact does not render it legitimate; and, consequently, it is not on this account alone worthy of respect. The robber who has stolen does not acquire a right to the thing stolen; the incendiary who reduces a house to ashes is no less deserving of punishment, of being forced to make reparation, than if he had been arrested in the attempt. This is so evident and clear, that it cannot be called in question. To assert the contrary, is to become the enemy of all morality, of all justice, of all right; and to proclaim the exclusive rule of force and cunning. Consummated facts, appertaining to social and political order, do not change their nature; the usurper, who seizes upon the crown of his lawful predecessor; the conqueror, who, by mere force of arms, has subdued a nation, does not thereby acquire a right to its possession; the government, which by gross iniquities has despoiled entire classes of citizens, exacted undue contributions, abolished legitimate rights, cannot justify its acts by the simple fact of its having sufficient strength to execute these iniquities. That is equally evident; and if there is here any difference at all, the crime is only the greater, from the greater gravity and extent of the wrongs committed, and of the scandal given to the public. Such are the principles of sound morality—individual morality, social morality; morality of the whole human race; immutable, eternal morality.

Let us now examine the question of public expediency. In some instances, a consummated fact, in spite of all its injustice, all its immorality and atrocity, acquires such an ascendency, that by not accepting it, or by being determined to destroy it, we should let loose a train of troubles and commotions, and perhaps without effect. Every government is bound to respect justice, and to act in such a manner that its subjects may also respect it; but it should not command what will not be obeyed, when it is deprived of the means of enforcing obedience. In such a case, we should not commit an injustice by not attacking the illegal interests, or by not endeavoring to obtain redress for the victims; the government, in such a case, may be compared to a man who, beholding robbers loaded with the fruit of their theft, is without the means of forcing them to make restitution. If you suppose an impossibility, what does it avail to say that the government is not a single individual, but a defender of all legitimate interests? No one is bound to impossibilities.

Observe, also, that this remark applies not only to a physical impossibility, but also to a moral one. Whenever, therefore, the government possesses the material means of obtaining reparation, a moral impossibility will be constituted, when the employing of those means would cause serious difficulties to the state, endanger the public peace, or sow the seeds of future insurrection. Order and public interest require the preference, for these are the primary objects of all government; consequently, that which cannot be accomplished without endangering them, ought to be considered as impossible. The application of these doctrines will always be a question of prudence, that cannot be subjected to any general rule. Depending as it *does* upon a thousand circumstances, it cannot be decided upon abstract principles; but by the consideration of existing facts, duly appreciated and considered by political tact. Such is the case of the respect due to consummated facts; the injustice of these facts is apparent; but we must not overlook their force. Not to attack them is not, necessarily, to sanction them. The legislator is bound to diminish the evil as far as possible; but not to risk an aggravation of it by attempting an impracticable reparation. As it is particularly injurious to society for great interests to remain insecure, and uncertain for the future, just means must be adopted, which, without occasioning complicity in the evil, may prevent the dangers of a doubtful situation, resulting from injustice itself. A just policy does not sanction injustice; but a wise policy never despises the importance of established facts. If such facts exist, and appear indestructible, it tolerates them; but without affording them the sanction of its participation or approval. Acting with dignity, it makes the best of difficulties; and in some sort allies the principles of eternal justice with the views of public expediency. We have a very striking case in point, which will place this matter in the clearest possible light. After the great evils, and the enormous acts of injustice perpetrated during the French Revolution, what possibility was there of making a complete reparation? In 1814, could every thing be restored to the position in which it stood in 1789? The throne overturned, all social distinctions levelled, and property broken up; who could reconstruct the ancient social edifice? No one.

Such is the respect to be entertained for consummated facts, which might be more properly termed *indestructible* ones. To illustrate my idea still further, I will give it a very simple exemplification. A proprietor, driven from his possessions by a powerful neighbor, has not the means of repossessing himself of them. He has neither wealth nor influence; and his spoliator abounds in both. If he have recourse to force, he will be vanquished; if to the tribunal, he will lose his cause; what, therefore, is he to do? To negotiate for an accommodation, to obtain what he can, and be resigned to his fate. This is all that can be said; and it is remarkable, that such are the principles adopted by governments. History and experience teach us, that consummated facts are respected when they are indestructible; that is, when they possess in themselves sufficient force to make them respected; in any other case, they are not so. And nothing is more natural. Whatever is not founded upon right, can only be maintained by force. (32)

CHAPTER LVI.

HOW THE CIVIL POWER MAY BE LAWFULLY RESISTED.

FROM what has been said in the foregoing chapters it follows, that it is allowable to resist illegitimate power by force. The Catholic religion does not enjoin obedience to governments existing merely *de facto*; for morality does not admit a mere fact, unsupported by right and justice. However, when power is in itself lawful, but in its exercise tyrannical, does our religion prohibit, in every instance, resistance by physical force; so that not to resist at all, forms a part of her dogmas? Is insurrection never allowable, in any supposition, for any motive? Although I have already eliminated many questions, it is necessary to draw here a fresh distinction, in order to fix exactly the point at which dogma ends, and opinions begin. It is evident, in the first place, that an individual has no right to kill a tyrant on his own authority. The Council of Constance, in its 15th session, condemned the following proposition as heretical: "Any vassal or subject may and should, lawfully and meritoriously, kill any tyrant. He may even, for this purpose, avail himself of ambushes, and wily expressions of affection or adulation; notwithstanding any oath or pact imposed upon him by the tyrant; and without waiting for the sentence or order of any judge." "Quilibet tyrannus potest et debet licite et meritorie occidi per quemcumque vassallum suum vel subditum, etiam per clanculares insidias, et subtiles blanditias vel adulationes, non obstante quocumque præstito juramento, seu confœderatione factis cum eo, non expectata sententia vel mandato judicis cujuscumque."

But does this decision of the Council of Constance constitute a prohibition of every kind of insurrection? No; it speaks of the murder of a tyrant by any particular individual; but every case of resistance is not maintained by a single individual; neither is it the aim of every insurrection to destroy a tyrant. This doctrine only serves to prevent murder, and a train of evils which would overwhelm society if it were established that any individual had a right of his own authority to kill the supreme ruler. Who will venture to accuse this doctrine of being favorable to tyranny? The liberty of the people should not be based upon the horrid right of assassination; the defence of the rights of society should not be confided to the dagger of a fanatic. The attributes of public power are so extensive and various, that their exercise must necessarily and frequently inconvenience some individuals. Man, inclined to extremes and revenge, easily enlarges upon the grievances which he suffers; passing from a particular to a general, he is inclined to look upon those who injure or oppose him as villains. At the slightest shock which he receives from government, he cries out that tyranny is insupportable; the act of arbitrary power, real or imaginary, committed against him, becomes, in his mouth, one of the many iniquities perpetrated, or the commencement of those that are to be. Grant, therefore, to the individual the right of killing a tyrant; proclaim to the people that, to render such an act lawful and meritorious, there is no need of a sentence, or any judicial condemnation; and from that time this horrible crime will become frequent. The wisest, the justest kings will fall victims to the parricidal dagger, or the poisoned cup. You will have furnished no guarantee to the liberty of the people, and you will have exposed the dearest interests of society to dreadful hazards.

The Catholic Church, by this solemn declaration, has conferred an immense service on humanity. The violent death of him who holds the supreme power seldom happens without causing bloodshed and great commotion. It provokes measures of suspicious precaution, easily converted into tyranny. It follows, then, that any crime instigated by excessive hatred of tyranny contributes to establish it in a form still more absolute and cruel. Modern nations should feel grateful to the Catholic Church for having established this sacred and saving principle. A person must be possessed of very mean sentiments, or very ferocious instincts, not to appreciate it, or to regret the bloody scenes of the Roman Empire and the barbarian monarchy. We have seen, and we still see, powerful nations delivered up to dreadful troubles, by the neglect of this Catholic maxim. The history of the last three centuries, and the experience of this, prove that this august precept of the Church was given to the people in anticipation of the dangers which were threatening them. In it we find no flattery for kings; for they are not the only ones benefited by it; it is a general proposition, including all others, whatever be their titles, who exercise supreme authority, whatever be the form of government, from the Russian autocrat to the most democratical republic.

It is worthy of remark, that modern constitutions, proceeding from the bosom of revolutions, have universally rendered a solemn homage to this Catholic maxim; they have declared the person of the monarch *sacred and inviolable.* What does this mean, but that this person should be placed under an impenetrable safeguard? You reproach the Catholic Church with placing a sort of shield before the person of kings, and yet you yourselves declare that person inviolable. The anointing of kings you ridicule, and yet you yourself declare that the king is sacred. Since you are forced to imitate the Church, her dogmas and her discipline must have contained an eternal truth, and high political principles; with this difference, however, that you represent as the work of the will of man what she esteems the work of the will of God. But if supreme power makes a scandalous abuse of its faculties, if it outsteps its just bounds, if it tramples under foot fundamental laws, if it persecutes religion, corrupts morality, outrages public dignity, attacks the honor of citizens, exacts illegal and disproportionate contributions, alienates national property, dismembers provinces, inflicts death and ignominy upon the people: in such cases, does Catholicity also prescribe obedience? does it forbid resistance? does it command subjects to remain tranquil, like a lamb in the claws of a wild beast? May there not exist, either in an individual, or in the principal bodies, or in the most distinguished classes of society, or in the entire mass of the nation, somewhere, in fine, the right of opposing, of resisting, after all means of mildness, representation, counsel, and entreaty have failed? In such disastrous circumstances, does the Church leave the people without hope, and tyrants without restraint?

In such extremities, certain very renowned theologians think that resistance is allowable; but the dogmas of the Church do not descend to these details. The Church abstains from condemning the opposite doctrines. In such extreme circumstances, non-resistance is not a dogmatical prescription. The Church has never taught such a doctrine; if any one will maintain that she has, let him bring forward a decision of a Council or of a Sovereign Pontiff to that effect. St. Thomas of Aquin, Cardinal Bellarmin, Suarez, and other eminent theologians, were well versed in the dogmas of the Church; and yet, if you consult their works, so far from finding this doctrine in them, you will find the opposite one. Now the Church has not condemned them, she has not confounded them with those seditious writers in whom Protestantism abounds, nor with modern revolutionists, who are continually disturbing social order. Bossuet and other authors of repute differ from St. Thomas, Bellarmin, Suarez; and this gives credit to the opposite opinion, but does not convert it into a dogma. Upon certain points of the highest import, the opinions of the illustrious Bishop of Meaux suffered contradiction; and we know that upon this case of an excess of tyranny, the Pope at another period was acknowledged to possess faculties which Bossuet refuses him.

The Abbé de Lamennais, in his impotent and obstinate resistance to the Holy see, adduced the doctrines of St. Thomas, and those of some other theologians, pretending that to condemn his own works was to condemn schools hitherto held irreproachable. (*Affaires de Rome.*) The Abbé Gerbet, in his excellent refutation of M. de Lamennais, after having very judiciously remarked, that the Sovereign Pontiff's object in reproving modern doctrines was, to prevent a renewal of the errors of Wickliffe, observes, at the epoch of this heresiarch's condemnation, the doctrines of St. Thomas and of other theologians were well known, and that, nevertheless, no one believed that they were included in the condemnation. The excellent author of this refutation deemed this sufficient to deprive M. de Lamennais of the shield under which he sought to defend and cover his apostacy; and for this reason, he abstains from drawing a parallel between the two doctrines. In fact, this reflection alone is sufficient to convince any judicious man that the doctrines of St. Thomas bear no resemblance to those of M. de Lamennais. It may, however, be useful to give in few words a comparison of the two doctrines. At the present time, and in these matters, it is very proper to know, not only that these doctrines differ, but likewise wherein they differ. M. de Lamennais' theory may be stated in the following terms: A natural equality among men, and, as necessary consequences, 1. Equality of rights, political rights included; 2. The injustice of every social and political organization not establishing this equality completely, as is the case in Europe and in the whole universe; 3. Expediency and legitimacy of insurrection, to destroy governments, and change social organization; 4. Abolition of all government, as the object of the progress of the human race.

The doctrines of St. Thomas on the same points may be thus expressed: *A natural equality among men;* that is to say, an essential equality, but exclusive of physical, intellectual, and moral gifts—an equality among men in the eyes of God—an equality in their destination, inasmuch as they are all created to enjoy God—an equality of means, inasmuch as they are all redeemed by Christ, and may all receive His grace; but exclusive of the inequalities which it may please God to establish by gifts of grace and glory. 1. *An equality of social and political rights.* According to the holy doctor, such an equality is impossible. He rather supports the utility and legitimacy of certain hierarchies; the respect due to those established by law; the necessity of there being some to command and others to obey; the obligation of being subject to the established laws of the country, whatever be the form of government; the preference for monarchical governments. 2. *The injustice of every social and political organization not establishing a complete equality.* St. Thomas looks upon this as an error opposed to reason and to faith. Nay, more; not only is it true that the inequality founded upon the very nature of man and of society is an effect and punishment of original sin, in as far as it entails upon man injury or inconvenience; but, according to the holy Doctor, this inequality would have existed among men even in a state of innocence. 3. *Expediency and legitimacy of insurrection, to destroy governments, and to change the social organization.* An erroneous and fatal opinion. We ought to submit to legitimate governments;

it is expedient even to tolerate such as make an improper use of their power; we must exhaust every means of entreaty, of counsel and representation, before we have recourse to others. We can only appeal to force in the greatest extremities, on rare occasions, and then only under many restrictions, as will be seen elsewhere. 4. *Abolition of all government, as the object of the progress of the human race.* An absurd proposition—a dream that cannot be realized. The necessity of government in every society; arguments founded upon the nature of man; analogies from the human body, from the very order of the universe; the existence of government even in a state of innocence. Such are the doctrines of De Lamennais and St. Thomas respectively. Let the reader compare them, and judge for himself.

It is impossible to adduce the words of the holy Doctor—they would fill the volume. Should any reader wish to consult them himself, let him read, in addition to the passages inserted in this work, the whole treatise, *De Regimine Principum*, the commentaries on the Epistle to the Romans, and those passages of the *Summa* in which the holy Doctor treats of the soul, of the creation of man, of the state of innocence, of the angels and of their hierarchy, of original sin and its effects, and, above all, his valuable Treatise on Laws and that on Justice, in which he discusses the origin of the right of property and of inflicting punishments. After that he will be convinced of the truth of what I have just advanced; he will then see the injustice of M. de Lamennais in attempting to make the illustrious writers and saints venerated on our altars the accomplices of his apostacy. In grave and delicate matters confusion produces error, the enemies of truth are interested in spreading darkness, in establishing general and vague propositions susceptible of various interpretations. They seek with anxiety a text favorable to some one of the numerous interpretations that are possible, and proudly exclaim, "How unjust it is in you to condemn us; what we maintain was asserted centuries ago, by the most respected and celebrated writers." The Abbé de Lamennais must have reckoned in a singular manner upon the credulity of his readers, to think of making them believe that there was no honest man to be found at Rome capable of informing the Pope, that in condemning the doctrines of the apostle of revolution, he was condemning also those of the angel of the schools, and other distinguished theologians. It is possible that M. de Lamennais never read the authors except in haste and in fragments, but many persons at Rome have spent their lives in studying them.

We are not ignorant of the violent declamations of Luther, Zwinglius, Knox, Jurieu, and other leaders of Protestantism, to stir up the people to revolt against princes; we are not ignorant of the gross and violent invectives made use of by these sectaries to excite the multitude. Catholics look upon such extravagances with horror. In like manner, they look with dread upon the anarchical doctrine of Rousseau, establishing that "the clauses of the *social contract* are so determined by the very nature of the act, that the *least modification* of them would render them *vain and null;* so that every one then resumes his former rights and regains his natural liberty. (*Contrat Social*, l. i. c. 6.) The doctrine of the theologians above cited does not contain this fruitful germ of insurrection and disaster; but, on the other hand, they are not found timid and pusillanimous in the last extremities. They preach up resignation, patience, and longanimity; but there is a point at which they stop and exclaim, *Enough*. If they do not advocate insurrection, they do not prohibit it; it would be in vain to require them to teach as a dogmatical truth the obligation of not resisting in extreme cases. They cannot teach the people to consider as a dogma what they do not acknowledge as such. It is not their fault if the tempest bursts, if the roaring waves arise; no other hand can control them than that of God, who rides upon the north wind and sports with the tempest.

For many centuries there has been inculcated in Europe a doctrine much criticised by those who do not understand it, the intervention of the Pontifical authority between the people and their sovereigns. This doctrine was nothing less than Heaven descending as an arbiter and judge, to put an end to the disputes of the earth.

The temporal power of the Popes has served as a wonderful theme to the enemies of the Church to create alarm, and declaim against Rome; but this power is no less an historical fact and a social phenomenon, which has filled with admiration the most renowned men of modern times, including some Protestants. The Scriptures make it a duty for slaves to obey their masters, even when they are oppressive and unjust. All that can be inferred from this is, that a prince, by the simple fact of his being wicked, does not lose his authority over his subjects, which condemns beforehand the errors of those who make the right of commanding dependent upon the sanctity of its possessor. Such a principle is anarchical, and incompatible with the existence of every society. When it is once established, power remains unsafe and tottering; every disturber declares all those divested of authority whom he may deem culpable. But our question is of a different nature, and the opinion of theologians cited by us has nothing to do with this error. These theologians also on their part advocate obedience to rulers, even though they be oppressive and unjust; they also condemn insurrection, when founded on no other pretext than the vices of persons exercising supreme power; they do not admit that any abuse of power justifies resistance; but they do not consider that they impugn the sacred text by admitting that in extreme cases it is allowable to place a barrier against the excesses of a tyrant. "If governments do not lose their power by the simple fact of their being wicked, how," it will be said, "can we conceive resistance to them lawful?" This is certainly not allowable, so long as they do not outstep the bounds of their faculties; but when they do so, their commands, as St. Thomas says, are rather acts of violence than laws. "No one has the right of judging the supreme power." This is true; but above this power exist the principles of reason, morality, religion. Power, although supreme, is bound to the execution of its promises, to keep its oaths. Society is not formed upon the model of Rousseau's ideal *contract*; but there exist, in certain cases, real pacts between the rulers and the people, to which both are bound to adhere.

In the celebrated *Catholic Proclamation to his pious Majesty Philip the Great, King of Spain and Emperor of the Indies by the Counsellors and the Council of One Hundred of the city of Barcelona*, in 1640, an epoch so profoundly religious that the Counsellors quote, as a high title of glory, *the zeal of the Catalonians for the Catholic faith, the devotion of the Catalonians to our lady the Blessed Virgin and the most holy Sacrament*;—at that time, which pride and ignorance have so often taxed with fanaticism, these counsellors said to the king, "Besides civil obligation, the customs, constitutions, and acts of the court of Catalonia are binding on conscience, and to violate them would be a mortal sin; for the prince has no right to annul a contract; it is made freely, but cannot be revoked without injustice. If a contract is not subject to the civil law, it is subject to the law of reason; and although the prince may be the master of the laws, the contracts he makes with his vassals are inviolable, for in making them he is a mere individual, and the vassal acquires a right equal to his. A contract, in fine, should be made between equals. Hence, as the vassal cannot be unfaithful to his lord, the latter, in like manner, is bound to keep the promise he has made by solemn engagement; and indeed, the rupture of a pact ought least of all to be expected on the part of a prince. If the word of a king is law, that word given in a solemn contract is still more binding. (*Catholic Proclamation*, sect. 27.) The courtiers urged the monarch to measures of coercion to reduce the Catalonians to submission; the Castilian army was preparing to enter the principality. In this extremity, after exhausting all means of representation and entreaty, the counsellors thus expressed themselves: "Finally, men who have vowed an inveterate hatred against the Catalonians have been so successful in their continual persuasions, that the uprightness and equity of your majesty have been turned from the means of peace and tranquillity proposed by us, and which should have been admitted, were it only on the grounds of experience; and to fill up the cup of their malice, they now lay your majesty under an obligation of oppressing the principality still further, by sending an army to sack and pillage wherever the caprice of the soldier may lead him; which would place this country in a position to say (were it not for the love it has borne, still bears, and ever will bear to your majesty) that such a breach of sworn faith would leave it free, a thing of which the province is unwilling to think, and prays God to avert. Nevertheless, the principality knows from experience that these soldiers have neither respect nor pity for any thing or person, married women and innocent virgins, temples, or God Himself, images of the Saints or the sacred vessels of our churches, nay, even the blessed Sacrament has twice this year been committed to the flames by these soldiers. *The principality is, therefore, everywhere in arms to defend, in such an urgent and irremediable extremity, fortune, life, honor, liberty, home, laws, and above all the sacred temples, the sacred images, and the holy Sacrament of the altar (be the same for ever praised). In such a case, the holy theologians do not merely affirm that resistance is lawful, but still further, that all persons, whether lay or clerical, may take up arms to avert the evil; that both secular and ecclesiastical property may and ought to contribute to the defence; that the nations invaded may, as the cause is universal, unite, confederate, and form juntas with a view to prevent such evils.*" (§ 36)

Such was the language addressed to kings, at a time when religion predominated over all things. The counsellors, according to the usage of the time, took care to make marginal notes of the sources of their information; and we are not aware that their doctrines have ever been condemned as heretical. These doctrines cannot, without manifest dishonesty, be confounded with those of many Protestants and modern revolutionists. A cursory perusal of these writings will enable any one to discover how widely they differ. By maintaining that it is not allowable in any case, in the greatest extremities, not even when the most precious and sacred interests are at stake, to offer resistance to the civil power, the thrones of kings are thought to be strengthened; for it is generally kings that are spoken of. But it should be remembered, that this doctrine affects every other supreme power, under every form of government. Since the texts of Scripture recommending obedience "to the powers that be," do not allude to kings only, but to all supreme powers, without exception or distinction, it follows that resistance cannot in any case be offered to the president of a republic. Will it be said that the faculties of a president are determined? Are not the faculties of a king also determined? Are there not, in absolute governments, laws fixing the limits of these faculties? And is not this the distinction constantly employed by the supporters of monarchy to repel the errors of their adversaries, who confound monarchy with despotism? "But," it will be said, "the president of a republic is only temporary." And what if he were perpetual? Besides, the faculties are neither increased nor diminished by the simple fact of their having to last a long or short period. If a council, a man, a family, is invested with a certain right, by virtue of a certain law; with certain restrictions, but with certain contracts and oaths; such a council, such a man or such a family is bound to adhere to the oath taken, whatever be the extent of its duration, temporary or perpetual. Such are the principles of natural right; so certain and simple, that they cannot present any difficulty.

Theologians, even those most attached to the Sovereign Pontiff, teach a doctrine which we must notice here, on account of the analogy it bears to the point under discussion. It is known that the Pope, when speaking *ex cathedra*, is acknowledged to be infallible, but not as a simple individual; and that, in this latter capacity, he might fall into heresy. In this case, theologians are of opinion that he would forfeit his dignity; some maintaining that he ought to be deposed, others that his deposition is the consequence of his having fallen from the faith. Whichever of these opinions be admitted, in this case resistance would become allowable, for this reason, that the Pope would have shamefully departed from the object of his institution, would have trampled on the basis of the laws of the Church, which is her dogmas, and would consequently have nullified the promises and oaths of obedience made to him. Spedalieri, in adducing this argument, observes, that kings are certainly not of higher rank than Popes,—that power has been granted to both *in ædificationem non in destructionem;* adding, that if Sovereign Pontiffs authorize this doctrine with relation to themselves, temporal sovereigns cannot object to its application to them.

It is strange that the monarchical zeal of Protestants and incredulous philosophers imputes to the Catholic religion as a crime, that she has allowed it to be maintained within her bosom, that, in certain cases, the subject may be released from his oath of allegiance; whilst other philosophers of the same school reproach it with having sanctioned despotism by its *detestable doctrine of non-resistance*, as Dr. Beatty expresses it. *The direct, indirect, and declaratory powers of the Popes* have served as an admirable bugbear to intimidate kings; the dangerous principles of theological works formed an excellent pretext for raising the cry of alarm, for representing Catholicity as a nest of seditious maxims. The hour of revolutions was struck,—circumstances were changed,—fresh necessities arose, and men adapted their language to the times. The Catholics, a short time before seditious and regicidal, were then declared abettors of despotism, fulsome adulators of civil power. Recently, the Jesuits, leagued with the infernal policy of Rome, were everywhere undermining thrones, to establish on their ruins the universal monarchy of the Pope; but the secret of this horrid plot was discovered, and fortunately so, for the world was otherwise about to experience a frightful catastrophe. But now that the Jesuits are expelled, and are expiating their crimes in exile, the French Revolution, the prelude to so many others, breaks out, and the aspect of affairs changes immediately. Protestants and unbelievers, the *supporters of ancient discipline, the zealous adversaries of the abuses of the Court of Rome*, fully comprehending the new situation of affairs, hasten to conform to it. From that moment, the Jesuits, the Catholics, the Pope, are no longer seditious or tyrannicides, but Machiavelian supporters of tyranny, enemies of the liberty of the people; and just as a league had been supposed to exist between the Jesuits and the Pope for the foundation of a universal theocracy, there is now discovered, thanks to the investigations of these eminent philosophers and *strict, incorruptible Christians, an infamous pact between the Pope and kings* to oppress, enslave, and degrade the unfortunate human race.

The answer to this enigma may be thus briefly expressed. So long as kings maintain their power and the peaceable possession of their thrones, so long as Providence restrains the tempest, and the monarch, raising his proud head towards heaven, commands the people with a lofty air, the Catholic Church does not flatter him. "Thou art dust," she says to him, "and into dust thou shalt return; power was given thee not unto destruction, but unto edification;

thy faculties are great, but not boundless. God is thy judge, as well as that of the lowest of thy subjects." The Church is then accused of insolence; and if any theologian should venture to investigate the origin of civil power, to point out, with generous freedom, the duties to which this power is subject; to write, in a word, with prudence upon public right, but without servility, the Catholics are then declared seditious. But the tempest bursts, thrones are overturned, revolution prevails, spills the blood of the people in torrents, cuts off royal heads, and all in the name of liberty. The Church says: "This is no liberty, but a succession of crimes; the fraternity and equality which I have taught, were never your orgies and guillotines." The Church then becomes a vile flatterer; her words, her actions, have indubitably revealed that the Sovereign Pontiff is the surest anchor of despotism; it has been proved that the Court of Rome has been polluted by an infamous pact. (33)

CHAPTER LVII.

POLITICAL SOCIETY IN THE SIXTEENTH CENTURY.

WE have already seen what has been the conduct of the Christian religion with respect to society; that is to say, that not caring whether such or such political forms were established in a country, she has ever addressed herself to man, seeking to enlighten his understanding and to purify his heart, fully confident that when these objects were attained, society would naturally pursue a safe course. This is sufficient to obliterate the reproach imputed to her of being an enemy to the liberty of the people.

Protestantism has certainly never revealed to the world a single dogma which exalts the dignity of man, nor created fresh motives of consideration and respect, or closer bonds of fraternity. The Reformation cannot, therefore, boast of having given the least impetus to the progress of modern nations; it cannot, consequently, lay the least claim to the gratitude of the people in this respect. But as it frequently happens that people lay aside main points and set a great value on appearances; and as Protestantism has been supposed to accord much better than Catholicity with those institutions in which it is usual to find guarantees for a high degree of liberty; we must draw a parallel. Besides, we cannot omit it without betraying an ignorance of the genius of this age, and authorizing the suspicion that Catholicity cannot derive any advantage from such a comparison. In the first place, I will observe, that those who look upon Protestantism as inseparable from public liberty do not in this respect agree with M. Guizot, who cannot certainly be accused of any want of sympathy for the Reformation. "In Germany," says this celebrated publicist, "far from demanding political liberty, it has accepted, I should not like to say political servitude, *but the absence of liberty.*" (*Hist. Gén. de la Civil. en Eur.* leç. 12.)

I quote M. Guizot, because in Spain we are so accustomed to translations, because we Spaniards have been led to suppose, that the best thing for us is to believe foreigners on their bare word; because amongst us, in questions of importance, it is necessary to have recourse to foreign authorities; and hence, a writer who appears to slight such authorities, exposes himself to the risk of being treated as an ignoramus, as one behind the age. Besides, with a certain class of writers, the authority of M. Guizot is decisive. In fact, a multitude of publications have appeared amongst us bearing the title of "Philosophy of History," whose authors it is quite clear, have used the works of that French writer as their text-books. Is this assertion, that Protestantism is the natural bulwark of liberty, true or false, accurate or inaccurate? What do history and philosophy teach us on this point? Has Protestantism advanced the popular cause, by contributing to the establishment and development of liberal forms of government? To place the question in its true light, and discuss it thoroughly, we must take a view of the state of Europe at the close of the fifteenth century, and at the beginning of the sixteenth. It is incontestable that individuals and society were then making rapid progress towards perfection. We have sufficient evidence of this fact in the wonderful march of intellect at this period, in the numerous measures of improvement effected at that epoch, and in the better organization everywhere introduced. This organization is doubtless still imperfect; but it is nevertheless such as cannot be likened to that of former times. If we carefully examine into the state of society at that epoch, as represented either in the writings or in the events of the time, we shall observe a certain restlessness, anxiety, and fermentation, which, while they indicated the existence of vast wants not yet satisfied, were evidence also of a tolerably distinct knowledge of those wants. Far from discovering in the men of that period a contempt or forgetfulness of their rights and dignity, or any discouragement and pusillanimity at the sight of obstacles, we find them abounding in foresight and ingenuity, swayed by lofty and sublime thoughts, fired with noble sentiments, and animated with intrepid and ardent courage. The progress of European society at that epoch was very rapid; three very remarkable circumstances contributed to render it so: 1. The introduction of the whole body of men to the rank of citizens, as a necessary consequence of the abolition of slavery and the decline of feudality; 2. The very nature of civilization, in which every thing advances together and abreast; 3. In fine, the existence of a means for increasing its development and rapidity—this means was the art of printing. To make use of a physico-mathematical expression, we may say, that the amount of motion must have been very considerable, since it was the product of the mass by the rapidity, and that the mass, as well as the rapidity, were then very considerable.

This powerful movement, which proceeds from good, is in itself good, and is productive of good, is, however, accompanied by inconveniences and perils; it raises flattering hopes, but it also inspires apprehensions and fears. The people of Europe are an ancient people, but they may be said to have become young again; their inclinations, their wants, urge them to great enterprises; and they enter upon them with the ardor of an impetuous and inexperienced young man, feeling in his breast a great heart, and in his head the lively spark of genius. In this situation, a great problem presents itself for solution, viz., to find the most proper means for directing society without impeding its progress; and for conducting it by a way free from precipices to the objects of its aim, *intelligence, morality, felicity*. A slight glance at this problem startles us at its immense extent; so numerous are the objects it embraces, the relations it bears, the obstacles and difficulties with which it is beset. Considering this question attentively, and comparing it with man's weakness, the mind is ready to lose courage and despond. The problem, however, exists, not as a scientific speculation, but as a real and urgent necessity. In such a case, society is like individuals; it attempts, essays, and makes efforts to get clear of the difficulty as well as possible.

Man's civil state improves daily; but to maintain this improvement, and to perfect it, requires a means: and this is the problem of *political forms*. What ought these forms to be? And, above all, what elements can we make use of? What is the respective force of these elements? What are their tendencies, their relations, their affinities? How shall they be combined? *Monarchy, Aristocracy, Democracy*—these three powers present themselves at the same time to dispute for the direction and government of society. They are certainly not equal, either in force, means of action, or in practical intelligence; but they all command our respect, they have all pretensions to a preponderance more or less decisive, and none of them are without the probability of obtaining it. This simultaneons concurrrence of pretensions, this rivalship of three powers so different in their nature and aim, forms one of the leading features of this epoch. It is, as it were, in a great measure the key to the principal events; and, in spite of the various aspects presented by this feature, it may be signalized as a general fact among all the civilized portion of the nations of Europe.

Before proceeding further in our examination of this subject, the mere indication of such a fact suggests the reflection, that it must be very incorrect to say that Catholicity has tendencies opposed to the true liberty of the people; for we see that European civilization, which, during so many ages, was under the influence and guardianship of this religion, did not then present one single principle of government exclusively predominating. Survey the whole of Europe at this period, and you will not find one country in which the same fact did not exist. In Spain, France, England, Germany, under the names of Cortes, States-General, Parliaments, or Diets; the same thing everywhere, with the simple modifications which necessarily result from circumstances adapted to each people. What is very remarkable in this case is, that if there be a single exception, it is in favor of liberty; and, strange to say, it exists precisely in Italy, where the influence of the Popes is immediately felt. The names of the Republics of Genoa, Pisa, Sienna, Florence, Venice, are familiar to all. It is well known that Italy is the country in which popular forms at that period gained most ground, and in which they were put in practice, whilst in other countries they had already abandoned the field. I do not mean to say that the Italian Republics were a model worthy of being imitated by the other nations of Europe. I am well aware that these forms of government were attended with grave inconveniences; but since so much is said of *spirit* and *tendencies*, since the Catholic Church is reproached with her affinity to despotism, and the Popes with a *taste* for oppression, it is well to adduce those facts which may serve to throw some doubt upon certain authoritative assertions, adduced as so many philosophico-historical dogmas. If Italy preserved her independence in spite of the efforts of the Emperors of Germany to wrest it from her, she owed it in a great part to the firmness and energy of the Popes.

In order to comprehend fully the relations which Catholicity bears to political institutions, in order to ascertain what degree of affinity it bears to such and such forms, and to form a correct idea of the influence of Protestantism in this respect over European civilization, we must examine carefully and in detail each of the elements claiming preponderance. When we examine them afterwards in their relations with each other, we will ascertain, as far as possible, where the truth lies in this shapeless mass. Every one of these three may be considered in two ways: 1. According to the ideas formed of them at the period we are speaking of; 2. According to the interests these elements represent, and the part they play in society. We must lay particular stress upon this distinction, without which we should expose ourselves to the commission of serious errors. In fact, the ideas which were entertained upon such or such principles of government did not coincide with the interest represented by this same element, and with the part it acted in society; and although it is clear that these two things must have had very close relations with each other, and could not be disengaged from a real and reciprocal influence, yet it is most certain that they differ considerably, and that this difference, the source of very various considerations, shows the subject in points of view quite dissimilar.

CHAPTER LVIII.

MONARCHY IN THE SIXTEENTH CENTURY.

THE idea of monarchy has ever existed in the bosom of European society, even at the time when the least use was made of it; and it is worthy of remark, that at the time when its energy was taken away, and it was destroyed in practice, it still retained its force in theory. We cannot say that our ancestors had any very fixed notions upon the nature of the object represented by this idea; nor can we wonder at it, since the continual variations and modifications which they witnessed must have prevented them from forming any very correct knowledge of it. Nevertheless, if we peruse the codes in places where monarchy is treated of, and if we consult the writings which have been preserved upon this matter, we shall find that their ideas on this point were more fixed than might have been imagined. By studying the manner of thinking of this period, we find that men in general were almost destitute of analytical knowledge, being more erudite than philosophical; so much so, that they scarcely ventured to express an idea without supporting it by a multitude of authorities. This taste for erudition, which is visible at the first glance into their writings—a mere tissue of quotations—and which must have been very natural, since it was so general and lasting, had very advantageous results; not the least of which was the uniting of ancient with modern society, by the preservation of a great number of records and memorials, which, had it not been for this public taste, must have been destroyed, and by exhuming from the dust the remains of antiquity about to perish. But, on the other hand, it produced many evils; amongst others, a sort of stifling of thought, which could no longer indulge in its own inspirations, although they may have been more happy than the ancient ones on some points.

However it may be, such is the fact: on examining it in relation to the matter under discussion, we find that monarchy was represented at that time as one single picture, in which there appeared at the same time the kings of the Jews and the Roman emperors, whose features had been corrected by the hand of Christianity. That is to say, the principles of monarchy were composed of the teachings of Scripture and the Roman codes. Seek every where the idea of emperor, king, or prince, you will always find the same thing, whether you look for the origin of power, its extent, its exercise, or its object. But what ideas were entertained of monarchy? What was the acceptation of this word? Taken in a general sense, abstractedly from the various modifications which a variety of circumstances gave to its signification, it meant, *the supreme command over society, vested in the hands of one man, who was to exercise it according to reason and justice.* This was the leading idea, the only one fixed, as a sort of pole, round which all other questions revolved. Did the monarch possess in himself the faculty of making laws without consulting general assemblies, which, under different names, represented the different classes of the kingdom? From the moment that we propose this question we come upon new ground. We have descended from theory to practice; we have brought our ideas into contact with the object to which they are to be applied. From that moment, we must allow, every thing vacillates and becomes obscure; a thousand incoherent, strange, and contradictory facts pass before our eyes; the parchments upon which are inscribed the rights, liberties, and laws of the people give rise to a variety of interpretations, which multiply doubts and increase difficulties. We see, in the first place, that the relations of the monarch with the subject, or, more properly speaking, the mode in which government should be exercised, was not very well defined. The confusion from which society was emerging was still felt, and was inevitable in an aggregation of heterogeneous bodies, in a combination of rival and hostile elements; that is, we discover an embryo, and consequently it is impossible as yet to find regular and well-defined forms.

Did this idea of monarchy contain any thing of despotism, any thing that subjected one man to the dominion of another by setting aside the eternal laws of reason and justice? No; from the moment that we touch upon this point we discover a new horizon, clear and transparent, upon which objects present themselves distinctly, without a shade of dimness or obscurity. The answer of all writers is decisive: Rule ought to be conformable to reason and justice; if it is not, it is mere tyranny. So that the principle maintained by M. Guizot, in his *Discours sur la Democratie moderne*, and in his *History of Civilisation in Europe*, viz. that the will alone does not constitute a right; that laws, to be laws, should accord with those of eternal reason, the only source of all legitimate power;—that this principle, I say, which we might imagine to be newly applied to society, is as ancient as the world. Acknowledged by ancient philosophers, developed, inculcated, and applied by Christianity, we find it in every page of jurists and theologians.

But we know what this principle was worth in the monarchies of antiquity, and also in our own days in countries where Christianity has not yet been established. Who, in such countries, presumes continually to remind kings of their obligation to be just? Observe, on the contrary, what is the case among Christians: the words 'reason' and 'justice' are constantly in the mouth of the subject, because he knows that no one has a right to treat him unreasonably or unjustly; and this he knows, because Christianity has impressed him with a profound idea of his own dignity, because it has accustomed him to look upon reason and justice, not as vain words, but as eternal characters engraven on the heart of man by the hand of God, perpetually reminding man that, although he is a frail creature, subject to error and to weakness, he is, nevertheless, stamped with the image of eternal truth and of immutable justice. If any one should question the truth of what I have advanced, it will suffice, to convince him, to remind him of the numerous texts previously cited in this work, and in which the most eminent Catholic writers bear testimony to their manner of thinking on the origin and faculties of civil power.

So much for ideas; as for facts, they vary according to times and countries. During the incursions of the barbarians, and so long as the feudal system prevailed, monarchy remained much beneath its typical idea; but during the course of the sixteenth century, matters assumed a different aspect. In Germany, France, England, and Spain, powerful monarchs were reigning, who filled the world with the fame of their names; in their presence aristocracy and democracy bowed with humility; or if by chance they ventured to raise their heads, it was only to suffer still greater degradation. The throne, it is true, had not yet attained that ascendency of power and importance which it acquired in the following century; but its destiny was irrevocably fixed—power and glory awaited it. Aristocracy and democracy might have labored to take part in future events; but it would have been labor in vain for them to attempt to appropriate them. A fixed and powerful centre was essential to European society, and monarchy completely satisfied this imperative necessity. The people understood and felt it; hence we find them eagerly grasping at this saving principle, and placing themselves under the safeguard of the throne.

The question is not, therefore, whether or not the throne ought to exist, or whether it ought to preponderate over aristocracy and democracy: these two questions have been already resolved. At the commencement of the sixteenth century, its existence and preponderance were already necessary. The question to be resolved is, whether the throne ought so decisively to have prevailed, that the two elements, aristocracy and democracy, should be erased from the political world; whether the combination which had hitherto existed was still to exist: or, whether these two elements should disappear; whether monarchical power should be absolute. The Church resisted royal power when it attempted to lay hands upon sacred things; but her zeal never carried her so far as to depreciate, in the eys of the people, an authority which was so essential to them. On the contrary, besides continually giving to the power of kings a more solid basis, by her doctrines favorable to all legitimate authority, she endeavored to give them a still more sacred character by the august ceremonies displayed at their coronations. The Church has been sometimes accused of anarchical tendencies, for having energetically struggled against the pretensions of sovereigns; by some, on the contrary, she has been reproached with favoring despotism, because she preached up to the people the duty of obedience to the *lawful* authorities. If I mistake not, these accusations, so opposite to each other, prove that the Church has neither been adulatory nor anarchical; she has maintained the balance even, by telling the truth both to kings and their subjects.

Let the spirit of sectarianism seek, on all sides, historical facts, to prove that the Popes have attempted to destroy civil monarchy by confiscating it to their own profit. But let us bear in mind what the Protestant Müller says, that the Father of the faithful was, during the barbarous ages, a tutor sent by God to the European nations; and let us not be astonished to find that differences have sometimes occurred between him and his pupils. To discover the intention which dictated these reproaches against the Court of Rome, relative to monarchy, we need only reflect upon the following question. All writers consider as a great benefit the creation of a strong central authority, and yet circumscribed within just limits that it may not abuse its power; they laud to the skies every thing tending, directly or indirectly, among all the nations of Europe, to establish such an authority. Why, then, when speaking of the conduct of Popes, do they attribute to a pretended taste for despotism the support which they give to royal authority, whilst they qualify with anarchical usurpation their efforts to restrain, upon certain points, the faculties of sovereigns? The answer is not difficult. (34)

CHAPTER LIX.

THE ARISTOCRACY OF THE SIXTEENTH CENTURY.

The aristocracy, as including the privileged portion of society, comprehended two classes very distinct in their origin and nature, the nobility and the clergy. Both abounded in power and riches; both were placed far above the people, and were important wheels in the political machine. There was, however, this remarkable difference between them, that the principal basis of the power and grandeur of the Clergy was religious ideas—ideas which circulated throughout society, which animated it, gave it life, and consequently insured for a long time the preponderance of the ecclesiastical power; whilst the grandeur and influence of the nobles rested solely upon a fact necessarily transient, viz. the social organization of the epoch—an organization which was becoming rapidly modified, since the people were then struggling to liberate themselves from the bonds of feudalism. I do not mean, that the nobles did not possess legitimate rights to the power and influence which they exercised; but merely that the principal portion of these rights, even supposing them founded upon the most just laws and titles, was not necessarily connected with any of the great conservative principles of society—those principles which invest with an immense force and ascendency the person or class which in any way represents them. But we touch here upon a subject little investigated, and upon the explanation of which depends the comprehension of great social facts. It is well, therefore, to develope it fully, and to examine it attentively.

Of what was monarchy the representative? Of a principle eminently conservative of society—a principle which has withstood all the attacks of theories and revolutions, and to which have been attached, as the only anchor of safety, those very nations in the bosom of which democratical ideas were diffused, and in which liberal institutions originated. This is one of the causes why monarchy, even in its most calamitous times, triumphed over its disasters. Feudal pride, and the unsettled state of the times, with the agitation of rising democracy, united to oppress it; scarcely was its power distinguishable amid the troubled waves of society, like the broken mast of a shipwrecked vessel. But, even at this time, we find the ideas of force and power bound to those of monarchy. Regal dignity was trampled under foot and outraged in various ways, but still held sacred and recognised as inviolable. Theory was not in accordance with practice; the idea was more forcible than the fact which it expressed: but we need not be astonished at this phenomenon, since such is always the character of ideas producing great changes. They are, at first, merely visible in society; they spread, take root, and penetrate into all institutions; time continues to prepare the way; and if the idea is just and moral, if it point to the satisfaction of a want, the moment at length comes in which facts give way, the idea triumphs, and bends and humbles all before it. This was the case, in the sixteenth century, with regard to monarchy; under one form or another, with greater or less modifications, it was actually essential to the people, as it is still; and for this reason it naturally prevailed over all its adversaries, and survived all accidents.

With respect to the clergy, we need not attempt to show that they were the representatives of the religious principle—a real social necessity for all the nations of the earth, when taken in its general sense; and a real social necessity for the nations of Europe, when taken in its Christian sense.

We have already seen that the nobility could not be compared either to monarchy or to the clergy, since they were destitute of the high principles represented by each of these bodies. Extensive privileges, and the ancient possession of great estates, with the guarantee of the laws and customs of the time; glorious traditions of military feats, pompous names, titles, and escutcheons of illustrious ancestors; such were the insignia of the lay aristocracy. But nothing of all this had any direct and essential relation with the great wants of society. The nobility depended upon a particular organization, necessarily transient; they were too nearly allied to a law purely positive and human, to be able to reckon upon a long duration, or to flatter themselves with success in all their pretensions and exigencies. It will be objected, perhaps, that the existence of an intermediate class between the monarch and the people is an essential necessity, acknowledged by all publicists, and founded upon the very nature of things. In fact, we have seen that in nations from which the ancient aristocracy has disappeared, a new one has been formed, either by the course of events or by the action of governments. But this objection is not applicable to the question in the point of view under which I consider it. I do not deny the necessity of an intermediate class; I merely affirm that the ancient nobility, such as it was, did not contain elements to ensure its duration, since it was liable to be replaced by another, as it has been in effect. The classes of the laity acquire their political and social importance from a superiority of intellect and force; this superiority no longer existing in the nobility, its fall was inevitable. At the beginning of the sixteenth century the throne and the people daily acquired a greater ascendency; the former became the centre of all social forces, and the people were constantly enriching themselves by industry and commerce. With regard to learning, the discovery of printing, as it became general, prevented it from being henceforth the exclusive patrimony of any particular class.

It was evident, therefore, that the nobility perceived, at this epoch, their ancient power escaping, and possessed no other means of preserving a part of it than to struggle to preserve the titles which it had given them. Unfortunately for them, their wealth was daily decreasing, not only from the dilapidations occasioned by luxury, but also from the extraordinary increase of non-territorial riches; the profound changes wrought in the value of every thing by means of the re-organization of society and the discovery of America caused immovable property to lose much of its importance. If the force of landed property was gradually diminishing, the rights of jurisdiction were marching still more rapidly towards their ruin. On one hand, these rights were opposed by the power of kings; and, on the other, by municipalities and other centres of action possessed by the popular element; so that, in spite of the most profound respect for acquired rights, and merely by allowing things to take their ordinary course, the ancient nobility was inevitably sunk to that point of depression in which it now exists. This could not happen to the clergy. Despoiled of their wealth, entirely or partially deprived of their privileges, there still remained for them the ministry of religion. No one could exercise this ministry without them; which was sufficient to insure them great influence in spite of all commotions and changes.

CHAPTER LX.

ON DEMOCRACY.

SUCH was the situation of Europe during the centuries preceding the sixteenth, that it appears difficult to find for democracy a well-defined place in political theories. Stifled by the established powers, deprived as yet of the resources which, in time, gave it the ascendency, it was natural it should be almost unobserved by politicians. It was in reality very feeble; and it was not, therefore, surprising that, owing to the influence of reality over ideas, theorists should regard the people merely as an abject portion of society, unworthy of honors or happiness, and fit only to labor and to serve. It is, however, worthy of remark, that ideas from that time took a new direction; it may even be affirmed that they were infinitely more elevated and more generous than facts. This is one of the most convincing proofs of the intellectual development that Christianity had operated amongst men—one of the most unexceptionable testimonies in favor of that profound sentiment of reason and justice which it had deposited in the heart of society. Now these elements were not to be stifled by events the most unfavorable, nor by the rudest shocks; for they were supported upon the very dogmas of religion, which still remain firm, in spite of all commotion, as an immovable axis remains fixed in the midst of broken machinery.

In perusing the writings of this epoch, we find established, as an indubitable fact, the right of the people to the administration of justice; they were not to be irritated by any vexatious regulations; the public imposts were to be equally divided; no one was to be forced to do any thing contrary to reason or the well-being of society: that is to say, these writers acknowledged and established all those principles upon which were to be based the laws and customs destined one day to produce civil liberty. This is so true, that, in proportion as circumstances permitted, these principles were rapidly and extensively developed;

vast and numerous applications were immediately made of them; and civil liberty took such deep root among the people of modern Europe, that it has never been erased from their bosoms; and we see it preserved in forms of absolute government as well as in the mixed forms.

To complete my demonstration, that the ideas in favor of the people proceeded from Christianity, I will adduce a reason which appears to me decisive. The philosophy adopted by the schools of that period was that of Aristotle. Aristotle's authority was of great weight; he was called by an autonomasia, *the Philosopher*; a good commentary of his works was considered the highest point to be attained in these matters. And yet, so far as the relations of society were concerned, the doctrines of the Stagyrite were not adopted; Christian writers took a higher and more generous view of mankind. Aristotle's degrading doctrines upon man born to servitude, destined to this end even by nature, anterior to all legislation; his horrible doctrines upon infanticide; his theories, which at one blow deprived all those who professed the mechanical arts of the title of citizen; in a word, those monstrous systems, which the ancient philosophers unconsciously learned from the society which surrounded them, were utterly rejected by Christian philosophers. The man who had just perused Aristotle's work on Politics took up his Bible, or the works of the Fathers: the authority of Aristotle was great, but that of the Church was still greater; the works of the pagan philosopher must be interpreted piously, or abandoned; in either case the rights of humanity were saved, and this was an effect of the preponderating force of the Catholic faith.

The system of castes most forcibly contributes to arrest the development of the popular element, by condemning the majority of the people of a country to a state of perpetual abjection and slavery. In this system, honors, riches, and command are confined and transferred from father to son; a barrier separates men from each other, and ends in causing the most powerful to be considered as belonging to a superior class of beings. The Church has ever opposed the introduction of so fatal a system, and to apply the word *caste* to the clergy would betray an ignorance of its meaning. On this subject M. Guizot has done ample justice to the cause of truth. He expresses himself in the following manner in the fifth lecture of his *Histoire générale de la Civilisation en Europe*: "With regard to the mode of formation and transmission of power in the Church, there is a word," says he, "much used in speaking of the Christian clergy, and which I am under the obligation of discarding; it is the word *caste*. The body of ecclesiastical magistrates has often been called a caste. This expression is not correct; the idea of heirship is inherent in that of *caste*. Travel over the world; take all those countries in which the system of *castes* exists, in India, in Egypt, you will find everywhere the *caste* essentially hereditary; it is the transmission of the same situation, of the same power, from father to son. Where heirship does not exist, there is no caste, there is a corporation; the spirit of corporate bodies has its inconveniences, but it is very different from that of castes. The word caste cannot be applied to the Christian Church. The celibacy of the clergy has prevented them from becoming a caste. You perceive already the consequences of this difference. A system of *caste*, and the existence of hereditary succession, inevitably involve the idea of privileges. The very definition of a *caste* implies privileges. When the same functions, the same powers, become hereditary in the same families, it is evident that privileges follow, and that no one can acquire such functions and powers unless he is born to them. This, in fact, is what has taken place: wherever religious government has fallen into the hands of a caste, it has become a privilege; no one has been permitted to enter it but the members of families belonging to the caste. Nothing of this has ever occurred in the Christian Church; on the contrary, she has ever maintained the equal admissibility of all men, whatever their origin, to all her functions, to all her dignities The ecclesiastical state, particularly from the fifth to the twelfth century, was open to all. The Church was recruited from all ranks, from the inferior as well as from the superior,—more commonly even from the inferior. She alone resisted the system of castes; she alone maintained the principle of equality of competition; she alone called all legitimate superiors to the possession of power. This is the first grand result naturally produced by the fact that she was a corporation, and not a caste."

This splendid passage of the French writer completely vindicates the Catholic Church from the reproach of exclusiveness with which it had been attempted to stain her; it presents to me also the opportunity of making some reflections upon the beneficial effects of Catholicity upon the development of civilization in favor of the plebeian classes. We are not ignorant of the numerous declamations against religious celibacy which have proceeded from the mouths of the pretended defenders of the rights of humanity; but is it not strange that they forget, as M. Guizot justly observes, that celibacy is exactly what has prevented the Christian clergy from becoming a caste? Let us examine, in fact, what would have been the case on the contrary supposition. At the time to which we refer, the ascendency of religious power was unlimited, and the wealth of the Church considerable; that is to say, she possessed every thing necessary for enabling a caste to establish its preponderance and stability. What further was needful, therefore? Hereditary succession, nothing more; and this would have been established by the marriage of the clergy. What I here affirm is no vain conjecture, it is a positive fact, which I can render evident by bringing forward historical proof. From certain remarkable regulations in ecclesiastical legislation, we learn that it required all the energy of pontifical authority to prevent this succession from being introduced. Every thing, in fine, tended to such an end; and if the Church preserved itself from such a calamity, it was owing to the horror which she always entertained of this fatal custom. Read the 17th chapter of the first book of the Decretals of Gregory IX.; the pontifical regulations therein contained prove, that the evil here spoken of presented alarming symptoms. The pope makes use of the strongest terms possible to be found: "*Ad enormitatem istam eradicandam,*" "observato Apostolici rescripti decreto *quod successionem in Ecclesia Dei hereditariam detestatur.*" "*Ad extirpandas successiones a sanctis Dei Ecclesiis studio totius sollicitudinis debemus intendere.*" "Quia igitur in Ecclesia successiones, et in prælaturis et dignitatibus ecclesiasticis *statutis canonicis damnantur.*" These expressions, and others of a like nature, clearly show that the danger was already considered serious, and justify the prudence of the Holy See in reserving to itself the exclusive right of granting dispensations on this point.

It required the continual vigilance of the pontifical authority to prevent this abuse from making daily progress, for it was urged on by the most powerful feelings of nature. Four centuries had elapsed since these measures had been taken, and yet we find that, in 1533, Pope Clement VII. was obliged to restrict a canon of Alexander III. in order to prevent grave scandals, grievously lamented by the pious Pontiff. Suppose that the Church had not opposed such an abuse with all her force, and that the custom had become general; bear in mind also, that in those ages of the grossest ignorance, the privileged classes were every thing, and the people had scarcely a civil existence; and see whether there would not have been formed an ecclesiastical caste along with that of the nobility, and whether both, united by the bonds of family and common interest, would not have opposed an invincible obstacle to the ulterior development of the plebeian class, plunging European society into that degradation in which Asiatic society now exists. Such would have been the consequence of the marriage of the clergy, if the pretended reform had been realized a few centuries sooner. When it came, at the beginning of the sixteenth century, it found European society in a great measure formed; it had to contend against an adult, who could not easily be made to forget his ideas and change his habits. What has actually taken place may lead us to infer what would have taken place. In England, a close alliance was formed between the lay aristocracy and the Protestant clergy; and what is very remarkable, we have seen, and we still see, in that country, something resembling castes, with the modifications which must necessarily ensue from the great development of a certain kind of civilization and liberty at which Great Britain has arrived.

If the clergy in the middle age, establishing their perpetuity by hereditary succession, had constituted themselves an exclusive class, would not the aristocratic alliance of which we are speaking have been a natural consequence? And who would thenceforth have been able to break this alliance? The enemies of the Church interpret all her discipline, and even some of her dogmas, by imputing to her ulterior designs; and hence they consider the law of celibacy as the result of an interested design. It was easy to see, however, that if the Church had entertained worldly views, she might have selected as a model those priests of other religions who have formed a separate, preponderating, and exclusive class, for which the severity of duty did not form a brazen wall against the enjoyments of nature. Europe, it will be objected, is not Asia. This is true; but the Europe of our days, and even that of the sixteenth century, is no longer the Europe of the middle ages. In those centuries, in which none but the clergy could read and write, and in which knowledge was exclusively in their possession, had they wished to plunge the world into darkness, they had only to extinguish the torch with which they were enlightening it. It is also very certain, that celibacy has given to the clergy a moral force and ascendency which they could not have attained by any other means. But this only proves that the Church has preferred moral to physical power, and that the spirit of her institutions is to act by exercising a direct influence upon the intelligence and heart of man. Now, is it not eminently praiseworthy to use all possible moral means for the direction of mankind? Is it not an honor to the Catholic clergy to have accomplished, by institutions severe against themselves, what they might have realized in part by systems indulgent to their own passions and degrading to others? Oh, we see here the work of Him who will remain with His Church till the end of the world.

Whatever may be the value of these reflections, it cannot be contested, that where Christianity has not existed, the people have been the victims of a small number, whose contempt and insults have been the only recompense of their labors. Consult history and experience; the fact is general and constant; there is not an exception even in those ancient republics so vaunted for their liberty. Under liberal forms, slavery existed; a slavery properly so called for some men; a slavery glossed over with fine appearances for that turbulent multitude who served the caprice of the Tribunes, and believed they were exercising their sublime rights by condemning to ostracism or to death the most virtuous citizens. It has sometimes happened that, among the Christians, appearances were not in favor of liberty, but things were so in reality, if we understand by the word liberty the empire of just laws, aiming at the well-being of the multitude, and founded upon the consideration and profound respect due to the rights of mankind. Observe the grand phases of European society at the time when Catholicity exclusively predominated. With various forms, distinct origins, different inclinations, they all follow the same course; all tend to favor the cause of the multitude; whatever has this for its aim, endures; whatever has not, perishes. Whence comes it that this was not the case in other countries? If evident reasons and palpable facts, moreover, did not manifest the salutary influence of the religion of Jesus Christ, so remarkable a coincidence would suffice to suggest grave reflections to those, who meditate upon the cause and character of the events which change or modify the destiny of mankind. Let those who represent Catholicity as the enemy of the people, point out to us a single doctrine of the Church sanctioning the abuses under which the people were suffering, or the injustice which oppressed them. Let them show us whether, at the commencement of the sixteenth century, when Europe was under the exclusive domination of the Catholic religion, the people were not as far advanced as they could be, considering the ordinary course of things. They certainly did not possess so much wealth as they have since acquired, and their knowledge was not so extensive as in modern times; but is the progress which has been made in this respect attributable to Protestantism? Was not the sixteenth century commenced under more favorable auspices than the fifteenth, and the latter under better auspices than the fourteenth? This proves that Europe, under the shield of Catholicity, continued in a progressive march; that the cause of the multitude suffered no prejudice from the influence of Catholicity; and that if great ameliorations have since been effected, they have not been a consequence of what is called the Reformation.

It is the development of industry and commerce that has most powerfully contributed to elevate modern democracy, by diminishing the preponderance of the aristocratic classes. I do not touch upon the events which took place in Europe before the appearance of Protestantism; but I see at a glance that, far from impeding such a movement, Catholic doctrines and institutions must have favored it, since, under their shield and protection, the manufacturing and mercantile interests were surprisingly developed. No one is ignorant of their astonishing success in Spain: and we cannot attribute this progress to the Moors; for Catalonia, subject exclusively to the Catholic influence, evinced such activity, prosperity, and intelligence in industry and commerce, that we could scarcely believe to what a state of perfection they had arrived, did not unexceptionable documents bear ample testimony to the fact. Read the *Historical Memoirs of the Marine, Commerce, and Arts of the ancient City of Barcelona*, by our celebrated Capmany. May we not account it an honor to belong to this Catalonian nation, whose ancestors displayed such zeal in all things, never allowing other nations to surpass them in the march of civilization and improvement? Whilst this phenomenon was advancing in the south of Europe, the association of the Hanseatic towns, the origin of which is lost in the centuries of the middle ages, was created in the north. It obtained in time such an amount of power as to measure its force with that of kings. Its rich factories, established all over Europe, and favored with many advantageous privileges, elevated it to the rank of a real power. Not satisfied with the power which it enjoyed in its own country, and in Sweden, Norway, and Denmark, it extended it to England and Russia. London and Novogorod admired the splendid establishments of those intrepid merchants, who, by means of their wealth, obtained exorbitant privileges; who had their own magistrates, and formed an independent state in the centre of foreign countries.

It is very remarkable that the Hanseatic league selected religious communities as their model, in all that concerned the system of life of the clerks in their counting-houses. Their clerks ate in common, had common dormitories, and none of them were allowed to marry. Any one of them transgressing this law, forfeited his rights to remain a member or a citizen of the Hanseatic Confederation. In France, the manufacturing classes were also organized, the better to resist the elements of dissolution existing in their bosom; and this change, so fruitful in results, is entirely due to a king venerated upon the altars of the Catholic Church. *The Establishment for the Trades of Paris* gave a powerful impetus to the industrial classes, by augmenting their intelligence and improving their morals; and whatever were the abuses that crept into that organization, it cannot be denied that St. Louis satisfactorily supplied a great want, by organizing the trades in the best manner possible, considering how little progress had at that time been made. What shall we say of Italy, containing within its bosom the powerful republics of Venice, Florence, Genoa, and Pisa? It is difficult to conceive what progress industry had made in this peninsula, and, as a natural consequence, what a development the democratical element received. Had the influence in itself been so oppressive, had the breath of the Roman court been fatal to the progress of the people, is it not evident that its effects would have been particularly felt in those countries which were the scene of its actions? Whence comes it, then, that whilst a great part of Europe was groaning under feudal oppression, the middle class, whose only title to nobility was the fruit of their intelligence and labor, appeared in Italy so powerful, so brilliant and flourishing? I will not contend that this development was attributable to the Popes; but, at least, we must grant that they never opposed it.

Now, if we observe a similar phenomenon in Spain, and particularly in Aragon, where the Pontifical influence was great; if the same thing is observable in the north of Europe, inhabited by people whom Catholicity alone has civilized; if, in fine, the same phenomenon is realized, with greater or less rapidity, in all countries exclusively subject to the belief and authority of the Church, we may conclude that Catholicity contains nothing opposed to the movement of civilization, and that it is not opposed to a just and legitimate development of the popular element.

I cannot think how it is possible for any one who has read history to accord to Protestantism the honor of being favorable to the interests of the multitude. Its origin was essentially aristocratic; and in those countries in which it has succeeded in taking root, it has established aristocracy upon such firm foundations, that the revolutions of three centuries have not been able to overturn it. Witness, for a proof of this, what has taken place in Germany, England, and all the north of Europe. It has been said that Calvinism is more favorable to the democratical element; and that if it had prevailed in France it would have established a system of federative republic in place of monarchy. Whatever may be the value of this conjecture upon a change which would certainly not have been very beneficial to the future prospects of that nation, it is perfectly certain that no other system than that of aristocracy would have been found practicable in France; for circumstances at that period would admit of nothing else; and the aristocrats who were at the head of religious innovation, would admit of no other organization. Had Protestantism triumphed in France, it is probable that the poor of that country, in imitation of their brethren in Germany, would have claimed a share in the rich booty; but they certainly would not have found Calvin's proverbial harshness more advantageous to them than the furious rashness of Luther was to the Germans. It is probable that these wretched villagers, who, according to contemporary writers, had nothing to eat but rye-bread, with no animal food, and slept upon a bundle of straw, with a board for their pillow, would not have felt themselves more comfortable than their brethren in Germany, had they thought proper to participate in the effects of the new doctrines. In this case, they would not have been punished, but exterminated, like their brethren beyond the Rhine. In England, the sudden disappearance of the monasteries produced pauperism. Their property having fallen into the hands of laymen, the religious being driven from their abodes, the poor who subsisted upon the alms of these holy establishments were left without the means of subsistence. And observe, that the evil was not temporary; it has continued to our own days, and is now one of the greatest evils afflicting Great Britain. I am aware that almsgiving is said to encourage indolence; but it is very certain that England, with her poor-laws and her legal charity, contains a far greater number of destitute poor than Catholic countries. It will be difficult to convince me, that to let people die of hunger is a good means of developing the popular element. Protestantism must have contained something very repulsive to the democrats of that period, since we find it rejected in Spain and Italy, the two countries in which the people enjoyed the greatest share of prosperity and rights. And this becomes still more worthy of attention, when we remark that religious innovation took root wherever the feudal aristocracy predominated. Look, it will be said, at the United Provinces; but this example only proves that Protestantism, determined to find supporters, willingly took part with the mal-contents. If Philip II. had been a zealous Protestant, the United Provinces would probably have alleged that they were unwilling to remain any longer subject to an heretical prince. These provinces were for a long time under the exclusive influence of Catholicity, and yet they were prosperous; the popular element was developed in their bosom, without meeting any obstacle on the part of religion. Exactly at the beginning of the sixteenth century they made the discovery, that they could no longer prosper without abjuring the faith of their ancestors. Observe the geographical position of the United Provinces; see them surrounded by reformists offering to assist them; and you will find in political considerations the reason which you may seek in vain in imaginary affinity between the Protestant system and the interests of the people. (35)

CHAPTER LXI.

ON THE VALUE OF THE DIFFERENT POLITICAL FORMS—CHARACTER OF MONARCHY IN EUROPE.

THE enthusiasm enkindled in Europe in latter times, has cooled down by degrees; experience has shown that a political organization not in accordance with the social organization is of no advantage to a nation, but rather overwhelms it with evil. Men also understand, and not without difficulty, simple as the matter is, that political systems should be regarded solely as a means of ameliorating the condition of the people, and that political liberty, to be at all rational, must be made a medium for the acquisition of civil liberty. Amongst enlightened men, these are ordinary ideas; fanaticism for such or such political forms, considered abstractly from their civil results, is now abandoned as a thing denoting ignorance, or as a discreditable means hypocritically made use of by the ambitious, devoid of real merit, whose only way to fortune is disturbance and revolution. It cannot, however, be denied that, considered as simple instruments, certain political forms, such as mixed, moderate, constitutional, or representative governments, or whatever they be designated, have acquired in some countries consideration and solidity; and that, in many countries, any principle which might be considered opposed to representative forms, and only favorable to absolute ones, would be repudiated beforehand. Civil liberty has become necessary to the people of Europe; and in some nations the idea of this liberty is so identified with that of political liberty, that it is difficult to explain how civil liberty can exist under an absolute monarchy. We must therefore examine what are the tendencies of the Catholic and those of the Protestant religions. I will proceed so as to discover these tendencies by an impartial analysis of historical facts. Never, perhaps, as M. Guizot felicitously observes, were the natural course of things, and the hidden ways of Providence, less understood. Wheresoever we meet not with assemblies, elections, urns, and votes, we imagine power must be absolute, and liberty unprotected. I have an express design in making use of the word tendencies, because it is clear that Catholicity has no dogma on this point—it does not pronounce upon the advantages of any particular form of government. The Roman Pontiff acknowledges equally as his son the Catholic seated upon the bench of an American Assembly, and the most humble subject of the most powerful monarch. The Catholic religion is too prudent to descend upon any such ground. Emanating from heaven itself, she diffuses herself, like the light of the sun, over all things, enlightens and strengthens all, and is never obscured or tarnished. Her object is to conduct man to heaven, by furnishing him on his passage with great assistance and consolation upon earth; she ceases not to point out to him eternal truths; she gives him in all his affairs, salutary counsels; but the moment we come to mere details, she has no obligation to impose, no duty to enjoin. She impresses upon his mind her sacred maxims of morality, admonishing him never to depart from them; like a tender mother speaking to her son, she says to him, "Provided you depart not from my instructions, do what you consider most expedient."

But is it true that there is in Catholicity at least a tendency to obstruct liberty? What has been the result of Protestantism in Europe with regard to political forms? In what has it corrected or ameliorated the work of Catholicity? In the centuries preceding the sixteenth, the organization of European society was so complicated, the development of all the intellectual faculties had arrived at such a point, the contention of interests was so lively, in fine, every nation was so enlarged by the successive agglomeration of provinces, that a central, forcible, energetic power, predominating over all individual pretensions and those of classes, was indispensable to the peace and prosperity of the people. Europe had no other hope for peace; for wherever there exists a great number of various, opposite, and all powerful elements, a regulating action is necessary to prevent violent shocks, to calm excessive ardor, to moderate the rapidity of motion, to prevent a continual war, which would necessarily lead to destruction and chaos. This immediately gave to the monarchical principle a fresh and irresistible impulse; and as this impulse was felt in every European country, even in those possessing republican institutions, it evidently resulted from causes that lay deep in the social condition of the times. At the present day there is not a publicist of any note who would question these truths. During the last half century, in fact, events have occurred well calculated to demonstrate that in Europe monarchy is something more than *usurpation* and *tyranny*. In the very countries in which democratical ideas have taken root, it has been found necessary to modify them, and in some degree to depart from them, in order to preserve the throne, which is regarded as the best safeguard of the great interests of society.

It is the infirmity of all things human, however good and salutary they may be, always to bring with them an accompaniment of inconveniences and evils. Monarchy could not evidently be exempt from this general rule; in other words, the great extension of force and power was sure to produce abuse and excess. The European nations are not of a sufficiently patient character, nor of a sufficiently moderate temperament, to endure with resignation all sorts of disorders. The European entertains so profound an idea of his dignity, that he cannot comprehend the quietism of the Oriental nations, living in the midst of degradation, bowing their slavish heads before the despot who despises and oppresses them. Hence, whilst we in Europe acknowledge and feel the necessity of a very strong power, we have always endeavored to take measures for restraining and preventing the abuse of this power. Nothing exalts so much the grandeur and dignity of the European nations as the comparison of them with those of Asia. The latter have no better means of delivering themselves from oppres sion than the assassination of their sovereigns. Whilst the blood of one monarch is still warm, another ascends his throne, trampling with a disdainful foot on the heads of nations as cruel as they are degraded. Not so in Europe; we have always recourse to intellectual means; we have established institutions which lastingly protect the people from oppression and excesses. We cannot deny that our efforts have cost torrents of blood, or affirm that we have always adopted the most expedient means; but on this point Europe, guided by the same spirit as in all other matters, has become anxious to substitute right in the place of mere might. This is no recent problem; it existed when European society was in its infancy, and in these latter times has been overlooked. Great efforts were made many centuries ago to resolve it. Observe how Count de Maistre states his opinions on this difficult problem:

"Although the greatest and most general interest of sovereignty consists in its being just, and although the cases in which it transgresses this condition are incomparably fewer than the others, unfortunately it does, however, frequently transgress it; and the particular character of certain sovereigns may so far augment these inconveniences, that in order to render them supportable, it is necessary to compare them with those which would exist if there were no sovereign. It was therefore impossible that men should not, from time to time, make efforts to secure themselves against the excess of this enormous prerogative; but on this point the world has adopted two widely different systems. *The daring tribe of Japheth has at all times been gravitating* (if we may use the expression) *towards what is termed liberty;* that is, towards that social condition in which the influence of the governing powers is least sensibly felt. Ever jealous of his rights and liberties, the European has sought to preserve them, sometimes by expelling his rulers, and at other times by opposing to them the barrier of law. He has tried every thing, every imaginable form of government, to set himself free from his rulers, or to restrain their power.

"The *immense posterity of Shem and Cham* have pursued another course. From the earliest ages down to our own time they have always said to their fellow-men, *Do whatever you please, and when we are tired we will put you to death.* Besides, they have never been able or willing to comprehend the nature of a republic; the balance of power, all those privileges, all those fundamental laws of which we are so proud, are totally unknown to them. Among them, the richest and most independent man, the possessor of immense movable wealth, absolutely at liberty to transport it whither he pleases, sure, moreover, of entire protection upon European ground, and threatened at home with the rope or the dagger, prefers them, nevertheless, to the misery of dying of ennui among us. But no one will ever think of recommending to Europe the public law of Asia and Africa, so short and clear; but as power in Europe is always so much feared, discussed, attacked, or transferred, since nothing so much wounds our pride as despotic government, the most general European problem is to know *how sovereign power may be restrained without being destroyed.*" (*Du Pape*, liv. ii. chap. 2.)

This spirit of political liberty, this desire of limiting power by means of institutions, did not originate with the French philosophers; before their time and long before the appearance of Protestantism, it was circulating in the veins of the European people. History has left us irrefragable testimonies of this truth. What institutions were deemed suitable for the accomplishment of this object? Certain assemblies, in which the voice of the nation's interests and opinions might be heard—assemblies formed in various ways, and meeting from time to time around the throne to make their complaints and assert their claims. As it was impossible for these assemblies to constitute the government without destroying the monarchy, it was necessary, in one way or another, to secure their influence in state affairs; and I do not see that anything better has hitherto been devised for attaining this object than the right of intervention in the enactment of laws, a right guaranteed to them by another, that may be justly termed the right arm of national representation,—the right of voting the supplies. Much has been written respecting constitutions and representative governments, but this is the essential point. Many and various modifications may be introduced, but in reality all consists in the establishment of the throne as the centre of power and of action, surrounded by assemblies that shall deliberate upon the laws and the taxes.

Does political liberty in this point of view originate in Protestant ideas? Is it under any obligation to them? Has it, in fine, any reproach against Catholicity? I open the works of Catholic writers anterior to Protestantism, in order to ascertain their sentiments on this subject, and I find that they take a clear view of the problem to be solved. I examine rigidly whether they teach anything opposed to the progress of the world, to the dignity or the rights of man; I examine, again, whether they bear any affinity to despotism or to tyranny, and I find them full of sympathy for the progress of enlightenment and of mankind, inflamed with noble and generous sentiments, and zealous for the happiness of the multitude. I remark, indeed, that their hearts swell with indignation at the mere names of tyranny and despotism. I open the records of history; I study the opinions and customs of the nations, and the predominating institutions; I behold on all sides nothing but *fueros*, privileges, liberty, cortes, states-general, municipalities, and juries. All this appears in the greatest confusion, but I see it; and I am not astonished to discover an absence of order, for it is a new world just arisen from chaos. I ask myself if the monarch possesses in himself the faculty of making laws; and upon this question I very naturally find variety, uncertainty, and confusion; but I observe that the assemblies representing the different classes of the nation take part in the enactment of the laws. I ask whether they have any interference in the great affairs of the state; and I find it stated in the codes that they are to be consulted on all grave and important affairs: I see monarchs frequently observing this precept. I ask whether these assemblies possess any guarantees for their existence and their influence; and the codes inform me by the most decisive texts, and a thousand facts are at hand to convince me, that these institutions were deeply rooted in the customs and manners of the people.

Now what was then the predominating religion? Catholicity. Were the people much attached to religion? So much so that the spirit of religion predominated over all. Did the clergy possess great influence? Very great. What was the power of the Popes? It was immense. Where do you find the clergy attempting to extend the power of kings to the prejudice of the people? Where are the pontifical decrees against such or such forms? Where are the measures and plans of the Popes for the restriction of one single legitimate right? No reply. Then I say indignantly, Europe, under the influence of Catholicity, arose from chaos to order, civilization advanced at a firm and steady pace, the grand problem of political forms engaged the attention of men of wisdom, questions of morality and laws were receiving a solution favorable to liberty, and yet the influence of the clergy was never greater even in temporal matters, and the power of the Popes was in every sense quite colossal.

What! one word from the Sovereign Pontiff would have smitten unto death every form of popular government; and yet such forms were receiving a rapid development. Where, then, is the tendency of the Catholic religion to enslave the people? Where the infamous alliance between kings and Popes to oppress and harass the people, to establish on the throne a ferocious despotism, and to rejoice under its gloomy shades over the misfortune and tears of mankind? When the Popes had a quarrel with any kingdom, was it usually with the king or the people? When it was necessary to oppose a firm front against tyranny and oppression, who stood forward more promptly or more firmly than the Sovereign Pontiff? Does not Voltaire himself admit that the Popes restrained princes, *protected the people*, put an end to the quarrels of the time by a wise intervention, reminded both kings and people of their duties, and hurled anathemas against those enormities which they could not prevent? (Quoted by M. de Maistre, *Du Pape.*)

It is very remarkable that the Bull *In Cœna Domini*, which created so much alarm, contains in its fifth article an excommunication against *"those who should levy new taxes upon their estates, or should increase those already existing beyond the bounds marked out by right."* The spirit of deliberation, so common even at this period, and which formed so singular a contrast with the tendency to violent measures, arose in a great measure from the example given by the Catholic Church during so many centuries. In fact, it is impossible to point out a society in which more assemblies have been held, combining in them every thing distinguished by science and virtue. General, national, provincial Councils and diocesan synods are to be met with in every page of the Church's history. Such an example, exposed during centuries to the view of the people, could not fail to influence and affect customs and laws. In Spain the greatest part of the Councils of Toledo were also national congresses; whilst the episcopal authority performed its functions in them, watching over the purity of dogmas, and providing for the wants of discipline, the great affairs of the state were also discussed in them in harmony with the secular power. In them were enacted those laws which are still an object of admiration to modern observers. The utopias of Rousseau are now fallen into complete disrepute among the best publicists. Representative governments are no longer to be defended as a means of bringing the general will into action, but as an instrument, through the medium of which reason and good sense may be consulted, which would otherwise remain dispersed throughout the nation. Legislative assemblies are now represented to us, in works upon constitutional law, as the foci in which all knowledge serving to throw light on the difficulties of public affairs may be concentrated; they are held up to us as the representatives of all legitimate interests, as the organ of all reasonable opinions, the voice of all just complaints, a channel of perpetual communication between governors and their subjects, a measure of justice in the laws, a means of rendering the laws respectable and venerable in the eyes of the people; in short, as a permanent guarantee that a government, never consulting its own interests, should study only public utility and expediency. At a time when we are informed in such fine terms what these assemblies ought to be, not what they are, it will not be uninteresting to refer to the Councils; for we see at a glance that the Councils must in a certain manner explain the nature and spirit, and point out the motives and aim, of political assemblies.

I am aware of the fundamental differences existing between these two assemblies; men who receive their powers from popular election cannot, in fact, be placed in the same rank as those who have been appointed by the Holy Ghost to govern the Church of God; neither can the monarch, who derives his right to the throne from the fundamental laws of the nation, be confounded with that rock upon which the Church of Christ is built. I grant also that, whether with regard to the subjects discussed in the Councils, or with regard to the persons engaged in these discussions, and to the extension of the Church over the whole earth, there must necessarily be a great dissimilarity between the Councils and political assemblies, with respect to the epoch of their being assembled, and the mode of their organization and of their proceedings. But we are not here about to imagine an ingenious parallel, and to seek with subtilty resemblances which do not exist; my only aim is to show the influence which the lessons of prudence and maturity given for so long a time by the

Church must have exercised upon political laws and customs. If we consult the annals of the nations of antiquity, or those of modern times, we shall discover that all deliberative assemblies are composed of persons who have a right to sit in them by a regulation stated in the laws. But to admit into them a man of knowledge, simply because he is so, is to pay a noble tribute to merit—to proclaim in the most solemn manner, that the care of ruling the world belongs properly to intelligence. This the Church alone has done.

I make this observation to prove that society is indebted mainly to the Church for the progress it has made in this respect. I will adduce on this point a fact that has not perhaps been sufficiently attended to, but which clearly shows that the Catholic Church was the first to seek out men of talent wherever they were to be found, and unhesitatingly to allow them influence in public affairs. I will not speak of that spirit which forms one of her distinctive characteristics among all other societies, which has ever led her to seek merit, and nothing but merit, and to raise it to the highest functions—a spirit which no one can deny her, and which has eminently contributed to her splendor and preponderance. But it is very remarkable that the influence of this spirit has been felt where, at first sight, it might have been least expected. In fact, it is well known that, according to the doctrines of the Church, no private individual has any right to interfere in the decisions and deliberations of the Councils; hence, however learned a theologian or jurist may be, his knowledge gives him no right whatever to take part in those august assemblies. Nevertheless, it is well known that the Church has ever taken care to call to them men who, whatever might be their titles, excelled most by their talents or their learning. Who does not read with pleasure the list of learned men who, although not Bishops, were present at the Council of Trent?

In modern society, do not talent, wisdom, and genius carry the highest head, command the greatest consideration and respect, and present the best claims to the direction of public affairs, and to the exercise of a preponderating influence? These should know that nowhere have their claims been respected or their dignity acknowledged so well as in the Church. What society, in fact, has ever sought, as the Church has, to elevate them, to consult them in the most important affairs, and to afford them an opportunity of shining in grand assemblies? In the Church, birth and riches are of no importance. If you are a man of high merit, untarnished by misconduct, and at the same time conspicuous by your abilities and your knowledge, that is enough—she will look upon you as a great man, will always show you extreme consideration, treat you with respect, and listen to you with deference. And since your brow, though sprung from obscurity, is radiant with fame, it will be held worthy to bear the mitre, the Cardinal's hat, or the tiara. To speak in the language of the day, I may remark, that the aristocracy of knowledge owes much of its importance to the ideas and discipline of the Church. (36)

CHAPTER LXII.

THE DEVELOPMENT OF MONARCHY IN EUROPE.

A SINGLE glance at the state of Europe in the fifteenth century enables us to discover that such a state of things could not long exist, and that of the three elements claiming preference, the monarchical must necessarily prevail. And it could not be otherwise; for we have always seen that societies, after a long period of trouble and agitation, place themselves at last under the protection of that power which offers them the greatest security and well-being. Beholding, on the one hand, those great feudatories, so proud, so exacting, so turbulent, enemies to each other, and rivals of the king as well as of the people; on the other hand, the commons, whose existence appears under so many different forms—whose rights, privileges, *fueros* and liberties present so various and complex an aspect—whose ideas have no constant and well defined direction;—we conclude at once, that neither were possessed of sufficient force to struggle against the royal power, already acting by a fixed plan and a determinate system, seizing every opportunity which might serve to forward its views. Who is not aware of the sagacity displayed by Ferdinand the Catholic in developing and implanting his prominent idea—that of centralizing power, giving it vigor, and rendering its action forcible and universal; that is, the idea of founding a true monarchy? And why not acknowledge in the immortal Ximenes a worthy and more eminent continuator of this policy? It would be erroneous to consider this as an evil to nations. All publicists agree that it was necessary to give strength and stability to power, and prevent its action from becoming weak or intermittent; but the only representative of real power at that time was the throne. Hence, to fortify and aggrandize royal power was of real necessity; all plans and efforts of man would have failed to place an obstacle in its way. But it remains, nevertheless, to be seen, whether this aggrandizement of royal power outstepped its due bounds; and this is the place for contrasting Protestantism with Catholicity, that we may ascertain which of them was culpable, if either, and to what extent. This is a very important and curious subject, but at the same time one of difficulty and delicacy. In fact, such a change has taken place of late in the meaning of words, the aversion which parties profess for each other is so profound, each one repels with such impetuosity every thing which bears the most remote resemblance to what is esteemed by his adversaries, that it is an arduous undertaking to render the state of the question and the meaning of words comprehensible. I ask one thing of my readers of all opinions; that is, that they will suspend their judgment until they have read the whole of what I have to adduce on this point. If they consent to this, and do not quarrel with the first word that shocks them—in a word, if they have sufficient patience to hear before they judge, I am confident that, if we do not altogether agree, which is impossible amid such a variety of opinions, they will at least grant that I have taken an apparently reasonable view of the subject, and that my conjectures are not altogether unfounded.

I shall commence, in the first place, by completely laying aside the question whether it was advantageous or not to society that, in the greatest part of European monarchies, royal power should have any other limits than those naturally imposed upon it by the state of ideas and customs. This question some will answer in the affirmative, others in the negative; and I need not observe to what party they respectively belong. To many people the word *liberty* is a scandal, just as the term absolute power is with others synonymous with despotism. But what is that liberty which the former repel with so much force? what meaning is attached to this word in their dictionaries? They have witnessed the French Revolution, with its iniquities and frightful crimes, and they have heard it continually crying out for liberty: they have witnessed the Spanish Revolution, with its vociferations of death, and its sanguinary excesses—its injustice, its disdain for every thing that Spaniards had been accustomed to esteem the most valuable and sacred; and yet they have heard the cries of this Revolution also for *liberty*. What was to be expected? Why, what we now witness. They confounded the name of liberty with all sorts of impieties and crimes; and, in consequence, they hated it, they repelled it, they fought against it sword in hand. In vain were they informed that the cortes was an ancient institution; they replied, that the ancient cortes was not like that of their times. In vain were they reminded that our laws ordained the nation's right of interference by its vote on the levying of taxes. They replied: "We are well aware of it; but the nation is not now represented by those who interfere in its affairs; they only avail themselves of this pretended title to enslave both the king and the people." They were told that the representatives of the different classes had formerly the right of intervention in the important affairs of the state. "What class do you represent," they replied; "you who degrade the monarch, insult and persecute the nobility, abuse and plunder the clergy, despising the people, and making their customs and their religious belief a subject for your sneers? What, then, do you represent? Is it the Spanish nation, when you trample on her religion and laws, when you excite social dissolution on all sides, and make blood flow in torrents? How can you call yourselves the restorers of our fundamental laws, when we find nothing either in you or in your acts which marks the true Spaniard; when all your theories, plans, and projects are only miserable copies of foreign books but too well known, while you have forgotten your own language?"

I pray the reader will cast his eyes over the files of the journals, the bulletins of the cortes, and other documents that remain of the two epochs of 1812 and 1820; let him also call to mind the events we have recently witnessed; let him afterwards peruse the records and memorials of anterior epochs,—our codes, our books, every thing, in fine, capable of throwing light upon the character, the ideas, and the customs of the Spanish people; then let him lay his hand upon his heart, and, whatever be his political opinions, let him tell us, upon his honor, if he finds the least resemblance between the past and the present; if he does not, at the very first glance, perceive a striking and violent contrast between the two epochs—a chasm, in fact, to fill up which, I say it with grief, would require heaps of fresh ruins, ashes, dead bodies, and torrents of blood. Were we to place the question beyond the influence of the empoisoned atmosphere of human passions and of bitter recollections, we might, it is true, very well examine the expediency of allowing the royal authority to attain to a growth that set it free from every kind of check or restraint, even in affairs of the most essential importance and in the voting of the government supplies. The question would then have merely a historico-political aspect, could not be confounded with actual practice, and, consequently, would not affect either the interests or the opinions of our time. However that might be, I will not stop to consider or to notice what has been thought and said upon the subject, but will take up the hypothesis, that the disappearance from the body politic, at that time, of every element save the monarchical, was a misfortune to the people, and an obstacle to the progress of true civilization. And whose was the fault? let me ask.

It is remarkable that the greatest increase of royal power in Europe dates precisely from the commencement of Protestantism. In England, from the time of Henry VIII., not only did monarchy prevail, but a despotism so cruel that no vain appearances of impotent forms have availed to disguise its excesses. In France, after the Huguenot war, royal power became more absolute than ever; in Sweden, Gustavus ascended the throne, and from that time kings began to exercise an almost unlimited power; in Denmark, monarchy continued, and became stronger; in Germany, the kingdom of Prussia was formed, and absolute forms generally prevailed; in Austria, the empire of Charles V. arose in all its power and splendor; in Italy, the small republics were fast disappearing, and the people, under some title or another, became subject to princes; in Spain, in fine, the ancient cortes of Castile, Aragon, Valencia, and Catalonia fell into disuse: that is to say, instead of seeing, by the accession of Protestantism, the people take one step towards representative forms, we find, on the contrary, that they rapidly advanced towards absolute government. This is a certain, incontestable fact. Sufficient attention has not perhaps been paid to so singular a coincidence; but it is not the less real, and is certainly of a nature to suggest numerous and interesting reflections. Was this coincidence purely accidental? Was there any hidden connection between Protestantism and the development and definitive establishment of absolutism? I think there was; and I will even add, that, had Catholicism retained an exclusive sway in Europe, the power of the throne would have been gradually diminished—that representative forms would probably not have disappeared altogether—that the people would have continued to take part in national affairs—that we should have been much farther advanced in civilization, much better fitted for the enjoyment of true liberty—and that this liberty would not be associated in our minds with scenes of horror. Yes, the fatal Reformation has given a wrong direction to European society, injured civilization, created necessities that previously had no existence, and opened chasms which it cannot close. It destroyed many elements of good, and consequently produced a radical change in the conditions of the political problem. This I think I can demonstrate.

CHAPTER LXIII.

TWO KINDS OF DEMOCRACY.

There is in the history of Europe one leading fact contained in all its pages, and still visible in our days, viz. the parallel march of two democracies, which, although sometimes apparently alike, are, in reality, very different in their nature, origin, and aim. The one is based upon the knowledge and dignity of man, and on the right which he possesses of enjoying a certain amount of liberty conformable to reason and justice. With ideas more or less clear, more or less uniform, upon the real origin of society and of power, it entertains at least very clear, precise, and fixed ones upon the real object and aim of both. Whether the right of commanding proceeds directly and immediately from God, or whether we suppose it communicated previously to society, and transmitted afterwards to those who govern, it always grants that power is for the common weal, and that, if it does not direct its actions to this end, it falls into tyranny. To privileges, honors, and distinctions of every kind, it applies its favorite touchstone—the public good; whatever is opposed to this, is rejected as noxious; whatever does not tend to promote it, is repudiated as superfluous. Convinced that knowledge and virtue are the only things of real worth, and deserving of consideration in the distribution of the social functions, this democracy requires them to be sought without ceasing, that they may be elevated to the summit of power and of glory; it goes to seek them in the midst of the deepest obscurity. A nobleman, proud of his titles and his heraldry, and boasting of the glorious deeds of his ancestors, without being able to imitate them, is, in its estimation, an object of ridicule; it will allow such a man to enjoy his riches, that the sacred right of property may not be violated; but it will remove from his grasp, by all lawful means, the influence he might derive from the nobility of his blood. In fine, if it takes nobility, birth or riches into consideration, it is not for any intrinsic worth of these advantages, but because they are signs which lead us to expect a more accomplished education, more knowledge and probity.

Full of generous ideas, this democracy, placing the dignity of man in the highest degree, reminding man of his rights, and also of his duties, is indignant at the very name of tyranny. It hates tyranny, condemns it, repels it, and is perpetually employed in discovering the best means for preventing it. Wise and calm, as the inseparable companion of reason and good sense must ever be, it agrees very well with monarchy; but we may rest assured that its desires have generally been, that the laws of the country should, in one way or another, place a restraint upon the excesses of kings. Aware that the rock against which they ran the risk of being wrecked, was the excess of contributions levied upon the people, its favorite idea, which it has never abandoned, even when it was impracticable, has been to restrain the unlimited faculties of power with respect to contributions. Another of its predominating ideas has been to prevent the will of man from prevailing in the formation or application of the laws. It has ever sought to guarantee and secure in some way, that the will should not usurp the place of reason. Such has been the force of this universal desire, that it has been indelibly stamped upon European manners, and the most absolute monarchs have been compelled to gratify it. Hence one thing very worthy of remark is, that the throne has ever been surrounded by respectable counsellors, whose existence was insured either by the laws or by the national customs. These counsellors certainly could not preserve, in all circumstances, the independence necessary for the accomplishment of their object, but they did not fail to be of great service; for their mere existence was an eloquent protest against unjust and arbitrary regulations; it was a noble personification of reason and justice, pointing out the sacred limits ever to be regarded as inviolable by the most powerful monarch. This is also the reason why sovereigns in Europe never exercise themselves the faculty of pronouncing judgment, differing in this respect from the sultans. The laws and customs of Europe energetically repulse this faculty, as fatal to the people as it is to the monarch; and the mere recital of such an attempt would excite public indignation against its author.

The meaning of all this is, that this principle, so much extolled, that it is not the monarch but the law that commands, has been received in Europe for many centuries; it was in full force in all the European nations long before modern publicists emphatically enunciated it. It will be said, perhaps, that if this was the case in theory, it was not so in practice. I do not deny that there were reprehensible exceptions, but the principle was generally respected. As a case in point, let us take the most absolute reign of modern times, with the most unlimited royal power in all its splendor, in its apogee,—the reign in which the king could exclaim with too much pride, but yet with truth, "I am the state"—that of Louis the Fourteenth. It lasted more than half a century, with an astonishing variety and complication of events. How many deaths, confiscations, and banishments took place in it, executed by the royal command, without any judicial ordeal! Perhaps some arbitrary acts of this time may be cited; but let them be compared with what was passing under equivalent circumstances amongst the nations out of Europe: let any one recall to mind what took place at the time of the Roman empire, and the excesses of absolute royalty wherever Christianity did not exist, and he will see that the excesses committed in European monarchies are scarcely worthy of being mentioned. This is a proof that the distinction made between monarchical governments, whether absolute or despotic, is not arbitrary and fictitious. Any one acquainted with the legislation and history of Europe must be well aware that this distinction is correct, and he will be forced to smile at those boisterous declamations in which malice or ignorance endeavors to confound the two systems of government.

This limit imposed upon power, this circle of reason and justice which we always find traced around it, derives its origin principally from the ideas disseminated by Christianity, whether it have its guarantee in ideas and manners or in political forms. It is Christianity that has proclaimed, "Reason and justice, knowledge and virtue, are every thing; the mere will of man, his birth, his titles, are of no intrinsic value." These words have penetrated every where, from the palace of kings to the poor man's cottage; and, from the moment that the mind of an entire people became imbued with such ideas, Asiatic despotism became impracticable. In fact, in the absence of every political form limiting the power of the monarch, a voice resounds in his ears on all sides, exclaiming, "We are not thy slaves, we are thy subjects; thou art a king, but thou art a man, and a man who, like ourselves, must appear one day before the Supreme Judge; thou hast the power of making laws, but merely for our interests; thou canst exact tributes from us, but only such as are necessary for the common weal; thou canst not judge us according to thy caprice, but only conformably to the laws; thou canst not seize our property without rendering thyself more culpable than the common robber, nor make an attempt on our lives, of thy own will, without becoming an assassin; the power thou hast received is not for thy comfort or pleasure, nor for the gratification of thy passions, but solely for our happiness; thou art a person exclusively devoted to the public weal; if thou forgettest this, thou art a tyrant."

Unfortunately, however, together with this spirit of lawful independence, of rational liberty,—together with this just, noble, and generous democracy, there has ever been another accompanying it, and forming with it the most lively contrast. The latter has been extremely injurious to the former, by preventing it from attaining the object of its just pretensions; erroneous in its principles and perverse in its intentions, violent and unjust in its mode of acting, its traces have been everywhere marked by a stream of blood. Instead of obtaining true liberty for the people, it has merely served to deprive them of that which they already possessed; or if it actually found them groaning under the yoke of slavery, it has only served to rivet their chains. Allying itself on all occasions with the basest passions, it has attracted to its standard all that was most vile and abject in society, and gathered together the most turbulent and ill-disposed men. By cheating its miserable followers with delusive promises, and exciting them with the prospect of plunder and pillage, it has been a perpetual source of commotions, scandals, and bitter animosities, that have at length produced their natural results—persecutions, proscriptions, and executions. Its fundamental dogma was the rejection of all authority of every description, to overturn which was its constant aim; the reward it expected for its labors was to seat itself upon a throne established amidst universal ruin, to glut itself with the blood of thousands of victims, and to revel in the grossest orgies during the distribution of its blood-stained spoil. In all times, in all countries, riots, popular insurrections, and revolutions have taken place; but, for the last seven centuries, Europe presents these scenes in so singular a character, that it forms a most fitting subject for the reflection of philosophers. In fact, these tendencies towards social dissolution—tendencies, the origin of which it is not difficult to discover in the very heart of man—have not only existed in the bosom of Europe, but have been formed into a theory; as ideas, they have been defended with all the obstinacy and infatuation of a sectarian spirit; and, wherever an opportunity occurred, reduced to practice with unyielding pertinacity and unbridled fury. The system was made up of folly and fanaticism, and carried out with obstinacy, a spirit of proselytism, and monstrous crimes. In every page of its history this truth is attested in characters of blood. Happy our nation, had she not tried the experiment!

Europe may be compared to those men of great capacity and of active and intrepid characters, who are either the very best or the very worst of men. Scarcely can a single fact of any weight remain isolated in Europe: there is not a truth that is not useful, nor an error that is not fatal. Ideas have a tendency to become realized, and facts, in their turn, incessantly call in the aid of ideas. If virtues exist, they are explained, and their foundation is sought for in elevated theories. If crimes are met with, their vindication is attempted on the authority of perverse theories. Nations do not rest satisfied with the practice either of good or evil—they strive to propagate it, and are restless till they have induced their neighbors to imitate them. Nay, there is something beyond a mere spirit of proselytism limited to a few countries—ideas, in our times, aim at nothing short of universal empire. The spirit of propagandism does not date from the French Revolution, nor even from the sixteenth century; from the very dawn of civilization, from the times when the minds of men began to evince symptoms of activity, this phenomenon is apparent, and in a very striking manner. In the agitated Europe of the twelfth and thirteenth centuries, we behold the Europe of the nineteenth century, just as the imperfectly defined lineaments of the germ contain forms of the future being.

A great part of the sects which assailed the Church, dating from the tenth century, were decidedly revolutionary; they either proceeded from the fatal democracy which I have just mentioned, or derived their support from it. Unfortunately this democracy, restless, unjust and turbulent, having compromised the tranquillity of Europe in the centuries anterior to the sixteenth, found in Protestantism its most fervent propagators. Among the numerous sects into which the pretended reform was immediately divided, some opened the way for it, and others adopted it as their standard. And what must have been the result in the political organization of Europe? I will say it candidly: the disappearance of those political institutions which enabled the different classes of the state to take part in its affairs, was inevitable. Now, as it was very difficult for the European people, considering their character, ideas and customs, to submit for ever to their new condition, as their predominant inclination must have urged them to place bounds upon the extension of power, it was natural that revolutions should ensue; it was natural that future generations should have to witness great catastrophes, such as the English Revolution of the seventeenth century and the French Revolution of the eighteenth. There was a time when it might have been difficult to comprehend these truths; that time is past. The revolutions in which for some centuries the different nations of Europe have been successively involved, have brought within the reach of the least intelligent that social law so frequently realized, viz. that anarchy leads to despotism, and that despotism begets anarchy. Never, at any time, in any nation (history and experience prove the fact), have anti-social ideas been inculcated, the minds of the people been imbued with the spirit of insubordination and rebellion, without almost immediately provoking the application of the only remedy at the command of nations in such conflicts, the establishment of a very strong government, which justly or unjustly, legally or not, lifts up its iron arm over every one, and makes all heads bend under its yoke. To clamor and tumult succeeds the most profound silence; the people then easily become resigned to their new condition, for reflection and instinct teach them that although it is well to possess a certain amount of liberty, the first want of society is self-preservation.

What was the case in Germany, after the introduction of Protestantism by a succession of religious revolutions? Maxims destructive of all society were propagated, factions formed, insurrections took place; upon the field of battle and upon the scaffolds blood flowed in torrents; but no sooner did the instinct of social preservation begin to operate, than, instead of popular forms being established and taking root, every thing tended towards the opposite extreme. And was not this the country in which the people had been flattered by the prospect of unrestrained liberty, of a re-partition and even a community of property; in fine, by the promise of the most absolute equality in every thing. Yet, in this same country, the most striking inequality prevailed, and the feudal aristocracy preserved its full force. In other countries, in which no such hopes of liberty and equality had been held out, we can scarcely discover the limits which separated the nobility from the people. In Germany, the nobility still retained their wealth and their preponderance, were still surrounded by titles, privileges, and distinctions of every description. In that very country, in which there were such outcries against the power of kings, in which the name of king was declared synonymous with tyrant, the most absolute monarchy was established; and the apostate of the Teutonic order founded that kingdom of Prussia, from which representative forms are still excluded.* In Denmark, Protestantism was established, and with it absolute power immediately took deep root; in Sweden we find, at the very same time, the power of Gustavus established.

What was the case in England? Representative forms were not introduced into that country by Protestantism; they existed centuries before, as well as in other nations of Europe. But the monarch who founded the Anglican Church was distinguished for his despotism, and the Parliament, which ought to have restrained him, was most shamefully degraded. What idea can we form of the liberty of a country whose legislators and representatives debased themselves so far as to declare, that any one obtaining a knowledge of the illicit amours of the Queen is bound, under pain of high treason, to bring an accusation against her? What can we think of the liberty of a country, in which the very men who ought to defend that liberty, cringe with so much baseness to the unruly passions of the monarch, that they are not ashamed, in order to flatter the jealousy of the sovereign, to establish that any young female who should marry a king of England, should, under a pain of high treason, be compelled before her marriage to reveal any stain there might be on her virtue? Such ignominious enactments are certainly a stronger proof of abject servility than the declaration of that same Parliament, establishing that the mere will of the monarch should have the force of law. Representative forms preserved in that country at a time when they had disappeared from almost every other nation of Europe, were not, however, a guarantee against tyranny; for the English cannot assuredly boast of the liberty they enjoyed under the reigns of Henry VIII. and Elizabeth. Perhaps in no country in Europe was less liberty enjoyed, in no country were the people more oppressed under popular forms, in no country did despotism prevail to a greater extent. If there be anything which can convince us of these truths, in case the facts already cited should be found insufficient, it is undoubtedly the efforts made by the English to acquire liberty. And if the efforts made to shake off the yoke of oppression are to be regarded as a sure sign of its galling effects, we are justified in thinking that the oppression under which England was groaning must have been very severe, since that country has passed through so long and terrible a revolution, in which so many tears and so much blood has been shed.

When we consider what has taken place in France, we remark that religious wars have always given an ascendency to royal power. After such long agitations, so many troubles and civil wars, we see the reign of Louis XIV., and we hear that proud monarch exclaim, "*I am the state.*" We have here the most complete personification of the absolute power which always follows anarchy. Have the European nations had to complain of the unlimited power exercised by monarchs? have they had to regret that all the representative forms which could ensure their liberties perished under the ascendency of the throne? Let them blame Protestantism for it, which spreading the germs of anarchy all over Europe, created an imperious, urgent, and inevitable necessity for centralizing rule, for fortifying royal power: it was necessary to stop up every source from which dissolvent principles might flow, and to keep within narrow bounds all the elements which, by contact and vicinity, were ready to ignite and produce a fatal conflagration.

* When this was written.—Tr.

Every reflecting man will agree with me on this point. Considering the aggrandizement of absolute power, they will discover in it nothing but the realization of a fact already long ago everywhere observed. Assuredly, the monarchs of Europe cannot be compared, either by the fact of their origin or the character of their measures, to those despots who, under different titles, have usurped the command of society at the critical moment when it was near its dissolution; but it may be said with reason, that the unlimited extent of their power has been caused by a great social necessity, viz. that of one sole and forcible authority, without which the preservation of public order was impossible. We cannot without dismay take a view of Europe after the appearance of Protestantism. What frightful dissolution! What erroneous ideas! What relaxation of morals! What a multitude of sects! What animosity in men's minds! What rage, what ferocity! Violent disputes, interminable debates, accusations, recriminations without end; troubles, rebellion, intestine and foreign wars, sanguinary battles, and atrocious punishments. Such is the picture that Europe presents; such are the effects of this apple of discord thrown among men who are brethren. And what was sure to be the result of this confusion, of this retrograde movement, by which society seemed returning to violent means, to the tyranny of might over right? The result was sure to be what it has in fact been: the instinct of preservation, stronger than the passions and the frenzy of man, was sure to prevail; it suggested to Europe the only means of self-preservation; royal power, already in the ascendant, and verging towards its highest point, was sure to end by attaining it in reality; there to become isolated and completely separated from the people, and to impose silence on popular passions. What ought to have been effected by a wise direction of ideas, was accomplished by the force of a very powerful institution; the vigor of the sceptre had to neutralize the impulse given to society towards its ruin. If we consider attentively, we shall find that such is the meaning of the event of 1680 in Sweden, when that country was subjected to the fierce will of Charles XI.; such the meaning of the event of 1669 in Denmark, when that nation, wearied with anarchy, supplicated King Frederick III. to declare the monarchy hereditary and absolute, which he in fact did; such, in fine, is the meaning of what took place in Holland in 1747, and of the creation of an hereditary stadtholder. If we require more convincing examples, we have the despotism of Cromwell in England after such terrible revolutions, and that of Napoleon in France after the republic. (37)

CHAPTER LXIV.

STRUGGLE BETWEEN THE THREE SOCIAL ELEMENTS.

When once these three elements of government, monarchy, aristocracy, and democracy, began each to contend for the ascendency, the most certain means of securing the victory to monarchy, to the exclusion of the other two elements, was to drive one of these latter into acts of turbulence and outrage; for it thus became absolutely necessary to establish one sole, powerful, unfettered centre of action, that would be able to awe the turbulent and to insure public order. Now, just at this time, the position of the popular element was full of hope, but also beset with dangers; and hence, to preserve the influence it had already acquired, and to increase its ascendency and power, the greatest moderation and circumspection were requisite. Monarchy had already acquired great power, and, having obtained it in part by espousing the cause of the people against the lords, it came to be regarded as the natural protector of popular interests. It certainly had some claims to this title, but no less certainly did it find in this circumstance a most favorable opportunity for extending its power to an unlimited degree, at the expense of the rights and liberties of the people.

There existed a germ of division between the aristocracy and the commons, which afforded the monarchs an opportunity of curtailing the rights and powers of the lords, convinced, moreover, as they were, that any measure tending to such an object would be well received by the multitude. But, on the other hand, the monarch might rest assured that the lords would hail with delight any act tending to humble the people, who already had raised their heads so high when the feudal aristocracy was to be resisted; and, in this case, if the people committed any excesses, if they adopted maxims and doctrines subversive of public order, no one could prevent the monarch from putting a stop to their proceedings by all possible means. The lords, who were powerful enough to repress such disorders themselves, would very naturally be glad to leave such a work to the monarch, fearing lest the people, in their exasperation against them, might deprive them of their prerogatives, their honors, their property, and even of their lives; or from the secret satisfaction they would naturally feel at seeing that rival power brought down which had recently humbled themselves, and whose rivalry had been maintained through so many and such ferocious struggles. In such an undertaking, the lords would naturally bring the whole weight of their influence to the support of the monarch, thus taking advantage of the false direction given to the popular movement to revenge themselves upon the people, whilst veiling their vengeance under the pretext of public utility. The people, it is true, possessed various means of defence; but when isolated and opposed to the throne, they found these means too weak to afford them any hope of victory. Learning, indeed, was no longer the exclusive patrimony of any privileged class, but knowledge had not had time to become diffused so far as to form a public opinion strong enough to exercise any direct influence upon the affairs of government. The art of printing was already producing its results, but was not yet sufficiently developed to produce that rapid and extensive circulation of ideas which has subsequently been attained. Notwithstanding the efforts everywhere made at that time to promote the diffusion of knowledge, we need only understand correctly the nature and character of the knowledge of the period, to be convinced that neither in substance nor in form was it calculated to become, to any general extent, the property of the popular classes. Thanks to the progress of commerce and the arts, there arose, it is true, a new description of wealth, destined of necessity to become the patrimony of the people. But commerce and the arts were then in their infancy, and did not possess either the extent or the influence which, at a later period, connected them intimately with every branch of society. Except in some few countries of very little importance, the position of the merchant and the artizan could not secure them any great amount of influence of itself.

Considering the course of events, and the elevation which royal power had acquired on the ruins of feudalism, the only means for restricting monarchical power, until the democratic element should have acquired sufficient force to be respected, was the union of the aristocracy with the people. But such a coalition was not easily to be obtained, since between the aristocracy and the people there existed so much animosity and rivalry—a rivalry which, to a certain extent, was inevitable, owing to the opposition of their respective interests. We must bear in mind, however, that the nobility were not the only aristocracy; there was another much more powerful and influential than they—the clergy. This latter class was at that time possessed of all the ascendency and influence which both moral and material means can confer; in fact, besides the religious character, which insured the respect and veneration of the people, they were possessed at the same time, of abundant riches; which easily secured to them, on the one hand, gratitude and influence; and, on the other, made them feared by the great, and respected by monarchs. Now, here is one of the leading mistakes of Protestantism: to crush the power of the clergy at such a time, was to accelerate the complete victory of absolute monarchy, to leave the people defenceless, the monarch unrestrained, aristocracy without a bond of union, without a vital principle; it was to prevent the three elements—monarchy, aristocracy, and democracy—from uniting to form a limited government, towards which almost all the European nations appeared to be inclining. We have already seen that it was not at that time expedient to isolate the people, for their political existence was still feeble and precarious; and it is no less evident that the nobility, as a means of government, ought not to have been left to themselves. This class, possessing no other vital principle than that derived from their titles and privileges, were incapable of resisting the attacks continually aimed at them by the royal power. In spite of themselves, the nobility were under the necessity of yielding to the monarch's will, of abandoning their inaccessible castles, to resort to the sumptuous palaces of kings, and play the part of courtiers.

Protestantism crushed the power of the clergy, not only in the countries in which it succeeded in implanting its errors, but also in others. In fact, where it could not fully introduce itself, its ideas, when not in open opposition to the Catholic faith, exercised a certain degree of influence. From that time the power of the clergy lost its principal support in the political influence of the Popes, for whilst kings assumed a tone of greater boldness against the pretensions of the Holy See, the Popes, on their side, that they might give no pretext, no occasion for the declamations of Protestants, were obliged to act with great circumspection in every thing relating to temporal affairs. All this has been regarded as the progress of European civilization,—as one step towards liberty; however, the rapid sketch which I have just given of the political condition of that period, clearly proves that, instead of taking the surest way to the development of representative forms, the road to absolute monarchy was chosen. Protestantism, interested in crushing by all possible means the power of the Popes, exalted that of kings even in spiritual matters. By thus concentrating in their hands the spiritual and temporal powers, it left the throne without any sort of counterpoise. By destroying the hope of obtaining liberty by peaceable means, it led the people to have recourse to force, and opened the crater of those revolutions which have cost modern Europe so many tears.

In order that the forms of political liberty should take root and attain to perfection, they were not to be forced prematurely from the atmosphere which gave them birth; for in this atmosphere existed together the monarchical, aristocratical, and popular elements, all strengthened and directed by the Catholic religion; under the influence of this same religion, these elements were being gradually combined, politics were not to be separated from religion. Instead of regarding the clergy as a fatal element, it was important to look upon them as a mediator among all classes and powers, ready to calm the ardor of strife, to place bounds against excess, to prevent the exclusive preponderance of the monarch, the nobility, or the people. Whenever powers and interests of different natures are to be combined, a mediator is essential, or some sort of intervention to prevent violent shocks; if this mediator does not exist in the very nature of the circumstances, recourse must be had to the law for the creation of one. From this it is evident what an evil Protestantism inflicted upon Europe; since its first act was completely to isolate the temporal power, to place it in rivalship and hostility to the spiritual, and to leave no mediator between the monarch and the people. The lay aristocracy at once lost their political influence; for they had now lost their force and bond of union, which they derived from their connection with the ecclesiastical aristocracy. When once the nobles were reduced to mere courtiers, the power of the throne was entirely without a counterpoise.

I have said it, and I repeat it, that the strengthening of the royal power, even at the expense of the rights and liberties of the lords and of the commons, tended powerfully to the maintenance of public order, and consequently to the progress of civilization; but, at the same time, the extreme preponderance obtained by this power is much to be lamented; and it may be well to reflect, that one of the principal causes of this preponderance was the removal of the clergy from the sphere of politics. At the commencement of the sixteenth century, the question no longer was, whether those numerous castles should be left standing, from the heights of which proud barons gave the law to their vassals, and held themselves justified in despising the ordinances of the monarch; nor whether that long list of communal liberties should be preserved, which had no connection with each other, which were opposed to the pretensions of the great, and at the same time embarrassed the action of the sovereign, by preventing the formation of a central government capable of insuring order, of protecting legitimate interests, of giving an impulse to the movement of civilization, which had everywhere commenced with so much activity. This was no longer the question; on all sides the castles were being levelled, the great lords were descending from their fortresses, and becoming more humane towards the people; they were giving up their exactions, and beginning to show respect to the power of the monarch; and the commons, obliged to submit to an amalgamation of the multitude of petty states, to form extensive monarchies, were forced to part with so much of their rights and liberties as was opposed to the system of general centralization.

The question was, to discover whether there existed any means of limiting power, and yet securing to the people the benefits of its centralization and augmentation; whether it was possible, without embarrassing or weakening the action of power, to secure to the people a reasonable amount of influence over the progress of affairs, and, above all, the right they had already acquired of watching over the public revenues. That is, at once to prevent the sanguinary horrors of revolutions, and the abuses and disorders of court favorites. The people alone were incapable of preserving this influence, unless they had been furnished with a knowledge of the public affairs; an indispensable resource in such a case, but of which they were in general completely destitute. I do not mean to deny the existence of a certain kind of knowledge amongst the commons; but we must bear in mind that the term *public affairs* had acquired an extensive signification; for it was not merely applied to a municipality or a province; centralization becoming everywhere more general and triumphant, caused this term to be applied to whole kingdoms, not merely considered as isolated, but in the whole of their relations with other nations. From that time European civilization began to assume that character of *generality*, which still distinguishes it: from that time, to understand aright the private affairs of any one kingdom, it was necessary to look abroad over the whole of Europe, sometimes over the whole world. Men capable of such elevated views could not be very common in society; moreover, as the most exalted part of society was attracted by the splendor of the throne of the monarch, a focus of intelligence was sure to be formed there, with exclusive pretensions to the government. Compare with this centre of action and intelligence, the people alone, still weak and ignorant, and the result may be easily guessed. Weakness and ignorance never prevailed over force and intelligence. But, what remedy was there for this difficulty? The preservation of the Catholic religion all over Europe, and consequently the influence of the clergy; for it is well known that the clergy were still considered at this epoch as the centre of learning.

Those who have extolled Protestantism for having weakened the influence of the Catholic clergy, have not sufficiently reflected upon the nature of that influence. It would have been difficult to discover at that epoch a class of citizens connected with the three elements of power by common interests with each, and yet not exclusively allied to any. Monarchy had nothing to fear from the clergy. In fact, how can we imagine that the ministers of a religion regarding power as an emanation from Heaven would declare themselves the enemies of royal power, which was acknowledged to be at the head of all others? Neither had the aristocracy any thing to apprehend on the part of the clergy, so long as they did not outstep the bounds of reason. The titles, by virtue of which they claimed the possession of riches, their rights to a certain degree of consideration and of precedence were not likely to be combated by a class whose principles and interests were necessarily favorable to every thing within the bounds of reason, of justice, and of the laws. The democracy, comprising the generality of the people, found support and most generous protection in the Church. How could the Church, which had labored so much to emancipate them from the ancient slavery, and at a later period from feudal chains, declare herself the enemy of a class which might be considered as her creature? If the people experienced an amelioration in their civil condition, it was owing to the efforts of the clergy; if they acquired political influence, it was owing to the amelioration of their condition—another favor obtained through the influence of the clergy; and if the clergy had any where a sure support, it was natural to look for it in that popular class which, continually in contact with them, received from them their inspirations and instructions.

Besides, the Church selected her members indiscriminately from all classes. To elevate a man to the sacred ministry she required neither titles of nobility nor riches, and this alone was sufficient to insure intimate relations between the clergy and the people, and to prevent the latter from regarding them with aversion and estrangement. Hence the clergy, united to all classes, were an element perfectly adapted to prevent the exclusive preponderance of any of these classes, to maintain all social elements in a certain gentle and productive fermentation, which in time would have produced and matured a natural combination. I do not mean to assert that there would not have arisen differences, disputes, perhaps conflicts, inevitable occurrences so long as men shall be men; but who does not see that the terrible effusion of blood in the wars of Germany, in the revolutions of England and France, would have been impossible? It will be said, perhaps, that the spirit of European civilization necessarily tended to diminish the extreme inequality of classes; I grant it, and will even add, that this tendency was conformable to the principles and maxims of the Christian religion, continually reminding men of their equality before God, of their common origin and destination, of the emptiness of honors and riches, and proclaiming that virtue is the only thing solid upon earth, the only thing capable of rendering us pleasing in the eyes of God. But to reform is not to destroy; to cure the disease, we must not kill the patient. It was deemed better to overthrow at one blow what might have been corrected by legal means; European civilization having been corrupted by the fatal innovations of the sixteenth century, legitimate authority having been disregarded even in matters within its exclusive sphere, its mild and beneficent action has been replaced by the disastrous expedients of violence. Three centuries of calamity have more or less opened the eyes of nations, by teaching them how perilous it is, even for the success of an enterprise, to confide it to the cruel hazard of the employment of force; but it is probable that if Protestantism, like an apple of discord, had not been thrown into the middle of Europe, all these great social and political questions would, at the present time, be much nearer being solved in a safe, peaceable, and certain manner, if, indeed, they had not been already solved long since. (38)

CHAPTER LXV.

POLITICAL DOCTRINES BEFORE THE APPEARANCE OF PROTESTANTISM.

In matters appertaining to representative government, modern political science boasts of its great progress: we hear it continually asserting that the school in which the deputies of the Constituent Assembly imbibed their lessons was totally ignorant of political constitutions. Now when we compare the doctrines of the predominating school of the present day with those of the preceding school, what difference do we discover between them? On what points do they differ? Where is this boasted progress?

The school of the eighteenth century said: "The king is the natural enemy of the people; his power must either be totally destroyed, or at least so far restrained and limited, that he may only appear with his hands tied on the summit of the social edifice, merely invested with the faculty of approving the measures of the representatives of the people." And what says the modern school, which boasts of its progress, of the advantage it has derived from experience, and of having hit the exact point marked out by reason and good sense? "Monarchy," says this school, "is essential to the great European nations; the attempts at republicanism made in America, whatever may be their results, require, as yet, the test of time; besides, they were made under circumstances very different from those in which we are placed, and consequently, are not to be imitated by us. The king should not be regarded as the enemy of the people, but as their father; instead of presenting him to public view with his hands tied, he should be represented surrounded with power, grandeur, and even with majesty and pomp; without which it is impossible for the throne to fulfil the high functions with which it is invested. The king should be inviolable—not nominally, but really and effectually, so that his power cannot, under any pretext, be attacked. He should be placed in a sphere beyond the whirlwind of passion and party, like a tutelar divinity, a stranger to mean views and base passions; he ought to be, as it were, the representative of reason and justice." "Fools," exclaims this school to its adversaries, "can you not see that it would be better to have no king at all than such a one as you would have? Your king would always be an enemy to the constitution, for he would find this constitution always attacking, embarrassing, restricting, and humiliating him."

We will now compare this progress with the doctrines predominating in Europe long before the appearance of Protestantism. This comparison will enable us to show clearly that every thing reasonable, just, and useful, contained in these doctrines, was already known and generally propagated in Europe when society was under the exclusive influence of the Catholic Church.

A king is essential, says the modern school; and, thanks to the influence of the Catholic religion, all the great nations of Europe had a king: *the king must not be regarded as the enemy, but as the father of the people;* and he was already called the father of the people: *the power of the king should be great;* that power was great: *the king should be inviolable, his person sacred;* his person was sacred, and his prerogative insured to him by the Church from the earliest ages, in an august and solemn ceremony, that of his coronation. "The people are supreme," said the school of the last century; "the law is the expression of the general will, the representatives of the people are alone, therefore, invested with legislative faculties; the monarch cannot resist this will. The laws are submitted to his sanction through mere formality; if the king refuses this sanction, the laws are to undergo another examination; but if the will of the representatives of the people still remains the same, it shall be raised to the dignity of law; and the monarch who, by the refusal of his sanction, shall show that he regards this general will as detrimental to the public good, shall be compelled, at the expense of his dignity and independence, to give effect to it."

In reply to this, the modern school says: "The supremacy of the people is either unmeaning, or has a dangerous sense; the law should not be the expression of will, but of reason; mere will does not constitute a law; for this purpose, reason, justice, and public expediency are required." These ideas were general long before the sixteenth century, not only amongst educated men, but even among the most simple and ignorant classes. A doctor of the thirteenth century admirably expressed it in his habitual laconic language: "*It is a rule dictated by reason, and having the common weal for its aim.*" "Would you," continued the modern school, "have royal power a truth, you must assign it the first place among legislative powers; you must entrust it with an absolute *veto*. In the ancient cortes, in the ancient states-general and parliaments, the king did occupy this place among the legislative powers; nothing was done without his consent; he possessed *an absolute veto*."

"Away with classes!" exclaims the Constituent Assembly; "away with distinctions! The king face to face with the people, directly and immediately; the rest is an attempt against imprescriptible rights." "You are rash," replies the modern school; "if there are no distinctions, they must be created. If there are not in society classes forming in themselves a second legislative body a mediator between the king and the people, there must be artificial ones: through the medium of the law must be created what does not exist in society; if reality is wanting, recourse must be had to fiction." Now these classes existed in ancient society, they took part in public affairs, they were organized as active instruments, they formed the first legislative bodies. I ask now, whether this parallel does not show, as clear as the light of day, that what is now termed progress in matters of government, is, in fact, a true return towards what was every where taught and practised under the influence of the Catholic religion before the appearance of Protestantism? In addressing myself to men endowed with the least intelligence upon social and political questions, I may assuredly dispense with the differences which must necessarily result from the two epochs. I grant that the course of events would of itself have caused important modifications; political institutions were to be accommodated to the fresh wants to be satisfied. But I maintain, at the same time, that, so far as circumstances permitted, European civilization was advancing on the right road to a better state, containing within itself the means necessary for reforming without destroying. But for this purpose a spontaneous development of events was necessary to bear in mind that the mere action of man is of little avail, that sudden attempts are dangerous; that the great productions of society are like those of nature, both requiring an indispensable element, *time*.

There is one fact which appears to me to have been too little reflected upon, although including the explanation of some strange phenomena of the last three centuries. This fact is, that Protestantism has prevented civilization from becoming homogeneous, in spite of a strong tendency urging all the nations of Europe to homogeneity. The civilization of the nations without doubt receives its nature and its characteristics from the principles that have given it life and movement; now these principles being the same, or very nearly so, in all the nations of Europe, these nations must have borne a close resemblance to each other. History and philosophy agree on this point; therefore, so long as the European nations did not receive the inculcation of any germ of division, their civil and political institutions were developed with a very remarkable similarity. True, certain differences were observable in them, which were the inevitable consequences of a variety of circumstances; but we see that they were becoming more and more alike and forming Europe into one vast whole, of which we can scarcely form a correct idea, accustomed as we are to ideas of disunion. This homogeneity would have arrived at its perfection through the effect of the rapidity which the increase and prosperity of commerce and the arts gave to intellectual and material communications; the art of printing would have contributed to it more than anything else, for the ebb and flow of ideas would have dispersed the inequalities separating the nations one from another.

But unfortunately, Protestantism appeared and separated the European people into two great families, which, since their division, have professed a mortal hatred towards each other. This hatred has been the cause of furious wars, in which torrents of blood have been shed. One thing yet more fatal than these catastrophies was the germ of civil, political, and literary schism, introduced into the bosom of Europe by the absence of religious unity. Civil and political institutions, and all the branches of learning, had appeared and prospered in Europe under the influence of religion; the schism was religious; it affected even the root, and extended to the branches. Thus arose among the various nations those brazen walls which kept them separate; the spirit of suspicion and mistrust was everywhere spread; things which before would have been deemed innocent or without importance, from that time were looked upon as eminently dangerous.

What uneasiness, disquietude, and agitation must have been the result of these fatal complications! We may say that in this detestable germ is contained the history of the calamities with which Europe was afflicted during the last three centuries. To what may we attribute the Anabaptist wars in Germany, those of the empire, and the Thirty-years war; those of the Huguenots in France, and the bloody scenes of the League; and that profound source of division, that uninterrupted series of discord, which beginning with the Huguenots, was continued by the Jansenists, and then by philosophers, terminating in the Convention? Had England not contained in her bosom that nest of sects engendered by Protestantism, would she have had to suffer the disasters of a revolution which lasted so many years? Had Henry VIII. not seceded from the Catholic Church, Great Britain would not have passed two-thirds of the sixteenth century in the most atrocious religious persecutions, and under the most brutal despotism; she would not have been drowned during the greater part of the seventeenth in torrents of blood, shed by sectarian fanaticism. Had it not been for Protestantism, would England have been in the fatal position in which she is placed by the Irish question, scarcely leaving her a choice between a dismemberment of the empire and a terrible revolution? Would not nations of brethren have found the means of coming to an amicable understanding, if, during the last three centuries, religious discords had not separated them by a lake of blood? Those offensive and defensive confederations between nation and nation, which divided Europe into two parties, as inimical to each other as the Christians to the Mussulmans, that traditional hatred between the North and the South, that profound separation between Protestant and Catholic Germany, between Spain and England, between that country and France, were sure to have an extraordinary effect in retarding communications between European nations; and what would have been obtained much sooner by moral means, could only be obtained by material ones. Steam tends to convert Europe into one vast city; if men who were one day to live under the same roof hated one another for three centuries, what was the cause of it? If people's hearts had been united long before in mutual affection, would not the happy moment in which they were to join hands have been hastened?

CHAPTER LXVI.

POLITICAL DOCTRINES IN SPAIN.

My explanation of this matter would be incomplete, were I to leave the following difficulty unresolved: "In Spain, Catholicity has prevailed exclusively, and under it an absolute monarchy was established, a sufficient indication that Catholic doctrines are inimical to political liberty." The great majority of men never look deeply into the real nature of things, nor pay due attention to the true meaning of words. Present them with something in strong relief that will make a vivid impression on their imagination, and they take facts just as they appear at the first glance, thoughtlessly confounding *causality* with *coincidence.* It cannot be denied that the empire of the Catholic religion *coincided* in Spain with the final *preponderance* of absolute monarchy; but the question is, *Was the Catholic religion the true cause of this preponderance?* Was it she that overturned the ancient cortes, to establish the throne of absolute monarchs on the ruins of popular institutions?

Before we commence our examination into the cause that destroyed the influence of the nation on public affairs, it may be well to remind the reader that in Denmark, Sweden, and Germany, absolutism was established and upheld in juxtaposition with Protestantism. Hence the argument of coincidence is very little worth, as, owing to the exact identity of circumstances in the two cases, it could just as well be proved that Protestantism leads to absolutism. I will just observe here, that in my endeavors to demonstrate in the foregoing chapters that the pseudo-Reformation tended to the overthrow of political liberty, I have not rested my arguments upon coincidences only, however careful I may have been to point them out to the reader. I have said that Protestantism, by diffusing dissolvent doctrines, had occasioned a necessity for an extension of temporal power; that by destroying the political influence of the clergy and the Popes, it had destroyed the equilibrium between the social classes, left no counterpoise to the throne, and further augmented the power of the monarch, by granting him ecclesiastical supremacy in Protestant countries, and exaggerating his prerogatives in Catholic nations.

But we will dismiss these general considerations, and fix our attention upon Spain. This nation has the misfortune to be one of those that are least known; its history is not properly studied, nor are sound views taken of its present condition. Its troubles, its rebellions, its civil wars, proclaim that it has not yet received its true system of government, which proves that the nation to be governed is but imperfectly understood. Its history is, if possible, still less perfectly understood. The present influence of events already very remote, works secretly and almost imperceptibly; and hence the eye of the observer is satisfied with a superficial view of affairs, and he forms his opinions too hastily—opinions which too often, in consequence, take the place of facts and reality. In treating of the causes that have deprived Spain of her political liberty, almost all authors fix their attention principally or exclusively upon Castile, giving monarchs infinitely more credit for sagacity than the course of events would seem to justify. They generally select the war of the *Communeros* as their point of view, and, according to certain writers, but for the defeat at Villalar, the liberties of Spain would have been forever secure. I admit that the war of the *Communeros* affords an excellent point of view for the study of this matter; in fact, the field of Villalar was in some measure witness to the conclusion of the drama. Castile should be regarded as the centre of events; and it is here that the Spanish monarchs gave proof of great sagacity in the manner in which they brought the enterprise to a close. Nevertheless, I do not deem it just to give an exclusive preference to one of these considerations, and it does appear to me that the real state of the question is generally misconceived: effects are taken for causes, accessories for principals.

In my opinion, the ruin of free institutions resulted from the following causes:—1st, the premature and immoderately extensive development of these institutions; 2dly, the formation of the Spanish nation out of a successive reunion of very heterogeneous parts, all possessing institutions extremely popular; 3dly, the establishment of the centre of power in the middle of the provinces where these forms were most restricted, and where the authority of the crown was the greatest; 4thly, the extreme abundance of wealth, the power and the splendor which the Spanish people saw everywhere around them, and which lulled them to sleep in the arms of prosperity; 5thly, the exclusively military position of the Spanish monarchs, whose armies were everywhere victorious, their military power and prestige being at their height precisely at the critical time when the quarrel had to be decided. I will take a rapid view of these causes, although the nature of this work does not permit me to devote to them the space which the gravity and importance of the subject demand. The reader will pardon me this political digression on account of the close connection existing between this subject and the religious question.

As regards popular forms of government, Spain has been in advance of all monarchical nations. This is an indubitable fact. In Spain, these forms received a premature and extreme development; and this contributed to their ruin, as a child sickens and dies, if, in its tender years, its growth is too rapid, or its intellect too precocious. This active spirit of liberty, this multitude of *fueros* and of privileges, these impediments everywhere placed in the way of power, checking the rapidity and energy of its action—this great development of the popular element, in its very nature restless and turbulent, existing simultaneously with the wealth, the power, and the pride of the aristocracy, very naturally gave rise to many commotions. Elements so numerous, so various, and so opposite to each other, which, moreover, had not time to be combined so as to form a peaceable and harmonious whole, were not likely to work tranquilly together. Order is the prime necessity of society; it is essential to the growth of the ideas, the manners, and the laws of a nation. Wherever there exists a germ of continual disorder, how deep soever it may have struck its roots, it is sure to be extirpated, or at least crushed, so as no longer to keep public tranquillity in perpetual danger. The municipal and political organization of Spain had this inconvenience, and hence an imperative necessity for its modification. But the ideas and the manners of the time were such, that matters could not be expected to stop at a simple modification. The system of constituencies, which so easily creates numerous assemblies, either to enact new fundamental codes or to reform the old ones, was not then understood as it is in our days; neither were men's ideas at that time so generalized as to place them above all that exclusively and particularly relates to a people, at a point of elevation whence they could no longer observe every petty local object, but had their attention wholly engrossed by mankind, society, the nation, or the government. It was not so at that time: a charter of liberty granted by a king to a city or a town; an immunity wrested from a feudal lord by his armed vassals; some privilege obtained in reward of warlike achievements, or sometimes granted as a recompense for the bravery of a man's ancestors; a concession to the cortes, made by the monarch in exchange for the grant of a contribution, or, as it was then termed, of a *service*,—a law or custom, the antiquity of which lay hidden in the depths of the past, or confounded with the infancy of monarchy: such, to give a few instances, were the titles of which they were proud, and which they maintained with jealous ardor

Liberty now-a-days is more vague, and sometimes less positive, owing to the generalization and elevation which men's ideas have assumed; but then it is far less liable to destruction. Speaking a language well understood by the people, and appearing as the common cause of all nations, it awakens universal sympathies, and is in a position to found more extensive associations as a guarantee against the attacks of power. The words liberty, equality, rights of man, intervention of the people in public affairs, ministerial responsibility, public opinion, liberty of the press, toleration, and other similar ones, do undoubtedly contain a great diversity of meanings, which it would be difficult to determine and to classify when we come to make a specific application of them; and yet these words present to the mind certain ideas which, although complicated and confused, have a false appearance of clearness and simplicity. On the other hand, these words represent certain striking objects that dazzle the mind by their vivid and flattering colors, and hence they cannot be uttered without exciting a lively interest; they are understood by the masses, and hence every self-constituted champion of the ideas they convey is at once regarded as a defender of the rights of all mankind. But imagine yourself living among the people of the fourteenth and fifteenth centuries, and your position will be found very different. Take for your subject the franchises of Catalonia or of Castile, and address yourself to the Aragonese, who were so intractable on the subject of their *fueros*, and you will produce no effect—will not succeed in awakening either their zeal or their interest; a charter that does not contain the name of one of their towns or cities is, in their eyes, a thing of no importance, and foreign to their wishes. This inconvenience, originating in the ideas of the times, which were naturally confined to local circumstances, became very great in Spain, where, under the same sceptre, there was formed an amalgamation of people differing most widely in their manners, in their municipal and political organization, and divided, moreover, by rivalries and animosities. In such a state of things it was comparatively easy to curtail the liberties of one province without giving umbrage to the others, or exciting their apprehensions for their own liberties. If, at the period of the insurrections of the *Communeros* in Castile against Charles V., there had existed that communication of ideas and sentiments, and those lively sympathies, which at the present time unite people together, the defeat of Villalar would have been a simple defeat and nothing more; the cry of alarm, resounding throughout Aragon and Castile, would certainly have given more trouble to the young and ill-advised monarch. But such was not the case; all the efforts of the people were isolated, and consequently barren of results. The royal power, proceeding upon a fixed and steady plan, was able to beat down piecemeal these scattered forces, and the result was not doubtful. In 1521, Padilla, Bravo, and Maldonado perished on the scaffold; in 1591, D. Diego de Heredia, D. Juan de Luna, and the Justiciary himself, D. Antonio de Lanuza, met the same fate; when, in 1640, the Catalonians rose in insurrection for the defence of their rights, notwithstanding the manifestos they issued to attract supporters, they found no one to assist them. There were then no flying sheets, coming every morning to fix the attention of the people upon all sorts of questions, and to stir up alarm at the least appearance of danger to their liberties. The people, warmly attached to their customs and usages, satisfied with the nominal confirmations which their monarchs were daily giving to their *fueros*, proud also of the respect shown to their ancient liberties, were little aware that they were confronted by a sagacious adversary, who never resorted to force but to effect a decisive blow, yet constantly held his powerful arm ready to crush them. An attentive study of the history of Spain will show that the concentration of the whole governing power in the hands of the monarch, to the exclusion, as far as was possible, of popular influence, dates from the reign of Ferdinand and Isabella. Nor is this surprising; for there was then a greater necessity for such a course, and it could be more easily adopted. There was a greater necessity; for, from that time, the action of government began to extend from one common center over the whole of Spain, the various portions of which differed so widely in their laws, their manners, and their customs; hence the central action naturally felt more sensibly the embarrassment occasioned by so great a diversity of cortes, of municipalities, of codes, and of privileges; and, as every government wishes its action to be rapid and efficacious, the idea of simplifying, uniting, and centralizing their power naturally took possession of the kings of Spain. It is, in fact, easy to understand that a monarch at the head of numerous armies, with magnificent fleets at his disposal, who had, on a hundred occasions, humbled his most powerful foes, and won the respect of foreign nations, would not like to be continually going to preside over the cortes in Castile, in Aragon, in Valencia, and in Catalonia. It would undoubtedly cost him dear to be constantly repeating the oath binding him to protect the rights and liberties of his subjects, and listening to the perpetual strain re-echoed in his ears by the *procuradores* of Castile, and the *brazos* of Aragon, Valencia, and Catalonia. It was hard for him to be obliged humbly to solicit from the cortes assistance for the expenses of the state, and particularly for almost continual wars. If he submitted to this, it was only from the dread of those resolute men, real lions in the battle-field when fighting in defence of their religion, their country, and their king, and who would have fought with no less intrepidity in their streets and houses, had an attempt been made to despoil them of those rights and franchises which they inherited from their forefathers.

The union of the crowns of Aragon and Castile alone so far prepared the way for the ruin of popular institutions, that it followed almost necessarily. From that time, in fact, the throne had obtained too great a preponderance for the *fueros* of the kingdoms recently united to oppose it with success. To imagine the existence at that period of a political power capable of resisting the crown, we must suppose all the assemblies held from time to time in the different kingdoms under the name of cortes united into one grand national representative body, with a power analogous to that of the king; we must suppose this central assembly actuated by a zeal equal to that of the ancient assemblies for the preservation of their *fueros* and privileges, ready to sacrifice all their rivalries to the public good, and advancing towards their object with a firm step, in one compact mass, and never giving an advantage to their adversary. In other words, we must suppose what was utterly impossible at that period; impossible, on account of the ideas, the habits, and the rivalries of the people; impossible, at a time when the people were incapable of comprehending the question in so lofty a sense; impossible, owing to the resistance which it would have met with from the monarchs; to the embarrassment and complication, arising from the municipal, social, and political organization. In a word, it was something impossible to effect or even to conceive.

Every circumstance was in favor of the aggrandizement of the royal power. The monarch being no longer merely king of Aragon or of Castile, but of Spain, the ancient kingdoms dwindled into insignificance before the majesty and the splendor of the throne, and sank by degrees to the rank which alone suited them, that of provinces. From that moment the action of the monarch became more extensive and complicated, and consequently he could not come so frequently into contact with his vassals. The celebration of the cortes in each of the recently united kingdoms, would have occasioned long delays; for the king was oftentimes engaged at another part of the empire. When sedition was to be chastised, abuses to be checked, or excesses to be repressed, he was no longer obliged to have recourse to the forces of the particular kingdom in which these things occurred, as he could employ the arms of Castile to subdue insurrection in the kingdom of Aragon, and those of Aragon to put down the rebels of Castile. Grenada lay at his feet; Italy yielded to one of his victorious captains; in his fleet was Columbus, who had just discovered a new world; under these circumstances, it was in vain to listen for the murmurs of the cortes and of *ayuntamientos,*—these were no longer heard, they had totally disappeared.

Had the national manners had a peaceable tendency, had not Spain been habituated to war, democratic institutions would probably have been preserved with less difficulty. Had the attention of the people been fixed exclusively upon their municipal and political affairs, they would have better understood their real interests; kings themselves would not have been so ready to rush into war, and the throne would in some degree have lost the prestige it obtained from the splendor and success of its armies; the administration would not have been imbued with that blunt harshness for which military habits are always more or less remarkable; and the ancient *fueros* would thus have more easily retained some consideration. But precisely at that period Spain was the most warlike nation in the world; it was in its element on the battle-field; seven centuries of combats had made it a nation of soldiers. Its recent victories over the Moors; the exploits of its armies in Italy; the discoveries of Columbus; every thing, in fine, contributed to its exaltation, and to inspire it with that spirit of chivalry which, for so long a time, was one of its distinguishing characteristics. It was necessary for the king to be a captain; and he was certain to captivate the minds of Spaniards, so long as he won renown by brilliant feats of arms. Now, arms are the bane of popular institutions. After a victory on the field of battle, the order and discipline of the camp are usually transferred to the city.

From the time of Ferdinand and Isabella, the throne rose to such a height of power that liberal institutions were almost lost sight of. The people and the grandees, it is true, re-appeared upon the scene after the death of Isabella; but this was entirely owing to the misunderstanding between Ferdinand the Catholic and Philip le Bel, which impaired the unity, and consequently the strength of the throne; and hence, as soon as these circumstances disappeared, the throne again resumed its full preponderance, and that not only during the last days of Ferdinand, but even under the regency of Ximenes. The men of Castile, exasperated by the excesses of the Flemish, and encouraged perhaps by the hope, that the rule of a young monarch would be, as it usually is, only feeble, again raised their voices; their remonstrances and complaints speedily ended in commotions and in open insurrection. Notwithstanding many circumstances highly favorable to the *Communeros,* and the probability that their conduct would be followed by all the provinces of the monarchy, we find that the insurrection, although considerable, did not assume either the importance or extent of a national movement; a great portion of the Peninsula preserved a strict neutrality, and the rest inclined to the cause of monarchy. If I am not mistaken, this fact indicates that the throne had already obtained an immense prestige, and was regarded as the highest and most powerful institution. The entire reign of Charles V. was extremely well calculated to perfect this beginning. Commenced under the auspices of the battle of Villalar, this reign continued through an uninterrupted series of wars, in which the treasures and the blood of Spain were spent with incredible profusion in all the countries of Europe, Africa, and America. The nation was not allowed time even to think of its affairs: almost always deprived of the presence of its king, it had become a province at the diposal of the Emperor of Germany, the ruler of Europe. True, the cortes of 1538 boldly gave Charles a severe lecture instead of the succor he demanded. But it was already too late; the clergy and the nobility were expelled from the cortes, and the representation of Castile was restricted for the future to the *procuradores* alone; that is, it was doomed to be no more than the shadow of what it had been—a mere instrument of the royal will.

Much has been said against Philip II.; but, in my opinion, this monarch merely kept his place, and allowed things to take their natural course. The crisis was already past; the question already decided; the Spanish nation could not regain its lost influence, save by the regenerating action of centuries. Still, we must not imagine that absolute power was so fully and completely established as to leave not a vestige of ancient liberty; but this liberty could do nothing from its asylum in Aragon and Catalonia against the giant that held it in check from the midst of a country entirely subject to his sway, from the capital of Castile. The monarchs might probably, by one bold and heavy blow, have struck down every thing that opposed them; but whatever probabilities of success they had in the vast means at their disposal, they were very careful not to make the attempt, but left the inhabitants of Navarre, the subjects of the crown of Aragon, in the tranquil enjoyment of their franchises, rights, and privileges. At the same time, they were careful to prevent the contagion spreading to the other provinces. By means of partial attacks, and more especially by leading the people to allow their ancient liberties to fall into desuetude, they gradually diminished their zeal for them, and insensibly brought them to a habit of tamely bending under the action of a central power. (39)

CHAPTER LXVII.

POLITICAL LIBERTY AND RELIGIOUS INTOLERANCE.

In the sketch I have here drawn, the rigorous accuracy of which no one can question, we have not discovered any thing like oppression in Catholicity, nor any alliance between the clergy and the throne for the destruction of liberty: what we *have* discovered is merely the regular and natural order of things,—a successive development of events contained in each other, as the plant is contained in the germ. As for the Inquisition, I think I have said enough respecting it in the chapters that treat of it: in this place I will merely observe, that it was not a political instrument in the hands of kings, ready to be used at their beck. Religion was its object; and as we have seen, far from losing sight of this object to suit the wishes of the sovereign, it unhesitatingly condemned the doctrines that would have unjustly extended the powers of the monarch. Shall I be told, that the Inquisition was in its very nature intolerant, and consequently opposed to the growth of liberty? I answer, that toleration, as now understood, had at that time no existence in any European country. Besides, it was under the direct and full influence of religious intolerance that the people were emancipated, municipalities organized, the system of large representative assemblies established, which, under different names, and more or less directly, interfered in public affairs.

Men's ideas were not yet so far perverted as to lead them to believe that religion was favorable and conducive to the oppression of the people; on the contrary, we observe in the hearts of these people a vehement desire for liberty and progress, whilst at the same time they clung with enthusiasm to a faith, in the sight of which it appeared to them just and salutary to refuse toleration to any doctrine at variance with the teaching of the Church of Rome. Unity of faith does not fetter the people—does not impede their movements in any direction—as well, indeed, might it be said, that the mariner is fettered by the compass that guides him in safety through the wide expanse of waters. Was the ancient unity of European civilization wanting in grandeur, in variety, or in beauty? Did Catholic unity, presiding over the destinies of society, arrest its progress, even in the ages of barbarism? Let us fix our eyes upon the grand and delightful spectacle exhibited in the centuries preceding the sixteenth, and pause a moment to reflect; we shall all the better understand in what manner Protestantism has given a wrong direction to the course of civilization.

The immense agitation occasioned by the gigantic enterprise of the Crusades shows in what a state of fermentation were the elements deposited in the bosom of society. The shock excited them to activity—union augmented their force—every where, and in every sense, was to be seen a vigorous and active movement, a sure presage of the high degree of civilization and refinement which Europe was about to attain. The arts and sciences, as if called into life by some powerful voice, reappeared, loudly asserting their claim to protection and an honorable reception. On the feudal castles, those heirlooms of the manners of the period of conquest, a ray of light suddenly gleamed, that illuminated with the rapidity of lightning all climates and all people. Those masses of men, who had hitherto bent in painful toil for the benefit of their masters, now lifted up their heads, and, with bold hearts and enfranchised lips, demanded a share in social advantages. Addressing each other with a look of intelligence, they combined together, and insisted in common that the law should be substituted for caprice. Then towns sprang up, increased in size and importance, and were surrounded with ramparts; municipal institutions arose, and began to develop themselves; kings, till then the sport of the pride, ambition or stubbornness of the feudal lords, seized upon an opportunity so favorable, and made common cause with the people. Threatened with destruction, feudalism entered valiantly into the contest, but in vain; and, restrained by a power even more irresistible than the weapons of its adversaries, and, as if oppressed by the air it breathed, it felt its action impeded, its energies enfeebled, and, despairing of victory, it gave itself up to the enjoyment to be found in the patronage of the arts.

To the coat of mail now succeeded elegance of dress; to the powerful shield, the pompous escutcheon; to the bearing and address of the warrior, the manners of the courtier:—thus was the whole power of feudalism undermined; the popular element was left completely at liberty to develop itself; and the powers of monarchs became every day more extensive. Royalty thus strengthened, municipal institutions in full vigor, and feudalism undermined, the remnants of barbarism and oppression still existing in the laws fell one by one beneath the attacks of so many adversaries; and, for the first time in the world's history, there was seen a considerable number of great nations presenting the peaceful spectacle of many millions of men living in social union, and enjoying together the rights of men and of citizens. Until this period, public tranquillity, and even the very existence of society, had to be secured by carefully excluding from the working of the political machine a great number of individuals by means of slavery—a system that proved at once the intrinsic inferiority and weakness of the governments of antiquity. The Christian religion, with the courage inspired by the consciousness of strength, and with an ardent love for humanity, had never doubted that she held in her hands other means of restraining men than a recourse to degradation and violence, and had, in fact, resolved the problem in a manner the most noble and generous. She had said to society: "Dost thou dread this immense multitude, that have no sufficient titles to thy confidence? I will stand security for them. Thou enslavest them; thou puttest chains around their necks; I will subdue their hearts. Leave them free; and this multitude, before which thou tremblest as before a herd of wild beasts, will become a class of men serviceable to themselves and to thee." This voice had been heard, and all men were freed from the yoke of slavery—

all entered upon this noble struggle, which was to place society in equilibrium, without destroying or shaking its foundations. We have already said above, that there existed powerful adversaries. Shocks more or less violent were inevitable; but there was no cause for anticipating any serious catastrophe, unless some fatal combination of circumstances arose to overthrow the only power capable of moderating the inflamed, and sometimes exasperated, passions of men—to impose silence upon that powerful voice, ever ready to say to the combatants, *That is enough.* That voice—the voice of Christianity—might have been heard with greater or less docility; but it would always have sufficed to calm down the fury of the passions, to moderate the fierceness of their conflicts, and thus to prevent scenes of bloodshed.

If we take a glance at Europe at the end of the fifteenth and beginning of the sixteenth centuries, with a view to discover the social elements, whose struggle seemed likely to disturb public tranquillity, we shall find the power of the throne already far superior to that of the lords and of the people; we shall see it endeavoring to please its rivals, lending its aid to one for the subjugation of the others: but already this power was evidently indestructible. Held more or less in check by the proud remnants of feudalism, and by the ever-growing and encroaching power of the people, monarchy nevertheless maintained its position as a central force for the protection of society against violence and excess. This tendency was so strong, that we every where meet with the same phenomenon, manifested with more or less distinctness, and with characters of greater or less identity. The nations of Europe were great both in numbers and extent; the abolition of slavery gave a sanction to the principle, that man ought to live free in the midst of society, enjoying its most essential advantages, and with sufficient room to enable him to take a more or less elevated rank, according to the means he employs to gain it. Thus society had said to each individual: "I acknowledge thee as a man and a citizen; from this moment I guarantee to thee the possession of these titles. If thou desirest to lead a quiet life in the bosom of thy family—labor and be careful; no one shall wrest from thee the rewards of thy labors, nor trammel the free exercise of thy faculties. Dost thou aspire to the possession of wealth—consider how others have acquired it, and display a similar activity and intelligence. Art thou ambitious of fame, of rising to an elevated rank, to splendid titles—the sciences and the military profession are before thee. If thou hast inherited an illustrious name, thou mayest still increase its lustre; if thou art not in possession of such a name, thou art free to acquire one."

Such was the condition of the social problem at the end of the fifteenth century. Every thing was made public, all the great means of action were openly developing themselves with rapidity; the art of printing already transmitted men's thoughts from one end of the world to the other with the speed of lightning, and insured their preservation for the benefit of future generations. The frequent intercourse between nations, the revival of literature and the arts, the cultivation of the sciences, the inclination for travelling and commerce, the discovery of a new passage to the East Indies, the discovery of America, the preference given to political negotiations for effecting the arrangements of international relations,—every thing combined to give to the minds of men that strong impulse, that shock which at once arouses and develops all their faculties, and gives new life. It is difficult to understand by what process of reasoning, in the face of facts so positive and certain,—facts that stand so prominently forward in every page of history, any man could ever seriously maintain that Protestantism aided human progress. If previous to Luther's reform society had been found stationary, and still submerged in the chaos into which it had been plunged by the irruptions of the barbarians; if the people had not succeeded, previously to that reform, in forming themselves into great nations, and in providing themselves with systems of government more or less perfectly organized, but all unquestionably superior to any that had hitherto existed,—the assertion might carry with it a degree of plausibility, or, at all events, it would not stand, as it unfortunately does, in direct opposition to the most authentic and notorious facts. But what, on the contrary, was the actual state of Europe at the time of Luther's appearance? The administration of justice, exercised with more or less perfection, already possessed a highly moral, rational, and equitable system of legislation for the guidance of its decisions; the people had in great part shaken off the yoke of feudalism, and had acquired abundant resources for the preservation and defence of their liberties; the executive had made immense progress, owing to the establishment, extension, and amelioration of municipalities; the royal authority, enlarged, fortified, and consolidated, formed in the midst of society a central force powerful to work good, to prevent evil, to restrain the passions, to preserve the balance of interests, to prevent ruinous social contests, and to watch over the general welfare of society by constant protection and effectual encouragement; in fine, at that period nations were seen to fix a look of great foresight and sagacity on the rock upon which the vessel of society is in danger of being wrecked, whenever the power of royalty is left without any sort of counterpoise. Such was already the condition of Europe before the religious revolution of the sixteenth century.

I promptly concede that great progress has been made since that period in all matters of a social, political and administrative nature; but does it follow that this progress is owing to the Protestant Reformation? To prove that it is, it would be necessary to produce two societies absolutely similar in position and circumstances, but separated by a long space of time, that would render all reciprocal influence between them impossible, and subjected, one to the influence of the Catholic, the other to the Protestant principle; then each of the two religions might come forward and say to the world, "This is my work." But it is absurd to compare, as is often done, times so widely different, circumstances so utterly dissimilar and exceptional with ordinary cases; it should also be remembered, that, in every thing, the first step is always the most difficult, and the greatest merit is always due to invention; in a word, after so many other violations of the rules of logic, our opponents should not obstinately persist in deducing from one single fact all other facts, simply because the latter happen to be posterior to the former, otherwise they will fall under suspicion of insincerity in their search after truth, and of a wish to falsify history.

The organization of European society, such as Protestantism found it, was, assuredly not perfect, but it was, at all events, as perfect as was possible. Unless Providence had vouchsafed to govern the world by prodigies, Europe, at this period, could not have attained to a more advantageous position. The elements of progress, of happiness, of civilization and refinement, were in her bosom; they were numerous and powerful; time was developing them by degrees in a manner truly wonderful; and as mournful experience is every day lessening the prestige and credit of destructive doctrines, the time is perhaps not far distant, when philosophers, examining dispassionately this period of history, will agree that society had even then received the most fortunate impulse. It will be seen that Protestantism, by giving a wrong direction to the march of society, only precipitated it upon a perilous route, where it has been on the brink of ruin; and would perhaps have been ruined altogether, had not the hand of the Most High been stronger than the feeble arm of man. Protestants boast of having rendered great service to society by having destroyed in some countries, and impaired in others, the power of the Popes. As regards the Papal supremacy in relation to matters of faith, what I have elsewhere said will suffice to demonstrate the disastrous consequences of the exercise of private judgment; as to discipline, I am unwilling to enter upon questions that would indefinitely extend the limits of this work. I will merely ask my opponents, whether they deem it prudent to leave a society co-extensive with the world without a legislator, without a judge, without an arbitrator, without a counsellor, without a chief?

Temporal power.—This term has long been the bugbear of kings—the watchword of the anti-Catholic party—a snare into which many upright men have fallen—a butt for the shafts of discontented statesmen, disappointed writers, and snarling canonists; and nothing more natural, seeing that the subject afforded them an opportunity of pouring out their resentments, and of giving currency to their suspicious doctrines, well assured that, by affecting zeal for the power of the monarch, they would find, in case of danger, a ready asylum in the palaces of kings. The present is not the place for the discussion of a question that has been the subject of so many vehement and learned disputes; and it would be the more inopportune, as, in the existing state of things, assuredly no power apprehends the least temporal usurpation on the part of the Holy See, which, whatever its enemies may say, has evinced at all times, and even humanly speaking, more prudence, tact, patience, and wisdom than any other power upon earth; and amidst the extreme difficulties of modern times, has taken up a position that enables it to yield to the various exigencies of the times without any compromise of its high dignity, without any deviation from its sublime obligations. It is certain that the temporal power of the Popes had risen in the course of time to such a height, that the successor of St. Peter had become a universal counsellor, arbitrator, and judge, from whose sentence it was dangerous to appeal, even in purely political matters. The general movement throughout Europe had somewhat weakened this power; but yet, at the moment when Protestantism made its appearance, it still had such an ascendency over the minds of men, it commanded so much veneration and respect, and was possessed of such vast means for defending its rights, enforcing its pretensions, supporting its decisions, and making its counsels respected, that the most powerful monarchs of Europe considered it a very serious matter to have the Court of Rome opposed to them in any affair whatever; and consequently they eagerly sought on all occasions, to secure its favor and friendship. Rome had thus become a general centre of negotiation, and no affair of importance could escape its influence.

Such have been the outcries raised against the colossal power, against this pretended usurpation of rights, that one might suppose the Popes to have been a succession of deep conspirators, who, by their intrigues and artifices, aimed at nothing short of universal monarchy. As our opponents plume themselves on their spirit of observation and historical analysis, I felt it necessary to observe, that the temporal power of the Popes was strengthened and extended at a time when no other power was as yet really constituted. To call that power usurpation therefore, is not merely an inaccuracy—it is an anachronism. In the general confusion brought upon all European society by the irruptions of the barbarians, in that strange medley of races, laws, manners, and traditions, there remained only one solid foundation for the structure of the edifice of civilization and refinement, only one luminous body to shine upon the chaos, only one element capable of giving life to the germ of regeneration that lay buried in blood-stained ruins—Christianity, predominant over and annihilating the remains of other religions, arose, in this age of desolation, like a solitary column in the center of a ruined city, or like a bright beacon amid darkness.

Barbarians, and proud of their triumphs as they were, the conquering people bowed their heads beneath the pastoral staff that governs the flock of Jesus Christ. The spiritual pastors, a body of men quite new to these barbarians, and speaking a lofty and divine language, obtained over the chiefs of the ferocious hordes from the north a complete and permanent ascendency, which the course of ages could not destroy. Such was the foundation of the temporal power in the Church; and it will be easily conceived that as the Pope towered above all the other pastors in the ecclesiastical edifice, like a superb cupola above the other parts of a magnificent temple, his temporal power must have risen far higher than that of ordinary bishops; and must also have had a deeper, more solid, and more lasting foundation. All the principles of legislation, all the foundations of society, all the elements of intellectual culture, all that remained of the arts and sciences, all was in the hands of religion; and all very naturally sought protection from the pontifical throne, the only power acting with order, concert, and regularity, and the only one that offered any guarantee for stability and permanence. Wars succeeded to wars, convulsions to convulsions, the forms of society were continually changing; but the one great, general, and dominant fact, the stability and influence of religion, remained still the same: and it is ridiculous in any man to declaim against a phenomenon so natural, so inevitable, and, above all, so advantageous, designating it, "A succession of usurpations of temporal power."

Power, ere it can be usurped, must exist; and where, I pray, did temporal power then exist? Was it in kings?—the sport, and frequently the victims of the haughty barons? In the feudal lords?—continually engaged in contests amongst themselves, with kings, and with the people? In fine, was it in the people?—a troop of slaves, who, thanks to the efforts of religion, were slowly working out their freedom? The people, it is true, united against the lords—they raised their voices to demand protection from the monarch, or to solicit the aid of the Church against the vexations and outrages inflicted on them by both; still, however, they as yet formed but an unorganized embryo of society, without any fixed rule, without government, and without laws. Could we honestly compare modern times with these? Could we apply to these bygone ages restrictions and distinctions of authority that are admissible only in a state of society in which the elements of life and civilization have been developed, in which solid and permanent foundations have been laid, in which, consequently, the functions of social authority could be, and have in effect been, regulated, after a minute analysis of the limits of their respective jurisdictions? To reason otherwise, would be to seek order in chaos, smoothness on the surface of a tempest-tossed ocean. We should not forget, either, a general and unvarying fact, founded on the very nature of things,—a fact, moreover, to which the history of all times and all countries is continually calling our attention, and which has received a striking confirmation from the revolutions of modern times,—viz. that whenever society is deeply diseased, there is always at hand a principle of life to stay the progress of the malady. A contest takes place—collisions occur one after another—they become more frequent and more violent; but ultimately the principle of order prevails over that of disorder, and continues long afterwards to predominate in society. This principle may be more or less just, more or less rational, more or less violent, more or less adequate to attain its object; but whatever it be in these respects, it always prevails in the end, unless, during the struggle, another, a better and more powerful principle takes its place.

Now, in the middle ages, this principle was the Christian Church. She alone could be this principle, for she had truth in her doctrines, justice in her laws, and regularity and prudence in her government. She was the only element of life that existed at this period—the only depository of the grand idea upon which the reorganization of society depended; and this idea was not vague and abstract, but positive and practicable, for it proceeded from the lips of Him whose word calls forth worlds out of nothing, and makes light to shine forth in the midst of darkness. When once the sublime doctrines of the Church had penetrated into the heart of society, her pure, fraternal, and consoling morality necessarily influenced its manners. Forms of government also, and systems of legislation were, in like manner, more or less affected by her mild and powerful influence. These are facts—undeniable facts. Now, the Roman Pontiffs were the center of this happy preponderance which religion so legitimately obtained and so justly deserved; hence it is clear that the power of the Holy See very naturally rose above all other powers.

After having contemplated this sublime picture, drawn from the plain and authentic records of history, why dwell on the defects or the vices of some few individuals? Why drag to light the excesses, the errors, the disorders ever incident to humanity? Why maliciously seek out facts through a long succession of obscure ages, collecting them together and placing them in a light most calculated to make an impression, and to mislead the ignorant? Why, in fine, urge, exaggerate, disfigure, and paint these facts in the darkest possible colors? To do so, is to betray a very shallow understanding of the philosophy of history, a spirit of great partiality, low views, grovelling sentiments, and miserable spleen. It should be loudly proclaimed to the whole world, and a thousand times repeated, that it may never be forgotten, that limits which have no existence cannot be respected—that to create power is not to usurp it—that to make laws is not to violate them—that to reduce to order the chaos in which society is overwhelmed is not to disturb society. Now this was the work of the Church—this is what was done by the Popes. (40)

CHAPTER LXVIII.

UNITY IN FAITH NOT ADVERSE TO POLITICAL LIBERTY.

THE supposed incompatibility of unity in faith with political liberty is an invention of the irreligious philosophy of the last century. Whatever political opinions be adopted, it is of extreme importance that we be on our guard against such a doctrine. We must not forget that the Catholic religion occupies a sphere far above all forms of government—she does not reject from her bosom either the citizen of the United States, or the inhabitant of Russia, but embraces all men with equal tenderness, commanding all to obey the legitimate governments of their respective countries. She considers them all as children of the same father, participators in the same redemption, heirs to the same glory. It is very important to bear in mind that irreligion allies itself to liberty or to despotism, according as its interests incline; lavish of its applause when an infuriated populace are burning temples and massacring the ministers of the altar, it is ever ready to flatter monarchs, to exaggerate their power beyond measure, whenever they win its favor by despoiling the clergy, subverting discipline, and insulting the Pope. Caring little what instruments it employs, provided it accomplishes its work, it is royalist when in a position to sway the minds of kings, to expel the Jesuits from France, from Spain, from Portugal, to pursue them to the four quarters of the globe without allowing them either respite or repose; liberal in the midst of popular assemblies that exact sacrilegious oaths from the clergy, and send into exile or to the scaffold the ministers of religion who remain faithful to their duty.

The man who cannot see that what I have advanced is strictly true, must have forgotten history, and paid little attention to very recent occurrences. With religion and morality, all forms of government are good; without them, none can be good. An absolute monarch, imbued with religious ideas, surrounded by counsellors of sound doctrines, and reigning over a people amongst whom the same doctrines prevail, may make his subjects happy, and will be sure to do so as far as circumstances of time and place permit. A wicked monarch, or one surrounded by wicked counsellors, will do mischief in proportion to the extent of his powers; he will be even more to be dreaded than revolution itself, because better able to arrange his plans, and to carry them out more rapidly, with fewer obstacles, a greater appearance of legality, more pretensions to public utility, and consequently with more certainty of success and of permanent results. Revolutions have undoubtedly done great injury to the Church; but persecuting monarchs have done equally as much. A freak of Henry VIII. established Protestantism in England; the cupidity of certain other princes produced a like result in the nations of the north; and in our own days, a decree of the Autocrat of Russia drives millions of souls into schism. It follows that an unmixed monarchy, if it be not religious, is not desirable; for irreligion, immoral in its nature, naturally tends to injustice, and consequently to tyranny. If irreligion be seated on an absolute throne, or if she hold possession of the mind of its occupant, her powers are unlimited; and, for my part, I know nothing more horrible than the omnipotence of wickedness.

In recent times, European democracy has signalized itself lamentably by its attacks upon religion; a circumstance which, far from favoring its cause, has injured it extremely. We can indeed form an idea of a government more or less free, when society is virtuous, moral, and religious; but not when these conditions are wanting. In the latter case, the only form of government that remains is despotism, the rule of force, for force alone can govern men who are without conscience and without God. If we attentively consider the points of difference between the revolution of the United States and that of France, we shall find that one of the principal points of difference consists in this, that the American revolution was essentially democratic, that of France essentially impious. In the manifestos by which the former was inaugurated, the name of God, of Providence, is every where seen; the men engaged in the perilous enterprise of shaking off the yoke of Great Britain, far from blaspheming the Almighty, invoke his assistance, convinced that the cause of independence was the cause of reason and of justice. The French began by deifying the leaders of irreligion, overthrowing altars, watering with the blood of priests the temples, the streets, and the scaffolds—the only emblem of revolution recognized by the people is Atheism hand in hand with liberty. This folly has borne its fruits—it communicated its fatal contagion to other revolutions in recent times—the new order of things has been inaugurated with sacrilegious crimes; and the proclamation of the rights of man was begun by the profanation of the temples of Him from whom all rights emanate.

Modern demagogues, it is true, have only imitated their predecessors the Protestants, the Hussites, the Albigenses; with this difference, however, that in our days irreligion has manifested itself openly, side by side with its companion, the democracy of blood and baseness; whilst the democracy of former times was allied with sectarian fanaticism. The dissolving doctrines of Protestantism rendered a stronger power necessary, precipitated the overthrow of ancient liberties, and obliged authority to hold itself continually on the alert, and ready to strike. When the influence of Catholicity had been enfeebled, the void had to be filled up by a system of espionage and force. Do not forget this, you who make war upon religion in the name of liberty; do not forget that like causes produce like effects. Where moral influences do not exist, their absence must be supplied by physical force: if you take from the people the sweet yoke of religion, you leave governments no other resource than the vigilance of police, and the force of bayonets. Reflect, and choose. Before the advent of Protestantism, European civilization, under the ægis of the Catholic religion, was evidently tending towards that general harmony, the absence of which has rendered necessary an excessive employment of force. Unity of faith disappeared, opening the way to an unrestrained liberty of opinion and religious discord; the influence of the clergy was in some countries destroyed, in others weakened: thus was the equilibrium between different classes put an end to, and the class naturally destined to fill the office of mediator rendered powerless. By abridging the power of the Popes, both people and governments were let loose from that gentle curb which restrained without oppressing, and corrected without degrading; kings and people were arrayed against each other, without any body of men possessed of authority to interpose between them in case of a conflict; without a single judge, who, the friend of both parties, and disinterested in the quarrel, might have settled their differences with impartiality, governments began to place their reliance upon standing armies, and the people upon insurrections.

And it is of no avail to allege that in countries where Catholicity prevailed, a political phenomenon arose similar to that which we observe in Protestant nations; for I maintain that amongst Catholics themselves events did not follow the course which they naturally would have followed, had not the fatal Reformation intervened. To attain its complete development, European civilization required the unity from which it had sprung; it could not by any other means establish harmony amongst the diverse elements which it sheltered in its bosom. Its homogeneity was gone the moment unity of faith disappeared. From that hour no nation could adequately effect its organization without taking into account, not only its own internal wants, but also the principles that prevailed in other countries, against the influence of which it had to be on its guard. Do you suppose, for instance, that the policy of the Spanish government, constituted as it was the protector of Catholicity against powerful Protestant nations, was not powerfully influenced by the peculiar and very dangerous position of the country?

I think I have shown that the Church has never been opposed to the legitimate development of any form of government; that she has taken them all under her protection, and consequently that to assert that she is the enemy of popular institutions is a calumny. I have also placed it equally beyond a doubt, that the sects hostile to the Catholic Church, by encouraging a democracy either irreligious or blinded by fanaticism, so far from aiding in the establishment of just and rational liberty, have, in fact, left the people no alternative between unbridled licentiousness and unrestrained despotism. The lesson thus furnished by history is confirmed by experience; and the future will serve only to corroborate its truth. The more religious and moral men are, the more deserving they are of liberty; for they have then less need of external restraints, having a most powerful one in their own consciences. An irreligious and immoral people stand in need of some authority to keep them in order, otherwise they will be constantly abusing their rights, and will consequently deserve to lose them. St. Augustine perfectly understood these truths, and explains briefly and beautifully the conditions necessary for all forms of government. The holy Doctor shows that popular forms are good where the people are moral and conscientious; where they are corrupt, they require either an oligarchy or an unmixed monarchy.

I have no doubt that an interesting passage, in the form of a dialogue, that we meet with in his first book on Free Will, chap. vi., will be read with pleasure.

"*Augustine.* You would not maintain, for instance, that men or people are so constituted by nature as to be absolutely eternal, and subject neither to destruction nor change?—*Evodius.* Who can doubt that they are changeable, and subject to the influence of time?—*Augustine.* If the people are serious and temperate; and if, moreover, they have such a concern for the public good that each one would prefer the public interest to his own, *is it not true that* *would be advisable to enact that such a people should choose their own authorities for the administration of their affairs?*—*Evodius.* Certainly.—*Augustine.* But, in case these same people become so corrupt that *the citizens prefer their own to the public good; if they sell their votes; if, corrupted by ambitious men, they intrust the government of the state to men as criminal and corrupt as themselves;* is it not true that, in such a case, if there be amongst them a man of integrity, and possessing sufficient power for the purpose, he will do well to take from these people the power of conferring honors, and concentrate it in the hands of a small number of upright men, or even in the hands of one man?—*Evodius.* Undoubtedly.—*Augustine.* Yet, since these laws appear very much opposed to each other, the one granting the people the right of conferring honors, the other depriving them of that right; since, moreover, they cannot both be in force at once, *are we to affirm that one of these laws is unjust, or that it should not have been enacted?*—*Evodius.* By no means."*

The whole question is here comprised in a few words: Can monarchy, aristocracy, and democracy, be one and all legitimate and proper? Yes. By what considerations are we to be guided in our decision as to which of these forms is legitimate and proper in any given case? By the consideration of existing rights, and of the condition of the people to whom such form is to be applied. Can a form once good become bad? Certainly it may; for all human things are subject to change. These reflections, as solid as they are simple, will prevent all excessive enthusiasm in favor of any particular form of government. This is not a mere question of theory, but one of prudence also. Now, prudence does not decide before having attentively considered and weighed all circumstances. But there is one predominant idea in this doctrine of St. Augustine: this idea I have already indicated, viz. that great virtue and disinterestedness are required under a free government. Those who are laboring to establish political liberty on the ruins of all religious belief would do well to reflect upon the words of the illustrious doctor.

How would you have people exercise extensive rights, if you disqualify them by perverting their ideas and corrupting their morals? You say that under representative forms of government reason and justice are secured by means of elections; and yet you labor to banish this reason and justice from the bosom of that society in which you talk of securing them. You sow the wind, and reap the whirlwind; instead of models of wisdom and prudence, you offer the people scandalous scenes. Do not say that we are condemning the age, and that it progresses in spite of us: we reject nothing that is good; but perversity and corruption we must reprobate. The age progresses—true; but neither you nor we know whither. Catholics know one thing—a thing which it needs not a prophet to tell, viz. that a good social condition cannot be formed out of bad men; that immoral men are bad; that where there is no religion, morality cannot take root. Firm in our faith, we shall leave you to try, if you choose, a thousand forms of government, to apply your palliatives to your own social patient, to impose upon him with deceitful words; his frequent

* *Aug.* Quid ipsi homines et populi, ejusne generis rerum sunt, ut interire mutarive non possint, æternique omnino sint?—*Evod.* Mutabile plane atque tempori obnoxium hoc genus esse quis dubitet?—*Aug.* Ergo, si populus sit bene moderatus et gravis, communisque utilitatis diligentissimus custos, in quo unusquisque minoris rem privatam quam publicam pendat, nonne recte lex fertur, qua huic ipsi populo liceat creare sibi magistratus, per quos sua res, id est publica, administretur?—*Evod.* Recte prorsus.—*Aug.* Porro, si paulatim depravatus idem populus rem privatam reipublicæ præferat, atque habeat venale suffragium, corruptusque ab eis qui honores amant, regimen in se flagitiosis consceleratisque committat, nonne item recte, si quis tunc extiterit vir bonus, qui plurimum possit, adimat huic populo potestatem dandi honores, et in paucorum bonorum vel etiam unius redigat arbitrium?—*Evod.* Et id recte.—*Aug.* Cum ergo duæ istæ leges ita sibi videantur esse contrariæ, ut una earum honorum [illegible] tribuat potestatem, auferat altera, et cum ista secunda ita lata sit, ut nullo [illegible] civitate simul esse possint, num dicemus aliquam earum injustam esse et ferri [illegible] —*Evod.* Nullo modo

convulsions—his continued restlessness—are evidences of your incapacity; and well is it for your patient that he still feels this anxiety: it is a sure sign that you have not entirely succeeded in securing his confidence. If ever you do secure it—if ever he fall asleep quietly in your arms—" all flesh will then have corrupted its way;" and it may also be feared lest God should resolve to sweep man from the face of the earth.

CHAPTER LXIX.

OF INTELLECTUAL DEVELOPMENT UNDER THE INFLUENCE OF CATHOLICITY.

It has been abundantly proved in the course of this work, that the pseudo-Reformation has not in any way contributed to the perfection either of individuals or of society; from which we may naturally infer that the case is the same as regards the development of the intellect. I am unwilling, however, to let this truth stand merely as a corollary, and I believe it to be susceptible of a special elucidation. We may freely examine what advantage Protestantism has conferred upon the various branches of human learning, without any fear of the result as regards Catholicity. When we are to examine objects naturally embracing a great many different relations, it is not enough merely to pronounce certain conspicuous names, or to cite with emphasis one or two facts. This is not the way to place a question in its proper light; and to treat it adequately, much more is required. A discussion, either confined within limits too narrow to admit of its full development, or allowed an indefinite range, carries with it, in the eyes of an observer of only slight penetration, an air of universality, elevation, and boldness, whilst in reality it is all uncertainty and vagueness, and is liable to be involved in endless contradictions.

To investigate this question satisfactorily, we must, it seems to me, grasp the Catholic and Protestant principles respectively, subject them to a most rigid scrutiny, and seize upon every point that appears favorable or inimical to the development of the human mind. Further, we should survey, in its widest range, the history of the intellect; pausing here and there at the epochs where the influence of the principle whose tendencies and effects we are studying has been most effectively exerted; then, rejecting anomalous exceptions, as proving nothing either one way or the other, and facts too insignificant and isolated to affect in any way the course of events, the mind, sufficiently elevated, and observing attentively, and with a sincere desire to know the truth, will be enabled to discover how far its philosophical deductions are in accordance with facts; and thus will it complete the solution of the problem.

One of the fundamental principles of Catholicity, one of its distinctive characteristics, is the submission of the intellect to authority in matters of faith. This is the point against which the attacks of Protestants have ever been and still are directed: and this is quite natural, seeing that Protestants profess resistance to authority as a fundamental and constituent principle. From this fatal source flow all their other errors. If there be in Catholicity any thing capable of arresting the march of the mind or of lowering its flight, it must unquestionably be the principle of submission to authority. With this principle must rest all the blame in this respect, if indeed the Catholic religion be chargeable with any.

Submission of the intellect to authority. These words, it cannot be denied, do, unless we have seized upon their true meaning, and ascertained the precise objects to which this submission is applicable, at first sight, convey an idea of antagonism to intellectual development. If you cherish an ardent affection for the dignity of our nature; if you are an enthusiastic advocate of scientific progress, and behold with delight the brilliant efforts of a bold, vigorous, and accomplished genius; you will discover something repulsive in a principle which appears to invoke slavery, since it checks the flight of the mind, clips the wings of the intellect, and casts it into the dust. But if you examine this principle in its essence, apply it to the various branches of learning, and observe what are the points of contact which it offers with the methods adopted for the cultivation of the mind, will you discover any foundation for these suspicions and apprehensions? What truth will you find in the reproaches of which Catholicity has been made the object? How vain and puerile will appear all the declamation published on this subject!

We will now enter fully into the examination of this difficulty; we will take the Catholic principle, and analyze it with the eye of impartial philosophy. With this principle before us, we will survey the whole field of science, and consult the testimony of the greatest men. If we find that it has ever been opposed to the genuine development of any one branch of learning; if, on visiting the tombs where repose the most illustrious, they tell us that the principle of submission to authority chained down their intellects, obscured their imaginations, and withered their hearts,—we will then acknowledge that Protestants are right in the reproaches which they are constantly directing against the Catholic religion on this subject. God, man, society, nature, the entire creation—such are the objects on which our minds can be occupied; beyond the sphere of these objects we cannot reach, for they embrace infinity—there is nothing beyond them. Well, then, the Catholic principle opposes no obstacle to the mind's progress. Whether as regards God or man, society or nature, it imposes no shackles, places no obstacle in the way of the human mind; instead of checking this progress, it rather serves as a lofty beacon, which, far from interfering with the mariner's liberty, guides him in safety amid the obscurity of night.

How does the Catholic principle oppose the freedom of the human mind in anything relating to the Divinity? Protestants surely will not tell us that there is anything at all wrong in the idea which the Catholic religion gives of God. Agreeing with us on the idea of a being eternal, immutable, infinite, the Creator of heaven and earth, just, holy, full of goodness, a rewarder of the good, and a punisher of the wicked, they admit this to be the only reasonable idea of God that can be presented to the mind of man. To this idea the Catholic religion unites an incomprehensible, profound, and ineffable mystery, veiled from the sight of weak mortals,—the august mystery of the Trinity; but on this point Protestants cannot reproach us, unless they are prepared to avow themselves Socinians. The Lutherans, the Calvinists, the Anglicans, and many other sects, condemn, as well as we do, those who deny this august mystery. We may remark here, that Calvin had Michael Servetus burned at Geneva for his heretical doctrines on the Trinity. I am well aware of the ravages that Socinianism has made among the separated Churches, where the spirit and the right of private judgment in matters of faith have converted Christians into unbelieving philosophers; but, notwithstanding this, the mystery of the Trinity was long respected by the leading Protestant sects, and is so yet, externally at least, by the greater part of them.

In any case, I cannot see how this mystery shackles human reason in its contemplation of the Divinity. Does it prevent it from going forth into immensity? What limit does it fix to the infinite ocean of light and being implied in the word *God?* Does it in the least obscure this splendor? When the mind of man, soaring above the regions of creation, and detaching itself from the body that would bear it down, abandons itself to the delights of sublime meditation on the infinite Being, Creator of heaven and earth, does this august mystery stop him in his heavenward flight? Ask the innumerable volumes written on the Divinity, eloquent and irrefragable testimonies of liberty enjoyed by the human mind wherever Catholicity prevails. The doctrines of Catholicity relative to the Divinity may be considered under two aspects; either as having reference to mysteries above our comprehension, or as touching what is within the reach of reason. As regards mysteries, their abode is in a region so sublime, they appertain to an order of things so superior to any created thought, that the mind, even after the most extensive, most profound, and, at the same time, most free investigations, is unable, without the aid of revelation, to form even the most remote idea of these ineffable wonders. How can things that never meet, which are of a totally distinct order, and which are an immense distance apart, interfere with each other? The intellect can fix upon one of them by means of meditation, can lose itself in contemplating it, without even thinking of the other. Can the moon's orbit come into contact with the remotest of the fixed stars?

Do you fear that the revelation of a mystery may limit the sphere of your reason's operations? Are you apprehensive lest, in wandering through immensity, you may be smothered in the narrowness of your reason? Was space wanted for the genius of Descartes, of Gassendi, of Mallebranche? Did these men complain that their intellects were limited, imprisoned? Why, indeed, should they complain (I speak not of them only, but of all the great minds of modern times who have treated of the Divinity), when they cannot but own that they are indebted to Catholicity for the most splendid and sublime ideas that enrich their writings? The philosophers of antiquity, in their treatises on the Divinity, are at an immense distance below the least eminent of our metaphysical theologians. What would Plato himself be compared to Lewis of Granada, Louis de Léon, Fenelon, or Bossuet? Before Christianity appeared upon earth, before the faith of the Chair of Peter had taken possession of the world, the primitive ideas on the Divinity having been effaced, the human mind wandered amongst a thousand errors, a thousand monstrous fancies; feeling the necessity of a God, man substituted for the Supreme Being the creation of his own imagination. But ever since the ineffable splendor, descending from the bosom of the Father of light, has shone upon the whole earth, ideas of the Divinity have remained so fixed, clear, and simple, and at the same time so lofty and sublime, that human reason has obtained a wider range; the veil which concealed the origin of the universe has been withdrawn; the world's destiny has been marked out, and man has received the key that explains the wonders which fill and surround him. Protestants have felt the force of this truth; their aversion for every thing Catholic was almost fanatical; yet, generally speaking, they may be said to have respected the idea of the Divinity. On this point, of all others, the spirit of innovation has been felt the least. How, indeed, could it be otherwise? The God of the Catholics was too great to be replaced by any other. Newton and Leibnitz, embracing heaven and earth in their speculations, could say nothing new of the Author of so many wonders, nothing but what had already been taught by the Catholic religion.

Well had it been for Protestants if, whilst in the midst of their wanderings they preserved this precious treasure, they had faithfully followed the example of their predecessors, and had rejected that monstrous philosophy which threatens us with the revival of all errors, ancient and modern, beginning with the substitution of a monstrous pantheism for the sublime Deity of Christianity. Let those Protestants who are friends of truth, jealous of the honor of their communion, devoted to their country's welfare, and interested in the future prospects of mankind, be warned in time. If pantheism should prevail, it will not be the spiritualist but the naturalist philosophers who will triumph. The German philosophers may in vain seek refuge in abstraction and enigmas, in vain condemn the sensualist philosophy of the last century; a God confounded with nature is not God, a God identified with every thing is nothing, pantheism is a deification of the universe, that is, a denial of God.

What sorrowful reflections suggest themselves to us when we consider the direction now taken by the minds of men in different parts of Europe, and more especially in Germany! Catholics long since told them they would begin with resistance to authority by denying a dogma, but would end by a denial of all, and fall into atheism; and the course of ideas during the last three centuries has fully confirmed the truth of the prediction. Strange, that German philosophy should aim at producing a reaction against the materialist school, and with all its spiritualism end in pantheism! Providence, it would seem, has ordained that the soil which has produced so many errors should be barren of truth. Out of the Church all is unsteadiness and confusion; materialism ending in atheism, wild idealism and fantastic spiritualism resulting in pantheism! Verily, God still abhors pride, and repeats the terrible chastisement of the confusion of tongues. Catholicity triumphs the while; but mourns in the midst of her triumphs. I do not see either how it can be that Catholicity impedes the operation of the intellect as regards the study of man. What does the Church require of us on this point? What does she teach on the subject? How far extends the circle embracing the doctrines we are forbidden to call in question?

Philosophers are divided into two schools, the materialists and the spiritualists. The former assert that the human soul is only a portion of matter, which, by a certain modification, produces in us what we call thought and will; the latter maintains that the energy accompanying thought and will is incompatible with the inertness of matter; that what is divisible, composed of divers parts, and consequently of divers entities, could not harmonize with the simple unity essential to a being that thinks, wills, reasons, with itself upon every thing, and possesses the profound consciousness of individuality. For these reasons they assert that the contrary opinion is false and absurd; and they ground their opinion upon a variety of considerations. The Catholic Church intervenes in the dispute, and says: "The soul of man is not corporeal, it is a spirit; you cannot be both a Catholic and a materialist." But ask the Catholic Church by what systems you are to explain the ideas, the sensations, the acts of the will, and human feelings,—and she will tell you that on these matters you are perfectly free to hold what you consider most in accordance with reason; that faith does not descend to particular questions appertaining to the affairs of this world, which God himself delivered to the consideration of men. Before the light of the Gospel shone upon the world, the schools of philosophy were in the most profound ignorance on the subject of our origin and our destiny; none of the philosophers could explain the profound contradictions that are found in man; none of them succeeded in pointing out the cause of that strange mixture of greatness and littleness, of goodness and malice, of knowledge and ignorance, of excellence and baseness. But religion came forth, and said: "Man is the work of God; his destiny is to be for evermore united with God; for him the earth is a place of exile only; man is no longer what he was when he came forth from the hands of his Creator; the whole human race is subjected to the consequences of a great fall." Now I would defy all philosophers, ancient and modern, to show wherein the obligation of believing these things militates in the slightest degree against the progress of true philosophy.

So far, indeed, are the doctrines of Catholicity from checking philosophical progress, that they are, on the contrary, a most fruitful source of this progress in every respect. If we wish to make progress in any of the sciences, it is no slight advantage for the intellect to have a safe and firm axis around which it may revolve; it is a fortunate thing to be enabled to avoid at the very outset in the intellectual race, a multitude of questions which would entangle us in inextricable labyrinths, or from which we could not escape without falling into most lamentable absurdities; in a word, when we approach the investigation of these questions, we ought to consider ourselves happy in finding them resolved beforehand in their most important points, and in knowing where the truth lies, and where the danger of falling into error. The philosopher's position is then that of a man who, sure of the existence of a mine in a certain spot, does not waste his time in searching after it, but, knowing his ground, all his researches and labors are profitable from the first. This is the cause of the vast advantage which in these matters modern philosophers possess over those of antiquity: the ancients had to grope in the dark; the moderns, preceded by brilliant lights, advance with a firm and sure step, and march straight to their destination. They may boast incessantly that they set aside revelation, that they hold it in disdain, perhaps that they even openly attack it. Even in this case religion enlightens them, and often guides their steps; for there are a thousand splendid ideas for which they are indebted to religion, and which they cannot erase from their minds; ideas which they have found in books, learned in catechisms, and imbibed with their milk; ideas which they hear uttered by every one around them; which are spread everywhere, and which impregnate with their vivifying and beneficent influence the atmosphere they breathe. In repudiating religion, these same moderns are carrying ingratitude to great lengths; for at the very moment they insult her, they are profiting by her favors.

This is not the place to enter into details on this matter, or numerous proofs might easily be adduced in support of the foregoing observations; a comparison between the first works of modern philosophy that came to hand and the works of the ancients would be decisive; but such a labor would still be incomplete for those who are not versed in these matters; and for those who are so, it would be superfluous. I leave the question with entire confidence to the perspicacity and impartiality of my readers; it will, I think, be acknowledged that whenever our modern philosophers have spoken of man with truth and dignity, their language has borne the impress of Christian ideas. Such is the influence of Catholicity upon those sciences which, confined to a purely speculative order, allow the genius of the philosopher the widest range and the greatest freedom possible; but if, as regards those sciences, the influence of Catholicity, instead of checking the mind in its flight, only enlarges its range, increases its sublimity, its daring, and at the same time its security, by preventing it from running astray, what shall we say of its influence on the study of ethics? Has the whole body of philosophers together ever discovered any thing beyond what is contained in the Gospel? What doctrine excels in purity, in sanctity, in sublimity that taught by the Catholic religion? On this point we will do justice to the philosophers, even to those most hostile to the Christian religion. They have attacked its doctrines, and smiled at the divinity of its origin; but have always evinced a profound respect for its morality. I know not what secret influence has constrained them into an avowal that must certainly have cost them dear. "Yes," they invariably say, "it cannot be denied that the morality of Catholicity is excellent."

There are certain doctrines of Catholicity which cannot be said to appertain directly either to God, to man, or to morality, in the sense generally given to this word. The Catholic religion is a revealed religion, of an order far superior to any thing that the human mind is capable of conceiving. Its object is to guide us to a destiny that we could neither attain nor even imagine by our own strength, and it is based upon this principle, that human nature, corrupted by the fall, requires to be restored and purified; evidently, therefore, it should contain certain doctrines explanatory of the mode in which this work of restoration and purification is to be effected, whether in a general or particular sense; and at the same time pointing out the means which God has chosen to lead man to happiness. Such are the doctrines of the Incarnation, of Redemption, of Grace, and of the Sacraments.

These dogmas embrace a wide field; the relations in which they stand to God and to man are very extensive; the doctrines of the Catholic Church are, and always have been, unchangeable. Well then! extensive as they are, they afford not a single point that can be said to have a tendency to embarrass the free action of the intellect in investigations of any kind. The cause of this fact is the same as that I have already indicated. Those who have attentively compared the sciences of philosophy and theology may have remarked that theology, in the sublime questions mentioned above, occupies a sphere so distinct and supereminent as scarcely to preserve a single point of contact with that in which philosophy moves. They are two vast and sublime orbits, occupying in the depths of space positions very distant from each other. Man sometimes tries to make them approximate, and would be glad if a ray of terrestrial light could penetrate into the region of incomprehensible mysteries; but he scarcely knows how to begin this, and we hear him avow, with a profound sense of his own weakness, that he is *speaking only conventionally* and *by analogy*, merely with a view to make himself better understood. The Church allows such attempts, owing to the good intentions they evince; sometimes she even prompts and encourages them, desiring, as far as possible, to accommodate what is incomprehensible in her doctrines to the feeble capacities of men.

After all their reasonings on the attributes of the Divinity and the relations of man to God, have philosophers discovered any thing incompatible with these doctrines of Catholicity? Have revealed truths stood in their way as a stumbling-block to their investigations? When Descartes, in the seventeenth century, effected a revolution in philosophy, a singular incident occurred that will throw a strong light on this subject. The Catholic doctrine respecting the august mystery of the Eucharist is known, and also in what the dogma of *transubstantiation* consists. Many theologians, the reader is also probably aware, in order to explain the supernatural phenomenon which takes place after the consummation of the miracle, had recourse to the doctrine of accidents, which they distinguished from the substance. Now the theory of Descartes, and of almost all other modern philosophers, was incompatible with this explanation, for they denied the existence of accidents distinct from the substance. It consequently appeared at first sight that a difficulty would here arise for the Catholic doctrine, and that the Church would have to oppose this system of philosophy. And did it so happen? Not at all. Upon a careful investigation of the matter, it was seen that the Catholic dogma belonged to a region infinitely above that uncertain one in which the philosophic doctrine was discovered, however closely they might have seemed to approximate. In vain theologians discussed the matter, indulged in mutual recriminations, drew from the new doctrine all sorts of inferences, in order to represent it as dangerous. The Church, always superior to the thoughts of men, kept aloof from these disputes, maintaining that grave, majestic, and impassive attitude so well becoming her to whom Jesus Christ confided the sacred deposit of His doctrine. Such is the liberty accorded by the Church to the genius of philosophers, that it is free in every sense. The Church has no need to be continually imposing restrictions and conditions; the sacred doctrines of which she is the depository dwelling in so elevated a region that the mind of man can scarcely ever meet them, at least so long as his investigations do not wander from the track of true philosophy.

But this human reason, at once so powerful and so feeble, sometimes becomes puffed up with arrogance and pride, and in the name of liberty and independence claims a right to blaspheme the Almighty, to deny man's free will, the immortality and spirituality of his soul, her sublime origin and her heavenly destiny. At such a time we avow, and we glory in the avowal, the Church does raise her voice, not to oppress or tyrannize over the human mind, but to defend the rights of the Supreme Being and the dignity of human nature; then, indeed, we behold her opposing, with unyielding firmness, that senseless liberty which consists in the fatal right of uttering all sorts of extravagances. This liberty Catholics neither possess nor desire, knowing that in these matters, as in others, there is a sacred line of demarcation between liberty and licentiousness. Happy slavery, that keeps us from atheism, materialism, and from doubting whether our souls come from God, whether they tend towards Him, and whether there exists for unhappy mortals, after the sufferings that weigh upon them in this life, a life of eternal happiness purchased by the merits of a God-man! As for the sciences which have society for their object, I think I need not vindicate the Catholic religion from the reproach of having in this respect oppressed the human mind. The long train of reflections in which I have set forth her doctrines and her influence, as regards the nature and extent of power, and the civil and political liberty of nations, proves to a demonstration that the Catholic religion, without descending to the arena in which the passions of men strive and contend, teaches a doctrine most favorable to true civilization and to the rightly-understood liberties of the people.

I will also touch briefly upon the relations of the Catholic principle with the study of the natural sciences. Assuredly it is not easy to see in what way this principle can be injurious to the progress of the human mind in this department of knowledge. I have said, it is not easy; I might have said impossible, and that for a very simple reason, founded upon a fact within the reach of every man; viz. the extreme reserve which the Catholic religion evinces in every thing relating to purely natural science. One might suppose that God had designed, on this matter, to read us a severe lesson on our excessive curiosity: you have only to read the Bible to be convinced of the truth of what I have advanced. I do not mean that nature is never noticed in the Bible; that divine book presents her to us in her grandest, noblest, and most sublime aspect; as a living whole, in fact, together with all her relations and her sublime destiny, but without any kind of analysis or decomposition. In these sacred pages the painter's pencil and the poet's fancy will meet with magnificent models; but the inquisitive philosopher will look in vain for the hints he is in quest of. The Holy Spirit did not aim at making naturalists, but virtuous men; hence, in describing the creation, He represents it solely in a light the best adapted to excite in us feelings of admiration and gratitude towards the Author of so many wonders and benefits. Nature, as she appears in the sacred text, has not much to gratify the curiosity of the philosopher; but then she delights and ennobles the imagination—she moves and penetrates the heart.

CHAPTER LXX.

HISTORICAL ANALYSIS OF INTELLECTUAL DEVELOPMENT.

FROM the rapid view we have taken of the several branches of learning in their relations to the authority of the Church, it is clear to a demonstration, that the alleged enslavement of the intellect amongst Catholics is nothing but a mere bugbear: in no respect does our faith either arrest or retard the progress of learning. Since, however, it not unfrequently happens that, in arguments apparently the most solid, a flaw is discovered when they are brought to the test of facts, it will be well to corroborate our assertion by historical testimony;

fully assured as we are, that the result must be favorable to the cause of truth. We will begin at the beginning.

M. Guizot maintains that the contest between the Church and the advocates of the freedom of thought originated in the middle ages. Noticing the efforts of John Erigena, Roscelin, Abelard, and the alarm they excited in the Church, he observes: "This was the great event that occurred at the end of the eleventh, and at the beginning of the twelfth centuries, at a time when the Church was under theocratic and monastic influence. It was then that, for the first time, a serious struggle was commenced between the clergy and the freethinkers." (*Hist. Générale de la Civilisation en Europe. Leçon* 6.) The entire scope of M. Guizot's work shows that, in his judgment, the best-founded reproach that could be cast upon the Catholic Church was, that she checked the freedom of thought. According to him, this is the point upon which the advantage of the Protestant system over Catholicity is the least controvertible. His object being the complete development of this idea, in treating of the religious revolution of the sixteenth century it was requisite for him to deposit it as a seed in his preliminary lectures; as otherwise the fact of the Reformation would have appeared isolated, and shorn of its importance. Besides, it was necessary that the resistance of Protestants to the Catholic Church should have a meaning; that it should carry with it the appearance of a noble and generous thought; that it should be regarded as the proclamation of the freedom of the human mind. To attain this end, the Church, on the one hand, must be represented as asserting claims in the middle ages to which she had not previously pretended; and, on the other, those writers who resisted these alleged pretensions of the Church must be held up as men of extraordinary penetration.

Now, such is precisely the thread of M. Guizot's discourse; and we hence infer his efforts to prepare beforehand the triumph of his opinions. His plan, however, is ill-concerted; for he appears to have overlooked the most palpable facts in the history of the Church; and not even to have known what were the doctrines of the three champions, whose names he invokes with so much complacency. That no one may accuse me of making inconsiderate assertions, I will here quote his words literally: "Thus every thing," says he, "seemed turning to the advantage of the Church, of her unity, and of her power. But whilst the Papacy was grasping at the government of the world, whilst the monasteries were undergoing a moral reformation, a few powerful but isolated individuals claimed for human reason the right of being something in man, the right to interfere in the formation of his opinions. Most of them refrained from attacking received opinions, or religious belief; they merely said that reason had a right to prove them; and that it was not enough that they were affirmed by authority. John Erigena, Roscelin, and Abelard were the interpreters, through whom individual reason began to lay claim to her inheritance —the first authors of that movement of liberty, which was associated with the reform movement of Hildebrand and St. Bernard If we seek the dominant feature of this movement, we shall find that it was not a change of opinion, a revolt against the system of public belief; it was simply the right of reasoning claimed for reason." (*Hist. Générale de la Civilisation en Europe. Leçon* 6.)

We will pass over the author's singular parallel between the efforts of John Erigena, Roscelin, and Abelard, and those of the great reformers, Hildebrand or St. Gregory VII., and St. Bernard. These latter sought to reform the Church by legitimate means, to render the clergy more venerable by making them more virtuous, and to win greater respect for authority by sanctifying the persons entrusted with its exercise: the others, according to M. Guizot, resisted this authority in matters of faith; that is, they aimed at its overthrow, and for this purpose laid the axe to the root; the former *were* reformers the latter devastators: and yet we are told that their efforts were directed to one and the same object, had one and the same tendency. Verily, the philosophy of history were a sorry thing, if it could allow of such a confusion of ideas! What progress can be made in this branch of knowledge, by men who have so strange a way of dealing with facts? But, I repeat, let us take leave of these aberrations, and fix our attention specially on two points: the worth of these three writers, so much vaunted, and the idea we are told to entertain of their resistance to authority. Doubtless the names of John Erigena and Roscelin are already pronounced with respect by those persons who would fain be thought well versed in the philosophy of history, without having ever read history, and who are obliged to content themselves with those easy lessons that are learned in an hour, and studied in an evening. With persons of this description, it is enough to have heard these names pronounced with emphasis, to have seen them coupled with epithets, such as *powerful men, advocates of human reason, interpreters of individual reason*, to make them fancy that learning is no less indebted to Erigena and Roscelin than to Descartes or Bacon.

Without bearing in mind the remarks I have already made on the peculiarity of M. Guizot's position, it would not be easy to conjecture why he should seek to represent as new and extraordinary, what was, in fact, neither new nor uncommon; how he could say that the Church first began the contest against liberty of thought, when she put down Erigena, Roscelin, and Abelard. He brings forward these three writers, as though their influence had been paramount; whereas they had no more influence than other sectarians, who abounded in preceding centuries. Who and what really was this John Erigena? A writer but imperfectly versed in theological science; but who, puffed up by the favor shown him by Charles the Bold, broached certain errors on the subject of the Eucharist, predestination and grace. In all that, I see only a man departing from the doctrine of the Church; and in Nicholas the First attempting to stop him in his career, I see only a Pope fulfilling his duty. What is there in all this either new or extraordinary? Does not the whole history of the Church, from the time of the Apostles, exhibit an unbroken succession of similar facts?

I repeat, it is impossible to conceive for what purpose the name of Erigena is brought forward. His errors produced no result of importance; and the age in which he lived cannot be considered as having exercised any great influence on the intellectual development of subsequent times. He lived in the ninth century. Now, this century had no share in the movement of those that followed; indeed, it is well known that the tenth century was the darkest period of ignorance during the middle ages; and that the intellectual movement commenced only at the close of the tenth, and at the opening of the eleventh century. Erigena and Roscelin are separated by two centuries. As for Roscelin and Abelard, it is easier to understand why their names are cited. Every one knows the noise that Abelard made in the world by his doctrines, and perhaps still more by his adventures. Roscelin may also command attention by his errors, and especially as the master of Abelard.

To give an idea of the spirit that guided these men, and of the opinion we are to form of their intentions, we must enter into some details touching their lives and their doctrines. Roscelin was one of the most crafty men of his time. A subtle dialectician and warm partizan of the sect of the Nominalists, he substituted his own opinions for the teaching of the Church; and ended by falling into the gravest errors on the sacred mystery of the Trinity. History has recorded a fact, that proves incontestably the notorious dishonesty of the man—his want of probity and of modesty. At the time that Roscelin was propagating his errors, St. Anselm, who was afterwards archbishop of Canterbury, was living, but at that time abbot of Beck. Lanfranc, archbishop of Canterbury, who died some time before, had left behind him the highest reputation for virtue and sound doctrine. Roscelin thought that the authority of so high a name would give currency and consideration to his errors; and, resorting to the foulest calumny, he affirmed that his opinions were the same as those of Archbishop Lanfranc, and Anselm, abbot of Beck. To this calumny Lanfranc could not reply, as he was already in the tomb; but the abbot of Beck vigorously repelled so unjust an imputation; and at the same time vindicated the reputation of Lanfranc, who had been his master. The works of St. Anselm leave no doubt as to the nature of Roscelin's errors. We find them recorded with the greatest precision. In fact, it were difficult to say why M. Guizot has conferred so much importance upon this man, or why he should be adduced as one of the principal champions of the freedom of thought. There is nothing in Roscelin to distinguish him from other heretics. He is a man who employs artifices and subtleties, and falls into error; but nothing is more common in the history of the Church; and it certainly cannot be considered matter of astonishment.

Abelard is more deserving of notice: his name has become so famous that no one is unacquainted with his sad adventures. A disciple of Roscelin, and as well skilled as his master in the dialectics of the age, endowed with great talents, and eager to parade them on the principal theatres of literature, Abelard earned a reputation never attained by the dialectician of Compiègne. His errors on points of very great importance produced much mischief in the Church, and drew upon himself many sorrows. But it is not true, as M. Guizot will have it, that his doctrines met with less reproof than his method; neither is it true that he and his master Roscelin had no intention of effecting a radical change in matters of doctrine. Evidence of a most unexceptionable kind fortunately places the matter beyond all doubt, and proves that it was not Roscelin's method, but his error on the Trinity, for which he was condemned. Nor have we less certainty in the case of Abelard; for the various errors taken from his works are preserved in the form of articles.

We learn from St. Bernard, that on the Trinity, Abelard held the opinions of Arius—on the Incarnation, those of Nestorius—on grace, those of Pelagius. All this did not merely *tend* to a radical change of doctrine, but actually was one. I do not know that Abelard ever protested against the truth of these accusations; and even if he had, we all know how to estimate such a protest. It is certain that, in the famous Assembly of Sens—convoked at the request of Abelard himself—he had not a word to say in reply to the sainted abbot of Clairvaux, who reproached him with his errors; and laying before him the very words of his propositions, extracted from his writings, urged him either to defend or abjure them Abelard, confronted with so formidable an adversary, was so embarrassed that he could only say, in reply, that he appealed to Rome. The Council of Sens, out of respect for the Holy See, abstained from condemning the person of the innovator, but did not fail to condemn his errors; and this condemnation was approved by the Sovereign Pontiff, and extended to his person also. Now, from the articles containing the errors of Abelard, it does not appear that his dominant idea was to proclaim the liberty of thought. He has, it is true, an overweening confidence in his own subtleties; but, beyond this, his only fault is an erroneous and dogmatizing spirit on points of the greatest importance; a fault which he had in common with all the heretics who preceded him.

All this M. Guizot ought to have known; how he can have overlooked it I cannot imagine, nor why he attaches to these authors an importance which they really do not deserve. Perhaps he was anxious to furnish Protestants with some illustrious predecessors, when he laid such stress on the names of Roscelin and Abelard. These two, after all, were not deficient in ability or in erudition.

and they lived precisely during the early period of the intellectual movement. Probably M. Guizot thought, that to bring these two innovators upon the scene would answer his purpose extremely well, as showing that, from the very dawn of intellectual development, men of the greatest fame had raised their voices in favor of freedom of thought. After all, had M. Guizot succeeded in proving that John Erigena, Roscelin, and Abelard aimed at nothing more than the assertion of the right of private examination in matters of faith, it would not follow that these innovators had not sought to effect a radical change in matters of doctrine. In fact, what can be more radical as regards matters of faith than that which strikes at authority, the root of all certainty? Neither would it follow, that in condemning the errors of these men the Church had taken alarm merely at their *method;* for if this method was to consist in withdrawing the intellect from the yoke of authority, even in matters of faith, it was itself a very grievous error, combated at all times by the Catholic Church, which never would consent to have her authority called in question on points of faith.

And yet, if these innovators had entered into the contest chiefly for the purpose of contending against authority in matters of faith, M. Guizot would have had some reason to notice their proceedings as constituting a new era; but, strange to say, their propositions do not appear to have been drawn up with a view to advocate the independence of thought, nor against authority in matters of faith; it was not for such an attempt, but for other errors, that the Church condemned them. Where, then, are the accuracy and historical truth which we should expect from such a man as M. Guizot? How could he venture, in addressing a numerous audience, thus to substitute his own thoughts for facts? The fact is, he well knew that these were matters generally treated very superficially; that to gain the sympathy of superficial men it would suffice to speak in pompous terms of the liberty of thought, to pronounce certain names probably heard by many for the first time, such as Erigena and Roscelin, and especially to mention the unfortunate lover of Heloïse.

M. Guizot, unable to conceal from himself that his observations upon this period were somewhat feeble, tries to apply a remedy by inserting a passage from the *Introduction to the Theology* of Abelard, which, in my opinion, is very far from answering the purpose of the publicist. His object, in fact, is to show that from that very period a vigorous spirit of resistance to the authority of the Church in matters of faith had sprung up, and that the human mind was even then longing to burst asunder the fetters in which it had been held. He would have us believe that Abelard, yielding to the importunities of his own disciples, had the courge to throw off the yoke of authority; and that his writings were, to a certain extent, the expression of a necessity long felt, of an idea with which many minds had long been agitated. The following is the passage referred to: "If we seek the dominant feature of this movement, we shall find that it was not a change of opinion, a revolt against the system of public belief; it was simply the right of reasoning claimed for reason."

We have already seen how utterly devoid of truth is this assertion of the publicist. The very attack upon authority was itself a radical change in opinions, and a revolution in received doctrines; for the authority of the Church was in itself a dogma, and formed the basis of all religious belief, as experience has satisfactorily shown, since the appearance of Protestantism at the commencement of the sixteenth century. But let us allow the historian to proceed: "The disciples of Abelard, as he himself tells us in his *Introduction to Theology,* required of him philosophical arguments, and such as would satisfy reason, requesting him to teach them not merely to repeat his instructions, but to understand them also; for no one can believe what he does not understand, and it is ridiculous to preach to others things that neither the teacher nor his pupils understand. 'What object can the study of philosophy have but that of leading the mind to the contemplation of God, to whom all things are to be referred? Why are the faithful allowed to read works treating of worldly affairs and the books of the Gentiles, except to prepare them to understand the sacred Scriptures, and to furnish them with the skill necessary for their defence?...... For this purpose alone we should avail ourselves of all our reasoning powers, lest, on questions so difficult and complicated as those that form the object of Christian faith, the subtilty of our opponents should too readily injure the purity of our faith.'"

It cannot be denied, that in Abelard's time a lively curiosity aroused men's minds to employ all their powers to be able to give a reason for what they believed; but it is not true that the Church threw any obstacle in the way of this movement, considering it as a scientific method, and so long as it did not overstep legitimate bounds, and attack or undermine the articles of faith. It is impossible to take a more unfavorable view of the Church than M. Guizot has here taken of her; nor could any one more completely overlook, I will even say distort, facts.

"The importance of this first attempt at liberty," says he, "of this revival of the spirit of inquiry, was soon felt. The Church, though engaged in effecting her own reform, took the alarm nevertheless, and at once declared war against the reformers, whose new methods menaced her with more evils than their doctrines."

Thus is the Church represented as conspiring against the progress of thought, repressing with a strong arm the first attempts of the mind to advance in the path of science, and laying aside questions of doctrine to contend against methods; and all this, we are told, as if it were something new and wonderful. "For," says M. Guizot, "this was the great event which occurred at the end of the eleventh and beginning of the twelfth centuries, at a time when the Church was under theocratic and monastic influence. It was now that, for the first time, a serious struggle commenced between the clergy and the freethinkers. The quarrels of Abelard and St. Bernard, the Councils of Soissons and Sens, in which Abelard was condemned, merely give expression to this event, which has occupied so large a space in the history of modern civilization."

Still the same confusion of ideas. I have said already, and must repeat here that the Church has condemned no method; it was not a *method,* but error, that the Church condemned, unless by a method be meant an assault upon the articles of faith, under pretence of breaking the fetters of authority, which is not merely a method, but an error of the very highest import. In reproving a pernicious doctrine, subversive of all faith, and denying the infallibility of the See of St. Peter in matters of doctrine, the Church did not put forth any new pretensions; her conduct has always been the same ever since the time of the Apostles, and is the same still. The moment a doctrine is propagated that appears in the least degree dangerous, the Church examines it, compares it with the sacred deposit of truth confided to her; if the doctrine is not inconsistent with divine truth, she allows it free circulation, for she is not ignorant that *God has given up the world to the controversies of men;* but if it is opposed to the faith, its condemnation is irremissible, without concern or regret. Were the Church to act otherwise, she would contradict herself, and cease to be what she is, the jealous depository of divine truth. If she allowed her infallible authority to be questioned, that moment she would forget one of her most sacred obligations, and would lose all claim on our belief; for, in betraying an indifference for truth, she would prove herself to be no longer a religion descended from heaven, but a mere delusion.

Precisely at the time of which M. Guizot speaks, we observe a fact which proves that the Church allows free scope to the exercise of thought. The high reputation which St. Anselm sustained during his whole career, and the great esteem in which he was held by the Sovereign Pontiffs of his time, are well known; yet St. Anselm philosophised with great freedom. In the introduction to his *Monologue,* he tells us that some persons entreated him to explain things by reason alone, without the aid of the sacred Scriptures. The Saint was not afraid to comply with their request, and he accordingly wrote the little work we have just named. In other parts of his works, too, St. Anselm adopts the same method. Very few persons concern themselves now-a-days about ancient writers, and doubtless very few have read the works of the holy Doctor of whom we are speaking. They display, however, such perspicuity of thought, such solid reasoning, and above all such a discreet and temperate judgment, that we are surprised to find the human mind, at the very commencement of the intellectual movement, attaining to so high an elevation. In him we find the greatest freedom of thought combined with the respect due to the authority of the Church; and far from impairing the vigor of his ideas, this respect augments their force and perspicuity. From his works we learn that Abelard was not the only one who taught, *not merely to repeat his lectures, but also to understand them;* for St. Anselm, some years previous, followed the same method with a clearness and solidity far beyond what could be expected at that time. We there discover, also, that in the bosom of the Catholic Church men carried the operations of reason to the greatest possible extent, though always within the bounds prescribed by its own weakness, and with reverential regard to the sacred veil that shrouds august mysteries.

The works of St. Anselm prove that Abelard was not exactly the man to teach the world that the end of philosophical studies is to lead the mind to the contemplation of God, to whom all things should be referred; and that we should avail ourselves of all our reasoning powers, lest on questions so difficult and complicated as those that form the object of Christian faith, the subtilties of our opponents should too readily injure the purity of our faith. But from the Saint's profound submission to the authority of the Church, from the candor and ingenuousness with which he acknowledges the limits of the human mind, we see that he was persuaded *that it is not impossible to believe what we do not comprehend;* and, in fact, there is a wide difference between the conviction that a thing exists, and a clear knowledge of the nature of the thing in the existence of which we believe.

CHAPTER LXXI.

RELIGION AND THE HUMAN MIND IN EUROPE.

As we are to examine what was, in the eleventh and twelfth centuries, the conduct of the Church in reference to innovators, we will avail ourselves of the excellent opportunity afforded by this epoch for noticing the progress of the human mind. It has been said that in Europe intellectual development was exclusively theological. This is true, and necessarily so; all the faculties of man receive their development according to the circumstances that surround him; and as his health, his temperament, his strength, his color even, and his stature depend upon climate, food, mode of life, and other circumstances affecting him, so in like manner his moral and intellectual faculties bear the stamp of the principles which predominate in the family and society of which he forms a constituent part. Now, in Europe, religion was the predominating element; in every thing religion made herself heard and felt; nowhere was there a principle of life or action discoverable unconnected with religion. It was quite natural, therefore, that in Europe all the faculties of man should have their development in a religious sense. A little attention will show us that this was the case not with the intellect only, but likewise with the heart, with the passions even, and with the whole moral man; just as, in whatever direction we go in Europe, we meet at every step with some monument of religion; so whatever faculty we examine in the individual European, we find upon it the impress of religion.

And the case was the same with families and society as with individuals; religion was equally predominant in both. Wherever man has progressed towards a state of perfection, we observe a similar phenomenon; and it is an invariable fact in the history of the human race, that no society ever entered on the road to civilization, save under the direction and impulse of religious principles. True or false, rational or absurd, wherever man is on the road to improvement, these principles are found. Some nations, indeed, may well excite our pity at the monstrous superstitions into which they have fallen; but we still must acknowledge, that, under these very superstitions, lay concealed germs of good that did not fail to produce considerable benefits. The Egyptians, Phœnicians, Greeks, and Romans were all extremely superstitious; yet the progress they made in civilization and intellectual culture was such, that their monuments and memorials strike us even yet with admiration. It is easy to smile at an extravagant observance or a senseless dogma; but we should remember that the growth and preservation of certain moral principles cannot be otherwise secured than under the protecting shade of religious belief. Now, these principles are most indispensably necessary to prevent individuals from being monstrously changed, and to maintain the social and family ties unbroken. Much has been said against the immorality tolerated, permitted, and sometimes even taught by certain forms of religion; and certainly nothing is more lamentable than to behold man thus led astray by that which ought to be his best guide. Let us, however, look for a reality beneath these shadows, which appear at first so gloomy, and we shall soon discover some rays of light that may lead us to regard false religions, not indeed with indulgence, but with less horror than those infamous systems which make matter self-existent, and pleasure the only divinity.

To preserve the idea of moral good and evil, an idea without meaning except in the supposition that there exists a divine power, is itself an inestimable advantage. Now this advantage adheres inseparably to every form of religion, even to those that make the most absurd and most criminal applications of the idea of good and evil. Doubtless, the people of antiquity, and those of our own time who have not received the light of Christianity, have gone most deplorably astray; but, in the midst of their very wanderings, there always remains a certain degree of light; and this light, however dimly it shines, however faint and feeble its rays, is incomparably better than the thick darkness of atheism. Between the nations of antiquity and those of Europe there is this very remarkable difference, that the former passed from a state of infancy to a state of civilization; while the latter advanced to this, in passing from that undefinable state which, in Europe, was the result of the invasion of the barbarians, of the confused mixture of a young with a decrepit society, of rude and ferocious nations with others that were civilized, cultivated, or rather effeminate. Hence, amongst the ancients the imagination was developed before the intellect, whilst amongst Europeans the intellect came before the imagination. With the former, poetry came first; with the latter, what is termed dialectics and metaphysics.

What is the reason of so striking a difference? When a people are yet in their infancy, either an infancy properly so called, or having lived long in ignorance, in a state similar to that of an infant people, we find them rich in sensations, but very poor in ideas. Nature, with her majesty, her wonders, and her mysteries, affects such a people the most; their language is grand, picturesque, and highly poetical; their passions are not refined, but, on the other hand, they are very energetic and violent. Now an intellect that ingenuously seeks the light, loves truth in its purity and simplicity, confesses and embraces it readily, lending itself neither to subtilties, artifices, nor disputes. The least thing that makes a vivid impression upon the senses or the imagination of such a people fills them with surprise and wonder; you cannot inspire them with enthusiasm without setting before them something heroic and sublime.

On the first glance at the state of the people of Europe in the middle ages, we perceive in them a certain resemblance to an infant people, but, at the same time, a very striking difference on several points. Their passions are very strong, they are pleased beyond every thing with the wonderful and the extraordinary, and, for want of realities, their imagination conjures up gigantic phantoms. The profession of arms is their favorite occupation; they rush eagerly into the most perilous adventures, and meet them with incredible courage. All this indicates a development of the feelings of sensibility and imagination, inasmuch as they produce intrepidity and valor; but, strange to say, together with these dispositions, we find a singular taste for things the most purely intellectual; with the most lively, ardent, and picturesque reality, we find associated a taste for the coldest and barest abstractions. A knight, with the cross on his shoulder, gorgeously clad, covered with trophies, beaming with glory won in a hundred combats; a subtile dialectician, disputing on the system of the Nominalists, and urging his subtilely devised abstractions till he becomes unintelligible;—these are certainly two characters very dissimilar, and yet they exist together in the same society; both have their prestige, receive the greatest homage, and are followed by enthusiastic admirers. Even when we have taken into account the singular position of the European nations at that period, it is not easy to assign a cause for this anomaly. We can easily understand how the people of Europe, emerging, for the most part, from the forests of the North, and engaged for a long time either in intestine wars or in conflicts with vanquished tribes, should have preserved, together with their warlike habits, a strong and lively imagination and violent passions; but it is not so easy to account for their taste for an order of ideas purely metaphysical and dialectical. When, however, we come to look deeply into the matter, we discover that this apparent anomaly had its origin in the very nature of things. How is it that a people in their infancy have so much imagination and sensibility? Because the objects by which these faculties are naturally excited abound around them; because individuals, being continually exposed to the influence of external things, these objects operate upon them more forcibly. Man first feels and imagines; later he understands and reflects: this is the natural order in which his faculties begin to operate. Hence, with every people the development of the imagination and of the passions precedes that of the intellect; the passions and the imagination finding their object and aliment before the intellect. This accounts, also, for the fact that the poetical always precedes the philosophical era. From this it follows, that nations in their infancy think little, as they want ideas; and this is the chief distinctive mark between them and the people of Europe at the period we are speaking of. In fact, *ideas* at that time *abounded in Europe;* and hence the purely intellectual was held in such repute even amidst the most profound ignorance. Hence, also, the intellect strove to shine even before its time appeared to have arrived. Sound ideas respecting God, respecting man and society, were already everywhere disseminated, thanks to the incessant teaching of Christianity; and as there still remained numerous traces of the wisdom of antiquity, both Christian and Pagan, the consequence was, that every man possessed of a little learning had, in fact, a great fund of ideas.

It is clear, however, that notwithstanding these advantages, the minds of men could not, amidst the chaos of erudition and philosophy that then presented itself, escape the confusion naturally resulting from the wide-spread ignorance, occasioned by a long succession of revolutions. They could not possess sufficient discrimination and judgment to pursue all at once, and with success, the study of the Bible, of the writings of the holy Fathers, of the civil and canon law, of the works of Aristotle, and of the Arabian commentaries. Yet these were all studied at the same time; on all these, disputes were zealously maintained; and the errors and extravagances which in such a state of things were inevitable were accompanied by the presumption that is invariably inherent in ignorance. To succeed in explaining certain passages of the Bible, of the Fathers, of the codes, and of the works of philosophers, great preparatory labors were necessary, as the experience of subsequent ages has proved. It was necessary to study languages, to examine archives and monuments, to collect together from all parts an immense mass of materials; then, to reduce these to order, to compare them together, and to discriminate between them; in a word, it was necessary to possess a rich fund of learning, enlightened by the torch of criticism. Now all this was then wanting, and could only be attained in the course of ages. The consequence was inevitable, considering the mania that existed for explaining every thing. If a difficulty arose, and the facts and knowledge requisite for its solution were wanting, they adopted a roundabout way; instead of seeking the support derivable from facts, the disputants took their stand upon an idea; substituting some subtle abstraction for solid reasoning; where they found it impossible to form a body of sound doctrine, they threw together a confused mass of ideas and words. Who could repress a smile, or not feel pity for Abelard, for instance, promising his disciples to explain to them the prophet Ezechiel, with very little time for preparation, and actually fulfilling his promise? I would ask the reader whether, in the middle of the thirteenth century, an explanation of Ezechiel, given with only a slight preparation, could have been successsful or interesting?

The study of dialectics and metaphysics was embraced with so much ardor, that in a short time these branches of knowledge superseded all others. The consequences were prejudicial to the minds of men; their attention being wholly engrossed by this object of their choice, the pursuit of more solid learning was regarded with indifference—history was neglected, literature unnoticed, in a word, the mind was only half developed. Every thing appertaining to the imagination and the feelings was sacrificed to the cultivation of the intellect; not, indeed, in its most useful operations,—the formation of a clear and perfect perception, of a mature judgment, of a habit of sound and accurate reasoning, —but in those which are astute, subtle, and extravagant.

Those who would reproach the Church for her conduct at that period in reference to innovators have a very imperfect understanding of the actual condition of Europe as regards science and religion. We have already seen that the intellectual development was religious; consequently, even when it deviated from the right path, it still retained this character, and the oddest subtilties were applied to mysteries the most sublime. Almost all the heretics of the time were renowned dialecticians, and their errors arose from an excess of subtilty. Roscelin, one of the leading dialecticians of his time, was the founder, or at least one of the leaders of the sect of the Nominalists. Abelard was celebrated for the readiness of his talents, his skill in disputation, and his address in explaining every thing to suit his thesis. The abuse of his intellect led him into the errors which we have already spoken of—errors which he would have avoided, had he not proudly yielded himself up to his own vain thoughts. The mania for subtilising every thing drew Gilbert de la Poirée into the most lamentable errors on the subject of the Divinity; Amaury, another celebrated philosopher, after the fashion of the time, took up so warmly the question of Aristotle's primordial matter, that he ended by declaring matter to be God. The Church strenuously opposed these errors, which arose in great numbers in minds led astray by vain arguments, and puffed up with foolish pride. It would argue a strange misconception of the true interests of science, to suppose that the Church's resistance to these raving innovators was not most favorable to intellectual progress.

These headstrong men, eager in the pursuit of knowledge, and captivated by the first chimera presented to their imagination, stood greatly in need of some discreet authority to restrain them within the bounds of reason and moderation. The intellect had scarcely taken the first steps in the career of knowledge, and yet fancied it already knew every thing, "pretending to know all things except the *nescio*, I know not," as St. Bernard reproaches the vain Abelard. Why should we not, for the good of humanity, and the credit of the human intellect, approve the condemnation pronounced by the Church against the errors of Gilbert, which aimed at nothing less than the overthrow of the ideas that we have of God? If Amaury and his disciple David de Dinant are smitten by the sentence of the Church, it is because they destroy the idea of the Divinity by confounding the Creator with *primordial matter.* Was it for the advantage of Europe that its intellectual movement should be commenced by precipitating itself at the very outset into the abyss of pantheism?

Had the human intellect followed in its development the way marked out for it by the Church, European civilization would have gained at least two centuries; the fourteenth century would have been as far advanced as the sixteenth was. To convince ourselves of the truth of this assertion, we have only to compare writings with writings, and men with men; the men most firmly attached to the faith of the Church attained to such eminence that they left the age in which they lived far behind them. Roscelin's antagonist was St. Anselm; the latter always remained faithful to the authority of the Church; the former rebelled against her: and who, let met ask, would have the hardihood to compare the dialectician of Compiègne with the learned Archbishop of Canterbury? How vast the difference between the profound and skilful metaphysician who composed the Monologue and the Prosologue, and the frivolous leader of the disputes of the Nominalists! Have the subtilties and cavillings of Roscelin any weight whatever against the lofty thoughts of the man who, in the eleventh century, to prove the existence of God, could reject all vain and captious reasonings, concentrate himself within himself, consult his own ideas, compare them with their object, and demonstrate the existence of God from the very idea of God, thus anticipating Descartes by five hundred years? Who best understood the true interests of science? Show me how the intellect of St. Anselm was degraded or shackled by the influence of the formidable authority of the Church, by any usurpation on the part of Popes of the rights of the human mind. And can Abelard himself be compared, either as a man, or as a writer, with his Catholic adversary, St. Bernard? Abelard was a perfect master of all the subtilties of the schools; noisy disputes were his amusement; he was intoxicated with the applause of his disciples, who were dazzled by their master's talents and courage, and still more by the learned follies of the age; yet what has become of his works? Who reads them? Who ever thinks of finding in them a single page of sound reasoning, the description of a single great event, or a picture of the manners of the time, in other words, the least matter of interest to science or history? On the contrary, what man of learning has not often sought this in the immortal works of St. Bernard?

It is impossible to find a more sublime personification of the Church combating against the heretics of his time than the illustrious Abbot of Clairvaux, contending against all innovators, and speaking, if we may use the term, in the name of the Catholic faith. No one could more worthily represent the ideas and sentiments which the Church endeavored to diffuse amongst mankind, nor more faithfully delineate the course through which Catholicity would have led the human mind. Let us pause for a moment in the presence of this gigantic mind, which attained to an eminence far beyond any of its contemporaries. This extraordinary man fills the world with his name—upheaves it by his words—sways it by his influence; in the midst of darkness he is its light; he forms, as it were, a mysterious link, connecting the two epochs of St. Jerome and St. Augustine, of Bossuet and Bourdaloue. In the midst of a general relaxation and corruption of morals, by the strictest observances and the most perfect purity he is proof against every assault. Ignorance prevails throughout all classes; he studies night and day to enlighten his mind. A false and counterfeit erudition usurps the place of true knowledge; he knows its unsoundness, disdains and despises it; and his eagle eye discovers at a glance that the star of truth moves at an immense distance from this false reflection, from this crude mass of subtilties and follies, which the men of his time termed philosophy. If at that period there existed any useful learning, it was to be sought in the Bible, and in the writings of the holy Fathers; to the study of these, therefore, St. Bernard devotes himself unremittingly. Far from consulting the vain babblers who are arguing and declaiming in the shools, St. Bernard seeks his inspirations in the silence of the cloister, or in the august sanctuary of the temple; if he goes out, it is to contemplate the great book of nature, to study eternal truths in the solitude of the desert, and, as he himself has expressed it, "in forests of beech-trees."

Thus did this great man, rising superior to the prejudices of his time, avoid the evil produced in his contemporaries by the method then prevailing. By this method the imagination and the feelings were stifled; the judgment warped; the intellect sharpened to excess; and learning converted into a labyrinth of confusion. Read the works of the sainted Abbot of Clairvaux, and you will find that all his faculties go, as it were, hand in hand. If you look for imagination, you will find the finest coloring, faithful portraits, and splendid descriptions. If you want feeling, you will learn how skilfully he finds his way into the heart, captivates, subdues, and fashions it to his will. Now he strikes a salutary fear into the hardened sinner, tracing with great force the formidable picture of the divine justice and the eternal vengeance; then he consoles and sustains the man who is sinking under worldly adversity, the assaults of his passions, the recollection of his transgressions, or an exaggerated fear of the divine justice. Do you want pathos? Listen to his colloquies with Jesus and Mary; hear him speaking of the blessed Virgin with such enrapturing sweetness, that he seems to exhaust all the epithets that the liveliest hope and the most pure and tender love can suggest. Would you have vigor and vehemence of style, and that irresistible torrent of eloquence which nothing can resist, which carries the mind beyond itself, fires it with enthusiasm, compels it to enter upon the most arduous paths, and to undertake the most heroic enterprises? See him with his burning words inflaming the zeal of the people, nobles, and kings; moving them to quit their homes, to take up arms, and to unite in numerous armies that pour into Asia to rescue the Holy Sepulchre. This extraordinary man is every where met with, every where heard. Entirely free from ambition, he possesses, nevertheless, a leading influence in the great affairs of Europe: though fond of solitude and retirement, he is continually obliged to quit the obscurity of the cloister to assist in the councils of kings and popes. He never flatters, never betrays the truth, never dissembles the sacred ardor which burns within his breast; and yet he is every where listened to with profound respect; his stern voice is heard in the cottages of the poor and in the palaces of kings; he admonishes with terrible severity the most obscure monk and the Sovereign Pontiff.

In the midst of so much ardor and activity, his mind loses none of its clearness or precision. His exposition of a point of doctrine is remarkable for ease and lucidity; his demonstrations are vigorous and conclusive; his reasoning is conducted with a force of logic that presses close upon his adversary, and leaves him no means of escape: in defence, his quickness and address are surprising. In his answers he is clear and precise; in repartee, quick and penetrating; and without dealing in the subtilties of the schools, he displays wonderful tact in disentangling truth from error, sound reason from artifice and fraud. Here is a man formed entirely and exclusively under the influence of Catholicity; a man who never strayed from the pale of the Church, who never dreamed of setting his intellect free from the yoke of authority; and yet he rises like a mighty pyramid above all the men of his time.

To the eternal honor of the Catholic Church, and utterly to disprove the accusation brought against her, of exerting an influence hostile to the freedom of the human mind, I must observe that St. Bernard was not the only man who rose superior to the age, and pointed out the way to genuine progress. It is unquestionably certain, that the most distinguished men of that period, those least influenced by the evils that so long kept the human mind in pursuit of mere vanities and shadows, were precisely the men most devotedly attached to Catholicity. These men set an example of what was necessary to be done for the advancement of learning; an example that for a long time had, it is true, but few followers, but which found some in subsequent ages: now it is to be observed that the progress of learning was due to the credit obtained by this method—I speak of the study of antiquity.

The sacred sciences were the chief object of attention at this period; as the intellect was theologically developed, dialectics and metaphysics were studied with a view to their application to theology. With Roscelin, Abelard, Gilbert de la Poirée, and Amaury, the phrase was: "Let us reason, subtilise, and apply our systems to all sorts of questions; let our reason be our rule and guide, without which knowledge is impossible." With St. Bernard, St. Anselm, Hugh and Richard de St. Victor, Peter Lombard, on the contrary, it was: "Let us see what antiquity teaches; let us study the works of the holy Fathers; let us analyse and compare their texts; we cannot place our dependence exclusively on arguments, which are sometime dangerous and sometimes futile." Which of these two judgments has been actually confirmed? Which of these methods was adopted when real progress was to be made? Was not recourse had to an unremitting study of ancient works? Was it not found necessary to throw aside the cavils of the dialecticians? Protestants themselves boast of having taken this way; their theologians consider it an honor to be versed in antiquity; and would be offended if treated as mere dialecticians. On which side, then, was reason? With the heretics, or with the Church? Who best understood the method most favorable to intellectual progress? The heretical dialectician, or the orthodox doctor? To these questions there can only be one reply. These are not mere opinions—they are facts; not an empty theory, but the actual history of learning, as known by all the world, and as represented to us in irrefragable documents. Unless prepossessed by the authority of M. Guizot, the reader certainly cannot complain that I have eschewed questions of history, or claimed his belief on my own bare word.

Unhappily, mankind seemed doomed never to find the true road without going a long way round; thus the intellect, taking the very worst way of all, went in pursuit of subtilties and cavils, forsaking the beaten track of reason and good sense. At the beginning of the twelfth century the evil had reached to such a height, that to apply a remedy was no slight undertaking; nor is it easy to say how far matters might have gone, nor what evils would have ensued in various ways, had not Providence, who never abandons the care of the moral, any more than of the physical universe, raised up an extraordinary genius, who, rising to an immense height above the men of his age, reduced the chaos to order. Out of the undigested mass, by retrenching here, adding there, classifying and explaining, this man collected a fund of real learning. Persons acquainted with the history of learning at that time will readily understand that I speak of St. Thomas Aquinas. Rightly to appreciate the extraordinary merit of this great Doctor, we must view him in connection with the times and circumstances of which we are treating. Beholding in St. Thomas Aquinas one of the most luminous, most comprehensive, and most penetrating intellects that have ever adorned the human race, we are almost tempted to think that his appearance in the thirteenth century was inopportune; we regret that he did not live in a more recent age, to enter the lists with the most illustrious men of whom modern Europe can boast. But, upon further reflection, we find that the human mind owes so much to him, we see so clearly the reason why his appearance at the time when Europe received his lectures was most opportune, that we have no other feeling left than one of profound admiration of the designs of Providence.

What was the philosophy of his time? Amidst the strange compound of Greek and Arabian philosophy and of Christian ideas, what would have become of dialectics, metaphysics, and morality? We have already seen what sort of fruit began to grow out of such combinations, favored by a degree of ignorance unable to distinguish the real nature of things, and encouraged by pride that pretended to a knowledge of every thing. And yet the evil was only beginning; its further development would have been attended with symptoms still more alarming. Fortunately, this great man appeared; the first touch of his powerful hand advanced learning two or three centuries. He could not root out the evil, but at least he applied a remedy; owing to his indisputable superiority, his method and his learning soon won their way everywhere. He became, as it were, the centre of a grand system, round which all other scholastic writers were forced to revolve; he thus prevented a multitude of errors that without his intervention would have been almost inevitable. He found the schools in a state of complete anarchy; he reduced them to order; and on account of his angelic intellect, and his eminent sanctity, was looked up to as their sublime dictator. This is the view I take of the mission of St. Thomas; it will be viewed in the same light by all those who study his works, and do not content themselves with a hasty perusal of a biographical article respecting him.

Now this man was a Catholic, and the Catholic Church venerates him upon her altars, and I do not see that his mind was shackled by authority in matters of faith; it goes abroad freely amongst all the branches of knowledge; he unites in his person such extensive and profound acquirements as to appear a prodigy for the age in which he lived. We observe in St. Thomas, notwithstanding the purely scholastic method which he adopted, the same characteristic that we discover in all the eminent Catholic writers of the times. He reasons much; but it is easy to see that he does not trust entirely to his reason, but proceeds with that wise diffidence which is an unequivocal sign of real learning. He avails himself of the doctrines of Aristotle; but evidently would have made less use of them, and more of the Fathers, but for his leading idea, which was, to make the philosophy of his time subservient to the defence of religion. The reader must not suppose that his metaphysics and moral philosophy are a congeries of inexplicable enigmas, as a knowledge of the period at which he wrote might lead us to apprehend. Nothing of the kind; and any one who entertains such an idea has evidently not spent much time in the study of his writings.

His metaphysical works, it must be acknowledged, make us perfectly acquainted with the dominant ideas of the time; but it is equally undeniable, that in every page we meet with the most luminous passages on the most complicated questions of ideology, ontology, cosmology, and psychology; so much so, that we almost imagine we are reading the works of a philosopher who wrote after the fullest development of the sciences had been attained

What his political ideas were, we have already seen; were it necessary, and did the nature of the present work permit, I might here produce many fragments from his *Treatise on Laws and on Justice*, distinguished for such solid principles, such lofty views, so profound a knowledge of the nature of society, that they would occupy an honorable position amongst the best works on legislation written in modern times. His treatises on virtues and vices, whether considered generally, or in detail, exhaust the subject, and defy all subsequent writers to produce a single idea of any importance that has not been already either developed, or at least suggested in them. Above all, his works are remarkable for moderation and extreme reserve in doctrinal expositions, in which respect they are eminently conformable to the spirit of Catholicity; and assuredly if all writers had followed in his footsteps, the field of science would have presented us with an assembly of sages, and would not have been converted into a blood-stained arena for furious combatants. Such is his modesty, that he does not relate a single incident in his life, private or public; from him we hear nothing but the language of enlightened reason, calmly dispensing its treasures: the man, with his fame, his misfortunes, his labors, and all his vain pretensions, with which other writers are wont to weary us, never appears for an instant. (41)

CHAPTER LXXII.

ON THE PROGRESS OF THE HUMAN MIND FROM THE ELEVENTH CENTURY TO THE PRESENT TIME.

I THINK I have satisfactorily vindicated the Catholic Church from the reproaches cast upon her by her enemies, for her conduct during the eleventh and twelfth centuries in reference to the development of the human mind. Let us now take a rapid survey of the march of intellect up to our own times, and see what titles Protestantism can produce to the gratitude of the friends of progress in human knowledge.

If I mistake not, the following are the phases through which the human mind has passed, since the revival of learning in the eleventh century. First came the epoch of subtilties, with its heaps of crude erudition; then the age of criticism, with appropriate attempts at grave controversies on the meaning of records and monuments; and finally came the reflecting age, and the inauguration of the philosophical period. The eleventh and succeeding centuries, to the sixteenth, were characterized by a fondness for dialectics and erudite trifles; criticism and controversy formed the distinctive characteristics of the sixteenth, and part of the seventeenth centuries; the philosophical spirit began to prevail towards the middle of the seventeenth, and continued to our own time. Now of what advantage was Protestantism to learning? None; Protestantism found learning already accumulated—this I can easily prove—Erasmus and Louis Vives shone in the time of Luther.

Did Protestantism promote the study of criticism? Yes; just as an epidemic that decimates nations aids the progress of the medicinal art. But we must not suppose that the taste for this kind of literary labor would not have been disseminated without the aid of the pseudo-Reformation. As monuments came to light, as a knowledge of languages became more general, as the public acquired clearer and more correct notions of history, people would naturally set themselves to discriminate between the apocryphal and the authentic. The necessary documents were at hand, and were studied unremittingly; for this was the favorite taste of the epoch. Under such circumstances, how is it possible there should have existed no desire to examine to what author, and to what age, such documents severally belonged; to investigate how far ignorance or dishonesty had falsified them, had taken from, or added to them? On this subject, I need only relate what took place relative to the famous decretals of Isidore Mercator. These decretals had been received, without opposition, during the centuries anterior to the fifteenth, owing to the want of antiquarian and critical research; but the moment that knowledge and facts began to accumulate, the edifice of imposture gave way. As early as the fifteenth century, Cardinal Cusa challenged the authenticity of certain decretals that had been supposed to be anterior to Pope Siricius; and the reflections of the learned Cardinal led the way to other attacks of a similar kind. A serious discussion arose, in which Protestants naturally took part; but it would unquestionably have been engaged in all the same, if Catholic writers had been left entirely to themselves. When the learned came to read the codes of Theodosius and Justinian, the works of antiquity, and collections of ecclesiastical records, they could not possibly fail to observe that the spurious decretals contained sentences and fragments belonging to an era posterior to the time to which they were referred; and when once such doubts had arisen, error was sure to be promptly exposed.

We may say of controversy, what we have just said of criticism. There would have been no want of controversy, even if the unity of the faith had never been violated. In support of this assertion, the recollection of what occurred amongst the different schools of Catholics is quite conclusive. These schools were engaged in controversy amongst themselves, in the presence even of the common opponent: and we may rest assured that, if their attention had not been partially diverted by that enemy, their polemical discussions would have been maintained only with the greater energy and warmth. Protestants have no more the advantage over Catholics, as regards controversy than as regards criticism. However true it be that some of our theologians did not see the necessity of opposing the enemy with arms superior to those taken from the arsenal of Aristotelian philosophy, it is quite certain that a great number of them took up a sufficiently lofty position, and were thoroughly impressed with the importance of the crisis, and urged the introduction of very great modifications into the course of theological studies. Bellarmin, Melchior Cano, Petau, and many others, were no way inferior to the most skilful Protestants, whatever may have been the boasted scientific merits of the defenders of error.

The knowledge of the learned languages must have contributed in an extraordinary degree to the progress of critical and controversial learning. Now I do not see that Catholics were behind others in the knowledge of Latin, Greek, and Hebrew. Anthony de Nebrija, Erasmus, Louis Vives, Lawrence Villa, Leonardus Aretinus, Cardinal Bembo, Sadolet, Poggio, Melchior Cano, and many others, too numerous to mention; were they, I ask, trained in Protestantism? Did not the Popes, moreover, take the lead in this literary movement? Who patronized the learned with greater liberality? Who supplied them with more abundant resources? Who incurred greater expenses in the purchase of the best manuscripts? Nor let it be forgotten, that such was the taste for pure Latinity, that some among the learned objected to read the Vulgate, for fear of acquiring inelegant phrases.

As regards Greek, we need only bear in mind the causes that led to its diffusion in Europe, to be convinced that the progress made in the knowledge of this language owes nothing whatever to the pseudo-Reformation. It is well known that, after the taking of Constantinople by the Turks, the literary remains of that unfortunate nation were brought to the coasts of Italy. In Italy the study of Greek was first seriously commenced; from Italy it spread to France, and to the other European states. Half a century before the appearance of Protestantism, this language was taught in Paris by the Italian Gregory de Tiferno. At the end of the fifteenth and beginning of the sixteenth centuries, Germany itself could boast of the celebrated John Reuchlin, who taught Greek with great applause, first at Orleans and Poictiers, and afterwards at Ingolstadt. Reuchlin, being on one occasion at Rome, so felicitously explained, and read with so pure an accent, a passage from Thucydides, in the presence of Argyropilus, that the latter, filled with admiration, exclaimed: "*Græcia nostra exilio transvolavit Alpes;* our exiled Greece has crossed the Alps."

Respecting Hebrew, I will transcribe a passage from the Abbé Goujet: "Protestants," says he, "would fain have it thought that they effected the revival of this language in Europe; but they are forced to acknowledge, that whatever they know of Hebrew they owe to the Catholics, who were their teachers, and the sources whence, even to this day, is obtained all that is most valuable in Oriental literature. John Reuchlin, who lived the greater part of his time in the fifteenth century, was unquestionably a Catholic, and one of the most skilful Hebrew scholars, and was also the first Christian who reduced the teaching of that language to a system. John Weissel of Groningen had taught him the elements of this language, and had himself pupils in whom he had awakened a love for this study. In like manner, it was by the exertions of Picus de Mirandula, who was a strict Catholic, that a taste for the study of Hebrew was revived in the West. At the time of the Council of Trent, most of the heretics who then knew that language had learned it in the bosom of the Church they had forsaken; and their vain subtilties respecting the meaning of the sacred text excited the faithful to still greater assiduity in the study of a language so well calculated to insure their own triumph and the defeat of their opponents. In devoting themselves to this branch of study, moreover, they were only following out the intentions of Pope Clement V., who, as early as the beginning of the fourteenth century, had ordained that Greek, and Hebrew, and even Arabic and Chaldean, should be publicly taught, for the benefit of foreigners, at Rome, at Paris, at Oxford, at Bologna, and at Salamanca. The design of this Pope, who so well knew the advantages resulting from well-conducted studies, was, to augment the learning of the Church by the study of languages, and to raise up doctors capable of defending her against every form of error. By means of these languages, and more especially of Hebrew, he intended to renew the study of the sacred books, that the latter, when read in the original, might appear more worthy of the Holy Spirit who inspired them, and by their combined grandeur and simplicity, when better known, awaken greater reverence for them; and that, without derogating from the respect due to the Latin version, it might be felt that an intimate acquaintance with the originals was peculiarly serviceable in confirming the faith of believers, and confuting heretics." (L'Abbé Goujet, *Discours sur le renouvellement des Etudes, et principalement des Etudes ecclésiastiques depuis le quatorzième siècle.*)

One of the causes which contributed the most to the development of the human mind was the creation of great centres of instruction, collecting the most illustrious talents and learning, and diffusing rays of light in all directions. I know not how men could forget that this idea was not due to the pretended Reformation, seeing that most of the universities of Europe were established long before the birth of Luther. That of Oxford was established in 895; Cambridge in 1280; that of Prague, in Bohemia, in 1358; that of Louvain, in

Belgium, in 1425; that of Vienna, in Austria, in 1365; that of Ingolstadt, in Germany, in 1372; that of Leipsic in 1408; that of Basle, in Switzerland, in 1469; that of Salamanca in 1200; that of Alcala in 1517. It would be superfluous to notice the antiquity of the universities of Paris, of Bologna, of Ferrara, and of a great many others, which attained the highest renown long before the advent of Protestantism. The Popes, it is well known, took an active part in the establishment of universities, granting them privileges, and bestowing upon them the highest honors and distinctions. How can any one, then, venture to assert, that Rome has opposed the progress of learning and the sciences, in order to keep the people in darkness and ignorance? As if Divine Providence had intended to confound these future calumniators of His Church, Protestantism made its appearance precisely at the time when, under the auspices of a renowned Pope, the progress in the science, in literature and the arts was most active. Posterity, judging of our disputes with impartiality, will undoubtedly pass a severe sentence upon those pretended philosophers, who are constantly endeavoring to prove from history, that Catholicity has impeded the progress of the human mind, and that scientific progress has been all owing to the cry of liberty raised in central Germany. Yes; sensible men in future ages, like those of our own times, will form a correct judgment upon this subject, when they reflect that Luther began to propagate his errors *in the age of Leo X.*

Certainly, the court of Rome could not at that time be reproached with obscurantism. Rome was at the head of all progress, which she urged onwards with the most active zeal, the most ardent enthusiasm; so much so, indeed, that if she were censurable at all—if there were in her conduct any thing of which history should disapprove—it was rather that her march was too quick than too slow. Had another St. Bernard addressed Leo X., he would assuredly not have blamed him for abusing his authority to impede the march of the human intellect and the progress of learning. "The Reformation," says M. de Chateaubriand, "deeply imbued with the spirit of its founder—a coarse and jealous monk—declared itself the enemy of the arts. By prohibiting the exercise of the imaginative faculties, it clipped the wings of genius, and made her plod on foot. It raised an outcry against certain alms destined for the erection of the basilica of St. Peter for the use of the Christian world. Would the Greeks have refused the assistance solicited from their piety for the building of a temple to Minerva? Had the Reformation been completely successful from the beginning, it would have established, for a time at least, another species of barbarism: viewing as superstition the pomp of divine worship; as idolatry the *chefs-d'œuvre* of sculpture, of architecture, and of painting, its tendency was to annihilate lofty eloquence and sublime poetry—to degrade taste, by repudiating its models—to introduce a dry, cold, and captious formality into the operations of the mind—to substitute in society affectation and materialism in lieu of ingenuousness and intellectuality, and to make machinery take the place of manual and mental operations. These are truths confirmed by every-day experience.

"Amongst the various branches of the reformed religion, their approximation to the beautiful and sublime is always found to be proportioned to the amount of Catholic truth they have retained. In England, where an ecclesiastical hierarchy has been upheld, literature has had its classic era. Lutheranism preserves some sparks of imagination, which Calvinism aims at utterly extinguishing; and so on, till we come to Quakerism, which would reduce social life to unpolished manners and the practice of trades. Shakspeare, in all probability, was a Catholic; Milton has evidently imitated some parts of the poems of St. Avitus and Masenius; Klopstock has borrowed very largely from the faith of Rome. In our own days, in Germany, the high imaginative powers have been put forth only when the spirit of Protestantism had begun to decline. It was in treating Catholic subjects that the genius of Goethe and Schiller was manifested; Rousseau and Madame de Staël are, indeed, illustrious exceptions to this rule; but were they Protestants after the model of the first disciples of Calvin? At this very day, painters, architects, and sculptors, of all the conflicting creeds, go to seek inspiration at Rome, where they find universal toleration. Europe, nay, the whole world, is covered with monuments of the Catholic religion. To it we are indebted for that Gothic architecture, which rivals in its details, and eclipses in its magnificence, the monuments of Greece. It is now three centuries since Protestantism arose,—it is powerful in England, in Germany, in America,—it is professed by millions of men,—and what has it erected? It can show only the ruins it has made; on which perhaps, it has planted gardens or built factories. Rebelling against the authority of tradition, the experience of centuries, and the venerable wisdom of ages, Protestantism let go its hold on the past, and planted a society without roots. Acknowledging for their founder a German monk of the sixteenth century, the reformers renounced the wonderful genealogy that unites Catholics, through a succession of great and holy men, with Jesus Christ Himself, and, through Him, with the patriarchs and the earliest of mankind. The Protestant era, from the first hours of its existence, refused all relationship with the era of that Leo who protected the civilized world against Attila, and also with the era of that other Leo, at whose coming barbarism vanished, and society, now no longer in need of defence, put on the ornaments of civilization." (*Etud. Histor.*, François I.)

It is much to be regretted that the author of such noble sentiments, who so accurately describes the effects of Protestantism on literature and the arts, should have said, that "the Reformation was, properly speaking, philosophic truth, under the guise of Christianity, attacking religious truth." (*Etud. Histor.*, Preface.) What is the meaning of these words? We shall best understand them from the illustrious author's own explanation. "Religious truth," says he, "is the knowledge of one God manifested in a form of worship. Philosophic truth is the threefold knowledge of things intellectual, moral, and natural." (*Etud. Histor.*, Exposition.) It is difficult to imagine how any one who admits the truth of the Catholic religion, and, as a necessary consequence, the falsehood of Protestantism, can define the latter to be, philosophic truth at war with religious truth. In the natural, as well as in the supernatural, order of things, in philosophy as in religion, all truths come from God, all end in Him. There cannot, therefore, be any antagonism between truths of one order and truths of another order; between religious and *true* philosophy, between nature and grace, no antagonism is possible. Truth is that which is; for truth resides in beings themselves; we should rather say, it consists of beings themselves such as they exist, such as they are in their substance; and hence it is quite incorrect to say that philosophic truth has ever stood in antagonism to religious truth.

According to the same author "Philosophic truth is neither more nor less than the independence of the human mind; its tendency being to make discoveries, and lead to perfection in the three sciences that come within its sphere, viz. the intellectual, the moral, and the natural. But philosophic truth," he continues, "looking forwards to the future, has stood in opposition to religious truth, which adheres to the past, owing to the immovable nature of the eternal principle upon which it is founded." (*Etud. Histor.*, Exposition.) With all the respect due to the immortal author of the *Génie du Christianisme* and of the *Martyrs*, I must take the liberty to observe, that we find here a lamentable confusion of ideas. The philosophic truth of which M. de Chateaubriand here treats, must be either science itself, considered as an aggregate of truths, or a general knowledge, in which truth and error are commingled; or, in fine, the whole body of men of learning, considered as constituting a very influential class in society. In the first case, it is impossible for philosophic truth to be in antagonism to religious truth,—that is, to Catholicity; in the second case, the alleged opposition is nothing extraordinary, for error being in this ease mixed up with truth, will on some points be found to be opposed to Catholic faith; and, finally, as regards the third hypothesis, it is unfortunately too true, that many men, distinguished by their talents and erudition, have been opposed to Catholicity; but, on the other hand, as great a number of men equally eminent have triumphantly maintained the truth of Catholicity; hence it would be extremely illogical to affirm that philosophic truth, even in this sense, is opposed to religious truth.

It is not my wish to give an unfavorable interpretation to the words of the illustrious writer; I rather incline to think, that, in his mind, philosophic truth is nothing but a spirit of independence considered in a general, vague, and undefined sense, and not as applied to any object in particular. This is the only way to reconcile assertions so different; for it is quite clear, that, after he had so severely condemned the Protestant Reformation, the writer could not proceed to admit that this same Reformation carried with it philosophic truth, properly so called, wherein it became opposed to Catholic doctrines. But, in this case, the language of the illustrious author is unquestionably wanting in precision; this, however, need not surprise us, as, upon reflection, we shall find that, in treating historico-philosophical subjects, precision is not to be expected from writers whose genius has been wont to soar into the highest regions on the wings of a sublime poetry.

It was not either in Germany or in England, but in Catholic France, that the philosophical movement advanced with the greatest freedom and daring. Descartes, the founder of a new era in philosophy, that superseded the Aristotelian, and gave a fresh impulse to the study of logic, of physics, and metaphysics, was a Frenchman and a Catholic. The greater part of his most distinguished followers were also in communion with the Roman Church. Philosophy, then, in the highest sense of the word, owes nothing to Protestantism. Before Leibnitz, Germany could scarcely reckon a single philosopher of any note; and the English shools that attained to any thing like celebrity arose after Descartes' time. We shall find, upon reflection, that France was the centre of the philosophical movement from the end of the sixteenth century; and at that period all the Protestant countries were so backward in this kind of study, that the active progress of philosophy amongst the Catholics was scarcely noticed by them. In like manner, it was in the bosom of the Catholic Church that the taste arose for profound meditations on the secrets of the heart, and on the relations of the human mind to God and nature, and that sublime abstraction which concentrates man's faculties, sets him free from the body, and elevates him to those exalted regions that appear destined to be visited exclusively by celestial spirits. Is not mysticism, in its pursest, most refined, and most elevated form, found in our Catholic writers of the golden age? Since that time, what has been published that may not be met with in the works of St. Teresa, in those of St. John of the Cross, in the venerable Avila, in Louis de Grenada, and in Louis de Leon?

And Pascal, that man of thought, one of the most vigorous geniuses of the seventeenth century, who was unhappily deceived for some time by a hypocritical and canting sect, was he a Protestant? Was it not he who laid the basis of that philosophico-religious school, whose investigations, directed at one time to the deepest questions of religion, at another to those of nature, or to the mysteries of the human heart, have surrounded truth with a flood of light? Do not the apologists of Christianity, whether Protestants or Catholics, when engaged in combating indifference or incredulity, avail themselves by preference of his *Pensées?* Authors who have written on the philosophy of history have perhaps surpassed all others in their eagerness to vilify the Church as the enemy of enlightenment, whilst they represent Protestantism as the great bulwark of the rights of the mind. Now, gratitude alone should have induced them to proceed more circumspectly; they should not forget that the real founder of the philosophy of history was a Catholic, and that the first and best work ever written on this subject came from the pen of a Catholic Bishop. It was Bossuet, in his immortal *Discours sur l'Histoire Universelle*, who first taught our modern thinkers to take a lofty survey of the human race; to embrace at one view all the events that have marked the course of ages, contemplating them in all their vastness and intimate connection, with all their phases, effects, and causes, and to draw from them salutary lessons for the instruction both of princes and people. Now, Bossuet was a Catholic, and, moreover, one of the most trenchant adversaries of the Protestant Reformation. His fame is heightened too by another work, in which he completely overthrows the doctrines of the innovators, by proving their continual variations, and demonstrating that theirs must be the way of error, seeing that variation is incompatible with truth. We may ask the abettors of Protestantism, if the Eagle of Meaux feels in his flight the fetters of the Catholic religion, when, glancing at the origin and destiny of mankind, at the fall of our first parents and its consequences, on the revolutions of the East and West, he traces with such wonderful sublimity the designs of Divine Providence?

As regards the literary movement, I might almost consider myself relieved from all necessity of combating the reproaches cast upon Catholicity by its enemies. What, in fact, was the literature of all the Protestant countries together, at the time when Italy produced those orators and poets, who, in succeeding ages, have been universally received as models? Various descriptions of literature were already quite common in Catholic countries, that were not even known in England or Germany; and when, at a later period, an attempt was made to fill up the hiatus, no better means could be found for the purpose than to take for models the Spanish writers, who had been subject *to Catholic obscurantism and the fires of the Inquisition.*

Neither the mind, the heart, nor the imagination of man owes any thing to Protestantism. Before the Reformation these were all in graceful and vigorous progress; after the Reformation, this progress continued in the bosom of the Catholic Church as successfully as before. Catholicity displays a bright array of illustrious men crowned with the glories they have won amidst the unanimous plaudits of all civilized nations. Whatever has been said of the tendency of our religion to enslave and hoodwink the mind, is but calumny. No; that which is born of light, cannot produce darkness; that which is the work of truth itself, need not fly from the sun's rays to conceal itself in the bowels of the earth. The daughter of heaven may walk in the brightness of day, may dare discussion, may gather around her all the brightest intellects; well assured that the more closely and attentively they see and contemplate her, the more pure, the more beauteous and enrapturing will she appear.

CHAPTER LXXIII.

SUMMARY. DECLARATION OF THE AUTHOR.

HAVING reached the end of my difficult enterprise, let me be allowed to take a retrospective view of the vast space over which I have but just passed, like the traveller who rests after his labor. The fear of seeing religious schism introduced into my country; the sight of the efforts which were made to inculcate Protestant errors amongst us; the perusal of certain writings, wherein it was stated that the pretended Reformation had been favorable to the progress of nations,—such were the motives which inspired me with the idea of undertaking this work. My object was, to show that neither individuals nor society owe any thing to Protestantism, either in a religious, social, political, or literary point of view. I undertook to examine what history tells us, and what philosophy teaches us, on this point. I was not ignorant of the immense extent of the questions which I had to enter upon; I was far from flattering myself that I was able to clear them up in a becoming manner; nevertheless I set forth upon my journey, with that courage which is inspired by the love of truth, and the confidence that one is defending its cause.

When considering the birth of Protestantism, I have endeavored to take as lofty a view as possible. I have rendered to men that justice which is due to them; I have attributed a large portion of the evil to the wretched condition of mankind, to the weakness of our minds, and to that inheritance of perverseness and ignorance which has been transmitted to us by the fall of our first parent. Luther, Calvin, and Zuinglius have disappeared from my eyes; placed in the immense picture of events, they have been viewed by me as small imperceptible figures, whose individuality was far from deserving the importance which was given to them at other periods. Honest in my convictions, and unreserved in my words, I have acknowledged with candor, but with sorrow, that there existed certain abuses, and that these abuses were taken as pretexts when it was wished to break the unity of the faith. I have allowed that a portion of the blame shall also fall upon men; but I have also pointed out, that the more you here lay stress upon the weakness and wickedness of man, the more do you illustrate the providence of Him who has promised to be with His Church till the consummation of ages.

By the aid of reasoning and irrefragable experience, I have proved that the fundamental dogmas of Protestantism show little knowledge of the human mind, and were a fruitful source of errors and catastrophes. Then, turning my attention to the development of European civilization, I have made a continued comparison between Protestantism and Catholicity; and I believe that I may assert, that I have not hazarded any proposition of importance without having supported it by the evidence of historical facts. I have found it necessary to take a survey of all ages, dating from the commencement of Christianity, and to observe the different phases under which civilization has appeared; without this, it would have been impossible to give a complete vindication of the Catholic religion.

The reader may have observed that the prevailing idea of the work is this: "Before Protestantism European civilization had reached all the development which was possible for it; Protestantism perverted the course of civilization, and produced immense evils in modern society; the progress which has been made since Protestantism, has been made not by it, but in spite of it." I have only consulted history, and I have taken extreme care not to pervert it; I have borne in mind this passage of holy writ: "Has God, then, need of thy falsehood?" The documents to which I refer are there; they are to be found in all libraries, ready to answer; read them, and judge for yourselves.

I am not aware, in the multitude of questions which have presented themselves to me, and which it has been indispensable for me to examine, that I have resolved any in a manner not in conformity with the dogmas of the religion which I was desirous of defending. I am not aware that, in any passage of my book, I have laid down erroneous propositions, or expressed myself in ill-sounding terms. Before publishing my work, I submitted it to the examination of ecclesiastical authority; and without hesitation, I complied with the slightest hint on its part, purifying, correcting, and modifying what had been pointed out as worthy of purification, correction, or modification. Notwithstanding that, I submit my whole work to the judgment of the Catholic, Apostolic, and Roman Church; as soon as the Sovereign Pontiff, the Vicar of Jesus Christ upon earth, shall pronounce sentence against any one of my opinions, I will hasten to declare that I consider that opinion erroneous, and cease to profess it.

NOTES.

Note 1, p. 26.

The *History of the Variations* is one of those works which exhaust their subject, and which do not admit of reply or addition. If this immortal *chef-d'œuvre* be read with attention, the cause of Protestantism, with respect to faith, is forever decided: there is no middle way left between Catholicity and infidelity. Gibbon read it in his youth, and he became a Catholic, abandoning the Protestant religion in which he had been brought up. When, at a later period, he left the Catholic Church, he did not become a Protestant, but an unbeliever. My readers will perhaps like to learn from the mouth of this famous writer what he thought of the work of Bossuet, and the effect which was produced on him by its perusal. These are his words: "In the *History of the Variations*, an attack equally vigorous and well-directed," says he, "Bossuet shows, by a happy mixture of reasoning and narration, the errors, mistakes, uncertainties, and contradictions of our first reformers, whose variations, as he learnedly maintains, bear the marks of error; *while the uninterrupted unity of the Catholic Church is a sign and testimony of infallible truth.* I read, approved, and believed." (Gibbon's *Memoirs*.)

Note 2, p. 27.

It has been wished to represent Luther to us as a man of lofty ideas, of noble and generous feelings, and as a defender of the rights of the human race. Yet he himself has left us in his writings the most striking testimony of the violence of his character, of his disgusting rudeness, and his savage intolerance. Henry VIII., king of England, undertook to refute the book of Luther called *De Captivitate Babylonica*; and behold the latter, irritated by such boldness, writes to the king, and calls him *sacrilegious, mad, senseless, the grossest of all pigs and of all asses.* It is evident that Luther paid but little regard to royalty; he did the same with respect to literary merit. Erasmus, who was perhaps the most learned man of his age, or who at least surpassed all others in the variety of his knowledge, in the refinement and *éclat* of his mind, was not better treated by the furious innovator, in spite of all the indulgence for which the latter was indebted to him. As soon as Luther saw that Erasmus did not think proper to be enrolled in the new sect, he attacked him with so much violence, that the latter complained of it, saying, "*that in his old age he was compelled to contend against a savage beast, a furious wild boar.*" Luther did not confine himself to mere words; he proceeded to acts. It was at his instigation that Carlostad was exiled from the states of the Duke of Saxony, and was reduced to such misery, that he was compelled to carry wood, and do other similar things, to gain his livelihood. In his many disputes with the Zwinglians, Luther did not belie his character; he called them *damned, fools, blasphemers.* As he lavished such epithets on his dissenting companions, we cannot be astonished that he called the doctors of Louvain *beasts, pigs, Pagans, Epicureans, Atheists;* and that he makes use of other expressions which decency will not allow us to cite; and that, launching forth against the Pope, he says, "*He is a mad wolf, against whom every one ought to take arms, without waiting even for the order of the magistrates; in this matter there can be no room left for repentance, except for not having been able to bury the sword in his breast;*" adding, "that all those who followed the Pope ought to be pursued like bandit-chiefs, were they kings or emperors." Such was the spirit of tolerance which animated Luther. And let it not be imagined that this intolerance was confined to him; it extended to all the party of the innovators, and its effects were cruelly felt. We have an unexceptionable witness of this truth in Melancthon, the beloved disciple of Luther, and one of the most distinguished men that Protestantism has had. "I find myself under such oppression," wrote Melancthon to his friend Camerarius, "that I seem to be in the cave of the Cyclops; it is almost impossible for me to explain to you my troubles; and every moment I feel myself tempted to take flight." "These are," he says, in another letter, "ignorant men, who know neither piety nor discipline; behold what they are who command, and you will understand that I am like Daniel in the lions' den." How, then, can it be maintained that such an enterprise was guided by a generous idea, and that it was really attempted to free the human mind? The intolerance of Calvin, sufficiently shown by the single fact mentioned in the text, is manifested in his works at every page, by the manner in which he treats his adversaries. *Wicked men, rogues, drunkards, fools, madmen, furies, beasts, bulls, pigs, asses, dogs,* and *vile slaves of Satan.* Such are the polite terms which abound in the writings of the famous reformer. And how many wretched things of the same kind could I not relate, if I did not fear to disgust my readers!

Note 3, p. 27.

The Diet of Spires had made a decree concerning the change of religion and worship, fourteen towns of the empire refused to submit to it, and presented a Protest; hence men began to call the dissenters *Protestants.* As this name is a condemnation of the separated churches, they have several times attempted to assume others, but always in vain; the names which they took were false, and false names do not last. What was their meaning when they called themselves *Evangelicals?* That they adhered to the Gospel alone? In that case they ought rather to call themselves *Biblicals;* for it was not to the Gospel that they professed to adhere, but to the *Bible.* They are also sometimes called *Reformers:* and many people have been accustomed to call *Protestantism, reformation;* but it is enough to pronounce this word, to feel how inappropriate it is; *religious revolution* would be much more proper.

Note 4, p. 27.

Count de Maistre, in his work *Du Pape*, has developed this question of names in an inimitable manner. Among his numerous observations, there is one very just one: it is, that the Catholic Church alone has a positive and proper name, which she gives to herself, and which is given to her by the whole world. The separated Churches have invented many, but without the power of appropriating them.—"Each one was free to take what name he pleased," says M. de Maistre; "*Lais*, in person, might be able to write upon her door, *Hôtel d'Artémise.* The great point is, to compel others to give us a particular name, which is not so easy as to take it of our own authority."

Moreover, it must not be imagined that Count de Maistre was the inventor of this argument; a long time before him St. Jerome and St. Augustin had used it. "If you," says St. Jerome, "hear them called Marcionites, Valentinians, Montanists, know that they are not the Church of Christ, but the synagogue of Antichrist.—Si audieris nuncupari Marcionitas, Valentinianos, Montanenses, scito, non Ecclesiam Christi, sed Antichristi esse synagogam." (Hieron. lib. *Adversus Luciferianos.*) "I am retained in the Church," says St. Augustin, "by her very name of Catholic; for it was not without a cause that she alone, amid so many heresies, obtained that name. All the heretics desire to be called Catholics; yet if a stranger asks them which is the church of the Catholics, none of them venture to point out their church or house.—Tenet me in Ecclesia ipsum Catholicæ nomen, quod non sine causa inter tam multas hæreses, sic ipsa sola obtinuit, ut cum omnes hæretici se Catholicos dici velint, quærenti tamen peregrino alicui, ubi ad Catholicam conveniatur, nullus hæreticorum, vel basilicam suam vel domum audeat ostendere." (St. Augustin.) What St. Augustin observed of his time is again realized with respect to the Protestants. I appeal to the testimony of those who have visited the countries where different communions exist. An illustrious Spaniard of the seventeenth century, who had lived a long time in Germany, tells us, "They all wish to be called Catholic and Apostolical; but notwithstanding this pretension, they are called Lutherans, or Calvinists.—Singuli volunt Catholici et Apostolici, sed volunt, et ab aliis non hoc prætenso illis nomine, sed Luterani potius aut Calviniani nominantur." (Caramuel.) "I have dwelt in the towns of heretics," continues the same writer, "and I have seen with my eyes and heard with my ears a thing on which the heterodox should reflect: *it is, that with the exception of the Protestant preacher, and a few others, who desire to know more of the thing than is necessary, all the crowd of heretics gave the name of Catholics to the Romans.*—Habitavi in hæreticorum civitatibus; et hoc propriis oculis vidi, propriis audivi auribus, quod deberet ab hæterodoxis ponderari, *præter prædicantem, et pauculos qui plus sapiunt quam oportet sapere, totum hæreticorum vulgus Catholicos vocat Romanos.*" Such is the force of truth. The ideologists know well that these phenomena have deep causes, and that these arguments are something more than subtilties.

Note 5, p. 38.

So much has been said of abuses, the influence which they may have had on the disasters which the Church suffered during the last centuries has been so much exaggerated, and at the same time so much care has been taken, by hypocritical praise, to exalt the purity of manners and strictness of discipline in the primitive Church, that some people have at last imagined a line of division between ancient and modern times. These persons see in the early times only truth and sanctity; they attribute to the others only corruption and falsehood; as if, in the early ages of the Church, all the faithful were angels—as if the Church, at all times, had not errors to correct and passions to control. With history in our hands, it would be easy to reduce these exaggerated ideas to their just value, to which Erasmus himself, certainly little disposed to exculpate his contemporaries, does justice. He clearly shows us, in a parallel between his own times and those of the early ages of the Church, how puerile and ill-founded was the desire, then so widely diffused, of exalting antiquity at the expense of the present time. We find a fragment of this parallel in the works of Marchetti, among his observations on Fleury's history.

It would not be less curious to pass in review the regulations made by the Church to check all kinds of abuses. The collections of councils would furnish us with so many materials thereupon, that many volumes would not suffice to make them known; or rather, these collections themselves, with alarming bulk, from one end to the other, are nothing but an evident proof of these two truths: 1st, that there have been at all times many abuses to be corrected, an effect, in some measure necessary, of the weakness and corruption of human nature; 2dly, that at all periods the Church has labored to correct these abuses, so that it may be affirmed without hesitation, that you cannot point out one without immediately finding a canonical regulation by its side to check or punish it. These observations clearly show that Protestantism was not caused by abuses, but that it was a great calamity, as it were, rendered unavoidable by the fickleness of the human mind, and the condition in which society was placed. In the same sense Jesus Christ has said, *that it was necessary that there should be scandal;* not that any one in particular is forced to give it, but because such is the corruption of the human heart, that the natural course of things must necessarily bring it.

NOTE 6, p. 42.

This concert and unity, which are found in Catholicity, are things which ought to fill every sensible man with admiration and astonishment, whatever his religious ideas may be. If we do not suppose that *the finger of God is here*, how can we explain or understand the continuance of the centre of unity in the see of Rome? So much has been said of the supremacy of the Pope, that it is very difficult to add any thing new; but perhaps our readers will not be displeased to see a passage of St. Francis de Sales, where the various remarkable titles given to the Sovereign Pontiff and to his see, by the Church in ancient times, are collected. This work of the holy Bishop is worthy of being introduced, not only because it interests the curiosity, but also because it furnishes matter for grave reflection, which we leave to the reader.

TITLES OF THE POPE.

Most Holy Bishop of the Catholic Church—Council of Soissons, of 300 Bishops.
Most Holy and Blessed Patriarch — Ibid., t. vii., Council.
Most Blessed Lord—St. Augustine, Ep. 95.
Universal Patriarch—St. Leo, P., Ep. 62.
Chief of the Church in the World—Innoc. ad P. P. Concil. Milevit.
The Bishop elevated to the Apostolic eminence—St. Cyprian, Ep. 3, 12.
Father of Fathers—Council of Chalcedon, Sess. iii.
Sovereign Pontiff of Bishops—Id.. in præf.
Sovereign Priest—Council of Chalcedon, Sess. xvi.
Prince of Priests—Stephen, Bishop of Carthage.
Prefect of the House of God and Guardian of the Lord's Vineyard—Council of Carthage, Ep. to Damasus.
Vicar of Jesus Christ. Confirmer of the Faith of Christians—St. Jerome, præf. in Evang. ad Damasum.
High-Priest — Valentinian, and all antiquity with him.
The Sovereign Pontiff — Council of Chalcedon, in Epist. ad Theodos. Imper.
The Prince of Bishops—Ibid.
The Heir of the Apostles—St. Bern., lib. de Consid.
Abraham by the Patriarchate—St. Ambrose, in 1 Tim iii.
Melchsedech by ordination—Council of Chalcedon, Epist. ad Leonem.
Moses by authority—St. Bernard, Epist. 190.
Samuel by jurisdiction—Id. ib., et in lib. de Consider.
Peter by power—Ibid.
Christ by unction—Ibid.
The Shepherd of the Fold of Jesus Christ—Id. lib. ii. de Consider.
Key-Bearer of the House of God—Id. ibid. c. viii.
The Shepherd of all Shepherds—Ibid.
The Pontiff called to the plentitude of power—Ibid.
St. Peter was the Mouth of Jesus Christ—St. Chrysost. Hom. ii., in Div. Serm.
The Mouth and Head of the Apostleship—Orig., Hom. lv. in Matth.
The Cathedra and Principal Church—St. Cypr., Ep. lv. ad Cornel.
The Source of Sacerdotal Unity—Id., Epist. iii. 2.
The Bond of Unity—Id. ibid. iv. 2.
The Church where resides the chief power (*potentior principalitas*)—Id. ibid. iii. 8.
The Church the Root and Mother of all the others—St. Anaclet. Papa, Epist. ad omnes Episc. et Fideles.
The See on which our Lord has built the Universal Church—St. Damasus, Epist. ad Univ. Episcop.
The Cardinal Point and Head of all the Churches—St. Marcellinus, R. Epist. ad Episc. Antioch.
The Refuge of Bishops—Conc. Alex., Epist. ad Felic. P.
The Supreme Apostolic See—St. Athanasius.
The Presiding Church—Emperor Justin., in lib. viii., Cod. de Sum. Trinit.
The Supreme See which cannot be judged by any other—St. Leo, in Nat. SS. Apost.
The Church set over and preferred to all the others —Victor d'Utiq., in lib. de Perfect.
The first of all the Sees—St. Prosper, in lib. de Ingrat.
The Apostolic Fountain—St. Ignatius, Epist. ad Rom. in Subscript.
The most secure Citadel of all Catholic Communion —Council of Rome under St. Gelasius.

NOTE 7, p. 45.

I have said that the most distinguished Protestants have felt the void which is found in all sects separated from the Catholic Church. I am about to give proofs of this assertion, which perhaps some persons may consider hazardous. Luther, writing to Zwinglius, said, "If the world lasts for a long time, it will be again necessary, on account of the different interpretations which are now given to the Scriptures, to receive the decrees of Councils, and take refuge in them, in order to preserve the unity of the faith.—Si diutius steterit mundus, iterum erit necessarium, propter diversas Scripturæ interpretationes quæ nunc sunt, ad conservandam fidei unitatem, ut conciliorum decreta recipiamus, atque ad ea confugiamus."

Melancthon, deploring the fatal results of the want of spiritual jurisdiction, said, "There will result from it a liberty useless to the world;" and in another place he utters these remarkable words: "There are required in the Church inspectors, to maintain order, to observe attentively those who are called to the ecclesiastical ministry, to watch over the doctrine of priests, and pronounce ecclesiastical judgments; so that if bishops did not exist, it would be necessary to create them. The *monarchy of the Pope would be of great utility to preserve among such various nations uniformity of doctrine.*"

Let us hear Calvin: "God has placed the seat of his worship in the centre of the earth, and has placed there only one Pontiff, whom all may regard, the better to preserve unity.—Cultus sui sedem in medio terræ collocavit, illi *unum* Antisticem præfecit, quem omnes respicerent, quo melius in unitate continerentur."—(Calvin, *Inst.* 6, § 11.)

"I have also," says Beza, "been long and greatly tormented by the same thoughts which you describe to me. I see our people wander at the mercy of every wind of doctrine, and after having been raised up, fall sometimes on one side, and sometimes on the other. What they think of religion to-day you may know; what they will think of it to-morrow you cannot affirm. *On what point of religion are the Churches which have declared war against the Pope agreed? Examine all, from beginning to end, you will hardly find one thing affirmed by the one which the other does not directly cry out against as impiety.*—Exercuerunt me diu et multum illæ ipsæ quas describis cogitationes. Video nostros palantes omni doctrinæ vento, et in altum sublatos, modo ad hanc, modo ad illam partem deferri. Horum, quæ sit hodie de religione sententia scire fortasse possis; sed quæ cras de eadem futura sit opinio, neque tu certo affirmare queas. In quo tandem religionis capite congruunt inter se Ecclesiæ, quæ Romano Pontifici bellum indixerunt? A capite ad calcem si percurras omnia, nihil prope modum reperias ab uno affirmari, quod alter statim non impium esse clamitet." (Th. Bez. *Epist. ad Andream Dudit.*)

Grotius, one of the most learned of Protestants, also felt the weakness of the foundation on which the separated sects repose. Many people have believed that he died a Catholic. The Protestants accused him of having the intention of embracing the Roman faith; and the Catholics, who had relations with him at Paris, thought the same thing. It is said that the celebrated Petau, the friend of Grotius, at the news of his death, said mass for him; an anecdote the truth of which I do not guarantee. It is certain that Grotius, in his work entitled *De Antichristo,* does not think, with other Protestants, that the Pope is Antichrist. It is certain that, in his work entitled *Votum pro Pace Ecclesiæ,* he says, without circumlocution, "that without the supremacy of the Pope, it is impossible to put an end to disputes;" and he alleges the example of the Protestants: "as it happens," says he, "among the Protestants." It is certain that, in his posthumous work, *Rivetiani Apologetici Discussio,* he openly lays down the fundamental principle of Catholicity, namely, that "the dogmas of faith should be decided by tradition and the authority of the Church, and not by the holy Scriptures only."

The conversion of the celebrated Protestant Papin, which made so much noise, is another proof of what we are endeavoring to show. Papin reflected on the fundamental principle of Protestantism, and on the contradiction which exists between this principle and the intolerance of Protestants, who, relying only on private judgment, yet have recourse to authority for self-preservation. He reasoned as follows: "If the principle of authority, which they attempt to adopt, is innocent and legitimate, it condemns their origin, wherein they refused to submit to the authority of the Catholic Church; but if the principle of private judgment, which they embraced in the beginning, was right and just, this is enough to condemn the principle of authority invented by them for the purpose of avoiding its excesses; for this principle opens and smooths the way to the greatest disorders of impiety."

Puffendorf, who will certainly not be accused of coldness when attacking Catholicity, could not help paying his tribute also to the truth, when, in a confession for which all Catholics ought to thank him, he says, "The suppression of the authority of the Pope has sowed endless germs of discord in the world: as there is no longer any sovereign authority to terminate the disputes which arise on all sides, we have seen the Protestants split among themselves, and tear their bowels with their own hands." (Puffendorf, *de Monarch. Pont. Roman.*)

Leibnitz, that great man, who, according to the expression of Fontenelle, advanced all sciences, also acknowledged the weakness of Protestantism, and the organizing power which belongs to the Catholic Church. We know that, far from participating in the anger of Protestants against the Pope, he regarded the religious supremacy of Rome with the most lively sympathy. He openly avows the superiority of the Catholic over the Protestant missions; the religious communities themselves, the objects of so much aversion to so many people, were to him highly respectable. These anticipations with respect to the religious ideas of this great man have been more and more confirmed by one of his posthumous works, published for the first time at Paris in 1819. *The Exposition of the Doctrine of Leibnitz on Religion, followed by Thoughts extracted from the writings of the same Author, by M. Emery, formerly General Superior of St. Sulpice,* contains the posthumous work of Leibnitz, whereof the title, in the original manuscript, is, *Theological System.* The commencement of this work, remarkable for its seriousness and simplicity, is certainly worthy of the great soul of this distinguished thinker. It is this: "After having long and profoundly studied religious controversies, after having implored the divine assistance, and laid aside, as far as it is possible for man, all spirit of party, I have considered myself as a neophyte come from the new world, and one who had not yet embraced an opinion; behold, therefore, the conclusions at which I have arrived, and what appeared to me, out of all that I have examined, worthy to be received by all unprejudiced men, as what is most conformable to the holy Scriptures and respectable antiquity; I will even say, to right reason and the most certain historical facts."

Leibnitz afterwards lays down the existence of God, the Incarnation, the Trinity, and the other dogmas of Christianity; he adopts with candor, and defends with much learning, the doctrine of the Catholic Church on tradition, the sacraments, the sacrifice of the Mass, the respect paid to relics and holy images, the Church hierarchy, and the supremacy of the Pope. He adds, "In all cases which do not admit the delay of the convocation of a general Council, or which do not deserve to be considered therein, it must be admitted that the first of the Bishops, or the Sovereign Pontiff, has the same power as the whole Church."

Note 8, p. 49.

Some persons may suppose that what we have said with respect to the emptiness of human knowledge and the weakness of our intellect, has been said only for the purpose of making the necessity of a rule in matters of faith more sensibly felt. It is not so. It would be easy for me to insert here a long list of texts, drawn from the writings of the most illustrious men of ancient and modern times, who have insisted upon this very point. I will only quote here an excellent passage from an illustrious Spaniard, one of the greatest men of the sixteenth century, Louis Vives. "*Jam mens ipsa, suprema animi et celsissima pars, videbit quantopere sit tum natura sua tarda ac præpedita, tum tenebris peccati cæca, et a doctrina, usu, ac solertia imperita et rudis, ut ne ea quidem quæ videt, quæque manibus contrectat, cujusmodi sint, aut quid fiant assequatur, nedum ut in abdito illa naturæ arcana possit penetrare; sapienterque ab Aristotele illa est posita sententia: Mentem nostram ad manifestissima naturæ non aliter habere se, quam noctuæ oculum ad lumen solis.* Ea omnia, quæ universum homi-rum genus novit, quota sunt pars eorum quæ ignoramus? Nec solum id in universitate artium est verum, sed in singulis earum, in quarum nulla tantum est humanum ingenium progressum, ut ad medium pervenerit, etiam in infimis illis ac villissimis; ut nihil existimetur verius esse dictum ab Academicis quam *Scire nihil.*" (Ludovic. Vives, *de Concordia et Discordia*, lib. iv. c. iii.) So thought this great man, who, to vast erudition in sacred and profane things, added profound meditation on the human intellect itself; who followed the progress of the sciences with an observant eye, and undertook to regenerate them, as his writings prove. I regret that I cannot copy his words at length, as well those in the passage which I have just cited, as those of his immortal work on the causes of the decline of the arts and sciences, and on the manner of teaching them. If any one complain that I have told some truths as to the weakness of our minds, and fear lest this should impede the progress of knowledge by checking its flights, I will remind him that the best way of promoting the progress of our minds is, to give them a knowledge of themselves. On this point, the profound sentence of Seneca may be quoted: "I know that many persons would have attained to wisdom, if they had not presumed that they already possessed it." "Puto multos ad sapientiam protuisse pervenire, nisi se jam crederent pervenisse."

NOTE 9, p. 53.

Dense clouds surround the intellect as soon as it approaches the first principles of the sciences. I have said that even the mathematics, the clearness and certainty of which have become proverbial, are not exempted from this universal rule. The infinitesimal calculation, which, in the present state of science, may be said to play the leading part, nevertheless depends on a few ideas which, up to this time, have not been well explained by any one—ideas with respect to *limits.* I do not wish to throw any doubt on the certainty of this calculation: I only wish to show, that, if it were attempted to examine the ideas which are as it were the elements of it, before the tribunal of metaphysical philosophy, the consequence would be, that shades would be cast upon their certainty. Without going further than the elementary part of science, we might discover some points which would not bear a continued metaphysical and ideological analysis without injury: a thing which it would be very easy to prove by example, if the nature of this work allowed it. We may recommend to the reader on this subject, the valuable letter addressed by the Spanish Jesuit, Eximeno, a distinguished philosopher and mathematician, to his friend, Juan Andres; he will there find some appropriate observations made by a man who certainly will not be rejected on the ground of incompetency. It is in Latin, and is called *Epistola ad clarissimum virum Joannem Andresium*

As to the other sciences, it is not necessary to say much to prove that their first principles are surrounded with darkness; and it may be said that the brilliant reveries of the most illustrious men have had no other source than this very obscurity. Led away by the feeling of their own strength, these men pursued truth even to the abyss; there, to use the expression of an illustrious contemporary poet, *the torch was extinguished in their hands;* lost in an obscure labyrinth, they were then abandoned to the mercy of their fancies and inspirations; it was thus that reality gave place to the beautiful dreams of their genius.

NOTE 10, p. 54.

Nothing is better for understanding and explaining the innate weakness of the human mind, than to survey the history of heresies; a history which we owe to the Church, to the extreme care which she has taken to define and classify errors. From Simon Magus, who called himself the legislator of the Jews, the renovator of the world, and the paraclete, while paying a worship of latria to his mistress Helena, under the name of Minerva, down to Hermann, preaching the massacre of all the priests and all the magistrates of the world, and affirming that he was the real son of God; a vast picture, very unpleasant to behold, I acknowledge, if it were only on account of the extravagances with which it abounds, presents itself to the observer, and suggests to him very grave and profound reflections on the real character of the human mind; there it is easy to see the wisdom of Catholicity, in attempting, in certain cases, to subject this inconstant spirit to rule.

NOTE 11, p. 57.

If any persons find difficulty in persuading themselves that illusion and fanaticism are, as it were, in their proper element among Protestants, behold the irresistible testimony of facts in aid of our assertion. This subject would furnish large volumes; but I must be content with a rapid glance. I begin with Luther. Is it possible to carry raving further than to pretend to have been taught by the devil, to boast of it, and to found new doctrines on so powerful an authority? Yet this was the raving of Luther himself, the founder of Protestantism, who has left us in his works the evidence of his interview with Satan.—Whether the apparition was real, or produced by the dreams of a night agitated by fever, it is impossible to carry fanaticism further than to boast of having had such a master. Luther tells us himself that he had many colloquies with the devil; but what is above all worthy of attention is, the vision in which, as he relates in the most serious manner, Satan, by his arguments, compelled him to proscribe private masses. He gives us a lively description of this adventure. He wakes in the middle of the night; Satan appears to him.—Luther is seized with horror; he sweats, he trembles; his heart beats in a fearful manner. Nevertheless the discussion begins, and the devil, like a good disputant, presses him so hard with his arguments, that he leaves him without reply. Luther is conquered; which ought not to astonish us, since he tells us that the logic of the devil was accompanied by a voice so alarming, that the blood froze in his veins. "I then understood," says this wretched being, "how it often happens that people die *at the break of day;* it is because the devil is able to kill or suffocate men; and without going so far as that, when he disputes with them, he places them in such embarrassment, that he can thus occasion their death. I have often experienced this myself." This passage is certainly curious.

The phantom which appeared to Zwinglius, the founder of Protestantism in Switzerland, affords us another example of extravagance no less absurd. This heresiarch wished to deny the real presence of Jesus Christ in the Eucharist; he pretended that what exists under the consecrated species is only a sign. As the authority of the sacred text, which clearly expresses the contrary, embarrassed him, behold, suddenly, at the moment when he imagined that he was disputing with the secretary of the town, a white or black phantom, so he tells us himself, appeared to him, and showed him a means. This pleasant anecdote we have from Zwinglius himself.

Who does not regret to see such a man as Melancthon also given up to the prejudices and manias of the most ridiculous superstition, stupidly credulous with respect to dreams, extraordinary phenomena, and astrological prognostics? Read his letters, which are filled with such pitiful things. At the time when the diet of Augsburg was held, Melancthon regarded as favourable presages for the new gospel an inundation of the Tiber, the birth at Rome of a monstrous mule with a crane's foot, and that of a calf with two heads in the territory of Augsburg,—events which to him were the undoubted announcements of a change in the universe, and particularly of the approaching ruin of Rome by the power of schism. He himself makes the horoscope of his daughter, and he trembles for her because Mars presents an alarming aspect; he is not the less alarmed at the tail of a comet appearing within the limits of the north. The astrologers had predicted that in autumn the stars would be more favorable to ecclesiastical disputes; this prognostic sufficed to console him for the slowness of the conferences of Augsburg on the subject of religion: we see, moreover, that his friends —that is, the leaders of the party—allowed themselves to be ruled by the same powerful reasons. As if he had not troubles enough, it is predicted that Melancthon will be shipwrecked in the Baltic; he avoids sailing on those fatal waters. Certain Franciscans had prophesied that the power of the Pope was about to decline, and then to fall for ever; also that, in the year 1600, the Turks were to become masters of Italy and Germany; Melancthon boasts of having the original prophecy in his possession; moreover, the earthquakes which occur confirm him in his belief.

The human mind had but just set itself up as the only judge of faith, when the atrocities of the most furious fanaticism already inundated Germany with blood. Mathias Harlem, the Anabaptist, at the head of a ferocious troop, orders the churches to be sacked, the sacred ornaments to be broken in pieces, and all books, except the Bible, to be burnt, as impious or useless. Established at Munster, which he calls Mont Sion, he causes all the gold, silver, and precious stones possessed by the inhabitants to be brought to him, and places them in a common treasury, and names deacons to distribute them. All his disciples are compelled to eat in common, to live in perfect equality, and to prepare for the war which they would have to undertake, *quitting Mount Sion*, as he himself said, *to subject all the nations of the earth to his power*. He at length dies in a rash attempt, wherein, like another Gideon, he undertook nothing less than to exterminate the army of the impious with a handful of men. Mathias immediately found an heir to his fanaticism in Becold, perhaps better known under the name of John of Leyden. This fanatic, a tailor by trade, ran naked through the streets of Munster, crying out, "*Behold, the king of Sion comes.*" He returned to his house, shut himself up there for three days; and when the people came to inquire for him, he pretended that he could not speak; like another Zachary, he made signs that he wanted writing materials, and wrote that it had been revealed to him by God, that the people should be governed by judges, in imitation of the people of Israel. He named twelve judges, choosing the men who were the most attached to himself; and until the authority of the new magistrates had been acknowledged, he took the precaution not to allow himself to be seen by any body. Already was the authority of the new prophet secured in a certain manner; but not content with the real command, he desired to surround himself with pomp and majesty; he proposed nothing less than to have himself proclaimed king. Now the blindness of the sectarian fanatics was so great, that it was not difficult for him to complete his mad enterprise; it was enough for him to play off a gross farce. A goldsmith who had an understanding with the aspirant to royalty, and was also initiated in the art of prophecy, presented himself before the judges of Israel, and spoke to them thus: "Behold, this is the will of the Lord God, the Eternal: as in other times I established Saul over Israel, and after him David, who was only a simple shepherd, so I now establish my prophet Becold king of Sion." The judges would not resolve on abdication; but Becold assured them that he also had had the same vision, that he had concealed it from humility, but that God having spoken by another prophet, it was necessary for him to resign himself to mount the throne, and *accomplish the orders of the Most High*. The judges persisted in wishing to call the people together; they assembled in the market-place; there a *prophet*, on the part of God, presented to Becold a drawn sword, as a sign of the *power of justice, which was conferred on him over all the earth, to extend to the four quarters of the world the empire of Sion;* he was proclaimed king with the most boisterous joy, and solemnly crowned on the 24th of June, 1534. As he had espoused the wife of his predecessor, he raised her to the royal dignity; but while reserving to her the exclusive privilege of being queen, he continued to have seventeen wives, in conformity with the *holy* liberty which he had proclaimed in this matter. The orgies, assassinations, atrocities, and ravings of all kinds which followed cannot be related; it may be affirmed that the sixteen months of the reign of this madman were only a series of crimes. The Catholics cried out against such horrible excesses. The Protestants cried out also; but who was to blame? Was it not they who, after having proclaimed resistance to the authority of the Church, had thrown the Bible into the midst of these wretched men, at the risk of their heads being turned by the ravings of individual interpretation, and of precipitating them into projects as criminal as they were senseless? The Anabaptists were well aware of this; and they were exceedingly indignant with Luther, who condemned them in his writings; and indeed, what right had he, who had established the principle, to desire to check its consequences? If Luther found in the Bible that the Pope was Antichrist, if he arrogated to himself, of his own authority, the mission of destroying the reign of the Pope, by exhorting all the world to conspire against him, why could not the Anabaptists say, in their turn, *that they had intercourse with God, and had received the order to exterminate all the wicked, and to establish a new kingdom, in which were to be seen only wise, pious, and innocent men, having become the masters of all things.*

Hermann preaching the massacre of all the priests and all the magistrates of the world; David George proclaiming that his doctrine alone was perfect, that that of the *Old and New Testaments was imperfect, and that he was the true Son of God;* Nicholas rejecting faith and worship as useless, treading under foot the fundamental precepts of morality, and teaching *that it was good to continue in sin, that grace might abound;* Hacket pretending that the spirit of the Messiah had descended upon him, and sending two of his disciples to cry out in the streets of London, *"Behold Christ coming here with a vase in his hand!"* Hacket himself crying out, at the sight of the gibbet, and in the agony of punishment, "Jehovah! Jehovah! do you not see that the heavens open, and that Jesus Christ comes to deliver me?" are not all these deplorable spectacles, and a hundred others that I might mention, proofs sufficiently evident that the Protestant system nourishes and inflames a fearful fanaticism? Venner, Fox, William Simpson, J. Naylor, Count Zinzendorf, Wesley, Baron Swedenborg, and other similar names, are sufficient to remind us of an assemblage of sects so extravagant, and a series of crimes such as would fill volumes, which would afford us the most ridiculous and the most odious pictures, the greatest miseries and the most deplorable errors of the human mind. I have not invented or exaggerated. Open history, consult authors—I do not mean Catholics, but Protestants, or whatever they may be—and you will every where find a multitude of witnesses who depose to the truth of these facts; notorious facts, which have taken place in the light of day, in great capitals, and in times bordering on our own; and let it not be supposed that this abundant source of illusion and fanaticism has been exhausted in the course of ages; it does not seem that it is yet near being dried up, and Europe appears condemned to hear the recital of visions, such as those of Baron Swedenborg in the inn in London; and we shall still see passports for heaven with three seals given out, like those of Johanna Southcote.

NOTE 12, p. 60.

Nothing is more palpable than the difference which exists on this point between Protestants and Catholics. On both sides there are persons who consider themselves to be favored with heavenly visions; but these visions render Protestants proud, turbulent, and raving mad, while among Catholics they increase the spirit of humility, peace, and love. Even in that very sixteenth century, in which the fanaticism of the Protestants agitated and stained Europe with blood, there lived in Spain a woman who, in the judgment of unbelievers and Protestants, is certainly one of those who have been the most deeply infected with illusion and fanaticism; but has the supposed fanaticism of this woman ever caused the spilling of a drop of blood, or the shedding of a tear? Were her visions, like those of Protestants, orders from heaven for the extermination of men? After the desolate and horrible picture which I have given in the preceding note, perhaps the reader will be glad to let his eyes rest upon a spectacle as peaceful as it is beautiful. It is St. Theresa writing her own life out of pure obedience, and relating to us her visions with angelic candor and ineffable sweetness. "The Lord (she says) willed that I should once have this vision: I saw near to me, on the left hand, an angel in a corporeal form; this is what I do not usually see, except by a prodigy; although angels often present themselves to me without my seeing them, as I have said in the preceding vision. In this the Lord willed that I should see him in the following manner: he was not tall, but small and very beautiful, his face all in a flame, and he seemed to be one of the angels very high in the hierarchy, who apparently are all on fire. Without doubt, he was one of those who are called seraphim.—These angels do not tell me their names; but I clearly see that there is so great a difference among the angels, between some and others, that I do not know how to express it. I saw in his hands a long dart of gold, which appeared to me to have some fire at the end of the point. It seemed to me that the angel buried this dart from time to time in my heart, and made it penetrate to my bowels, and that when withdrawing it, he carried them away, leaving me all inflamed with a great love of God." (*Vie de St. Thérèse*, c. xxix. no. 11.) Another example: "At this moment I see on my head a dove very different from those of earth; for this one had no feathers, but wings as it were of the shell of mother of pearl, which shone brightly. It was larger than a dove; it seemed to me that I heard the noise of its wings. It moved them almost for the time of an Ave Maria. The soul was already in such a condition that, herself swooning away, she also lost sight of this divine dove. The mind grew tranquil with the presence of such a guest, although it seemed to me that so wonderful a favor ought to fill it with perturbation and alarm; but as the soul began to enjoy it, fear departed, repose came with enjoyment, and the mind remained in ecstacy." (*Vie*, c. xxviii. no. 7.) It would be difficult to find any thing more beautiful, expressed in more lively colors, and with a more amiable simplicity. It will not be out of place to copy here two other passages of a different kind, which, while they enforce what we wish to shew, may contribute to awaken the taste of our nation for a certain class of Spanish writers, who are every day falling into oblivion with us, while foreigners seek for them with eagerness, and publish handsome editions of them. "I was once at office with all the rest; my soul was suddenly fixed in attention, and it seemed to me to be entirely as a clear mirror without reverse or side, neither high nor low, but shining every where. In the midst of it, Christ our Saviour presented himself to me, as I am accustomed to see Him. He appeared to me to be at once in all parts of my soul. I saw Him as in a clear mirror, and this mirror also (I cannot say how) was entirely imprinted on our Lord himself, by a communication which I cannot describe—a communication full of love. I know that this vision has been of great advantage to me every time that I recollect it, principally when I have just received communion. I was given to understand that when a soul is in a state of mortal sin, this mirror is covered with great darkness, and is extremely obscure, so that our Lord cannot appear or be seen therein, although He is always present as giving being; as to heretics, it is as if the mirror were broken, which is much worse than if it were obscured. There is a great difference between seeing this and telling it; it is difficult to make such a thing understood. I repeat, that this has been very profitable to me, and also very afflicting, on account of the view of the various offences by which I have obscured my soul, and have been deprived of seeing my Lord." (*Vie*, c. xi. no. 4.)

In another place she explains a manner of seeing things in God; she represents the idea by an image so brilliant and sublime, that we appear to be reading Malebranche, when developing his famous system.

"We say that the Divinity is like a bright diamond, infinitely larger than the world; or rather like a mirror, as I have said of the soul in another vision; except that here it is in a manner so sublime, that I know not how to exalt it sufficiently. All that we do is seen in this diamond, which contains all in itself; for there is nothing which is not comprised in so great a magnitude. It was alarming to me to see in so short a time so many things assembled in this bright diamond; and I am profoundly afflicted every time that I think that things so shocking as my sins appeared to me in this most pure brightness." (*Vie*, c. xl. no. 7.)

Let us now suppose, with Protestants, that all these visions were only pure illusions: at least it is evident that they do not pervert ideas, corrupt morals, or disturb public order; and assuredly, had they served only to inspire these beautiful pages, we should not know how to regret the illusion. This is a confirmation of what I have said of the salutary effects which the Catholic principle produces in souls, by preventing them from being blinded by pride, or throwing themselves into dangerous courses. This principle confines them to a sphere where it is impossible for them to injure any one; but it does not deprive them of any of their force or energy to do good, supposing that the inspiration is real. Although it would have been easy for me to cite a thousand examples, I was compelled, for the sake of brevity, to confine myself to one, when selecting St. Theresa as one of those who are the most distinguished in this respect, and because she was contemporary with the great aberrations of Protestantism. In fine, as she was a daughter of Spain, I seized the opportunity of recalling her to the memories of Spaniards, who begin too much to forget her.

NOTE 13, p. 64.

Some of the leaders of the Reformation have left suspicions that they taught with insincerity, that they did not themselves believe what they preached, and that they had no other object than to deceive their proselytes. As I am unwilling to have it imputed to me that I have made this accusation rashly, I will adduce some proofs in support of my assertion. Let us hear Luther himself. "Often," he says, "do I think within myself that I scarcely know where I am, and whether I teach the truth or not (Sæpe sic mecum cogito, propemodum nescio, quo loco sim, et utrum veritatem doceam, necne)." (Luther, *Col. Isleb. de Christo.*) And it is the same man who said: "It is certain that I have received my dogmas from heaven. I will not allow you to judge of my doctrine, neither you nor even the angels of heaven (Certum est dogmata mea habere me de cœlo. Non sinam vel vos vel ipsos angelos de cœlo de mea doctrina judicare)." (Luther, *contra Reg. Ang.*) John Matthei, the author of many writings on the life of Luther, and who is not scanty in eulogies on the heresiarch, has preserved a very curious anecdote touching the convictions of Luther. It is this: "A preacher called John Musa related to me that he one day complained to Luther that he could not prevail on himself to believe what he taught to others: '*Blessed be God* (said Luther) *that the same thing happens to others as to myself: I believed till now that* THAT *was a thing which happened only to me.*'" (Johann. Matthesius, *conc.* 12.)

The doctrines of infidelity were not long delayed; but would it be believed that they are found expressed in various parts of Luther's own works? "It is likely," says he, speaking of the dead, "that, except a few, they all sleep deprived of feeling." "I think that the dead are buried in so ineffable and wonderful a sleep, that they feel or see less than those who sleep an ordinary sleep." "The souls of the dead enter neither into purgatory nor into hell." "The human soul sleeps; all its senses buried." "There is no suffering in the abode of the dead." ("Verisimile est, exceptis paucis, omnes dormire insensibiles." "Ego puto mortuos sic ineffabili et miro somno sopitos, ut minus sentiant aut videant, quam hi qui alias dormiunt." "Animæ mortuorum non ingrediuntur in purgatorium nec infernum." "Anima humana dormit, omnibus sensibus sepultis." "Mortuorum locus cruciatus nullos habet.") (Tom. ii. *Epist. Lat. Isleb.* fol. 44; t. vi *Lat. Wittenberg.* in cap. ii., cap. xxiii., c. xxv., c. xlii. et xlix. *Genes.* et t. iv. *Lat. Wittenberg,* fol. 109.) Persons were not wanting ready to receive such doctrines; and this teaching caused such ravages, that the Lutheran Brentsen, disciple and successor of Luther, hesitates not to say: *"Although no one among us publicly professes that the soul perishes with the body, and that there is no resurrection of the dead, nevertheless the impure and wholly profane lives which they for the most part lead, show very clearly that they do not believe that there is another life. Some even allow words of this kind to escape them, not only in the intoxication of libations, but even when fasting, in their familiar intercourse.* (Et si inter nos nulla sit publica professio quod anima simul cum corpore intereat, et quod non sit mortuorum resurrectio, tamen impurissima et profanissima illa vita, quam maxima pars hominum sectatur, perspicue indicat quod non sentiat vitam post hanc. Nonnullis etiam tales voces, tam ebriis inter pocula, quam sobriis in familiaribus colloquiis.)" (Brentius, *Hom.* 35, in cap. 20, Luc.) There were in this same sixteenth century some men who cared not to give their names to this or that sect, but who professed infidelity and scepticism without disguise. We know that the famous Gruet paid with his head for his boldness in this way; and it was not the Catholics who cut it off, but the Calvinists, who were offended that this unhappy man had taken the liberty to paint the character and conduct of Calvin in their true colors. Gruet had also committed the crime of posting up placards at Geneva, in which he charged the pretended reformers with inconsistency, on account of the tyranny which they attempted to exercise over consciences, after having shaken off the yoke of authority on their own account. This took place soon after the birth of Protestantism, as the sentence on Gruet was executed in 1549.

Montaigne, who has been pointed out as one of the first sceptics who acquired reputation in Europe, carries the thing so far, that he does not even admit the natural law. *"They are not serious* (he says) *when, to give some certainty to laws, they say that there are any laws fixed, perpetual, and immutable, which they call natural, which are impressed on the human race by the condition of their peculiar essence."* (Montaigne, *Ess.* l. ii. c. 12.)

We have already seen what Luther thought of death, or at least the expression which escaped him on this subject; and we cannot be astonished after that, that Montaigne wished to die like a real unbeliever, and that he says, speaking of the terrible passage: *"I plunge my head, insensibly sunk in death, without considering or observing it, as in a silent and obscure depth, which swallows me up at once, stifles me in a moment with powerful sleep full of insipidity and indolence."* (Montaigne, l. iii. c. 9.) But this man, who wished that death should find him planting his cabbages, and without thinking of it (*Je veux que la mort me trouve plantant mes choux, mais sans me soucier d'elle*), was not of the same opinion in his last moments. When he was near breathing his last, he wished that the holy sacrifice of the Mass should be celebrated in his apartment, and he expired while making an effort to raise himself on his bed, in the act of adoring the sacred Host. We see that he had profited in his heart by some of his ideas with respect to the Christian religion. "It is pride," he had said, "that leads man out of the common path, and urges him to embrace novelties, loving rather to be the chief of a wandering and undisciplined band, than to be a disciple of the school of truth." In another place, at once condemning all the dissenting sects, he had said, "In religious matters it is necessary to adhere to those who are the established judges of doctrine, and who have legitimate authority, not to the most learned and the cleverest."

From all that I have just said, it is clear that if I accuse Protestantism of having been one of the principal causes of infidelity in Europe, I do not accuse it without reason. I repeat here, that it is by no means my intention to overlook the efforts of some Protestants to oppose infidelity; I do not assail *persons*, but *things*, and I honor merit wherever I find it. In fine, I will add, that if at the end of the seventeenth century a considerable number of Protestants displayed a tendency towards Catholicity, we must seek the reason for it in the progress which they saw infidelity making,—a progress which it was impossible to check, at least without holding fast to the anchor of authority which the Catholic Church offered to the whole world. I cannot, without exceeding the limits which I have marked out for myself, give a circumstantial detail of the correspondence between Molanus and the Bishop of Tyna, of Leibnitz and Bossuet. Readers who desire to become thoroughly acquainted with that affair, may examine it partly in the works of Bossuet himself, and partly in the interesting work of M. de Beausset, prefixed to some editions of Bossuet.

Note 14, p. 86.

In order to form an idea of the state of knowledge at the time of the appearance of Christianity, and become convinced that there was nothing to be expected from the human mind abandoned to its own strength, it is enough to recall to mind the monstrous sects which every where abounded in the first ages of the Church, the doctrines whereof formed the most shapeless, extravagant, and immoral compound that it is possible to conceive. The names of Cerinthus, Menander, Ebion, Saturninus, Basilides, Nicolas, Carpocrates, Valentinus, Marcion, Montanus, and so many others, remind us of the sects in which delirium was connected with immorality. When we throw a glance over these philosophico-religious sects, we see that they were capable neither of conceiving a philosophical system with any degree of concert, nor of imagining a collection of doctrines and practices to which the name of religion can be applied. These men overturned, mixed, and confounded all; Judaism, Christianity, and the recollections of the ancient schools, were all amalgamated in their deluded heads; what they never forgot was, to give a loose rein to all kinds of corruption and obscenity.

In the spectacle of these ages, a wide field is opened to the conjectures of true philosophy. What would have become of human knowledge, if Christianity had not come to enlighten the world with her celestial doctrines; if that divine religion, confounding the foolish pride of man, had not come to show him how vain and senseless were his thoughts, and how far he was removed from the path of truth? It is remarkable that these same men, whose aberrations make us shudder, gave themselves the name of Gnostics, on account of the superior knowledge with which they supposed themselves to be endowed. We see that man is at all times the same.

NOTE 15, p. 115.

I have thought that it would not be useless to transcribe here, word for word, the canons which I have mentioned in the text. My readers may thereby acquire for themselves a complete knowledge of what is found there; and there will be no room left to suppose that the real sense of the regulations has been perverted in the extracts which I have given.

CANONS AND OTHER DOCUMENTS,

Which show the solicitude of the Church to improve the lot of slaves, and the various means she has used to accomplish the abolition of slavery:

§ I.

A penance is imposed on the mistress who maltreats her slave (ancillam).

(Concilium Eliberitanum, anno 305.)

"Si qua domina furore zeli accensa flagris verberaverit ancillam suam, ita ut in tertium diem animam cum cruciatu effundat; eo quod incertum sit, voluntate an casu occiderit; si voluntate, post septem annos, si casu, post quinquennii tempora, acta legitima pœnitentia, ad communionem placuit admitti. Quod si infra tempora constituta fuerit infirmata, accipiat communionem." (Canon 5.)

It must be observed, that the word 'ancillam' means a slave properly so called, and not any kind of servant. This appears, indeed, from the words *flagris verberaverit,* which express a chastisement reserved for slaves.

They excommunicate the master who, of his own authority, beats his slave to death.

(Concilium Epaoense, anno 517.)

"Si quis servum proprium sine conscientia judicis occiderit, excommunicatione biennii effusionem sanguinis expiabit." (Canon 34.)

This same regulation is repeated in the 15th canon of the 17th Council of Toledo, held in 694; even the words of the Council of Epaon are there copied with very slight change.

(Ibid.) *The slave guilty of an atrocious crime was to escape corporeal punishments by taking refuge in a church.*

"Servus reatu atrociore culpabilis si ad ecclesiam confugerit, a corporabilibus tantum suppliciis excusetur. De capillis vero, vel quocumque opere, placuit, a dominis juramenta non exigi." (Canon 39.)

Very remarkable precautions to prevent masters from maltreating the slaves who had taken refuge in churches.

(Concilium Aurelianense quintum, anno 549.)

"De servis vero, qui pro qualibet culpa ad ecclesiæ septa confugerint, id statuimus observandum, ut, sicut in antiquis constitutionibus tenetur scriptum, pro concessa culpa datis a domino sacramentis, quisquis ille fuerit, expediatur de venia jam securus. Enim vero si immemor fidei dominus trascendisse convincitur quod juravit, ut is qui veniam acceperat, probetur postmodum pro ea culpa qualicumque supplicio cruciatus, dominus ille qui immemor fuit datæ fidei, sit ab omnium communione suspensus. Iterum si servus de promissione veniæ datis sacramentis a domino jam securus exire noluerit, ne sub tali contumacia requirens locum fugæ, domino fortasse dispereat, egredi nolentem a domino cum liceat occupari, ut nullam, quasi pro retentatione servi, quibuslibet modis molestiam aut calumniam patiatur ecclesia: fidem tamen dominus, quam pro concessa venia dedit, nulla temeritate transcendat. Quod si aut gentilis dominus fuerit, aut alterius sectæ, qui a conventu ecclesiæ probatur extraneus, is qui servum repetit, personas requirat bonæ fidei Christianas, ut ipsi in persona domini servo præbeant sacramenta: quia ipsi possunt servare quod sacrum est, qui pro transgressione ecclesiasticum metuunt disciplinam." (Canon 22.)

It is difficult to carry solicitude for the lot of slaves further. This document is very curious.

They forbid bishops to mutilate their slaves: they order that the duty of chastising them should be left to the judge of the town, who, nevertheless, could not cut off their hair, a punishment which was considered too ignominious.

(Concilium Emeritense, anno 666.)

"Si regalis pietas pro salute omnium suarum legum dignata est ponere decreta, cur religio sancta per sancti concilii ordinem non habeat instituta, quæ omnino debent esse cavenda? Ideoque placuit huic sancto concilio, ut omnis potestas episcopalis modum suæ ponat iræ; nec pro quolibet excessu cuilibet ex familia, ecclesiæ aliquod corporis membrorum sua ordinatione præsumat extirpare aut auferre. Quod si talis emerserit culpa, advocato judice civitatis, ad examen ejus deducatur quod factum fuisse asseritur. Et quia omnino justum est, ut pontifex sævissimam non impendat vindictam; quidquid coram judice verius patuerit, per disciplinæ severitatem absque turpi decal vatione maneat emendatum." (Canon 15.)

Priests are forbidden to have their slaves mutilated.

(Concilium Toletanum undecimum, anno 675.)

"His a quibus domini sacramenta tractanda sunt, judicium sanguinis agitare non licet: et ideo magnopere talium excessibus prohibendum est, ne indiscretæ præsumptionis motibus agitati, aut quod morte plectendum est, sententia propria judicare præsumant, aut truncationes quaslibet membrorum quibuslibet personis aut per se inferant, aut inferendas præcipiant. Quod si quisquam horum immemor præceptorum, aut ecclesiæ suæ familiis, aut in quibuslibet personis tale quid fecerit, et concessi ordinis honore privatus, et loco suo, perpetuo damnationis teneatur religatus ergastulo: cui tamen communio exeunti ex hac vita non neganda est, propter domini misericordiam, *qui non vult peccatoris mortem, sed ut convertatur et vivat.*" (Canon 6.)

It should be remarked, that the word *familia*, employed in the two last canons which we have just cited, should be understood of slaves. The real meaning of this word is clearly shown us by the 74th canon of the 4th Council of Toledo.

"De *familiis* ecclesiæ constituere presbyteros et diaconos per parochias liceat..... ea tamen ratione ut *antea manumissi libertatem status sui percipiant.*

We see this word employed in the same sense by Pope St. Gregory. (Epist. xliv. l. 4.)

A penance is imposed on the master who kills his slave of his own authority.

(Concilium Wormatiense, anno 868.)

"Si quis servum proprium sine conscientia judicum qui tale quid commiserit, quod morte sit dignum, occiderit, excommunicatione vel pœnitentia biennii, reatum sanguinis emendabit." (Canon 38.)

"Si qua femina furore zeli accensa, flagris verberaverit ancillam suam, ita ut intra tertium diem animam suam cum cruciatu effundat, eo quod incertum sit voluntate, an casu occiderit ; si voluntate, septem annos, si casu, per quinque annorum tempora legitimam peragat pœnitentiam." (Canon 39.)

They check the violence of those who, to revenge themselves for the asylum granted to slaves, take possession of the goods of the Church.

(Concilium Arausicanum primum, anno 441.)

"Si quis autem mancipia clericorum pro suis mancipiis ad ecclesiam fugientibus crediderit occupanda, per omnes ecclesias districtissima damnatione feriatur." (Canon 6.)

§ II.

(Ibid.) *They check all attempts made against the liberty of slaves enfranchised by the Church, or who have been recommended to her by will.*

"In ecclesia manumissos, vel per testamentum ecclesiæ commendatos, si quis in servitutem, vel obsequium, vel ad colonariam conditionem imprimere tentaverit, animadversione ecclesiastica coerceatur." (Canon 7.)

They secure the liberty of those who have received the benefit of manumission in the Churches. The latter are enjoined to take upon themselves the defence of the enfranchised.

(Concilium quintum Aurelianense, anno 549.)

"Et quia plurimorum suggestione comperimus, eos qui in ecclesiis juxta patrioticam consuetudinem a servitiis fuerunt absoluti, pro libito quorumcumque iterum ad servitium revocari, impium esse tractavimus, ut quod in ecclesia Dei consideratione a vinculo servitutis absolvitur, irritum habeatur. Ideo pietatis causa communi concilio placuit observandum, ut quæcumque mancipia ab ingenuis dominis servitute laxantur, in ea libertate maneant, quam tunc a dominis perceperunt. Hujusmodi quoque libertas si a quocumque pulsata fuerit, cum justitia ab ecclesiis defendatur, præter eas culpas, pro quibus leges collatas servis revocare jusserunt libertates." (Canon 7.)

The Church is charged with the defence of the enfranchised, whether they have been emancipated within her enclosure, whether they have been so by letter or testament, or have gained their liberty by prescription. They restrain the arbitrariness of the judges towards these unfortunate persons. It is decided that the Bishops shall take cognizance of these causes.

(Concilium Matisconense secundum, anno 585.)

"Quæ dum postea universo cœtui secundum consuetudinem recitata innotescerent, Prætextatus et Pappulus viri beatissimi dixerunt: Decernat itaque, et de miseris libertis vestræ auctoritatis vigor insignis, qui ideo plus a judicibus affliguntur, quia sacris sunt commendati ecclesiis: ut si quas quispiam dixerit contra eos actiones habere, non audeat eos magistratus contradere ; sed in episcopi tantum judicio, in cujus præsentia litem contestans, quæ sunt justitiæ ac veritatis audiat. Indignum est enim, ut hi qui in sacrosancta ecclesia jure noscuntur legitimo manumissi, aut per epistolam, aut per testamentum, aut per longinquitatem temporis libertatis jure fruuntur, a quolibet injustissime inquietentur. Universa sacerdotalis Congregatio dixit: Justum est, ut contra calumniatorum omnium versutias defendantur, qui patrocinium immortalis ecclesiæ concupiscunt. Et quicumque a nobis de libertis latum decretum, superbiæ ausu prævaricare tentaverit, irreparabili damnationis suæ sententia feriatur. Sed si placuerit episcopo ordinarium judicem, aut quemlibet alium sæcularem, in audientiam eorum accersiri, cum libuerit fiat, et nullus alius audeat causas pertractare libertorum nisi episcopus cujus interest, aut is cui idem audiendum tradiderit." (Canon 7.)

The defence of the freed is confided to the priests.

(Concilium Parisiense quintum, anno 614.)

"Liberti quorumcumque ingenuorum a sacerdotibus defensentur, nec ad publicum ulterius revocentur. Quod si quis ausu temerario eos imprimere voluerit, aut ad publicum revocare, et admonitus per pontificem ad audientiam venire neglexerit, aut emendare quod perpetravit distulerit, communione privetur." (Canon 5.)

The enfranchised recommended to the Churches shall be protected by the Bishops.

(Concilium Toletanum tertium, anno 589.)

"De libertis autem id Dei præcipiunt sacerdotes, ut si qui ab episcopis facti sunt secundum modum quo canones antiqui dant licentiam, sint liberi ; et tantum a patrocinio ecclesiæ tam ipsi quam ab eis progeniti non recedant. Ab aliis quoque libertati traditi, et ecclesiis commendati, patrocinio episcopali tegantur, a principe hoc episcopus postulet." (Canon 6.)

The Church undertakes to defend the liberty and the property acquired by industry of the enfranchised who have been recommended to her.

(Concilium Toletanum quartum, anno 633.)

"Liberti qui a quibuscumque manumissi sunt, atque ecclesiæ patrocinio commendati existunt, sicut regulæ antiquorum patrum constituerunt.

sacerdotali defensione a cujuslibet insolentia protegantur; sive in statu libertatis eorum, seu in peculio quod habere noscuntur." (Cap. 72.)

The Church will defend the enfranchised: a regulation which does not distinguish whether they have been recommended to her or not.

(Concilium Agathense, anno 506.)

"Libertos legitime a dominis suis factos ecclesia, si necessitas exegerit, tueatur; quod si quis ante audientiam, aut pervadere, aut expoliare præsumpserit, ab ecclesia repellatur." (Canon 29.)

§ III.

The Church shall regard the ransom of captives as her first care; she shall give their interests the preference over her own, however bad may be the state of her affairs.

"Sicut omnino grave est, frustra ecclesiastica ministeria venundare, sic iterum culpa est, imminente hujusmodi necessitate, res maxime desolatæ Ecclesiæ captivis suis præponere, et in eorum redemptione cessare." (Caus. xii. q. 2, canon 16.)

Remarkable words of St. Ambrose touching the ransom of captives. To perform this pious duty, the holy Bishop breaks up and sells the sacred vessels.

(S. Ambrosius de Off. lib ii. cap. 15.)

(§ 70.) "Summa etiam liberalitas captos redimere, eripere ex hostium manibus, subtrahere neci homines, et maxime feminas turpidini, reddere parentibus liberos, parentes liberis, cives patriæ, restituere. Nota sunt hæc nimis Illyriæ vastitate et Thraciæ: quanti ubique venales erant captivi orbe ....

Ibid. (§ 71.) "Præcipua est igitur liberalitas, redimere captivos et maxime ab hoste barbaro, qui nihil deferat humanitatis ad misericordiam, nisi quod avaritia reservaverit ad redempionem."

Ib. l. ii. c. 2 (§ 13.) "*Ut nos aliquando in invidiam incidimus, quod confregerimus vasa mystica, ut captivos redimeremus*; quod Arianis displicere potuerat, nec tam factum displiceret, quam ut esset quod in nobis reprehenderetur."

These noble and charitable sentiments were not those of St. Ambrose only; his words are but the expression of the feelings of the whole Church. Without referring to numberless proofs which I might adduce here, and before I pass to the canons which I mean to insert, I will copy some passages from a touching letter of St. Cyprian, which contains the motives which animated the Church in her pious enterprise, and gives a lively description of her zeal and charity in these admirable efforts.

"Cyprianus Januario, Maximo, Proculo, Victori, Modiano, Nemesiano, Nampulo, et Honorato, fratribus salutem. Cum maximo animi nostri gemitu et non sine lacrymis legimus litteras vestras, fratres carissimi, quas ad nos pro dilectionis vestræ sollicitudine de fratrum nostrorum et sororum captivitate fecistis. Quis enim non doleat in ejusmodi casibus, aut quis non dolorem fratris sui suum proprium computet cum loquatur apostolus Paulus et dicat: *Si patitur unum membrum, compatiuntur et cætera membra: si lætatur membrum unum, collætantur et cætera membra.* (1 ad Cor. xii. 26.) Et alio loco: *Quis infirmatur*, inquit, *et non ego infirmor?* (2 ad Cor. xi. 29.) Quare nunc et nobis captivitas fratrum nostra captivitas computanda est, et periclitantium dolor pro nostro dolore numerandus est, cum sit scilicet adunationis nostræ corpus unum, et non tantum dilectio sed et religio instigare nos debeat et confortare ad fratrum membra redimenda. Nam cum denuo apostolus Paulus dicat: *Nescitis quia templum Dei estis, et Spiritus Dei habitat in vobis?* (1 ad Cor. iii. 16), etiamsi charitas nos minus adigeret ad opem fratribus ferendam, considerandum tamen hoc in loco fuit, Dei templum esse quæ capta sunt, nec pati nos longa cessatione et neglecto dolore debere, ut diu Dei templa captiva sint; sed quibus possumus viribus elaborare et velociter gerere ut Christum judicem et Dominum et Deum nostrum promereamur obsequiis nostris. Nam cum dicat Paulus apostolus, *Quotquot in Christo baptizati estis, Christum induistis* (ad Gal. iii. 27,) in captivis fratribus nostrus contemplandus est Christus et redimendus de periculo captivitatis, qui nos de diaboli faucibus exuit, nunc ipse qui manet et habitat in nobis de barbarorum manibus exuatur, et redimatur nummaria quantitate qui nos cruce redemit et sanguine.

. . . .

Quantus vero communis omnibus nobis mœror atque cruciatus est de periculo virginum quæ illic tenentur? pro quibus non tantum libertatis, sed et pudoris jactura plangenda est, nec tam vincula barbarorum quam lenonum et lupanarium stupra deflenda sunt, ne membra Christo dicata et in æternum continentiæ honorum pudica virtute devota, insultantium libidine et contagione fœdentur? Quæ omnia istic secundum litteras vestras fraternitas nostra cogitans et dolenter examinans, prompte omnes et libenter ac largiter subsidia nummaria fratribus contulerunt.

. . . .

Misimus autem sestertia centum millia nummorum, quæ istic in ecclesia cui de Domini indulgentia præsumus, cleri et plebis apud nos consistentis collatione, collecta sunt, quæ vos illic pro vestra diligentia dispensabitis.

. . . .

Si tamen ad explorandam nostri anima charitatem, et examinandi nostri pectoris fidem tale aliquid acciderit, nolite cunctari nuntiare hæc nobis litteris vestris, pro certo habentes ecclesiam nostram et fraternitatem istic universam, ne hæc ultra fiant precibus orare, si facta fuerint, libenter et largiter subsidia præstare." (Epist. 60.)

Thus the zeal for the redemption of captives, a zeal which was exerted with so much ardor in later ages, had appeared in the earliest times of the Church; this zeal was founded on grand and sublime motives, which render this work in some measure divine. and secure to those who devote themselves to it an unfading crown. Important information on this subject will be found also in the works of St. Gregory. (V. lib. iii. ep. 16; lib. iv. ep. 17; lib. vi. ep. 35; lib. vii. ep. 26, 28, and 38; lib. ix. ep. 17.)

The property of the Church employed for the redemption of captives.

(Concilium Matisconense secundum, anno 585.)

"Unde statuimus ac decernimus, ut mos antiquus a fidelibus reparetur; et decimas ecclesiasticis famulantibus ceremoniis populus omnis inferat, quas sacerdotes aut in pauperum usum *aut in captivorum redemptionem prœrogantes*, suis orationibus pacem populo ac salutem impetrent: si quis autem contumax nostris statutis saluberrimis fuerit, a membris ecclesiæ omni tempore separetur." (Canon 5.)

It is allowed to break up the sacred vessels, in order to devote the price of them to the redemption of captives.

(Concilium Rhemense, anno 625 vel. 630.)

"Si quis episcopus, excepto si evenerit ardua necessitas pro redemptione captivorum ministeria sancta frangere pro qualicumque conditione presumpserit, ab officio cessabit ecclesiæ." (Canon 22.)

The following canon informs us that the Bishops gave letters of recommendation to the captives; they are desired to state therein the date and price of the ransom; they are requested also to mention there the wants of those who are thus restored to liberty.

(Concilium Lugdunense tertium, anno 583.)

"Id etiam de epistolis placuit captivorum, ut ita sint sancti pontifices cauti, ut in servitio pontificibus consistentibus qui eorum manu vel subscriptione agnoscat epistolæ aut quælibet insinuationum litteræ dari debeant, quatenus de subscriptionibus nulla ratione possit Deo propitio dubitari: et epistola commendationis pro necessitate cujuslibet promulgata dies datarum et pretia constituta, vel necessitates captivorum quos cum epistolis dirigunt, ibidem inserantur." (Canon 2.)

Excess into which some ecclesiastics allowed themselves to fall, by an indiscreet zeal in favor of captives.

(Synodus S. Patricii, Auxilii et Isernini Episcoporum in Hibernia celebrata, circa annum Christi 450 vel 456.)

"Si quis clericorum voluerit juvare captivo cum suo pretio illi subveniat, nam si per furtum illum inviolaverit, blasphemantur multi clerici per unum latronem, qui sic fecerit excommunionis sit." (Canon 32.)

The church employed her property in the ransom of captives; and when the latter had afterwards acquired the means of repaying the sums advanced for them, she refused all reimbursement and graciously gave up the price of the ransom.

(Ex epistolis S. Gregorii.)

"Sacrorum canonum statuta et legalis permittit auctoritates, lici res ecclesiasticas in redemptionem captivorum impendi. Et ideo, quia edocti a vobis sumus, ante annos fere 18, virum reverendissimum quemdam Fabium, Episcopum Ecclesiæ Firmanæ, libras 11 argenti de eadem ecclesia pro redemptione vestra, ac patris vestri Passivi, fratris et coepiscopi nostri, tunc vero clerici, necnon matris vestræ, hostibus impendisse, atque ex hoc quamdam formidinem vos habere, ne hoc quod datum est, a vobis quolibet tempore repetatur, hujus præcepti auctoritate suspicionem vestram prævidimus auferendam; constituentes, nullam vos exinde, hæredesque vestros quolibet tempore repetitionis molestiam sustinere, nec a quoquam vobis aliquam objici quæstionem." (L. 7, ep. 14, et hab. Cuas. 12, q. 2, c. 15.)

The property of the Church served to ransom captives.

(Concilium Vernense secundum, anno 844.)

"Ecclesiæ facultates quas reges et reliqui christiani Deo voverunt, ad alimentum servorum Dei et pauperum, ad exceptionem hospitum, *redemptionis captivorum*, atque templorum Dei instaurationem, nunc in usu sæcularium detinentur. Hinc multi servi Dei penuriam cibi et potus ac vestimentorum patiuntur, pauperes consuetam eleemosynam non accipiunt, negliguntur hospites, *fraudantur captivi*, et fama omnium merito laceratur." (Canon 12.)

Let us observe in this canon the use which the Church made of her property; after having supported the clergy, and maintained divine worship, she devoted it to succor the poor, travellers or pilgrims, and to redeem captives. I make this observation here, because the opportunity offers; not because this canon is the only proof of the excellent use which the Church made of her property. Indeed, a great number of others might be cited, beginning with the canons called Apostolical. It is necessary also to remark the expression which is sometimes made use of to stigmatize the wickedness of the spoilers of the Church, or of those who administer her property badly; they are called *pauperum necatores*, 'murderers of the poor;' to make it well understood that one of the principal objects of this property is the support of the necessitous.

§ IV.

Those who attempt to take away the liberty of persons are excommunicated.

(Concilium Lugdunense secundum, anno 566.)

"Et qui peccatis facientibus multi in perniciem animæ suæ ita conati sunt, aut conantur assurgere, ut animas longa temporis quiete sine ulla status sui competitione viventes, nunc improba proditione atque traditione, aut captivaverint aut captivare conentur, si juxta præceptum domini regis emendare distulerint, quousque hos quos obduxerunt, in loco in quo longum tempus quiete vixerint, restaurare debeant, ecclesiæ communione priventur." (Canon 3.)

We see in this canon that private individuals, by too frequent attempts, employed violence to reduce free persons to slavery. At this time, on account of the irruptions of the barbarians, the state of Europe was such, that public authority, weak in the extreme, did not, properly speaking, exist. This is the reason why it is so noble to see the Church struggling every where to support public order, to defend liberty, and excommunicating those who attacked that liberty, in contempt of the commands of the king.

The same abuse repressed.

(Concilium Rhemense, anno 625 vel 630.)

"Si quis ingenuum aut liberum ad servitium

inclinare voluerit, aut fortasse jam fecit, et commonitus ab episcopo se de inquietudine ejus revocare neglexerit, aut emendare noluerit, tamquam calumniæ reum placuit sequestrari." (Canon 17.)

It is declared that he who leads away a Christian to sell him, is guilty of homicide.

(Concilium Confluentinum, anno 922.)

"Item interrogatum est, quid de eo faciendum sit qui christianum hominem seduxerit, et sic vendiderit: responsumque est ab omnibus, homicidii reatum, ipsum hominem sibi contrahere." (Canon 7.)

The traffic in men, practised at that time in England, is proscribed; it is forbidden to sell men like ignoble animals.

(Concilium Londinense, anno 1102.)

"Ne quis illud *nefarium negotium* quo hactenus in Anglia solebant homines sicut bruta animalia venundari, deinceps ullatenus facere præsumat."

We see, from the canon which I have just cited, to what point the Church had attained in all that affects true civilization. We are in the nineteenth century, and it is considered that a great step has been gained in modern civilization by the consent of the great European nations to sign treaties to suppress the slave-trade; now the canon which we have just cited tells us, that at the beginning of the twelfth century, and in that very town of London, where the famous Convention was lately held, the traffic in men was forbidden, and stigmatized as it deserves. *Nefarium negotium*—detestable trade—it is called by the Council: *infamous traffic*, it is called by modern civilization, the unconscious heir of the thoughts and even the words of those men who are treated by it as barbarians, of those Bishops, whom calumny has more or less represented as a band of conspirators against the liberty and happiness of the human race.

It is ordered that persons who have been sold or pledged, shall immediately recover their liberty by restoring the price received it is ordained that more shall not be required of them than they shall have received for their liberty.

(Synodus incerti loci, circa annum 616.)

"De ingenuis qui se pro pecunia aut alia revendiderint, vel oppignoraverint, placuit ut quandoquidem pretium, quantum pro ipsis datum est, invenire potuerunt, absque dilatione ad statum suæ conditionis reddito pretio reformentur, nec amplius quam pro eis datum est requiratur. Et interim, si vir ex ipsis, uxorem ingenuam habuerit, aut mulier ingenuum habuerit maritum, filii qui ex ipsis nati fuerint, in ingenuitate permaneant." (Canon 14.)

The text of this Council, held, according to some, at Boneuil, well deserves to have some remarks made on it. The beneficial regulation which allowed a man who had been sold to regain his liberty by paying the sum received, checked an evil which was deeply rooted in the customs of Gaul at that time, for we find it at a very early period. We know, indeed, from Cæsar, whose testimony we have cited in the text, that many men of that country sold their liberty to relieve themselves from difficulties. Let us also remark the regulation contained in the same canon with respect to the children of the person who was sold; whether it be the father or mother, the canon prescribes, in both cases, that the children shall be free; and it here departs from the well known rule of civil law: *partus sequitur ventrem.*

§ V.

It is forbidden to give up to the Jews the slaves who have taken refuge in the churches; it matters little whether they have chosen that asylum because their masters obliged them to things contrary to the Christian faith, or because they have been maltreated by them after having been once withdrawn from the sacred asylum under the promise of pardon.

(Concilium Aurelianense tertium, anno 538.)

"De mancipiis Christianis, quæ in Judæorum servitio detinentur, si eis quod Christiana religio vetat, a dominis imponitur, aut si eos quos de ecclesia excusatos tollent, pro culpa quæ remissa est, affligere aut cædere fortasse præsumpserint, et ad ecclesiam iterato confugerint, nullatenus a sacerdote reddantur, nisi pretium offeratur ac detur, quod mancipia ipsa valere pronuntiaverit justa taxatio." (Canon 13.)

The precept given in the preceding canon is renewed; a precept contained in the canon which we have just cited.

(Concilium Aurelianense quartum, anno 541.)

"Cum prioribus canonibus jam fuerit definitum ut de mancipiis Christianis, quæ apud Judæos sunt, si ad ecclesiam confugerint, et redimi se postulaverint, etiam ad quoscumque Christianos refugerint, et servire Judæis noluerint, taxato et oblato a fidelibus justo pretio, ab eorum dominio liberentur, ideo statuimus, ut tam justa constitutio ab omnibus catholicis conservetur." (Canon 30.)

The Jew who perverts a Christian slave is punished with the loss of all his slaves. (Ibid.)

"Hoc etiam decernimus observandum, ut quicumque Judæus proselytum, qui advena dicitur, Judæum facere præsumpserit, aut Christianum factum ad Judaicam superstitionem adducere; vel si Judæus Christianam ancillam suam sibi crediderit sociandam; vel si de parentibus Christianis natum, Judæum sub promissione fecerit libertatis, mancipiorum amissione mulctetur." (Canon 31.)

Jews are forbidden to have Christian slaves henceforth; as to those who are in their power, all Christians are allowed to ransom them by paying their Jewish masters twelve solidi.

(Concilium Matisconense primum, anno 581.)

"Et liceat quid de Christianis qui aut de captivitatis incursu, aut fraudibus Judæorum servitio implicantur, debeat observari, non solum canonicis statutis, sed et legum beneficio pridem fuerit constitutum; tamen quia nunc item quo rumdam querela exorta est, quosdam Judæos, per civitates aut municipia consistentes, in tantam insolentiam et proterviam prorupisse, ut nec reclamantes Christianos liceat vel pretio de eorum servitute absolvi: idcirco præsenti concilio, Deo auctore, sancimus, ut nullus Christianus Judæos deinceps debeat deservire; sed datis pro quolibet bono mancipio 12 solidis, ipsum mancipium quicumque Christianus, seu ad ingenuitatem, seu ad servitium, licentiam habeat redimendi; quia nefas est, ut quos Christus Dominus sanguinis sui effusione redemit, persecutorum vinculis maneant irretiti. Quod si acquiescere his quæ statuimus quicumque Judæus noluerit, quamdiu ad pecuniam constitutam venire distulerit, liceat mancipio ipsi cum Christianis ubicumque voluerit habitare. Illud etiam specialiter sancientes, quod si quis Judæus Christianum mancipium ad errorem Judaicum convictus fuerit suasisse, ut ipse mancipio careat, et legandi damnatione plectatur." (Canon 16.)

The preceding canon is almost equivalent to a decree for the entire emancipation of Christian slaves; for if, on the one hand, Jews were forbidden to acquire new Christian slaves, and, on the other, those who were in their possession could be redeemed by the first Christian who came, it is clear that the charity of the faithful thus finding a door open to it, the number of Christian slaves who groaned in the power of the Jews must have diminished in an extraordinary manner. It is not said that these canonical regulations of the Church from the first moment obtained all the result which was intended; but, as she was the only power that remained standing at that time, and the only one that exercised influence on the nations, it cannot be doubted that her regulations were infinitely advantageous to those in whose favor they were established.

Jews are forbidden to acquire Christian slaves. If a Jew perverts to Judaism, or circumcises a Christian slave, the latter becomes free without having any thing to pay to his master.

(Concilium Toletanum tertium, anno 589.)

"Suggerente concilio, id gloriossimus dominus noster canonibus inserendum præcipit, ut Judæis non liceat Christianas habere uxores, *neque mancipia comparare in usus proprios*. . .

"Si qui vero Christiani ab eis Judaico ritu sunt maculati, vel etiam circumcisi, non reddito pretio ad libertatem et religionem redeant Christianam." (Canon 14.)

This canon is remarkable, both because it protects the conscience of the slave, and imposes on masters a punishment favorable to liberty. This manner of checking the arbitrary power of those who violated the consciences of their slaves, is found, during the following century, in a curious example contained in the collection of the laws of Ina, queen of the West Saxons. It is this:

If a master makes his slave work on Sunday, the slave becomes free.

(Leges Ynæ reginæ Saxonum Occiduorum, anno 692.)

"Si servus operetur die dominica per præceptum domini sui, sit liber." (Leg. iii.)

Another curious example:

If a master gives meat to a slave on a fasting-day, the slave becomes free.

(Concilium Berghamstedæ anno 5° Withredi regis Cantii, id est Christi 697: sub Bertualdo Cantuariensi archiepiscopo celebratum. Hæc sunt judicia Withredi regis Cantuariorum.)

"Si quis servo suo carnem in jejunio dederit comedendam, servus liber exeat." (Canon 15.)

It is definitively forbidden for Jews to have Christian slaves; all contravention of this order shall deprive the Jews of all their slaves, who shall obtain their liberty from the prince.

(Concilium Toletanum quartum, anno 633.)

"Ex decreto gloriosissimi principis hoc sanctum elegit concilium, ut Judæis non liceat Christianos servos habere, nec Christiana mancipia emere, nec cujusquam consequi largitate: nefas est enim ut membra Christi serviant Antichristi ministris. Quod si deinceps servos Christianos, vel ancillas Judæi habere præsumpserint, sublati ab eorum dominatu libertatem a principe consequantur." (Canon 66.)

It is forbidden to sell Christian slaves to Jews or Gentiles; if such sales have been made, they shall be annulled.

(Concilium Rhemense, anno 625.)

"Ut Christiani Judæis vel Gentilibus non vendantur; et si quis Christianorum necessitate cogente mancipia sua Christiana elegerit venundanda, non aliis nisi tantum Christianis expendat. Nam si paganis aut Judæis vendiderit, communione privetur, et emptio careat firmitate." (Canon 11.)

No precaution was too great in those unhappy times. It might appear at first that such regulations were an effect of the intolerance of the Church with respect to the Jews and Pagans; and yet, in reality, they were a barrier against the barbarism which invaded all; they were a guarantee of the most sacred rights of man; so much the more necessary, as all the others, it may be said, had disappeared. Read the document which we are about to transcribe; you will there see that barbarism was carried so far, that slaves were sold to the Pagans to be sacrificed.

(Gregorius Papa III. ep. ad Bonifacium Archiepiscopum, anno 731.)

"Hoc quoque inter alia crimina agi in partibus illis dixisti, quod quidam ex fidelibus ad *immolandum* paganis sua venundent mancipia. Quod ut magnopere corrigere debeas, frater, commonemus, nec sinas fieri ultra; scelus est enim et impietas. Eis ergo qui hæc perpetraverunt, similem homicidæ indices pœnitentiam."

These excesses must have occupied the active attention of the Church, as we see the Council of Liptines, held in 743, again insist on this point, and forbid Christian slaves to be given up to the Gentiles.

"Et ut mancipia Christiana paganis non tradantur." (Canon 7.)

It is forbidden to sell a Christian slave out of the territory comprised within the kingdom of Clovis.

(Concilium Cabilonense, anno 650.)

"Pietatis est maximæ et religionis intuitus, ut captivitatis vinculum omnino a Christianis redimatur. Unde sancta Synodus noscitur censuisse, ut nullus mancipium extra fines vel terminos, qui ad regnum domini Clodovei regis pertinent, debeat venundare, ne quod absit, per tale commercium, aut captivitatis vinculo, vel quod pejus est, Judaica servitute mancipia Christiana teneantur implicita." (Canon 9.)

This canon, which forbids the selling of Christian slaves out of the kingdom of Clovis, for fear that they should fall into the power of the Pagans and Jews, and the other of the Council of Rheims, cited above, which contains a similar regulation, are worthy of remark, under two aspects; they show, 1st, the high respect which we ought to have for the soul of man, even of him who is a slave, since it is forbidden to sell him where his conscience might be in danger: a respect which it was very important to maintain, both in order to eradicate the erroneous maxims of antiquity on this point, and because it was the first step towards emancipation. 2d. By limiting the power of sale, there was introduced into that kind of property a law which distinguished it from others, and placed it in a different and more elevated category. This was a great step made towards declaring open war against this property itself, and abolishing it by legitimate means.

Clerics who sold their slaves to Jews are severely reproved: they are threatened with alarming punishments.

(Concilium decimum Toletanum, anno 656.)

"Septimæ collationis immane satis et infandum operationis studium nunc sanctum nostrum adiit concilium; quod plerique ex sacerdotibus et levitis, qui pro sacris ministeriis, et pietatis studio, gubernationisque augmento sanctæ ecclesiæ deputati sunt officio, malunt imitari turbam malorum, potius quam sanctorum patrum insistere mandatis: ut ipsi etiam qui redimere debuerunt, venditiones facere intendant, quos Christi sanguine præsciunt esse redemptos; ita duntaxat, ut eorum dominio qui sunt empti in ritu Judaismo convertantur oppressi, et fit execrabile commercium, ubi nitente Deo justum est sanctum adesse conventum; quia majorum canones vetuerunt ut nullus Judæorum conjugia vel servitia habere præsumat de Christianorum cœtu."

Here the Council eloquently reprimands the guilty; it continues:

"Si quis enim post hanc definitionem talia agere tentaverit, noverit se extra ecclesiam fieri, et præsenti, et futuro judicio cum Juda simili pœna percelli, dum modo Dominum denuo proditionis pretio malunt ad iracundiam provocare." (Canon 7.)

§ VI.

Pope St. Gregory the First gives freedom to two slaves of the Church of Rome. Remarkable passage, in which this holy pope explains the motives which induced the Christians to enfranchise their slaves.

"Cum Redemptor noster totius conditor creaturæ ad hoc propitiatus humanam voluerit carnem assumere, ut divinitatis suæ gratia, diruto quo tenebamur captivi vinculo servitutis, pristinæ nos restitueret libertati; salubriter agiter, si homines quos ab initio natura creavit liberos et protulit, et jus gentium jugo substituit servitutis, in ea natura in qua nati fuerant, manumittentis beneficio, libertati reddantur. Atque ideo pietatis intuitu, et hujus rei consideratione permoti, vos Montanam atque Thomam famulos sanctæ Romanæ Ecclesiæ, cui Deo adjutore deservimus, liberos ex hac die civesque Romanos efficimus, omneque vestrum vobis relaxamus servitutis peculium." (S. Greg. 1. v. ep. 12.)

Bishops are directed to respect the liberty of those who have been enfranchised by their predecessors. Mention is made of the power given to Bishops to free their slaves who deserve well, and the sum is fixed which they may give them to aid them in living.

(Concilium Agathense, anno 506.)

"Sane si quos de servis ecclesiæ benemeritos sibi episcopus libertate donaverit, collatam libertatem a successoribus placuit custodiri, cum hoc quod eis manumissor in libertate contulerit, quod tamen jubemus viginti solidorum numerum, et modum in terrula, vineola, vel hospitiolo tenere. Quod amplius datum fuerit, post manumissoris mortem ecclesia revocabit." (Canon 7.)

What has been mortaged or alienated from the property of the Church by a Bishop who has left nothing of his own, must be restored; but enfranchised slaves are excepted from this rule: they shall preserve their liberty.

(Concilium Aurelianense quartum, anno 541.)

"Ut episcopus qui de facultate propria ecclesiæ nihil relinquit, de ecclesiæ facultate si quid aliter quam canones eloquunter obligaverit, vendiderit, aut distraxerit, ad ecclesiam revocetur. Sane si de servis ecclesiæ libertos fecerit numero competenti, in ingenuitate permaneant, ita ut ab officio ecclesiæ non recedant." (Canon 9.)

An English Council ordains that, at the death of each Bishop, all his English slaves shall be freed. The solemnization of the obsequies is regulated; to terminate the funeral ceremonies, each Bishop and abbot shall enfranchise three slaves, by giving them each three solidi.

(Synodus Cellichytensis, anno 816.)

"Decimo jubetur, et hoc firmiter statuimus asservandum, tam in nostris diebus, quamque etiam futuris temporibus, omnibus successoribus nostris qui post nos illis sedibus ordinentur quibus ordinati sumus: ut quandocumque aliquis ex numero episcoporum migraverit de sæculo, hoc pro anima illius præcipimus, ex substantia uniuscumque rei decimam partem dividere, ac distribuere pauperibus in eleemosynam, sive in pecoribus, et armentis, seu de ovibus et porcis, vel etiam in cellariis, *nec nom omnem hominem Anglicum liberare, qui in diebus suis sit servituti subjectus*, ut per illud sui proprii laboris fructum retributionis percipere mereatur, et indulgentiam peccatorum. Nec ullatenus ab aliqua persona huic capitulo contradicatur, sed magis, prout condecet, a successoribus augeatur, et ejus memoria semper in posterum per universas ecclesias nostræ ditioni subjectas cum Dei laudibus habeatur et honoretur. Prorsus orationes et eleemosynas quæ inter nos specialiter condictam habemus, id est, ut statim per singulas parochias in singulis quibusque ecclesiis, pulsato signo, omnis famulorum Dei cœtus ad basilicam conveniant, ibique pariter xxx psalmos pro defuncti animæ decantent. Et postea unusquisque antistes et abbas sexcentos psalmos, et centum viginti missas celebrare faciat, *et tres homines liberet et eorum cuilibet tres solidos distribuat.*" (Canon 10.)

A curious document, which shows the generous resolution made by the Council of Armagh in Ireland, to give liberty to all the English slaves.

(Concilium Ardamachiense in Hibernia celebratum, anno 1171: ex Giraldo Cambrensi, cap. xxviii. Hiberniæ expugnatæ.)

"His completis convocato apud Ardamachiam totius Hiberniæ clero, et super advenarum in insulam adventu tractato diutius et deliberato, tandem communis omnium in hoc sententia resedit: propter peccata scilicet populi sui, eoque præcipue quod Anglos olim, tam a mercatoribus, quam prædonibus atque piratis, emere passim, et in servitutem redigere consueverant, divinæ censura vindictæ hoc eis incommodum accidisse, ut et ipsi quoque ab eadem gente in servitutem vice reciproca jam redigantur. Anglorum namque populus adhuc integro eorum regno, communi gentis vitio, liberos suos venales exponere, et priusquam inopiam ullam aut inediam sustinerent, filios proprios et cognatos in Hiberniam vendere consueverant. Unde et probabiliter credi potest, sicut venditores olim, ita et emptores, tam enormi delicto juga servitutis jam meruisse. Decretum est itaque in prædicto concilio, et cum universitatis consensu publice statutum, ut Angli ubique per insulam, servitutis vinculo mancipati, in pristinam revocentur libertatem."

It is thus that religious ideas influence and soften the ferocious manners of nations. When a public calamity occurs, they immediately find its cause in the divine anger, justly excited by the traffic which the Irish carried on by buying English slaves of merchants, robbers, and pirates. It is not less curious to learn, that at that time the English were barbarous enough to sell their children and relations, like the Africans of our days. This frightful custom must have been pretty general, as we read in the passage quoted, that it was the common vice of those nations: *communi gentis vitio.* This makes us better understand the necessity of a regulation inserted above, that of the Council of London, held in 1102, which proscribes this infamous traffic in men.

It is forbidden to change the slaves of the Church for other slaves, unless the exchange procured their liberty.

(Ex concilio apud Sylvanectum, anno 864.)

"Mancipia ecclesiastica, nisi ad libertatem non convenit commutari; videlicet ut mancipia, quæ pro ecclesiastico homine dabuntur, in ecclesiæ servitute permaneant, et ecclesiasticus homo, qui commutatur, fruatur perpetua libertate. Quod enim semel Deo consecratum est, ad humanos usus transferri non decet." (V. Decret. Greg. IX., l. iii. tit. 19, cap. 3.)

A Canon containing the same regulation as the preceding; and whence, moreover, it appears, that the faithful, for the salvation of their souls, were accustomed to offer their slaves to God and the Saints.

(Ex eodem, anno 864.)

"Injustum videtur et impium, ut mancipia, quæ fideles Deo et sanctis ejus pro remedio animæ suæ consecrarunt, cujuscumque muneris mancipio, vel commutationis commercio iterum in servitutem secularium redigantur, cum canonica auctoritas servos tantummodo permittat distrahi fugitivos. Et ideo ecclesiarum rectores summopere caveant, ne eleemosyna unius, alterius peccatum fiat. Et est absurdum, ut ab ecclesiastica dignitate servus discedens, humanæ sit obnoxius servituti." (Ibid. cap. 4.)

Freedom shall be granted to slaves who wish to embrace the monastic state, yet without neglecting useful precautions to ascertain the reality of their vocation.

(Concilium Romanum sub S. Gregorio I., anno 597.)

"Multos de ecclesiastica seu sæculari familia, novimus ad omnipotentis Dei servitium festinare, ut ab humana servitute liberi in divino servitio valeant familiarius in monasteriis conversari, quos si passim dimittimus, omnibus fugiendi ecclesiastici juris dominium occasionem præbemus: si vero festinantes ad omnipotentis Dei servitium, incaute retinemus, illi invenimur negare quædam qui dedit omnia. Unde necesse est, ut quisquis ex juris ecclesiastici vel sæcularis militiæ servitute ad Dei servitium converti desiderat, probetur prius in laico habitu constitutus: et si mores ejus atque conversatio bona desiderio ejus testimonium ferunt, absque retractatione servire in monasterio omnipotenti Domino permittatur, ut ab humano servitio liber recedat, qui in divino obsequio districtiorem appetit servitutem." (S. Greg. epist. 44. lib. iv).

The abuse of ordaining slaves without the consent of their masters had spread; this abuse is checked.

(Ex epistolis Gelasii Papæ.)

"Ex antiquis regulis et novella synodali explanatione comprehensum est, personas obnoxias servituti, cingulo cœlestis militiæ non præcingi. Sed nescio utrum ignorantia an voluntate rapiamini, *ita ut ex hac causa nullus pene Episcoporum videatur extorris.* Ita enim nos frequens et plurimorum querela nos circumstrepit, ut ex hac parte nihil penitus putetur constitutum." (Distin. 54. c. 9.)

"*Frequens equidem, et assidua nos querela circumstrepit* de his pontificibus, qui nec antiquas regulas nec decreta nostra noviter directa cogitantes, obnoxias possessionibus obligatasque personas, venientes ad clericalis officii cingulum non recusant." (Ibid. c. 10.)

"Actores siquidem filiæ nostræ illustris et magnificæ feminæ, Maximæ, petitorii nobis insinuatione conquesti sunt, Sylvestrum atque Candidum, originarios suos, contra constitutiones, quæ supradictæ sunt, et contradictione præeunte a Lucerino Pontifice diaconos ordinatos." (Ibid c. 11.)

"*Generalis etiam querelæ vitanda præsumptio est, qua propemodum causantur universi;*

passim servos et originarios, dominorum jura, possessionumque fugientes, sub religiosæ conversationis obtentu, vel ad monasteria sese conferre, vel ad ecclesiasticum famulatum, conniventibus quippe præsulibus, indifferenter admitti. Quæ modis omnibus est amovenda pernicies, ne per Christiani nominis institutum aut aliena pervadi, aut publica videatur disciplina subverti." (Ibid. c. 12.)

The parish priests are allowed to choose some clerics from the slaves of the Church.

(Concilium Emeritense, anno 666.)

"Quidquid unanimiter digne disponitur in sancta Dei ecclesia, necessarium est ut a parochitanis presbyteris custoditum maneat. Sunt enim nonnulli, qui ecclesiarum suarum res ad plenitudinem habent, et sollicitudo illis nulla est habendi clericos, cum quibus omnipotenti Deo laudum debita persolvant officia. Proinde instituit hæc sancta synodus, ut omnes parochitani presbyteri, juxta ut in rebus sibi a Deo creditis sentiunt habere virtutem, de ecclesiæ suæ familia clericos sibi faciant; quos per bonam voluntatem ita nutriant, ut et officium sanctum digne paragant, et ad servitium suum aptos eos habeant. Hi etiam victum et vestitum dispensatione presbyteri merebuntur, et domino et presbytero suo, atque utilitati ecclesiæ fideles esse debent. Quod si inutiles apparuerint ut culpa patuerit, correptione disciplinæ feriantur; si quis presbyterorum hanc sententiam minime custodierit, et non adimpleverit, ab episcopo suo corrigatur: ut plenissime custodiat, quod digne jubetur." (Canon 18.)

It is prescribed to the Bishops to confer liberty on the slaves of the Church before they admit them into the clerical body.

(Concilium Toletanum nonum, anno 655.)

"Qui ex familiis ecclesiæ servituri devocantur in clerum ab episcopis suis, necesse est, ut libertatis percipiant donum: et si honestæ vitæ claruerint meritis, tunc demum majoribus fungantur officiis. (Canon 11.)

It is allowed to ordain the slaves of the Church, liberty having been previously conferred on them.

(Concilium quartem Toletanum, anno 633.)

"De familiis ecclesiæ constituere presbyteros ut diaconos per parochias liceat; quos tamen vitæ rectitudo et probitas morum commendat: ea tamen ratione, *ut antea manumissi libertatem status sui percipiant*, et denuo ad ecclesiasticos honores succedant; irreligiosum est enim obligatos existere servituti, qui sacri ordinis suscipiunt dignitatem."

§ VII.

We have shown in the text by what means, with what wisdom and perseverance Christianity abolished slavery in the ancient world; Christian and Catholic Europe was free at the time when Protestantism appeared. Let us now see what Catholicity has done in modern times, with respect to slaves in other parts of the world. We can present to our readers in one document, which is the evidence of the ideas and feelings of the Sovereign Pontiff Gregory XVI., an interesting history of the solicitude of the Roman See in favor of the slaves of the whole universe. I mean the apostolical letters published at Rome, November 3, 1839, against the slave-trade; and I recommend the perusal of them. It will be there seen, in the most authentic and decisive manner, that the Catholic Church, on this important subject of slavery, has always showed, and shows still, the most lively spirit of charity, without in the least offending against justice, or for a moment departing from the path of prudence.

"*Gregorius P. P.* XVI. *ad futuram rei memoriam.*

"Raised to the supreme degree of the apostolical dignity, and filling, although without any merit on our part, the place of Jesus Christ, the Son of God, who, by the excess of His charity, has deigned to become man, and die for the redemption of the world; we consider that it belongs to our pastoral solicitude to exert all our efforts to prevent Christians from engaging in the trade in blacks or any other men, whoever they may be.

"As soon as the light of the Gospel began to spread, the unfortunate men who fell into the hard fate of slavery during the numerous wars of that period, felt their condition improved; for the apostles, inspired by the Spirit of God, on the one hand, taught slaves to obey their earthly masters, as Jesus Christ Himself, and to be resigned from the bottom of their heart to the will of God; but, on the other, they commanded masters to behave well to their slaves, to grant them what was just and equitable, and not to treat them with anger, knowing that the Lord of both is in heaven, and that with Him there is no distinction of persons.

"The law of the Gospel having very soon universally and fundamentally ordained sincere charity towards all, and the Lord Jesus having declared that He would regard as done or refused to Himself all the acts of beneficence and mercy done or refused to the poor and little ones—it naturally followed that Christians not only regarded their slaves as brethren, above all when they were become Christians, but that they were more inclined to give liberty to those who rendered themselves worthy of it. This usually took place particularly on the solemn feasts of Easter, as St. Gregory of Nyssa relates. There were even found some who, inflamed with more ardent charity, *embraced slavery for the redemption of their brethren;* and an apostolic man, our predecessor, Pope Gregory I., of sacred memory, attests that he had known a great many who performed this work of mercy. Wherefore the darkness of Pagan superstition being entirely dissipated in the progress of time, and the manners of the most barbarous nations being softened,—thanks to the benefit of faith working by charity,—things advanced so far, that for many centuries there have been no slaves among the greater part of Christian nations. Yet (we say it with profound sorrow) men have been since found, even among Christians, who, shamefully blinded by the desire of sordid gain, have not hesitated to reduce into slavery, in distant countries, Indians, Negroes, and other unfortunate races; or to assist in this scandalous crime, by instituting and organizing a traffic in these unfortunate beings, who had been loaded with chains by others. A great number of the Roman Pontiffs, our predecessors of glorious memory, have not forgotten to stigmatize, throughout the extent of their jurisdiction, the conduct of these men as injurious to their salvation, and disgraceful to the Christian name; for they clearly saw that it was one of the causes which tended most powerfully to make infidel nations continue in their hatred to the true religion.

"This was the object of the apostolical letters of Paul III., of the 29th of May, 1537, addressed to the Cardinal Archbishop of Toledo, under the ring of the fisherman, and other letters, much more copious, of Urban VIII., of the 22d April, 1639, addressed to the collector of the rights of the Apostolic Chamber in Portugal,—letters, in which the most severe censures are cast upon those who venture to reduce the inhabitants of the East or West Indies into slavery, buy, sell, give, or exchange them, separate them from their wives and children, strip them of their property, take or send them into strange places, or deprive them of their liberty in any way; to retain them in slavery; or aid, counsel, succor, or favor those who do these things under any color or pretence whatever; or preach or teach that this is lawful, and, in fine, co-operate therewith in any way whatever. Benedict XIV. has since confirmed and renewed these pontifical ordinances before mentioned by new apostolical letters to the Bishops of Brazil and some other countries, dated the 20th December, 1741, by means of which he calls forth the solicitude of the Bishops for the same purpose. A long time before, another of our more ancient predecessors, Pius II., whose pontificate saw the empire of the Portuguese extended in Guinea and in the country of the blacks, addressed letters, dated the 7th of October, 1482, to the Bishop of Ruvo, who was ready to depart for those countries: in these letters he did not confine himself to giving to this prelate the means requisite for exercising the sacred ministry in those countries with the greatest fruit, but he took occasion very severely to blame the conduct of those who reduced the neophytes into slavery. In fine, in our days, Pius VII., animated by the same spirit of charity and religion as his predecessors, zealously interposed his good offices with men of authority for the entire abolition of the slave-trade among Christians.

"These ordinances, and this solicitude of our predecessors, have availed not a little, with the aid of God, in defending the Indians, and other nations who have just been mentioned, against the barbarity of conquest, and the cupidity of Christian merchants; but the Holy See is far from being able to boast of the complete success of its efforts and zeal, for, if the slave-trade has been partially abolished, it is still carried on by a great many Christians. Wherefore, desiring to remove such a disgrace from all Christian countries, after having maturely considered the matter with many of our venerable brethren, the Cardinals of the Holy Roman Church, assembled in Council, following the example of our predecessors, by virtue of the apostolic office, we warn and admonish in the Lord all Christians, of whatever condition they may be, and enjoin upon them that, for the future, no one shall venture unjustly to oppress the Indians, Negroes, or other men, whoever they may be; to strip them of their property or reduce them into servitude: or give aid or support to those who commit such excesses, or carry on that infamous traffic, by which the blacks, as if they were not men, but mere impure animals, reduced like them into servitude, without any distinction, contrary to the laws of justice and humanity, are bought, sold, and devoted to endure the hardest labors; and on account of which dissensions are excited and almost continual wars are fomented among nations by the allurements of gain offered to those who first carry away the Negroes.

"Wherefore, by virtue of the apostolical authority, we condemn all these things aforesaid, as absolutely unworthy of the Christian name; and, by the same authority, we absolutely prohibit and interdict all ecclesiastics and laymen from venturing to maintain that this traffic in blacks is permitted, under any pretext or color whatsoever; or to preach or teach in public or in private, in any way whatever, anything, contrary to these apostolic letters. And in order that these letters may come to the knowledge of all, and that no one may pretend ignorance, we ordain and decree that they be published and posted up, according to custom, by one of our officers, on the doors of the basilica of the Prince of the Apostles, of the Apostolic Chancery, of the Palace of Justice, of Monte Citorio, and at the Campo di Fiori. Given at Rome, at St. Mary Major's, under the seal of the fisherman, the 3d of November, 1839, the ninth year of our Pontificate.

LOUIS, CARDINAL LAMBRUSCHINI."

I again particularly invite attention to the document which I have just inserted—to these letters which magnificently crown the united efforts of the Church for the abolition of slavery. As the abolition of the slave-trade—the object of a treaty recently made between the great powers—is at this moment one of the affairs which occupy the chief attention of Europe, it is proper to pause a few moments, to reflect on the contents of the apostolic letters of the Sovereign Pontiff Gregory XVI. Let us observe, in the first place, that in the year 1482, Pope Pius II. addressed apostolical letters to the Bishop of Ruvo, about to depart for the newly discovered countries—letters, in which he did not exclusively confine himself to giving the prelate the powers necessary to exercise his holy ministry with the greatest fruit in those countries, but in which he takes occasion to censure very severely the conduct of Christians who reduced the neophytes into slavery. Exactly at the end of the fifteenth century, at the time when it may be said that the Church gathering the last fruit of her long labors, at length saw Europe emerge from the chaos in which the irruption of the barbarians had plunged her; at the time when the social and political institutions were developed with daily increasing ardor, and began to form a regular and coherent body; at this moment the Church resumes her secular contest with another barbarism which reappeared in distant countries; she opposes the abuse of the superiority of strength and intelligence, which the conquerors possessed over the conquered nations.

This fact alone proves that, for the true liberty and well-being of nations, for the just pre-eminence of right over might, and for the triumph of justice over force, the intelligence and refinement of nations are not enough—religion also is required. In ancient times, we see nations cultivated to the highest point commit unheard of atrocities; and in modern times, Europeans, so proud of their knowledge and advancement, introduce slavery among the unfortunate nations who have fallen under their dominion. Now, who was the first to raise a voice against such injustice—against such horrible barbarity? It was not policy, which perhaps rejoiced to see its conquests consolidated by slavery; it was not commerce which found in this infamous traffic an easy means of making shameful but abundant profits; it was not philosophy, which, fully explaining the doctrines of Plato and Aristotle, would perhaps have seen without concern the resuscitation of the degrading theory of *races born for slavery;* but it was the Catholic religion, expressing herself by the mouth of the Vicar of Jesus Christ.

It is certainly a consolatory spectacle for Catholics to see a Roman Pontiff, four centuries ago, condemn what Europe, with all her civilization and refinement, condemns only at the present day. Still, Europe only does so with difficulty; and all those who take part in this tardy condemnation are not exempt from the suspicion of being actuated by motives of interest. No doubt the Roman Pontiff did not effect all the good he intended; but doctrines do not remain sterile when they emanate from a high quarter, whence, diffusing themselves to great distances, they descend on persons who receive them with veneration, if it were only on account of him who teaches them. The conquering nations were then Christians, and sincere ones; it is therefore indubitable, that the admonitions of the Pope, transmitted by the mouths of Bishops and other priests, must have had very salutary effects. If, in cases like this, where we see a measure taken against an evil, the evil nevertheless resists and continues, we imagine, by a grievous mistake, that the measure has been vain, and that its author has produced no effect. It is one thing to extirpate, and another to diminish an evil; and it cannot be doubted that, if the Bulls of the Popes had not all the effect intended, they must nevertheless have served to diminish the evil, by improving the lot of nations fallen under the yoke. The evil prevented and avoided is not seen; the preservative has hindered its existence; but the existing evil is palpable—it affects us, it excites our regret, and we often forget the gratitude due to the hand which has preserved us from greater evils. How often is it thus with respect to religion! She cures many things, but she prevents still more. If she takes possession of the heart of man, it is in order to destroy there even the very roots of a thousand evils.

Let us imagine the Europeans of the fifteenth century invading the East and West Indies, without any check, guided only by the inspirations of cupidity, and by the caprices of arbitrary power, full of the pride of conquerors, and of the contempt with which the Indians must have inspired them, on account of the inferiority of their knowledge, and of their backwardness in civilization and refinement: what must have happened? If, in spite of the incessant cries of religion, in spite of the influence which she had on laws and manners, the conquered nations have had so much to suffer, would not the evil have been carried to an intolerable extent, without those powerful causes which incessantly combated, prevented or diminished it? The conquered would have been reduced into slavery *en masse;* they would have been condemned *en masse* to perpetual degradation; they would have been deprived even of the hope of one day entering on the career of civilization.

If the conduct of Europeans at that time with respect to men of other races—if the conduct of some nations of our own days is to be deplored, it cannot be said at least that the Catholic religion has not opposed such excesses with all her strength; it cannot be said that the Head of the Church has ever allowed these evils to pass without raising his voice to recall to mind the rights of men, to stigmatize injustice, to excite abhorrence of cruelty, and energetically to plead the cause of humanity, without distinction of races, climates, or colors.

Whence does Europe derive this lofty idea and this generous feeling, which urge her to declare herself so strongly against the traffic in men, and to demand the complete abolition of slavery in the colonies? When posterity shall call to mind these glorious facts; when it shall adopt them as marking a new era in the annals of civilization; when, studying and analyzing the causes which have conducted European legislation and manners to so high a pitch, and, passing over temporary and unimportant motives, insignificant circumstances, and secondary agents, it shall seek for the vital principle which impelled European civilization towards so glorious an end, it will find that this principle was Christianity; and if, desiring to fathom the question more and more, it should inquire whether this was Christianity, under a vague and general form—Christianity without authority—Christianity without Catholicity—the answer of history will be this: Catholicity, exclusively prevailing in Europe, abolished slavery among the European races; she introduced the principle of the abolition of slavery into European civilization, by showing practically, and in opposition to the opinion of antiquity, that slavery was not necessary for society; and she made it understood, that the sacred work of enfranchisement was the foundation of all great and life-giving civilization. She has therefore inoculated European civilization with the principle of the abolition of slavery; it is owing to her that, wherever this civilization has come into contact with slavery, it has been profoundly disturbed—an evident proof that there were at the bottom two opposite elements, two contending principles, which were compelled to struggle incessantly, until the more powerful, noble, and fruitful prevailing, and reducing the other under the yoke, in the end annihilated it. I will say more: by searching whether facts really confirm this influence of Catholicity, not only in all that concerns the civilization of Europe, but also in the countries which Europeans have conquered two centuries ago, in the East and West, we shall meet with Catholic Bishops and priests working without intermission in improving the lot of colonial slaves; we shall call to mind what is due to the Catholic missions; we shall read and understand the apostolical letters of Pius II., issued in 1482, and mentioned above; those of Paul III., in 1537; those of Urban VIII., in 1639; those of Benedict XIV., in 1741; and those of Gregory XVI., in 1839.

In these letters there is taught and defined all that has been or can be said on this point in favor of humanity. We shall there find blamed, condemned, and punished, all that European civilization has at length resolved to condemn and punish; and when calling to mind also that it was Pius VII., who, at the beginning of this century, *zealously interposed his good offices with men in power for the complete abolition of slavery among Christians*, we shall not be able to avoid acknowledging and confessing that Catholicity has had the principal share in this great work. It is she indeed who has laid down the principle on which the work rests, who has established the precedents which guide it, who has constantly proclaimed the principles which have suggested it and has constantly condemned those who have opposed it; it is she, in fine, who at all times has declared open war against cruelty and cupidity, —the support and perpetual motives for injustice and inhumanity. Let us hear the testimony of a celebrated Protestant author, Robertson, the historian of America: "From the time that ecclesiastics were sent as instructors into America, they perceived that the rigor with which their countrymen treated the natives rendered their ministry altogether fruitless. The missionaries, in conformity with the mild spirit of that religion which they were employed to publish, soon remonstrated against the maxims of the planters with respect to the Americans, and condemned the *repartimientos*, or distributions, by which they were given up as slaves to their conquerors, as no less contrary to natural justice and the precepts of Christianity, than to sound policy. The Dominicans, to whom the instruction of the Americans was originally committed, were the most vehement in attacking the *repartimientos*. In the year 1511, Motesino, one of their most eminent preachers, inveighed against this practice in the great church at St. Domingo, with all the impetuosity of his natural eloquence. Don Diego Columbus, the principal officers of the colony, and all the laymen who had been his hearers, complained of the monk to his superiors; but they, instead of condemning, applauded his doctrine, as equally pious and seasonable. The Franciscans, influenced by the spirit of opposition and rivalship which subsists between the two orders, discovered some inclination to take part with the laity, and to espouse the defence of the *repartimientos*. But as they could not with decency give their approbation to a system of oppression so repugnant to the spirit of religion, they endeavored to palliate what they could not justify, and alleged in excuse for the conduct of their countrymen, that it was impossible to carry on any improvement in the colony, unless the Spaniards possessed such dominion over the natives, that they could compel them to labor. The Dominicans, regardless of such political and interested considerations, would not relax in any degree the rigor of their sentiments, and even refused to absolve, or admit to the sacrament, such of their countrymen as continued to hold the natives in servitude. Both parties applied to the king for his decision in a matter of such importance. Ferdinand empowered a committee of his Privy Council, assisted by some of the most eminent civilians and divines in Spain, to hear the deputies sent from Hispaniola in support of their respective opinions. After a long discussion, the speculative point in controversy was determined in favor of the Dominicans; the Indians were declared to be a free people, entitled to all the natural rights of man; but notwithstanding this decision, the *repartimientos* were continued upon their ancient footing. As this determination admitted the principle upon which the Dominicans founded their opinion, they renewed their efforts to obtain relief for the Indians with additional boldness and zeal. At length, in order to quiet the colony, which was alarmed by their remonstrances and censures, Ferdinand issued a decree of his Privy Council (1513), declaring that after mature consideration of the apostolic Bull, and other titles by which the Crown of Castile claimed a right to its possessions, in the new world, the servitude of the Indians was warranted both by the laws of God and man; that unless they were subjected to the dominion of the Spaniards, and compelled to reside under their inspection, it would be impossible to reclaim them from idolatry, or to instruct them in the Christian faith; that no further scruple ought to be entertained concerning the lawfulness of the *repartimientos*, as the King and Council were willing to take the charge of that upon their own consciences; and that therefore the Dominicans, and monks of other religious orders, should abstain for the future from those invectives which, from an excess of charitable but ill-informed zeal, they had uttered against the practice. That his intention of adhering to this decree might be fully understood, Ferdinand conferred new grants of Indians upon several of his courtiers. But in order that he might not seem altogether inattentive to the rights of humanity, he published an edict, in which he endeavored to provide for the mild treatment of the Indians under the yoke to which he subjected them; he regulated the nature of the work which they should be required to perform; he prescribed the mode in which they should be clothed and fed, and gave directions with respect to their instruction in the principles of Christianity. But the Dominicans, who, from their experience of what had passed, judged concerning the future, soon perceived the inefficacy of those provisions, and foretold that, as long as it was the interest of individuals to treat the Indians with rigor, no public regulations would render their servitude mild or tolerable. They considered it as vain to waste their own time and strength in attempting to communicate the sublime truths to men whose spirits were broken, and their faculties impaired by oppression. Some of them, in despair, requested the permission of their superiors to remove to the continent, and pursue the object of their mission among such of the natives as were not hitherto corrupted by the example of the Spaniards, or alienated by their cruelty from the Christian faith. Such as remained in Hispaniola continued to remonstrate, with decent firmness, against the servitude of the Indians.

"The violent operations of Albuquerque, the new distributor of the Indians, revived the zeal of the Dominicans against the *repartimientos*, and called forth an advocate for that oppressed people who possessed all the courage, the talents, and the activity requisite in supporting such a desperate cause. This was Bartholomew de las Casas, a native of Seville, and one of the clergymen sent out with Columbus in his second voyage to Hispaniola, in order to settle in that Island. He early adopted the opinion prevalent among ecclesiastics with respect to the unlawfulness of reducing the natives to servitude; and that he might demonstrate the sincerity of his conviction, he relinquished all the Indians who had fallen to his share in the division of the inhabitants among their conquerors, declaring that he should ever bewail his own misfortune and guilt, in having exercised for a moment this impious dominion over his fellow-creatures. From that time he became the avowed patron of the Indians; and by his bold interpositions in their behalf, as well as by the respect due to his abilities and character, he had often the merit of setting some bounds to the excesses of his countrymen." (*History of America*, book 3.)

It would be too long to relate here the energetic efforts of De las Casas in favor of the colonies of the new world; all know them—all must know that, filled with zeal for the liberty of the Indians, he conceived and undertook an attempt at civilization analogous to that which was realized later, to the immortal honor of the Catholic clergy, in Paraguay. If the efforts of De las Casas had not all the success that might naturally have been expected, we find the cause of this in the thousand passions with which history makes us acquainted, and perhaps also in the impetuosity of this man, whose sublime zeal was not always accompanied by the consummate prudence which the Church displays.

However this may be, Catholicity has completely accomplished her mission of peace and love; without injustice or catastrophe, she has broken the chains under which a large portion of the human race groaned; and if it had been given her to prevail for some time in Asia and Africa, she would have achieved their destruction in the four quarters of the globe, by banishing the degradations and the abominations introduced and established in those countries by Mahometanism and idolatry. It is melancholy, no doubt, that Christianity has not yet exercised over these latter countries all the influence which would have been necessary to ameliorate the social and political condition of those nations, by changing their ideas and manners. But if we seek for the causes of this lamentable delay, we certainly shall not find them in the conduct of Catholicity. This is not the place to point out these causes; nevertheless, while reserving the analysis and complete examination of this matter for another part of the work, I will make the remark *en passant*, that Protestantism may justly criminate itself for the obstacles which, during three centuries, it has opposed to the universality and efficacy of the Christian influence on infidel nations. These few words will suffice here; we shall return to this important subject later.

Note 16, p. 131.

We can scarcely believe how far the ideas of the ancients went astray with regard to the respect which is due to man. Can it be believed that they went so far, as to regard the lives of all who could not be useful to society as of no value? and yet nothing is more certain. We might lament that this or that city had adopted a barbarous law; that a ferocious custom was introduced among a people by the effect of particular circumstances; yet as long as philosophy protested against such attempts, human reason would have been unstained, and could not have been accused without injustice of taking part in infamous attempts at abortion or infanticide. But when we find crime defended and taught by the most important philosophers of antiquity; when we see it triumph in the minds of the most illustrious men, who, with fearful calmness and serenity, prescribe the atrocities which we have named, we are confounded, and our blood runs cold; we would fain shut our eyes, not to see so much infamy thrown upon philosophy and human reason. Let us hear Plato in his *Republic*, in that book in which he undertook to collect all the theories in his opinion the most distinguished and the best adapted to lead human society towards its *beau ideal*. This is his scandalous language: "Oportet profecto secundum ea quæ supra concessimus, optimos viros mulieribus optimis ut plurimum congredi: deterrimos autem contra, deterrimis. Et illorem quidem prolem nutrire, horum minime, si armentum excellentissimum sit futurum. Et hæc omnia dum agantur, ab omnibus præterquam a principibus ignorari, si modo armentum custodum debeat seditione carere." "Prope admodum;" "Very good," replies another speaker. (*Plat. Rep.* l. v.)

Behold, then, the human race reduced to the condition of mere brutes; in truth, the philosopher had reason to use the word flock (*armentum*)! There is this difference, however, that magistrates imbued with such feelings must have been more harsh towards their subjects than a shepherd towards his flock. If the shepherd finds among the lambs which have just been born a weak and lame one, he does not kill it or allow it to die of hunger; he carries it to the sheep who ought to nourish it, he caresses it to stop its cries.

But perhaps the expressions which we have just quoted escaped the philosopher in a moment of inadvertence; perhaps the idea which they reveal was only one of those sinister inspirations which glide into the mind of a man, and pass away without leaving any more impression than is made by a reptile moving through the grass. We wish it were so, for the fame of Plato; but unhappily he returns to it so often, and insists on the point with so systematic a coldness, that no means of justifying him are left. "With respect," he says lower down, "to the children of citizens of inferior rank, and even those of other citizens, if they are born deformed, the magistrates shall hide them, as is proper, in some secure place, which it shall be forbidden to reveal." "Yes," replies one of the interlocutors; "if we desire to preserve the race of warriors in its purity."

Plato also lays down various rules with respect to the relations of the two sexes; he speaks of the case in which the man and woman shall have reached an advanced age: "Quando igitur jam mulieres et viri ætatem generationi aptam egressi fuerint, licere viris dicemus, cuicumque voluerint, præterquam filiæ atque matri et filiarum natis matrisve majoribus: licere et mulieribus cuilibet, præterquam filio atque patri, ac superioribus et inferioribus eorumdem. Cum vero hæc omnia mandaverimus, interdicemus fœtum talem (si contigeret) edi et in lucem produci. Si quid autem matrem parere coegerit, ita exponere præcipiemus, quasi ei nulla nutritio sit."

Plato seems to have been very well pleased with his doctrine; for, in the very book in which he writes what we have just seen, he lays down the famous maxim, that the evils of states will never be remedied, that societies will never be well governed, until philosophers shall become kings, or kings become philosophers. God preserve us from seeing on the throne a philosophy such as his! Moreover, his wish for the reign of philosophy has been realized in modern times. What do I say? It has had more than empire; it has been deified, and divine honors have been paid to it in public temples. I do not believe, however, that the happy days of the worship of reason are now much regretted.

The horrible doctrine which we have just seen in Plato was transmitted with fidelity to future schools. Aristotle, who on so many points took the liberty of departing from the doctrines of his master, did not think of correcting those which regard abortion and infanticide. In his *Politics* he teaches the same crimes with the same calmness as Plato: "In order," he says, "to avoid nourishing weak or lame children, the law should direct them to be exposed or made away with." "Propter multitudinem autem liberorum, ne plures sint quam expediat, si gentium instituta et leges vetent procreata exponi, definitum esse oportet procreandorum liberorum numerum. Quod si quibus inter se copulatis et congressis, plures liberi, quam definitum sit, nascantur, priusquam sensus et vita inseratur, abortus est fœtui inferendus." (*Polit.* l. vii. c. 16.)

It will be seen how much reason I had to say that man, *as man*, was esteemed as nothing among the ancients; that society entirely absorbed him; that it claimed unjust rights over him, and regarded him as an instrument to be used when of service, and which it had a right to destroy.

We observe in the writings of the ancient philosophers, that they make of society a kind of *whole*, consisting of individuals, as the mass of iron consists of the atoms that compose it; they make of it a sort of unity, to which all must be sacrificed; they have no consideration for the sphere of individual liberty; they do not appear to dream that the object of society is the good, the happiness of individuals and families. According to them, this unity is the principal good, with which nothing else can be compared; the greatest evil that can happen is, that this unity should be broken—an evil which must be avoided by all imaginable means. "Is not the worst evil of a state," says Plato, "that which divides it, and *makes many out of one?* and is not the greatest excellence of a state, that which binds all its parts together, and makes it *one?*" Relying on this principle, and pursuing the development of his theory, he takes individuals and families, and kneads them, as it were, in order to form them into ONE compact whole. Thus, besides education and life in common, he wishes also to have women and children in common; he considers it injurious that there should be personal enjoyments or sufferings; he desires that all should be common and social; he allows individuals to live, think, feel, and act only as parts of a great whole. If you read his *Republic* with attention, and particularly the fifth book, you will see that the prevailing idea of this philosopher is what we have just explained. Let us hear Aristotle on the same point: "As the object of society," he says, "is *one*, it is clear that the education of all its members ought necessarily to be one and identical. Education ought to be public, and not private; as things now are, each one takes care of his children as he thinks proper, and teaches them as he pleases. Each citizen is a particle of society, and the care to be given to a particle ought naturally to extend to what the whole requires." (*Polit.* l. viii. c. 1.) In order to explain to us what he means by this common education, he concludes by quoting with honor the education which was given at Sparta, which every one knows consisted in stifling all feelings except a ferocious patriotism, the traits of which still make us shudder.

With our ideas and customs, we do not know how to confine ourselves to considering society in this way. Individuals among us are attached to the social body, forming a part of it, but without losing their own sphere—that of the family; and they preserve around them a vast career, where they are allowed to exert themselves, without coming into collision with the colossus of society. Nevertheless, patriotism exists; but it is no longer a blind instinctive passion, urging man on to the sacrifice, like a victim, with bandaged eyes, but it is no reasonable, noble, and exalted feeling, which forms heroes like those of Lepanto and Baylen; which converts peaceful citizens, like those of Gyronna and Saragossa, into lions; which, as by an electric spark, makes a whole people rise on a sudden without arms, and brave death from the artillery of a numerous and disciplined army: such was Madrid, following the sublime *Mourons* of Daoiz and of Velarda.

I have already hinted, in the text, that society among the ancients claimed the right of interfering in all that regards individuals. I will add, that the thing went to a ridiculous extent. Who would imagine that the law ought to interfere in the food of a woman who was *enceinte*, or in the exercise which she should take every day? This is what Aristotle gravely says: "It is necessary that women who are *enceinte* should take particular care of their bodies; that they should avoid indulgence in luxury, and using food which is too light and weak. The legislator easily attains his end by prescribing and ordering them a daily walk, in order to go to honor and venerate the gods, to whom it has been confided by fate to watch over the formation of beings. Atque hoc facile assequitur scriptor legum, si eis iter aliquod quotidianum ad cultum venerationemque deorum eorum, quibus sorte obtigit, ut præsint gignendis animantibus, injunxerit ac mandaverit." (*Polit.* l. vii. c. 16.)

The action of laws extended to every thing; it seems that, in certain cases, even the tears of children could not escape this severity. "Those," says Aristotle, "who, by means of laws, forbid children to cry and weep, are wrong: cries and tears serve as exercise for children, and assist them in growing; they are an effort of nature, which relieves and invigorates those who are in pain." (*Polit.* l. vii. c. 17.)

These doctrines of the ancients—this manner of considering the relations of individuals with society—very well explain how castes and slavery could be regarded as natural among them. Who can be astonished at seeing whole races deprived of liberty, or regarded as incapable of partaking of the rights of other superior classes, when we see generations of innocent beings condemned to death, and these conscientious philosophers not having the slightest scruple with respect to the legitimacy of so inhuman an act? It was not that these philosophers had not happiness in view as the object of society; but they had monstrous ideas with respect to the means of obtaining that happiness.

Note 17, p. 146.

The reader will easily dispense with my entering into details on the abject and shameful condition of women among the ancients, and in which they still are among the moderns where Christianity does not prevail; moreover, my pen would be checked every moment by strict laws of modesty, if I were to attempt to represent the characteristic features of this wretched picture. The *inversion* of ideas was such, that we hear men the most renowned for their gravity and moderation rave in the most incredible manner on this point. We will lay aside hundreds of examples which it would be easy to adduce; but who is ignorant of the scandalous advice of the *sage* Solon, with respect to the lending of women for the purpose of improving the race? Who has not blushed to read what the *divine* Plato, in his *Republic*, says of the propriety and manner of making women share in the public games? Let us throw a veil over recollections so dishonourable to human wisdom. When the chief legislators and sages so far forgot the first elements of morality, and the most ordinary inspirations of nature, what must have been the case with the vulgar? How fearfully true those words of the sacred text which represent to us the nations deprived of the light of Christianity as sitting *in darkness and in the shadow of death!*

There is nothing more fatal to woman, nothing more apt to degrade her, than that which is injurious to modesty; and yet we see that the unlimited power granted to man over woman contributed to this degradation, and reduced her, among certain nations, to be nothing but a slave. Losing sight of the manners of other nations, let us consider those of the Romans for a moment. Among them the formula, *ubi tu Cayus ego Caya*, seemed to indicate a subjection so slight, that it might almost be called an equality; but in order to appreciate this equality, it is enough to recollect that, at Rome, a husband could put his wife to death by his own authority, and that not only in the case of adultery, but for offences infinitely less serious. In the time of Romulus, Egnacius Menecius was acquitted of a similar crime, although his wife had done nothing more than drink wine from a cask. These traits describe a nation, whatever importance you may besides think proper to attach to the solicitude of the Romans to prevent their matrons from becoming addicted to wine. When Cato directed an embrace, as a proof of affection, among relations, for the purpose, as Pliny relates, of ascertaining whether the women smelt of wine, *an temetum olerent*, it is true he showed his strictness; but it was an unworthy outrage offered to the honor of the women themselves whose virtue it pretended to preserve. There are some remedies worse than the disease.

Note 18, p. 157.

The antichristian philosophy must have had considerable influence on the desire to find among the barbarians the origin of the elevation of the female character in Europe, and of some other principles of our civilization. Indeed as soon as you discover the source of these admirable qualities in the forests of Germany, Christianity is stripped of a portion of its honors; and what was its own and peculiar glory is divided among many. I will not deny that the Germans of Tacitus are sufficiently poetical; but it is difficult to believe that the real Germans were so to any extent. Some passages inserted in the text add great force to our conjecture; but what appears to me eminently calculated to dissipate all these illusions is, the history of the invasion by the barbarians, above all that which has been written by eyewitnesses. The picture, far from continuing poetical, then becomes disgusting in the extreme. This interminable succession of nations passes before the eyes of the reader, like an alarming vision in an evil dream; and certainly the first idea which occurs to us at the sight of this picture is, not to seek for any of the qualities of modern civilization in these invading hordes; but the great difficulty is, to know how this chaos has been reduced to order, and how it has been possible to produce from such barbarism the noblest and most brilliant civilization that has ever been seen on earth. Tacitus appears to be an enthusiast; but Sidonius, who wrote at no great distance from the barbarians, who saw them, and suffered from meeting them, does not partake of this enthusiasm. "I find myself," he said, "among long-haired nations, compelled to hear the German language, and to applaud, at whatever cost, the song of the drunken Burgundian, with hair plastered with rancid grease. *Happy your eyes who do not see them; happy your ears who do not hear them!*" If space permitted, it would be easy for me to accumulate a thousand passages which would evidently show what the barbarians were, and what could be expected from them in all respects. It is as clear as the light of day, that it was the design of Providence to employ these nations to destroy the Roman empire, and change the face of the world. The invaders seem to have had a feeling of their terrible mission. They march, they advance, they know not whither they go; but they know well that they go to destroy. Attila called himself the scourge of God. The same barbarian himself defined his formidable duty in these words: "*The star falls, the sea is moved; I am the hammer of the earth.* Where my horse passes, the grass never grows." Alaric, marching towards the capital of the world, said: "*I cannot stop; there is some one urges me, who excites me to sack Rome.*" Genseric prepares a naval expedition; his troops are on board, he himself embarks: no one knows the point towards which he will direct his sails. The pilot approaches the barbarian, and asks him; "*My lord, against what nations will you wage war?*" "*Against those who have provoked the anger of God,*" replies Genseric.

If Christianity, in the midst of this catastrophe, had not existed in Europe, civilization would have been lost and annihilated, perhaps forever. But a religion of light and love was sure to triumph over ignorance and violence. Even during the times of the calamities of the invasion, that religion prevented many disasters, owing to the ascendency which it began to exercise over the barbarians; the most critical moment being past, the conquerors having become in some degree settled, she immediately employed a system so vast, so efficacious, so decisive, that the conquerors found themselves conquered, not by arms, but by charity. It was not in the power of the Church to prevent the invasion; God had decreed it, and His decree must be accomplished. Thus the pious monk who went to meet Alaric approaching Rome, could not stop him on his march, because the barbarian answered him, that he could not stop,—that there was some one who urged him on, and that he advanced against his own will. But the Church awaited the barbarians after the conquest, knowing that Providence would not abandon His own work, that the hope of the future lot of nations was left in the hands of the spouse of Jesus Christ; on this account does Alaric advance on Rome, sack, and destroy it; but on a sudden, finding himself in presence of religion, he stops, becomes mollified, and appoints the Churches of St. Peter and St. Paul as places of refuge. A remarkable fact, and an admirable symbol of the Christian religion preserving the universe from total ruin.

NOTE 19, p. 165.

The great benefit conferred on modern society by the formation of a pure and correct public conscience, would acquire extraordinary value in our eyes, if we compared our moral ideas with those of all other nations, ancient and modern; the result of such an examination would be, to show in how lamentable a manner good principles become corrupted, when they are confided to the reason of man. I will content myself, however, with a few words on the ancients, in order to show how correct I was in saying that our manners, however corrupt they may be, would have appeared a model of morality and dignity to the heathens.

The temples consecrated to Venus in Babylon and Corinth are connected with abominations such as to be even incomprehensible. Deified passion required sacrifices worthy of it; a divinity without modesty required the sacrifice of modesty; and the sacred name of Temple was applied to asylums of the most unbridled licentiousness. There was not a veil even for the greatest crimes. It is known how the daughters of Chypre gained a dowry for their marriage; all have heard of the mysteries of Adonis, Priapus, and other impure divinities. There are vices which, as it were, want a name among the moderns; or if they have one, it is accompanied by the recollection of a terrible chastisement inflicted on some criminal cities. In reading the histories of antiquity descriptive of the manners of their times, the book falls from our hands. On this subject we must be content with these few hints, calculated to awaken in the minds of our readers the recollection of what has a thousand times excited their indignation in reading the history and studying the literature of pagan antiquity. The author is compelled to be satisfied with a recollection: he abstains from a description.

NOTE 20, p. 171.

It is now so common to exalt beyond measure the power of ideas, that some persons will perhaps consider exaggerated what I have said with respect to their want of power, not only to influence society, but even to preserve themselves, while, remaining in the mere sphere of ideas, they do not become realized in institutions, which are their organ, and at the same time their rampart and defence.

I am very far, as I have clearly stated in the text, from denying or calling in question what is called the power of ideas: I only mean to show that, alone and by themselves, ideas have little power; and that science, properly so called, as far as the organization of society is concerned, is a much less important thing than is generally supposed. This doctrine has an intimate connection with the system followed by the Catholic Church, which, while constantly endeavoring to develope the human mind by means of the propagation of the sciences, has nevertheless assigned to them a secondary part in the regulation of society. While religion has never been opposed to true science, never, on the other hand, has she ceased to show a certain degree of mistrust with respect to all that was the exclusive production of human thought; and observe that this is one of the chief differences between religion and the philosophy of the last age; or, we should rather say, it was the cause of their violent antipathy. Religion did not condemn science; on the contrary, she loved, protected, and encouraged it; but at the same time she marked out its limits, warned it that it was blind on some points, announced to it that it would be powerless in some of its labors, and that in others its action would be destructive and fatal. Philosophy, on the contrary, loudly proclaimed the sovereignty of science, declared it to be all-powerful, and deified it; it attributed to it strength and courage to change the face of the world, and wisdom and foresight enough to work this change for the good of humanity. This pride of knowledge, this deification of thought, is, if you observe closely, the foundation of Protestant doctrine. All authority being taken away, reason is the only competent judge, the intellect receives directly and immediately from God all the light which is necessary. This is the fundamental doctrine of Protestantism, that is to say, the pride of the mind.

If we closely observe, even the triumph of revolutions has in no degree nullified the wise anticipations of religion; and knowledge, properly so called, instead of gaining any credit from this triumph, has entirely lost what it had: there remains nothing of the revolutionary knowledge; what remains is the effects of the revolution, the interests created by it, the institutions which have arisen from those interests, and which, since that time, have sought in the department of science itself our principles to support them,—principles altogether different from those which had been proclaimed in the beginning.

I have said that every idea has need of being realized in an institution; this is so true, that revolutions themselves, warned by the instinct which leads them to preserve, with more or less integrity, the principles whence they have arisen, tend from the first to create those institutions in which the revolutionary doctrines may be perpetuated, or to constitute successors to represent them when they shall have disappeared from the schools. This may lead to many reflections on the origin and present condition of several forms of governments in different countries of Europe.

When speaking of the rapidity with which scientific theories succeed each other, when pointing out the immense development which the press has given to the field of discussion, I have shown that this was not an infallible sign of scientific progress, still less a guarantee for the fertility of human thought in realizing great things in the material and social order. I have said that grand conceptions proceed rather from *intuition* than from *discourses;* and on this subject I have recalled to mind historical events and personages which place this matter beyond a doubt. In support of this assertion, ideology might have furnished us with abundant proofs, if it were necessary to have recourse to science itself to prove its own sterility. But mere good sense, taught by the essons of experience daily, is enough to convince us that the men who are the most able in theory are, often enough, not only mediocre, but even weak in the exercise of authority. With regard to the hints which I have thrown out with respect to "intuition" and "discourses," I leave them to the judgment of any one who has applied to the study of the human mind. I am confident that the opinion of those who have reflected will not differ from my own.

NOTE 21, p. 175.

I have attributed to Christianity the gentleness of manners which Europe now enjoys. Yet, in spite of the decline of religious belief in the last century, this gentleness of manners, instead of being destroyed, has only been raised to a higher degree. This contrast, the effect of which, at first sight, is to destroy what I have established, requires some explanation. First of all, we must recollect the distinction pointed out in the text between effeminacy and gentleness of manners. The first is a fault, the second a valuable quality; the first emanates from enervation of the mind and weakening of the body; the second is owing to the preponderance of reason, the empire of the mind over the body, the triumph of justice over force, of right over might. There is a large portion of real gentleness in manners at the present day, but luxury has also a considerable part therein. This luxury of manners has certainly not arisen from religion, but from infidelity; the latter, never extending its view beyond the present life, causes the lofty destinies, and even the very existence of the soul, to be forgotten, puts egotism upon the throne, constantly excites and keeps alive the love of pleasure, and makes man the vile slave of his passions. On the contrary, at the first sight, we perceive that our manners owe all their gentleness to Christianity; all the ideas, all the feelings, on which this gentleness is founded, bear the mark of Christianity. The dignity of man, his rights, the obligation of treating him with the respect which is due to him, and of appealing to his mind by reason rather than to his body by violence, the necessity imposed on every one of keeping within the line of his duty, of respecting the property and the persons of others,—all this body of principles, to which real gentleness of manners is owing, is due, in Europe, to the influence of Christianity, which, after a struggle of many centuries against the barbarism and ferocity of invading nations, succeeded in destroying the system of violence which these same nations had made general.

As philosophy has taken care to change the ancient names consecrated by religion, and authorized by the usage of a succession of ages, it happens that some ideas, although the produce of Christianity, are scarcely acknowledged as such, only because they are disguised under a worldly dress. Who does not know that mutual love among men and fraternal charity are ideas entirely due to Christianity? Who does not know that pagan antiquity did not acknowledge them, that it even despised them? And nevertheless, this affection, which was formerly called *charity,* because charity was the virtue from which it took its legitimate origin, has constantly taken care to assume other names, as if it were ashamed to be seen in public with any appearance of religion. The mania for attacking the Christian religion being passed, it is openly confessed that the principle of universal charity is owing to her; but language remains infected with Voltairian philosophy even since the discredit into which that philosophy has fallen. Whence it follows, that we very often do not appreciate as we ought the influence of Christianity on the society which surrounds us, and that we attribute to other ideas and other causes the phenomena which are evidently owing to religion. Society at present, in spite of all its indifference, is more indebted to religion than is commonly supposed; it resembles those men, who, born of an illustrious family, in which good principles and a careful education are transmitted as an inheritance from generation to generation, preserve in their manners and behavior, even in the midst of their disorders, their crimes, and I will even venture to say, their degradation, some traits which denote their noble origin.

Note 22, p. 183.

A few regulations of Councils, quoted in the text, are sufficient to give an idea of the system pursued by the Church for the purpose of reforming and softening manners. It may be remarked that, on previous occasions during this work, I have a strong inclination to call to mind monuments of this kind; I will state here that I have two reasons for doing this: 1. When having to compare Protestantism with Catholicity, I believe that the best means of representing the real spirit of the latter is, to show it at work; this is done when we bring to light the measures which were adopted, according to different circumstances, by Popes and Councils. 2. Considering the direction which historical studies take in Europe, and the taste, which is daily becoming more general, not for histories, but for historical documents, it is proper always to bear in mind that the proceedings of Councils are of the highest importance, not only in historical and ecclesiastical matters, but also in political and social ones; so that to pay no attention to the data which are found in the records of Councils, is monstrously to mutilate, or rather wholly to destroy, the history of Europe.

On this account it is very useful, and even necessary in many things, to consult these records, although it may be painful to our indolence, on account of their enormous extent and the *ennui* of finding many things devoid of interest for our times. The sciences, above all those which have society for their object, lead to satisfactory results only by means of painful labors. What is useful is frequently mixed and confounded with what is not. The most valuable things are sometimes found by the side of repulsive objects; but in nature, do we find gold without having removed rude masses of earth?

Those who have attempted to find the germ of the precious qualities of European civilization among the barbarians of the north, should undoubtedly have attributed the gentleness of our manners to the same barbarians; they would have had in support of this paradox a fact certainly more specious than that which they have relied on to give the honor of elevating European women to the Germans. I allude to the well-known custom of avoiding the infliction of corporal punishments, and of chastising the gravest offences by fines only. Nothing is more likely to make us believe that these nations were happily inclined to gentleness of manners, since, in the midst of their barbarism, they used the right of punishment with a moderation which is not found even among the most civilized and refined nations. If we regard the thing in this point of view, it seems as if the influence of Christianity on the barbarians had the effect of rendering their manners more harsh instead of more gentle; indeed, after Christianity was introduced, the infliction of corporal punishments became general, and even that of death was not excluded.

But when we attentively consider this peculiarity of the criminal code of the barbarians, we shall see that, far from showing the advancement of their civilization and the gentleness of their manners, it is, on the contrary, the most evident proof that they were behind-hand; it is the strongest index of the harshness and barbarism which reigned among them. In the first place, inasmuch as crimes among them were punished by means of fines, or, as it was called, by *composition*, it is clear that the law paid much more attention to *repairing an injury* than to *punishing a crime;* a circumstance which clearly shows us how little they thought about the morality of the action, as they attended not so much to the action itself, as to the wrong which it inflicted. Therefore this was not an element of civilization but of barbarism; this tended to nothing less than the banishment of morality from the world. The Church combated this principle, as fatal in public as in private affairs; she introduced into criminal legislation a new set of ideas, which completely changed its spirit. On this point M. Guizot has done full justice to the Catholic Church. I am delighted to acknowledge and to insert this homage here by transcribing his own words. After having pointed out the difference which existed between the laws of the Visigoths, derived in great part from the Councils of Toledo, and the other barbarian laws, M. Guizot signalizes the immense superiority of the ideas of the Church in matters of legislation, of justice, and in all that concerns the search after truth and the lot of men; he adds: "In criminal matters, the relation of crimes to punishments is fixed (in the laws of the Visigoths) according to sufficiently just, philosophical, and moral notions. We there perceive the efforts of an enlightened legislator, who contends against the violence and rashness of barbarian manners. The chapter *De cœde et morte hominum*, compared with the corresponding laws of other nations, is a very remarkable example of this. Elsewhere, it is almost exclusively the injury which seems to constitute the crime, and the punishment is sought in that material reparation which is the result of composition. Here, the crime is referred to its real and moral element, the intention. The different shades of criminality, absolutely voluntary homicide, homicide by inadvertence, provoked homicide, homicide with or without premeditation, are distinguished and defined almost as well as in our own codes, and the punishments vary in a proportion equally just. The justice of the legislator has gone still further. He has attempted, if not to abolish, at least to diminish the diversity of legal value established among men by the other barbarian laws. The only distinction which it preserves is that of freeman and slave. With respect to freeman, the punishment varies neither with the origin nor the rank of the deceased, but only according to the different degrees of the culpability of the murderer. With regard to slaves, not venturing completely to withdraw from the masters the right of life and death, it has been attempted at least to restrain it by subjecting it to a public and regular procedure. The text of the law deserves to be cited.

"'If no one guilty of, or an accomplice in, a crime ought to remain unpunished, with how much more reason ought he to be condemned who has wickedly and rashly committed a homicide! Thus, as masters, in their pride, often put their slaves to death without any fault of the latter, it is proper altogether to extirpate this license, and to ordain that the present law shall be forever observed by all. No master or mistress shall put to death, without public trial, any of their slaves, male or female, or any person dependent on them. If a slave or any other servant shall commit a crime which may subject him to capital punishment, his master or his accuser shall immediately inform the judge or the count or duke of the place where the deed has been committed. After the affair has been inquired into, if the crime be proved, let the criminal undergo, either by the judge or his own master, the sentence of death which he has deserved; so that, nevertheless, if the judge be unwilling to put the accused to death, he shall draw up in writing a capital sentence, and then it shall be in the power of the master to put him to death or not. Indeed, if the slave, with a fatal audacity, resisting his master, has struck, or attempted to strike, him with a weapon, with a stone, or with any other kind of blow, and if the master, in defending himself, has killed the slave in his passion, the master shall be in no way subject to the punishment of homicide. But it shall be necessary to prove that the event took place thus, and that by the testimony or oath of the slaves, male or female, who shall have been present, and by the oath of the author of the deed himself. Whoever from mere malice, either by his own hand or that of another, shall have killed his slave without public trial, shall be marked with infamy, declared incapable of appearing as a witness, shall be obliged to pass the rest of his life in exile and penance, and his goods shall go to the nearest relations to whom they are given by the law.'—*For. Jud.* liv. vi. tit. xv. l. 12." (*Hist. Génér. de la Civilisation en Europe*, leçon 6.)

I have copied this passage from M. Guizot with pleasure, because I find there a confirmation of what I have just said on the subject of the influence of the Church in softening manners, and of what I have before stated with respect to the great amelioration which the Church made in the condition of slaves, by limiting the excessive power of their masters. This truth is proved in its place by so many documents, that it seems useless to revert to it here; it is enough now for my purpose, to point out that M. Guizot fully allows that the Church gave morality to the legislation of the barbarians, by making them consider the wickedness of the crime, whereas they had previously attended only to the injury of which it was the cause; she has thus transferred the action from the physical to the moral order, giving to punishments their real character, and not allowing them to remain reduced to the level of a mere material reparation. Hence we see that the criminal system of the barbarians, which, at the first *view*, seemed to indicate progress in civilization, was, in reality, owing to the little ascendency which moral principles exercised over these nations, and to the fact, that the views of the legislator were very slightly raised above the purely material order.

There is another observation to be made on this point, viz. that the mildness with which crimes were punished is the best proof of the frequency with which they were committed. When in a country assassinations, mutilations, and other similar attempts are very rare, they are regarded with horror; those who are guilty of them are chastised with severity. But when crimes are very frequently committed, they insensibly lose their enormity; not only those who commit them, but all the world become accustomed to their hideous aspect, and the legislator is then naturally induced to treat them with indulgence. This is shown us by the experience of every day; and the reader will have no difficulty in finding in society at the present time more than one crime to which the remark which I have just made is applicable. Among the barbarians, it was common to appeal to force, not only with respect to property, but also to persons; wherefore it was natural that crimes of this kind should not be regarded by them with the same aversion, it may be said with the same horror, as among a people where the triumph of the ideas of reason, justice, right, and law, render it impossible to conceive even the existence of a society where each individual should believe himself self-entitled to do justice to himself. Thus the laws against these crimes naturally became milder, the legislator contenting himself with repairing the injury, without paying much attention to the culpability of the delinquent. And this is intimately connected with what I have said above with respect to public conscience; for the legislator is always more or less the organ of this public conscience. Where an action, in any society whatever, is regarded as a heinous offence, the legislator cannot decree a mild punishment for it; on the other hand, it is not possble for him to chastise with great severity what the society absolves or excuses. It will sometimes happen that this proportion will be altered, that this harmony will be destroyed; but things soon quitting the path into which violence forced them, will not be long in returning to their ordinary course. Manners being chaste and pure, offences against them will be covered with abhorrence and infamy; but if morals be corrupted, the same acts will be regarded with indifference; at the most they will be denominated slight weaknesses. Among a people where religious ideas exercise great influence, the violation of all that is consecrated to God is regarded as a horrible outrage, worthy of the greatest chastisements: among another people, where infidelity has made its ravages, the same violation is not even placed on the list of ordinary offences; instead of drawing on the guilty the justice of the law, scarcely does it draw on them the slight correction of the police. The reader will understand the appropriateness of this digression on the criminal legislation of the barbarians, when he reflects that, in order to examine the influence of Catholicity on the civilization of Europe, it is indispensable to take into consideration the other elements which have concurred in forming that civilization. Without this, it would be impossible properly to appreciate the respective action of each of these elements, either for good or evil; impossible to bring to light the share which the Church can exclusively claim in the great work of our civilization; impossible to resolve the high question which has been raised by the partisans of Protestantism on the subject of the assumed advantages which the religious revolution of the sixteenth century has conferred on modern society. It is because the barbarian nations are one of these elements, that it is so often necessary to attend to them.

Note 23, p. 189.

In the middle ages, almost all the monasteries and colleges of canons had a hospital annexed to them, not only to receive pilgrims, but also to aid in the support and consolation of the poor and the sick. If you desire to see the noblest symbol of religion sheltering all kinds of misfortune, consider the houses devoted to prayer and the most sublime virtues converted into asylums for the miserable. This was exactly what took place at that time, when the public authority not only wanted the strength and knowledge necessary to establish a good administration for the relief of the unfortunate, but did not even succeed in covering with her ægis the most sacred interests of society; this shows us that when all was powerless, religion was still strong and fruitful; that when all perished, religion not only preserved herself, but even founded immortal establishments. And pay attention to what we have so many times pointed out, viz. that the religion which worked these prodigies was not a vague and abstract religion—the Christianity of the Protestants; but religion with all her dogmas, her discipline, her hierarchy, her supreme Pontiff, in a word, the Catholic Church.

They were far from thinking in ancient times that the support of the unfortunate could be confided to the civil administration alone, or to individual charity; it was then thought, as I have already said, that it was a very proper thing that the hospitals should be subjected to the Bishops; that is to say, that there should be a kind of assimilation made between the system of public beneficence and the hierarchy of the Church. Hence it was that, by virtue of an ancient regulation, the hospitals were under the control of the Bishops as well in temporals as in spirituals, whether the persons appointed to the care of the establishments were clerical or lay, whether the hospital had been erected by order of the Bishop or not.

This is not the place to relate the vicissitudes which this discipline underwent, nor the different causes which produced the successive changes; it is enough to observe, that the fundamental principle, that is, the interference of the ecclesiastical authority in establishments of beneficence, always remained unimpaired, and that the Church never allowed herself to be entirely deprived of so noble a privilege. Never did she think that it was allowable for her to regard with indifference the abuses which were introduced on this point to the prejudice of the unfortunate; wherefore she has reserved at least the right to remedy the evils which might result from the wickedness or the indolence of the administrators. The Council of Vienne ordains, that if the administrators of a hospital, lay or clerical, become relaxed in the exercise of their charge, proceedings shall be taken against them by the Bishops, who shall reform and restore the hospital of their own authority, if it has no privilege of exemption, and by delegation, if it has one. The Council of Trent also granted to Bishops the power of visiting the hospitals, even with the power of delegates of the Apostolic See in the cases fixed by law; it ordains, moreover, that the administrators, lay or clerical, shall be obliged every year to render their accounts to the ordinary of the place, unless the contrary has been provided in the foundation; and that if, by virtue of a particular privilege, custom, or statute, the accounts must be presented to any other than the ordinary, at least he shall be added to those who are appointed to receive them.

Without paying attention to the different modifications which the laws and customs of various countries may have introduced in this matter, we will say that one thing remains manifest, viz. the vigilance of the Church in all that regards beneficence; it is her constant tendency, by virtue of her spirit and maxims, to take part in affairs of this kind, sometimes to direct them exclusively, sometimes to remedy the evils which may have crept in. The civil power acknowledged the motives of this holy and charitable ambition; we see that the Emperor Justinian does not hesitate to give public authority over the hospitals to the Bishops, thereby conforming to the discipline of the Church and the general good.

On this point there is a remarkable fact, which it is necessary to mention here, in order to signalize its beneficent influence; I mean, the regulation by which the property of hospitals was looked upon as Church property,—a regulation which was very far from being a matter of indifference, although at first sight it might appear so. Their property, thereby invested with the same privileges as that of the Church, was protected by an inviolability so much the more necessary as the times were the more difficult, and the more abounding in outrages and usurpations. The Church which, notwithstanding all the public troubles, preserved great authority and a powerful ascendency over governments and nations, had thus a simple and powerful claim to extend her protection over the property of hospitals, and to withdraw them as much as possible from the cupidity and the rapacity of the powerful. And it must not be supposed that this doctrine was introduced with any indirect design, nor that this kind of community, this assimilation between the Church and the poor, was an unheard-of novelty; on the contrary, this assimilation was so well suited to the common order of things, it was so entirely founded on the relations between the Church and the poor, that if the property of the hospitals had the privilege of being considered as the property of the Church, that of the Church, on the other hand, was called the property of the poor. It is in these terms that the holy Fathers express themselves on this point: these doctrines had so much affected the ordinary language, that when, at a later period, the canonical question with respect to the ownership of the goods of the Church had to be solved, there were found by the side of those who directly attributed this property to God, to the Pope, to the clergy, some who pointed out the poor as being the real proprietors. It is true that this opinion was not the most conformable to the principles of law; but the mere fact of its appearing on the field of controversy is a matter for grave consideration.

NOTE 24, p. 196.

A few reflections, in the form of a note, on a certain maxim of toleration professed by a philosopher of the last century, Rousseau, would not be out of place here; but the analogy of the following chapter with that which we have just finished induces us to reserve them for note 25. The considerations to which the opinion of Rousseau will lead, apply to the question of toleration in religious matters, as well as to the right of coercion exercised by the civil and political power; I therefore beg my reader to reserve for the following note the attention which he might be willing to afford me now.

NOTE 25, p. 203.

For the purpose of clearing up ideas on toleration as far as lay in my power, I have presented this matter in a point of view but little known; in order to throw still more light upon it, I will say a few words on religious and civil intolerance,—things which are entirely different, although Rousseau absolutely affirms the contrary. Religious or theological intolerance consists in the conviction, that the only true religion is the Catholic,—a conviction common to all Catholics. Civil intolerance consists in not allowing in society any other religions than the Catholic. These two definitions are sufficient to make every man of common sense understand that the two kinds of intolerance are not inseparable; indeed, we may very easily conceive that men firmly convinced of the truth of Catholicity may tolerate those who profess another religion, or none at all. Religious intolerance is an act of the mind, an act inseparable from faith; indeed, whoever has a firm belief that his own religion is true, must necessarily be convinced that it is the only true one; for the truth is one. Civil intolerance is an act whereby the will rejects those who do not profess the same religion; this act has different results, according as the intolerance is in the individuals or in the government. On the other hand, religious tolerance consists in believing that all religions are true; which, when rightly understood, means that none are true, since it is impossible for contradictory things to be true at the same time. Civil tolerance is, to allow men who entertain a different religion to live in peace. This tolerance, as well as the co-relative intolerance, produces different effects, according as it exists in individuals or in the government.

This distinction, which, from its clearness and simplicity, is within the reach of the most ordinary minds, has nevertheless been mistaken by Rousseau, who affirms that it is a vain fiction, a chimera, which cannot be realized, and that the two kinds of intolerance cannot be separated from each other. Rousseau might have been content with observing, that religious intolerance, that is to say, as I have explained above, the firm conviction that a religion is true, if it is general in a country, must produce, in the ordinary intercourse of life as well as in legislation, a certain tendency not to tolerate any one who thinks differently, principally when those who dissent are very limited in number; his observation would then have been well founded, and would have agreed with the opinion which I have expressed on this point, when I attempted to represent the natural course of ideas and events in this matter. But Rousseau does not consider things under this aspect: desiring to attack Catholicity, he affirms that the two kinds of intolerance are inseparable; "for," says he, "it is impossible to live in peace with those whom one believes to be damned; to love them would be to hate God, who punishes them." It is impossible to carry misrepresentation further: who told Rousseau that the Catholics believe in the damnation of any man, whoever he may be, as long as he lives; and that they think that to love a man who is in error would be to hate God? On the contrary, could he be ignorant that it is a duty, an indispensable precept, a dogma, for Catholics to love all men? Could he be ignorant that even children, in the first rudiments of Christian doctrine, learn that we are obliged to love our neighbor as ourselves, and that by this word neighbor is meant whoever has gained heaven, or may gain it; so that no man, so long as he lives, is excluded from this number? But Rousseau will say, you are at least convinced that those who die in that fatal state are condemned. Rousseau does not observe that we think exactly the same with respect to sinners, although their sin be not that of heresy; now, it has not come into the head of any body that good Catholics cannot tolerate sinners, and that they consider themselves under the obligation of hating them. What religion shows more eagerness to convert the wicked? The Catholic Church is so far from teaching that we ought to hate them, that she causes to be repeated a thousand times, in pulpits, in books, and in conversations, those words whereby God shows that it is His will that sinners shall not perish, that He wills that they shall be converted and live, that there is more joy in heaven when one of them has done penance, than upon the ninety-nine just who need not penance. And let it not be imagined that the man who thus expresses himself against the intolerance of Catholics was the partizan of complete toleration; on the contrary, in society, such as he imagined it, he did not desire toleration for those who did not belong to the religion which the civil power thought proper to establish. It is true that he is not at all anxious that the citizens should belong to the true religion. "Laying aside," he says, "political considerations, let us return to the right, and let us lay down principles on this important point. The right which the social pact gives to the sovereign over his subject does not exceed, as I have said, the bounds of public utility. Subjects, therefore, are accountable to their sovereign for their opinions, inasmuch as those opinions are of importance to the community. Now, it is of great importance to the state, that every citizen should have a religion which shall make him love his duties; but the dogmas of that religion interest the state and its members only inasmuch as those dogmas affect morality and the duties which those who profess it are bound to perform towards others. As for the rest, each one may have what opinions he pleases, without being subject to the cognizance of the sovereign, for he has no power in the other world; it is not his affair what may be the lot of his subjects in the life to come, provided they be good citizens in this. There is, therefore, a profession of faith purely civil, the articles whereof it belongs to the sovereign to fix, not exactly as dogmas of religion, but as social sentiments, without which it is impossible to be a good citizen or a faithful subject. Without being able to compel any one to believe them, it can banish from the state him who does not believe them; it can banish him, not as wicked, but as anti-social, as incapable of sincerely loving the laws and justice, and of sacrificing his life to his duty. If any one, after having publicly acknowledged these dogmas, conducts himself as if he did not believe them, let him be punished with death; he has committed the greatest of crimes, he has lied against the laws." (*Du Contrat Social*, l. iv. c. 8.)

Such, then, is the final result of the toleration of Rousseau, viz. to give to the sovereign the power of fixing articles of faith, to grant to him the right of punishing with banishment, or even death, those who will not conform to the decisions of this new Pope, or who shall violate after having embraced them. However strange the doctrine of Rousseau may appear, it is not excluded from the general system of those who do not acknowledge the supremacy of authority in religious matters. When this supremacy is to be attributed to the Catholic Church, or its head, it is rejected; and, by the most striking contradiction, it is granted to the civil power. It is very singular that Rousseau, when banishing or putting to death the man who quits the religion fashioned by the sovereign, does not wish him to be punished as impious, but as anti-social. Rousseau, following an impulse very natural in him, did not wish that impiety should be at all taken into account when punishments were to be inflicted; but of what consequence is the name given to his crime to the man who is banished or put to death? In the same chapter, he allows an expression to escape him, which reveals at once the object which he had in view in all this show of philosophy: "Whoever dares to affirm that *out of the Church there is no salvation*, ought to be driven from the state." Which means, in other words, that toleration ought to be given to all except Catholics. It has been said, that the *Contrat Social* was the code of the French revolution; and, indeed, the latter did not forget what the tolerant legislator has prescribed with respect to Catholics. Few persons now venture to declare themselves the disciples of the philosopher of Geneva, although some of his timid partisans still lavish on him unmeasured eulogies. Let us have sufficient confidence in the good sense of the human race, to hope that all posterity, with a unanimous voice, will confirm the stamp of ignominy with which all men of sense have already marked that turbulent sophist, the impudent author of the *Confessions*.

When comparing Protestantism with Catholicity, I was obliged to treat of intolerance, as it is one of the reproaches which are most frequently made against the Catholic religion; but my respect for truth compels me to state, that all Protestants have not preached universal toleration; and that many of them have acknowledged the right of checking and punishing certain errors. Grotius, Puffendorf, and some more of the wisest men that Protestantism can boast of, are agreed on this point; therein they have followed the example of all antiquity, which, in theory as well as in practice, has constantly conformed to these principles. A cry has been raised against the intolerance of Catholics, as if they had been the first to teach it to the world; as if intolerance was a cursed monster, which was engendered only where the Catholic Church prevailed. In default of any other reason, good faith at least required that it should not be forgotten that the principle of universal toleration was never acknowledged in any part of the world; the books of philosophers, and the codes of legislators, contain the principle of intolerance with more or less rigor. Whether it were desired to condemn this principle as false, or to limit it, or to leave it without application, it is clear that an accusation ought not to have been made against the Catholic Church in particular, on account of a doctrine and conduct, wherein she only conformed to the example of the whole human race. Refined as well as barbarous nations would be culpable therein, if there were any crime; and the stigma, far from deserving to fall upon governments directed by Catholicity, or on Catholic writers, ought to be inflicted on all the governments of antiquity, including those of Greece and Rome; on all the ancient sages, including Plato, Cicero, and Seneca; on modern governments and sages, including Protestants. If men had had this present to their minds, the doctrine would not have appeared so erroneous, nor the facts so black; they would have seen that intolerance, as old as the world, was not the invention of Catholics, and that the whole world, ought to bear the responsibility of it.

Assuredly the toleration which, in our days, has become so general, from causes previously pointed out, will not be affected by the doctrines, more or less severe, more or less indulgent, which shall be proclaimed in this matter; but for the very reason, that intolerance, such as it was practised in other times, has at last become a mere historical fact, whereof no one can fear the re-appearance, it is proper to enter into an attentive examination of questions of this kind, in order to remove the reproach which her enemies have attempted to cast upon the Catholic Church.

The recollection of the encyclical letter of the Pope against the doctrines of M. de Lamennais, and the profound wisdom contained therein appropriately presents itself here. That writer maintained that universal toleration, the absolute liberty of worship, is the normal and legitimate state of society,—a state which cannot be changed without injury to the rights of the man and the citizen. M. de Lamennais, combatting the encyclical letter, attempted to show that it established new doctrines, and attacked the liberty of nations. No; the Pope, in his encyclical letter, does not maintain any other doctrines than those which have been professed up to this time by the Church—we may say by all governments—with respect to toleration. No government can sustain itself if it is refused the right of repressing doctrines dangerous to social order, whether those doctrines are covered with the mantle of philosophy, or disguised under the veil of religion. The liberty of man is not thereby assailed; for the only liberty which is worthy of the name, is liberty in conformity with reason. The Pope did not say that governments cannot, in certain cases, tolerate different religions; but he did not allow it to be established as a principle, that absolute toleration is an obligation on all governments. This proposition is contrary to sound religious doctrines, to reason, to the practice of all governments, in all times and countries, and the good sense of mankind. The talent and eloquence of the unfortunate author have not availed against this, and the Pope has obtained the most solemn assent of all sensible men of all creeds; while the man of genius, covering his brow with the shades of obstinacy, has not feared to seize upon the ignoble arms of sophistry. Unhappy genius! who scarcely preserves a shadow of himself, who has folded up the splendid wings on which he sailed through the azure sky, and now, like a bird of evil omen, broods over the impure waters of a solitary lake.

Note 26, p. 219.

When speaking of the Spanish Inquisition, I do not undertake to defend all its acts either in point of justice, or of the public advantage. Without denying the peculiar circumstances in which this institution was placed, I think that it would have done much better, after the example of the Inquisition of Rome, to avoid as much as possible the effusion of blood. It might have perfectly watched over the preservation of the faith, prevented the evils wherewith religion was threatened by the Moors and the Jews, and preserved Spain from Protestantism, without employing that excessive rigor, which drew upon it the severe and deserved reprimands and admonitions of the Sovereign Pontiffs, provoked the complaints of the people, made so many accused and condemned persons appeal to Rome, and furnished the adversaries of Catholicity with a pretext for charging *that* religion with being sanguinary which has a horror of the effusion of blood. I repeat, that the Catholic religion is not responsible for any of the excesses which have been committed in her name; and when men speak of the Inquisition, they ought not to fix their eyes principally on that of Spain, but on that of Rome. There, where the Sovereign Pontiff resides, and where they best understand how the principle of intolerance should be understood, and what use ought to be made of it, the Inquisition has been mild and indulgent in the extreme. Rome is the part of the world where humanity has suffered the least for the sake of religion; and that, without the exception of any countries, either of those where the Inquisition has existed, or of those where it has been unknown; of those where Catholicity has been predominant, or where Protestantism has triumphed. This fact, which cannot be denied, should suffice to convince every sincere man what is the spirit of Catholicity in this matter.

I make these remarks in order to show my impartiality, to prove that I am not ignorant of evils, and that I do not hesitate to admit them wherever I find them. Notwithstanding this, I am desirous that the facts and the observations contained in the text, as well with respect to the Inquisition itself, and to the different epochs of its duration, as to the policy of the kings who founded and established it, shall not be forgotten. The same desire makes me transcribe here a few documents likely to throw a stronger light upon this important subject. In the first place, I will quote the preamble of the Pragmatic Sanction of the Catholic princes Ferdinand and Isabella, for the explusion of the Jews; we there find stated in a few words, the outrages which the Jews inflicted on religion, and the dangers with which they threatened the state.

"Book viii. chap. 2, second law of the new *Recopilacion.* Don Ferdinand and Donna Isabella, at Granada, 30th March, 1492. Pragmatic Sanction.

"Having been informed that there existed in these kingdoms bad Christians, who judaized and apostatized from our holy Catholic faith, whereof the communication between the Jews and Christians was in great part the cause, we ordained, in the Cortes held by us in Toledo, in 1480, that the Jews in all the cities, towns, and other places of our kingdoms and lordships, should be confined in the Juiferies and places appointed for them to live and dwell in, hoping that this separation would serve as a remedy; we also provided and gave orders that an Inquisition should be appointed in our said kingdoms; which Inquisition, as you know, is and has been practised for more than twelve years, and has discovered a great number of delinquents, as is notorious. As we have been informed by the Inquisitors, and many other religious persons, lay and ecclesiastical, it is certain that great injury to the Christians had been and is the result of the participation, intercourse, and communication which they have had, and still have, with the Jews; it has been proved that the latter, by all the means in their power, constantly labor to subvert the faith of Christians, to withdraw them from our holy Catholic faith, to lead them away from it, to attract them, and to pervert them to their own noxious creed and opinions; instructing them in the ceremonies and observances of their own law; holding meetings to teach them what they ought to believe and observe according to that law; taking care to circumcise them and their children, giving them books in order to recite their prayers, teaching them the fasts which they ought to observe, assembling to read with them, teaching them the histories of their laws; notifying to them the Paschal times before they arrive, admonishing them as to what they ought to do and observe during those times; giving them, bringing for them, from their own homes, the bread of azimes, meats killed according to their ceremonies; instructing them as to the things from which they ought to abstain, in order to obey the law, as well in eating as in other things; persuading them, as far as they can, to adopt and keep the Law of Moses, and making them understand that no other law than that is true. All these things are certain from numerous testimonies, from the acknowledgments of the Jews themselves, and of those who have been perverted and deceived by them, which has inflicted great injury, detriment, and dishonor on our holy Catholic faith. Although we were already informed of these things from many quarters, and although we were aware that the real remedy for all these evils and inconveniences was to place an insurmountable barrier to the communication of the Jews with the Christians, and to banish the Jews from our kingdoms, we wished to be satisfied with enjoining them to quit all the cities, towns, and places of Andalusia, where it seemed that they had done the most mischief, believing that that would be enough to hinder those of the other cities, towns, and places of our kingdoms and lordships from doing and committing what has been mentioned. But being informed that this measure, as well as the acts of justice exercised on some of the Jews who were found guilty of these offences and crimes against our holy Catholic faith, do not suffice to remedy the evil thoroughly; for the purpose of obviating and abolishing so great an opprobrium, such an offence against the faith and the Christian religion, since it appears that the same Jews, with a fatal ardor, redouble their perverse attempts wherever they live and associate; wishing to suppress the occasion of offending more against our holy Catholic faith, as well on account of those persons whom it has pleased God up to this time to preserve, as of those who, after having fallen, have repented and returned to our holy mother the Church; wishing to prevent the offences which, on account of the weakness of our human nature, and the suggestions of the devil, which continually make war on us, might easily occur, if the principal cause of the evil were not removed by the expulsion of the Jews from our kingdoms; considering, besides, that when a great and detestable crime has been committed by some members of a college or university, it is reasonable that that college or that university should be dissolved and destroyed, that some may be punished on account of the others, and the lesser number on account of the greater; that those who pervert the good and virtuous mode of life of cities and towns, by a contagion which may injure others, may be banished from those towns; and that if it be allowed to act thus for other slight causes prejudicial to the state, there is still more reason to allow it for the greatest, the most dangerous, the most contagious of crimes, that which is in question: for all these reasons we, having consulted our Council, and taken the advice of some prelates," &c.

We are not now examining whether or not there is any exaggeration in these imputations against the Jews, although, according to all appearances, there must have been a great deal of foundation for them, in consequence of the situation in which the two rival nations were placed. Observe, besides, that if the preamble of the Pragmatic Sanction is silent with respect to a hundred accusations brought against the Jews by the generality of the people, the report of these crimes had not the less weight with the public; consequently, the situation of the Jews was aggravated in an extraordinary degree, and the princes were so much the more inclined to treat them with severity.

With respect to the mistrust with which the Moors and their descendants must have been regarded, besides the facts pointed out above, others might be related which show the disposition of men's minds to see in the presence of these men a permanent conspiracy against the Christians. Almost a century had elapsed since the conquest of Granada, and it was still feared that this kingdom might be the centre of plots contrived by the Moors against the Christians, the source of perfidious projects, and the place whence came the means of maltreating in all ways the defenceless persons upon our coasts.

Thus spoke Philip II. in 1567:

"Book viii. chap. 2, of the new *Recopilacion*.

"Law xx., which decrees severe punishments against the inhabitants of the kingdom of Granada who shall have hidden, received, or favored the Turks, Moors, or Jews, or given them intelligence, or corresponded with them.

"D. Philip II., Madrid, 10 December, 1567.

"Having been informed that, notwithstanding what has been ordained by us, as well by sea as by land, particularly for the kingdom of Granada, for the purpose of insuring the defence and security of our kingdoms, the Turks, Moors, and corsairs have already committed, and still commit, in the ports of this kingdom, on the coasts, in maritime places, and those bordering on the sea, robberies, misdeeds, injuries, and seizures of Christians; evils which are notorious, and which, it is said, have been, and are, committed with ease and security, by favor of the intercourse and understanding which the ravishers have had, and still have, with some of the inhabitants of the country, who give them intelligence, guide them, receive them, hide them, and lend them favor and assistance; some of them even going away with the Moors and Turks, leading away and carrying with them their wives, their children, their goods, Christian captives, and the things which they were able to ravish from the Christians; while other inhabitants of the same kingdom, who have participated in these projects, or have been acquainted with them, remain in the country, without having been or being punished; for it appears that measures are not executed with due severity, nor as completely, or with as much care as they ought to be: as, moreover, it seems very difficult to get accurate information, as it appears that even the justices and the judges, to whom it belongs to make inquiries and to punish, have displayed remissness and negligence in their employment;—this having been agitated and discussed in our Council, with the view of providing, as is proper in a thing of such great importance, for the service of God our Master, for our own and the public good; the thing having been consulted upon by us, it has been agreed that we ought to publish this present letter," &c.

Years passed away; the hatred between the two nations still endured; in spite of the numerous checks which the Mahometan race had received, the Christians were not satisfied. It was very probable that a nation who had suffered, and might still suffer, such great humiliations, would attempt to avenge them. It is also by no means difficult to believe in the reality of the conspiracies which were charged against the Moors. However this may be, the report of these conspiracies was general, and the government was seriously alarmed by them. Those who desire a proof of this, may read what Philip III. said, in 1609, in the law which expelled the Moriscoes.

"Book viii. chap. 2, of the new *Recopilacion.*

"Law xxv. By virtue of which the Moriscoes were banished from the kingdom: causes of this expulsion—means which were adopted for the execution of the measure.

"D. Philip III., Madrid, 9 December, 1609.

"For a long time it has been endeavored to save the Moriscoes in these kingdoms: the holy office of the Inquisition has inflicted divers punishments; numerous edicts of mercy have been granted; neither means nor diligence have been spared to instruct them in our holy faith, without being able to obtain the desired result, for none of them have been converted. On the contrary, their obstinacy has increased; the peril which threatens our kingdoms, if we keep the Moriscoes, has been represented to us by persons very well informed and full of the fear of God, who, thinking it proper that a prompt remedy should be applied to this evil, have represented to us that the delay might be charged upon our royal conscience, considering the grave offences which our Lord receives from that people. We have been assured that we might, without scruple, punish them in their lives and properties, since they were convicted by their continued offences of being heretics, apostates, and traitors of *lèse-majesté* divine and human. Although it would have been allowable to proceed against them with the rigor which their offences deserve, nevertheless, desiring to bring them back by means of mildness and mercy, I ordained, in the city and kingdom of Valencia, an assembly of the patriarchs, and other prelates and wise men, in order to ascertain what could be resolved upon and settled; but having learned that, at the very time they were engaged in remedying the evil, the Moriscoes of the said kingdom of Valencia, and of our other domains, continued to urge forward their pernicious projects; knowing, moreover, from correct and certain intelligence, that they had sent to treat at Constantinople with the Turks, and at Morocco with the king, Muley Fidon, in order that there might be sent into the kingdom of Spain the greatest number of forces possible to aid and assist them; being sure that there would be found in our kingdom more than 150,000 men, as good Moors as those from the coasts of Barbary, all ready to assist them with their lives and fortunes, whereby they were persuaded of the facility of the enterprise; knowing that the same treaties have been attempted with heretics and other princes our enemies: considering all that we have just said, and to fulfill the obligation which we are under of preserving and maintaining the holy Roman Catholic faith in our kingdoms, as well as the security, peace, and repose of the said kingdoms, with the counsel and advice of learned men, and others, very zealous for the service of God and for our own, we ordain that all the Moriscoes, inhabitants of these kingdoms, men, women, and children, of all conditions," &c.

I have said that the Popes labored, from the commencement, to soften the rigors of the Spanish Inquisition, sometimes by admonishing the kings and inquisitors, sometimes by giving the accused and condemned a right of appeal. The kings feared that the religious innovations would produce a public disturbance; I add, that their policy embarrassed the Popes, and prevented them from carrying as far as they would have wished their measures of mildness and indulgence. Among the other documents which support this assertion, I will cite one which proves the irritation of the Spanish kings at the assistance which the accused found at Rome.

"Book viii. chap. 3, law 2, of the new *Recopilacion,* enjoining persons condemned by the Inquisition, and absent from these kingdoms, not to return there under pain of death and losing their goods.

"D. Ferdinand and D. Isabella, at Saragossa, 2d August, 1498. Pragmatic Sanction.

"Some persons condemned as heretics by the Inquisition have absented themselves from our kingdoms, and have gone to other countries, where, by means of false reports and undue formalities, they have surreptitiously obtained exemptions, absolutions, mandates, securities, and other privileges, in order to be exempt from the condemnations and punishments which they had incurred, and to remain in their errors, which, nevertheless, does not prevent their attempting to return to these kingdoms, wherefore, wishing to extirpate so great an evil, we command these condemned persons not to be so bold as to return. Let them not return into our kingdoms and lordships, by any way, in any manner, for any cause or reason whatsoever, under pain of death and the loss of their goods; which punishment we will and ordain to be incurred by the act itself. One-third of the property shall be for the persons who shall have denounced, another for the courts, and the third for our exchequer. Whenever the said justices, in their own places and jurisdiction, shall know that any of the said persons are in any part of their jurisdiction, we order all and each of them, without exception, to go to the place where such persons are, without being otherwise called upon, to apprehend them forcibly and immediately, and without delay to execute, and cause to be executed, on them and their properties the punishments which we have appointed; and this notwithstanding all exemption, reconciliation, securities, and other privileges which they may have, these privileges, in the present case, and with respect to the said penalties, not availing them

We order them to do and accomplish this under pain of the loss and confiscation of all their property. The same penalty shall be incurred by all other persons who shall have hidden or received the said condemned persons, and who knowing that they were so, shall not have given information to our courts. We order all great men and councillors, and other persons of our kingdoms, to give favor and assistance to our courts, whenever it shall be demanded and required from them, to accomplish and execute what has been said above, under the penalties which the courts themselves shall appoint on this subject."

We see from this document, that, after the year 1498, things had reached such a point, that the kings attempted to maintain against every one all the rigor of the Inquisition, and that they were offended that the Popes interfered to soften it. It will be understood thereby whence proceeded the harshness with which the guilty were treated; and this shows us one of the causes which made the Inquisition sometimes use its power with excessive severity. Although it was not a mere instrument of the policy of kings, as some have said, the Inquisition felt more or less the influence of that policy; and we know that policy, when about to defeat an adversary, does not commonly display an excess of compassion. If the Spanish Inquisition had been at that time under the exclusive authority and direction of the Popes, it would have been infinitely milder and more moderate in its method of acting.

At that time the object ardently desired by the kings of Spain was, to obtain that the judgments of the Inquisition should be definitive in Spain, without appeal to Rome; Queen Isabella had expressly demanded this of the Pope. The Sovereign Pontiffs would not accede to these solicitations, no doubt fearing the abuse which might be made of so fearful an arm when the restraint of the moderating power should become wanting.

It will be understood from the facts which I have just quoted, how much reason I had to say that, if you excuse the conduct of Ferdinand and Isabella with respect to the Inquisition, you must not condemn that of Philip II., since the Catholic sovereigns showed themselves still more harsh and severe than the latter monarch. I have already pointed out the reason why the conduct of Philip II. has been so rigorously condemned; but it is also necessary to show why there has been a sort of obstinacy in excusing that of Ferdinand and Isabella.

When it is wished to falsify an historical fact by calumniating a person or an institution, it is necessary to begin with an affectation of impartiality and good faith; great success is obtained in this by manifesting indulgence for the same thing which it is desired to condemn, but taking care that this indulgence has strongly the appearance of being a concession gratuitously made to our adversaries, or of a sacrifice of our opinions, of our feelings, on the altars of reason and justice, which are our guide and our idol. We thus predispose our hearers or readers to regard the condemnation which we are about to pronounce as a judgment dictated by the strictest justice; a judgment in which neither passion, nor partiality, nor perverse views, have any part. How can we doubt the good faith, the love of truth, the impartiality of the man who begins by excusing what, according to all appearances, and considering his opinions, ought to be the object of his anathemas? Such is the situation of the men of whom we speak. They intended to attack the Inquisition; now it happened that the protectress, and, in some sort, the foundress of that tribunal was Queen Isabella,—that distinguished name which Spaniards have always pronounced with respect, that immortal queen, one of the noblest ornaments of our history. What was to be done in this difficulty? The means were simple. Although the Jews and heretics had been treated with the greatest severity in the time of the Catholic sovereigns, and although they had carried severity further than all those who have succeeded them, it was necessary to close the eye to these facts, to excuse the conduct of these sovereigns, and to point out the important matters which urged them to employ the rigors of justice. They thus avoided the difficulty,—for it was one to cast a stigma on the memory of a great queen cherished and respected by all Spaniards,—and they thus prepared the way for merciless accusations against Philip II. That monarch had the unanimous cry of all Protestants against him, for the simple reason that he had been their most powerful adversary; it would therefore cost nothing to make all the weight of execration fall upon him. The enigma is thus explained. Such is the cause of a partiality so unjust,—such is the hypocrisy of that opinion which, while excusing the Catholic sovereigns, condemns Philip II. without appeal.

I have not attempted to justify the policy of this monarch in all respects; but I have presented a few considerations which may serve to mitigate the violent attacks made upon him by his adversaries: it only remains for me to transcribe here the documents to which I alluded when I said that the Inquisition was not a mere instrument of the policy of Philip II., and that this prince did not intend to establish a system of *obscurantisme* in Spain.

Don Antonio Perez, in his *Relations*, gives a letter of the confessor of the king, Fray Diego de Chaves, in which letter the latter affirms that the secular prince has power over the lives of his subjects and vassals, and adds in a note: "I shall not undertake to relate all that I have heard said on the subject of the condemnation of some of these propositions; this is not within my province. Those who are concerned in this will at once understand the import of my words. I shall content myself with saying that, at the time when I was at Madrid, the Inquisition condemned the following proposition: a preacher —it matters not that I should mention his name—maintained in a sermon, at St. Jerome's, in Madrid, in presence of the Catholic king, *that kings have an absolute power over the persons of their subjects, as well as over their properties.* Besides some other separate matters, the preacher was condemned to retract this publicly, in the same place, with all the ceremonies of a juridical act, which he did in the same pulpit, saying that he had advanced such a proposition on such a day, and that he retracted it as erroneous 'For, messieurs,' said he, reading literally from a paper, '*kings have no other power over their subjects than what is given them by the divine and human law; they have none proceeding from their own free and absolute will.*' I even know who condemned the proposition, and appointed the words which the accused, to the great gratification of the former, was obliged to pronounce; indeed, he rejoiced to see torn up so poisonous a weed, which he felt was increasing, as the event proved. Master Fray Hernando del Castillo (I will mention his name) was the one who prescribed what the accused was to say; he was consultee of the holy office, and preacher to the king; he was a man of singular learning and eloquence, very well known and esteemed by his own nation, and especially by the Italians. Dr. Velasco, an important personage of that time, said of him, that the guitar in the hands of Fabricio Dentici was not so sweet as the tongue of Master Fray Hernandez del Castillo to the ears of those who heard him." And at page 47 in the text: "I know," says Don Antonio Perez, "that they were denominated very scandalous by persons very important by their rank, their learning, and their Christian purity of heart; there was one among them who had held supreme rank in the spiritual order in Spain, and had previously filled an office in the tribunal of the Inquisition." Perez afterwards says, that this person was the nuncio of his Holiness. (*Relaciones de Anton. Perez.* Paris, 1624.)

The letter of Philip II. to Doctor D. Benito Arias Montano contains the following, in addition to the remarkable passage which we have quoted.

"Concerning what you, Dr. &c., my chaplain, will have to do at Antwerp, whither we send you. Dated at Madrid, 25th March, 1568.

"Besides that you will render this good office and service to the said Plantinus, know that, from this time, in proportion as the six thousand crowns are recovered from his hands, I apply them to buy books for the monastery of St. Laurent-le-Royal, of the order of St. Jerome, which I am building near the Escurial, as you know. Thus you are admonished that such is my intention; you will comply with this, and will be diligent in collecting all the choice books, printed and MS., that your excellent discernment shall think proper, in order to bring them and place them in the library of the said monastery. Indeed, it is one of the chief possessions which I would wish to leave to the religious who are intended to dwell there, for it is the most useful and necessary. Wherefore I have also commanded my ambassador in France, D. Francis de Alaba, to collect the best books which he shall be able in that kingdom: you will communicate with him on that subject. I will direct him to communicate in writing also with you, to send you a list of the books which are to be had, as well as their price, before buying them; you will advise him as to which he had better take or leave, and what he may give for such. He will send to you at Antwerp those which he has thus bought; you will acknowledge them, and forward them here, all at once, at the proper time."

During the reign of Philip II.,—of that prince who is represented to us as one of the principal authors of *obscurantisme,*—choice works, both printed and MS., were sought in foreign countries, in order to enrich the Spanish libraries; in our age, which we call that of enlightenment, the libraries of Spain have been plundered, and their treasures have gone to add to those of foreigners. Who is ignorant of the collections which have been made of our books and MS., in England? Consult the catalogues of the British Museum and other private libraries. The author of these lines states only what he has seen with his own eyes —what he has heard lamented by persons worthy of respect. While we show so much negligence in preserving our treasures, let us not be so unjust and so puerile as to lose our time in vain declamation against those who have bequeathed them to us.

APPENDIX.

A few words on Puigblanch, Villeneuve, and Llorente.

Here, in the Spanish edition, the notes relating to the Inquisition terminate; but I think it may not be useless in the French edition to add a few words, to explain the matter to my foreign readers: little versed as they are in the knowledge of our affairs, they might often happen to drink at corrupted sources, which they imagine to be pure and salutary. Le Compte de Maistre, with respect to the Spanish Inquisition, cites *L' Inquisition dévoilée de Natanaël Jomtob:* I will say a few words, lest the authority of the author who quotes should give too much importance to him who is quoted. This Natanaël Jomtob is no other than Dr. D. Antonio Puigblanch, a Spaniard, who died not long ago in London. This author, in the prologue to his works published in London, himself explains the reason which made him adopt a strange name. "These Hebrew words," he says, "are two proper significative names, which, together, form the inscription, *Dedit Deus diem bonum.* I wished thus to express the happiness of being able to speak and write freely against the tribunal of the Inquisition, and the happiness of seeing it abolished." (*Prolog.* p. cxv.)

In order that the reader may judge of the value that belongs to this work, I will observe, that the first qualification in an historian, especially on a matter so delicate, is complete impartiality united to a great fund of moderation: these two qualifications were wanting in M. Puigblanch, who was lamentably infected with the contrary faults. It is impossible to be more violent than he is against all that he meets with; his ill-humor and anger blind him; he attacks institutions and men with perfect fury; he respects nothing: add to this a pitiable vanity. It would be easy for me to produce here various proofs of the impiety of Puigblanch; but I should fear to soil my paper by transcribing the impious satires of this man. This is enough to give an idea of the point of view in which he could regard things relating to religious affairs and to the clergy. He misses no opportunity of ridiculing the ministers of religion, of indulging in invectives against them, and of giving vent to the incomprehensible rage which he has against them. The unbecoming manner in which he treats his adversaries, real or imaginary, even when they have more or less sympathy with his opinions, is a good apology for the things which he combats on the other hand. I cannot repeat his words here, so coarse are they; besides, they attack persons who are still living; suffice it to say, that not content with insulting them in the most disgusting way, Puigblanch descends so low as to reproach them with their physical defects, after the manner of a market-woman. What was to be hoped from such a mind in a matter so important and delicate? Were such dispositions suitable for an historian of the Inquisition, who published his work precisely in the year 1811, that is to say, at a time of reaction and effervescence? With respect to talent and knowledge, I will not refuse to M. Puigblanch either reading or erudition, or a certain aptitude for criticism, yet it must not be forgotten that his mind was far from being so cultivated as it ought to have been, in order to keep pace with our age. A work like his required that he should have followed the march of the times, that he should not have been altogether devoid of the philosophy of history, that he should not have relied exclusively upon certain books, while accumulating crude erudition, and incessantly perusing etymologies and grammatical questions: this is what was wanting in M. Puigblanch. To sum up all in one sentence, I have found the following description, which I heard in London, from the mouth of a distinguished man who had intercourse with Puigblanch for a long time, to be perfectly correct: "Puigblanch," he told me, "knew what a learned man of the seventeenth century in Spain might have known." The Christian reader may imagine what was the result of the amalgamation of this kind of instruction with all the bile of Voltairian passion.

D. Joaquin Lorenzo Villanueva is another of those Spaniards who have distinguished themselves by declaiming against the Inquisition; in his Literary Life (*Vida Literaria*) he had asserted that the public information on this question, and the abolition of that famous tribunal, were in great part owing to him. Puigblanch strongly recriminates against Villanueva, who attempted to usurp his glory by availing himself of his work without acknowledging it, and other similar things, which do as little honor to the one as to the other. Villanueva has been already judged in Spain by all sensible men; foreigners who desire to understand this question will be under the unpleasant obligation of reading the two large volumes in 8vo, in which he has written his literary life. The bile of Villanueva against all the clergy who are not of his coterie, and, above all, his hatred against Rome, show themselves at every page of his book, and from time to time produce explosions which are much too violent to accord with the extreme mildness which he is pleased to affect. Moreover, let the reader prepare and arm himself with patience, if he undertake to get through these two large volumes, which contain, written by the man himself, who so well deserved it, the most complete panegyric of his profound knowledge, his vast erudition, his great humility, and his virtues of all kinds. It certainly would have been very well, if the author, with a slight recollection of modesty, had not candidly told us, that they went so far as to call him the *father of the poor*, that his poetic fire was not cooled by age, that his activity in labor did not allow him to remain idle, even in the midst of the greatest persecutions; in fine, if he had not undertaken to make us believe that all his life was a continual sacrifice on the altars of knowledge and virtue. To those who desire to derive their information from Villanueva, we have a right to say: Do not forget that you must beware of believing all—that the tree is known by its fruits—that the wolf often assumes sheep's clothing.

Among those who have made the most noise with respect to the Inquisition, is Llorente, the author of a history of that famous institution. The impartiality which may be expected from this writer shows itself every moment in his book, which has evidently been written for the purpose of blackening, as much as possible, the Catholic clergy and the Holy See. Happily the author has made himself too well known by his other works, for any Catholic to allow himself to be deceived by his insidious writings. No one, especially in Spain, is ignorant of the project of the religious constitution with which Llorente attempted to disturb consciences, and introduce schism and heresy into our country. Does he who attempts to destroy the universal discipline established from the earliest ages, who expresses doubts on the most sacred mysteries of our holy religion, who contests the infallible authority of the Church, and does not hold the first four Œcumenical Councils to be legitimate, deserve the least credit when writing the history of the Inquisition,—that history which affords so many opportunities of declaiming against the clergy and against Rome? Here is a proof of his impartiality. In his history of the Inquisition, he could not avoid relating the conduct of the Apostolic See in the early times of the Inquisition in Spain, and the efforts made by the Holy See for the purpose of softening the rigors of that tribunal, the appeals which were made, and the merciful judgments which were almost always obtained at Rome; all these facts clearly showed that Rome, far from being, as he pretended, a monster of cruelty, was rather a model of mildness and prudence. How do you think he gets out of this difficulty? By saying, that what the Court of Rome wanted was, to extort money from us. An explanation as unworthy as it is impudent—an odious means of depriving the most beneficent and generous actions of their lustre, and which shows a fixed design to find evil every where, even to the extent of assigning evil motives for benefits which are the most worthy of gratitude.

With respect to Llorente, I am unwilling to pass over in silence a remarkable fact which he has had the kindness to communicate to the public in the same work. King Joseph, the intruder, intrusted Llorente, by express orders, with the archives of the Supreme Council and the Tribunal of the Inquisition of the capital. This excellent man was so perfect an archivist, that he burnt all the reports of proceedings, with the approbation of his master (as he himself tells us), with the exception of those which could appertain to history, by the celebrity or the renown of the persons who figured in them, such as those of Caranza, of Macanaz, and a few others; although he preserved entire, he adds, the registers of the decisions of the Council, the royal ordinances, and the bulls and briefs from Rome. (Edition Française, 1818, t. 4, p. 145.) After having heard this remarkable confession, we will ask every impartial man, whether there is not room for greatly mistrusting an historian who claims to be sole and *unique*, because he has had the opportunity of consulting the original documents whereon he founds his history, and who, nevertheless, burns and destroys these same documents? Was there no place to be found in Madrid to place them, where they could be examined by those who, after Llorente, might wish to write the history of the Inquisition from the original documents? Llorente has preserved, he tells us, those which belonged to history; but the history of the Inquisition had equally need of others, even the most obscure —even the most apparently insignificant; for it not seldom happens that a fact, a circumstance, a word, shows us an institution, and paints for us an age. And observe, that this destruction took place at a critical moment of public disturbance, when the whole nation, devoted to an immortal struggle in defence of her independence, could not fix her attention on such matters. The most remarkable men, scattered on all sides, then led their fellow-citizens in arms, or were engaged in the most important interests of the country; consequently they could not watch over the conduct of an archivist, who, after having left his brethren, whose blood was flowing upon the battle-field, accepted employment under a foreign intruder, and burned the documents of an institution whereof he undertook to write the history.

Note 27, p. 281.

The plan of my work required that questions relating to the religious communities should be examined at some length but it did not allow me to give to this matter all the development of which it is susceptible. Indeed, it would be possible, in my opinion, in writing the history of religious communities, to give side by side that of the nations among whom these communities arose, so as to show in detail a truth we have now proved, viz. that the establishment of religious institutions, besides the superior and divine object which they have had in view, has been at all times the fulfilment of a social and religious necessity. Although my strength does not enable me to aspire to such an enterprise, by which the courage may well be daunted, even by contemplating the immense extent of such a work, I wish to suggest the idea of it here; perhaps a man may be found with sufficient capacity, learning, and leisure, to undertake it, and enrich our age with this new monument of history and philosophy. By conceiving the plan in this point of view, and making it subordinate to this unity of object, whereof the foundation, which shows itself in well-known facts, is discovered in obscure and conjectured in hidden ones, there would be no difficulty in giving all desirable variety to this work. The subject itself leads to variety; for it invites the writer to descend to extremely interesting particulars, which will be like the episodes of a grand and unique poem. The disposition of men's minds, now become favorable to religious institutions, thanks to the deceptions which are the consequence of vain theories, and to the lessons of experience, which destroy the calumnies invented by philosophy, render the road every day more easy. The path is already sufficiently beaten; it is only required to enlarge and extend it, in order to conduct a greater number of men towards the region of truth.

Having pointed out this, it only remains for me to state here, in conclusion, divers facts which could not be given in the text, and which I have preferred to collect in a note: As these facts belonged to the same subject, it appeared to me proper to collect them apart, while leaving the reader to pay full attention to the observations which form the body of my work.

There were known among the pagans, under the name of ascetics, persons who devoted themselves to abstinence and the practice of the austere virtues; so that, even before Christianity, there already existed the idea of those virtues which have been since exercised in Christianity. The lives of the philosophers are full of examples which prove the truth of my assertion. Yet it will be understood that, deprived of the light of faith and the aid of grace, the pagan philosophers afforded but a very faint shadow of what was afterwards realized in the lives of the Christian ascetics. We have stated that the monastic life is founded on the Gospel, inasmuch as the Gospel contains asceticism. From the foundation of the Church we see the monastic life established under one form or another. Origen tells us of certain men, who, in order to reduce their bodies into subjection, abstained from eating meat and from all that had life. (Origen, *Contr. Celsum*, lib. v.) Tertullian makes mention of some Christians who abstained from marriage, not because they condemned it, but in order to gain the kingdom of heaven. (Tertul. *De Cult. Femin.* lib. ii.)

It is remarkable, that the weaker sex participated in a singular manner in that strength of mind which Christianity communicated for the exercise of the heroic virtues. In the early ages of the Church there were already reckoned, in great numbers, virgins and widows consecrated to the Lord, bound by a vow of perpetual chastity; and we see that special care was taken in the ancient Councils of the Church of that chosen portion of her flock. It is one of the objects of the solicitude of the Fathers to regulate discipline on this point in a proper manner. The virgins made their public profession in the church; they received the veil from the hands of the bishop, and, for greater solemnity, they were distinguished by a kind of consecration. This ceremony required a certain age in the person who was consecrated to God; we also observe that discipline has been very different on this point. In the East they received persons seventeen years old, and even sixteen, as we learn from St. Basil (*Epist.* can. 18); in Africa at twenty-five, as we see from the fourth canon of the third Council of Carthage; in France at forty, as appears from the nineteenth canon of the

Council of Agde. Even when the virgins and widows dwelt in the houses of their fathers, they did not cease to be reckoned among ecclesiastical persons; they received the support of the Church by this title, in cases of necessity. If they violated their vow of chastity, they were excommunicated, and could not return to the communion of the faithful, except by submitting to public penance. (For these details, see the thirty-third canon of the third Council of Carthage, the nineteenth canon of the Council of Ancyra, and the sixteenth canon of that of Chalcedon.)

In the first three centuries, the state of the Church, subject to an almost continual persecution, must naturally have hindered persons who loved the ascetic life, men or women, from assembling in the towns to observe it in common. Some think that the propagation of the ascetic life in the desert is in great part due to the persecution of Decius, which was very cruel in Egypt, and made a great number of Christians retire into the deserts of the Thebais, or other solitudes in the neighbourhood. Thus commenced the establishment of that method of life which, in the end, was to gain so prodigious an extension. St. Paul, if we are to believe St. Jerome, was the founder of the solitary life.

It appears that some abuses were introduced into the monastic life from the earliest ages, as we see certain monks detested at Rome in the time of Jerome. *Quousque genus detestabile monacorum urbe non pellitur,* says the saint by the mouth of the Romans in a letter to Paula; but the reputation of the monks, which had perhaps been compromised by the Sarabaïtes and the Gyrovagues, a kind of vagabonds whose last care was the practice of the virtues of their state, and who indulged in gluttony and other pleasures with shameful licentiousness, was soon restored. St. Athanasius, St. Jerome himself, St. Martin, and other celebrated men, among whom St. Bennet distinguished himself in a particular manner, renewed the splendor of the monastic life by the most eloquent apology, that which consisted in giving, as they did, the most sublime example of the most austere virtues.

It is remarkable that, in spite of the multiplication of monks in the east and west, they were not divided into different orders, so that, during the first six centuries, all, as Mabillon observes, were considered as forming one institute. There was something noble in this unity, which, as it were, formed all the monasteries into one family; but it must be acknowledged that the diversity of orders afterwards introduced was essentially calculated to attain the various and numerous objects which successively attracted the attention of religious institutions.

The discipline, by virtue whereof no new order could be instituted without the previous approbation of the sovereign Pontiff, it may be said, was very necessary, considering the ardor which afterwards urged many persons to establish new institutions; so that, without this prudent check, disorder would have been introduced in consequence of the exaggerated transports which urged some imaginations to exceed all bounds.

Some people take delight in relating the excesses into which some individuals of the mendicant orders fell; and they borrow the narratives of Matthew Paris, without forgetting the lamentations of St. Bonaventura himself. I wish not to excuse evil, wherever it is found; but I will observe, that the circumstances of the times when the mendicant orders were established, and the kind of life they were obliged to embrace, in order to fulfill the purpose for which they were intended, as I have pointed out in the text, rendered almost inevitable those evils which pious men sincerely deplored, and which the enemies of the Church lament with no less affectation than exaggeration.

Note 28, p. 305.

I have already shown, by numerous testimonies of scholastic theologians, how the divine origin of the civil power is to be understood; and it is evident that it contains nothing but what is perfectly conformable to sound reason, and adapted, at the same time, to the high aims of society. It would have been easy for me to accumulate testimonies; but I think I have adduced a sufficient number to throw light on the subject, and to satisfy every reader who, free from unjust prejudices, is sincerely desirous of listening to truth. In order, however, to view this subject under every aspect, I will add a few explanations on that celebrated passage of St. Paul to the Romans, chap. xiii., in which the Apostle speaks of the origin of powers, and of the submission and obedience due to them. Let it not be thought, however, that I purpose attaining this end by any reasoning more or less specious. Whenever a passage of Scripture is to be expounded in its true sense, we should not rely principally upon what our wavering reason suggests to us, but rather upon the interpretation of the Catholic Church; for this reason we should consult those writers whose high authority, founded on their wisdom and their virtue, leads us to hope that they have not deviated from the maxim, *Quod semper, quod ubique, quod ab omnibus traditum est.*

We have already seen a remarkable passage of St. John Chrysostom, explaining this point with as much clearness as solidity; we have also learned, from the testimony of the Fathers, what motives induced the Apostles to inculcate so pressingly the obligation of obedience to the lawful authorities. It only remains for us to insert here the commentaries of some illustrious writers on the text of the Apostle. In them we shall find, as it were, a code of doctrine; and when we come to appreciate the reasons on which the precepts inculcated in the sacred text are founded, we shall more easily discover their true meaning.

Observe, in the first place, with what wisdom, prudence, and piety this important subject is expounded by a writer who was not of the golden era, but, on the contrary, who lived in what is generally termed the barbarous age—St. Anselm. In his commentaries on the 13th chapter of the Epistle to the Romans, this doctor thus expresses himself:

" Omnis anima potestatibus sublimioribus subdita sit. Non est enim potestas nisi a Deo. Quæ autem sunt, a Deo ordinatæ sunt. Itaque qui resistit potestati, Dei ordinationi resistit. Qui autem resistunt, ipsi sibi damnationem acquirunt.

"Sicut superius reprehendit illos, qui gloriabantur de meritis, ita nunc ingreditur illos redarguere, qui postquam erant ad fidem conversi nolebant subjici alicui potestati. Videbatur enim quod infideles, Dei fidelibus non deberent dominari, etsi fideles deberent esse pares. Quam superbiam removet, dicens: *Omnis anima*, id est, *omnis* homo, *sit* humiliter *subdita potestatibus* vel secularibus, vel ecclesiasticis, sublimioribus se: hoc est, omnis homo sit subjectus superpositis sibi potestatibus. A parte enim majore significat totum hominem, sicut rursum a parte inferiore totus homo significatur ubi Propheta dicit: *Quia videbit omnis caro salutare Dei.* Et recte admonet, ne quis ex eo quod in libertatem vocatus est, factusque Christianus, extollatur in superbiam, et non arbitretur in hujus vitæ itinere servandum esse ordinem suum, et *potestatibus*, quibus pro tempore rerum temporalium gubernatio tradita est, non se putet esse subdendum. Cum enim constemus ex anima et corpore, et quamdiu in hac vita temporali sumus, etiam rebus temporalibus ad subsidium ejusdem vitæ utamur, oportet nos ex ea parte, quæ ad hanc vitam pertinet, subditos esse *potestatibus*, id est, res humanas cum aliquo honore administrantibus: ex illa vero parte, qua Deo credimus, et in regnum ejus vocamur, non debemus subditi esse cuiquam homini, id ipsum in nobis evertere cupienti, quod Deus ad vitam æternam donare dignatus est. Si quis ergo putat quoniam Christianus est, non sibi esse vectigal reddendum, sive tributum, aut non esse honorem exhibendum debitum eis quæ hæc curant *potestatibus*, in magno errore versatur. Item si quis sic se putat esse subdendum, ut etiam in suam fidem habere potestatem arbitretur eum, qui temporalibus administrandis aliqua sublimitate præcellit, in majorem errorem labitur. Sed modus iste servandus est, quem Dominus ipse præcipit, ut reddamus *Cæsari quæ sunt Cesaris, et Deo quæ sunt Dei.* Quamvis enim ad illud regnum vocati simus, ubi nulla erit potestas hujusmodi, in hoc tamen itinere conditionem nostram pro ipso rerum humanarum ordine debemus tolerare, nihil simulate facientes, et in hoc non tam hominibus, quam Deo, qui hoc jubet, obtemperantes. Itaque *omnis anima sit subdita sublimioribus potestatibus*, id est, omnis homo sit subditus primum divinæ potestati, deinde mundanæ. Nam si mundana potestas jusserit quod non debes facere, contemne potestatem, timendo sublimiorem potestatem. Ipsos humanarum rerum gradus adverte. Si aliquid jusserit procurator, nonne faciendum est? Tamen si contra proconsulem jubeat, non utique contemnis potestatem, sed eligis majore servire. Non hinc debet minor irasci, si major prælata est. Rursus si aliquid proconsul jubeat, et aliud imperator, numquid dubitatur, illo contempto huic esse serviendum. Ergo si aliud imperator, et aliud Deus jubeat, quid faciemus? Numquid non Deus imperatori est præferendus? Ita ergo *sublimioribus potestatibus anima* subjiciatur, id est, homo. Sive idcirco ponitur *anima* pro homine, qui secundum hanc discernit, cui subdi debeat, et cui non. Vel homo, qui promotione virtutem sublimatus est, *anima* vocatur a digniore parte. Vel, non solum corpus sit subditum, sed *anima*, id est, voluntas: hoc est, non solum corpore, sed et voluntate serviatis. Ideo debetis subjici, quia *non est potestas nisi a Deo.* Numquam enim posset fieri nisi operatione solius Dei, ut tot homines uni servirent, quem considerant unius secum esse fragilitatis et naturæ. Sed quia Deus subditis inspirat timorem et obediendi voluntatem, contigit ita. Nec valet quisquam aliquid posse, *nisi* divinitus ei *datum* fuerit. *Potestas* omnis *est a Deo.* Sed ea *quæ sunt, a Deo ordinatæ sunt.* Ergo potestas est ordinata, id est, rationabiliter a Deo disposita. *Itaque qui resistit potestati*, nolens tributa dare, honorem deferre, et his similia, *Dei ordinationi resistit*, qui hoc ordinavit, ut talibus subjiciamur. *Hoc enim contra illos dicitur, qui se putabant ita debere uti libertate Christiana, ut nulli vel honorem deferrent, vel tributa redderent.* Unde magnum poterat adversus *Christianam religionem scandalum nasci a principibus seculi.* De bona potestate patet, quod eam perfecit Deus rationabiliter. De mala quoque videri potest, dum et boni per eam purgantur, et mali damnantur, et ipsa deterius præcipitatur. *Qui potestati resistit*, cum Deus eam ordinaverit, *Dei ordinationi resistit.* Sed hóc tam grave peccatum est, *quod qui resistunt, ipsi* pro contumacia et perversitate *sibi damnationem* æternæ mortis acquirunt. Et ideo non debet quis resistere, sed subjici."

This remarkable passage contains all—the origin of power, its object, its duties, and its limits. We must observe, that St. Anselm expressly confirms what I have hinted in the text on the subject of the wrong meaning sometimes given in the first centuries to Christian liberty; many imagining that this liberty carried with it the abolition of the civil powers, and particularly of those which were infidel. He also shows the scandal which this doctrine might cause; thus explaining how the Apostles, without attempting to attribute to the civil power any extraordinary and supernatural origin, like that of the ecclesiastical power, had nevertheless powerful reasons for inculcating that this power emanates from God, and that whoever resists it, resists the ordinance of God.

Passing on to centuries nearer our own time, we find the same doctrines in the most eminent commentators. Cornelius a Lapide interprets the passage of St. Paul in the same way as St. Anselm, and explains, by the same reasons, the solicitude with which the Apostles recommended obedience to the civil powers. These are his words:

"*Omnis anima* (omnis homo) *potestatibus sublimioribus*, id est principibus et magistratibus, qui potestate regendi et imperandi sunt præditi; ponitur enim abstractum pro concreto; *potestatibus*, hoc est potestate præditis, *subdita sit*, scilicet iis in rebus, in quibus potestas illa sublimior et superior est, habetque jus et jurisdictionem, puta in temporalibus, subdita sit regi et potestati civili, quod propie hic intendit Apostolus; per potestatem enim, civilem intelligit; in spiritualibus vero subdita sit Prælatis, Episcopis et Pontifici.

"Nota.—Pro *potestatibus sublimioribus*, *potestatibus* supereminentibus vel *præcellentibus*, ut, Noster vertit, 1 Pet. ii., *sive regi quasi præcellenti*, Syrus vertit, *potestatibus dignitate præditis:* id est magistratibus secularibus, qui potestate regendi præditi sunt, sive duces, sive gubernatores, sive consules, prætores, &c.

"Seculares enim magistratus hic intelligere

Apostolum patet, quia his solvuntur tributa et vectigalia quæ hisce potestatibus solvi jubet ipse v. 7, ita Sanctus Basilius de *Constit. Monast.* c. 23.

"Nota.—Ex Clemente Alexand. lib. iv. *Stromatum*, et S. Aug. in Psal. cxviii. cont. 31, *Initio Ecclesiæ, puta tempore Christi et Pauli, rumor erat, per Evangelium politias humanas, regna et respublicas seculares everti;* uti jam fit ab hæreticis prætendentibus libertatem Evangelii: unde contrarium docent, et studiose inculcant Christus, cum solvit didrachma, et cum jussit Cæsari reddi ea quæ Cæsaris sunt; et Apostoli: idque ne in odium traheretur Christiana religio, et ne Christiani abuterentur libertate fidei ad omnem malitiam.

"Ortus est hic rumor ex secta Judæ et Galilæorum de qua Actor. 5, in fine, qui pro libertate sua tuenda omne dominium Cæsaris et vectigal, etiam morte proposita abnuebant, de quo Josephus, libr. xviii. *Antiqu.* 1. Quæ secta diu inter Judæos viguit; adeoque Christus et Apostoli in ejus suspicionem vocati sunt, quia origine erant Galilæi, et rerum novarum præcones. Hos Galilæos secuti sunt Judæi omnes, et de facto Romanis rebellarunt: quod dicerent populum Dei liberum non debere subjici et servire infidelibus Romanis; ideoque a Tito excisi sunt. Hinc etiam eadem calumnia in Christianos, qui origine erant et habebantur Judæi, derivata est: unde Apostoli, ut eam amoliantur, sæpe docent principibus dandum esse honorem et tributum.

"Quare octo argumentis probat hic Apostolus principibus et magistratibus deberi obedientiam. . . . . .

"His rationibus probat Apostolus Evangelium, et Christianismum, regna et magistratus non evertere, sed firmare et stabilire: quia nil regna et principes ita confirmat, ac subditorum bona, Christiana et sancta vita. Adeo, ut etiam nunc principes Japones et Indi Gentiles ament Christianos, et suis copiam faciant baptismi et Christianismi suscipiendi, quia subditos Christianos, magis quam Ethnicos, faciles et obsequentes, regnaque sua per eos magis firmari, pacari et florere experiuntur."

With regard to the mode in which civil power proceeds from God, the celebrated commentator agrees with the other theologians. Like them, he distinguishes between direct and indirect communication, and takes care to define the particular meaning of the term, *divine origin* of power, when applied to ecclesiastical authority.

In his explanation of these words, *all power is from God,* he thus expresses himself:

"*Non est enim potestas, nisi a Deo;* quasi diceret principatus et magistratus non a diabolo, nec a solo homine, sed a Deo ejusque divina ordinatione et dispositione conditi et instituti sunt: eis ergo obediendum est.

"Nota primo.—*Potestas sæcularis est a Deo mediate; quia natura et recta ratio, quæ a Deo est, dicat, et hominibus persuasit præficere reipublicæ magistratus, a quibus regantur. Potestas vero ecclesiastica immediate est a Deo instituta; quia Christus ipse Petrum et Apostolos Ecclesiæ præfecit.*"

The celebrated Dom Calmet explains the same passage with no less learning; he quotes numerous passages from the holy Fathers, showing what ideas the first Christians held on the subject of civil power, and how calumniously they have been accused of being the disturbers of public order.

"*Omnis anima potestatibus,* &c. Pergit hic Apostolus docere Fideles vitæ ac morum officia. Quæ superiori capite vidimus, eo desinunt, ut bonus ordo et pax in Ecclesia interque Fideles servetur. Hæc potissimum spectant ad obedientiam, quam unusquisque superioribus potestatibus debet. Christianorum libertatem atque a Mosaicis legibus immunitatem commendaverat Apostolus; at ne quis monitis abutatur, docet hic, quæ debeat esse subditorum subjectio erga Reges et Magistratus.

"Hoc ipsum gravissime monuerant primos Ecclesiæ discipulos Petrus et Jacobus; repetitque Paulus ad Titum scribens, sive ut Christianos, insectantium injuriis undique obnoxios, in patientia contineret, *sive ut vulgi opinionem deleret, qua discipuli Jesu Christi, omnes ferme Galilæi, sententiam Judæ Gaulonitæ sequi, et principum authoritati repugnare censebantur.*

"*Omnis anima,* quilibet, quavis conditione aut dignitate, *potestatibus sublimioribus subdita sit;* Regibus, Principibus, Magistratibus, iis denique quibus legitima est authoritas, sive absoluta, sive alteri obnoxia. Neminem excipit Apostolus, non Presbyteros, non Præsules, non Monachos, ait Theodoretus; illæsa tamen Ecclesiasticorum immunitate. Tunc solum modo parere non debes, cum aliquid Divinæ Legi contrarium imperatur: tunc enim præferenda est debita Deo obedientia; quin tamen vel arma capere adversus Principes, vel in seditionem abire liceat. Repugnandum est in iis tantum, quæ justitiam, ac Dei legem violant; in cæteris parendum. Si imperaverint aut idolorum cultum aut justitiæ violationem cum necis vel bonorum jacturæ interminatione, vitam et fortunas discrimini objicito, ac repugnato; in reliquis autem obtempera.

"*Non est enim potestas nisi a Deo.* Absolutissima in libertate conditus est homo, nulli creatæ rei, at uni Deo subditus. Nisi mundum invasisset una cum Adami transgressione peccatum, mutuam æqualitatem libertatemque homines servassent. At libertate abusos damnavit Deus, ut parerent iis, quos ipse principes illis daret, ob pœnam arrogantiæ, qua pares Conditori effici voluerunt. At, inquies, quis nesciat, quorumdam veterum Imperiorum initia et incrementa ex injuria atque ambitione profecta. Nemrod, exempli causa, Ninus, Nabuchodonosor, aliique quamplures, an Principes erant a Deo constituti? Nonne similius vero est, violenta Imperia primum exorta esse ab imperandi libidine? liberorum vero Imperiorum originem fuisse hominum metum, qui sese impares propulsandæ externorum injuriæ sentientes, aliquem sibi Principem creavere, datamque sibi a Deo naturalem ulciscendi injurias potestatem, volentes libentesque alteri tradiderunt? Quam vere igitur docet Apostolus, quamlibet potestatem a Deo esse, eumque esse positæ inter homines authoritatis institutorem?"

He points out four ways in which power may be said to emanate from God, and it is remarkable that none of them are extraordinary or supernatural; all of them serve to confirm more and more what reason and the very nature of things teach us.

"Omnino Deus potestatis autor et causa est.

I. Quod, hominibus tacite inspiraverit consilium subjiciendi se uni, a quo defenderentur. II. Quod imperia inter homines utilissima sint servandæ concordiæ, disciplinæ, ac religioni. Porro quicquid boni est, a Deo ceu fonte proficisciter. III. Cum potestas tuendi ab aggressore vitam vel opes, hominibus a Deo tradita, atque ab ipsis in Principem conversa, a Deo primum proveniat, Principes ea potestate ab hominibus donati, hanc ab ipso Deo accepisse jure dicuntur; quamobrem Petrus humanam creaturam nuncupat, quam Paulus potestatem a Deo institutam: humana igitur et divina est, varia ratione spectata, uti diximus. IV. Denique suprema authoritas a Deo est, utpote quam Deus, a sapientibus institutam, probavit.

"Nulla unquam gens sæcularibus potestatibus magis paruit, quam primæ ætatis Christiani, qui a Christo Jesu et ab Apostolis edocti, nunquam ausi sunt Principibus a Providentia sibi datis repugnare. Discipulos fugere tantum jubet Christus. Ait Petrus, Christum nobis exemplum reliquisse, cum sese Judicum iniquitate pessime agi passus est. Monet hic Paulus, resistere te Dei voluntati, atque æternæ damnationis reum effici, si potestati repugnas. 'Quamvis nimius et copiosus noster populus, non tamen adversus violentiam se ulciscitur: patitur,' ait sanctus Cyprianus. 'Satis virium est ad pugnam; at omnia perpeti ex Christo didicimus. Cui bello non idonei, non prompti fuissemus, etiam copiis impares, qui tam libenter trucidamur? si non apud istam disciplinam magis occidi liceret, quam occidere,' inquit Tertullianus. 'Cum nefanda patimur, ne verbo quidem reluctamur, sed Deo remittimus ultionem,' scribebat Lactantius. Sanctus Ambrosius: 'coactus, repugnare non novi. Dolere potero, potero flere, potero gemere: abversus arma, milites, Gothos quoque; lacrymæ meæ arma sunt. Talia enim sunt munimenta Sacerdotis. Aliter ne debeo nec possum resistere.'"

I have said in the text, that there was to be remarked a singular coincidence of opinions on the origin of society between the philosophers of antiquity, deprived of the light of faith, and those of our days who have abandoned this light; both wanting the only guide, which is the Mosaic history, have found in their researches after the origin of things, nothing more than chaos, in the physical as well as in the moral order. In support of my assertion, I will insert passages from two celebrated men, in which the reader will find, with very little difference, the same language as in Hobbes, Rousseau, and other writers of the same school.

"There was a time," says Cicero, "when men wandered in the fields like the brutes, feeding on prey like wild beasts, deciding nothing by reason, but every thing by force. No religion was then professed, no morality observed; there were no laws of marriage; the father could not distinguish his own children, and the possession of property by virtue of principles of equity was unknown. Hence the blind, unrestrained passions ruled tyrannically in the midst of error and ignorance, and used the powers of the body for their gratification as their most injurious satellites."

"Nam fuit quoddam tempus cum in agris homines passim bestiarum more vagabantur, et sibi victu ferino vitam propagabant; nec ratione animi quidquam, sed pleraque viribus corporis administrabant. Nondum divinæ religionis, non humani officii ratio colebatur; nemo nuptias viderat legitimas, non certos quisquam inspexerat liberos; non jus æquabile quid utilitatis haberet, acceperat. Ita propter errorem atque inscitiam, cæca ac temeraria dominatrix animi cupiditas ad se explendam viribus corporis abutebatur, perniciosissimis satellitibus." (*De Inv.* 1.)

The same doctrine is to be found in Horace:

"Cum prorepserunt primis animalia terris,
Mutum et turpe pecus, glandem atque cubilia propter
Unguibus et pugnis, dein fustibus, atque ita porro
Pugnabant armis, quæ post fabricaverat usus:
Donec verba, quibus voces sensusque notarent,
Nominaque invenere: dehinc absistere bello,
Oppida cœperunt munire et ponere leges,
Neu quis fur esset, neu latro, neu quis adulter.
Nam fuit ante Helenam mulier teterrima belli
Causa: sed ignotis perierunt mortibus illi,
Quos Venerem incertam rapientes, more ferarum,
Viribus editior cædebat, ut in grege taurus.
Jura inventa metu injusti fateare necesse est,
Tempora si fastosque velis evolvere mundi,
Nec natura potest justo secernere iniquum,
Dividit ut bona diversis, fugienda petendis."
Satir. lib. i. sat. 3.

"When men first began to crawl upon the earth, they were only like a herd of brute and speechless animals, contending with their nails or their fists for a few acorns or for a den. They afterwards contended with sticks and such arms as experience taught them to invent. At length they discovered the use of words to express their thoughts; gradually they became weary of fighting, and built cities, and made laws to prevent theft, robbery, and adultery; for, before Helen, women had been the cause of terrible wars. He who was the strongest, abusing his power, after the manner of brutes, attacked the weak, like a bull among a subject herd; they thus contended for the favors of inconstant Venus; but their end was inglorious. If you consult the origin of things, you will acknowledge that laws have been made in apprehension of injustice. Nature enables us to discern good from evil, what is to be sought after from what is to be avoided, but she is incapable of distinguishing justice from injustice."

NOTE 29, p. 311.

Concerning this question, as to the direct or indirect origin of civil power, it is remarkable, that, in the time of Louis of Bavaria, the imperial princes solemly sanctioned the opinion that power emanates directly from God. In an imperial Constitution, published against the Roman Pontiff, they established the following proposition: "In order to avoid so great an evil, we declare that imperial dignity and power proceed directly from God.—Ad tantum malum evitandum, declaramus, quod imperialis dignitas et potestas est immediate a Deo solo." That we may form an idea of the spirit and tendency of this doctrine, let us see what kind of man this Louis of Bavaria was. Excommunicated by John XXII., and at a later period by Clement VI., he went so far as to depose this latter Pontiff, in order to exalt to the Pontifical Chair the antipope Peter, for which reason the Pope, after repeated admonitions, divested him of his imperial dignity, substituting Charles IV. in his stead.

Ziegler the Lutheran, a zealous supporter of direct communication, in order to explain his doctrine, compares the election of a prince to that of a minister of the Church. The latter, says he, does not receive his spiritual authority from the people, but immediately from God. From this explanation it is evident with how much reason I have said, that such a doctrine tended to place the temporal and spiritual powers on a level, by making it appear that the latter could not claim, by reason of its origin, any superiority over the former. I do not mean, however, to assert, that this declaration, made in the time of Louis of Bavaria, had directly this aim, since it may rather be regarded as a sort of weapon employed against the pontifical authority, the ascendency of which was dreaded. But it is well known that doctrines, besides the influence resulting immediately from them, possess a peculiar force, which continues to develope itself as opportunities occur. Some time after, we see the kings of England defenders of the religious supremacy which they had just usurped, supporting the proposition advanced in the imperial Constitution.

I know not with what foundation it can be said that Ziegler's opinion was general before the time of Puffendorf; in consulting ecclesiastical and secular writers, we do not find the least support for such an assertion. Let us be just even to our adversaries. Ziegler's opinion, defended by Boecler and others, was attacked by certain Lutherans, amongst others by Boehmer, who observes, that this opinion is not favorable, as its partisans pretend, to the security of states and princes. To repeat what I have already explained in the text, I do not consider that the opinion of *direct communication*, rightly understood, is so inadmissible and dangerous as some have imagined; but as it lay open to an evil interpretation, Catholic theologians have done well to combat its tendency to encroach upon the divine origin of ecclesiastical power.

Note 30, p. 317.

I might quote a thousand remarkable passages showing the reader how unjust it is in the enemies of the clergy to accuse them of being favorable to despotism. But, to be brief, and to spare him the fatigue of perusing so many texts and quotations, I shall merely present to him a specimen of the current opinions on this point in Spain at the beginning of the 17th century, a few years after the death of Philip. II., the monarch who is represented to us as the personification of religious fanaticism and political tyranny. Among the numerous books published at that time on these delicate points, there is a very singular one, which does not appear to be very well known; its title is as follows:

A Treatise on the State and Christian Politics, for the use of Kings and Princes, and those holding government appointments, by Brother John de Ste.-Marie, a religious in the province of St. Joseph, of the order of our glorious Father St. Francis.

This book, printed at Madrid in 1615, furnished with all the privileges, approbations, and other formalities in use, must have been well received at that epoch, since it was reprinted at Barcelona in 1616, by Sebastian de Cormellas. Who shall say whether this work did not inspire Bossuet with the idea of that intituled *Politics derived from the very words of Scripture?* The title is certainly analogous, and the idea is in fact the same, although differently carried out. "I think," says Brother John de Ste.-Marie, "I shall escape all difficulty, by laying before kings in this work, not my own reasonings, nor those afforded by eminent philosophers and the records of profane history, but the words of God and His saints, and the divine and canonical histories, whose teaching commands respect, and whose authority cannot be prejudicial to any one, however powerful a sovereign he may be; in fact, to these a Christian cannot but submit, since every thing in them is dictated by the Holy Ghost, the author of these divine maxims. If I cite examples of Gentile kings, if I appeal to antiquity, and adduce passages from philosophers unconnected with the people of God, I shall do so incidentally only, and as we resume possession of what of right belongs to us, and has been unjustly usurped by others." (Chap. 2.)

The work is dedicated to the king. Addressing him, and praying him to read it, and not to allow himself to be imposed upon by those who would dissuade him from its perusal, the good religious says, with a pleasing candor, "Let no one tell you that these things are metaphysical, impracticable, and all but impossible."

The following inscription is placed at the head of the 1st chapter: "Ad vos (O Reges) sunt hi sermones mei, ut discatis sapientiam et non excidatis: qui enim custodierint justa juste, justificabuntur: et qui didiscerint ista, invenient quid respondeant." (*Sap.* 6, v. 10.)

In the first chapter, the title of which is, "A treatise in which the import and definition of this word commonwealth are briefly discussed," we read these remarkable words: "So that monarchy must degenerate if it be absolute and without restraint (for power and authority thus become unreasonable); in all things falling under the cognizance of law, it should be bound by the law; and in special and incidental matters it should be subject to advice, from the connection which it ought to have with the aristocracy, which is its assistant, and forms a council of learned and powerful men. Without this wise modification, monarchy will create great errors of government, will give but little satisfaction, but, on the contrary, will cause great discontent among the governed. The wisest and most enlightened men of every age have invariably considered this form of government the best; and without such a modification no city or kingdom has ever been considered well governed. Good kings and the wisest statesmen have always been in favor of this system; bad kings, on the contrary, elated by their power, have pursued the opposite course. Hence, if a monarch, whoever he be, decides by himself, without taking advice, or against the advice of his councillors, he passes the legitimate bounds of monarchy, and even when his decisions are fortunate, he is a tyrant. History is full of these examples and of their disastrous consequences; it will be enough to adduce one only, that of Tarquin the Proud, as related in the 1st book of Livy, a king whose pride was unbounded, and who, to render himself absolute, and to put every thing under his feet, strove to weaken the authority of the Roman Senate by diminishing the number of Senators, thus arrogating to himself an absolute right of decision in all the affairs of the empire."

In chapter 2, in which the author treats of "the meaning of the word king," we read as follows: "We meet here very opportunely with the third meaning of the word king, which is the same as that of father; as we find in Genesis, when the Sichemites gave to their king the name of Abimelech, which means 'Father and Lord.' Kings were formerly styled the fathers of their states. Whence King Theodoric, defining royal majesty (as Cassiodorus relates), makes use of these words: '*Princeps et Pastor publicus et communis.*—The king is the public and common father of the state.' From the extreme resemblance between the office of a king and that of a father, Plato was induced to call the king the father of a family; and the philosopher Xenophon says: *Bonus Princeps nihil differt a bono Patre.* The difference solely consists in one having few and the other a great number of persons under his dominion. And it is certainly very reasonable to give kings this title of father; for they ought to be the fathers of their subjects and of their kingdoms, watching over their welfare and preservation with the love and solicitude of a Father. Royalty, says Homer, is nothing else than a paternal government, like that of a father over his children: '*Ipsum namque regnum imperium est suapte natura paternum.*' *The best manner of governing well is, for the king to be possessed with the love of a father, and to regard his subjects as his own children. The love of a father for his children, his solicitude that they should want for nothing, his devotedness to each of them, all this bears the greatest resemblance to the love of a king for his subjects. He is called father, and this name lays him under the obligation of acting in accordance with the meaning it conveys.'* This name, so well adapted to kings, and which, when well considered, is the greatest of all titles and epithets of majesty and power, since it embraces all, the genus and the species, the father being alone the lord, the master, or the chief; this name, I say, is above all human names for expressing authority and solicitude. Antiquity, with a view to confer upon an emperor an extraordinary degree of honor, called him the Father of the State, which was greater than Cæsar, Augustus, or any other glorious name; it decreed him this title, either to flatter him, or to lay him under the weighty obligations required by the name of father. In fine, to give kings this name is to remind them of their duty, viz. to direct, govern, and maintain their states and kingdoms in justice; like good pastors, to feed their rational sheep; like physicians, to care for them and heal them; to take care of their subjects, as a father does of his children, with prudence, love, and solicitude; for the king is for *them*, rather than for himself. 'Kings are under greater obligations to their kingdoms and states than to themselves;' in fact, if we consider the institution of kings and monarchs, we shall find that the king was appointed for the good of the kingdom, and not the kingdom for the good of the king."

In his 3d chapter, of which the following is the title, "Whether the name of king necessarily implies an office," he thus expresses himself:—"Besides what we have advanced, it may be proved that the name of a king is the name of an office, by the common maxim, 'the benefice is the reward of the office.' Since, therefore, kings receive such great benefices, not only from the considerable tributes they receive from the State, but also from the advantage they derive from benefices and ecclesiastical rents, they certainly do hold an office, and that the greatest of all, for which reason the entire kingdom so bountifully assists them. This is what St. Paul says in his Epistle to the Romans: *Ideo et tributa præstatis*, &c. Kingdoms do not contribute for nothing; all those states, taxes, and great revenues, that name, that high authority and eminent dignity, are not given gratuitously. They would have their title of king for nothing if they had no subjects to rule and govern, and if they were freed from this obligation: *In multitudine populi dignitas regis.* This great dignity, wealth, rank, majesty, and honor, are possessed by them with the perpetual obligation of ruling and governing their states, so as to preserve them in peace and justice. *Let kings bear in mind, therefore, that they are only invested with this title to serve their kingdoms; and the latter, that kings ought to be paid.* They hold an office requiring them to labor: *Qui præest in sollicitudine*, says St. Paul. Such is the title and the name of king, and of him who rules: one who is the first not only as regards honors and enjoyments, but also as regards cares and solicitude. *Let them not imagine that they are kings merely in name and representation, and appointed only to make themselves honored;* merely to exhibit their royal person and sovereign dignity in a pompous manner, like some of the kings of the Persians and Medes, who were mere shadows of kings, forgetful of their office, as though they had never received it. Nothing is more destitute of life and substance than the shadowy image which stirs its arm or its head only when some one acts upon it. God forbade the Israelites to have statues or painted images, representing a hand where there was none, and a face that did not exist, exhibiting to the eye an imaginary body, and feigning by apparently living actions to see and to speak; for God loves not feigned images, painted men, or sculptured kings, like those spoken of by David: *Os habent et non loquentur, oculos habent et non videbunt.* What does it avail to have a tongue that speaks not, eyes that see not, ears that hear not, or hands which do not work? Is it any thing more than an idol of stone, bearing only the external representation of a king? To bear the supreme name and all authority, and not to be capable of any thing, sounds badly. The names which God has given to things are like the title of a book, which, in a few words, contains every thing that is included in the book. This name of king was given to kings by God himself, and contains every thing to which they are obliged by virtue of their office. If their actions are not in accordance with the name, it is as if the mouth should affirm what the head denies, like a buffoon, whom no one believes in earnest. Every one would regard as a mockery and a delusion a signboard bearing the inscription, 'Pure gold sold here,' if, in reality, nothing but tinsel was sold. The name of king should not be an empty thing, a mere superfluity in the royal person—it should be what it implies and gives itself out for. Your name indicates that you rule and govern; rule and govern, therefore, in reality. Do not be mere pasteboard kings, to use a common expression, that is, kings in name only. In France, there was a time when kings had nothing but the name, and the government was entirely in the hands of their generals, whilst they, like animals, were occupied only with gluttony and luxurious living. That it might be known they were living, for they never went out, they used to appear in public once a year, on the 1st of May, in the squares of Paris, seated on a throne, as kings in a dramatic representation, and there they were saluted, gifts were presented to them, and they, on their part, granted certain favors to whomsoever they thought proper. In order to show to what a degree of degradation they had fallen, Eginard tells us, in the beginning of his Life of Charlemagne, that they were devoid of courage and incapable of great actions; they merely held the empty name of king; for, in reality they were not kings, neither had they any participation in the government or riches of the kingdom; every thing was entrusted to the mayors of the palace, styled majors-domo of the royal household; and the latter usurped every thing to such a degree, that they left the wretched king nothing but his title. Seated on his throne, with his long hair and beard, the monarch played his part, pretending to give audiences to ambassadors arriving from all parts, and to furnish them with answers to convey to their masters; whilst in reality they merely answered according to the instructions they had received, either by word or writing, although they appeared to answer on their own responsibility. So that royal power for such a king was reduced to the mere name, to this throne and this ridiculous majesty; the real kings and masters were those favorites by whom the monarch was oppressed. God said of one of the kings of Samaria, that he was merely to be compared to a little vapor, which, seen from afar, appeared something, but when touched was no longer any thing. Simia in tecto rex fatuus in solio suo. (St. Bernard, *de Consider ad Eug.* cap. 7.) *A monkey on a housetop, which, presenting the appearance of a man, is taken for such by those who know not what it is; such is a useless king upon a throne. Monkeys also serve to amuse children, and the king is a laughing-stock to him who looks upon him apart from any royal act, invested with authority, and making no use of it. A king dressed in purple, seated on a throne with great majesty, suited to his grandeur, grave, severe, and terrible in appearance, but in reality an absolute nonentity. Like a painting* de la main du Greco, *which, placed in an elevated position, and seen from a distance, looks very beautiful, and produces a great effect, but when nearly approached is but a rough sketch.* All pomp and majesty, properly considered, are a mere sketch and shadow of a king. *Simulacra gentium,* says David, speaking of kings who have nothing but the name; and according to the Hebrew text: *Imago fictilis et contrita.* A figure of pounded earth, crumbling on all sides; an empty phantom, great in appearance, but a mere piece of deception. The name which Elifaz unjustly applied to Job is perfectly applicable here, when he designated this good and just king, a man void of foundation and substance, bearing only external appearances; he styled him *Myrmicoleon,* that is, the name of the animal which, in Latin, is called Formica-leo, because it is a monstrous conformation, one half of its body, in fact, representing a fearful lion, an animal always used as an emblem of a king, and the other half an ant, that is, a most feeble and insignificant thing. Such are the authority, the name, throne, and majesty of a fierce lion and of a powerful monarch; but as regards the essence, you will find only that of an ant. There have been kings whose very name filled the world with terror; but these kings were void of substance in themselves, in their kingdoms they were as mere ants; their names and offices were very great, but without effect. Let the king, therefore, bear in mind that he has an office to fulfill, and not only an office, but that he is obliged to speak and labor on all offices, of which he is the general superintendent. St. Augustine and St. Thomas, explaining that passage of St. Paul which treats of episcopal dignity, say, that the word *bishop,* in Greek, is composed of two roots signifying the same thing as *superintendent.* The name of bishop, king, and every other superior, are names signifying superintendence over, and co-operation with, every office. This is what is expressed by the sceptre used by kings in public acts, a ceremony used by the Egyptians, who borrowed it from the Israelites. The latter, in order to point out the duty of a good king, painted an open eye placed in an elevated position on the point of a rod in the form of a sceptre, representing, on the one hand, the great power of the king, the solicitude and vigilance which he ought to exercise; on the other, that he ought not to be satisfied with holding the supreme power, with occupying the most exalted and most eminent position, and, in possession of these, passing his life in sleep and repose; on the contrary, he should be the first in commanding and counselling, he should appear in every office, incessantly watching and inspecting, like a man doing the business in which he is engaged. Jeremiah also understands it in this sense, for when God asked him what he saw, he answered: *Virgam vigilantem ego video.* Thou hast seen well; and verily I tell thee, that I who am supreme, will watch over my flock; I who am a shepherd, will watch over my sheep; I who am a king and a monarch, will watch without ceasing over all my inferiors. *Regem festinantem,* says the Chaldean, a king who is in haste; for, although he has eyes and sees, if he remains in repose, in his pleasures and amusements, if he does not go about from place to place; if he does not act so as to become acquainted with all the good and evil that is going on in his kingdom, he is as though he did not exist. Let him consider that he is the head, and even the head of the lion, which even in its sleep keeps its eyes open; that he is the rod with eyes, that he is the torch; let him open his eyes, therefore, and sleep no longer, trusting to those who are blinded, and see no better than moles: who, if they have eyes, only employ them to see their own interest, and to distinguish at a greater distance what may conduce to their own profit and aggrandizement. Such persons have eyes for themselves, and it would be better if they had them not, for their eyes are those of birds of prey—of vultures."

In his fourth chapter, the title of which is, "On the office of kings," the author thus explains the origin of royal power and its obligations:—"From this it follows," says he, "that the institution of the state of royalty, or king, represented by the head, was not merely for the use and profit of the king himself, but for that of his whole kingdom. Hence he ought to see, hear, feel, and understand, not only by himself and for himself, but by all and for all. He ought not merely to fix his regards upon his own greatness, but on the good of his subjects, since it is for them, and not for himself, that he was born a king. *Adverte*, said Seneca to the Emperor Nero, *rempublicam non esse tuam, sed te reipublicæ.*—When men first issued from solitude, and united to live in common, they knew that every one would naturally labor for himself or his own family, and that no one would take an interest in all; they agreed to select a man of great merit, that all might have recourse to him; a man who, distinguished above all the rest by his virtue, his prudence, and courage, should be the chief over all, should govern all, watch over all, and should exert himself for the advantage of all — for the common weal—like a father for his children, or a shepherd for his sheep. Now, considering that this man, abandoning his own affairs to look after those of others, could not maintain himself and his family (every one was then maintained by the labor of his hands), it was agreed that all should contribute to his support, in order that he might not be distracted by any other occupations than those of the common weal and the public government. Such was the end for which kings were instituted—such was their beginning. The good king ought to be more solicitous for the public than for his own private interest. He possesses his grandeur at the expense of great solicitude; the anxiety, the disquietude of mind and body, which is fatigue for him, is repose, support, and protection for others. Thus smiling flowers and fruits, whilst they adorn the tree, exist not so much for the tree, nor on account of the tree, as for the sake of others. Do not imagine that all happiness is in the beauty and grace of the flower, and in those who are the flowers of the world: powerful kings and princes may be termed the flowers of the world, but flowers who consume their lives, who are full of solicitude, and whose fruit will rather contribute to the enjoyment of others than to their own. 'For,' says the Jew Philo, 'the king is to the kingdom what the wise is to the ignorant man, what the shepherd is to his sheep, the father to his children, light to darkness, and what God is upon earth to all his creatures.' The investiture he gave to Moses, when he appointed him the chief and king over his people, was to tell him that he ought to be as God, the common father of all: for the office and dignity of a king require all this. *Omnium domos illius vigila defendit, omnium otium illius industria, omnium vacationem illius occupatio.* (Seneca, *Lib. de Consol.*) This is what the prophet Samuel says to Saul, recently elected king, when he expounds to him the obligations of his office: 'Consider, Saul, that God has this day constituted thee king over all this kingdom; thou art bound by the office to govern the whole of it. Thou hast not been made a king to enjoy repose, to become proud, and to glory in the dignity of a king; but to govern thy kingdom, to maintain it in peace and justice, to defend and protect it against its enemies.' *Rex eligitur, non, ut sui ipsius curam habeat*, says Socrates, *et sese molliter curet, sed ut per ipsum ii, qui elegerunt, bene beateque vivant.* They were not created and introduced into the world for their own convenience and pleasure or to be fed upon every dainty morsel of food (if such were the case, no one would willingly submit to them); but they were appointed for the advantage and common good of all their subjects, to govern them, protect them, enrich them, preserve and serve them. All this is perfectly admissible; for although the sceptre and crown appear to be the emblems of domination, the office of a king is, strictly speaking, that of a slave. *Servus communis, sive servus honoratus*, are words which have sometimes been applied to a king, *quia a tota republica stipendia accipit ut serviat omnibus.* And the Supreme Pontiff glories in this title, *Servus servorum Dei.* In ancient times this name of slave was one of infamy; but since Christ bore it it has become a name full of honor. Now, since it is neither repugnant nor derogatory to the essence nor nature of the Son of God, neither can it be derogatory to the nature and grandeur of the king.

"Antigonus, king of Macedon, was perfectly aware of this, and said candidly to his son, when he rebuked him for the severity with which he governed his subjects: *An ignoras, fili mi, regnum nostrum nobilem esse servitutem?* Before his time Agamemnon expressed himself in the same manner: 'We live apparently in the midst of grandeur and exaltation; but in reality we are the servants and slaves of our subjects.' Such is the office of good kings —an honorable servitude. From the moment of their being created kings, their actions no longer depend upon their own will, but on the laws and rules which have been given them, and on the conditions upon which they have undertaken their office. And although they may fail to comply with these conditions (which are the effects of a human convention), they may not fail to comply with that dictated by natural and divine law, the mistress of kings as well as of subjects. Now, these rules are almost all included in the words of Jeremiah, which God, according to St. Jerome, addresses to kings on giving them the command:—*Facite judicium et justitiam, liberate vi oppressum de manu calumniatoris, et advenam, et pupillum, et viduam nolite contristare, neque opprimatis inique, et sanguinem innocentum non effundatis.* Such is the summary of the obligations of a king; such the laws of his institution, which lay him under the obligation of maintaining in peace and justice the orphan, the widow, the poor, the rich and the powerful man, and him who can do nothing for himself. Upon him rest the wrongs of his ministers towards some, the injustice suffered by others, the sorrows of the afflicted, the tears of those who weep, not to mention many other burdens—a flood of cares and obligations—imposed upon every prince or chief of a state. For if he is the head to command and govern, and to bear the burdens of others, he should also be the feet upon which the whole weight of the state is sustained. Kings and monarchs, says the holy man Job, as we have seen, bear and carry the world upon their shoulders, on account of their office. Hence the figure we meet with in the Book of Wisdom: *In veste poderis, quam habebat summus sacerdos, totus erat orbis terrarum.* From the moment a man is created king, let him consider himself loaded with a burden so heavy that a strong carriage would not support it. Moses felt this strongly; for God having made him His viceroy, His captain-general, His lieutenant in the government, instead of returning thanks for so distinguished a favor, he complains that so heavy a burden should be placed upon him. *Cur afflixisti servum tuum? Cur imposuisti pondus universi populi hujus super me?* Again, continuing his complaint, he says, *Numquid ego concepi omnem hanc multitudinem? Aut genui eam, ut dicas mihi: Porta eos?*—'Lord, have I conceived all this multitude, or begotten them, and thou shouldst say to me, Carry them on thy shoulders?' Now, it is remarkable that God said nothing of that to Moses; he merely tells him to rule and govern them, to fulfill towards them the office of captain and chief. Nevertheless, what says Moses? That God commanded him to bear them on his shoulders—*Porta eos.* It appears, then, that he has no reason to complain, since he is merely told to be the captain, to direct, rule, and govern. It is a common expression, 'A word to the wise is sufficient.' He who knows and understands what it is to govern and to be the chief, knows also that government and obligation are the same thing. The very words *regere* and *portare* are synonymous, and have the same meaning: there is no government nor employment without obligation and labor. In the distribution of the offices which Jacob made among his children, he appointed Reuben to be the first in his inheritance and the highest in command—*prior in donis, major in imperio.* And St. Jerome translates *major ad portandum,* for command and obligation are the same thing; and the obligation and the labor are so much more considerable as the command is more exalted. St. Gregory, in his *Morales,* says, that the power, domination, and rule of kings over the whole world should not be looked upon as an honor but as a labor. *Potestas accepta non honor, sed onus æstimatur.* And this truth was ever received by the blindest among the Gentiles. One of them, taking the same view of the subject, says, speaking of another Pagan, that his god Apollo had made him all glorious and happy by the gift of a certain office: *Lœtus erat, mixtoque oneri gaudebat honore.* So that power and command is composed of a little honor and weighty obligations. The Latin word for honor only differs from that for burden by one letter—*onos* and *onus.* Besides, there always were and always will be persons willing to undertake the responsibility for the sake of the honor, although every one avoids as much as possible any thing that lays him under an obligation, and seeks after what is glorious; a dangerous choice, for the latter is not always the most secure."

If such language is taxed with flattery, it would be difficult to comprehend what is meant by *telling the truth.* And observe, that the above truths are not told without reflection; the good religious takes such pains to inculcate them, that were it not for the childlike candor of his language, which discloses the purest of intentions, we might accuse him of irreverence. This passage is long, but exceedingly interesting, for it faithfully reflects the spirit of the age. Innumerable other texts might be adduced to prove how unjustly the Catholic clergy are accused of being favorable to despotism. I cannot conclude without inserting here two excellent passages from the learned Father Fr. Ferdinand de Zeballos, a religious of the order of St. Jerome in the Monastery of St. Isidore del Campo, and known by a work intituled, "False Philosophy, or Atheism, Deism, Materialism, and other new sects convicted of State Crimes against their Sovereigns and Rulers, against the Magistrates and Lawful Authorities." Madrid, 1776. Observe with what tact the learned writer appreciates the influence of religion upon society. (Book ii. dissertation 12, art. 2.)

"A mild and moderate government is most agreeable to the spirit of the gospel.

§ I.

"One excellent and estimable point in our holy religion is, that she offers to human policy, in her important truths, assistance in preserving good order among men with less trouble. 'The Christian religion,' says Montesquieu, with much truth, 'is far removed from pure despotism. Mildness being so strongly recommended in the gospel, it is opposed to the despotic fury with which princes might administer justice and practise cruelties.' This opposition on the part of Christianity to the cruelty of the monarch should not be active, but passive and full of mildness, which Christianity can never lose sight of without losing its character. This is the difference between Catholic Christians and the Calvinists and other Protestants. Basnages and Jurieu, in the name of all their reformation, wrote that it is allowable for the people to wage war against their princes whenever they are oppressed by them, or their conduct appears tyrannical.

"The Catholic Church has never changed the doctrines she received from Jesus Christ and His Apostles. She loves moderation, she rejoices in good: but she does not resist evil, she overcomes it by patience. Governments established under the direction of false religions cannot be satisfied with a moderate policy. With them the despotism or tyranny of princes, the ferocity of penalties, the rigor of an inflexible and cruel legislation, are so many necessary evils. But why has it been given to the Catholic religion only to purge human governments from such inhumanity? First, on account of the forcible impression produced by her dogmas; secondly, through the effect of the grace of Jesus Christ, which renders men docile in doing good, and energetic in combating evil. Wherever false religion predominates, and where, in consequence, these two means of aid are wanting, the government is under the necessity of supplying them as far as possible by efforts of a severe, harsh, and terror-inspiring policy, in default of that virtue which ought to exist in religion to restrain citizens.

"Hence the Catholic religion, by the influence of her dogmas over human affairs, relieves governments from the necessity of being harsh. In Japan, where the prevailing religion has no dogmas, and gives no idea of heaven or hell, laws are made to supply this defect—laws rendered useful by the cruelty with which they are conceived and the punctuality with which they are executed. In every society in which deists, fatalists, and philosophers have promulgated this error, that our actions are unavoidable, it is impossible to prevent laws from becoming more terrible and sanguinary than any we have known among barbarian nations; for in such a society, men, after the manner of brutes, being urged by palpable motives to do what they are commanded and omit what they are forbidden, these motives, with chastisements, must be daily more formidable, in order to avoid losing from habit the power of making themselves felt. The Christian religion, which admirably teaches and explains the dogmas of rational liberty, has no need of an iron rod to govern mankind. The fear of the pains of hell, whether eternal, to punish crimes unrepented of, or temporal, to wash away the stains of sins confessed, relieves judges from the necessity of augmenting punishments. On the other hand, the hope of gaining heaven, as a reward for laudable actions, words, and thoughts, induces men to be just, not only in public but also in the secrecy of the heart. What laws or penalties would avail governments not possessed of this dogma of hell and of glory, to make their citizens men of real merit? Materialists, denying the dogma of a future state, and deists, holding out to the wicked the flattering security of paradise, place governments under the painful necessity of arming themselves with all the instruments of terror, and of always inflicting the most cruel punishments, to restrain the people from destroying one another.

"Protestants have already come to this point by rejecting the dogma of the eternity of hell, or, at least, by preserving merely the fear of a temporary pain. The first reformers, as d'Alembert observes to the clergy of Geneva, denied the doctrine of purgatory, and retained that of hell; but the Calvinists, and modern reformers, by their limitation of the duration of hell, leave only what may be properly termed purgatory. Is not the dogma of the last judgment, when each one's secret offences, however small, shall be exposed to the whole world, of singular efficacy in restraining the thoughts and desires, and all the perversity of the heart and of the passions? It is evident that this dogma so far relieves political governments from the painful and continual vigilance which it would have to exercise over a town in which the idea of this judgment has perished, together with the thoughts which it inspires."

§ II.

"There are certain aberrations observable among philosophers, which lead us to think that these men were possessed of some true discernment in their lucid moments, or whilst they were in the Catholic religion. Hence they have said, 'that religion was invented for a political purpose, to spare sovereigns the necessity of being just, of making good laws, and of governing well.' This folly, which stands self-condemned when we come to speak of religion previously formed, supposes, nevertheless, the truth we are speaking of. It is evident to every one, even to the philosophers whose extravagant assertion we have just adduced, that the Christian religion, by her dogmas, is serviceable to human governments, and aids in making good citizens, even in this world. Yet they avail themselves of this very point to put forth their insane malice: but, in reality, and in spite of themselves, they mean to say, that the dogmas of religion are of such service to governments, and so efficacious in facilitating a great part of their work, that they appear to be formed on purpose, and according to the designs of a magistrate or a political government. We cannot say, on this account, that religion alone is sufficient to govern men, without any judicial aid, without the intervention of the laws and of penalties. In speaking of this efficacy of the dogmas inculcated by religion, we are not rash and presumptuous; we do not reject as superfluous the office of law and police. We are told by the Apostle, that for the just there would have been no need of laws; but there are so many wicked, who, through their forgetfulness of their destiny and the terrible judgments of God, live under the exclusive rule of their passions, that it has been found necessary to make laws and institute punishments, in order to restrain them. Hence, the Catholic religion does not reject the wise vigilance of police, nor abrogate its office; she seconds it, on the contrary, and receives assistance from it, to the very great advantage of good governments; the people, through its influence, are ruled better, and with less austerity and severity."

§ III.

"The second reason which renders the most mild and moderate governments sufficient in Catholic States is, the assistance which the grace of the gospel affords for doing good and avoiding evil,—an assistance imparted by the use of the sacraments, or other means employed by the Spirit from above. Without this, every law is harsh; this unction softens every yoke, renders every burden light."

In his third article, Father Zeballos repels the accusation of despotism with which the enemies of monarchy reproach it. On this occasion he points out the just limits of royal authority, and overthrows an argument which some persons have pretended to found on the Scriptures, for the exaggeration of the prerogatives of the throne. He expresses himself as follows:

"When the objection, that the sovereign had the power of seizing the property of every citizen, was made against monarchy, it was rather an argument against the nature of despotism than against the form of monarchical government. 'What does it avail,' says Theseus in Euripides, 'to amass riches for our heirs, to bring up our daughters with care, if we are to be deprived of the greater portion of these riches by a tyrant, if our daughters are to serve the most unruly passions?' You perceive, then clearly, that in pretending to argue against the office of a monarch, it is a tyrant only that is spoken of. True, the frequent abuse of power resorted to by kings has caused these names and forms to be confounded. Others have already observed that the ancients were scarcely acquainted with the nature of true monarchy; this was very natural, since they never witnessed any thing but the abuse of it. This gives me the opportunity of making a remark upon the circumstance of the Hebrews asking to be governed by kings. 'Make us a king to judge us, as all nations have,' said they to the prophet. Samuel saw with grief this levity, which was about to cause a total revolution in the government appointed by God. Nevertheless, God commands the prophet to take no notice of this affront, which was principally offered to the Lord; for they were abandoning Him, being unwilling that He should rule over them any longer. 'As they have forsaken Me, and served strange gods, so do they also unto thee,' and ask for kings like unto those of the nations. Observe what an intimate connection always exists between a change of government and a change in religion, especially when the change is from a true to a false one.

"But what is particularly deserving of notice is, the acquiescence granted to the people's demand. They wish to be ruled by kings, exactly as all other nations were. The Lord chastises their spirit of revolt by leaving them to their desires. He commands Samuel to comply with their request, but to point out to them, at the same time, *the rights of the king* who was to rule over them like unto the nations, and said: 'This will be the right of the king that shall reign over you: he will take your sons, and will put them in his chariots, and will make them his horsemen, and his running footmen, to run before his chariots; and he will appoint them to be his tribunes, and his centurions, and to plough his fields, and to reap his corn, and to make him arms and chariots. Your daughters also will he take to make him ointments, and to be his cooks and bakers; and he will take your fields, and your vineyards, and your best olive-yards, and give them to his servants. Moreover, he will take the tenth of your corn, and of the revenues of your vineyards, to give to his eunuchs and servants. Your servants also, and hand-maids, and your goodliest young men, and your asses, he will take away, and put them to his work. Your flocks also he will tithe, and you shall be his servants; and you shall cry out in that day from the face of the king whom you have chosen to yourselves; and the Lord will not hear you in that day, because you desired unto youselves a king. And the people would not hear the voice of Samuel, and they said, Nay, but there shall be a king over us, and we also will be like all nations.' (1st Kings, chap. viii., from verse 11 to middle of verse 20 inclusively.)

"Some persons, being determined to extend the power of kings beyond its limits, draw from these words the formula of royal right. A blind pretension, and reflecting little honor on legitimate monarchs such as the Catholic sovereigns. Unless a person wishes knowingly to deceive himself on this portion of the Scripture, or is blind, he may see by the context, and by comparing this passage with others, that it is not legitimate right that is here meant, but *de facto* right. I mean to say, that the Holy Spirit does not explain what just monarchs ought to do; but what had been done, and was still done, by the kings of Pagan nations, mere tyrants, and commonly so called. Observe, that the people demanded nothing but to be placed on an equality with the Pagan nations in a political point of view. They had not the prudence to demand a king such as he ought to be, but such as was common in those days; and this was what God granted them. If God, as the prophet observes, has sometimes given the people kings in His wrath, what people were more deserving of this than those who had abandoned God himself, and refused to be ruled by Him? Indeed, God did chastise His people severely by granting them their foolish demand. He did give them a king, but a king who was to exercise what, according to the perverse custom of the times, formed the royal right described in the sacred text just quoted.

"What man in our days, conversant with what has been written upon the different natures of governments, upon their abuse, and without even understanding what is said in the Scriptures, could imagine that the text of Samuel contains the legitimate form of royalty or of monarchy? Does this power impart the right of seizing the property of the subjects, their lands, their riches, their sons and daughters, and even their natural liberty? Is this the model of a monarchy, or of the most tyrannical despotism? To dispel every illusion on this point, we need only compare with what we have just read the 21st chap. of the third Book of Kings, in which the history of Naboth, an inhabitant of Jezrael, is narrated. Achab, the king of Israel, wished to enlarge the palace, or pleasure-house which he possessed in that town. A vineyard of Naboth's, near the palace, came within the plan of the gardens that were to be added. The king did not seize it at once, of his own authority, but asked the proprietor to let him have it on the honest condition of paying him the price at which he should value it, or giving him a better in another place. Naboth would not consent to this, because it was the inheritance of his ancestors. The king, not being accustomed to meet with a refusal, threw himself upon his couch oppressed with grief; the queen, Jezabel, came, and told him to calm his agitation: 'Thy authority is great indeed,' said she to him;

Grandis authoritatis es: she promises to put him in possession of the vineyard. This abominable woman wrote to the judges of Jezrael to commence an action against Naboth for a calumny, to be proved against him by two suborned witnesses; and she demanded that he should be condemned to death. The queen was obeyed; Naboth was stoned to death. All this was necessary that the vineyard might enter into the royal treasury, and that, watered by the blood of the proprietor, it might produce flowers for the palace of these princes. But, in reality, it produced none, neither for the king nor for the queen; it furnished them with nothing but briars and mortal poisons. Elias presents himself before Achab when he was going to take possession of Naboth's vineyard; he announces to him that he, and all his house, even to the dog that approacheth the wall, shall be erased from the face of the earth.

"You look upon royal right as explained to the people by Samuel as legitimate; tell me, then why Achab and Jezabel are so severely punished for taking the vineyard and the life of Naboth, *since the king had a right to take from his subjects their most valuable vineyards and olive trees,* according to the declaration of the prophet. If Achab possesses this right after he is established the king of the people of God, whence comes it that he, so violent a prince, should entreat Naboth with so much civility? And why is it necessary to accuse Naboth of some calumny? His resistance to the king's right, by refusing to accept the just value of what was suitable to the enlargement of the palace and gardens, would have been a sufficient motive for instituting an action against him. We find, however, that Naboth committed no injustice against the king by refusing to sell his patrimony, not even in the estimation of the queen, who boasted of her husband's *great authority.* This great authority, which Jezabel admitted in the king, was neither more nor less than the royal right spoken of by Samuel to the people; it was, as I have said, a *de facto* right to take and seize upon every thing by mere force, as Montesquieu says of the tyrant.

"*Do not therefore, mention this passage, nor any other of the Scriptures, to justify the idea of a government so ill-conceived. The doctrine of the Catholic religion is attached to legitimate monarchy, with its suitable characteristics, and in accordance with the qualities which modern publicists recognise, viz. as a paternal and sovereign power, but conformable to the fundamental laws of the state. Within limits so suitable, nothing can be more regular than this power, the most extensive of all temporal powers, and that which is most favored and supported by the Catholic Church.*"

Such is the horrible despotism taught by these men so basely calumniated! Happy the people who are ruled by a prince whose government is regulated by these doctrines!

NOTE 31, p. 330.

The importance of the matter treated of in this part of my work obliges me to insert here, at some length, passages proving the truth of what I have advanced. I did not think it advisable to give a translation of the Latin passages, that I might avoid augmenting excessively the number of pages; besides, among the persons who may wish to make themselves thoroughly acquainted with the subject, and who will consequently take an interest in consulting the original texts, there are few ignorant of the Latin language.

Observe how St. Thomas expresses himself on royal power, and with what solid and generous doctrine he points out its duties in the third book, chap. 11, of his treatise *De Regimine Principum.*

DIVUS THOMAS.

"*De Regimine Principum,* liber iii. caput xi.

"Hic Sanctus Doctor declarat de dominio regali, in quo consistit, et in quo differt a politico, et quo modo distinguitur diversimodo secundum diversas rationes.

"Nunc autem ad regale dominium est procedendum, ubi est distinguendum de ipso secundum diversas regiones, et prout a diversis varie invenitur traditum. Et primo quidem, in Sacra Scriptura aliter leges regalis dominii traduntur in Deuteronomio per Moysen, aliter in 1 Regum per Samuelem prophetam, uterque tamen in persona Dei differenter ordinat regem ad utilitatem subditorum, quod est proprium regum, ut Philosophus tradit in 8 ethic. Cum, inquit, constitutus fuerit rex, non multiplicabit sibi equos, nec reducet populum in Ægyptum, equitatus numero sublevatus, non habebit uxores plurimas, quæ alliciant animam ejus, neque argenti, aut auri immensa pondera: quod quidem qualiter habet intelligi, supra traditur in hoc lib. describetque sibi Deuteronomium legis hujus, et habebit secum, legetque illud omnibus diebus vitæ suæ, ut discat timere dominum Deum suum, et custodire verba ejus et cæremonias, et ut videlicet possit populum dirigere secundum legem divinam, unde et rex Salomon in principio sui regiminis hanc sapientiam a Deo petivit, ad directionem sui regiminis pro utilitate subditorum, sicut scribitur in 3 lib. Regum. Subdit vero dictus Moyses in eodem lib. Nec elevetur cor ejus in superfluum super fratres suos, neque declinet in partem dexteram, vel sinistram, ut longo tempore regat ipse et filius ejus super Israel. Sed in primo Regum, traduntur leges regni, magis ad utilitatem Regis, ut supra patuit in lib. 2 hujus operis, ubi ponuntur verba omnino pertinentia ad conditionem servilem, et tamen Samuel leges quas tradit cum sint penitus despoticæ dicit esse regales. Philosophus autem in 8 ethic. magis concordat cum primis legibus. Tria enim ponit de rege in eo. 4, videlicet, quod ille legitimus est rex qui principaliter bonum subditorum intendit. Item, ille rex est, qui curam subditorum habet, ut bene operentur quemadmodum pastor ovium. Ex quibus omnibus manifestum est, quod juxta istum, modum despoticum multum differat a regali, ut idem Philosophus videtur dicere in 1 politic. Item, *quod regnum non est propter regem, sed rex propter regnum,* quia ad hoc Deus *providit de eis, ut regnum regant et gubernent, et unumquemque in suo jure conservent:* et hic est *finis regiminis, quod si ad aliud faciunt in seipsos commodum retorquendo, non sunt reges sed tyranni.* Contra *quos dicit Dominus in Ezech.*

Væ pastoribus Israel, qui pascunt semetipsos. Nonne greges pascuntur a pastoribus? Lac comedebatis, et lanis operiebamini, et quod crassum erat occidebatis: gregem autem meum non pascebatis: quod infirmum fuit, non consolidastis, et quod ægrotum non sanastis, quod confractum non alligastis, quod abjectum non reduxistis, et quod perierat non quæsistis; sed cum austeritate imperabatis eis et cum potentia. In quibus verbis nobis sufficienter forma regiminis traditur redarguendo contrarium. Amplius autem regnum ex hominibus constituitur, sicut domus ex parietibus, et corpus humanum ex membris, ut Philos. dicit in 3 politic. Finis *ergo regis est, ut regimen prosperetur, quod homines conserventur per regem.* Et hinc habet commune bonum cujuslibet principatus participationem divinæ bonitatis: unde bonum commune dicitur a Philosopho in 1 ethic. esse quod omnia appetunt, et esse bonum divinum, *ut sicut Deus qui est rex regum, et dominus dominantium, cujus virtute principes imperant, ut probatum est supra, nos regit et gubernat non propter seipsum, sed propter nostram salutem: ita et reges faciant et alii dominatores in orbe.*"

Note 32, p. 336.

I have noticed the opinion of D. Felix Amat, Archbishop of Palmyra, with respect to the obedience due to *de facto* governments. I have remarked, that this writer's principles, besides being false, are opposed to the rights of the people. The Archbishop of Palmyra appears to have been at a loss to discover a maxim to which it is possible to conform under all circumstances that may occur, and which do occur but too often. He dreaded the obscurity and confusion of ideas when the legitimacy of a given case was to be defined; he wished to remedy an evil, but he appears to have aggravated it to an extraordinary degree. Observe how he sets forth his opinion in his work entitled *Idea of the Church Militant,* chap. iii. art. 2:

"The more I reflect," says he, "on the difficulties I have just pointed out, the more I am convinced that it is impossible to resolve them, even those which are ancient, with any degree of certainty; and it is equally impossible to derive any light from them to aid us in resolving those which are formed at the present day by the struggle between the prevailing spirit of insubordination in opposition to the judgment and will of the governor, and the contrary effort made to limit more and more the liberty of those who obey. Starting from the divers points and notions that I have laid down relative to the supreme power in all really civil societies, it appears to me, that, instead of losing time in mere speculative discussions, it will be more useful to propose a practical, just, and opportune maxim for the preservation of public tranquillity, especially in Christian kingdoms and states, and for affording the means of re-establishing it when it has been troubled or destroyed.

"The *Maxim.*—No one can doubt the legitimacy of the obligation of every member of any civil society whatever to obey the government which is de facto and unquestionably established. I say '*unquestionably established,*' because there is here no question of a mere invasion or temporary occupation in time of war. From this maxim follow two consequences: 1st, to take part in insurrections, or assemblages of people, addressing themselves to the constituted authorities with a view to compel them to grant what they consider unjust, is always an act contrary to right reason; always unlawful, condemned by the natural law and by the Gospel. 2dly, individual members of society, who combine together and take up arms, in small or large numbers, for the purpose of attacking the established government by physical force, are always guilty of rebellion, a crime strongly opposed to the spirit of our divine religion."

I will not here repeat what I have already said on the unsoundness, the inconveniences, and the dangers of such a doctrine, but merely add, that with respect to governments only established *de facto,* to grant them the right of commanding and exacting obedience involves a contradiction. To say that a *de facto* government is bound, whilst it does exist, to protect justice, to avoid crimes, to prevent the dissolution of society, is merely to maintain truths universally admitted, and denied by no one; but to add, that it is unlawful, and contrary to our holy religion, to combine together and raise forces for the overthrow of a *de facto* government, is a doctrine which Catholic theologians have never professed, which true philosophy has never admitted, and which no nation has ever observed.

Note 33, p. 343.

I insert here certain remarkable passages from St. Thomas and Suarez, in which these authors explain the opinions to which I have alluded in the text, respecting the differences which may arise between governors and the governed. I refer to what I have already pointed out in another place; we are not about to examine so much whether such or such doctrines are true, as to discover what were the doctrines at the time we are speaking of, and what opinion the most distinguished doctors formed on the delicate questions of which we are treating.

D. THOMAS.

(2. 2. Q. 42. art. 2° ad tertium.—Utrum seditio sit semper pecatum mortale?)

3. Arg. Laudantur qui multitudinem a potestate tyrannica liberant, sed hoc non de facili potest fieri sine aliqua dissensione multitudinis, dum una pars multitudinis nititur retinere tyrannum, alia vero nititur eum abjicere, ergo seditio potest fieri sine peccato.

Ad tertium dicendum; quod regimen tyrannicum non est justum quia non ordinatur ad bonum commune, sed ad bonum privatum regentis ut patet per Philosophum; et ideo perturbatio hujus regiminis non habet rationem seditionis, nisi forte quando sic inordinate perturbatur tyranni regimen, quod multitudo subjecta majus detrimentum patitur ex perturbatione consequenti quam ex tyranni regimine; magis autem tyrannus seditiosus est, qui in populo sibi subjecto discordias et seditiones nutrit, ut tutius dominari possit; hoc enim tyrannicum est, cum sit ordinatum ad bonum proprium præsidentis cum multitudinis nocumento.

Cardinalis Cayetanus in hunc textum. "Quis sit autem modus ordinatus perturbandi tyrannum et qualem tyrannum, puta secundum regimen tantum, vel secundum regimen et titulum, non est præsentis intentionis: sat est nunc, quod utrumque tyrannum licet ordinate perturbare absque seditione quandoque; illum ut bono reipublicæ vacet, istum ut expellatur."

LIB. I.

De Regimine Principum. (Cap. x.)

Quod rex et princeps studere debet ad bonum regimen propter bonum sui ipsius, et utile quod inde sequitur, cujus contrarium sequitur regimen tyrannicum.

Tyrannorum vero dominium diuturnum esse non potest, cum sit multitudini odiosum. Non potest enim diu conservari, quod votis multorum repugnat. Vix enim a quoquam præsens vita transigitur quin aliquas adversitates patiatur. Adversitatis autem tempore occasio deesse non potest contra tyrannum insurgendi; et ubi adsit occasio, non deerit ex multis vel unus qui occasione non utatur. Insurgentem autem populus votive prosequitur: nec de facili carebit effectu, quod cum favore multitudinis attentatur. Vix ergo potest contingere, quod tyranni dominium protendatur in longum. Hoc etiam manifeste patet, si quis consideret unde tyranni dominium conservatur. Non n. conservatur amore, cum parva, vel nulla sit amicitia subjectæ multitudinis ad tyrannum ut ex præhabitis patet: de subditorum autem fide tyrannis confidendum non est. Non n. invenitur tanta virtus in multis, ut fidelitatis virtute reprimantur, ne indebitæ servitutis jugum, si possint, excutiant. Fortassis autem nec fidelitati contrarium reputabitur secundum opinionem multorum, si tyrannicæ nequitiæ qualitercumque obvietur. Restat ergo ut solo timore tyranni regimen sustentetur; unde et timeri se a subditis tota intentione procurant. Timor autem est debile fundamentum. Nam qui timore subduntur, si occurrat occasio qua possint impunitatem sperare, contra præsidentes insurgunt eo ardentius, quo magis contra voluntatem ex solo timore cohibebantur. Sicut si aqua per violentiam includatur, cum aditum invenerit, impetuosius fluit. Sed nec ipse timor caret periculo, cum ex nimio timore plerique in desperationem inciderint. Salutis autem desperatio audacter ad quælibet attentanda præcipitat. Non potest igitur tyranni dominium esse diuturnum. Hec etiam non minus exemplis, quam rationibus apparet.

LIB. I. CAP. VI.

Conclusio; quod regimen unius simpliciter sit optimum; ostendit qualiter multitudo se debet habere circa ipsum, quia auferenda est ei occasio ne tyrannizet, ei quod etiam in hoc est tolerandus propter majus malum vitandum.

Quia ergo unius regimen præ eligendum est, quod est optimum, et contingit ipsum in tyrannidem converti, quod est pessimum, ut ex dictis patet, laborandum est diligenti studio, ut sic multitudini provideatur de rege, ut non incidat in tyrannum. Primum autem est necessarium, ut talis conditionis homo ab illis ad quos hoc spectat officium, promoveatur in regem, quod non sit probabile in tyrannidem declinare. Unde Samuel Dei providentiam erga institutionem regis commendans, ait, 1 Regum xiii.: Quæsivit sibi Dominus, virum secundum cor suum: deinde sic disponenda est regni gubernatio, ut regi jam instituto tyrannidis subtrahatur occasio. Simul etiam sic ejus temperetur potestas, ut in tyrannidem de facili declinare non possit. Quæ quidem ut fiant, insequentibus considerandum erit. Demum vero curandum est, si rex in tyrannidem diverteret, qualiter posset occuri. Et quidem si non fuerit excessus tyrannidis, utilius est remissam tyrannidem tolerare ad tempus, quam tyrannum agendo multis implicari periculis, quæ sunt graviora ipsa tyrannide. Potest, n. contingere ut qui contra tyrannum agunt prævalere non possint, et sic provocatus tyrannus magis desæviat. Quod si prævalere quis possit adversus tyrannum, ex hoc ipso proveniunt multoties gravissimæ dissensiones in populo, sive dum in tyrannum insurgitur, sive post dejectionem tyranni erga ordinationem regiminis multitudo separatur in partes. Contingit etiam ut interdum dum alicujus auxilio multitudo expellit tyrannum, ille potestate accepta tyrannidem arripiat, et timens pati ab alio quod ipse in alium fecit, graviori servitute subditos opprimat. Sic enim in tyrannide solet contingere, ut posterior gravior fiat quam præcedens, dum præcedentia gravamina non deserit, et ipse ex sui cordis malitia nova excogitat: unde Syracusis quondam Dyonisii mortem omnibus desiderantibus, anus quædem ut incolumnis et sibi superstes esset, continue orabat: quod ut tyrannus cognovit, cur hoc faceret interrogavit. Tum illa, puella, inquit, existens cum gravem tyrannum haberemus, mortem ejus cupiebam, quo interfecto, aliquantulum durior successit; ejus quoque dominationem finiri magnum existimabam, tertium te importuniorem habere cœpimus rectorem; itaque si tu fueris absumptus, deterior in locum tuum succedet. Et si sit intolerabilis excessus tyrannidis, quibusdam visum fuit, ut ad fortium virorum virtutem pertineat tyrannum interimere, seque pro liberatione multitudinis exponere periculis mortis: cujus rei exemplum etiam in veteri Testamento habetur. Nam Ajoth quidam Eglon regem Moab, qui gravi servitute populum Dei premebat, sica infixa in ejus femore interemit, et factus est populi judex. Sed hoc Apostolicæ doctrinæ non congruit. Docet n. nos Petrus, non bonis tantum et modestis, verum etiam discolis Dominis reverenter subditos esse. 2 Petr. ii. Hæc est enim gratia, si propter conscientiam Dei sustineat quis tristitias patiens injuste: unde cum multi Romani Imperatores fidem Christi persequerentur tyrannice, magnaque multitudo tam nobilium, quam populi esset ad fidem conversa, non resistendo, sed mortem patienter et armati sustinentes pro Christo laudantur, ut in sacra Thebæorum legione manifeste apparet; magisque Ajoth judicandus est hostem interemisse, quam populi rectorem, licet tyrannum; unde et in veteri Testamento leguntur occisi fuisse hi qui occiderunt Joas regem Juda, quamvis a cultu Dei recedentem, eorumque filiis reservatis secundum legis præceptum. Esset autem hoc multitudini periculosum et ejus rectoribus, si privata præsumptione aliqui attentarent præsidentium necem etiam tyrannorum. Plerumque enim hujusmodi periculis magis exponunt se mali quam boni. Malis autem solet esse grave dominium non minus regum quam tyrannorum, quia secundum sententiam Salomonis: Dissipat impios rex sapiens. Magis igitur ex hujus præsumptione immineret periculum multitudini de amissione regis, quam remedium de subtractione tyranni. Videtur autem magis contra tyrannorum sævitiam non privata præsumptione aliquorum, sed auctoritate publica procedendum. Primo quidem, si ad jus multitudinis alicujus pertineat sibi providere de rege, non injuste ab eadem rex institutus potest destitui, vel refrænari ejus potestas, si potestate regia tyrannice abutatur. Nec putanda est talis multitudo infideliter agere tyrannum destituens, etiamsi eidem in perpetuo se ante subjecerat: quia hoc ipse meruit in multitudinis regimine se non fideliter gerens, ut exigit regis officium, quod ei pactum a subditis non reservetur. Sic Romani Tarquinium superbum quem in regem susceperant, propter ejus et filiorum tyrannidem a regno ejecerunt substituta minori, scilicet consularia potestate. Sic etiam Domitianus, qui modestissimis Imperatoribus Vespasiano patri, et Tito fratri ejus successerat, dum tyrannidem exercet, a senatu Romano interemptus est, omnibus quæ perverse Romanis fecerat per Senatusconsultum juste et salubriter in irritum revocatis. Quo factum est, ut beatus Joannes Evangelista dilectus Dei discipulus, qui per ipsum Domitianum in Pathmos insulam fuerat exilio relegatus, ad Ephesum per Senatusconsultum remitteretur. Si vero ad jus alicujus superioris pertineat multitudini providere de rege, spectandum est ab eo remedium contra tyranni nequitiam. Sic Archelai, qui in Judæa pro Herode patre suo regnare jam cœperat, paternam malitiam imitantis, Judæis contra eum querimoniam ad Cesarem Augustum deferentibus, primo quidem potestas diminuitur, ablato sibi regio nomine, et medietate regni sui inter duos fratres suos divisa: deinde cum nec sic a tyrannide compesceretur a Tiberio Cesare relegatus est in exilium apud Lugdunum Galliæ civitatem. Quod si omnino contra tyrannum auxilium humanum haberi non potest, recurrendum est ad regem omnium Deum, quid est adjutor in opportunitatibus in tribulatione. Ejus enim potentiæ subest, ut cor tyranni crudele convertat in mansuetudinem, secundum Salomonis sententiam. Proverb. xii. Cor regis in manu Dei quocumque voluerit inclinavit illud. Ipse enim regis Assueri crudelitatem, qui Judæis mortem parabat, in mansuetudinem vertit. Ipse est qui ita Nabuchodonosor, crudelem regem convertit, quod factus est divinæ potentiæ prædicator. Nunc igitur, inquit, ego Nabuchodonosor laudo, et magnifico, et glorifico regem cœli, quia opera ejus vera et viæ ejus judicia, et gradientes in superbia potest humiliare. Dan. iv. Tyrannos vero quos reputat conversione indignos, potest auferre de medio vel ad infimum statum reducere, secundum illud Sapientes Eccles. x. Sedem ducum superborum destruxit Deus, et sedere fecit mites pro eis. Ipse enim qui videns afflictionem populi sui in Ægypto, et audiens eorum clamorem Pharaonem tyrannum dejecit cum exercitu suo in mare; ipse est qui memoratum Nabuchodonosor prius superbientem non solum ejectum de regni solio, sed etiam de hominum consortio, in similitudinem bestiæ commutavit. Nec enim abreviata manus ejus est, ut populum suum a tyrannis liberare non possit. Promittit enim populo suo per Isaiam, requiem se daturum a labore et confusione, ac servitute dura, qua ante servierat, et per Ezech. xxxiv. dicit: Liberabo meum gregem de ore eorum pastorum, qui pascunt seipsos. Sed ud hoc beneficium populus a Deo consequi mereatur, debet a peccatis cessare, quia in ultionem peccati divina permissione impii accipiunt principatum, dicente Domino per Osee xiii.: Dabo tibi regem in furore meo, et in Job. xxxiv. dicitur, quod regnare facit hominem hypocritam propter peccata populi. Tollenda est igitur culpa, ut cesset a tyrannorum plaga.

SUAREZ.

(Disp. 13. De Bello. sect. 8.—Utrum seditio sit intrinsece mala?)

Seditio dicitur bellum commune intra eamdem Rempublicam, quod geri potest, vel inter duas partes ejus, vel inter Principem et Rempublicam. Dico primo: Seditio inter duas partes Reipublicæ semper est mala ex parte aggressoris: ex parte vero defendentis se justa est. Hoc secundum per se est notum. Primum ostenditur: quia nulla cernitur ibi legitima auctoritas ad indicendum bellum; hæc enim residet in supremo Principe, ut vidimus sect. 2. Dices, interdum poterit Princeps eam auctoritatem concedere, si magna necessitas publica urgeat. At tunc jam non censetur aggredi pars Reipublicæ, sed Princeps ipse; sicque nulla erit seditio de qua loquimur. Sed, quid si illa Reipublicæ pars sit vere offensa ab alia neque possit per Principem jus suum obtinere? Respondeo, non posse plus efficere, quam possit persona privata, ut ex superioribus constare facile potest.

Dico secundo: Bellum Reipublicæ contra Principem, etiamsi aggressivum, non est intrinsece malum: habere tamen debet conditiones justi alias belli, ut honestetur. Conclusio solum habet locum, quando Princeps est tyrannus; quod duobus modis contingit, ut Cajet. not. 2. 2. q. 64 articulo primo ad tertium: primo si tyrannus sit quoad dominium, et potestatem: secundo solum quoad regimen. Quando priori modo accidit tyrannus, tota Respublica, et quodlibet ejus membrum jus habet contra illum; unde quilibet potest se ac Rempublicam a tyrannide vindicare. Ratio est; quia tyrannus ille aggressor est, et inique bellum movet contra Rempublicam, et singula membra; unde omnibus competit jus defensionis. Ita Cajetanus eo loco, sumique potest ex D. Thom. in secundo, distinctione 44, quæstione secunda, articulo secundo. De posteriori tyranno idem docuit Joann. Hus, imo de omni iniquo superiore; quod damnatum est in Concilio Constant. Sessione 8 et 15. Unde certa veritas est, contra hujusmodi tyrannum nullam privatam personam, aut potestatem imperfectam posse juste movere bellum aggressivum, atque illud esset propie seditio. Probatur, quoniam ille, ut supponitur, verus est Dominus: inferiores autem jus non habent indicendi bellum, sed defendendi se tantum; quod non habet locum in hoc tyranno: namque ille non semper singulis facit injuriam, atque si invaderent, id solum possent efficere, quod ad suam defensionem sufficeret. At vero tota Respublica posset bello insurgere contra ejusmodi tyrannum, neque tunc excitaretur propia seditio (hoc siquidem nomen in malam partem sumi consuevit). Ratio est: quia tunc tota Respublica superior est Rege: nam, cum ipsa dederit illi potestatem, ea conditione dedisse censetur, ut politice, non tyrannice regeret, alias ab ipsa posset deponi. Est tamen observandum, ut ille vere, et manifeste tyrannice agat; concurrantque aliæ conditiones ad honestatem belli positas. Lege Divum Thomum 1 de regimine Principum, cap. 6.

Dico tertio: Bellum Reipublicæ contra Regem neutro modo tyrannum, est propiissime seditio, et intrinsece malum. Est certa, et inde constat: quia deest tunc et causa justa, et potestas. Ex quo etiam e contrario constat, bellum Principis contra Rempublicam sibi subditam, ex parte potestatis posse esse justum, si adsint aliæ conditiones; si vero desint, injustum omnino esse.*

Listen to the language of P. Marquez in Spain, in the so-called despotic times: it is well known that his work intituled *El Gobernador Cristiano* was not one of those obscure books which are never widely circulated; it met with such success that it went through several editions, as well in Spain as in foreign countries. I will give the title at length, and I will add, at the same time, a note of the editions published at different epochs, in different countries, in different languages,—a note which is to be found in the edition of Madrid in 1773.

"The Christian Magistrate (*El Gobernador Cristiano*), according to the Life of Moses, the Ruler of the People of God, by the R. P. M. J. R. John Marquez, O. S. A., preacher to his Majesty King Philip III., Examiner of the Holy Office of the Inquisition, and Evening Professor of Theology at the University of Salamanca. New and sixth edition, with permission. Madrid, 1773."

"The Christian Magistrate, composed at the request and in honor of His Excellency the Duke of Feria, first published at Salamanca, in the year 1612; a second edition in the same town in 1619; a third edition at Alcala in 1634, and a fourth at Madrid in 1640; the fifth edition was published out of Spain, at Brussels, in 1664. This is the masterpiece among works of this nature which have been written among us.

"Father Martin of St. Bernard, of the Order of Cîteaux, translated this work into Italian, and had it printed at Naples, in 1646. It was also translated into French by M. de Virion, counsellor to the Duke of Lorraine, and it was printed at Nancy in 1621."

BOOK I. CHAP. 8.

"We have now to answer the contrary objections. We maintain that neither the divine nor the natural law has given to states the power of arresting the progress of tyranny by means so violent as that of shedding the blood of princes, they being the vicars of God, divinely invested with the right of life and death over other men. But so far as resisting their cruelty is concerned, it is incontestable that it may and ought to be done. They are not to be obeyed in any thing opposed to the law of God; we must, therefore, escape from their wicked commands, and prevent their blows, as Jonathan did with regard to Saul, his father, when he saw him take his spear to smite David, and when, rising from the table, he went in search of the latter, and warned him of his danger. It is also sometimes allowable to resist princes by force of arms, in order to prevent them from executing notoriously rash and cruel determinations; for, according to the words of St. Thomas, this is not to excite sedition, but to stop and prevent it. Tertullian affirms the same thing when he says: 'Illis nomen factionis accommodandum est, qui in odium bonorum et proborum conspirant, cum boni, cum pii congregantur, non est factio dicenda, sed curia.'

"This is the reason why the blessed St. Hermenegildus, a glorious Spanish martyr, took up arms and entered the field against King Leovigildus, an Arian, to resist the great persecution directed by this prince against the Catholics. This fact is related by the contemporary historians. True, St. Gregory of Tours condemns this act of our king-martyr, not for having resisted his sovereign, but because the former was both his king and his father: and he maintains that although he was a heretic, his son ought not to have resisted him. This reply, however, is not well founded, as Baronius observes. Moreover, the authority of this Gregory was combated by another Gregory, greater than he, St. Gregory the Great, who, in the preface to his book of *Morales*, approves of the embassy of Leander, sent to Constantinople by St. Hermenegildus, to solicit the aid of Tiberius against Leovigildus, his father. It is indubitable that however strong may be the obligation of filial piety, that of religion is still stronger. The latter obliges us to sacrifice every thing if it be necessary; and it is on account of cases of this nature, that it is written of the tribe of Levi: 'Qui dixerunt patri suo et matri suæ, necio vos, et fratribus suis ignoro vos, nescierunt filios suos.' Such was the conduct of the Levites when they took up arms, by the command of Moses, to punish their relations for the sin of idolatry.

"If the prince should go so far as personally to make an attempt upon the life of the subject who has no other means of defending himself than killing him,—as when Nero, parading the streets of Rome, followed by a troop of armed men, attacked the quiet and unsuspecting citizens; I say, that in such a case it would be allowable to kill him; for if it is true, as Fr. Dominic de Soto observes, that the subject in this extremity is to suffer himself to be killed, and so prefer the monarch's life to his own, it is solely in the case when the death of the monarch would give rise to great troubles and civil wars in the state; in any other case it would be monstrously inhuman to force men to a thing so insupportable. But when the subject's property is merely to be defended against the cupidity of the monarch, it should not be allowable to lay hands on him; for it is a privilege granted to princes by divine and human laws, that their blood shall not be spilt for any outrage which, committed by any other violator of private property, would be a sufficient

* An extract from Bellarmine de Romano Pont. is here omitted.

motive for taking away his life. The reason of this is, that the life of the king is the soul and bond of the state; that it is of more importance than the property of individuals; that it is better to tolerate grievances of this nature, than to destroy the head of the state."

NOTE 34, p. 348.

In order to give an idea of the means employed at this epoch to limit the power of the monarch, by forming associations, whether among the people themselves, or between the people, the grandees, and the clergy, I insert here the letter, or *Charter of Fraternity* (*Hermandad*), which the kingdoms of Leon and Galicia made with Castile. I have extracted this piece literally from the collection intituled *Bullarium ordinis militiæ santi Jacobi Gloriosissimi Hispaniarum patroni*, p. 223. It will prove to us the existence already, at a remote epoch of our history, of a lively instinct for liberty, although ideas were still limited to a secondary order.

"1. In the name of God and of the blessed Virgin. Amen.

"Be it known to all those who shall read this letter, that on account of the innumerable acts of injustice, injuries, deeds of violence, murders, imprisonments, insolent refusals of audience, opprobriums, and other outrages without measure, committed against us by the king D. Alphonso, to the contempt of God, of justice, of right, and to the great detriment of all these kingdoms; we, the infantes, the prelates, the rich men, the councils, the orders, the knights of the kingdoms of Leon and Galicia, seeing ourselves overwhelmed with injustice and ill-treatment, as we have stated above, and finding it insupportable; our lord the infante Don Sancho has thought good and appointed that we should be of one mind and of one heart, he with us and we with him, to maintain our laws, our privileges, and our charters, in our usages, our manners, our liberties, and franchises, which we enjoyed under king Don Alphonso, his great-grandfather, the conqueror at the battle of Merida, and under king Don Ferdinand, his grand-father; under the emperor and all the other kings of Spain, their predecessors; and under the king Don Alphonso, his father,—all princes who have best merited our gratitude; and our said lord the infante Don Sancho has bound us to this effect by oath and promise, as it is certain by letters between him and us. Considering that it is agreeable to the service of God, of the blessed Virgin, of the court of Heaven, to the defence and honor of the holy Church, of the infante Don Sancho, and of the kings who shall succeed him, in fine, to the advantage of the whole country, we ordain and establish fraternity (*hermandad*), now and for ever, we the whole of the kingdoms above named, with the councils of the kingdom of Castile, with the infantes, the rich men, the hidalgos, the prelates, the orders, the knights, and all others who are in this kingdom, and who are willing to be with us, as it has just been said.

"2. Be it known to them, that we will insure to our lord the infante Don Sancho, and to all other kings who shall succeed him, all their rights, all their suzerainty, wholly and entirely, as we have promised, and as they are contained in the privilege which he has given us to this effect. Justice shall continue to be decreed by the suzerainty. The Martiniega* shall be paid in the place and in the manner in which it was customary to pay it, according to right, to Don Alphonso, the conqueror at the battle of Merida. The money † shall be paid at the end of seven years in the usual place and manner, the kings not enjoining the coining of money. The repast (*yantar*) ‡ shall be taken in the place in which it was usual for the kings to take it, according to the *fuero*, once a year, while visiting the very place, as it was given to the king Don Alphonso, his great-grandfather, and to the king Don Ferdinand, his grandfather. The *fonsadera*, § when the king is with the army, in the customary place, according to the *fuero* and right in the days of the abovenamed kings, guaranteeing to each the privileges, charters, liberties, and franchises appertaining to us.

"3. Be it known to them moreover, that we will maintain all our rights, usages, customs, privileges, charters, all our liberties and franchises, always and in such a manner, that should the king, the infante Don Sancho, or the kings who shall succeed them, or any of the lords, alcades, merinos, or any other persons, attempt to infringe upon them, in whole or in part, in any way or at any time, we will unite into one entire whole, and inform the king, the infante Don Sancho, or those who shall succeed them, of the nature of our complaint, and ask them if they are willing to reform; and if not, we will unite into one entire body to defend and protect ourselves, as it is ordained in the charter granted us by the infante Don Sancho.

"4. Moreover, be it known to them that no member of this *hermandad* shall be chastised, and nothing shall be taken from him contrary to right and the custom of the place, in the councils of the said *hermandad;* and it shall not be allowable to take from him more than is demanded by the *fuero*, in the place in which he shall be.

"5. We protest, that if an alcade, a merino, or any other person, on the authority of a letter of the king, of the infante Don Sancho, by his command, or that of the kings who shall succeed him, shall kill a man of our *hermandad* without hearing him and judging him according to law, that we, the *hermandad*, will take away his life for such an act. And if we cannot arrest him, he shall be declared an enemy to the *hermandad;* every member of the *hermandad* who shall have concealed him shall fall under the penalty of perjury and felony, and shall be treated in his turn as an enemy to this *hermandad*.

"6. We declare, moreover, that the port-duties shall be paid by us only in conformity to the rights and usages of the times of Don Alphonso, or the king Don Ferdinand, and the councils of the *hermandad* will not permit any person to receive them beyond this measure.

* Tribute that was paid on St. Martin's day.

† Another tribute.

‡ A tribute for the king's repast during his journeys.

§ Tribute for maintaining the ditches of the castles in Castile, and the armies.

"7. Moreover, no infante or rich man shall be a merino or grand bailiff in the kingdoms of Leon and Galicia. Neither can these functions be exercised by an infançon, or a knight having notoriously a great number of knights or other men of the country in vassalage; neither can they be exercised by a stranger to the country. And we so will it, because such was the custom in the days of the king Don Alphonso and of the king Don Ferdinand.

"8. All those who may wish to appeal from the judgment of the king, or of Don Sancho, or of other kings who shall succeed him, may do so; they shall have recourse to the book of the *Fuero Juzgo,* in the kingdom of Leon, as was usual in the days of the kings who preceded this. That if the right of appeal be refused to any who may wish to invoke it, we, on our part, will act according to the injunctions contained in the charters granted us by Don Sancho.

"9. That we may guarantee and execute all the acts of this *hermandad,* we make a seal of two plates, bearing the following impressions: upon one of the plates, the figure of a lion; and upon the other, the figure of St. James on horseback, with a sword in his right hand; in his left, a standard with a cross at the top, and shells. The inscription shall be thus expressed: '*The Seal of the Hermandad of the Kingdoms of Leon and Galicia.*' This seal shall be affixed to the documents which shall be required by this *hermandad.*

"10. We the whole *hermandad* of Castile, make a promise and render homage to all the *hermandad* of the kingdoms of Leon and Galicia, that we will assist each other well and loyally to keep and maintain every one of the above-named things. That if we fail to do so, we are traitors for this alone, like him who slays his lord or surrenders a castle; and may we never in that case have either hands, or tongues, or arms to protect ourselves.

"11. But lest there should be any doubt about the pact we are now making, in order that this pact may be for ever inviolate, we seal this letter with the two seals of the *hermandad* of Castile, Leon, and Galicia, and place it in the hands of D. Pedro Nunez, and the Order of the Knights of St. John, who are united with us in this *hermandad.* Given at Valladolid, the 8th day of July, in the year one thousand three hundred and twenty."

Spain had passed through many centuries without knowing of any other religion than the Catholic. She still preserved in all its force and vigor, the idea that the king should be the first to observe the laws; that he could not rule the people according to his caprice; that he ought to govern by principles of justice and views of public expediency. Saavedra, in his *Devises,* thus expressed himself:—

"1st. Laws are vain when the prince who promulgates them does not confirm and uphold them by his own life and example. A law will appear lenient to the people when observed by its author.

"In commune jubes si quid, censesve tenendum,
Primus jussa sibi, tunc observantior æqui
Fit populus, nec ferre vetat, cum videri ipsum
Auctorem parere sibi.

"The laws promulgated by Servius Tullius were not only intended for the people, but also for kings. The disputes between the monarch and his subjects were to be settled in conformity with these laws, as Tacitus relates of Tiberius: 'Although we are not subject to the laws,' said the emperors Severus and Antonius, 'let us conform our lives to these laws.' The monarch is bound by the law not merely from the fact of its being a law, but from the very reason upon which it is founded, when it is natural and common to all, and not particular and exclusively destined to the right government of subjects; for in this case the observance of the law merely concerns the subject, although the monarch, if it should so happen, is bound to obey it, in order to render it tolerable to others. Such appears to have been the meaning of the mysterious command given by God to Ezechiel, *to eat the volume,* that others seeing him the first to taste the laws and declare them good, might be induced to imitate him. The kings of Spain are so far subject to the laws, that the Treasury, in causes relating to the royal patrimony, is absolutely subject to the same laws as the least of his subjects; and in doubtful cases, the Treasury is condemned. Philip II. thus ordained it; and on an occasion in which his grandson Philip IV., the glorious father of V. A., was personally brought to judgment in an important trial of the Chamber, before the royal council, the judges had the noble determination to condemn him, and his majesty had the rectitude to hear the sentence without expressing any indignation. Happy empire, in which the cause of the monarch is always the least favored!"

Note 35, p. 356.

Sufficient attention has not perhaps been paid to the merit of the industrial organization introduced into Europe from the earliest ages, and which became more and more diffused after the twelfth century. I allude to the trades-unions, and other associations, which, established under the influence of the Catholic religion, commonly placed themselves under the patronage of some Saint, and had pious foundations for the celebration of their feasts, and for assisting each other in their necessities. Our celebrated Capmany, in his *Historical memoirs on the Marine, Commerce, and the Arts of the ancient City of Barcelona,* has published a collection of documents, very valuable for the history of the working classes and of the development of their influence on politics. Few works have appeared in foreign countries, in the latter part of the last century, of such great merit as that of our fellow-countryman, published in 1779. One very interesting chapter of this work is devoted to the institution of trades-corporations. I give here a copy of the chapter, which I particularly recommend to the perusal of those persons who imagine that nothing had been thought of in Europe for the benefit of the laboring classes, of those who are so foolish as to look upon that as a means of slavery and exclusivism, which was in reality a means of encouragement and of mutual support. It also appears to me that, by reading the philosophical remarks of Capmany, every sensible man will be convinced that Europe, from the earliest ages, has possessed systems adapted to the encouragement of industry, to the preservation of it from the fatal agitations of those times, to secure esteem for it, and to the legitimate and salutary development of the popular element. It will be no less useful to present this sketch to certain foreign writers, continually occupied with social and political economy, and who, nevertheless, in compiling the history of that science, have not even been acquainted with a work so important for every thing connected with the middle ages of Europe, from the eleventh to the eighteenth century.

"*Of the institution of the Trades-Corporations and other Associations of Artisans at Barcelona.*

"No memoir has hitherto been discovered which might serve to enlighten and guide us in fixing the exact epoch of the institution of the trades-associations at Barcelona.* But according to all the conjectures furnished by ancient monuments, it is very probable that the political erection or formation of the bodies of laborers took place in the time of Don Jaime I., under whose glorious reign the arts were developed under a favorable influence; whilst commerce and navigation took a higher flight, owing to the expeditions of the Aragonese arms beyond the seas. Increased facilities in the means of transport have given an impetus to industry; and an increasing population, the natural result of labor, by its reaction apon labor, augmented the demand for it. At Barcelona, as every where else, trades-corporations naturally arose when the wants and the tastes of society had, of necessity, grown so multifarious, that artisans were forced, with a view to secure protection to their industry, to form themselves into communities. Luxury, and the tastes of society, like every other object of commerce, are subject to continual change; hence, new branches of trade are continually springing up and displacing others; so that at one period each separate art runs into various branches, whilst at another, several arts are combined into one. At Barcelona, corporate industry has passed through all these vicissitudes in the course of five centuries. The hardware trade has comprised at different periods eleven or twelve branches, and consequently afforded subsistence to as many classes of families, whilst at the present time these same branches are reduced to eight, in consequence of certain changes in fashions and customs.

"In accordance with the social system which generally prevailed at that time in most European countries, it was found necessary to bestow liberty and privileges upon an industrious and mercantile people, who thus became a great source of strength and support to kings; and this could not be effected without classifying the citizens. But these lines of demarcation could not be maintained distinct and inviolate without a political division of the various corporations in which both men and their occupations were classified. This division was the more necessary in a city like Barcelona, which, ever since the middle of the thirteenth century, had assumed a sort of democratic independence in its mode of government. Thus, in Italy, the first country in the West that reestablished the name and the influence of the people, after these had been effaced in the iron ages by Gothic rule, the industrial classes had already been formed into corporations, which gave stability to the arts and trades, and conferred great honors upon them in those free cities, where, amidst the flux and reflux of invasions, the artisan became a senator, and the senator an artisan. Wars and factions, endemic evils in that delightful country at the time of which we are speaking, could not, in spite of all their ravages, effect the destruction of the associated trades, whose political existence, when once their members were admitted to a share in the government, formed the very basis of the constitution of both nations, inasmuch as both were industrial and mercantile. At Barcelona the trades were well regulated, prosperous, and flourishing, under that municipal system, and that consular jurisprudence, of which commerce, and its invariable concomitant, industry, have always stood in need. It was thus that this capital became one of the most celebrated centres of the manufacturing industry of the middle ages—a reputation which it has maintained and increased up to the present time. In like manner, it was under the name and rule of corporations and brotherhoods that trades were established in Flanders, in France, and in England, countries in which the arts have been carried to their highest degree of perfection and renown. The trades-corporations of Barcelona, even when viewed merely as a necessary institution for the due regulation of the primitive form of municipal government, should be regarded as most important, whether for the preservation of the arts, or as forming the basis of the influence of the artisans themselves. It is at once evident, from the experience of five centuries, that trades-unions have effected unspeakable good in Barcelona, were it only by preserving, as an imperishable deposite, the love, the tradition, and the memory of the arts. They have formed so many rallying points, so many banners, as it were, under which more than once the shattered forces of industry have found refuge; and have thus been enabled to recover their energy and activity, and to perpetuate their existence to our own days, in spite of pestilence, wars, factions, and a multitude of other calamities, which exhaust men's energies, overthrow their habitations, and change their manners. If Barcelona, so often visited by these physical and political plagues, had possessed no community, no bond, no common interest among its artisans, it would certainly have witnessed the destruction of their skill, their economy, and their activity, as is the case with beavers, when their communities have been broken up and dispersed by the hunters.*

* "It is extremely difficult to ascertain the origin of the trades-corporations, even in those towns which have been the longest and the best disciplined.—Sandi, in his *Civil History of Venice* (t. ii part 1, lib. iv. p. 767), after having reckoned sixty-one trades-corporations existing in that capital at the beginning of his century, declares that it is impossible to assign to each of these corporations the date of its origin, or that of its first statutes. This historian nevertheless consulted all the archives of the republic; he contents himself with observing, that none of the corporations are anterior to the fourteenth century." (*The notes which accompany this chapt r are those of Capmany himself.*)

* We here recognise many ideas taken from a

"By a happy effect of the security enjoyed by families in their different trades, and thanks to the aid, or *mont-de-piete*, established in the very bosom of the corporation for its necessitous members, who, without this assistance, might have been plunged into misery, these economical establishments at Barcelona have directly contributed to maintain the prosperity of the arts, by shutting out misery from the workshop, and preserving the operatives from indigence. Without this corporate police, by which each trade is surrounded, the property and the fortune of the artisan would have been exposed to the greatest risks; moreover, the credit and stability of the trades themselves would have been perilled; for then the quack, the unskilled operative, and the obscure adventurer, might have imposed upon the public with impunity, and a pernicious latitude might have taken the place of liberty. On the other hand, the trades-corporations being powerful associations, each one by itself being governed by a unanimity of intelligence and a community of interests, could purchase their stocks of raw materials seasonably and advantageously. They supplied the wants of the masters; they made advances, or stood security, for those of their members who lacked either time or funds for making great preliminary disbursements of capital at their own cost. Besides, these corporations, comprehending and representing the industry of the nation, and consequently feeling an interest in its maintenance, addressed from time to time memorials to the Municipal Council, or to the Cortes, relative to the injuries they were sustaining, or the approach of which they, as it often happened, foresaw from the introduction of counterfeit goods, or of foreign productions, which is a cause of ruin to our industry. In fine, without the institution of trades-corporations, instruction would have been void of order and fixed rules; for where there are no masters duly authorized and permanently established, neither will there be any disciples; and all regulations, in default of an executive power to see them observed, will be disregarded and trodden under foot. Trades-corporations are so necessary to the preservation of the arts, that the various trades known at the present day in this capital have derived their appellations and their origin from the economical divisions, and from the arts established by these corporations. When the blacksmith in his shop made ploughshares, nails, keys, knives, swords, &c., the names of the trades of the blacksmith, the nailer, the cutler, the armorer, &c. were unknown; and as there was no special and particular instruction in each of these branches of labor, the separation of which afterwards formed so many new arts maintained by their respective communities, these trades were unknown.

"The second political advantage resulting from the institution of trades-corporations at Barcelona was, the esteem and consideration in which at all times these establishments caused both the artisans and the arts to be held. This wise institution won respect for the operative classes, by constituting them a visible and permanent order in the state. Hence it is that the conduct and the mode of life of the Barcelonians have ever been such as are to be found only amongst an honorable people. Never having been confounded with any exempted and privileged body (for the trades-corporations draw a circle around their members, and let them know what they are, and what they are worth), these people learned that there was honor and virtue within their own sphere, and labored to preserve these qualities; so certain is it that social distinctions in a nation have more influence than is sometimes believed in upholding the spirit of each social class.

"Another view of this question shows us that trades-corporations form communities, governed by an economic code, which assigns to each corporation certain employments and certain honors, to which every individual member may aspire. Even men's prejudices, when wisely directed, sometimes produce admirable effects. Thus the government, the administration of these bodies, in which the artisan always enjoyed the prerogative of managing the resources and the interests of his trade and of his fellow-members, with the title of Counsellor, or Elder (*Prohombre*), won for the mechanical arts of Barcelona public and general esteem; whilst the pre-eminence in a festival or an assembly serves with these men to soften the rigors of manual labor, and the disadvantages of their inferior condition. At the same time that the trades of Barcelona, formed into well-organized bodies, fixed and preserved the arts in that capital, they had the further credit, by acting as political bodies of the most numerous class of the people, of gaining a high esteem for their members. The obscure artisan, without matriculation, or a common bond, continues isolated and wandering; he dies, and with him perishes his art; or at the first reverse of fortune, he emigrates and abandons his craft. What consideration can wretched wandering followers of any trade obtain in a country? Just such as knife-grinders and tinkers possess in the provinces of Spain. At Barcelona, all the trades have constantly enjoyed the same general esteem, because all have been established and governed upon a system which has rendered them fixed, respectable, and prosperous.

"The esteem in which the trades of Barcelona were held from the time when the municipal government had formed them into national corporations, the agents of public economy, gave rise to the laudable and useful custom of perpetuating trades in the same families. In fact the people having learned that, without quitting the class to which they belonged, they could preserve the respect and consideration due to useful and honorable citizens, no longer desired to quit it, and were no longer ashamed of their condition. When trades are held in honor, which is the consequence of the stability and civil properties of corporations, they naturally become hereditary. Now, the advantages both to the artisan and the arts, resulting from this transmission of trades,

work which saw the light in 1774, from the press of Sancha, under the title of *Dicours economique-politique pour la defensedu travail mecanique des ouvriers, par D. Ramon Miguel Palacio.* The author of these memoirs, fearing to be accused of a gross plagiarism, observes that, being obliged here to treat of this same matter, he was forced to adopt many of the ideas contained in this work, which at that time he thought it proper to publish without affixing his real name."

are so real and so well known, that it is needless to specify them here, or to dwell upon their salutary effects. This demarcation and classification of trades caused many of the arts to become sure possessions for those who adopted them. Hence fathers aimed at transmitting their trade to their sons; and thus was formed an indestructible mass of national industry, which made labor honorable, by implanting steady and homogeneous manners, if we may so speak, in the bosom of the class of artisans.

"Another circumstance contributed still more to render the exercise of the mechanical arts honorable at Barcelona, not only more than in most other parts of Spain, but more than in any other state, ancient or modern. This was the admission of the trades-corporations upon the register of municipal offices in this city, which enjoyed so many royal grants and extraordinary privileges of independence. Thus the nobility—that Gothic nobility—with their great domains, sought to be incorporated with the operatives in the *Ayuntamiento,* there to fill the offices and supreme stations in the political government, which, during more than five hundred years, continued in Barcelona under a form and in a spirit truly democratic.* All mechanical offices, without any odious distinction or exclusion, were held worthy to be declared qualified for the consistorial council of magistrates; all had a voice and a vote among the conscript fathers who represented this city, the most highly privileged perhaps that ever existed; one of the most renowned for its laws, its power, and its influence; one of the most respected in the middle ages amongst all the states and monarchies of Europe, Asia, and Africa.†

"This political system, and this municipal form of government, resembled that which prevailed in the middle ages amongst all the principal towns of Italy, whence Catalonia borrowed many of its customs and usages. Genoa, Pisa, Milan, Pavia, Florence, Sienna, and other towns, had a municipal government composed of the leading men in commerce, and the arts, under the name of consuls, counsellors, &c. *Priores Artium*—such was the name of a popular form of elective government, distributed among the different classes of citizens, without excluding the artisans, who, in the thirteenth and fourteenth centuries, were in their most flourishing condition, forming the most respectable part of the population, and consequently the richest, the most powerful, and the most independent. This democratic liberty, besides giving stability and permanency to industry in the towns of Italy, conferred a singular degree of honor on the mechanical professions. The grand council of these towns was summoned by the tolling of the bell, when the artisans arranged themselves under the banners or gonfalons of their respective trades. Such was also the political constitution of Barcelona from the middle of the thirteenth to the commencement of the present century. With these facts before us, need we feel surprise that, in our own days, arts and artisans in Barcelona still retain undiminished esteem and consideration: that a love for mechanical professions has become hereditary; that the dignity and self-respect of the artisan class have become traditional, even to the last generations, in which the customs of their ancestors have been transmitted by the succession of example, even after the extinction of the political reasons in which these customs had their origin? Several trades-corporations still preserve in the halls of their *juntas* the portraits of those of their members who formerly obtained the first employments in the state. Must not this laudable practice have engraven on the memory of the members of the corporation all the ideas of honor and dignity consistent with the condition of an artisan? Assuredly the popular form of the ancient government of Barcelona could not fail to imprint itself generally and forcibly on the manners of the people; indeed, where all the citizens were equal in the participation of honors, it is easy to see that no one would willingly remain inferior to another in virtue or in merit, although inferior, in other respects, by his condition and fortune. This noble emulation, which must naturally have been awakened to activity in the concourse of all orders in the state, gave birth to the dignity, the lofty and inviolate probity of the artisans of Barcelona; and this character they have maintained to our own times, to the admiration of Spain and of foreign nations. Such has been the negligence of our national authors, that this narrative will have the appearance of a discovery: up to the present time Barcelona and the Principality had not attracted the scrutinizing notice of the political historian, so that a dark shadow still concealed the real principles (always unknown to the crowd) from which in all times, have sprung the virtues and the vices of nations.

"To these causes may be attributed, in great part, the esteem which the artisans have acquired. Nothing could be more salutary than this obligation they were always under of comporting themselves with dignity and distinction in public employments, whether in the corporation or the municipal government. Moreover the constant example of the master of the house, who, up to the present time, has always lived in common with his apprentices in a praiseworthy manner, has confirmed the children in ideas of order and dignity; for the manners and habits of a people, which are as powerful as law, must be inculcated from the tenderest age. Thus, in Barcelona, the operative has never been confounded by the slovenliness of his dress with the mendicant, whose idle and dissipated habits, says an illustrious writer, are easily contracted when the dress of the man of respectability is in no way distinguished from that of the rabble. Nor are the laboring population ever seen wearing those cumbersome garments which, serving as a cover for rags and a cloak for idleness, cramp the movements and activity of the body, and

* "Consult the Appendix of Notes, Nos. 28 and 30. You will there see what respect and power the town of Barcelona enjoyed at another period, by means of the municipal magistrates, who represented it under the ordinary name of councillors."

† "In the diplomatic collection of these memoirs, we find a multitude of letters and other documents proving the direct and mutual relations which existed between the city of Barcelona and the emperors of the East, of Germany, the sultans of Egypt, the kings of Tunis, of Morocco, and various monarchs and states, or other great powers of Europe."

invite to a life of indolent ease. The people have not contracted a habit of frequenting taverns, where example leads to drunkenness and moral disorders. Their amusements, so necessary for working people to render their daily toils supportable, have always been innocent recreations, which either afforded them repose from their fatigues or varied them. The games formerly permitted were either the ring (*la bague*), nine pins, bowls, ball, shooting at a mark, fencing, and public dancing, authorized and watched over by the authorities; an amusement which from time immemorial has been general amongst the Catalans, in certain seasons and on certain festivals of the year.

"The respect for the artisan of Barcelona has never been diminished on account of the material on which his art was exercised, whether it was silver, steel, iron, copper, wood, or wool. We have seen that all the trades were equally eligible to the municipal offices of the state; none were excluded—not even butchers. Ancient Barcelona did not commit the political error of establishing preferences that might have produced some odious distinctions of trades. The inhabitants considered that all the citizens were in themselves worthy of esteem, since all contributed to the growth and maintenance of the property of a capital whose opulence and power were founded upon the industry of the artisan and the merchant. In fact, Barcelona has ever been free from that idea, so generally entertained, that every mechanical profession is low and vulgar—a mischievous and very common prejudice, which, in the provinces of Spain, has made an irreparable breach in the progress of the arts. At Barcelona, admission into certain trades-corporations has never been refused to the members of other trades: in this city all the trades are held in the same estimation. In a word, neither Barcelona nor any other town in Catalonia has ever entertained those vulgar prejudices that are enough to prevent honorable men from devoting themselves to the arts, or to cause the son to forsake the art practised by the father."*

Note 36, p. 361.

I have spoken of the numerous Councils held by the Church at different epochs; why, it will be asked, does she not hold them more frequently now? I will answer this question by quoting a judicious passage from Count de Maistre, in his work *On the Pope,* book i. chap. 2:—

"In the first ages of Christianity," says he, "it was more easy to assemble Councils, because the Church was not so numerous as now, and because the emperors possessed powers that enabled a sufficient number of Bishops to assemble, so that their decisions needed only the assent of other Bishops. Yet these Councils were not assembled without much difficulty and embarrassment. But in modern times, since the civilized world has been divided into so many sovereignties, and immeasurably increased by our intrepid navigators, an Œcumenical Council has become a chimera.† Simply to convoke all the Bishops, and to bring legally together such a convocation, five or six years would not suffice."

Note 37, p. 369.

That my readers may be convinced of the truth and accuracy of what I here affirm, I invite them to read the history of the heresies that have afflicted the Church since the first ages, but particularly from the tenth century down to our own days.

Note 38, p. 373.

It was not, I have said, without prejudice to the liberty of the people that the influence of the clergy was withdrawn from the working of the political machine. In order to ascertain how far this is true, it may be well to remark, that a great number of theologians were favorable to tolerably liberal doctrines in political matters, and that it was the clergy who exercised the greatest freedom in speaking to kings, even after the people had almost entirely lost the right of intervention in political affairs. Observe what opinions St. Thomas held on forms of government.

(Quest. cv. 1a 2æ.)

De ratione judicialium præceptorum art. 1. Respondeo dicendum, quod circa bonam ordinationem principum in aliqua civitate, vel gente, duo sunt attendenda, quorum unum est, ut omnes aliquam partem habeant in principatu; per hoc enim conservatur pax populi et omnes talem ordinationem amant et custodiunt ut dicitur (II. *Polit.,* cap. i.); aliud est quod attenditur secundum speciem regiminis vel ordinationis principatum, cujus cum sint diversæ species, ut philosophus tradit in III. *Polit.* cap. v., præcipue tamen unum regimen est, in quo unus principatur secundum virtutem: et aristocratia, id est potestas optimorum, in qua aliqui pauci principantur secundum virtutem. Unde optima ordinatio principum est in aliqua civitate vel regno, in quo unus præficitur secundum virtutem qui omnibus præsit et sub ipso sunt aliqui principantes secundum virtutem, et tamen talis principatus ad omnes pertinet, tum quia ex omnibus eligi possunt, tum quia etiam ab omnibus eliguntur. Talis vero est omnis politia bene commixta ex regno in quantam unus præest, et aristocratia in quantum multi principantur secundum virtutem, et ex democratia, id est potestate populi in quantum ex popularibus possunt eligi principes, et ad populum pertinet electio principum, et hoc fuit institutum secundum legem divinam.

Divus Thomas. (1a 2æ Q. 90, art. 4o.)

Et sic ex quatuor prædictis potest colligi definitio legis quæ nihil est aliud quam quædam rationis ordinatio ad bonum commune ab eo qui curam communitatis habet promulgata. Q. 95, art. 4.

* See the remarks of his Excellency M. Campomanes on these abuses and false principles of policy, in his *Discourse on the Popular Education of Artisans,* from page 119 to 160.

† We ordinarily call a chimera, or an impossibility, that which offers great difficulties. On this occasion we cannot help observing to sincere persons, that, from these great difficulties, they may judge of the lawfulness and sincerity of the desires manifested by the *soi-disant* reformers and appellants to Councils. They do not wish for Councils; but, under the shadow of this word, they wish to escape the authority of their legitimate superiors. (Note by the authors of the *Bibliothèque de Religion,* published in Spain.)

Tertio est de ratione legis humanæ ut instituatur a gubernante communitatem civitatis: sicut supra dictum est. (Quest. 90, art. 3.) Et secundum hoc distinguuntur leges humanæ secundum diversa regimina civitatum, quorum unum, secundum philosophum in III. *Polit.*, cap. xi., est regnum, quando scilicet civitas gubernatur ab uno, et secundum hoc accipiuntur constitutiones principum; aliud vero regimen est aristocratia, id est principatus optimorum vel optimatum, et secundum hoc sumuntur responsa prudentum et etiam senatusconsulta. Aliud regimen est oligarchia, id est principatus paucorum divitum et potentum; et secundum hoc sumitur jus prætorium, quod etiam honorarium dicitur. Aliud autem regimen est populi, quod nominatur democratia; et secundum hoc sumuntur plebiscita. Aliud autem est tyrannicum, quod est omnino corruptum unde ex hoc non sumitur aliqua lex. Est etiam et aliquod regimen ex istis commixtum, quod est optimum, et secundum hoc sumitur lex quam majores natu simul cum plebibus sanxerunt, ut Isidorus dicit lib. 5, *Etym. C.* cap. x.

If certain declaimers are to be believed, it would seem that the principle, that it is the law which governs, and not the will of man, is quite a recent discovery. But observe with what solidity and perspicuity the angelic doctor expounds this doctrine.

(1ª 2æ Q. 93, art. 1.)

Utrum fuerit utile aliquas leges poni ab hominibus.

Ad 2m dicendum, quod sicut Philosophus dicit. 1. Rhetor. Melius est omnia ordinari lege, quam dimittere judicum arbitrio, et hoc propter tria. Primo quidem, quia facilius est invenire paucos sapientes, qui sufficiant ad rectas leges ponendas, quam multos; qui requirerentur ad recte judicandum de singulis. Secundo, quia illi qui leges ponunt, ex multo tempore considerant quid lege ferendum sit: sed judicia de singularibus factis fiunt ex casibus subito exortis. Facilius autem ex multis consideratis potest homo videre quid rectum sit, quam solum ex aliquo uno facto. Tertio, quia legislatores judicant in universali, et de futuris: sed homines judiciis præsidentes judicant de præsentibus; ad quæ afficientur amore vel odio, aut aliqua cupiditate; et sic eorum depravatur judicium. Quia ergo justitia animata judicis non invenitur in multis, et quia flexibilis est: ideo necessarium fuit in quibuscumque est possibile, legem determinare quid judicandum sit, et paucissima arbitrio hominum committere.

In Spain, the *Procuradores* of the Cortes dared not raise their voices against the excesses of power; and their timidity drew down the keen reproaches of P. Mariana. In the examination to which he was subjected in the celebrated suit commenced against him on the subject of the *seven treatises*, he confesses having applied to the *Procuradores* the epithets of *vile, superficial, and utterly venal*, only striving to obtain the favor of the prince, and their own particular interests, without solicitude for the public good. He added, that such was the public cry, the general complaint, at least at Toledo, where he was residing.

I will leave unnoticed his work intituled *De Rege et Regis institutione*, of which I have spoken elsewhere. Confining myself to his *History of Spain*, I will observe with what liberty he expresses himself on the most delicate points, without meeting with any opposition, either from the civil or from the ecclesiastical authority. In his 1st book, chap. 4, speaking of the Aragonese, in his usual grave and severe tone, he says: "The Aragonese possess and enjoy laws and *fueros* very different from those of the other people of Spain; they possess every thing most adapted for preserving liberty against the excessive power of kings, for preventing this power from degenerating and changing, by its natural tendency, into tyranny; for they are not ignorant of this truth, that the right of liberty is generally lost by degrees."

It was precisely at this epoch that the clergy expressed themselves with the greatest freedom on the most delicate of all subjects, that of contributions. The venerable Palafox, in his memorial or petition to the king for ecclesiastical immunity, said: "According to St. Augustine, to the great Tostat, and other weighty authors, the Son of God appointed that the children of God—that is the ministers of the Church, his priests—should not pay tribute to the pagan princes. In fact, he addressed to St. Peter the following question, already resolved by the eternal wisdom of the Father: *Reges gentium a quibus accipiunt tributum, a filiis, an ab alienis?* St. Peter answered, *Ab alienis;* and our Lord concluded with these words: *Ergo liberi sunt filii.* I may be allowed, sire, to make this delicate observation, that the Divine Majesty does not say, *Reges gentium a quibus capiunt tributum*, but *a quibus accipiunt.* By this word *accipiunt*, we understand the mildness and mansuetude with which the payment of a tribute should always be exacted, in order to diminish the bitterness and repugnance accompanying a tribute.

"46. It is doubtless useful for the preservation of the state, that, in the first place, subjects should give, in order that princes may then receive. It is proper that kings should receive, and employ the tribute paid them, for on this depends the safety of crowns; but it is well that subjects should first give it voluntarily. It is doubtless from this passage of Scripture, from this expression of the Eternal Word, that the Catholic Crown, always so pious, has received the holy doctrine, by virtue of which neither your majesty nor your illustrious predecessors have ever permitted a tribute to be levied without its having first received the consent of the kingdoms themselves, and been offered by them; and your majesty is incomparably more exalted by limiting and moderating your power, than by exercising it to its utmost extent.

"47. Sire, if laymen, who have no exemption in matters of tribute, enjoy that which the kindness of your majesty and of the most Catholic kings grant them; if they do not pay till they choose to make a voluntary offering; if nothing is received from them except on this condition, will religion, your majesty's renowned piety, and the devoted zeal of the Council, allow the clergy—the sons, the ministers of God, the privileged, those who are exempt by divine and human law in all the nations of the world, and among the very pagans—to enjoy less favor than strangers, who are not, like them, either ministers of the Church or priests of God? Is the word *capiunt*, sire, to be applied exclusively to the ministers of God, and the word *accipiunt* to men of the world?"

In his work intituled *Historia Real Sagrada*, the same writer raises his voice against tyranny with extreme severity:

"12. *Such*," says he, "*is the law which the king whom you wish for will maintain in your regard.* The word law is here employed ironically, as if God should say: 'You imagine, without doubt, that this king of yours would govern according to law; on this supposition you asked for him, since you complained that my tribunal did not govern you. Now, the law which this king will exercise towards you will be, to disregard all law; and his law will eventually be tyranny respected.' The politician who, relying upon this passage, should attribute as a right to the monarch a power which is merely pointed out by God to the people as a chastisement, would be an uncivilized being, unworthy of being treated as a rational creature. The Lord, in this instance, does not define what is the best; he does not say what he is giving them; these words are no appreciation of power; he merely declares what would be the case, and what he condemns. Who shall dare to found the origin of tyranny on justice itself? God says, that he whom they desire for a king will be a tyrant—not a tyrant approved of by him, but a tyrant that he reprobates and chastises. And subsequent events clearly shewed it, since there were in Israel wicked kings, by whom the prophecy was fulfilled, and Saints who obtained on the throne the mercy of God. The wicked kings literally accomplished the divine threat, by doing what they were forbidden; the good ones established their dignity upon propriety and justice within prescribed limits."

Father Marquez, in his *Christian Prince or Magistrate* (*Gobernador Cristiano*), also enlarges on the same question; he expounds his opinion both theoretically and practically.

(Chapter xvi. 53.)

"Thus far we have heard the words of Philo, writing on this event. As these words afforded me an opportunity of reasoning on the obligations of Christian kings, I have taken care to quote them at length. I will not expect these kings to act like Moses; for they have not the miraculous aid which the Hebrew legislator received for the relief of the people, nor the rod which God gave him to make water flow from the rock at need. But I will recommend them to reflect maturely on the additional services they shall attempt to exact from their subjects, and the burdens they shall impose on them. Let them reflect that they are bound to justify the motive of their request in all truth, and without any false coloring; always and constantly aware that they are in the presence of God, that the eyes of God are fixed on their hands, that He will require from them a strict account of their actions. For, as the holy doctor of Nazianzen says, the Son of God came designedly into the world at the taking of a census and a resettlement of the imposts, in order to confound kings who would have appointed them through caprice; so that kings may now know that the Son of God takes account of every item, and weighs in the balance of his strict justice things which we should account of little moment.

"The above reflection will serve to dispel the false ideas of certain flatterers, who, to obtain the favor of princes, persuade them that they are perfectly independent and the masters of the lives and property of their subjects, free to dispose of them as they may think proper. In support of this pretended maxim, they allege, as we have seen, the history of Samuel, who answered the people on the part of God, when they were demanding a king, 'You shall have one, but on terrible conditions.' This king was to take from them their fields, their vineyards, their oliveyards, to give them to his servants; he was to take their daughters for slaves, 'to make him ointments, and to be his cooks and bakers.' And they have not observed that, as John Bodin says, this is the interpretation of Philip Melancthon, which alone is sufficient to render it suspicious. Moreover, as St. Gregory, and after him other doctors, have observed, this passage of Scripture does not establish the just right of kings, but rather announces beforehand the tyranny of a great number of princes; in fine, these words do not explain what good princes might do, but merely what bad ones would usually do. Hence, when Achab seized upon the vineyard of Naboth, God was angry with him, and we know how He treated him. When David, the elect of God, demanded a spot whereon to set up the altar of Jebusee, he only asked it on condition of paying the value of the land.

"For this reason princes should examine with scrupulous attention whether contributions are just; for if they are not, doctors decide that they cannot, without manifest injustice, thus more or less infringe on the rights of their subjects. This doctrine is so Catholic and certain, that men holding sound doctrine affirm that, in this case, princes cannot impose fresh tributes, even though necessary, without the consent of the nation. For, say they, the prince not being (which he certainly is not) the master of his subjects' property, cannot make use of it without the consent of those from whom he is to receive it. This custom has been long in practice in the kingdom of Castile, where the laws of royalty prohibit the levying of any new impost without the intervention of the Cortes: after having received the sanction of the Cortes, the impost is submitted to the vote of the towns; and the prince does not consider his demand granted till it has received the sanction of the majority of the towns. Edward I. of England made a similar law, according to many authors of weight; and Philip of Commines says, that it was the same in France till the time of Charles VII., who, urged by an extreme necessity, suppressed these formalities, and levied a tax without waiting for the consent of the States, and this inflicted on the kingdom so deep a wound, that it will long continue unhealed. If we may credit certain affirmations, this author reports, that it was then asserted that the king had escaped from the guardianship exercised by the kingdom; but that his own opinion is, that kings cannot, without the consent of their people, exact a single farthing; princes acting otherwise, says he, fall under the Pope's excommunication; no doubt that of the bull *In Cœna Domini.* For my own part, I ought to confess that I do not find this in Philip de Commines. . . . . With respect to this second point, it is evident, that the prince cannot, on his own authority, impose new tributes without the consent of the nation, whenever this nation shall have acquired by any of the reasons mentioned a contrary right, which I consider to be the case in Castile. No one, in fact, will deny that kingdoms at their commencement have a right to choose their kings on this condition, or render them such services as to obtain in return that no new imposts shall be laid on them without their consent. Now, in either case, there will be a compact made, from which kings cannot depart; and it is of no consequence, as some imagine it to be, whether they have obtained their kingdoms through the election of their subjects, or by mere force of arms. Although it is probable, indeed, that a State yielding itself of its own accord, will obtain greater privileges and better conditions than those acquired by a just war, it would not, however, be impossible for a State, in choosing a king, to confer upon him all its power in an absolute manner, and without this restriction, with a view to lay him under greater obligations, and to testify to him a greater degree of devotedness; and, on the other hand, a king, who had subjected a kingdom by force of arms, might nevertheless voluntarily grant it this privilege, with a view to obtain its gratitude, and more affectionate obedience on its part. The positive rule, therefore, for this particular right, will be the contract made, whether virtually or expressly, between the State and the prince; a contract which should be inviolable, especially if it is sealed by an oath."

The Prince, or Christian Magistrate.

(Liv. ii. ch. xxxix. § 2.)

"Princes, it is said, may compel their subjects to sell at half-price, or to give gratuitously, a part of their property. This opinion is generally founded on the law which ordains that, when a ship in a tempest has been saved by throwing overboard a part of the cargo, the proprietors of the remaining part are obliged to make a proportionate contribution to indemnify the sufferers for the loss they have sustained. Bartholus and other authors have inferred from this, that in a time of necessity and famine the monarch may require his subjects to give gratuitously, and *a fortiori* to sell at a lower price, a portion of their property to those in need. The monarch, say they, might, without any doubt, render property common, as it was before the establishment of social rights; he may consequently take it from one of his subjects and give it to another.

"It is certainly said in the laws of the kings of Israel, that he who should be chosen by God might seize upon the vineyards and property of his subjects, to confer them on his own servants; but the doctors do not support their arguments on this text. In fact, as we have said in chapter 16th, book i., the question does not concern the rights of a good prince, but the tyrannical acts of a bad one. Now, a careful study of the Scriptures will shew, that this passage must be favourable to one or other of the two opinions; for, if it were intended to establish that kings would possess in conscience the authority set forth in this passage, they would certainly have the right of seizing the property of one of their subjects to give it to another. If this passage is merely meant as a declaration of the injustices, of the extortions, and the tyrannies of wicked monarchs, it is no less certain that in Scripture the deed is considered unjust; for this deed is alleged as an example of what tyrants would do; now if it had been permitted to a good king, it would not have been quoted as an example of tyranny, as the Scriptures suppose it.

"Thus, this text alone, even were there no other in support of this doctrine, would satisfy me, that kings cannot lawfully compel their subjects to relinquish their property for less than its value, not even under pretext of the public good. In fact, were this pretext valid, it would not have been difficult for the kings of Israel to find an excuse for their tyranny; they might have alleged, that it was important to the public good to reward servants whose fidelity was so advantageous to the interests of the kingdom. Further, King Achab might have urged, that the amusements of the prince formed a part of the public good, since the people are so much interested in the health of the prince; and under this pretext might have deprived Naboth of his vineyard in order to enlarge his gardens. We find, however, that this pretext did not justify him in compelling Naboth even to sell his vineyard; the king, although grieved, was not offended by this man's refusal, neither was it his intention to seize the vineyard, had not the impious Jezabel furnished him with the means of doing so.

"Reason is evidently in favour of this opinion. Kings are the ministers of justice, and have been appointed to administer and uphold justice among the people. As St. Thomas teaches, the contract in buying and selling is only just in proportion as the price is equivalent to the thing purchased. Public, it is true, should be preferred to individual interest; in case, therefore, that a State is in danger of dissolution, the monarch might demand property at a less price, or even for nothing, just as he might compel the citizen to expose his life, which is of still greater value, in defending the common cause in a just war. This case, however, as P. Molina observes, is impossible, since the monarch would always be able to indemnify the individual for the loss he sustained, by levying for this purpose a general tax, a just tribute, and one that the State would be bound to pay. To prove this still more clearly, let us imagine the most urgent case possible; let us suppose that the king is besieged in his capital by a tyrant; the tyrant is about to enter sword and torch in hand; he offers to raise the siege on condition of receiving a statue of gold of great value, formerly the property of his ancestors, which a subject of the besieged king, the commander-in-chief of his armies, had taken in the plunder of a town, and made the inalienable property of the eldest son of his family. To render the case still more pressing, let us suppose that the tyrant has a dearly-cherished relation in the service of the besieged king, and that he will be satisfied if a rich lord of the kingdom, possessing a great number of estates, be despoiled, and his property conferred on his relation. It cannot be doubted that, in order to purchase the lives of all, this arrangement might be entered into; and that the king would be justified in acceding to the demand, in taking the statue, or even the whole of this property, to confer it on the tyrant's relation. But no one will assert that the lord should suffer the whole loss. The State would be under the obligation of indemnifying him for the loss, by taking upon itself the indemnification, the lord merely contributing his quota; for this reason, that it would be opposed to natural justice for the burdens of the whole body to fall upon a single member, which would be the case according to the law proposed by the opponents. If, in a case of shipwreck, all the cargo were thrown overboard to save the ship and the lives and fortunes of all, the obligation being common to all, it would not be just that it should fall exclusively upon the owners; because the cargo could best be thrown overboard and most endangered the ship's safety: the loss should be borne by all, even by those who had with them things only of little weight, as jewels or diamonds, for instance; since neither these latter proprietors nor the vessel herself could be saved without lightening her by throwing overboard the heavier portion of the cargo.

"The law decrees also that the owner of the vessel shall pay his quota. Not that he is obliged to indemnify the owners of the merchandise lost, because he sees them in need; it may be supposed, indeed, that these parties are rich, and, although their present loss is extreme, they will nevertheless be under the obligation of returning what would then have been lent to them; for, as the doctors decide, there is no obligation of giving to the rich man when he suffers a heavy loss, when a loan will answer the same end. But it is said that the obligation of the master of a ship is founded on the fact, that all the passengers and the proprietors being interested in saving their lives and their property, the risk and the loss of what was thrown overboard ought to fall on all, and not exclusively on the owners of what was lost. As a proof that this is the correct interpretation, it will be sufficient to notice the summary of the title, and the very words of the law, which are: *Eo quod id tributum servatæ mercedes deberent.*

"But, except in this case, or in others equally pressing, if the ruin of the State would not result from the mere fact of an individual refusing to yield up his house to the prince, the latter could not compel the proprietor to give it up for a less price than its just value, and still less for nothing; for so long as the persons and the property of the State are safe, it is of no importance to the body corporate whether such or such persons are rich or poor; no one, in fact, in the general community possesses a fixed degree from which he can neither descend nor rise. This instability observable among the members of the same State, some losing what others gain, and *vice versa*, is inseparable from the state of society, such is the instability of temporal affairs; and the public good generally speaking, neither loses nor gains by it.'

NOTE 39, p. 382.

Some persons imagine, that in speaking of the loss of liberty in Spain, the question may be readily reduced to one point of view, as if the kingdom had always possessed the unity which it only acquired in the eighteenth century, and only then in an incomplete manner. A perusal of history, and especially of the codes of the different provinces of which the monarchy was composed, will convince us that the central power has been created and fortified among us very slowly; and that at the time when this difficult task was nearly accomplished in Castile, much still remained to be done in Aragon and Catalonia. Our constitutions, our customs, our manners, in the seventeenth century, evidently prove that the monarchy of Philip II., such as we conceive it, strong and irresistible, was not yet established in the crown of Aragon. I will abstain from adducing here documents and quoting facts with which every one is acquainted; the dimensions of this volume require me to be brief.

NOTE 40, p. 388.

The immortal work of Count de Maistre, in which he so ably refutes the calumnies of the enemies of the Apostolic See, is well known. Among so many and such profound observations, there is one deserving of particular attention: that on the moderation of the Popes in every thing relating to the extension of their dominions, when he points out the difference between the Roman and the other European Courts. "It is," says he, "a very remarkable circumstance, but either disregarded or not sufficiently attended to, that the Popes have never taken advantage of the great power in their possession for the aggrandisement of their States. What could have been more natural, for instance, or more tempting to human nature, than to reserve a portion of the provinces conquered from the Saracens, and which they gave up to the first occupant, to repel the Turkish ascendency, always on the increase? But this, however, they never did, not even with regard to the adjacent countries, as in the instance of the Two Sicilies, to which they had incontestable rights, at least according to the ideas then prevailing, and over which they were nevertheless contented with an empty sovereignty, which soon ended in the *haquenée*, a slight tribute, and merely nominal, which the bad taste of the age still disputes with them.

"The Popes may have made too much, at the time, of this universal sovereignty, which an opinion equally universal allowed them. They may have exacted homage; may indeed, if you will, have too arbitrarily imposed taxes. I do not wish to enter into these points here, but it still remains certain that they have never sought to increase their dominions at the expense of justice, whilst all other governments fell under this anathema; and, at the present time even, with all our philosophy, our civilization, and our fine books, there is not perhaps one of the European powers in a condition to justify all its possessions before God and reason." (*Du Pape*, book ii. chap. 6.)

Note 41, p. 350.

I will here insert some passages in which St. Anselm explains the motives that induced him to write, and the method which he intended to follow in his writings.

Præfatio beati Anselmi Episcopi Cantuariensis in Monologuium.

Quidam fratres sæpe me studioseque precati sunt, ut quædam de illis, quæ de meditanda divinitatis essentia, et quibusdam aliis hujus meditationi cohærentibus, usitato sermone colloquendo protuleram, sub quodam eis meditationis exemplo describerem. Cujus scilicet scribendæ meditationis magis secundum suam voluntatem quam secundum rei facilitatem aut meam possibilitatem hanc mihi formam præstituerunt: quatenus auctoritate scripturæ penitus nihil in ea persuaderetur. Sed quidquid per singulas investigationes finis assereret, id ita esse plano stylo et vulgaribus argumentis simplicique disputatione, et rationis necessitas breviter cogeret, et veritatis claritas patenter ostenderet. Voluerunt etiam ut nec simplicibus peneque fatuis objectionibus mihi occurrentibus obviare contemnerem, quod quidem diu tentare recusavi, atque me cum re ipsa comparans, multis me rationibus excusare tentavi. Quanto enim id quod petebant, usu sibi optabant facilius: tanto mihi illud actu injungebant difficilius. Tandem tamen victus, tum precum modesta importunitate, tum studii eorum non contemnenda honestate, invitus quidem propter rei difficultatem, et ingenii mei imbecillitatem, quod precabantur incæpi, sed libenter propter eorum caritatem, quantum potui secundum ipsorum definitionem effeci. Ad quod cum ea spe sim adductus, ut quidquid facerem illis solis a quibus exigebatur, esset notum, et paulo post idipsum ut vilem rem fastidientibus, contemptu esset obruendum, scio enim me in eo non tam precantibus satisfacere potuisse, quam precibus me prosequentibus finem posuisse. Nescio tamen quomodo sic præter spem evenit, ut non solum prædicti fratres sed et plures alii scripturam ipsam, quisque eam sibi transcribendo in longum memoriæ commendare satagerent, quam ego sæpe tractans nihil potui invenire me in ea dixisse, quod non catholicorum patrum, et maxime beati Augustini scriptis cohæreat.

Idem. *Quod hoc licet inexplicabile sit, tamen credendum sit.* (Cap. lxii.)

Videtur mihi hujus tam sublimis rei secretum transcendere omnem intellectus aciem humani: et idcirco conatum explicandi qualiter hoc sit, continendum puto. Sufficere namque debere existimo rem incomprehensibilem indaganti si ad hoc rationando pervenerit, ut eam certissime esse cognoscat, etiamsi penetrare nequeat intellectu quomodo ita sit, nec idcirco minus his adhibendam fidei certitudinem, quæ probationibus necessariis nulla alia repugnante ratione asseruntur, si suæ naturalis altitudinis incomprehensibilitate explicari non patiantur. Quid autem tam incomprehensibile, quam id quod supra omnia est? Quapropter si ea quæ de sua essentia hactenus disputata sunt necessariis rationibus sunt asserta, quamvis sic intellectu penetrari non possint ut quæ verbis valeant explicari: nullatenus tamen certitudinis eorum nutat soliditas. Nam si superior consideratio rationabiliter comprehendit incomprehensibile esse, quomodo eadem summa sapientia sciat ea quæ fecit de quibus tam multa non scire necesse est; quis explicet quomodo sciat aut dicat se ipsam, de qua aut nihil, aut vix aliquid homini sciri possibile est?

Incipit prœmium in Prosologuion librum Anselmi, Abbatis Beccensis, et Archiepiscopi Cantuariensis.

Postquam opusculum quoddam velut exemplum meditandi de ratione fidei, cogentibus me precibus quorumdam fratrum in persona alicujus tacite secum ratiocinando quæ nesciat investigantis edidi, considerans illud esse multorum concathenatione contextum argumentorum, cœpi mecum quærere: si forte posset invenire unum argumentum, quod nullo alio ad se probandum, quam se solo indigeret, et solum ad astruendum quia Deus vere est; et quia est summum bonum nullo alio indigens, et quo omnia indigent ut sint et bene sint, et quæcumque credimus de divina substantia sufficeret. Ad quod cum sæpe studioseque cogitationes converterem, atque aliquando mihi videretur jam capi posse quod quærebam, aliquando mentis aciem omnino fugeret: tandem desperans volui cessare, velut ab inquisitione rei quam inveniri esset impossibile. Sed cum illam cogitationem, ne mentem meam frustra occupando ab aliis in quibus proficere possem impediret, penitus a me vellem excludere, tunc magis ac magis nolenti et defendenti, se cœpit cum importunitate quadam ingerere. Quadam igitur die cum vehementer ejus importunitati resistendo fatigarer, in ipso cogitationum conflictu sic se obtulit quod desperabam, ut studiose cogitationem amplecterer, quam sollicitus repellebam. Æstimans igitur quod me gaudebam invenisse, si scriptum esset alicui, legenti placiturum. De hoc ipso et quibusdam aliis sub persona conantis erigere mentem suam ad contemplandum Deum, et quærentis intelligere quod credit, subditum scripsi opusculum. Et quoniam nec istud nec illud cujus supra memini, dignum libri nomine, aut cui auctoris præponeretur nomen judicabam: nec tamen sine aliquo titulo, quo aliquem in cujus manus venirent, quodammodo ad se legendum invitarent, dimittenda putabam, unicuique dedi titulum: ut prius exemplum meditandi de ratione fidei, et sequens fides quærens intellectum diceretur. Sed cum jam a pluribus et his titulis utrumque transumptum esset, coegerunt me plures et maxime reverendus Archiepiscopus Lugdunensis Hugo nomine, fungens in Gallia legatione apostolica, prœcepit auctoritate, ut nomen meum illis præscriberem. Quod ut aptius fieret illud quidem Monologuium, id est Soliloquium, istud vero Prosologuion, id est Alloquium nominavi.

I have said that St. Anselm excelled Descartes in his manner of proving the existence of God: let the reader, indeed, peruse the following passages. I do not, however, intend to pronounce an opinion on the merits of this demonstration; my business is, to notice the progress of the human mind, and not to resolve philosophical questions.

PROSOLOGUIUM D. ANSELMI.

Quod Deus non possit cogitari non esse.

Quod utique sic vere est, ut nec cogitari possit non esse. Nam potest cogitari esse aliquid, quod non possit cogitari non esse, quod majus est quam quod non esse cogitari potest. Quare si id, quo majus nequit cogitari, potest cogitari non esse: id ipsum, quo majus cogitari nequit, non est id quo majus cogitari nequit; quod convenire non potest. Sic ergo vere est aliquid, quo majus cogitari non potest, ut nec cogitari possit non esse. Et hoc es tu, Domine Deus noster. Sic ergo vere es, Domine Deus meus, ut nec cogitari possis non esse. Et merito. Si enim aliqua mens posset cogitare aliquid melius te, ascenderet creatura super Creatorem; et judicaret de Creatore, quod valde est absurdum. Et quidem quidquid est aliud præter solum te, potest cogitari non esse. Solus igitur verissime omnium, et ideo maxime omnium habes esse, quia quidquid aliud est non sic vere est, et idcirco minus habet esse. Cur itaque, *dixit insipiens in corde suo non est Deus?* Cum causa in promptu sit rationali menti, te maxime omnium esse? Cur, nisi stultus et insipiens?

Quomodo insipiens dixit in corde suo quod cogitari non potest. (Cap. iv.)

Verum quomodo dixit insipiens in corde suo quod cogitare non potuit, aut quomodo cogitare non potuit quod dixit in corde, cum idem sit dicere in corde, et cogitare. Quod si vere, imo quia vere, et cogitavit: quia dixit in corde et non dixit in corde, quia cogitare non potuit; non uno tantum modo dicitur aliquid in corde vel cogitatur. Aliter enim cogitatur res, cum vox eam significans cogitatur: aliter cum idipsum, quod res est, intelligitur. Illo itaque modo, potest cogitari Deus non esse: isto vero, minime. Nullus quippe intelligens id quod Deus est, potest cogitare quia Deus non est; licet hæc verba dicat in corde, aut sine ulla, aut cum aliqua extranea significatione. Deus enim, est id quo majus cogitari non potest. Quod qui bene intelligit, utique intelligit id ipsum sic esse, ut nec cogitatione queat non esse. Qui ergo intelligit sic esse Deum, nequit eum non esse cogitare. Gratias tibi, bone Domine, gratias tibi, quia quod prius credidi te donante, jam sic intelligo te illuminante; ut si te esse nolim credere, non possim non intelligere.

Ejusdem beati Anselmi liber pro insipiente incipit.

Dubitanti, utrum sit; vel neganti quod sit aliqua talis natura, qua nihil majus cogitari possit; tamen esse illam, huic dicitur primo probari; quod ipse negans vel ambigens de illa, jam habeat eam in intellectu, cum audiens illam dici, id quod dicitur intelligit: deinde, quia quod intelligit necesse est, ut non in solo intellectu, sed etiam in re sit. Et hoc ita probatur; quia majus est esse in intellectu et in re, quam in solo intellectu. Et si illud in solo est intellectu, majus illo erit quidquid etiam fuerit in re, at si majus omnibus, minus erit aliquo, et non erit majus omnibus quod utique repugnat. Et ideo necesse est ut, majus omnibus, quod est jam probatum esse in intellectu, et in re sit; quoniam aliter majus omnibus esse non poterit. Responderi potest, quod hoc jam esse dicitur in intellectu meo, non ob aliud, nisi quia id quod dicitur intelligo.

The passages I have just quoted will have shewn to my readers that thought was not oppressed in the Catholic Church. The most eminent doctors were accustomed to reason on the most important subjects with a just and reasonable independence; and although with profound respect for the teaching of the Catholic Church, they nevertheless surveyed, as well as Abelard and better, the field of true philosophy. We cannot expect from human intelligence at this epoch more than is to be found in St. Anselm. How is it, therefore, that such eulogiums have been passed upon Roscelin and Abelard, without ever mentioning this holy doctor? Why present a picture of the intellectual movement so incomplete, and not insert in it so noble and beautiful a figure?

If you would know how incorrect it is that Abelard, as M. Guizot affirms, abstained from attacking the doctrines of the Church—how incorrect M. Guizot is in his statement of the causes which excited the zeal of the pastors of the Church against Abelard, read the letter of the Bishops of Gaul to Pope Innocent, in which you will find a complete recital of the origin and cause of this important affair. Here is the letter:

EPISTOLA CCCLXX.

Reverendissimo Patri et Domino, INNOCENTIO, *Dei gratia summo Pontifici, Henricus Senonensium Archiepiscopus, Carnotensis Episcopus, Sanctæ Sedis Apostolicæ famulus, Aurelianensis, Antissiodorensis, Trecensis, Meldensis Episcopi, devotas orationes et debitam obedientiam.*

Nulli dubium est quod ea quæ Apostolica firmantur auctoritate, rata semper existunt; nec alicujus possunt deinceps mutilari cavillatione, vel invidia depravari. Ea propter ad vestram Apostolicam Sedem, Beatissime Pater, referre dignum censuimus quædam quæ nuper in nostra contigit tractari præsentia. Quæ quoniam et nobis, et multis religiosis ac sapientibus viris rationabiliter acta visa sunt, vestræ serenitatis expectant comprobari judicio, simul et auctoritate perpetuo roborari. Itaque cum per totam fere Galliam in civitatibus, vicis, et castellis, a Scholaribus non solum intra Scholas, sed etiam triviatim: nec a litteratis, aut provectis tantum, sed a pueris et simplicibus, aut certe stultis, de Sancta Trinitate, quæ Deus est, disputaretur: insuper alia multa ab eisdem, absona prorsus et absurda, et plane fidei catholicæ, sanctorumque Patrum auctoritatibus obviantia proferrentur; cumque ab his qui sane sentiebant, et eas ineptias rejiciendas esse censebant, sæpius admoniti corriperentur, vehementius convalescebant, et auctoritate magistri sui Petri Abailardi, et cujusdam ipsius libri, cui *Theologiæ* indiderat nomen; nec non et aliorum ejusdem opusculorum freti ad astruendas profanas adinventiones illas, non sine multarum animarum dispendio, sese magis ac magis armabant. Quæ enim et nos, et alios plures non parum moverant ac læserant; inde tamen quæstionem facere verebantur.

Verum Dominus Abbas Claræ-vallis, his a diversis et sæpius auditis, immo certe in prætaxato magistri Petri *Theologiæ* libro, nec non et aliis ejusdem libris, in quorum forte lectionem inciderat, diligenter inspectis; secreto prius; ac deinde secum duobus aut tribus adhibitis testibus, juxta Evangelicum præceptum, hominem convenit: Et ut auditores suos a talibus compesceret, librosque suos corrigeret, amicabiliter satis ac familiariter illum admonuit. Plures etiam Scholarium adhortatus est, ut et libros venenis plenos repudiarent et rejicerent: et a doctrina, quæ fidem lædebat Catholicam, caverent et abstinerent. Quod magister Petrus minus patienter et nimium ægre ferens, crebro nos pulsare cœpit, nec ante voluit desistere, quoad Dominum Clara-vellensem Abbatem super hoc scribentes, assignato die, scilicet octavo Pentecostes, Senonis ante nostram submonuimus venire præsentiam: quo se vocabat et offerebat paratum magister Petrus ad probandas et defendendas de quibus illum Dominus Abbas Clara-vallensis, quomodo prætaxatum est, reprehenderat sententias. Cæterum Dominus Abbas, nec ad assignatum diem se venturum, nec contra Petrum sese disceptaturum nobis remandavit. Sed quia magister Petrus interim suos nihilominus cœpit undequaque convocare discipulos; et obsecrare, ut ad futuram inter se, Dominumque Abbatem Clara-vallensem disputationem, una cum illo suam sententiam simul et scientiam defensuri venirent; Et hoc Dominum Clara-vallensem minime lateret; veritus ipse, ne propter occasionem absentiæ suæ tot profanæ, non sententiæ sed insaniæ, tam apud minus intelligentes, quam earumdem defensores majore dignæ viderentur auctoritate, prædicto quem sibi designaveramus die, licet eum minime suscepisset, tactus zelo pii fervoris, imo certe Sancti Spiritus igne succensus, sese nobis ultro Senonis præsentavit. Illa vero die, scilicet octava Pentecostes, convenerant ad nos Senonis Fratres et Suffraganei nostri Episcopi, ob honorem et reverentiam sanctarum, quas in Ecclesia nostra populo revelaturos nos indixeramus, Reliquiarum.

Itaque præsente glorioso Rege Francorum Ludovico cum Wilhelmo religioso Nivernis Comite, Domino quoque Rhemensi Archiepiscopo, cum quibusdam suis suffraganeis Episcopis nobis etiam, et suffraganeis nostris, exceptis Parisiis et Nivernis, Episcopis præsentibus, cum multis religiosis Abbatibus et sapientibus, valdeque litteratis clericis adfuit Dominus Abbas Clara-vallensis; adfuit magister Petrus cum fautoribus suis. Quid multa? Dominus Abbas cum librum Theologiæ magistri Petri proferret in medium, et quæ annotaverat absurda, imo hæretica plane capitula de libro eodem proponeret, ut ea magister Petrus vel a se scripta negaret, vel si sua fateretur, aut probaret, aut corrigeret: visus est diffidere magister Petrus Abailardus, et subterfugere, respondere noluit, sed quamvis libera sibi daretur audientia, tutumque locum, et æquos haberet judices, ad vestram tamen, sanctissime Pater, appellans præsentiam, cum suis a conventu discessit.

Nos autem licet appellatio ista, minus Canonica videretur, Sedi tamen Apostolicæ deferentes, in personam hominis nullam voluimus proferre sententiam: Cæterum sententias pravi dogmatis ipsius, quia multo infecerant, et sui contagione adusque cordium intima penetraverant, sæpe in audientia publica lectas et relectas, et tam verissimis rationibus, quam Beati Augustini, aliorumque Sanctorum Patrum inductis a Domino Clara-vallensi auctoritatibus, non solum falsas, sed et hæreticas esse evidentissime comprobatas, pridie ante factam ad vos appellationem damnavimus. Et quia multos in errorem perniciosissimum et plane damnabilem pertrahunt, eas auctoritate vestra, dilectissime Domine, perpetua damnatione notari; et omnes qui pervicaciter et contentiose illas defenderint, a vobis, æquissime Pater, juxta pœna mulctari unanimiter et multa precum instantia postulamus.

Sæpe dicto vero Petro, si Reverentia vestra silentium imponeret, et tam legendi, quam scribendi prorsus interrumperet facultatem, et libros ejus perverso sine dubio dogmate respersos condemnaret, avulsis spinis et tribulis ab Ecclesia Dei, prevaleret adhuc læta Christi seges succrescere, florere, fructificare. Quædam autem de condemnatis a nobis capitulis vobis, Reverende Pater, conscripta transmisimus, ut per hæc audita reliqui corpus operis facilius æstimetis.

Observe how St Bernard explains the system and errors of the celebrated Abelard. In chapter 1 of the treatise which he wrote, *De erroribus Petri Abailardi*, he says:

"Habemus in Francia novum de veteri magistro Theologum, qui ab ineunte ætate sua in arte dialectica lusit; et nunc in scripturis sanctis insanit. Olim damnata et sopita dogmata, tam sua videlicet quam aliena suscitare conatur, insuper et nova addit. Qui dum omnium quæ sunt cœlo sursum, et quæ in terra deorsum, nihil præter solum Nescio nescire dignatur; ponit in cœlum os suum, et scrutatur alta Dei, rediensque ad nos refert verba ineffabilia, quæ non licet homini loqui. Et dum paratus est de omnibus reddere rationem, etiam quæ sunt supra rationem, et contra rationem præsumit, et contra fidem. Quid enim magis contra rationem, quam ratione rationem conari transcendere? Et quid magis contra fidem, quam credere nolle, quidquid non possit ratione attingere?"

In chapter 4, he sums up, in a few words, the aberrations of the dialectician:

"Sed advertite cætera. Omitto quod dicit spiritum timoris Domini non fuisse in Domino: timorem Domini castum in futuro seculo non futurum: post consecrationem panis et calicis priora accidentia quæ remanent pendere in aere: dæmonum in nobis suggestiones contactu fieri lapidum et herbarum, prout illorum sagax malitia novit; harum rerum vires diversas, diversis incitandis et incendendis vitiis, convenire: Spiritum Sanctum esse animam mundi: mundum juxta Platonem tanto excellentius animal esse, quanto meliorem animam habet Spiritum Sanctum. Ubi dum multum sudat quomodo Platonem faciat Christianum, se probat ethnicum. Hæc inquam omnia, aliasque istiusmodi nænias ejus non paucas prætereo, venio ad graviora. Non quod vel ad ipsa cuncta respondeam, magnis enim opus voluminibus esset. Illa loquor quæ tacere non possum.

"Cum de Trinitate loquitur," says he in his letter 192, "sapit Arium, cum de Gratia sapit Pelagium, cum de persona Christi sapit Nestorium."

Pope Innocent, condemning the doctrines of Abelard, says: "In Petri Abailardi perniciosa doctrina, et prædictorum hæreses, et alia perversa dogmata catholicæ fidei obviantia pullulare cœperunt."

APPENDIX.

Note (*a*), p. 289.

Quod necesse est homines simul viventes ab aliquo diligenter regi.

Et siquidem homini conveniret singulariter vivere, sicut multis animalium, nullo alio dirigente indigeret ad finem, sed ipse sibi unusquisque esset rex sub Deo summo rege, in quantum per lumen rationis divinitus datum sibi, in suis actibus seipsum dirigeret. Naturale autem est homini ut sit animal sociale, et politicum, in multitudine vivens, magis etiam quam omnia alia animalia; quod quidem naturalis necessitas declarat. Aliis enim animalibus natura præparavit cibum, tegumenta pilorum, defensionem, ut dentes, cornua, ungues, vel saltem velocitatem ad fugam. Homo autem institutus est nullo horum sibi a natura præparato, sed loco omnium data est ei ratio, per quam sibi hæc omnia officio manuum posset præparare, ad quæ omnia præparanda unus homo non sufficit. Nam unus homo per se sufficienter vitam transigere non posset. Est igitur homini naturale, quod in societate multorum vivat. Amplius, aliis animalibus insita est naturalis industria ad omnia ea quæ sunt eis utilia vel nociva, sicut ovis naturaliter extimet lupum inimicum. Quædam etiam animalia ex naturali industria cognoscunt aliquas herbas medicinales, et alia eorum vitæ necessaria. Homo autem horum, quæ sunt suæ vitæ necessaria, naturalem cognitionem habet solum in communi, quasi eo per rationem valente ex universalibus principiis ad cognitionem singulorum, quæ necessaria sunt humanæ vitæ, pervenire. Non est autem possibile, quod unus homo ad omnia hujusmodi per suam rationem pertingat. Est igitur necessarium homini, quod in multitudine vivat, et unus ab alio adjuvetur, et diversi diversis inveniendis per rationem occuparentur, puta, unus in medicina, alius in hoc, alius in alio. Hoc etiam evidentissime declaratur per hoc, quod est proprium hominis locutione uti, per quam unus homo aliis suum conceptum totaliter potest exprimere. Alia quidem animalia exprimunt mutuo passiones suas, in communi, ut canis in latratu iram, et alia animalia passiones suas diversis modis. Magis igitur homo est communicativus alteri, quam quodcumque aliud animal, quod gregale videtur, ut grus, formica, et apis. Hoc ergo considerans Salomon in Ecclesiaste ait: "Melius est esse duos, quam unum. Habent enim emolumentum mutuæ societatis." Si ergo naturale est homini quod in societate multorum vivat, necesse est in hominibus esse, per quod multitudo regatur. Multis enim existentibus hominibus et uno quoque id quod est sibi congruum providente, multitudo in diversa dispergeretur, nisi etiam esset aliquis de eo quod ad bonum multitudinis pertinet, curam habens, sicut et corpus hominis, et cujuslibet animalis deflueret, nisi esset aliqua vis regitiva communis in corpore, quæ ad bonum commune omnium membrorum intenderet. Quod considerans Salomon dicit: "Ubi non est gubernator, dissipabitur populus." Hoc autem rationabiliter accidit: non enim idem est quod propium, et quod commune. Secundum propria quidem differunt, secundum autem commune uniuntur: diversorum autem diversæ sunt causæ. Oportet igitur præter id quod movet ad propium bonum uniuscujusque, esse aliquid, quod movet ad bonum commune multorum. Propter quod et in omnibus quæ in unum ordinantur, aliquid invenitur alterius regitivum. In universitate enim corporum, per primum corpus, scilicet celeste, alia corpora ordine quodam divinæ providentiæ reguntur, omniaque corpora, per creaturam rationalem. In uno etiam homine anima regit corpus, atque inter animæ partes irascibilis et concupiscibilis ratione reguntur. Itemque inter membra corporis unum est principale, quod omnia movet, ut cor, aut caput. Oportet igitur esse in omni multitudine aliquod regitivum. (D. Th., Opusc. de Regimine Principum, l. i. cap. 1.)

Note (*b*), p. 290.

Ubi considerandum est, quod dominium, vel prælatio introducta sunt ex jure humano: distinctio autem fidelium et infidelium est ex jure divino. Jus autem divinum quod est ex gratia, non tollit jus humanum quod est ex naturali ratione; ideo distinctio fidelium et infidelium secundum se considerata, non tollit dominium, et prælationem infidelium supra fideles. (2. 2. quest. 10, art 10.)

Note (*c*), p. 290.

Respondeo dicendum quod sicut supra dictum est (quest. 10, art. 10), infidelitas secundum se ipsam non repugnat dominio, eo quod dominium introductum est de jure gentium, quod est jus humanum, Distinctio autem fidelium et infidelium est secundum jus divinum, per quod non tollitur jus humanum. (2. 2. quest. 12, art. 2.)

Note (*d*), p. 290.

Respondeo dicendum quod sicut actiones rerum naturalium procedunt ex potentiis naturalibus: ita etiam operationes humanæ procedunt ex humana voluntate. Oportuit autem in rebus naturalibus, ut superiora moverent inferiora ad suas actiones per excellentiam naturalis virtutis collatæ divinitus. Unde et oportet in rebus humanis, quod superiores moveant inferiores per suam voluntatem ex vi auctoritatis divinitus ordinatæ. Movere autem per rationem et voluntatem est præcipere; et ideo sicut ex ipso ordine naturali divinitus instituto inferiora in rebus naturalibus necesse habent subjici motioni superiorum, ita etiam in rebus humanis ex ordine juris naturalis et divini, tenentur inferiores suis superioribus obedire. (2. 2 quest. 105, art. 1.)

NOTE (*e*), p. 291.

Obedire autem superiori debitum est secundum divinum ordinem rebus inditum ut ostensum est. (2. 2. quest. 104, art. 2.)

NOTE (*f*), p. 291.

Respondeo dicendum quod fides Christi est justitiæ principium, et causa, secundum illud Rom. iii. "Justitia Dei per fidem Jesu Christi;" et ideo per fidem Christi non tollitur ordo justitiæ sed magis firmatur. Ordo autem justitiæ requirit, ut inferiores suis superioribus obediant: aliter enim non posset humanarum rerum status conservari. Et ideo per fidem Christi non excusantur fideles, quin principibus secularibus obedire teneantur. (2. 2. quest. 105, art. 6.)

NOTE (*g*), p. 291.

Certum est politicam potestatem a Deo esse a quo non nisi res bonæ et licitæ procedunt, et quod probat Aug. in toto fere 4 et 5 libr. de Civit. Dei. Nam sapientia Dei clamat, Proverb. viii.: Per me reges regnant; et infra: Per me principes imperant. Et Daniel ii.: Deus cœli regnum et imperium dedit tibi, &c.; et Daniel iv.: Cum bestiis ferisque erit habitatio tua, et fenum, ut bos comedes, et rore cœli infunderis: septem quoque tempora mutabuntur super te, donec scias quod dominetur Excelsus super regnum hominum, et cuicumque voluerit, det illud. (Bell. de Laicis, l. iii. c. 6.)

NOTE (*h*), p. 291.

Sed hic observanda sunt aliqua. Primo politicam potestatem in universum consideratam, non descendendo in particulari ad monarchiam, aristocratiam, vel democratiam immediate esse a solo Deo; nam consequitur necessario naturam hominis, proinde esse ab illo, qui fecit naturam hominis; præterea hæc potestas est de jure naturæ, non enim pendet ex consensu hominum, nam velint, nolint, debent regi ab aliquo, nisi velint perire humanum genus, quod est contra naturæ inclinationem. At jus naturæ est jus divinum, jure igitur divino introducta est gubernatio, et hoc videtur proprie velle Apostolus, cum dicit Rom. xiii: Qui potestati resistit, Dei ordinationi resistit. (Ib.)

NOTE (*i*), p. 292.

Secundo nota, hanc potestatem immediate esse tanquam in subjecto, in tota multitudine, nam hæc potestas est de jure divino. At jus divinum nulli homini particulari dedit hanc potestatem, ergo dedit multitudini; præterea sublato jure positivo, non est major ratio cur ex multis æqualibus unus potius, quam alius dominetur: igitur potestas totius est multitudinis. Denique humana societas debet esse perfecta respublica, ergo debet habere potestatem se ipsam conservandi, et proinde puniendi perturbatores pacis, &c. (Ib.)

NOTE (*k*), p. 293.

Tertio nota, hanc potestatem transferri a multitudine in unum vel plures eodem jure naturæ: nam Respub. non potest per seipsam exercere hanc potestatem, ergo tenetur eam transferre in aliquem unum vel aliquos paucos; et hoc modo potestas principum in genere considerata, est etiam de jure naturæ, et divino; nec posset genus humanum, etiamsi totum simul conveniret, contrarium statuere, nimirum, ut nulli essent principes vel rectores. (Ib.)

NOTE (*l*), p. 293.

Quarto nota, in particulari singulas species regiminis esse de jure gentium, non de jure naturæ; nam pendet a consensu multitudinis, constituere super se regem vel consules, vel alios magistratus, ut patet: et si causa legitima adsit, potest multitudo mutare regnum in aristocratiam, aut democratiam, et e contrario ut Romæ factum legimus.

Quinto nota, ex dictis sequi, hanc potestatam in particulari esse quidem a Deo, sed mediante consilio, et electione humana, ut alia omnia, quæ ad jus gentium pertinent, jus enim gentium est quasi conclusio deducta ex jure naturæ per humanum discursum. Ex quo colliguntur duæ differentiæ inter potestatem politicam, et ecclesiasticam: una ex parte subjecti, nam politica est in multitudine, ecclesiastica in uno homine tanquam in subjecto immediate; altera ex parte efficientis, quod politica universe considerata est de jure divino, in particulari considerata est de jure gentium; ecclesiastica omnibus modis est de jure divino, et immediate a Deo. (Ib.)

NOTE (*m*), p. 294.

In hac re communis sententia videtur esse, hanc potestatem dari immediate a Deo ut auctore naturæ, ita ut homines quasi disponant materiam et efficiant subjectum capax hujus potestatis; Deus autem quasi tribuat formam dando hanc potestatem. Cita a Cajet. Covar. Victor. y Soto. (De Leg. l. iii. c. 3.)

NOTE (*n*), p. 294.

Secundo sequitur ex edictis, potestatem civilem, quoties in uno homine, vel principe reperitur, legitimo, ac ordinario jure, a populo, et communitate manasse, vel proxime vel remote, nec posse aliter haberi, ut justa sit. (Ibid. cap. 4.)

NOTE (*o*), p. 294.

Defensio Fidei Catholicæ et Apostolicæ adversus Anglicanæ sectæ errores, cum responsione ad apologiam pro juramento fidelitatis et præfationem monitoriam serenissimi Jacobi Angliæ Regis, Authore P. D. Francisco Suario Gratanensi, e Societate Jesu, Sacræ Theologiæ in celebri Conimbricensi Academia Primario Professore, ad serenissimos totius Christiani orbis Catholicos Reges ac Principes.

Lib. 3. De Primatu Summi Pontificis, cap. 2. Utrum Principatus politicus sit immediate a Deo, seu ex divina institutione.

..... In qua rex serenissimus non solum novo, et singulari modo opinatur, sed etiam acriter invehitur in Cardinalem Bellarminum, eo quod asseruerit, non regibus authoritatem a Deo *immediate*, perinde ac pontificibus esse concessam. Asserit ergo ipse, regem non a populo, sed *immediate* a Deo suam potestatem habere; suam vero sententiam quibusdam argumentis, et exemplis suadere conatur, quorum efficaciam in sequenti capite expendemus.

Sed quamquam controversia hæc ad fidei dogmata directe non pertineat (*nihil enim ex divina Scriptura, aut Patrum traditione in illa definitum ostendi potest*), nihilominus diligenter tractanda, et explicanda est. Tum quia potest esse occasio errandi in aliis dogmatibus; tum etiam quia prædicta regis sententia, prout ab ipso asseritur et intenditur, nova et singularis est, et ad exaggerandam temporalem potestatem, et spiritualem extenuandam videtur inventa. Tum denique quia sententiam illustrissimi Bellarmini *antiquam, receptam, veram, ac necessariam esse censemus.*

NOTE (*p*), p. 295.

R. P. Hermanni Busembaum Societatis Jesu Theologia Moralis, nunc pluribus partibus aucta a R. P. D. Alphonso de Ligorio Rectore majore congregationis SS. Redemptoris; adjuncta in calce operis, præter indicem rerum, et verborum locupletissimum, perutili instructione ad praxim confessariorium Latine reddita.

Lib. 1, Tract 2. De legibus, cap. 1. De natura, et obligatione legis. Dub. 2.

104. Certum est dari in hominibus potestatem ferendi leges; sed potestas hæc quoad leges civiles a natura nemini competit, nisi communitati hominum, et ab hac transfertur in unum, vel in plures, a quibus communitas regatur.

NOTE (*q*), p. 295.

Theologia Christiana Dogmatico-Moralis Auctore P. F. Daniele Concina ordinis Prædicatorum. Editio novissima, tomus sextus, de Jure nat. et gent., &c. Romæ, 1768.

Lib. 1. De Jure natur. et gent., &c. Dissertatio 4, De leg. hum. C. 2.

Summæ potestatis originem a Deo communiter arcessunt scriptores omnes. Idque declaravit Salomon, Prov. viii. "Per me reges regnant, et legum conditores justa decernunt." Et profecto quemadmodum inferiores principes a summa majestate, ita summa majestas terrena a supremo Rege, Dominoque dominantium pendeat necesse est. Illud in disputationem vocant tum theologi, tum jurisconsulti, sit ne a Deo proxime, an tantum remote hæc potestas summa? Immediate a Deo haberi contendunt plures, quod ab hominibus neque conjunctim, neque sigillatim acceptis haberi possit. Omnes enim patres familias æquales sunt, solaque œconomica in propias familias potestate fruuntur. Ergo civilem politicamque potestatem, qua ipsi carent, conferre aliis nequeunt. Tum si potestas summa a communitate, tanquam a superiore, uni, aut pluribus collata esset, revocari ad nutum ejusdem communitatis posset; cum superior pro arbitrio retractare communicatam potestatem valeat; quod in magnum societatis detrimentum recideret.

Contra disputant alii, et *quidem probabilius ac verius*, advertentes omnem quidem potestatem a Deo esse; sed addunt, non transferri in particulares homines immediate, sed mediante societatis civilis consensu. Quod hæc potestas sit immediate, non in aliquo singulari, sed in tota hominum collectione, docet conceptis verbis S. Thomas 1. 2. qu. 90. art. 3 ad 2. et qu. 97. art. 3 ad 3 quem sequuntur Dominicus Soto, lib. 1. qu. 1. art. 3. Ledesma 2. Part. qu. 18. art. 3. Covarruvias in pract. cap. 1. Ratio evidens est: quia omnes homines nascuntur liberi, respectu civilis imperii; ergo nemo in alterum civili potestate potitur. Neque ergo in singulis, neque in aliquo determinato potestas hæc reperitur. Consequitur ergo in tota hominum collectione eamdem extare. Quæ potestas non confertur a Deo per aliquam actionem pecuiarem a creatione distinctam; sed est veluti proprietas ipsam rectam rationem consequens, quatenus recta ratio præscribit ut homines in unum moraliter congregati, expresso aut tacito concensu modum dirigendæ, conservandæ, propugnandæque societatis præscribant.

NOTE (*r*), p. 296.

Hinc infertur, potestatem residentem in principe, rege, vel in pluribus, aut optimatibus, aut plebeiis, ab ipsa communitate aut proxime, aut remote proficisci. Nam potestas hæc. a Deo immediate non est. Id enim nobis constare peculiari revelatione deberet; quemadmodum scimus, Saulem et Davidem electos a Deo fuisse. Ab ipsa ergo communitate dimanet oportet.

Falsam itaque reputamus opinionem illam quæ asserit, potestatem hanc immediate et proxime a Deo conferri regi, principi, et cuique supremæ potestati, excluso Reipublicæ tacito, aut expresso consensu. Quamquam lis hæc verborum potius quam rei est. Nam potestas hæc a Deo auctore naturæ est, quatenus disposuit, et ordinavit ut ipsa Respublica pro societatis conservatione, et defensione, uni, aut pluribus supremam regiminis potestatem conferret. Immo facta designatione imperantis, aut imperantium, potestas hæc a Deo manare dicitur, quatenus jure naturali, et divino tenetur, societas ipsa parere imperanti. Quoniam reipsa Deus ordinavit ut per unum, aut per plures hominum societas regatur. Et hac via omnia conciliantur placita: et oracula Scripturarum vero in sensu exponuntur. Qui resistit potestati, Dei ordinationi resistit. Et iterum: Non est potestas nisi a Deo: ad Rom. viii. Et Petrus Epist. 1, cap. ii. Subjecti igitur estote omni humanæ creaturæ propter Deum: sive Regi, &c. Item Joan. xix. Non haberes potestatem adversum me ullam, nisi tibi datum esset desuper. Quæ, alia testimonia evincunt, omnia a Deo, supremo rerum omnium moderatore, disponi, et ordinari. At non propterea humana consilia, et operationes excluduntur; ut sapienter interpretantur S. Augustinus tract. 6, in Joan. et lib. 22. cont. Faustum, cap. 47, et S. Joannes Chrysostomus Hom. 23, in Epist. ad Rom.

NOTE (*s*), p. 296.

Quinam possint ferre leges? Dico 1. Potestas legislativa competit communitati vel illi, qui curam communitatis gerit. (Ibid. art. 3. 0.)

Prob. 1. Ex Isidoro L. 5. Etymol. C. 10 et refertur C. Lex, Dist. 4. ubi dicit: Lex est constitutio populi, secundum quam majores natu simul cum plebibus aliquid sanxerunt. (Ibid in art. 1. 0.)

Prob. 1. Ratione. (Ibid. 0.) Illius est condere legem, cujus est prospicere bono communi; quia, ut dictum est, leges feruntur propter bonum commune: atqui est communis, vel illius, cui curam communitatis habet, prospicere bono communi: sicut enim bonum particulare est finis proportionatus agenti particulari, ita bonum commune est finis proportionatus communitati, vel ejus vices gerenti; ergo. Confirmatur: (Ibid. ad 2.) lex habet vim imperandi et coercendi; atqui nemo privatus habet vim imperandi multitudini et eam coercendi, sed sola ipsa multitudo, vel ejus Rector: Ergo. (Tract. de Legi. Art. 4.)

NOTE (*t*), p. 296.

Dices: Superioris est imperare et coercere; atqui communitas non est sibi superior: Ergo R. D. Min. Communitas, sub eodem respectu considerata, non est sibi superior, C. Sub diverso respectu, N. Potest itaque communitas considerari collective, per modum unius corporis moralis, et sic considerata est superior sibi consideratæ distributive in singulis membris. Item potest considerari vel ut gerit vices Dei, a quo omnis potestas legislativa descendit, juxta illud Proverb. Per me reges regnant, et legum conditores justa decernunt; vel ut est gubernabilis in ordine ad bonum commune: primo modo considerata est superior et legislativa; secundo modo considerata est inferior et legis susceptiva.

NOTE (*u*), p. 297.

Quod ut clarius percipiatur, observandum est hominem inter animalia nasci maxime destitutum pluribus tum corporis cum animæ necessariis, pro quibus indiget aliorum consortio et adjutorio, consequenter eum ipsapte natura nasci animal sociale: societas autem quam natura, naturalisve ratio dictat ipsi necessariam, diu subsistere non potest, nisi aliqua publica potestate gubernetur; juxta illud Proverb. Ubi non est gubernator, populus corruet. Ex quo sequitur, quod Deus, qui dedit talem naturam, simul ei dederit potestatem gubernativam et legislativam, qui enim dat formam, dat etiam ea, quæ hæc forma necessario exigit. Verum, quia hæc potestas gubernativa et legislativa non potest exerceri a tota multitudine; difficile namque foret, omnes et singulos simul convenire toties quoties providendum est de necessariis bono communi, et de legibus ferendis; ideo solet multitudo transferre suum jus seu potestatem gubernativam, vel in aliquos de populo ex omni conditione, et dicitur Democratia; vel in paucos optimates, et dicitur Aristocratia; vel in unum tantum, sive pro se solo, sive pro successoribus jure hæreditario, et dicitur Monarchia. Ex quo sequitur, omnem potestatem esse a Deo, ut dicit Apost. Rom. xiii. immediate quidem et jure naturæ in communitate, mediate autem tantum et jure humano in Regibus et aliis Rectoribus: nisi Deus ipse immediate aliquibus hanc potestatem conferat, ut contulit Moysi in populum Israel, et Christus SS. Pontifici in totam Ecclesiam.

Hanc potestatem legislativam in Christianos, *maxime justos, non agnoscunt, Lutherani et Calvinistæ, secuti in hoc Valdenses, Wicleffum, et Joan. Hus. damnatos in Conc. Constant. sess.* 6. *can.* 15. *Et quamvis Joannes Hus eam agnosceret in principibus bonis, eam tamen denegabat malis, pariter ideo damnatus in eodem Concil. sess.* 8.

NOTE (*x*), p. 297.

Compendium Salmatic. authore R. P. F. R. Antonio a S. Joseph olim Lectore, priore ac examinatore Synodali in suo collegio Burgensi, nunc procuratore generali in Romana Curia pro Carmelitarum Discalceatorum Hispanica Congregatione. Romæ, 1779. Superiorum permissu. Tractatus 3, De Legibus, cap. 2. De potestate ferendi leges.

Punctum I. De potestate legislativa civili.

Inq. 1. An detur in hominibus potestas condendi leges civiles? R. Affirm. constat ex illo Prov. viii. Per me reges regnant, et legum conditores justa decernunt. Idem patet ex Apost. ad Rom. xiii. et tanquam de fide est definitum in Conc. Const. sess. 8, et ultima. Prob. ration. quia ad conservationem boni communis requiritur publica potestas, qua communitas gubernetur: nam ubi non est gubernator, corruet populus, sed nequid gubernator communitatem nisi mediis legibus gubernare: ergo certum est dari in hominibus potestatem condendi leges, quibus populus possit gubernari. Ita D. Th. lib. i. de regim. princip. c. 1 et 2.

Inq. 2. An potestas legislativa civilis conveniat principi immediate a Deo? R. omnes asserunt dictam potestatem habere principes a Deo. Verius tamen dicitur, non *immediate* sed *mediante* populi consensu illam eos a Deo recipere. Nam omnes homines sunt in natura æquales, nec unus est superior, nec alius inferior ex natura, nulli enim dedit natura supra alterum potestatem, sed hæc a Deo data est hominum communitati, quæ judicans rectius fore gubernandum per unam vel per plures personas determinatas, suam transtulit potestatem in unam, vel plures, a quibus regeretur, ut ait D. Th. 1. 2. q. 90. a. 3. ad. 2.

Ex hoc naturali principio oritur discrimen regiminis civilis. Nam si Respublica transtulit omnem suam potestatem in unum solum, appellatur Regimen Monarchicum; si illam contulit Optimatibus populi, nuncupatur Regimen Aristocraticum; si vero populus, aut Respublica sibi retineat talem potestatem, dicitur Regimen Democraticum. Habent igitur Principes regendi potestatem a Deo, quia supposita electione a Republica facta, Deus illam potestatem, quæ in communitate erat, Principi confert. Unde ipse nomine Dei regit, et gubernat, et qui illi resistit, Dei ordinationi resistit, ut dicit Apost. loco supra laudato.

INDEX.

THE END.

www.ingramcontent.com/pod-product-compliance
Lightning Source LLC
LaVergne TN
LVHW021318110826
845150LV00003B/610
* 9 7 8 1 4 2 5 5 5 7 1 6 4 *